MW01532388

the
BEER
log
By James D. Robertson

Perfect Bound Version Released 1995

All inquiries should be addressed to Bosak Publishing Co.
4764 Galicia Way, Oceanside, CA. 92056, (619) 724-4447

ISBN: 0-9635332-5-8

Printed in the United States of America

This book is dedicated to
the memory of Sheldon Wasserman,
expert on Italian wines, writer of extraordinary
books on wine, and good friend.
It was his encouragement that started my writing career.

ACKNOWLEDGEMENTS

In the sixteen years that I have been tasting, writing, and constantly thinking about beer, there have been hundreds of people who helped me with the task. I would like to list them all, but they are legion. I do, however, want them to know that I am grateful for their assistance.

I would like to name some of those whose contribution transcends the norm. Jim Peabody of Simi Valley, CA; Alan Follett of So. San Francisco, CA; and Bob Remalia of Cleveland, OH, have worked hard to keep me supplied with brews as they appear in their area. There have been many others, to be sure, but those three have done the most, and for a long time.

I also want to mention the current regular members of the taste panel: Bill Geiger, Ken Orey, Don Lambrecht, Fred Taylor, Kent Sabin, Sal Manno, Tony Langon, Mike Weber, and Tom Clark. They are necessary to the process and are my reality checkers. For this they get to say to their wives: "Dear, I have to go out drinking beer tonight," and their wives say (knowing that it is the taste panel meeting): "Fine, have a good time." If you think about it, they have a really good thing going.

I must extend my appreciation to the brewers of the world, particularly in the United States, who make that wonderful stuff and who frequently provide me with samples, information, guidance, etc. Without their help, this book would be a shadow of what it is.

Lastly, I have to acknowledge the assistance and encouragement of Mike Bosak of Bosak Publishing Company (*All About Beer* and *Suds 'n Stuff*) and his staff. Mike keeps flogging me onward, and I sometimes need that.

ABOUT THE AUTHOR

James D. Robertson is a retired electronics engineer, having worked for the Department of the Army and the Department of Defense for thirty-four years following his graduation from MIT in 1956. His worldwide travels associated with his career exposed him to much of the world's bounty, and he discovered that he had a taste for it all. Most important, he felt a need to bring the appreciation of food, wine, and beer to others.

When at home, he wrote about wine, beer, food, and restaurants. He has been published over 200 times in fifteen publications, including *Cosmopolitan* and *Consumer's Digest*. To date, he has written four books: *The Great American Beer Book* and three editions of *The Connoisseurs Guide to Beer*. *The Beer Log* brings that total to five.

He attributes his tasting talent to an extraordinary palate memory, which was honed to a sharp edge in many years of wine tasting. In those days of wine discovery (1960s and 1970s), parlor games included naming the exact growers and vintages of a selection of wines. The talent developed at that time carried through into the world of beer.

Since retirement in 1990, he has traveled twice to the West Coast and to Chicago, Ontario, and Germany specifically to taste beer. In the fall of 1992, he intends to attend the Great American Beer Fest in Colorado and then travel on to Australia, New Zealand, and Indonesia. Plans for 1993 call for a comprehensive study of beers of the American northwestern states, British Columbia, and Belgium.

ABOUT THIS BOOK

GENERAL

The Beer Log is designed to be the living document for beer lovers. By providing space for the owner's beer notes, it becomes the personal beer log of the owner. The notes provided on the sheets of the log only provide a starting point for the user. It won't be much of a book to read in front of the fire on a cold winter's evening. Rather, it will be a reference and personal log book for the serious beer drinker, one to carry with you on adventures in beer hunting. The looseleaf format will allow for additional and change pages to be made available on a continuing basis. When the binder becomes full, a second binder can be obtained, and there are few serious limitations. Once you start using *The Beer Log*, you have the opportunity to stay in step with developments in the world of beer as they happen.

The other side of assuring that *The Beer Log* becomes that living document is to promise that there will be annual issues of addendum and change pages that will update and refine the log. The first set of such sheets is already in preparation.

The initial issue of *The Beer Log* is primarily composed of beers available in the United States. The imports reported are items that are or have been available in the U.S. for the past fifteen years. Domestic American brews reported are beers produced over that same time period, but only those which are believed to still be in production at the time of writing. The same is true of Canadian beers. I have deviated from this philosophy in a very few places, mostly including some foreign beers, to avoid having to issue a change page in the future for a single additional brand of a brewer that already has an extensive list of export labels to the United States.

The planned addendum pages to be released in 1993 will report on brews that have been imported in very limited batches and may not available to the general public, domestic brews of Panama, Japan, Belgium, England, and Germany, and newly arrived domestic contract, micro, and brew-pub beers. I expect there to be some additional 1000 brews to be described and rated in the first update.

BEER TYPES

We who deal with beer on an everyday basis sometimes forget that there are new people reading our stuff all the time. It is therefore useful for us to stop our headlong plunge into new and interesting turf to look back and define the basics so we are playing with the same deck. So this ding-dong school doesn't get too pedantic, we will offer it in short segments to remind

OVER ▶

our old readers and to educate our new ones in a painless manner.

First, there are only two distinctly different sorts of beer. There is beer made from bottom-fermenting yeast (the yeast goes to the bottom during fermentation) and there is beer made from top-fermenting yeast(which goes to the top during fermentation). The top-fermenting yeast was discovered centuries ago and is used to make ale. Bottom-fermenting yeast was simultaneously discovered by Gabriel Sedlmayr and Anton Dreher about 1830 and is the yeast used to make lager or pilsener beer.

Lager Beer

The term *lager* is derived from a German word that means to store or stock. It refers to the long period of lagering, wherein the beer is stored in cellars to undergo the slow second fermentation. It is bottom-fermented and "long" aged. The aging of a better lager will last for several months, but all too many of our domestic products see little more than a week of cellar time, so great is the rush to the marketplace.

In America, fermentation takes place at temperatures of 45°-55° F. (and sometimes higher) and proceeds slowly over a period of five to eight days. European lager brewers usually ferment at a slightly lower temperature, and less-vigorous fermentation occurs over a longer period of time, often as long as ten to fourteen days. Better domestic beers may also be brewed according to European practice. The aging is done very near the freezing temperature for water and proceeds very slowly. The longer the beer is aged, the more "complete" will be the flavor, and the resultant brew will have more body and a longer shelf life.

Light lagers are pale gold in color, light in body, are flavored with a medium to light hop taste, and are fairly high in carbonation. They generally have a soft, mellow, dry taste. They are best served cold, at around 40°-45° F. The two most popular types, pilsener and Dortmunder, make up the major volume of U.S. beer production. These two styles, which differ only slightly, best match the definition of light lager given above, with the malt having more influence in aroma and taste than the hops. The term *pilsener* is used interchangeably with the word *lager* in most of the world today, whereas the use of *Dortmunder* has almost disappeared as a beer adjective in the U.S. With the utilization of corn or rice as an adjunct to the barley malt, the appearance of many domestic beers is becoming paler and paler, with some already nearly as pale as water.

The Vienna type is characterized by an amber color and a very mild hop taste. It is usually brewed with less hops than the Dortmunder or pilsener type, but is not less flavorful because the malt contribution is increased by this particular brewing method.

The Munich type, or dark lager, has a dark-brown color, and is full-bodied with a sweet malt flavor and slight hop taste. It is more aromatic and "creamy" than a light lager. The color of a true dark lager comes from the addition of roasted barley. Imitation dark lagers are made with caramel or with a roasted barley malt extract, a much less expensive process. The alcohol content in these dark lagers approaches 5 percent by weight. Light Munich beers are Dortmunder types and, like many of the current Dortmunder brews, have more of a hop flavor. The color of these German light lagers is darker than the corresponding American brews because of the slower fermentation. They can be likened to the Bohemian beers with their fine and strongly noticeable hop flavor, pronounced bitter taste, and vinous character.

Oktoberfest beer was once brewed only for the autumn festivals (usually held in September). Originally a light lager with high alcoholic content available only on draft for serving at the festival, it is now readily found year round in bottles. Packaged Oktoberfest beer differs very little from the regular export lager, including its alcohol content.

In Germany, Festbier (festival beer) is produced by many brewers, large and small, in conjunction with Christmas, Easter, and local folk festivals and for Kirchweihen, the celebration for the patron saint of the local church. These beers are usually brewed the month before the festival, mostly only draft, but sometimes packaged. For example, Märzen and Ostern (March beer and Easter beer) are brewed in January, lagered outside in winter, and tapped (traditionally by the mayor) when it is very cold, so that some of the water is frozen and the beer is higher in alcohol.

Bock beer is believed to have originated in the once-famous beer capital of Einbeck. A heavy dark beer with a slightly sweet malt flavor and strong hop background, bock is brewed in the winter for consumption in the spring. True bock derives its color from the heat treatment given to the barley in the malting process and may have as much as 10 percent alcohol by weight. Many artificial bocks produced today are colored and flavored with a prepared syrup containing caramelized sugar.

Steam beer, another bottom-fermented brew, originated on the West Coast of the United States as a direct result of the desire for malt beverages and the extreme shortage of ice. It is a development in beer brewing that is peculiar to America. Fermentation proceeds at a relatively higher temperature (60°-68° F.) and barley malt is used exclusively. Within twelve to eighteen hours after the yeast has been added to the wort in the fermenting tubs, the beer comes into "krausen," where it is kept from six to eight hours. It is then run into the clarifier for two to three days (depending on the ambient temperature) for completion of fermentation. If fermentation has been proper, at the end of this stage the beer will undergo a reduction of 50-60 percent and will be quite clear in appearance. From the clarifier, the beer is racked directly into barrels, where it receives an addition of about 20 percent of krausen, together with some fining. In four to six days the beer has raised a sufficient amount of "steam" in the barrels (some fifty pounds per square inch), and some bleeding of pressure is required. In olden times, these barrels were shipped to saloons, rested a few days, and then tapped for the trade. Steam beer is made today by only one West Coast firm, and the product is bottled. Total refrigeration may not be necessary because of the strength of the brew, but it must be kept cool, for it is not pasteurized. Steam beer has a golden-brown color, sharp hoppy taste, full body, and a lingering malt finish.

Ales

The ales have been around for a very long time and fought a losing battle to the lagers for most of the nineteenth and twentieth centuries. Even in England and Canada, where ales held sway until the last decade, they have begun to yield their market share to the lagers. Even many of the brews labeled ales are bottom-fermented beer made in an ale-like style.

Ale is more vinous in nature, possesses a greater percentage of alcohol (4 to 5 percent by weight) and extract than a lager, is more aromatic, and full bodied, and has a more pronounced hop flavor and tartness.

Ale is fermented at a higher temperature than lager for a lesser period of time and, when maturing, is stored at temperatures in the range of 40°-45° F. (as opposed to lager, which matures at temperatures near 32° F.). Ale requires additional aging in the bottle to develop its best strength and flavor.

There are a number of different types of ale produced today. Common or stock ales are characterized by lower levels of carbonation. Cream ales and sparkling ales have relatively high levels of carbonation, resulting in a rich foam and strong effervescence. The "bitter" of England is brewed from pale-ale malts, with corn and rice added in small amounts to make the beer clear and brilliant. It is more heavily hopped than "mild," the other staple of British pubs, a brown-hued smooth ale beverage with a dominant malt flavor.

The strong or brown ales are quite dark and may be tawny brown, ruby red or brown with a reddish tinge in their coloring. Some are highly carbonated; others have just the slightest touch of bubble. The alcohol level is usually quite high, some approaching the equivalent of a wine. These will keep for several years in a bottle, just like a wine. All have the characteristic full malt flavor and a vinous character, and some are hopped quite heavily. Included in this type are the barley wines, which are notably vinous and well hopped. These may be matured for up to eighteen months, often in oak casks, which imparts a tannin to the brew, making it seem even more like a wine.

Stout & Porter

There is no rule that says what kind of yeast is used to make a stout or a porter, so they can be either.

Stout has a dark color (some are almost black), a rich malty flavor usually combined with a rather strong bitter hop taste, and a high alcohol content (5-6.5 percent by weight). Stout usually has low to medium carbonation and is best served at temperatures above 45° F. Stout is a heavy beer with barley added as its main ingredient. Although rarely seen today, milk stout was once popular with the sick and elderly for its reputed restorative properties. It is a sweet stout so named for the lactose used as a nonfermentable sugar in the brew.

Porter originated in England about 1722 to satisfy the market that had arisen from a public demand for a brew that was drawn equally from casks of ale and beer. Originally it was a heavy beverage, but it is more lightly brewed today and has a more bitter and dry taste than it had in the eighteenth century. Porter is made with charcoal or colored malt and is a dark-brown, heavy-bodied, malty-flavored brew with a slightly sweet taste and a less pronounced hop flavor than ale. It is usually about 5 percent alcohol by weight. All early porter was top-fermented, and many of the better ones still are; a few domestic American ones are bottom-fermented.

Malt Liquor

In America, as in the rest of the world, the term *malt liquor* is loosely defined with no legal or accepted meaning. In general, malt liquor has higher alcohol and warmer fermentation. An average American malt liquor has 4.5-5 percent alcohol by weight (compared to 3.6-3.8 percent for lagers); 12-13 percent original gravity, strength of the wort before fermentation in percent solids (lagers are 11-11.5 percent); and 65-75 percent real degree of fermentation, the percentage of original gravity lost during fermentation to alcohol (lagers are 60-64 percent). In many American states and in some foreign countries, a brew cannot be called beer or ale if its alcoholic content exceeds specified limits. Malt liquor is one of the allowed terms, and it is hung on many higher-alcohol brews, particularly imports, just to satisfy local labeling laws.

The major producers of malt liquor in the United States are convinced that its market is predominantly black, and much of the malt liquor marketing is clearly oriented in that direction. Some malt liquor is designed to compete with "pop" wines, and there are beer and wine and beer and soda combinations offered as malt liquor. Others are dry, malty, and very beerlike. There are many good malt liquors, and they come in a wide variety of styles and flavors.

The first American malt liquor was Colt .45, developed by the Altes Brewery in Detroit. It was later sold to the National Brewery of Baltimore, which promoted it into a national brand.

Lights and Drys

In 1964, true light and dry beer became possible with the development and commercial availability of an enzyme called amyloglucosidase. This enzyme completed the work of the malt amylases and rendered all the dextrins in beer completely fermentable. All the starchy content could be converted to alcohol. The real extract of a beer made with amyloglucosidase in the fermenter consists only of protein, minerals, by-products of fermentation (e.g., lactic acid), and some pentose sugars, which are neither fermentable nor caloric.

The alcohol level resulting from the amyloglucosidase fermentation is greater than for regular beer. The higher alcohol comes from the dextrins that are broken down by the enzyme to fermentable sugars and which are then fermented by the yeast that is already present. The level of alcohol is usually about 1 percent higher than for regular beer, but there is an interesting effect concerning it. Because this low-calorie beer has no dextrins remaining, the alcohol in it can be more rapidly absorbed by the bloodstream, significantly increasing its intoxicating potential. To mitigate this undesired fringe benefit, the brewer adjusts the light beer to an alcohol level slightly below that of regular beer by adding water. This low-calorie beer, when packaged, will have about 0.3 percent less alcohol than regular beer but will have the same potential for intoxication.

So, a true light or dry beer has fewer calories, no carbohydrates, and as much intoxicating effect as regular beer. There is a loss of body because the dextrins are no longer there. Because of the need for alcohol reduction by dilution, there also may be less aroma and flavor. This loss of flavor and aroma can be avoided to a great degree by the brewer's use of high-quality ingredients that would make a brew with character sufficient to stand out even with the dilution to reduce alcohol.

Weissbier

Wheat beer or white beer was first made in England, but its major markets developed on the continent of Europe, especially in Germany and Belgium. It came into prominence in Germany as Hamburg Wheat Beer in the sixteenth century. Made from wheat and barley malt, it has a distinctive yeasty or bready aroma and a taste frequently made very complex by the formation of lactic acid and its unique spicy flavor. Since that time several styles evolved, including the white effervescent Berliner Weiss served in bowl-shaped stemware with a dash of woodruff or fruit syrup.

In southern Germany, wheat beer was the leading seller among malt beverages prior to the discovery of bottom-fermenting yeast and the invention of lager, and today it is experiencing a revival. There are two distinct styles, each with its vociferous following of adherents. Some prefer the Hefe-weizen (or Hefe-weiss, as it is sometimes labeled), a wheat beer with the yeast left in the bottle, extolling its virtues as a source of vitamins, nourishment, and enhanced flavor. Others prefer the filtered version called kristall-klar, which is more like a lager. The Kristall-klar is frequently served with a twist of lemon, which tends to cut the head and mitigate any sharpness of flavor, making it even more like a lager.The Belgian white beer looks more like Berliner Weiss but usually has a sharper flavor than the Hefe-weizen. It is another unique style of wheat beer and in a class by itself, being very full-flavored, and extremely dry and thirst quenching.

So that, in a nutshell, is a description of the basic styles of beer. To be sure, there are many other finer divisions within those categories.

DESCRIPTION & RATING

The beers are named according to the label, without regard to the accuracy of that labeling. Whatever the brewer says is what is reported. The visual appearance is given, followed by any interesting visual features such as the head, etc. Next is a description of the aromatic features of the product—what does it smell like? Features of the "nose" consisting of the aroma (smells produced by the ingredients) and bouquet(smells produced as a result of fermentation) are presented. As to mouth sensations (the effect of the beer in the mouth or on the palate), the notable effects are described as appropriate. There may be a single palate sensation, one notable taste or flavor, or complexities involving the front of the palate (the initial taste-like sensation on the front of the tongue), the mid-palate (taste experienced on the middle or sides of the tongue), and the finish (the taste experienced at the point of swallowing). Lastly, the aftertaste is described as a function of time, taste value, and intensity.

In rating the beers, they were judged first on how well they fit their definition, and second on how pleasing they were to beer drinkers. If a beer totally failed to match the standard of its type, it might well suffer some loss of points, but if it were an excellent example of some other type, it could still attain a high rating score. Over 90 percent of the beers rated herein were judged by a taste panel of six or more tasters. All features (appearance, nose, palate, and aftertaste) were considered in the rating. Dry, low-calorie, and non-alcoholic beers were judged as lagers and, because most of them have attenuated features, suffered accordingly.

Scoring is to be interpreted as follows:

0-18 Poor. Atypical of type. Has unpleasant features, flawed aroma or taste, or both. Badly mishandled, gone off with age. Improperly made. Unforgivable faults. Undrinkable, or tastes like carbonated water or soda pop. A beer you would not purchase again.

19-36 Fair. May not be true to type. Noticeable faults, but not overwhelming. Poorly balanced. May have some good features, like thirst quenching, but inferior to most other beers or lacking what other readily available beers offer. Not a beer you would prefer to purchase again.

37-54 Good. Typical of type. Faults are small and forgiveable. Good balance. Pleasant and enjoyable. Good serviceable beer for thirst quenching and regular enjoyment, if obtainable at a good price.

55-72 Very Good. True to type. No significant faults or offensive features. Well balanced. Aroma, flavor, and aftertaste all present to the appropriate degree, but short of excellent. A beer you would be willing to pay some premium to purchase or to go out of your way to obtain.

73-90 Excellent. Characteristic of the best of type. No faults or offensive features. All components of aroma and taste in harmony. Aroma, flavor, and aftertaste very much present and appropriate. A beer that deserves a premium price and one that you would go out of your way to obtain.

Whenever possible, beers previously listed in *The Great American Beer Book* and the various editions of *The Connoisseurs Guide to Beer* were retasted and newly rated.

Whenever there was an opportunity to retaste a brand that had performed below an average standard of acceptability, it was submitted to the taste panel again. In all cases, the best performance is reported and the best score listed. The example of any brew you may try could be better or worse than that reported herein. Some brews have a short shelf life, and others are fragile and cannot withstand exposure to high or low temperatures or other mishandling. Stores well versed in proper handling of malt beverages are few and far between.

It must be noted that the rating list contains items that are not described in the text. In some cases, these are brews no longer offered for sale in the United States or Canada. They have been included because one never knows when they may reappear. Most others included in the rating list, but not currently described, will be reported in detail in the upcoming set of change pages scheduled for 1993. Purging them from my current data base would require extensive work and is not warranted in view of the fact that they would soon have to be added back in. Also, the rating list has been intentionally separated from the descriptive text to allow the ability to change scores without necessarily changing the descriptions and to provide a quick look-up capability. It also allows easy addition to the rating list for new beers using a SORT command.

DETAILS

In describing thousands of brews, accuracy is not the only objective. There is a need for a certain degree of precision, but this must not be carried out to the point where it becomes pedantic. After all, this is basically a notebook, a record of beer-tasting experience.

Where there are multiple features, the most prominent is named first. For example, a brew that is described as having a nose of hops and malt will smell most noticeably of hops, but there will be malt in there as well. Rarely will I mention a specific variety of hops, for the hops used in the recipe may change because of supply problems or simply because the brewer wishes to change the style. Although the types of malt, yeast, and fermentation times and temperatures have an effect, the hops used in making the brew are the most notable feature in establishing a style. If you want to make an English-style ale, Golding and Fuggle hops will give you a good start. Hallertau and Tettnanger will give a German style lager, and so forth. In those few cases where I have found significant differences in the taste (or aroma) of different batches of brew, they are noted, but this happens rarely after a brand has become established.

I place great stock in balance and aftertaste. The balance is the measure of just how well the various components (hops, malt, carbonation, etc.) fit together when they are on your palate. Nothing should clash. The aftertaste is very important because it is the last thing about the beer you will experience and may be the only thing you will remember about the brew. Some features (such as carbonation level) are mentioned only when they are noticeable, as when overdone or lacking.

Lactic acid, which presents itself as a spiciness in wheat beer, is not necessarily viewed as a bad feature. In fact, when intended it can be most attractive if it is balanced in with the other flavors, giving great depth of character. It is a dominant (and intended) feature of many Belgian beers. There are times, however, when it is not intentional, too strong, or out of control. In those cases the excess acid will be noted as a flaw.

There are other flavor and aroma features of beer worth a brief comment. The citrus quality of many West Coast beers comes from the hops. It is intentional. Hops can also give interesting, complex odors of clover, verbena, sage, and parsley in addition to the orange, lemon, and grapefruit. Vinousness, or a wine-like quality, indicates the presence of esters formed by the reaction of an acid and an alcohol. While it may be attractive in an ale, it is rarely attractive in a pilsener. High alcohol content may also give beer a wine-like quality.

Leather, paper, cardboard, and woody smells and tastes indicate that the beer has oxidized. This is almost never helpful. Soapiness is the presence of octanoic or capryilic acid and is tolerable only if so weak it is barely noticeable. A cheese-like feature is caused by the presence of isovaleric acid resulting from the oxidation of amyl alcohol. A smell or taste of banana indicates that there is amyl acetate in the brew. Corn is the presence of dimethyl sulfide. Green apple tells us that there is acetylaldehyde and that the beer is oxidizing. Butter or butterscotch comes from diacetyl, a diketone. An aroma like nail polish remover is just that: acetone, probably caused by bacterial fermentation of corn mash. Rancid butter smell is from butyric acid and may be caused by oxidation or the action of anaerobic bacteria on lactic acid. A wet, moldy-basement smell comes from the same source as the rancidity. Mercaptans cause rubber, boot, and skunk smells. These result from complex chemical processes involving the sulfhydril bodies present in hop resins. Medicinal smells come from phenolics, soluble acidic compounds derived from the actions of a phenol with an aldehyde. As you can imagine, none of the above are considered desirable, and brewmasters expend considerable effort in avoiding them. Where I found them, however, I was obliged to mention them, since they may be the result of shoddy workmanship or a short shelf life (which means that unless you are certain that the beer is fresh on the shelf, you are likely to get a faulty product).

To fulfill the objective of this book, the reader should add his or her own notes to complete it. Since it is in looseleaf format, it can be reconfigured in any manner desired. It is highly recommended that the owner of *The Beer Log* obtain the annual update issues to keep the book current. If you have access to brews not listed, and wish to supply me with samples for inclusion in future updating efforts, I will be happy to provide you in return with brews you cannot obtain where you are. Please write to me first, however, since I am doing my best to stay ahead of you and we need not waste each other's funds shipping items back and forth unnecessarily. Write me at 57 Heights Terrace, Fair Haven, NJ 07704. I reside in New Jersey, California, and Nova Scotia, Canada, depending on the time of year, so the preferred shipping destination will vary according to season.

The Beer Log should bring great satisfaction and pleasure to beer lovers. It can be carried on beer-hunting trips, serving as the owner's personal log of beers tasted, adding one's own perceptions of the brews (no matter what the author says!). It is a great gift for the beer lover who has everything else. It may give a new direction to beer fans—variety and appreciation, rather than mere quantity.

CANARY ISLANDS

Sical, S.A.

Brewery in **Las Palmas**

TROPICAL EXPORT PILS BEER — bright gold, hop aroma, all hop palate, sour finish and aftertaste.

ETHIOPIA

Almaza Brewery

Brewery in **Almaza**

ALMAZA PILSENER — gold, a little skunky first, but this soon clears to a malt and hop nose, light body, light malt and hop flavor, dull malty aftertaste.

Asmara Brewery

Brewery in **Asmara**

ASMARA LAGER BEER — deep bright gold, big malt nose, good body, big malt flavor, long dry hop aftertaste.

Notes:

Ethiopian Beverage Co.

Brewery in **Harar**

HARAR BEER — pale gold, slightly toasted malt aroma and flavor, burnt malt appears in the fairly long aftertaste.

GAMBIA

Banjul Breweries, Ltd.

Brewery in **Banjul**

JULBREW LAGER — yellow-gold, caramel-malt aroma, malt flavor reflects some of the caramel, medium to good body, light off-dry malt aftertaste.

IVORY COAST

Solibra Abidjan

Brewery in **Abidjan**

MAMBA MALT LIQUOR — bright gold, fine carbonation, beautiful malt nose, pleasant-tasting complex malt flavor, big body, long off-sweet malt aftertaste.

KENYA

Kenya Breweries, Ltd.

Brewery in **Nairobi**

TUSKER MALT LAGER — pale gold, dry malt nose, lightly sweet malt flavor, candy and hop finish, strong dry and bitter hop aftertaste.

LIBERIA

Monrovia Breweries, Inc.

Brewery in **Monrovia**

MONROVIA CLUB BEER — bright deep gold, hop nose, vegetal malt flavor, improves to just plain malt at the finish, dry hop aftertaste has a sour component.

Notes:

MALTA

Simonds Farsons Cisk, Ltd.

Brewery in **Valletta**

FARSONS SHANDY — bright gold, cointreau-like nose, light fruit flavor, really no beer taste at all, light body, pleasant, but not really like a shandy, which is fruit juice (like lemonade) added to beer. The beer taste should still come through.

NIGERIA

Nigerian Breweries, Ltd.

Brewery in **Lagos**

GULDER LAGER BEER — gold, grape soda nose, grapey hop flavor and aftertaste, a very strange beer with a chemical background in the aftertaste.

STAR LAGER BEER — hazy gold, skunky hop nose and taste, long aftertaste like the flavor.

SOUTH AFRICA

South African Breweries, Ltd.

Brewery in **Johannesburg**

CASTLE LAGER — deep gold, bright hop nose and pronounced hop flavor, finely carbonated with small bubbles, straightforward hop palate lacks complexity, slightly bitter dry hop aftertaste.

HANSA PILSENER — pale gold, lovely malt and hop aroma, lots of carbonation, good balance between the hops and the malt on the palate but the flavor is marred by excessive carbonation, finishes quite tasty though, and the aftertaste is long and good with both malt and hops, excellent except for the carbonation.

ROGUE LONG BREW BEER — gold, apple-malt nose, highly carbonated, faint malt flavor, faint short hop aftertaste.

LION LAGER — pale amber, pleasant lightly malted nose, faint off-dry fruit-like flavor, little complexity, medium length off-dry malt aftertaste, very drinkable, but it has little zest.

AMSTEL LAGER — bright medium deep gold, balanced malt-hop aroma, good dry malt palate in front, becomes a little sweeter at the finish but is pleasant, some bitter hops appear in the aftertaste, which is long and good, excellent except for being too highly carbonated.

SWAZILAND

Swaziland Brewers, Ltd.

Brewery in Mbabane

SIMBA IMPORTED LAGER — pale yellow-gold, nose like Concord grapes, fairly sweet grapey flavor, highly carbonated, grapey aftertaste, like a New York wine cooler.

TOGO

B.B. Brewery

Brewery in Lome

NGOMA TOGO PILS — hazy gold, skunky nose, big hop flavor, smooth and balanced (despite the poor nose), dry hop finish and aftertaste.

NGOMA AWOOYO SPECIAL — amber, malt nose is lightly toasted but has a dank component, off-dry malt flavor has a touch of sour that is more noticeable in the finish and in the back of the long dry hop aftertaste.

Notes:

ZAIRE

SBK Brewery

Brewery in Kinshasa

NGOMA CASTEL BEER — hazy yellow-gold, fruity malt aroma, palate has an off-dry malt front, a dry middle, and an off-dry malt finish, medium body, short dry malt aftertaste.

Notes:

CHINA

Beijing Brewery

Brewery in **Beijing (Peking)**

MON-LEI BEER — gold, off-dry malt nose and flavor, fairly dry hop finish, long dry aftertaste, good balance, good body.

FIVE STAR BEER — pale gold, off-dry malt nose, toasted (a bit burnt) malt flavor and long aftertaste. Also has been seen as SPECIALLY BREWED FIVE STAR BEER.

NINE STAR PREMIUM BEER — gold, hop nose, good malt and hop flavor, good body, some complexity, off-dry finish, long dry hop aftertaste. Brewery named as being Five Star Brewery.

Chu Jiang Brewery

Brewery in **Guangzhou (Canton)**

CHU SING BEER — pale gold, light off-dry grainy malt aroma, off-dry malt flavor has a papery finish, long dull malt and sour hop aftertaste.

Feng Shon Brewery

Brewery in **Beijing (Peking)**

PEKING BEER — pale gold, clean malt aroma, fruity malt flavor, hop finish, off-dry malt aftertaste, pleasant but without much complexity.

Guang Dong Brewery

Brewery in **Sanshui**

CHANGLEE BEER — brilliant medium deep gold, faint off-dry malt nose, light body, light malt flavor, brief malt aftertaste.

Guangzhou Brewery

Brewery in **Guangzhou (Canton)**

Labels also mention Pijiuchang Brewery, Pearl River Brewery.

DOUBLE HAPPINESS GUANGZHOU BEER — pale gold, hop nose is almost skunky, high carbonation, light malt flavor in front, hops develop in the middle to finish, light body, dry hop aftertaste.

SONG HAY DOUBLE HAPPINESS BEER — gold, beautiful malt nose, mild dry malt flavor, faintly buttery in back, short dry malt aftertaste.

HUA NAN BEER — yellow-gold, pleasant malt nose, malt flavor has hops in back, hop finish and aftertaste, fairly refreshing.

BAIYUN BEER — hazy yellow, off-dry malt nose and front palate, sour hop finish and aftertaste.

CANTON LAGER BEER — gold, faint malt nose, malt flavor, big body, long malt aftertaste.

SWEET CHINA — yellow-gold, pineapple nose and flavor, smooth and round, faint finish and aftertaste, seems a bit artificial, but is flavored with real pineapple.

Huaguang Brewery

Brewery in Shanghai

PANDA BEER — bright tawny-gold, malt and light hop nose, sharp malt flavor that turns somewhat sour at the finish, this continues into the aftertaste.

Shenyang Brewery

Brewery in Shenyang

CHINA GOLD BEER — bright deep gold, hoppy ale-like nose, bright hop and malt flavor, good balance, low carbonation, good balance, some hop bite in the finish and long malt aftertaste.

SNOWFLAKE BEER — yellow-gold, hop nose has a trace of skunk, hop flavor, finish, and aftertaste is just a tad sour.

SHENYANG EXPORT SPECIAL BEER — deep gold, malt nose, lightly toasted off-dry malt flavor, light body, long off-dry malt aftertaste.

Tientan Brewery

Brewery in Beijing (Peking)

TIENTAN BEER — hazy yellow-gold, strong hop nose, big hop flavor, off-dry malt in finish, dry bitter hop aftertaste, could use more malt for better balance.

Tientsin Brewery

Brewery in Tientsin

GREAT WALL BEER — deep gold, toasted caramel malt nose, light body, good hop and malt flavor up front, but finish is bitter and burnt.

Notes:

Tsing-Tao Brewery

Brewery in Tsing-Tao

TSING-TAO BEER — tawny-yellow, malt nose, malt and hop flavor, good body, medium dry malt finish and aftertaste with plenty of hop backing.

TSING-TAO PORTER — deep brown, big roasted malt flavor with a hop finish, big body, long roasted malt and hop aftertaste.

CHINA CLIPPER BEER — pale gold, malt aroma with a hop background, dry malt flavor, hop middle, malt finish and aftertaste, pleasant and balanced.

Zhujiang Brewery

Brewery in Zhujiang (Shanghai)

YI KING CHINESE BEER — medium gold, malt nose, off-dry malt front palate, hop middle and finish, good body, dry hop aftertaste.

GOLDEN DRAGON BEER — pale gold, light fruity-malt aroma, off-dry light malt flavor, almost no hops, off-dry malt aftertaste.

ZHU JIANG BEER — pale gold, faint malt aroma, clean crisp pleasant dry malt flavor, light to medium body, dry hop aftertaste.

SHANGHAI BEER — brilliant gold, toasted malt aroma and flavor, creamy, light body, unbalanced sweet-sour aftertaste, overall pleasant. Also seen as SHANGHAI GOLDEN BEER.

YUCHUAN BEER — yellow-gold, pleasant hop nose and taste, off-dry malt finish, hops return in the long aftertaste.

CHUNG HUA BEER — pale gold, faint malt and hop nose, hops start off the palate yielding soon to off-dry malt with a spicy background, the finish and aftertaste are almost too sweet malt. Brewery named is Cian Jiang Brewery of Zhe Jiang. I feel there may be something amiss with the spelling.

CYPRUS

Cyprus, Keo, Ltd.

Brewery in Cyprus

KEO PILSENER BEER — deep cloudy yellow, tart malty aroma reminds you of rhubarb, malt flavor, low carbonation, short malt aftertaste.

FIJI

Carlton Brewery Ltd.

Brewery in Suva

FIJI BITTER BEER — tawny, faint apple and malt nose, malt flavor with a candy background, woody middle, grainy finish and aftertaste.

HONG KONG

Hong Kong Brewery, Ltd.

Brewery in Kowloon

MON-LEI BEER — pale bright yellow, malt aroma and flavor, some sour hops in the finish and aftertaste.

SUN-LIK BEER — bright yellow-gold, faint malt nose, malt and hop flavor, dry hop finish, light dry hop aftertaste.

INDIA / PAKISTAN

High Range Breweries, Ltd.

Breweries in Voranad and Kerala

KINGFISHER LAGER BEER — brilliant pale gold, big aromatic hop nose with plenty of malt, sprightly malt and hop flavor, short sour malt aftertaste.

Hindustan Breweries & Bottling, Ltd.

Brewery in Thana

BOMBAY BEER — clear tawny-gold, faint malt nose, light body, off-dry and vegetal malt palate, dull malt finish and aftertaste.

Kalyani Breweries, Ltd.

Brewery in Calcutta

TAJ MAHAL LAGER BEER — deep gold, highly carbonated, pleasant malt palate, medium body, pleasant malt aftertaste of medium length.

TAJ MAHAL PREMIUM LAGER BEER — gold, skunky/soapy nose, dull malt flavor, dry short malt aftertaste. Brewed and bottled in England for UB Ltd., Bangalore, India.

Khoday Brewing & Distilling Industries Private, Ltd.

Brewery in **Bangalore**

SOVEREIGN LAGER BEER — tawny-gold, aroma of ferruginous spring water and toasted malt, watery body, flavor like the nose, finishes good toasted malt, but there is little aftertaste.

Mohan Meakin Breweries, Ltd.

Mohan Nagar Brewery in **Ghaziabad**

GOLDEN EAGLE LAGER BEER — deep gold, pleasant off-dry malt aroma, smoky-salty malt flavor that is not unpleasant, short dry malt aftertaste, hops are faint at best.

Mohan Rocky Springwater Breweries, Ltd.

Brewery in **Khopoli**

EAGLE LAGER BEER — brilliant amber-gold, dank toasted malt nose, weak toasted malt flavor, watery body, brief malt aftertaste.

Murree Brewery Co., Ltd.

Brewery in **Rawalpindi, Pakistan**

MURREE EXPORT LAGER — pale yellow-gold, off-dry malt nose, dry sour malt flavor, long dry and bitter hop aftertaste.

Notes:

Sheeba Breweries (P.V.) Ltd.

Breweries in **India**

INDIAN GURU LAGER BEER — bright gold, aroma is almost skunky, but not quite, instead is hops and banana, hop flavor with malt in back and good complexity, long dry hop and malt aftertaste. Brewed and bottled in England for Sheeba Breweries.

INDONESIA

P.T. San Miguel Brewery

Brewery in **Tambun, Bekasi**

One of the San Miguel, Manila, breweries.

SAN MIGUEL BEER — deep gold, pleasant malt aroma with good hop background, palate to match, long dry hop aftertaste.

SAN MIGUEL DARK BEER — deep red-brown, rich off-dry toasted malt nose, complex toasted malt and licorice flavor, pleasant long malt aftertaste.

Notes:

ISRAEL

National Breweries, Ltd.

A national amalgamation of breweries in **Tel Aviv, Bat Yam,** and **Netanza**

MACCABEE PREMIUM BEER — gold, creamy head, soft malt nose, crisp malt and hop flavor is fairly dry at finish, high carbonation, pleasant dry brief malt and hop aftertaste. Tempo Beer Industries, Ltd., Netyana.

GOLD STAR — amber, big off-dry malt nose at first, but it quickly fades, flavor starts out off-dry as well, but dries at the middle, dry malt finish, medium body, medium to long dry malt aftertaste. Tempo Beer Ind.

BEERSHEBA PREMIUM — gold, hop nose, sour hop flavor, high carbonation, medium body, light malt aftertaste with little duration.

Notes:

JAPAN

Asahi Breweries

Brewery in **Tokyo, Japan**

ASAHI LAGER BEER — very pale gold, clean fresh spring water and malt nose, flavor like the nose, very light and inoffensive, little aftertaste.

ASAHI DRAFT BEER — bright gold, light hop and malt aroma, light grapey hop flavor, dry hop finish and aftertaste.

ASAHI SUPER DRY — light gold, faint apple malt nose, light body, weak malt flavor, short weak dull malt aftertaste.

ASAHI "Z" DRAFT BEER — deep gold, hop and malt nose, light malt flavor, dry hop finish, long dry hop aftertaste.

COORS BEER — light gold, clean light grainy nose, pleasant off-dry malt flavor, light body, long pleasant malt aftertaste.

Kirin Brewery Co., Ltd.

Twelve breweries in Japan, including **Tokyo** and **Kyobashi**

KIRIN BEER — pale yellow-gold, off-dry malt nose, flavor has more hops than malt, hop finish and aftertaste are light and long, medium body, clean tasting.

KIRIN LIGHT BEER — bright gold, faint off-dry malt and hop nose, very light hop and malt flavor, light dry malt finish, brief dry malt aftertaste.

KIRIN DRAFT BEER — bright gold, faint malt aroma and flavor, faint dry hop finish and aftertaste.

KIRIN FINE MALT — deep gold, big hop and malt nose, good body, flavor is malt in front, hops in back, medium dry long malt aftertaste.

KIRIN ICHIBAN — hazy gold, grainy malt nose, malt flavor, hop finish, medium length.

KIRIN DRY DRAFT BEER — brilliant gold, light perfumy malt nose, very dry malt flavor, finish, and aftertaste.

BUDWEISER BEER — pale yellow-gold, almost no aroma at all, light body, very dry malt flavor with hops in back, brief faint malt aftertaste.

HEINEKEN BEER — bright gold, faint malt nose, malt flavor with hops faintly in back, hop finish, brief dry hop aftertaste.

Orion Breweries

Brewery in Nago, Okinawa

ORION LAGER BEER — deep yellow-gold, malt aroma and flavor, light hops in the finish and aftertaste.

Sapporo Breweries, Ltd.

Brewery in Tokyo

SAPPORO LAGER BEER — medium gold, mellow hoppy nose, pleasant hop flavor has good malt in support, brief dry hop aftertaste.

SAPPORO DRAFT BEER — hazy gold, fruity malt and apple peel nose, plenty of malt throughout palate, dry hop aftertaste.

SAPPORO BLACK BEER — opaque red-brown, heavy malt aroma with a tang in back, flavor like the nose, medium body, creamy texture, faintly sour malt aftertaste.

NEXT ONE LIGHT AND TASTY DRAFT BEER — pale gold, sour hop nose, high carbonation, light body, faint malt and hop palate, faint dry hop aftertaste.

YEBISU DRAFT BEER — deep gold, good beery nose with plenty of hops, zesty dry flavor has more hops than malt, additional malt would help the balance, hop finish, long dry hop aftertaste.

YEBISU PREMIUM DRAFT BEER — deep hazy gold, big malt and hop nose, big body, hefty malt flavor, long, long dry malt and hop aftertaste.

SAPPORO DRAFT DRY — brilliant gold, very light perfumy malt aroma, very dry malt flavor, dry malt finish and aftertaste, not much to it.

SAPPORO DRAFT THE WINTER'S TALE — gold, dank malt nose, crisp dry malt flavor tastes better as you continue to drink it, dry malt finish and aftertaste.

YEBISU DRAFT STOUT — deep gold, pleasant malt nose, alcoholic malt flavor, medium body, smooth, dry malt aftertaste.

SAPPORO SPECIAL CLEAN MALT DRAFT BEER — gold, hop nose, medium dry malt flavor, dry hop finish and aftertaste, good length.

SAPPORO MALT 100 ALL MALT BEER — medium deep gold, big grainy malt and hop nose, good body, clean malt flavor, long malt aftertaste with hops faintly in back.

Suntory, Ltd.

Breweries in Osaka and Tokyo

SUNTORY REAL DRAFT BEER — gold, faint malt aroma, medium body, carbonation dominates the flavor which is malt and apple peel, dull dry malt finish and aftertaste.

SUNTORY BEER — bright pale gold, dull faintly hopped nose is a little stinky, flavor is dull malt and hops, dry hop finish, and the aftertaste is dry sour hops.

SUNTORY MALT'S ALL MALT BEER — very deep gold, big grainy malt nose, good body, slightly off malt flavor, long dry hop aftertaste.

KOREA

Chosun Brewery Co., Ltd.

Brewery in Seoul

CROWN LAGER BEER — pale gold, faint malt and hop nose, faint sweetness way in back, flavor is off-dry malt with hops, medium body, fair duration.

CROWN DRY — hazy yellow, faint malt and hop nose, light papery malt flavor, short dry aftertaste.

Notes:

Oriental Brewery Co., Ltd.

Brewery in Seoul

ORIENTAL OB LAGER BEER — pale gold, light malt and apple peel aroma and flavor, mostly a dry malt finish and aftertaste.

OB DRY BEER — bright gold, hop nose, palate is sweet malt up front, watery hop finish, light short dry hop aftertaste.

MALAYA

Malayan Breweries Pte., Ltd.

Brewery in Singapore

Archipelago Brewery Co. (1947), Ltd.

ANCHOR PILSENER BEER — deep gold, hop and malt nose, slightly roasted malt flavor, malt-hop finish, decent balance, good body, long malt and hop aftertaste.

TIGER GOLD MEDAL LAGER BEER — gold, good malt and hop nose, light malt flavor with apple peel in finish, dull malt and hop aftertaste.

NEW GUINEA

Papua New Guinea Pty, Ltd.

Brewery in Port Moresby

One of the San Miguel, Manila-owned breweries.

SAN MIGUEL PILSNER BEER — medium gold, malt nose, woody malt flavor, faint dry hop aftertaste.

SAN MIGUEL NEGRA DARK BEER — pale red-brown, dry roasted malt nose and similar but drier flavor, dry hop finish and aftertaste.

SP Brewery, Ltd.

Brewery in Papua

SOUTH PACIFIC SPECIAL EXPORT LAGER — pale gold, pleasant malt aroma with hops in back, palate is off-dry malt in front, dry in the middle and finish, off-dry malt aftertaste.

Notes:

PHILIPPINES

Asia Brewery, Inc.

Brewery in **Manila**

MANILA GOLD PALE PILSEN BEER — pale bright gold, sweet fruit-like aroma, very dry hop flavor, finish, and aftertaste.

San Miguel Brewery

Brewery in **Manila** is one of three in the Philippines.

SAN MIGUEL BEER — pale yellow-gold, complex malt and strong hop nose, creamy and fresh tasting, excellent balance, good fresh malt and hop flavor, long refreshing dry hop aftertaste.

SAN MIGUEL PALE PILSEN — pale straw yellow, malt nose is a bit grainy, malt flavor with light hop background, medium body, light dry hop aftertaste.

SAN MIGUEL DARK BEER — deep red-brown, light rich toasted malt aroma, well-balanced rich malt and hop flavor, toffee-mint finish, long refreshing malt and hop aftertaste, marvelous big-bodied brew is very satisfying.

RED HORSE MALT LIQUOR — pale gold, faint winey malt nose, fruity malt flavor is refreshing but not complex, slight hop tang in the aftertaste.

SAMOA

Western Samoa Breweries, Ltd.

Brewery in **Apia**

RAINMAKER IMPORTED PREMIUM BEER — tawny-gold, faintly skunky hop nose, complex flavor is hops at first, then light off-dry malt, long off-dry malt aftertaste.

Notes:

TAHITI

Brasserie de Tahiti

Brewery in **Papeete**

HINANO TAHITI LAGER BEER — pale gold, malt aroma with good hops, clean bright hop and off-dry malt flavor, light body, dry light hop finish and aftertaste.

TAIWAN

Taiwan Tobacco & Wine Monopoly Bureau

Brewery in **Taipeh**

DYNASTY TAIWAN BEER — deep yellow-gold, rich appetizing malt aroma, clean malt flavor is lightly toasted, long clean malt aftertaste, pleasant drinkable brew when fresh.

DYNASTY PREMIUM DRY BEER — pale gold, pleasant malt nose with good hops, good tasting off-dry malt flavor, light body, pleasant butterscotch and honeyed finish, clean long malt aftertaste.

CHINA BEER — hazy pale amber, toasted malt aroma, good toasted malt flavor, finish, and aftertaste, fairly well balanced. From Chien-Kuo Brewery.

THAILAND

Boon Rawd Brewery Co., Ltd.

Brewery in **Bangkok**

SINGHA LAGER BEER — brilliant gold, pleasant malt nose with good hop character, strong and bitter hop flavor, lingering hop aftertaste.

SINGHA LAGER STOUT — deep gold, sour grainy nose and taste with a large dose of hops that hang on into the long aftertaste, big body, strong brew.

Thai Amarit Brewery, Ltd.

Brewery in **Bangkok**

SIAM ALE — pale gold, skunky hop nose overwhelms any malt, off-dry malt front palate, hop finish, long strong hop aftertaste.

AMARIT LAGER BEER — pale gold, clean malt aroma with hops in back, too high carbonation, balanced malt and hop flavor, bitter hop aftertaste.

PAYAK LAGER BEER — medium pale gold, hop nose, dry hop and malt flavor, not balanced, dry hop finish and aftertaste.

BANGKOK BEER — pale gold, skunky nose at first but it yields to faint malt, faint malt flavor is very short.

QUALITY PRODUCT OF THAILAND
BANGKOK
BEER
NET CONTENT
11.2 FL. OZ.
(330 ML.)
FOR EXPORT ONLY
SPECIAL
BREWED
BREWED & BOTTLED BY T.A.B. BANGKOK THAILAND
IMPORTED BY LAPINEE TRADE INC. HOLLYWOOD, CA., U.S.A.
CA REDEMPTION VALUE * 5¢ REFUND NY-VT-MA-CT-

Notes:

TURKEY

Efes Breweries

Brewery in **Istanbul**

EPHESUS TURKISH PILSNER BEER — pale gold, off-dry malt aroma with the hops in back, light body, light malt flavor, light malt finish and aftertaste.

EFES PILS — deep gold, toasted malt and hop aroma, good balance, flavor like the nose, fairly complex, medium long dry malt-hop aftertaste.

EFES PILSEN — pale gold, light malt nose and taste, refreshing, long dry malt aftertaste, hops stay well in the back but are there.

Notes:

AUSTRALIA

The Brisbane Brewery Pty., Ltd.

Brewery in **Brisbane**

AUSTRALIA PREMIUM LAGER — deep gold, lovely beery malt nose, fruity malt and tart hop flavor, good body, short malt and hop aftertaste.

Carlton & United Breweries, Ltd.

Operates ten breweries.

Products export to the U.S. bear labels citing brewery of production being in Melbourne, Australia. Tooth labels (including Reschs) are from Sydney.

FOSTER'S LAGER — gold, fresh light hop and malt aroma, light body, fresh well-hopped flavor, pleasantly balanced, good finish, long dry hop aftertaste. Available on draft in the U.S., but that Foster's is made in Canada (see Molson).

FOSTER'S LIGHT LAGER — bright gold, light dry malt aroma, flavor is weak malt and carbonation, light body, faint malt aftertaste is short.

SHEAF STOUT
IMPORTED
AUSTRALIA
1 PT 9·6 FL OZ
BREWED & BOTTLED BY
CARLTON & UNITED BREWERIES (N.S.W.) PTY. LIMITED
26 BROADWAY • SYDNEY • N.S.W. • AUSTRALIA • PRODUCT OF AUSTRALIA
IMPORTED BY MISSION IMPORTS INC • LOS ANGELES • CALIF. • U.S.A.

VICTORIA BITTER ALE — yellow-gold, pungent hop nose, big hop flavor well backed with malt, big body, long dry hop aftertaste, a big hoppy brew.

ABBOTS LAGER — yellow-gold, apple-malt nose, light malt flavor, light body, finishes slightly sour, short malt aftertaste.

MELBOURNE BITTER — amber-gold, malt nose, light bitter hop flavor, light body, very sharp hop finish and aftertaste.

RESCHS SPECIAL EXPORT PILSENER — pale gold, light fresh light malt and hop aroma, good flavor is off-dry malt at first, then clean dry hops, short dry hop aftertaste. Has been labelled RESCHS PREMIUM LAGER.

TOOTHS KB LAGER — pale gold, faint malt nose, light body, light malt flavor, light dry hop finish and aftertaste.

TOOTH SHEAF STOUT — deep dark brown, almost opaque, toffee-coffee nose, big smoky coffee flavor, medium

Thos. Cooper & Sons, Ltd.

Breweries in **Upper Kensington, Burnside,** and **Leabrook**

BIG BARREL AUSTRALIAN LAGER — deep gold, faint malt aroma, light hop flavor, dry hop aftertaste, fairly dull and short.

THOS. COOPER ADELAIDE LAGER — medium bright gold, light malt and hop nose, malt flavor, fresh and zesty up front and in finish, weak in the middle, light body, off-dry malt and hop finish and aftertaste, fairly short. The description of this beer exactly matches my notes for COOPER GOLD CROWN BEER tasted here in the 1970s and early 1980s, and must be a new label for that product.

Note: Cooper has previously exported an excellent line of brews to the U.S. including a stout and a real ale. Both were excellent, but are not presently available.

Matilda Bay Brewing Co.

Brewery in **Fremantle**

RED BACK MALTED WHEAT BEER — bright gold, big head, fruity malt aroma, off-dry malt flavor with a sharp and spicy component that continues on into the aftertaste, light body.

Mildura Brewery, Ltd.

Brewery in **Mildura**

DOWN UNDER LAGER BEER — tawny-gold, vegetal malt nose, winey malt flavor up front, bitter hop finish, dull malt aftertaste.

Northern Breweries Pty., Ltd.

Brewery in **Mildura**

KANGAROO BEER — bright gold, grainy malt nose, off-dry malt flavor up front, hop middle is quite bitter, dry hop finish and aftertaste.

South Australia Brewing Company

Breweries in **Adelaide** and **Thebarton**

BROKEN HILL LAGER BEER — pale gold, faint malty cider nose, hop flavor, dry hop aftertaste with little length.

OLD AUSTRALIA STOUT — opaque brown, fruity-winey complex toasted malt nose, dry toasted malt flavor, off-dry malt finish, long dry malt aftertaste with concentration.

SOUTHWARK PREMIUM LAGER BEER — deep gold, off-dry apple peel and malt aroma, off-dry malt palate, some roasted malt in back. dry malt aftertaste, very little discernible hop character.

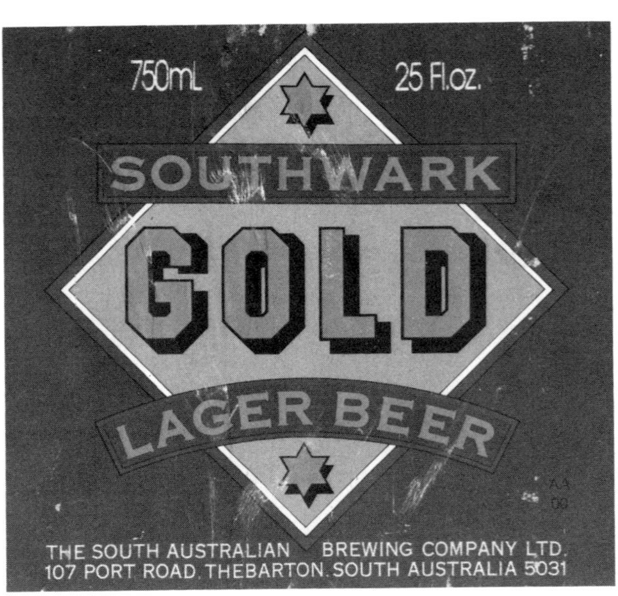

WEST END EXPORT BEER — gold, big hop nose, slightly roasted malt and hop flavor, dry hop finish and aftertaste, good length, good flavor.

SOUTHWARK GOLD LAGER BEER — gold, dusty buttery malt nose with a faint sense of vinegar in back, high carbonation, off chemical taste, bad, bad, bad.

Note: This brewery previously exported a wider line of brews to the U.S., but they are not currently available.

Swan Brewery Co., Ltd.

Brewery in **Perth**

Owned by Bond Brewing New South Wales, Ltd.

SWAN EXPORT LAGER — deep gold, light malt and hop nose, light hop palate, malt finish, fairly long hop aftertaste.

Tasmanian Breweries, Pty., Ltd.

Breweries in **Hobart** and **Launceston**

Also known as Cascade Brewery Co., Ltd.

BOAGS LAGER — pale gold, light malt and perfumy hop nose, good body, light malt flavor, hop finish, short dry hop aftertaste.

BOAGS DRAUGHT BEER — bright gold, faint apple nose, very little beer flavor, just some faint apple and malt fizzy water with a trace of hops in the finish, long faint dry hop aftertaste.

BOAGS XXX ALE — pale yellow, light malt nose, light off-dry malt flavor, light hop finish, short dry light hop aftertaste.

BOAGS PREMIUM LAGER — deep gold, hop nose, flavor is malt first, thence hops, light body, short dry hop aftertaste.

BOAGS PREMIUM LIGHT — bright gold, nice beery grainy malt nose, light body, light malt flavor with a slight vegetal character, light malt finish and aftertaste.

RAZOR'S EDGE LAGER BEER — gold, faint malt nose, high carbonation, hop flavor, finish, and aftertaste, end well but could use more flavor up front.

NEW ZEALAND

Dominion Breweries, Ltd.

Brewery in Auckland

DB EXPORT BEER — medium gold, dry but fruity malt nose, winey malt palate has a berry-like nature, hops come in at the finish, dry hop aftertaste.

DOUBLE BROWN BEER — hazy amber, apple-malt nose, off-dry malt flavor and finish, long malt aftertaste is a bit drier than the flavor.

KIWI LAGER — bright gold, perfumy clean malt nose, bright slightly off-dry malt flavor, medium body, clean light hop aftertaste with good duration.

Independent Breweries, Ltd.

Brewery in Auckland

NEW ZEALAND PREMIUM LAGER BEER — hazy gold, light malt nose, light malt flavor is a bit off-dry, seems to get sweeter in the finish and aftertaste.

Notes:

Leopard Breweries, Ltd.

Brewery in Hastings

LEOPARD LAGER — gold, sweet fruity malt nose reminds you of pineapple, off-dry malt flavor has hops in back, light body, flavor doesn't develop and ends weakly with carbonation and dry hops.

LEOPARD EXPORT LAGER BEER — pale gold, malt nose has a pine needle and sour background, fruity malt flavor, sour hop finish, dry sour hop aftertaste has an apple background.

LEOPARD STRONG BEER — tawny gold, sour fruity malt aroma, malt flavor has some apple-like tones, light sour malt aftertaste.

Lion Breweries, Ltd.

Brewery in Auckland

STEINLAGER NEW ZEALAND LAGER BEER — pale gold, lovely aroma is more hops than malt, good hop flavor up front, off-dry malt develops in the mid-palate, dry hop aftertaste with that malt in the background, good balance, good tasting, lots of character and very drinkable.

Notes:

AUSTRIA

Adambräu, G.M.B.H.

Brewery at **Innsbruck**

TIROL EXPORT LAGER — amber, off-dry roasted malt and caramel nose, lightly roasted malt palate, hops from middle-on, long hop aftertaste.

ADAM CLASSIC — gold, hop nose, malt flavor, high carbonation, hop finish, dry hop aftertaste.

ADAM HELLES EXPORT — gold, grainy nose seems a bit oat-like, malt flavor with hops in back, dull malt finish, long dry hop and malt aftertaste.

ADAM DUNKEL — brown, dry malt nose, off-dry malt flavor, medium body, off-dry malt finish, fairly dry malt aftertaste, reminds you of a malta (malz bier).

ADAM FESTBIER — brown color, big roasted malt nose, dry roasted malt flavor, finish and aftertaste like the flavor, smooth, balanced, and tasty.

EUROPE

Burgerbräu Kaiser

Brewery in **Innsbruck**

INNSBRUCK IMPORTED LAGER BEER — bright gold, big hop nose, flavor is hops and only hops all the way through to the long hop aftertaste. Not especially bitter, just hops and nothing but hops.

KAISER MÄRZEN FASSTYP — gold, big malt nose, malt flavor is dry, dry malt finish and aftertaste.

KAISER KÜR PILS — gold, hop nose, sour hop flavor, dry hop finish and aftertaste.

KAISER PREMIUM — gold, bright hop nose, good malt and hop flavor has a piquant-spicy-tangy nature, balanced and smooth, finishes malt, dry hop aftertaste.

Notes:

Brauerei Eggenberg

Brewery in **Vorchdorf**

EGGENBERGER SCHLOSSPILS BEER — bright gold, light hop nose, malt flavor, light hop and malt aftertaste, little duration.

EGGENBERGER URBOCK 17 — medium deep bright gold, good malt and hop nose, big hop flavor with plenty of malt, big body, complex, malt really develops well at the finish and into the long aftertaste. A very good bock.

EGGENBERGER URBOCK 23 — amber, lovely roasted malt nose, huge body, great malt flavor, really fills your mouth and senses, smooth despite its size, very long malt aftertaste, a great sipping beer.

MacQUEENS NESSIE WHISKEY MALT RED BEER — hazy amber, excellent lightly toasted malt nose, huge malt flavor, very heavy body, all malt and very, very long, can't call it dry but it is not at all sweet despite the large amount of malt, 7.5% alc/vol and a 17° density.

Notes:

Privatbrauerei Fritz Egger

Brewery in Unterradlberg

EGGER PILS — yellow-gold, roasted malt nose and taste, long roasted malt flavor.

EGGER NATUR-BRÄU — gold, hop nose with plenty of malt, big soapy malt and hop flavor, a very good-tasting flavor, high carbonation, dry malt and hop finish and aftertaste.

Gosser Brauerei A.G.

Brewery in Loeben-Goss

Affiliated with Steirische Brauindustrie, A.G.

GOSSER GOLDEN ROCK FAMOUS AUSTRIAN BEER — gold, light malt and hop aroma, malt and hop flavor, hop finish, dry hop aftertaste.

GOSSER BEER — pale gold, malt nose with hops in back, smooth malt and hop flavor, dry hop finish and aftertaste.

GOSSER EXPORT BEER — deep bright gold, big hop aroma, smooth hop flavor, aftertaste is hops and malt, medium body.

GOSSER STIFTSBRÄU — extremely deep red-brown, slightly toasted malt nose, off-dry roasted malt flavor, medium to good body, malt finish and aftertaste, could use a little more hops for better balance and complexity.

GOSSER HELLER BOCK — medium deep gold, light hop and malt aroma, balanced hop and malt flavor, more hops than malt, however; medium-length hop aftertaste. Very big and good-tasting brew.

GOSSER MAERZEN — gold, pleasant malt nose, big malt and hop flavor on the sour side, dry sour malt and hop aftertaste.

Notes:

Harmer K.G./ Ottakringer Brauerei

Brewery in Vienna

OTTAKRINGER FASSL GOLD EXPORT LAGER BEER — brilliant gold, lovely hop aroma, finely balanced hop and malt flavor, good body, clean bright taste throughout, pleasant hop finish, long appetizing hop aftertaste, a very good beer.

OTTAKRINGER GOLD FASSL PILS — pale bright gold, faint hop and malt aroma, hop flavor, finish, and aftertaste.

OTTAKRINGER BOCK — tawny gold, beautiful complex hop and malt nose, big malt flavor with a lot of hop character, big body, richly flavored, lingering aftertaste like the flavor.

OTTAKRINGER HELLES BIER — gold, huge hop nose, flavor is mostly malt, hop finish, dry light hop aftertaste.

Vereinigte Kärtner Brauereien A.G.

Brewery in Villach

VILLACHER GOLD EXPORT BEER — gold, good malt aroma with light hops, light body, hop flavor is best up front, flattens and weakens to the finish, light dry hop aftertaste.

Österreichische Brauerei A.G.

Breweries in Linz, Weiselburg, Kaltenhausen (Salzburg), et al.

AUSTRIAN GOLD LAGER BEER — gold, rising hop nose with an off-dry malt background, medium dry hop flavor, dull dry hop and malt aftertaste.

ADLER BRÄU EXPORT — amber, light toasted malt nose, hop flavor, bitter hop aftertaste.

EDELWEISS HEFETRUB-WEIZENBIER — hazy gold, very sweet malt nose, good-tasting bright malt flavor with a spicy background, toasted malt and spicy clove finish and long clean aftertaste, very refreshing Weizenbier. From Hofbräu Kaltenhausen.

EDELWEISS KRISTALLKLAR WEIZENBIER — hazy gold, fruity estery nose (banana?), refreshing light spicy flavor, zesty and bright, fairly long aftertaste. From Hofbräu Kaltenhausen.

EDELWEISS WEIZENBIER DUNKEL — hazy amber, fruity-berry aroma, with a faint estery character (again, banana?), this time the banana is in with the wheat and a spicy bite in the flavor, long spicy hop and malt aftertaste. From Hofbräu Kaltenhausen.

Brauerei Schwechat A.G.

Brewery in Vienna

STEFFL EXPORT — gold, malt nose and taste, hop finish, dry hop aftertaste.

VIENNA LAGER BEER — gold, lovely malt and hop nose, highly hopped palate, hop finish, long dry hop aftertaste, medium body, little complexity.

Steirische Brauindustrie, A.G./Br. Puntigam/ Bruder Reininghaus Brauerei A.G.

Breweries in Graz and Puntigam

PUNTIGAMER PANTHER GENUINE DRAFT BEER — gold, malt nose, malt and bitter hop flavor and finish, long bitter aftertaste.

PUNTIGAMER PANTHER DARK MALT BEER — deep brown, big malt nose, rich dark malt flavors, some chocolate and coffee notes, medium body, long dry malt aftertaste, good rich malt all the way across the palate, good balance, drinkable.

PUNTIGAM EXPORT BEER — deep gold, dry hop nose, flavor is dry hops in front, malt at the finish, long dry malt and hop aftertaste.

PUNTIGAMER MAERZENBIER — gold, big malt nose, very dry malt flavor and aftertaste.

Notes:

Privatbrauerei Josef Sigl

Brewery in Obertrum am See

WEIZEN GOLD DUNKELES HEFEWEIZEN — hazy amber, foamy, malt nose with a lactic acid background like cloves, off-dry malt front palate, spicy middle and finish, good body, too much carbonation as it interferes with the flavors which are otherwise balanced, long spicy malt aftertaste.

WEIZEN GOLD HEFEWEIZENBIER — slightly hazy gold, spicy complex clove nose and big spicy flavor, creamy, lively, tasty, a sprightly dry malt finish with the spiciness in back, long aftertaste like the finish.

WEIZEN GOLD CHAMPAGNER WEIZENBIER — pale gold, malt nose, spice is there but it is very faint, more a dry sparkling malt flavor, dry malt finish and aftertaste. It is Champagne-like.

Brauerei Stiegl

Brewery in Salzburg

STIEGL GOLDBRÄU — deep golden amber, big malt nose, big malt front palate, vanishes in the middle, dull malt finish and long dull malt aftertaste.

STIEGL WEIHNACHTSBOCK — deep gold, faint off-dry malt nose, huge malt flavor, heavy body, rich and full flavored, complex, rich malt finish, feels good in your mouth, long malt aftertaste holds the richness of the flavor, very satisfying, a marvelous brew.

COLUMBUS MÄRZEN — amber-gold, light clean hop and malt nose, flavor is strong hops at first, smooths out a bit, malt comes in at the middle and stays through the finish and into the aftertaste, good complexity, good balance.

COLUMBUS GOLDEN BOCK — bright deep gold, toasted malt and hop nose, hops dominate front palate, lacks a middle, malt at the finish and aftertaste, not much complexity, so-so balance.

COLUMBUS FESTIVAL DARK — deep ruby color, roast malt aroma and flavor, off-dry malt finish, medium body, long sweet malt aftertaste. It is luscious but heavy and filling; one would probably be enough.

Notes:

Zipfer Bräu/ Brauerei Zipf

Breweries identified as being in **Zipf, Austria,** on export labels and **Rezpt, Austria,** on domestic labels.

Older labels state affiliation with Österreichische Bräu A.G. and use the name Brauerei Zipf Vorm Wm. Schaup.

ZIPFER URTYP LAGER BEER — pale gold, bright hop nose, big hop flavor, overdone hops, bitter hop finish and aftertaste.

ZIPFER BIER IMPORTED LAGER BEER — gold, lovely hop nose that shows a lot of malt given some time, good hop flavor, especially in the middle, long bitter hop aftertaste, better balance than the beer above.

ZIPFER MÄRZEN — pale gold, mild hop nose, high carbonation, pleasant lightly hopped flavor with some malt, short hop and sour malt aftertaste. This was found in the U.S.; the version found in Austria had a malt nose, hefty malt flavor, medium body, dry malt finish and aftertaste. Not any better than the export version, but definitely more of a Maerzen in style.

ZIPFER JOSEFI BOCK — gold, big malt nose, hops are in back, huge malt flavor goes on and on, alcoholic, powerful, yet stays balanced, a really great brew at 7.1% alc/vol and a density of 16.2°.

AZORES

S. Miguel

Brewery in **Azores**

ESPECIAL — orange-gold color, off-dry slightly dank malt aroma, off-dry almost too sweet malt flavor, soft finish, slightly sweet malt aftertaste; if there are hops I couldn't find them.

Notes:

BELGIUM

Brasserie de Abbaye de Leffe

Abbey brewery in **Dinant**

Other Abbaye de Leffe brews are made by Brasserie St. Guibert.

ABBEY DE LEFFE BIERE LUXE — deep reddish orange-brown, good malt nose, off-dry malt flavor, clean and bright, not flabby or cloying, long sour malt aftertaste.

Brie de l'Ancre/ Brij Het Anker

Brewery in **Mechelen**

GOUDEN CAROLUS (CAROLUS D'OR) — deep red-brown, big clean roasted malt aroma, great complexity, sweet and delicious sipping beer, marvelous for dessert, 7.5% alcohol.

TOISON D'OR — hazy gold, tart ale nose, zesty ale flavor, plenty of hops, big body, long malt and hop aftertaste, balanced and sprightly, good brew.

TRIPLE TOISON D'OR — hazy yellow, great complex citrus hop nose, big strong flavor with lots of both hops and malt, big body, vinous, sour licorice aftertaste, very good brew with considerable alcohol (7%).

Bierbrouwerijen Arcense

Brewery in **Arcense**

MAGNUS — cloudy brown, light malt aroma, heavy body, winey, alcoholic (7%), creamy, tasty malt flavor, long on the palate and very good.

Notes:

Brouwerijen Artois Brasseries

Brewery in ten cities including **Leuven/Louvain**

STELLA ARTOIS — gold, sour malt aroma with good hops, big hop flavor and finish, clean dry hop aftertaste with good length.

LOBURG BIERE LUXE — yellow-gold, well-hopped malt nose, big hop flavor, bitter hop aftertaste, reasonably good balance and length.

S.A. Bass N.V.

Brewery in **Mechelen**

LAMOT PILSOR BEER — yellow-gold, more hops than malt in the nose, strong hop flavor with a sour malt background, aftertaste like the flavor.

BASS OLD BARLEY STOUT — opaque brown, brown head, off-dry malt nose, rich malt palate, nicely balanced, dry malt finish and aftertaste.

P.H. Vandenstock, S.A., Brasserie Belle-Vue

Brewery in **Brussels**

GUEZE BELLE-VUE — cloudy amber, sour summer sausage nose, strong sweet malt flavor, strong lambic background, long aftertaste like the flavor.

BELLE-VUE CREAM BEER — deep gold, good smooth lambic nose of grain, fruity wheat, and faint lactic acid, good citrus-like flavor and long aftertaste.

BELLE-VUE KRIEK BEER — cherry red, foamy, cherry-lambic nose with good cherry candy up front, clean but very sweet, very long on the palate like a liqueur, quite good of the type.

Bry de Block

Brewery in **Merchtem**

SATAN ALE — hazy amber, big head, lemony nose, strong sweet and sour palate, lots of lemony-lactic bite, long aftertaste.

Brouwerij Bockor

Brewery in **Grimbergen**

JACOBINS KRIEK LAMBIC — cherry-red color, clean fresh spicy cherry aroma, low carbonation, short aftertaste, sweet black cherry soda with a little bite.

GUEZE LAMBIC JACOBINS — brilliant amber, no nose, sour, sweet, and bitter flavor, finish, and aftertaste, no balance and no style.

Bosteels Family Brewery

Brewery in **Buggenhout**

KWAK PAUWEL — garnet, delicate and slightly sweet malt, licorice, and coffee bean nose, good tangy malt flavor, sour malt finish, long dry malt aftertaste, not complex but big and bright.

CUPIDO NATURAL ALE — bright deep amber, malt and fruity ester nose, thin body, weak flavor, faint lactic-salty malt palate, short aftertaste.

Brasserie Centrale S.A.

Brewery in **Marbaix-la-Tour**

SAISON REGAL BIERE LUXE — pale amber, foamy, nose starts out off-dry malt but builds in sweetness as it goes until it begins to clash with the hops, the flavor is strong and sweet, very long aftertaste like the flavor.

Brouwerij Corsendonk

Brewery at **Oud Turnhout**

CORSENDONK AGNUS — deep gold, complex beautiful aroma with fruit, anise, and herbs, big flavor of roasted malt with an anise background, interesting, complex, and zesty, really lasts a long time, fine sipping beer.

CORSENDONK PATER NOSTER — cloudy amber, malt nose, foamy, big palate starts out fruity malt, finishes spicy, long hop aftertaste, complex and very long, very likeable, has plenty of alcohol (7%), but it is barely noticeable.

CORSENDONK MONK'S PALE ALE — hazy gold, fruity malt nose, big strong malt flavor, noticeable alcohol, good spicy hop character in back and in the finish, long hop and malt aftertaste, a sensational sipping beer that will knock your socks off!

CORSENDONK MONK'S BROWN ALE — cloudy brown, big malt nose, complex big malt flavor, big body, subtle and balanced, very long lasting, easy to drink.

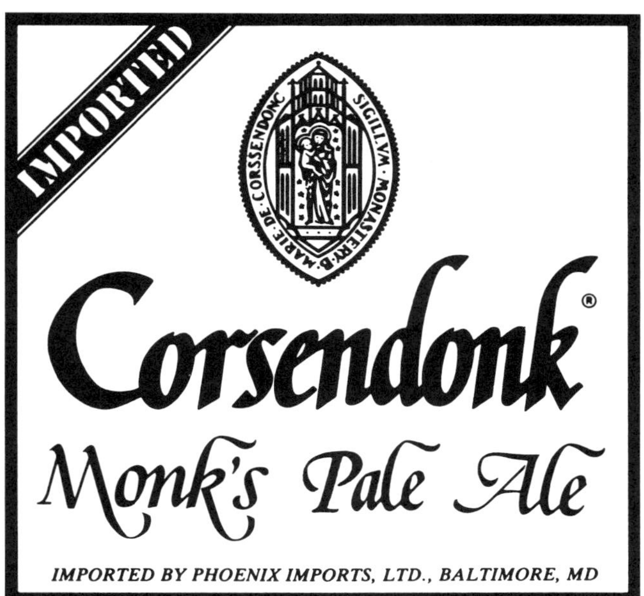

Brasserie/ Brouwerijen Dilbeek

Brewery in Itterbeek

Export labels read Timmerman's Breweries.

TIMMERMAN'S PECHE LAMBIC — hazy gold, sour peach nose, complex peach flavor with a lambic tang, very tasty, fairly dry medium long aftertaste, nicely done.

TIMMERMAN'S FRAMBOISE LAMBIC — hazy red-brown, raspberry nose, raspberry-lambic flavor, tasty, medium-length aftertaste like the flavor, nicely done as well.

N.V. De Keersmaeker S.A.

Brewery in Kobbegem

MORT SUBITE KRIEK LAMBIC — cherry-red, lightly carbonated, delicate sweet cherry aroma, tart cherry flavor, sweet and sharp at the same time, light body, good balance, lightly finished and little aftertaste.

Notes:

Brasserie de Kluis

Brewery in Hoegaarden

HOEGAARDEN WHITE ALE — cloudy yellow-white, foamy, tutti-frutti nose, sharp puckery taste, finish is softer, but the flavor obtains throughout and into the long aftertaste.

DIESTER'S BEER — fairly deep copper-red, creamy head, light fruity-malt nose, off-dry toasted malt flavor, smooth creamy texture, big body, winey and alcoholic (8%), very long aftertaste, off-dry to sweet malt throughout.

OUD HOEGAARDS BIER — hazy pale yellow, pleasant fruity-citrus nose, off-dry lemony palate, sour finish and aftertaste.

HOEGAARDEN GRAND CRU TRIPLE — hazy pale amber, lovely fruity-apple aroma, big complex grainy flavor is fruit-like in front, slightly acidic in the middle, grainy finish, strong and long, dry aftertaste, very interesting and very good, high alcohol (8.7%).

HOEGAARDEN GRAND CRU ALE — hazy gold, big foamy head, complex malt aroma with an almost citrus-like tang, big complex citrus, anise, malt, hops, alcohol, cherries, pine needles, fruit, and berry flavor, incredibly complex and the flavor really flows, balanced and very long, fascinating well-made brew, one of the most interesting beers I have ever tasted.

De Koninck Brewery

Brewery in Antwerp

DE KONINCK — bright copper, toasted malt nose, faint lactic in back, dry hop flavor is astringent on the palate, long, long dry hop aftertaste.

De Smedt Brewery

Brewery in Opwijk

AFFLIGEM TRIPLE ABBEY BEER — deep amber, tangy hop nose, big fruity hop flavor, huge and complex, very long and very good.

Notes:

Brie Dubusson Frères

Breweries in **Pipaix** and **Tournai**

BUSH BEER STRONG ALE — copper color, off-dry candy fruit nose, heavy body, concentrated flavor is off-dry up front, bitter in the middle, sour at the end, high alcohol (9.5-10%), great length, a fascinatingly complex sipping beer. When exported to the U.S., it was labelled SCALDIS to avoid incurring the wrath of Anheuser-Busch.

Flanders Family Brewers

Brewery in **Geel**

FLANDERS FARMERS ALE — hazy rose color, light chocolate malt nose, soft yet richly flavored, smooth chocolate malt flavor, big body, long malt aftertaste. If there are hops, I can't detect them.

FLANDERS GRAND CRU TRIPLE — hazy pale amber; strong spicy complex nose was thought at first to be chemical-banana oil-odd whatever, but as time passed it was realized that it was the senses that were being overwhelmed and it was complex malt, spice, honey, hops, alcohol, and almost anything that you could think up; the palate is complex toasted malt, spice, and in the back of the palate, salty, high alcohol is ever-present, right into the long dry malt aftertaste, a very interesting sipping beer.

EUROPE

Brasserie/Brouwerij de Gouden Boom

Brewery in **Bruges**

WHITE OF BRUGES — cloudy yellow-white, light ephemeral citrus nose, complex fruity flavor, dry finish, full body, off-dry malt aftertaste.

Grimbergen Abbey (Watou Prior)

Abbey brewery at **Grimbergen**

Labels indicate other secular breweries which may have made the brews under license, a common practice by Belgian abbeys. Examples seen are Brasserie Maes in Waarloos and Brasserie L'Union in Jumet.

GRIMBERGEN DOUBLE — deep ruby-amber, big malt aroma, big complex roasted malt and hop flavor, off-dry roasted malt finish, drops off quickly, however, and there is only a weak short aftertaste.

GRIMBERGEN TRIPLE — deep gold, light fruity-malt and lychee nut aroma, big strong hop and malt flavor, alcoholic (9%), off-dry malt and hop finish and aftertaste, long and delicious, a huge delicious brew.

HET KAPPITEL — cloudy-brown, mild malt aroma, intense sweet fruity-coffee flavor, big body, tangy yet smooth, complex, dry malt finish and long aftertaste.

Huyghe Brewery

Brewery in **Melle/Ghent**

BLANC DES NEIGES — hazy gold, perfumy lemon-grapefruit soda nose, light body, dry and sour malt flavor with a pine background, fairly long aftertaste like the flavor.

MATEEN TRIPLE — gold, big head, big fruity-malt aroma, quite lemony, huge rich malt flavor, heavy body, hops emerge at the finish but they were in back all along, long delicately spiced malt aftertaste, great sipping beer.

ARTEVELDE GRAND CRU — amber, big head, faint tangy citrus light malt nose, smooth likeable malt flavor, tasty and refreshing, a malty brew for the most part but there are plenty of hops from the middle on.

Liefmans Brewery

Brewery in **Oudenaarde**

LIEFMAN'S GOUDENBAND — hazy mahogany, a complex rich aroma that includes herbs, strong citrus, prunes, Worcestershire sauce, and black cherry flavor (though it is not

a kriek beer) that gradually becomes malty, acidic background, seems a bit winey, long sour malt aftertaste. Many of the samples I tasted were spoiled even though from a period of over four years; this one was at least interesting, although it too may have suffered mishandling.

LIEFMAN'S KRIEK BIER — opaque reddish-brown, fruity cherry aroma is both sweet and sharp, zesty semi-dry cherry flavor like an aperitif, finishes more malty, long and interesting, an ale with cherries, a very good kriek.

LIEFMAN'S FRAMBOZENBIER/BIERE DE FRAMBOISES — red-brown color, almost opaque, raspberry nose, raspberry flavor together with hops and malt, long surprisingly dry aftertaste, a very interesting, likeable, and very good brew of type.

Lindeman's Farm Brewery

Brewery in Viezenbeck

LINDEMAN'S GUEZE LAMBIC BEER — cloudy peach color, strong lemony aroma, strong complex flavor with citrus, cloves, honey, malt, and hops, extremely long aftertaste like the flavor, typical gueze.

LINDEMAN'S KRIEK LAMBIC BEER — pale pink color, aroma like faint cherries laid on a gueze, complex cherry, cinnamon, and citrus flavor, the cherries mitigate the intensity of the sour lambic flavors, light body, surprisingly dry finish and aftertaste, considerable length.

FARO LAMBIC BELGIAN ALE — medium to pale copper color, lactic nose, intense sweet malt and sour lactic flavor, medium body, long tenacious sweet malt aftertaste. Faro is a lambic sweetened with candy sugar, and that's just what it tastes like.

CONTENTS: 355ML (12 FL OZ)
SPONTANE GISTING
FERMENTATION SPONTANÉE
SOLE U.S. AGENTS
Merchant DuVin CORPORATION
SEATTLE WA 98121
PÊCHE
LAMBIC
PRODUCT OF
BELGIUM
NATURAL INGREDIENTS WATER · MALT · YEAST HOPS · PEACHES
ALE WITH FRESH PEACHES ADDED
BROUWERIJ
LINDEMANS
VLEZENBEEK BELGIUM
Sole U.S. Agents Merchant DuVin Corp. Seattle, WA 98121

GUEZE LAMBIC BELGIAN ALE — cloudy-orange, fruity-lactic nose, big head, dry tangy acidic taste, dry tangy aftertaste, overall the brew is quite dry.

LINDEMAN FRAMBOISE — rosy-orange, nose like Chambord with a lambic background, the raspberries show well, sour green apple and raspberry flavor, complex, the beer (malt and hops) shows up in the finish and aftertaste. Very interesting and quite pleasant.

LINDEMAN'S PECHE LAMBIC — amber-gold, clean peach nose, bright clean peach flavor, lambic tang is in the background, very tasty and pleasant, medium length. I suspect that they toned down the lambic character for the American market.

Brasserie Maes

Brewery in Waarloos

MAES PILS — medium deep gold, lots of malt and hops in the aroma, good body, big hop flavor well backed with malt, dry hop finish and aftertaste.

Martens Brewery

Brewery in Bocholt

BOCHOLTER KWIK PILS PREMIUM BEER — pale golden amber, complex hop and faint off-dry malt aroma, complex hop flavor and finish, good body, bitter hop aftertaste.

SEZOENS BOCHOLT BELGIAN ALE — pale golden amber, complex hop and malt nose with some charcoal and lactic acid in back, flavor is more malt than hops, the charcoal and lactic acid reappear in the finish, dry malt aftertaste.

Moorgat Breweries

Brewery in Breendonk

DUVEL BELGIAN BEER — creamy copper-gold, sweet clean malty aroma, huge complex flavor that is candy and toasted malt in front, smoky in the middle, and finishes clean bright malt, long malt aftertaste, a strongly flavored brew at 8% alcohol, this is a great sipping beer.

DUVEL BELGIAN ALE — cloudy gold, big off-dry malt aroma, huge body, big complex flavor that appears intensely sweet at first, but quickly takes on a sharp hop character, long tart aftertaste, a very big flavorful brew that shows a lot of both malt and hops.

MAREDSOUS 6% — cloudy orange-brown, huge head, tangy-spicy ale aroma, zesty fruity malt, hop, and citrus flavor, assertive but not offensive, complex, extremely long aftertaste like the flavor, a dynamite brew! The Maredsous brews are an abbey beer produced under license from Brasserie de Maredsous, Denee, Belgium.

MAREDSOUS 8% — deep amber, lovely roasted malt nose, big rich off-dry roasted malt flavor, long aftertaste like the flavor, big body, long off-dry malt aftertaste, delicious.

MAREDSOUS 9% — cream color, creamy head, complex citrus, berry, and nutty flavor (reminds me of a rum-topf), rich dry complex flavor that is mostly roasted malt, very mouth-filling and very long.

STEENDONK BRABANT WHITE ALE — pale whitish-gold, off-dry grapefruit nose, finely carbonated, lemony-grapefruit flavor, lemon finish and aftertaste.

Brasserie d'Orval

Abbey brewery in **Villers-Devant-Orvan**

ORVAL ABBEY'S ALE BIERE LUXE — deep foamy orange, soapy-sweet malt aroma, intense aromatic flavor fills the senses, alcoholic, resinous, hoppy, tangy, long aftertaste like the flavor, a very tasty brew with great complexity.

ORVAL TRAPPISTE ALE — pale orange, sharp hop nose, intense hop flavor, pungent sweet hop finish, long hop aftertaste, big and powerful, a real mouthful of good brew.

Notes:

Brasserie Palm

Brewery in **Londerzeel**

PALM ALE — amber, lovely malt aroma, zesty dry hop flavor, big body, malt finish, long dry hop aftertaste, excellent balance, a good-tasting, even-natured brew.

SPECIALE AERTS — bright copper, roasted malt aroma, rich off-dry malt flavor, dry hop aftertaste. Brasserie Aerts, Brussels.

AERTS 1900 — amber, big head, tangy malt aroma and flavor, the tang softens as it goes and leaves a smooth malt finish and aftertaste, good body, very good flavor with great malt character.

PALM BOCK PILS — bright tawny-gold, bright hop nose and palate, off-dry malt at finish, long smooth dry hop aftertaste.

Brewery Riva

Brewery in **Dentergem**

RIVA 2000 LAGER BEER — brilliant gold, well-carbonated, off-dry malt aroma with hops and toasted malt in back, complex flavor, bitter hop finish, long malt and dry hop aftertaste.

VONDEL TRIPLE — copper, piquant candy-citrus aroma, intense off-dry malt and tangy hop palate, long aftertaste like the flavor.

WITTEKOP BIERE BLANCHE — cloudy yellow, delicate fruity aroma with an acidic backtaste, lemony palate is forthright but delicate, interesting, pleasant, well-balanced, wine-like, and very long.

LUCIFER ALE — gold, big foamy head, perfumy winey fruity aroma, big strong zesty hop palate, good tasting, big body, lots of alcohol, off-dry malt finish with a mild licorice background, extremely long malt aftertaste, big and very good.

DENTERGEMS WHITE ALE — hazy yellow, huge head, soapy nose, wheaty-malt flavor, smooth, medium body, cuts off abruptly, little or no aftertaste.

Notes:

Brasserie Rodenbach

Brewery in Roselare

RODENBACH BELGIUM BEER — deep copper-red, strong roasted malt aroma with a sour background, very strong off-dry malt with an acidic background, long strong aftertaste like the flavor.

ALEXANDER RODENBACH — hazy amber, powerful acidic hop nose, complex malt and hop flavor with an acidic background, very strong with a lemony-cherry backtaste, fairly sweet malt finish and aftertaste with none of the acidity showing.

Abbaye de Scourmont

Abbey brewery at Scourmont, Chimay

CHIMAY RED CAP ALE — hazy deep brown, big head, chocolate and fruity malt and hop aroma with a faint lactic background, rich complex zesty roasted malt flavor, excellent balance, good body, smooth, long tasty aftertaste like the flavor. This bottle had a red capsule which denotes 7% alcohol. A white capsule denotes 8% and a blue capsule is 9%.

CHIMAY BLUE CAP SPECIAL — deep orange-brown, huge tan head, faint malt nose, big rich sweet and sharp flavor, plenty of both malt and hops, very long aftertaste like the flavor, good but not as complex as the red cap above.

CHIMAY ALE GRANDE RESERVE — deep orange-brown, big head, complex malt and citrus nose, assertive malty ale flavor is sweet, spicy, and fruity, smooth and well-balanced, very complex, spiciness is most pronounced in the finish, very long aftertaste.

CHIMAY CINQ CENTS ALE — faintly hazy-amber, highly carbonated, light lactic nose with malt in back, big malt flavor that is very complex with lactic acid, spice, pine needles, and fruit, big long aftertaste, a big pleasureful brew.

Brasserie de Silly

Brewery in Silly

SAISON SPECIALE ARTISANAL BELGIAN ALE — hazy orange, ephemeral lightly fruited nose, sweet complex powerful (startling considering the lack of warning from the nose) flavor, much like a sparkling Cognac and Grand Marnier combination, big body, long aftertaste like the flavor.

St. Bernardus Bry

Brewery in Wajou

ST. SIXTUS ABDY BIER — deep copper, sweet apple malt aroma, very sweet and very complex malt palate, finishes better than it starts, extremely pleasant malt aftertaste, huge body, great length, needs time to develop as this beer is meant to ferment in the bottle for five or more years. In Belgium this brew is labelled ST. SIXTUS ABT and is rated at 8.5% alc/vol.

ST. SIXTUS PRIOR — deep hazy-brown, faint malt aroma, slightly perfumy, big body, palate of malt, candy, and acid in a somewhat confused state, all three flavors go into the aftertaste, but the acid is the most noticeable. This brew is rated at 7.5% alc/vol.

ST. SIXTUS PATER — lightly hazy medium deep brown, light sweet malt nose, palate of off-dry malt, acid, hops, with a candy sweetness in back, complex aftertaste of all components has a questionable balance.

Notes:

Brasserie St. Guibert, S.A.

Brewery in **Mont St. Guibert**

ABBAYE DE LEFFE BLONDE ALE — deep gold, highly carbonated, light hop aroma, good hoppy ale-like flavor, long hop aftertaste.

LEFFE RADIEUSE BELGIAN ALE — deep copper, hop nose, complex hop palate with bitter and off-dry tones, very long hop aftertaste.

LEFFE BELGIAN DARK ALE — dark copper, good malt and hop aroma, fine malt flavor with hops in back, well-balanced, long aftertaste, pleasant to drink.

VIEUX TEMPS — medium deep amber, malt nose, big malt flavor with a touch of acidity in back, malt finish and aftertaste still have the acid backtaste.

Brasserie/ Bierbrouwerijen Sterkens

Brewery in **Meer**

STER ALE — medium amber, pleasant roasted malt aroma, a trace of dry mustard in back, dry malt flavor, creamy, medium body, fairly long malt aftertaste, pleasant drinking.

ORIGINAL ST. SEBASTIAAN CROCKALE — amber-brown, big rich malt aroma, big dry complex malt flavor, big and beautiful, off-dry malt finish, long rich malt aftertaste.

ST. SEBASTIAAN GOLDEN BELGIAN ALE — hazy gold, big toasted malt nose, big malt flavor, medium body, high alcohol, tangy cider-like bite at the finish, long hop aftertaste.

ST. SEBASTIAAN DARK BELGIAN ALE — deep ruby-amber, big complex nose with hops, malt, alcohol, lactic acid, and maybe even acetone, off-dry lightly acidic flavor, alcohol noticeable on the palate, spicy complex finish and aftertaste, very long, keeps changing as you drink it and becomes more drinkable, has to be served at room temperature to get the full effect, which is quite good.

ST. PAUL DOUBLE — hazy amber, malt and alcohol nose, strong malt flavor, alcohol on the palate, but well-balanced, big body, long malt aftertaste.

ST. PAUL TRIPLE — hazy gold, fruity-banana malt nose, big strong malt and lactic flavor, piney background, high alcohol, big body, extremely long aftertaste like the flavor, very good complex flavor.

Brasserie Union S.A.

Brewery in **Jumet**

CUVEE DE L'HERMITAGE — tawny-amber, rich malt aroma, off-dry toasted malt and bitter hop flavor, big wine-like body, strong malt flavor, big hop finish, smooth hop aftertaste with plenty of malt, a fine sipping beer with 8% alc/vol.

CUVEE DE L'HERMITAGE CHRISTMAS — deep amber, big candy caramel malt aroma, big malt and hop flavor, long hop and malt aftertaste, big body, fairly strong flavor, high alcohol (7.5%), strong stuff but not well put together.

Notes:

Brouwerij Van Honsebrouck

Brewery in Ingelmunster

BRIGAND BELGIAN ALE — hazy amber-gold, big head, strong off-dry lactic nose and flavor, complex, in some ways like a mead, high alcohol (9%), powerful in that you feel it in your nose from its volatile nature when you are sipping, long aftertaste like the flavor, strong sipping beer that is good of type.

GUEZE ST. LOUIS — pale amber, aroma like fruit, herbs, and sausage, a definite gueze palate, fruity and lactic, smooth and creamy, nothing offensive, medium long aftertaste like the flavor, a very good gueze.

KASTEEL BIER/BIERE DU CHATEAU — cloudy amber, off-dry roasted malt nose, high alcohol, interesting and complex, strong sweet malt flavor, sweet malt finish, long dry malt aftertaste.

Brewery Van Hougaerde

Brewery in Leuven/Louvain

LEOPOLD THREE STARS PILS — pale gold, good malt and hop nose with a fruity backtaste, sour malt finish, long sour hop aftertaste.

Notes:

Van Steenberge Brewery

Brewery in Ertvelde

The corporate name Brasserie Bios is still used on some labels.

AUGUSTIJN — amber, tangy-soapy aroma, grain and bitter hop flavor, tangy sweet finish, long off-dry hop aftertaste, very complex, very big and assertive, very long.

BIOS COPPER ALE — medium deep cloudy red-brown, sharp yeasty sweet spicy nose, sweet and sour lactic palate, tenacious long hop aftertaste.

Brasserie Weize

Brewery in Van Roy

WIEZE LAGER BEER — brilliant gold, medium hop nose with good malt, good clean malt-hop flavor with spring water background, slight metallic finish, good balance, very drinkable.

Westmalle Abbey

Cistercian Trappiste Abbey Brewery in Westmalle

WESTMALLE TRIPLE ABBEY BEER — bright gold, fine bitter hop aroma and bright hop flavor, full-bodied, good balance, dry hop and malt finish, long dry hop aftertaste, high alcohol (8%), delicious brew.

WESTMALLE DUBBEL ABBEY BEER — fairly deep cloudy orange-brown, delicious complex off-dry malt nose, rich and full bodied, big roasted malt flavor is quite complex and seems to change as it goes, very long aftertaste like the flavor, a truly great Trappiste brew.

Notes:

BULGARIA

Brewery Haskowo

Brewery in Haskowo

ASTICA — bright gold, sweet nose is like a banana popsicle with a malt, pear, and lactic background, lactic-malt flavor, loses the lactic and gains malt as it goes, aftertaste is almost all malt, not unlikeable, but a little rough.

Brewery Zagorka

Brewery in Stara Zagora

ZAGORKA IMPORTED PREMIUM LAGER — bright gold, faint malt and hop nose, good body, weak dry hop flavor, dry hop finish and short dry hop aftertaste.

CZECHOSLOVAKIA

Budvar Brewery

Brewery in Ceske Budejovice

BUDVAR BUDWEISER — bright tawny-gold, lively hop aroma, flavor is bright hops, there is malt but it is in the background, the hops are strongest at the finish, for the aftertaste is long light hops. Well-made, well-balanced, likeable brew. On draft, the hops seem less pronounced, the malt shows better, and this results in an improved balance and a more delicate hop aftertaste, making a good beer even better. This is the 12° density version, the best-known Budvar and the one exported to most of the world.

BUDVAR BUDWEISER — tawny-gold, off-dry malt aroma with hops in back, creamy off-dry malt flavor with the hops well in back, finish has more hops and a slight salty nature, long aftertaste is once again malty like the flavor. This is the 10° density version, available locally.

Chebski Starovar

Brewery in Cheb/Eger

EGER URBIER — gold, good malt nose with hops, smooth malt flavor, light and dry, good body, fairly long dry malt aftertaste.

Urquell Brewery

Brewery in Pilsen

PILSNER URQUELL — bright tawny-gold, good head, appetizing hop aroma, smooth well-balanced malt and hop flavor, refreshing and satisfying, long smooth dry hop aftertaste, excellent classic Pilsener beer. In Czechoslovakia it is called Prazdroj. Freshly bottled, it is almost not distinguishable from the fresh draft except for the thickness of the head, which is very dense on draft.

GAMBRINUS PILSEN — deep gold, appetizing hop nose, bright hop flavor with plenty of malt in support, malt emerges well at the finish, and stays to balance a long dry hop aftertaste. Gambrinus Brewery, Pilsen.

WENZEL'S BRÄU — bright gold, roasted malt and hop aroma, palate has an off-dry front, but this quickly becomes big hops, some malt rejoins the hops at the finish, but the long aftertaste is dry hops backed with faintly sour malt. This is a pleasant, lovely-tasting brew when fresh.

DENMARK

Albani Breweries, Ltd.

Brewery in Odense

ALBANI EXPORT BEER — yellow-gold, light malt nose with light hops in back, pleasant flavor with a good mix of hops and malt, malt finish, light dry malt and hop aftertaste.

ALBANI PILSNER — gold, medium hop nose, good hop and malt pils flavor, good balance, pleasant but not complex or long.

GIRAF MALT LIQUOR — fairly deep amber-gold, lovely malt and hop nose, bitter hops briefly on front of palate, but big off-dry malt comes quickly in for an overall malt flavor, hops reappear in the finish, long off-dry malt and hop aftertaste, complex, good body, good tasting.

ALBANI PORTER — deep molasses brown color, smooth light malt aroma, big rich malt flavor with a touch of sour malt in back, extended rich malt aftertaste, good body, smooth and delicious, extremely complex, tones of coffee, licorice, and chocolate weave in and out, balanced, delightful. This is one of my top ten all-time favorites. I recently tasted a bottle that was eight years old, and it received top scores in a blind tasting from everyone present.

ALBANI PÅSKEBRYG — deep pale amber, malt nose with slight hops, big malt and hop flavor, long malt-hop aftertaste, very drinkable. Paske is Danish for Easter and bryg is beer.

ALBANI JULE BRYG — medium amber, malt and light hop nose, big hop and malt flavor, palate is first malt then hops develop across it to dominate the finish, decent balance, long big dry hop aftertaste.

Albani
PORTER
BY APPOINTMENT TO THE ROYAL DANISH COURT
BREWED AND BOTTLED BY
ALBANI BREWERIES
ODENSE · DENMARK
℮ 33 CL.
5 701473 001109
DÄNISCHES STARKBIER
BIRRA DOPPIO MALTO SCURA PRODOTTA E CONFEZIONATA DALLA

Notes:

Carlsberg Breweries/ United Breweries, Ltd.

United Breweries is an amalgamation of Carlsberg Breweries and the Tuborg and Royal Breweries in **Copenhagen, Elsinore** and **Silkeborg**

CARLSBERG ROYAL LAGER BEER — deep gold, light pleasant and clean malt aroma, hops are in back, light dry good hop flavor, good balance, light off-dry malt aftertaste.

CARLSBERG ELEPHANT MALT LIQUOR — deep gold, light fruity malt aroma with some hops and apple peel, big pungent flavor with lots of character, almost a sense of menthol, there is so much volatility, big strong malt aftertaste with hops to support and give balance.

CARLSBERG SPECIAL DARK BEER — deep amber, light balanced malt and hop aroma, light body, light flavor with hops not arriving until the finish, short medium dry aftertaste.

TUBORG BEER — pale gold, pleasant malt nose with some hop character, big sharp hop flavor, touch of sour in the finish, strong and long dry hop aftertaste.

CARLSBERG BEER — bright gold, big hop nose, lovely bright hop flavor, good long dry hop aftertaste, balanced and fairly complex.

CARLSBERG LIGHT — bright gold, faintly skunky nose, off-dry malt and sour dry hop flavor, aftertaste like the flavor has medium length.

TUBORG ROYAL DANISH EXTRA STRONG BEER — brilliant deep gold, hop and malt nose, strong winey off-dry malt palate, long malt aftertaste, definitely strong flavored as promised and likely has high alcohol as well (probably on the order of 8%).

TUBORG PORTER DOUBLE STOUT — opaque, brown head, strong malt nose, slightly bitter, rich complex malt flavor, balanced and even stronger than the nose, big hops at the finish, long aftertaste has both hops and malt aplenty.

CARLSBERG SPECIAL BREW EXTRA STRONG EXPORT LAGER — bright gold, beautifully balanced big malt and hop aroma, a big mouthful of flavor with both malt and hops, big body, noticeable alcohol, long balanced malt and hop aftertaste, 8% alc/vol.

IMPERIAL STOUT — almost opaque-black, rich complex stout aroma hinting of all kinds of good things, luxurious malt flavor, good body, fairly dry, very long dry malt aftertaste. Wiibroes Brewery, Elsinore.

NEPTUN DANISH PILSNER — brilliant pale gold, malt nose, malt flavor, light hops in the finish, light dry hop aftertaste. Neptun Brewery, Silkeborg.

NEPTUN GOLDEN BROWN — brilliant gold, earthy hop nose, big hop and off-dry malt flavor, good body, doubtful balance, off-dry malt and bitter hop finish, long bitter and dry hop aftertaste.

NEPTUN PAASKE BRYG — gold, light malt and hop nose, strong hop flavor with too little malt in support, long dry bitter hop aftertaste. An Easter festival beer which is supposed to be a bock-style brew.

NEPTUN PINSE BRYG — bright lime green (colored green intentionally), malt and big hop aroma, very well-hopped flavor with just a little (too little) malt for balance, long dry bitter hop aftertaste, not unlike the Easter beer above. Pinse is Danish for Whitsuntide or Pentecost, a religious festival for the seventh Sunday after Easter.

GREEN ROOSTER MALT LIQUOR — another bright lime-green beer, delicious aromatic clover hop aroma, complex hop flavor, full-bodied, balanced, malt finish, long dry hop and malt aftertaste, a delicious well-hopped brew. This is a fantastic brew. Don't let the color put you off.

Ceres Breweries, Ltd.

Brewery in **Aarhus, Horsens**

CERES BEER — gold, faint apple-malt nose, light off-dry malt flavor, brief dry hop aftertaste.

RED ERIC MALT LIQUOR — yellow-gold, aroma of hops and off-dry toffee-malt, hops and toffee palate, good body, lots of character, long dry hop and malt aftertaste.

Harboes Brewery

Brewery in **Skaelskor**

HARBOE BEAR BEER — pale bright gold, fresh malt aroma, off-dry malt flavor in front, but by the finish it is all bitter hops, long dry and bitter hop aftertaste.

HARBOE GOLD EXPORT BEER — deep clear gold, light malt and hop aroma, light dry flavor at the start but the finish is off-dry malt, the aftertaste is good dry malt and hops, the balance stays good throughout.

Lolland-Falsters Bryghus

Brewery at **Nykobing, Falsters Island**

LOLLAND-FALSTERS EXPORT DANISH BEER — bright gold, clean malt nose, flavor is lightly toasted malt up front, bitter hops at the finish, complex, good body, long lightly hopped dry aftertaste with a smoked background.

DANISH DYNAMITE — hazy gold, light hop and malt nose, a trifle skunky at first, big rich malt flavor has a lot of hops in back and finishes "hot," big body, long bitter-dry hop aftertaste.

Thor Breweries

Brewery at **Randers**

THOR BEER — pale gold, light off-dry malt nose, malt-hop flavor, medium body, fair balance, medium to long dry hop aftertaste.

DANISH GOLD — pale bright gold, malt nose, strong hop flavor, dry hop aftertaste, medium body, fair length.

BUUR BEER DE LUXE — deep gold, fresh and clean malt-hop aroma, huge sweet hop flavor, big body, slightly soapy finish, long hop aftertaste, a wonderful brew with great taste.

Notes:

FINLAND

Hartwell Co., Inc.

Breweries in **Kaarina, Turku, Vaasa,** and **Karelia**

KARJALA EXPORT BEER — deep tawny gold, fine hop aroma, sprightly hop flavor, big body, spicy finish, long dry hop aftertaste, a satisfying and filling beer.

Osakeyhtio Mallasjuoma, Inc.

Breweries in **Lahti, Heinola,** and **Oulo**

FINLANDIA GOLD BEER — gold, lovely malt aroma, pleasant malt flavor with plenty of hop character, excellent balance, long dry hop aftertaste, fairly complex and very drinkable.

FINLANDIA LIGHT BEER -- bright tawny-gold, mild hop aroma, hop palate is shallow and not well balanced, malt aftertaste is a bit sour.

ERIKOIS EXPORT OLUT IVA LAHDEN — tawny gold, roasted malt, toffee, and molasses nose, toasted grainy malt flavor, very pleasant to sip, long dry malt aftertaste.

Sinebrychoff Brewery

Brewery in **Helsinki**

KOFF FINNISH BEER — bright gold, zesty hop nose, big hop flavor, fairly well balanced, long hop aftertaste, no shortage of hops here,

KOFF IMPERIAL STOUT — deep brown, caramel and hop aroma, dry rich malt and hop flavor, plenty of both, bitter and dry hop aftertaste with a herbaceous background.

Notes:

FRANCE

L'Alsacienne de Brasseries, S.A.

Brewery in **Schiltigheim**

Some labels identify brews as being made by Heineken in Schiltigheim.

MÜTZIG EXPORT BEER — pale gold, strong pefumy pine needle nose, hop and malt flavor, light body, dry malt aftertaste.

MÜTZIG — pale gold, hop nose, complex malt and hop flavor, hop finish and faint sour hop aftertaste.

Brasserie Amos

Brewery in **Metz**

AMOS IMPORTED FRENCH BEER — yellow-gold, malt nose is big at first but fades, pleasant off-dry malt flavor, heavy body, a bit winey, off-dry malt finish and aftertaste, lacks complexity.

Brasserie Benifontaine

Brewery in **Nord Pas de Calais**

CASTELAINE BLOND BIERE DE GARDE — gold, faint apple-malt nose, big bright fruity malt and hop flavor, long aftertaste like the flavor, very flavorful and smooth.

EUROPE

Brasserie Duyck

Brewery in **Jenlain**

JENLAIN FRENCH COUNTRY ALE — bright pale amber, fresh malt nose, finely carbonated, bright malt flavor like a delicate barley wine, fairly dry malt throughout, especially in the long aftertaste, very good with food.

LE MADELON FRENCH COUNTRY BEER — deep amber, roasted malt nose with a Kir-like background, winey dry roasted malt flavor, complex, soft, and smooth, a bit like a porter but not enough to be named one, few hops, if any.

Societé Européene de Brasseries

Brewery in **Sèvres**

SKANSEN SPECIAL LAGER — pale amber, roasted malt nose, off-dry toasted malt flavor, spicy hot component to the malt aftertaste.

KANTERBRAU GOLD BIERE SPECIALE — yellow-gold, malt nose, bit of an ale-like hop bite on the front of the palate, then roasted malt emerges and pushes the bitter hops to the background, long hop and roasted malt aftertaste, balance is a bit off.

Le Grands Chais de France

Brewery in **Schiltigheim**

CHIC ALSACE BEER — pale gold, light sweet hop and malt nose, light body, hop flavor, sour hop aftertaste, lacks body and complexity.

CHIC LITE ALSACE BEER — very pale gold, dank malt nose, grainy carbonated water flavor, somewhat gassy, metallic malt finish and aftertaste, little character.

Brasseries Kronenbourg, S.A.

Brewery in **Strasbourg**

KRONENBOURG 1664 IMPORTED BEER — medium gold, light malt aroma is almost fruity, vinous malt flavor, medium long dry hop aftertaste.

KRONENBOURG 1664 DARK BEER — deep copper color, extremely light malt aroma, malt flavor, light body, dull dry malt aftertaste.

KRONENBOURG 1664 MALT LIQUOR — bright amber-gold, good sour malt aroma, carbonation competes with the malt flavor, heavy body, long smooth malt aftertaste.

Brasseurs de Paris/ Brasserie Nouvelle de Lutèce

Brewery **B.N.L. Port Autonome de Paris, Bonneiul**

BIERE DE PARIS — beautiful brilliant pale amber, light fragrant toasted malt aroma with a tang, light body, delicate toasted malt flavor with a caramel background, balanced hop finish, long dry hop aftertaste. It is a barleywine of great delicacy and finesse. It is excellent with food. In France it is labelled Lutèce Bière de Paris.

Haag-Metzger & Cie., S.A./Brasserie Météor

Brewery in **Hochfelden**

METEOR PILS BIER DE LUXE — pale yellow-gold, faint pils style nose with more hops than malt, crisp hop flavor, long clean dry hop aftertaste.

Notes:

La Grande Brasserie Moderne

Brewery in **Roubaix**

SEPTANTE ROUGE — pale amber, strong aromatic nose with hops and malt, interesting palate that is first off-dry malt, hops join the malt at mid-palate, then a long dry aftertaste of hops and malt, medium body, complex, clean, long, and flavorful.

SEPTANTE 5 — pale copper-amber, off-dry malt aroma, strong dry malt flavor, big body, malt finish, pleasant malt aftertaste, well balanced, somewhat wine-like, noticeable alcohol, well made.

SEPTANTE VERTE — medium deep gold, weak hop and malt aroma, good big hop flavor with plenty of malt, faintly sour background to the long malt aftertaste, a good beer with food.

SUPER 49 GRANDE BIERE DE LUXE — hazy gold, pleasant hop and malt nose, sour malt palate, metallic background, long sour hop aftertaste with some fruity malt hiding somewhere.

TERKEN BRUNE — deep amber-brown, lightly toasted big malt nose, good body, good and big toasted malt flavor, long dry malt aftertaste, hops not noticeable if there, has complexity, however, and is a well-made malt brew with a good level of intensity.

TERKEN BIERE DE LUXE — deep gold, light malt nose, light and smooth malt flavor, good body, some noticeable alcohol, soft texture, tasty.

TRADER JOE'S SPECIAL DARK HOLIDAY ALE — deep amber, malt nose, big toasted malt flavor, finish has a scorched component, long toasted malt aftertaste is also a bit burnt.

Notes:

Brasserie Mattière du Pêcheur, S.A.

Breweries in **Schiltigheim** and **Strasbourg**

FISCHER BEER — pale gold, pleasant off-dry malt and hop nose, light body, pleasant slightly off-dry malt flavor, aftertaste is drier than the flavor and is still mostly malt, fairly short.

FISCHER ALE — pale gold, pleasant off-dry malt and hop nose is sweeter than above, but the malt flavor is nicely dry with the hops in back, good balance, long dry aftertaste like the flavor.

FISCHER D'ALSACE — bright gold, hop aroma, hop flavor has the malt sliding in from mid-palate on, very good balance, malt finish, good body, long dry malt and hop aftertaste, well-made beer.

FISCHER D'ALSACE BITTER — pale amber, hop nose, fairly bitter hop flavor that extends into a long dry aftertaste.

FISCHER D'ALSACE AMBER — light amber, aroma with plenty of off-dry malt and bright hops, flavor starts out with the malt, hops come in the middle and stay for the finish and long aftertaste, good hefty body, some complexity, a good, very drinkable brew.

FISCHER LA BELLE STRASBOURGEOISE — deep gold, grainy malt nose, malt flavor seems to gain strength as it crosses the palate, hops join the malt at the finish, leading into a good long aftertaste with both components in harmony.

FISCHER PILS — pale gold, light malt nose, malt flavor gets hops as it approaches the finish, long fairly dry hop aftertaste.

FISCHER GOLD — gold, off-dry fruity malt aroma, strong vinous malt flavor, long malt aftertaste, heavy body.

36.15 PECHEUR LA BIERE AMOREUSE — bright gold, flowery, fruity, herbal, complex aroma (has added myrrh, ginger, cardamom, ginseng, cola, cinnamon, mango, licorice, myrtle, and eleutherococque), fruity herbal flavor, almost cherry-like, good body, medium length, not beer-like.

ADELSHOFFEN BIERE SPECIALE D'ALSACE — deep yellow, off-dry fruity malt aroma with a touch of hops, very complex flavor of fruit and faint hops, a bit wine-like, not dry, long roasted malt aftertaste.

MÜNSTERHOF FRENCH BEER — deep gold, malt nose, light malt and hop flavor, sour malt finish and aftertaste. Br. Adelshoffen.

ADELSHOFFEN TRADITION — medium deep gold, very pleasant fruity aroma, light body, pleasant slightly burnt fruity malt flavor, little depth, pleasant malt finish and short aftertaste.

ADELSCOTT SMOKED MALT LIQUOR — bright orange, butterscotch and smoky barbecue nose, smoky sweet malt palate, light body, some alcohol noticeable, very pleasant and very drinkable.

ZELE — deep gold, lime aroma, light body, light lime flavor, not beer-like, flavored like the Canadian Zélé, light and brief.

Brasseries Pelforth, S.A.

Brewery in Lille

Also uses corporate name Brasseries Pelican on some labels.

PELFORTH PALE ALE — deep gold, good malt nose, pleasant tasting malt and hop flavor, excellent balance, good body, off-dry malt aftertaste. Labeled also LA BIERE BLONDE DE FRANCE.

GEORGE KILLIAN'S BIERE ROUSSE (RED ALE) — reddish brown, big nose with lots of hops and molasses-caramel malt, flavor starts out big hops and finishes dry roasted malt, good balance, big body, long clean dry malt aftertaste.

PELICAN EXPORT BEER — gold, fresh fruity-malt nose, papery malt flavor, medium body, dull hop finish and aftertaste.

Notes:

Brasserie Schutzenberger, S.A.

Brewery in Schiltigheim

SANT'OR MALT BEVERAGE — very pale bright gold, faint hop nose, vegetal malt flavor, weak body, malt finish and aftertaste like the flavor.

SCHUTZ PILS LUXE BIERE D'ALSACE — tawny-gold, good hop and malt nose, good hop flavor up front, good malt in the middle, aftertaste has an unpleasant overly sour component that is not in the flavor.

SCHUTZENBERGER JUBILATOR FRENCH BEER — yellow-gold, good hop nose with off-dry malt in back, palate is mostly sharp bitter hops except for some malt at the very beginning and some off-dry malt in the finish, complex flavor, long dry aftertaste shows both hops and malt.

Brasserie St. Leonard

Brewery in St. Leonard/St. Martin, Boulogne

BRASSIN DE GARDE DE SAINT LEONARD — bright amber-peach, very faint toasted malt flavor, touch of hops in the finish, is wine-like without being winey, long dry hop aftertaste still shows good malt, a very nice brew, especially good with food.

Brasserie de Saint Sylvestre

Brewery in St. Sylvestre

3 MONTS FLANDERS GOLDEN ALE — amber, malt nose with a citrus background, rich complex malt flavor, high alcohol, full bodied, long malt aftertaste.

Notes:

Union de Brasseries

France's largest brewery with five brew-plants in **Paris**

Other breweries at other locations such as St. Amand-les-eaux.

"33" EXPORT BEER — deep bright gold, clean bright malt aroma with good hops and some yeast, big hop flavor in front, malt in back, good body, sour malt finish, good balance, long dry well-hopped aftertaste, a lively tasty brew that wakes up your palate.

"33" EXTRA DRY BEER BLONDE SPECIALE — amber-gold, bright well-hopped aroma, big flavor with lots of hops and off-dry roasted malt, complex, good body, good balance, long dry aftertaste like the flavor.

"33" RECORD BEER — deep yellow-gold, clean off-dry malt aroma with some hops, big rich off-dry malt flavor with good hop support, pleasant dry hop finish and aftertaste.

SLAVIA EXTRA DRY — deep tawny-gold, off-dry fruit-like malt aroma with a spicy background of something resembling woodruff, big toasted malt and hop flavor, long dry hop aftertaste with malt holding well in the background.

ROEMER PILS — deep yellow-gold, hop nose, tart and sour palate, long aftertaste like the flavor, but the more unpleasant aspects mar the effect.

PORTER 39 — deep red-brown, clean sweet fruity-toasted malt aroma, roasted malt flavor, lingering aftertaste like the flavor, a good porter.

PANTHER MALT BEVERAGE — bright amber, nice malt nose, tastes like cereal grain soda pop, hop bite in the short aftertaste.

PANACH' BEER-tawny-gold, off tuna salad aroma, citrus soda pop flavor, reminds you of a French citron pressé, not much of a beer, this product is flavored.

GERMANY

Brauerei Aktien

Brewery in **Kaufbeuren**

AKTIEN EDEL AUSSTICH — bright gold, complex clean appetizing hop nose, smooth malt flavor with good hop support, good body and balance, long dry malt and hop aftertaste.

AKTIEN JUBILAUMS PILS — bright gold, complex and appetizing hop nose, nce hop flavor well backed with malt, good tasting, clean, balanced, and quite long.

STEINGADENER WEISSE DUNKEL — cloudy orange, grainy nose, malt and carbonation palate, dull and short.

AKTIEN FRUNDSBERG EXPORT DUNKEL — deep amber, nice malt nose, straightforward malt flavor, one dimensional, no character, no complexity, fairly brief malt aftertaste.

AKTIEN ST. MARTIN DUNKLER DOPPELBOCK — deep orange-amber, off dry grainy malt aroma, off-dry malt flavor, good body, hop finish, long dry malt aftertaste.

AKTIEN TÄNZELFEST-BIER — brilliant gold, complex malt and hop aroma, fairly rich malt flavor, medium body, dry malt finish and aftertaste.

AKTIEN HELL — gold, big malt and hop nose, big malt and dry hop flavor, light to medium body, long dry malt and hop aftertaste.

Allgäuer Brauhaus

Brewery in **Kempten**

MÖNCHSHOF KAPUZINER WEIZEN KRISTALLKLAR — medium deep gold, big head, wheaty nose with a touch of spicy lactic acid, some banana as well, spicy-malt palate, banana finish, short mellow aftertaste, fairly good balance, and a nice ending.

Brauhaus Altenmünster-Weissenbrunn

Brewery in **Altenmünster**

ALTENMÜNSTER BRAUER BEER — deep gold, complex hop aroma, big hop flavor, creamy texture, slightly sour hop finish and aftertaste, pretty good except that it could use a bit more malt, especially in the finish.

Altes Brauhaus Gmbh.

Brewery in **Lippstadt**

WESTFALEN PILS — gold, slightly toasted malt and hop aroma, pleasant bright hop flavor, lightly carbonated, slightly sour hop finish and aftertaste.

C.H. Andreas Westfälische Pils Brauerei

Brewery in **Hagen**

ANDREAS PILS — tawny-gold, clean aromatic hop nose with an off-dry malt background, bright hop flavor with an off-dry malt backing, burnt malt aftertaste.

Brauerei Arnold

Brewery in **Lauf**

ARNOLD PILSENER — medium to deep gold, low carbonation, light roasted malt nose and flavor, medium length dry roasted malt aftertaste, pleasant but lacks complexity.

ARNOLD BAVARIAN DARK BEER — deep copper-brown, beautiful roasted malt nose, tasty malt flavor, light body, pleasant but lacks depth and length.

BARON VON FUNK PREMIUM BEER COOLER — cloudy gold, malty-citrus flavor like a shandy, but with more fruit than beer, sweet and light, sticky-sweet finish, almost no aftertaste.

Notes:

Augustiner Brauerei, A.G.

Brewery in **Munich**

AUGUSTINER BRÄU MUNICH EXPORT LIGHT BEER — beautiful bright gold, clean but very light aroma, slightly off-dry malt flavor with delicate hop background, clean light malt and hop finish, long mild dry hop aftertaste, very smooth and tasty.

AUGUSTINER BRAÜ MUNICH MAXIMATOR DARK EXPORT BEER — pale brown with copper tones, strong malt and hop nose, rich complex malt flavor with plenty of zest and character, slightly bitter and dry hop finish and aftertaste, a lovely double bock with lots of gusto.

Brauerei Bavaria-St. Pauli

Brewery in **Hamburg**

GRENZQUELL GERMAN PILSNER — gold, good hop nose, bright well-hopped flavor well backed with malt, good body, lots of hop character, long dry hop aftertaste, a big tasty brew.

ASTRA EXCLUSIVE — bright gold, dry faintly toasted malt nose, lightly sour and bitter hop flavor, one dimensional (hops) taste, short dry hop aftertaste.

GRENZQUELL GERMAN DARK PILSNER — deep copper, good hop and roasted malt aroma and flavor, thin body, some molasses in the finish, virtually no aftertaste.

JEVER PILSENER — bright tawny-gold, aroma is more malt than hops, big body, flavor starts out malt but gradually turns to hops, building bitterness as it goes until it finishes quite bitter, lingering bitter hop aftertaste.

ASTRA ALE — pale amber, good malt nose, pleasant malt flavor, but is too sweet and it becomes cloying after a while, long, too-sweet malt aftertaste.

ASTRA MEISTER BOCK — medium gold, good hop and malt aroma, light body, light malt flavor, faint molasses aftertaste has little length.

Notes:

Bayerische Brauerei, A.G.

Brewery in **Kaiserslautern**

BARBAROSSA KAISER BIER — gold, very foamy, fruity malt nose, flavor is off-dry malt and sharp hops with a faint acidic background, complex and interesting, short dry aftertaste.

BARBAROSSA GOLD EXPORT — gold, complex toasted malt nose, malt palate briefly up front, then drops off to nothing immediately, wood and corn are behind the light malt aftertaste.

BBK PILS — pale bright gold, light hop nose, palate is mostly hops but there is some malt, fair balance but short and dull.

Brauerei Beck & Co.

Brewery in **Bremen**

BECK'S BEER — pale gold, mild malt nose, light body, pleasant light hop flavor, fine balance, light dry hop finish and aftertaste.

BECK'S DARK BEER — medium deep amber-brown, hop nose, big hop flavor, finish, and bitter hop aftertaste, plenty of hops for everyone.

ROLAND LIGHT LOW-CALORIE BEER — pale gold, light but good hop nose, weak body, hop and grainy malt palate, sour hop aftertaste.

DRIBECK'S LIGHT BEER — deep gold, grainy malt aroma, light body, good hop and malt flavor, hop finish, fairly long dry hop aftertaste.

HAAKE BECK NON-ALCOHOLIC MALT BEVERAGE — bright gold, malt aroma, flavor starts out dry malt, becomes big hops, grainy malt finish, and sour hop aftertaste, some complexity and fairly interesting.

Privatbrauerei Becker

Brewery in **St. Ingbert**

BECKER'S EXPORT —brilliant medium deep gold, faint hop nose, high carbonation, light body, light malt and hop flavor, pleasant, good balance, faint hop finish, and faint dry hop aftertaste.

BECKER'S PILS — pale yellow-gold, ample hop aroma, strong bitter hop flavor, sour hop finish and long sour-bitter hop aftertaste.

BECKER'S EXTRA HERB PREMIUM PILS — bright gold, beautiful hop aroma, strong bitter hop palate, long sour bitter metallic hop aftertaste.

Berliner Brewery

Brewery in **Berlin**

SCHUTER'S RED STAR SELECT — tawny-gold, faint malt aroma, sour hop flavor, dry hop finish, dry hop aftertaste with a sour background.

Exportbierbrauerei Berliner Bürgerbräu

Brewery in **Berlin**

BERLINER PILS EXPORT — deep tawny-gold, big hop nose, bitter hop palate, medium body, long sour hop aftertaste.

TÜRMER GERMAN BEER — gold, fresh malt nose, medium body, fruity-malt flavor, sour malt and hop aftertaste.

EUROPE

Burger Bräu Bernkastel

Brewery in **Bernkastel-Kues**

BERNKASTELER PILS — pale gold, strong sweet hop aroma, malt starts the flavor but it is dominated and finished with hops, long dry hop aftertaste, the hops and malt cross but seem to come together.

Binding Brauerei, A.G.

Brewery in **Frankfurt**

STEINHAUSER BEER — bright gold, light hop nose with good malt support, light body, smooth hop flavor and finish, good balance, long dry hop aftertaste.

RÖMER PILS — yellow-gold, sweet hop nose, brief off-dry malt flavor, light body, light medium dry malt aftertaste with hops in back.

CLAUSTHALER HERBFRISCHES SCHANKBIER — deep gold, grainy hop aroma, high carbonation, grainy hop and CO_2 flavor, long dry hop aftertaste. Version tasted in Europe.

CLAUSTHALER BIER — bright gold, fragrant honeyed malt aroma, off-dry malt palate, long off-dry malt aftertaste goes bitter at the end. Export version to the U.S.

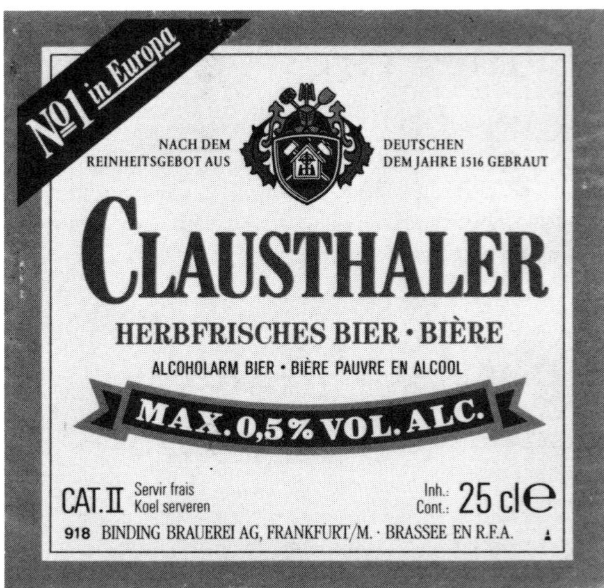

Brauerei Bischoff

Brewery in **Winnweiler**

BISCHOFF PREMIUM EXPORT BEER — gold, toasted malt nose, off-sweet toasted malt flavor, dull finish and aftertaste, not interesting.

BISCHOFF PILS — bright gold, light off-dry hop and malt aroma, off-sweet malt flavor, little finish, faint sour fruity apple aftertaste.

Bitburger Brauerei Thomas Simon

Brewery in **Bitburg**

BITBURGER PREMIUM PILS — gold, big hop nose, bright hop flavor, medium body, hop finish, long hop aftertaste. A nice straightforward pils.

Notes:

Schlossbrauerei Braunfels

Brewery in **Braunfels**

BRAUNFELS PILS — gold, tangy hop nose and taste, short dry hop aftertaste.

BRAUNFELSER 1868 — gold, hop nose and taste, some oxidation, long sour hop aftertaste.

Brauerei Brombach, Erdinger Weissbräu

Brewery in **Erding**

ERDINGER WEISSBIER — cloudy gold, foamy, piquant grainy nose, clean balanced wheaty flavor, pleasantly off-dry at the finish, long slightly off-dry malt aftertaste, smooth and mellow brew.

ERDINGER PIKANTUS STARKE WEISSBIER — reddish-brown, roasted malt and wheat grain aroma, off-dry complex malt flavor, highly carbonated, very long and likeable, seems more like a Weizenbock. Also exported to U.S. as **PIKANTUS** — dark amber, big head, tangy wheat beer nose with a light lactic-spice touch, tangy wheat-malt-lactic flavor, very light acid, adds rather than detracts, very tasty and quite long.

PREMINGER ALKOHOLFREI WEISSBIER — bright gold, grainy nose, light grainy flavor, touch of honey in the brief aftertaste.

ERDINGER WEISSBIER KRISTALLKLAR — gold, nice toasted malt nose, malt flavor has just a faint trace of spice, light body, light dry malt finish and aftertaste, very refreshing.

ERDINGER WEISSBIER DUNKEL — deep amber, faint malt aroma, light malt flavor with faint spice in back, light body, light and dry malt finish and aftertaste.

Deininger Kronenbräu A.G.

Brewery in Hof

EKU HEFE-WEIZEN — bright gold, big head, spicy lactic and wheat nose, flavor to match, good complexity, long and tasty.

EKU WEIZENBOCK DUNKEL — medium-deep amber-brown, toasted wheat nose, flavor has a lactic bite but it is overall a big malt taste, a candy Sen-Sen like aftertaste, very complex and very long, noticeable alcohol.

DEININGER PILS — bright pale gold, hop nose and big hop flavor, creamy texture, dusty background, long zesty hop aftertaste.

DEININGER EXPORT — bright deep gold, malt and hop nose, malt palate, smooth and balanced, brief dry hop aftertaste.

DEININGER KRISTALL WEIZEN — bright gold, big head, refreshing lactic clove nose, spicy with a clean fruit background, flavor like the nose, complex and balanced, long aftertaste is a continuation of the flavor, leaves your mouth clean and refreshed.

EKU WEIZEN KRISTALLKLAR — bright gold, big head, fruity lactic nose, light flavor like the nose, medium-length clean fruity-spicy aftertaste.

DEININGER HELL — brilliant gold, bright hop and malt aroma, clean appetizing hop flavor, dry malt and hop finish and aftertaste.

DEININGER HOFQUELL — brilliant pale gold, appetizing malt and hop nose, clean hop flavor, soapy hop finish and aftertaste.

DEININGER FESTBIER — medium bright gold, good malt and hop nose, pleasant malt flavor, good body, malt finish, medium long dry malt aftertaste.

DEININGER HEFE-WEISSBIER — hazy gold, spicy clove nose, spicy zesty malt flavor, smooth and refreshing, good balance between the spice and the malt, creamy, richly flavored, long medium dry spicy malt aftertaste, excellent wheat beer.

Dinkelacker Wülle, A.G.

Brewery in Stuttgart

DINKELACKER PRIVAT LIGHT BEER — gold, complex malt and hop aroma, great heft and plenty of zest, good body, plenty of character, good bright hop flavor, well-balanced, long dry hop aftertaste.

DINKELACKER BLACK FOREST LIGHT BEER — cloudy gold, blueberry, malt aroma, off-dry malt flavor, dank finish and aftertaste.

DINKELACKER BOCK C.D. EXTRA — dark brown, big malt aroma and flavor, big body, rich malt flavor, long dry malt aftertaste.

DINKELACKER DARK IMPORT PRIVAT — brown, big malt nose, rich malt flavor with a yeasty nature, sour malt finish, long dry malt aftertaste, also seen labeled as DINKELACKER DARK C.D. EXTRA.

DINKELACKER WEIZENKRONE — yellow, huge head, pleasant light malt aroma, highly carbonated, sour malt finish, dry malt aftertaste.

DINKELACKER DARK BREW — amber-brown, big roasted malt nose and flavor, sour malt finish, long dry malt and hop aftertaste, good balance, drinkable.

PRO NON-ALCOHOLIC BEER — bright gold, hops first in the aroma then grainy malt, bright hop and off-dry malt flavor, slightly sour malt aftertaste.

Dom Brauerei

Brewery in **Köln**

DOM KÖLSCH — deep gold, big hop nose backed with roasted malt, light body, tasty hop and roasted malt flavor, slightly bitter hop finish and aftertaste, highly carbonated and a bit too light, but tasty nevertheless.

Dortmunder Actien Brauerei/Dortmunder Hansa Brauerei

Merged breweries in **Dortmund**

DORTMUNDER HANSA EXPORT — deep gold, strongly hopped nose, heavy body, big hop flavor and finish, long dry hop aftertaste. Has reached the U.S. as **DORTMUNDER HANSA IMPORTED GERMAN BEER**.

ALT SEIDELBRÄU — deep gold, big hop nose with a sour malt background, big bitter hop flavor, big body, very well hopped to the point of being harsh, long dry hop aftertaste.

DAB MEISTER PILS — gold, clean malt aroma, fresh hop and malt flavor, good tasting, good body, has zest and character, long dry hop aftertaste.

DORTMUNDER ACTIEN ALT — deep amber, dry roasted malt nose, tangy malt flavor, light body, brief finish, faint aftertaste.

DAB EXPORT — medium deep gold, lightly hopped nose, heavy body, big flavor with plenty of hops and malt, good balance, stays off-dry throughout, including the finish and early aftertaste, bitterness arrives at the very end and almost clashes with the sweet character.

DAB KRAFT-PERLE CEREAL BEVERAGE — dark reddish-brown, burnt sugar aroma, tastes like fermented maple sugar and butter, a bit too sweet. Non-alcoholic.

DAB ORIGINAL SPECIAL RESERVE BEER — bright gold, lovely hop aroma, lively hop flavor, medium body, tasty and long.

DAB TRADITIONAL DARK — brilliant amber, yeasty sour malt nose, dry malt flavor, light dry malt finish and long aftertaste.

DAB LIGHT — brilliant pale gold, hop and grain nose, hop palate shows little, if any, malt, fairly long sour hop aftertaste.

Dortmunder Stifts Brewery

Brewery in **Dortmund**

DORTMUNDER STIFTS PREMIUM GERMAN PILSNER — bright gold, light sour hop aroma, sour well-hopped flavor, highly carbonated, finishes bitter hops, long dry hop aftertaste is more pleasant, not being as bitter as the flavor.

Dortmunder Union Schultheiss

Brewing conglomerate with breweries in **Dortmund and Berlin**

Includes Dortmunder Union Brauerei A.G., Dortmunder Ritterbrauerei, A.G., and The Schultheiss Brauerei, A.G.

DORTMUNDER UNION SIEGEL PILS — pale yellow-gold, good sour malt aroma with hops in back, fine malt and hop flavor, a very good pilsener-style beer, long dry hop aftertaste.

DORTMUNDER UNION PILSENER — tawny-gold, toasted malt aroma, pleasant toasted malt flavor, good balance, light body, a little sour malt in back but it doesn't mar the taste, toasted malt carries through the palate into the finish and aftertaste, light and not complex.

EUROPE

BERLINER WEISS SCHULTHEISS — pale cloudy white, foamy, yeasty nose and flavor, medium long semi-dry yeasty-malt aftertaste.

BERLINER UR-BOCK — hazy deep amber-gold, toasted malt nose and flavor, somewhat uninteresting dry malt aftertaste, lacks zest.

GERMANIA PREMIUM MALT BEVERAGE — yellow-gold, off-dry grainy malt nose, grainy palate is off-dry in front, dry in the middle-on, dry malt aftertaste has little duration, tastes like a light beer, which is good for a non-alcoholic brew.

DORTMUNDER UNION BEER — deep bright gold, toasted malt aroma and flavor, medium body, good flavor but not enough of it, fairly short dry malt aftertaste, lacks complexity and depth.

DORTMUNDER UNION MALT LIQUOR — bright tawny-gold, lovely rich roasted malt aroma, big malt flavor is especially good up front on the palate, finish is sour hops and this becomes the aftertaste, good length.

DORTMUNDER UNION SPECIAL — pale gold, intense and complex malt aroma, good malt flavor is strongly accented with hops, balanced, straightforward well-hopped beer, long dry hop aftertaste, an excellent pilsener.

DORTMUNDER UNION ORIGINAL — gold, hop nose, flavor starts out briefly as off-dry malt, then turns bitter hops with a metallic background, long aftertaste like the flavor.

DORTMUNDER UNION LIGHT BEER — bright gold, big hop nose, light body, flavor is carbonation and faintly sour malt, brief light dry aftertaste.

DORTMUNDER UNION DARK BEER — medium deep amber-brown, outstanding rich malt and hop aroma, medium body, finely carbonated, rich dark malt flavor, hops come in at the finish, pleasant dry malt and hop aftertaste, an excellent dark pilsener that goes very well with salamis and other cold wursts.

DORTMUNDER RITTER BRÄU LIGHT BEER — deep yellow, big hop and malt nose, huge hop flavor, big body, long sharp and dry hop aftertaste, a robust well-hopped brew.

DORTMUNDER RITTER PILS — gold, big hop nose, big hop flavor has a sour component in back, plenty of malt in back, good body, finishes dry hops without the bitterness, long dry hop aftertaste, a hearty brew, a good pils.

DORTMUNDER RITTER BRÄU BOCK — deep gold, beautiful toasted malt and hop aroma, very complex, delicious, rich toasted malt flavor, excellent balance, a blockbuster, long, long rich malt and hop aftertaste.

DORTMUNDER RITTER EXPORT — deep gold, malt and hop nose, vegetal malt flavor, short dry malt aftertaste has a sourness in back.

DORTMUNDER RITTER DARK — medium deep brown, heavy malt nose with complex vegetal components (like celery seed and sage), hops join in for the flavor but the malt holds dominance and is somewhat sour, the sourness does get in the way, long dry and slightly sour malt aftertaste.

GASTHAUS SPECIAL —medium gold, creamy texture, pleasant mild hop nose, good body, bright hop flavor, very short dry hop aftertaste.

DORTMUNDER WESTFÄLIA SPECIAL — gold, faint malt and hop nose, sour malt flavor, hops seem out of balance, sharp hop finish and aftertaste.

DORTMUNDER WESTFÄLIA EXPORT BEER — bright pale gold, light hop nose, off-dry malt flavor, bitter hop finish and aftertaste.

Privatbrauerei Eder

Brewery in Grossostheim

EDER PILS — hazy yellow, light hop nose, big hop flavor up front, sour malt in back, fair balance, long dry hop aftertaste.

BAVARIA BAYERISCH WEIZEN — gold, lactic spicy malt nose, clean wheat taste with only the faintest lactic spice, clean wheat and malt finish and aftertaste.

EDER PRIVAT EXPORT —hazy gold, grainy molasses nose, big body, big malt flavor, long and rich, ends dry malt.

EUROPE

Einbecker Brauhaus, A.G.

Brewery in Einbeck

EINBECKER UR-BOCK STARKBIER — amber-gold, sour hop nose, pleasant hop palate up front, sour hop finish that goes into a long sour hop aftertaste.

EINBECKER UR-BOCK — pale amber-gold, roasted malt and hop aroma, pleasant malt and hop flavor has licorice and caramel in back, big body, a pervasive saltiness comes in at the finish and stays through the aftertaste and is detrimental to the flavors.

Engel Brauerei

Brewery at Schwäbische Gmeund

TYROLIAN BRÄU BEER — bright gold, good malt and hop nose, malt and hop flavor up front, goes to slightly sweet malt in mid-palate, finishes dry malt, long dry malt and hop aftertaste.

ST. BERNARD BRÄU BEER — bright gold, light malt aroma with faint hops, balanced malt and hop flavor, long dry hop aftertaste.

ANGEL BREW BEER — gold, big toasted malt aroma, rich malt and hop flavor, really feels good in your mouth, big body, long dry hop aftertaste has good malt support, a delicious and beautiful beer.

TROMPE LA MORT DOUBLEBOCK — deep gold with an amber tinge, rich malt aroma, very rich malt flavor, big body, huge, very strong and very long dry malt aftertaste.

Erste Kulmbacher Actienbrauerei, A.G.

Brewery in Kulmbach

EKU BAVARIA SPECIAL RESERVE — bright gold, complex malt and hop nose, more hops than malt, medium body, good long dry malt finish, little aftertaste.

EKU KULMINATOR URTYP HELL 28 — brilliant deep amber, strong and complex malt aroma, big intense concentrated malt flavor, more than enough malt and alcohol, some hops but the flavor is mostly malt, very winey, long, long off-dry malt aftertaste, almost overwhelming, but actually is just a fantastically good monster brew.

EKU BAVARIA DARK RESERVE — deep copper-brown, faint vegetal malt aroma, dull dry malt flavor, finish, and short aftertaste.

EKU KULMINATOR DUNKLER DOPPELBOCK — bright deep amber, complex sweet toasted malt and licorice nose, malt is like Ovaltine, big grainy malt flavor, very heavy and filling, but very good and very long.

EKU JUBILÄUMSBIER — bright tawny-gold, appetizing malt and hop aroma that fills a room, marvelous malt and hop flavor starts out off-dry and finishes with bright hops, long dry hop aftertaste has a hint of roasted malt in back, good balance, wonderful Festbier.

EKU KULMBACHER EXPORT — brilliant gold, big head, absolutely beautiful apple-malt aroma, faint off-dry fruity malt flavor is masked with excessive carbonation, complex finish and long dry malt aftertaste, balance is hurt by the carbonation.

EKU PILS — medium deep gold, pleasant fruity-malt aroma, bitter hop palate, poor balance, medium long dry bitter hop aftertaste.

EKU KULMBACHER HELLER MAIBOCK — bright deep gold, creamy head, off-dry malt and hop nose, huge body, complex malt and hop flavor that is generally dry except the finish is off-dry, long fairly dry hop aftertaste, very good balance.

EKU ALT BAYERISCHES HEFE-WEIZEN DUNKEL — cloudy light brown, very foamy, huge head, aroma like fermented wheat, a bit off-dry but mostly just grainy on the palate, too much carbonation for the flavor, long dry malt aftertaste, reasonably pleasant and refreshing overall despite the carbonation.

EKU
28
CONT.
e 33 cl
ECHT KULMBACHER
BRAUEREI-FÜLLUNG
28%
STAMMWÜRZE
THE STRONGEST BEER IN THE WORLD · LA PIU FORTE BIRRA DEL MONDO
LA PLUS FORTE BIÈRE DU MONDE · LA MAS FUERTE CERVEZA DEL MUNDO
HET ZWAARSTE BIER TER WERELD
Erste Kulmbacher Actienbrauerei
KULMBACH W. GERMANY ALLEMAGNE GERMANIA ALEMANIA R.F.
month, mois, mes, mese
1 2 3 4 5 6 7 8 9 10 11 12 1988 1989

EKU HEFE-WEISSBIER DUNKEL — deep hazy amber, faint malt nose, clean and crisp malt flavor, dry but has a richness, long dry malt aftertaste.

EKU OKTOBERFEST — bright gold, good hop and malt aroma, not big but pleasant, light complex malt and hop flavor, dry hop finish and aftertaste with a touch of sour malt at the end.

EKU EDELBOCK — deep gold, flowery fruity off-dry malt and hop aroma, very appetizing, palate is big off-dry malt in front and middle, finishes caramel sweet, hops appear in the aftertaste behind the caramel, but way behind, long, long full and rich malt aftertaste, a little light on the hops, but very delicious.

EKU RUBIN DARK — dark amber-brown, very malty toasted aroma, very dry toasted malt flavor, light body, hops come in at the finish and stay into a long complex dry aftertaste, overall it is dry and malty, also it is a bit confused.

HOFBRÄU LIGHT RESERVE — tawny-gold, big malt-hop aroma and flavor, a bit clumsy as there is far too much hops for the malt, long dry hop aftertaste, lacking in balance and finesse.

HOFBRÄU BAVARIA DARK RESERVE — deep brownish-orange, light malt aroma, strong malt taste, finishes smoothly, however, leading into a fairly long dry malt aftertaste.

Erzquell Brauerei

Brewery in Erzquell

ERZQUELL EDELBRÄU BEER — deep copper-brown, light malt nose, pleasant off-dry malt palate in front, flat in the middle, flabby malt finish, off-dry malt aftertaste has little length or character.

Privatbrauerei Euler, GEBR

Brewery in Wetzlar

STRASSBRÄU PILSENER SPEZIAL HESSENLAND BIER — pale gold, yeast and malt aroma, flavor is mostly hops, complkex but not well-balanced, a burnt malt taste shows up in the finish and dominates the long aftertaste.

EULER LANDPILS — pale gold, lovely hop and malt aroma, big hop flavor, good body, sour hop finish, sharp bitter hop aftertaste.

KLOSTER ALTENBERG KLOSTER BIER — bright gold, smoky toasted and sour malt aroma, slightly sour malt flavor has plenty of hops, medium body, short hop aftertaste.

MAXIMILIAN TYP MÜNCHEN HELLER BOCK — medium deep tawny-gold, beautiful complex apple aroma, delicious strong malt flavor, complex, a little on the sweet side, but still well-balanced, long medium dry malt aftertaste. Also seen labeled more simply as **MAXIMILIAN HELLER BOCK.**

ALT WETZLAR DARK BEER — deep copper, light toasted malt nose, light body, palate is first malt, then bitter hops at the finish, sour, bitter and dry hop aftertaste.

Brauerei Faust

Brewery in Millenberg am Main

JOHANN GOTTRIED FORST PILS — yellow-gold, toasted malt nose and taste with a sharp hop background, finishes a bit sour, long dry hop aftertaste borders on bitter.

FORST HEFE-WEISSBIER — amber, sharp tangy aroma like ginger ale, smoky flavor with a lactic acid-spice background, some off-dry malt in the middle and in the aftertaste, balance is a bit shaky.

Brauerei Felsenkeller

Brewery in Herford

HERFORDER PILSNER — deep tawny-gold, bright hop nose, big sour hop palate, finish is harshly bitter, long bitter hop aftertaste.

HERFORDER PILS PREMIUM BEER — pale gold, faint malt and hop aroma with a trace of skunk, light hop palate, slightly bitter long dry hop aftertaste.

Notes:

Fiedler Gmbh.

Brewery in Koblenz

FIEDLERS BOCK — deep gold, faint fruity-sour malt nose, like cherry Kool-Aid, strong malt flavor with the hops in back, heavy body, noticeable alcohol, extremely long dry hop aftertaste.

FIEDLERS PILS IM STEIN — bright gold, toasted malt and hop nose, light smooth malt flavor, dry malt and hop finish and aftertaste.

Carl Funke, A.G.

Stern Brewery in Essen

GERMAN STAR NON-ALCOHOLIC MALT BEVERAGE — bright gold, sweet grainy malt nose, cereal-like grainy flavor, weak body, grainy-tinny aftertaste with little length.

STERN PREMIUM LAGER — bright gold, nice light malt and hop aroma, slightly toasted malt flavor, good balance, hops come in for the finish but it stays more malty, good body, long dry malt and hop aftertaste.

Notes:

Fürstlich Fürstenbergische Brauerei, K.G.

Brewery in Donauschingen

FÜRSTENBERG PILSENER — bright gold, malt aroma with hops in back, big hop flavor, nicely balanced, hops ease off a bit at the finish and the long aftertaste is smooth light dry hops, a nicely made, very serviceable pilsener.

FÜRSTENBERG IMPORTED GERMAN BEER — deep bright gold, smooth hop aroma with a little roasted malt in back, palate is mostly malt but there is good hop support, very good balance, complex and interesting, long dry hop aftertaste.

Privatbrauerei Gaffel

Brewery in Köln

GAFFEL KÖLSCH — light amber-gold, faint caramel nose, light body, slightly sweet front palate with a faint banana character, some hops at the finish, long dry malt aftertaste.

Gold Ochsen, Gmbh.

Brewery in Ulm

GOLD OCHSEN PREMIUM BEER — gold, roasted malt and hop nose, tasty roasted malt flavor, lovely up front but weak at the finish, short dry roasted malt aftertaste.

GOLD OCHSEN HEFE WEIZEN — deep gold, lovely lightly toasted malt aroma, creamy head, pleasant slightly sweet malt flavor with a wheaty background, very good duration and balance, lots of character.

Hacker-Pschorr, A.G.

Brewery in Munich

HACKER EDELHELL EXPORT — gold, medium hop aroma, bright hop flavor with an off-dry malt background, good body, excellent balance, plenty of character, long dry hop aftertaste with a hint of malt in back, very nicely done.

HACKER-PSCHORR OKTOBERFEST MÄRZEN — pale amber, light malt aroma, bright malt-hop flavor, well-balanced, tasty complex malt and hop finish and aftertaste.

HACKER-PSCHORR ORIGINAL OKTOBERFEST BIER BRÄUROSL-MÄRZEN — deep amber, big malty nose and taste, a beer to chew on, big in every way, but expertly balanced, long rich dry malt aftertaste, not to be missed.

HACKER-PSCHORR LIGHT BEER — pale gold, beautiful clean malt and hop aroma, big malt and hop flavor, very good balance, more hops appear at the finish and stay for the aftertaste, stays clean and good throughout.

HACKER-PSCHORR DARK BEER — medium dark amber-brown, malt-hop aroma with molasses in back, good-tasting toasted malt flavor, medium body, finish is a bit weak, but the medium long toasted malt aftertaste is excellent.

HACKER-PSCHORR WEISS BIER — foamy pale yellow-gold, yeasty nose, medium body, grainy dry flavor has a yeasty-spicy-smoky pine resin background, fairly bright, extremely complex, very pleasant and interesting, finish and aftertaste like the flavor but more dry, good duration.

PSCHORR-BRÄU WEISSE (WEISSBIER WITH YEAST) — cloudy gold, spicy clove nose, flavor starts tart and spicy, finishes a bit sweeter, good carbonation, medium body, fairly long off-dry malt aftertaste.

HACKER-PSCHORR MAIBOCK — brilliant deep tawny-gold, big smooth hop and malt aroma, good off-dry malt and hop flavor, extremely fine balance, very tasty, finish is off-dry malt and hops, and there is a long complex hop and malt aftertaste.

PSCHORR MUNICH — bright copper, caramel nose, light carbonation, wine-like malt flavor, heavy body, some hops show lightly in the finish and aftertaste, but they have trouble getting through the winy malt.

HACKER-PSCHORR FEST BEER — pale amber-gold, roasted malt and hop aroma, good hop and malt palate, but there is a faint sourness that carries through and does mar the aftertaste.

HACKER-PSCHORR BRAUMEISTER PILS — bright gold, toasted malt and hop nose, pleasant hop and toasted malt flavor, good body, finish is mostly malt, good long dry hop aftertaste.

HACKER-PSCHORR ANIMATOR DUNKLER DOPPELBOCK — deep ruby-amber-brown, rich malt aroma, fruity-malt flavor has a rich backtaste, complex, balanced, very satisfying, long, long dry and rich malt aftertaste.

Heidelberger Schlossquell Brauerei, A.G.

Brewery in Heidelberg

VALENTINS KLARES WEIZENBIER — bright gold, big head, clean grainy malt aroma with a touch of refreshing clove-lactic spice, clean fresh bright flavor is like the nose but better, lingering wheat and malt aftertaste, delicious and refreshing, very drinkable.

Notes:

Henninger Brauerei KGuA

Brewery in **Frankfurt**

HENNINGER INTERNATIONAL — gold, faint sweet malt aroma, highly carbonated, light off-dry malt flavor, little hop character, light off-dry malt aftertaste, needs more hops.

HENNINGER BIER — deep gold, clean hop aroma with a touch of roasted malt in back, good dry hop flavor, big body, good balance, excellent finish and dry hop aftertaste, fresh tasting and refreshing.

HENNINGER DARK BIER — rosy-amber, dry roasted malt nose yields some hops when swirled, good malt and hop flavor, complex, balanced, long roasted malt and hop aftertaste, good beer with lots of character. More recently labeled CHRISTIAN HENNINGER DARK BEER.

HENNINGER KAISER PILSENER — deep gold, appetizing hop aroma, excellent malt and hop flavor, extremely dry, pleasant dry finish and long dry hop aftertaste, finely balanced, bright and refreshing.

HENNINGER DOPPELBOCK DUNKLER BOCK — reddish-amber, aroma of hops, licorice, molasses, and roasted malt, big palate is mostly malt, quite complex, delicious, well-balanced, drinkable and satisfying.

GERSTEL BRÄU NON-ALCOHOLIC BEER — bright deep gold, rich grainy malt nose, pleasant grainy flavor, good but short, some hops appear in the aftertaste.

CHRISTIAN HENNINGER BEER — medium gold, soapy hop nose, bright hop flavor, good balance, good long dry hop aftertaste, but there is not much complexity.

KARAMALZ ALKOHOLFREIES MALZGETRÄNK — deep red, light smoky-sweet malt nose, slightly smoky sweet malt flavor, long sweet malt aftertaste.

Brauerei Herrenhausen

Brewery in **Hannover**

HERRENHAUSEN EXPORT LAGER BEER — medium gold, sharp hop and malt nose, flavor is malt in front, hops in the middle and finish, long malt aftertaste, good balance and good flavor.

HORSY DEUTSCHES QUALITÄTSBIER — bright tawny-gold, big hop aroma with a perfumy malt background, complex malt and hop palate, more malt than hops, complex and well-balanced, good hop finish, long malt aftertaste.

Brauerei Herrnbräu

Brewery in **Ingolstadt**

MÖNCHSHOF KAPUZINER WEISSE HEFETRÜB — cloudy amber, huge head, wheat and lactic acid nose, complex creamy off-sweet malt palate with lactic overtones, doesn't come off well at all, long acidic malt aftertaste.

Privatbrauerei Hildebrand Gmbh. & Co., K.H.

Brewery in **Pfungstadt**

PFUNGSTADTER — pale yellow-gold, hop and sour malt aroma, good flavor with a touch of roasted malt to give it richness, good-tasting finish, good balance, long malt aftertaste.

BOCKALE PREMIUM CLASS — pale gold, faint hop and roasted malt aroma, highly carbonated, big hop flavor, and long hop aftertaste, could use more malt for a better balance.

Notes:

Hofbräuhaus Munich

Brewery in Munich

HOFBRÄU OKTOBERFEST BEER — amber, big hop nose with plenty of malt, big chewy palate with lots of hops and malt, big body, good balance, long dry malt and hop aftertaste.

Hofmark Spezialitäten Brauerei

Brewery in Cham

HOFMARK HERRENPILS — pale yellow-gold, beautiful hop and roasted malt aroma, complex interesting dry malt flavor, brief malt finish, medium long dry malt aftertaste.

DAS FEINE HOFMARK LAGER BEER — hazy gold, faint off-dry malt aroma, light malt flavor, not exciting or long.

HOFMARK GOLD — gold, sour hop nose, hop flavor turns malty as it crosses the palate, good body, good complexity, long dry malt aftertaste.

DAS FEINE HOFMARK WÜRZIG HERB — gold, toasted malt nose has faint fruitiness and a tang, big hop flavor, big body, some off-dry malt appears at the finish and carries into the long aftertaste to lurk behind the hops, good balance, good beer.

DAS FEINE HOFMARK WÜRZIG MILD — gold, apple-malt nose, much like cider and hops, good flavor like the nose but more dry, highly carbonated, excellent balanced mid-palate and finish, long dry malt and hop aftertaste, very appetizing brew.

Holsten Brauerei

Brewery in Hamburg

SENATOR URBOCK MAIBOCK — pale amber, smoky caramel nose and taste, heavy body, long roasted malt aftertaste.

HOLSTEN LAGER — yellow-gold, hop nose has a little malt in back, big hop flavor, too much for the malt and balance, long strong dry bitter hop aftertaste.

HOLSTEN CERVEZA TIGRE — light gold, malt nose, sour and bitter hop palate, finishes quite sour, poor balance, long slightly sour hop aftertaste.

HOLSTEN EXPORT — bright gold, big roasted malt aroma, some hops in the back of the nose, lots of hops in the flavor, but they are neither sharp nor unpleasant, good toasted malt appears at the finish, and there is a pleasant long dry roasted malt aftertaste.

HOLSTEN DRY BIER— bright gold, rising malt aroma, dry malt flavor, dull dry hop finish and aftertaste.

HOLSTEN PREMIUM BEER — bright gold, vegetal malt nose, dry hop flavor, long dry hop aftertaste.

EXTRACTO DE MALTA HAMBURG MALT BEVERAGE — deep brown, lightly carbonated, malty ceral aroma, molasses-malt flavor, very heavy body, thick and chewy, sweet but not cloying, some hops creep in for the finish and aftertaste, but overall it stays malty, very long sweet malt aftertaste.

DRESSLER EXPORT BEER — yellow-gold, hop nose, strong bitter hop flavor, long dry and bitter hop aftertaste, very austere.

Brauerei Hümmer

Brewery in Dingolhausen

HÜMMER GERMAN EXPORT BEER — tawny-gold, mild hop and malt nose, smoky malt flavor, hops in the finish but well buried under the smoked flavor, long smoky aftertaste.

Privatbrauerei Franz Inselkammer

Brewery in Aying

CELEBRATOR DOPPELBOCK — deep red-brown, good caramel and toasted malt aroma, some sweetness in back, big body, complex off-dry toasted malt flavor, hop finish that gradually becomes dry, long dry hop aftertaste, good balance, especially in the middle, low carbonation.

AYINGER MAIBOCK — medium pale gold, good hop and toasted malt nose, complex hop flavor, plenty of malt backing, most of which doesn't appear until mid-palate, big body, off-dry malt finish, long dry malt and hop aftertaste, very complex throughout, and delicious.

AYINGER FEST-MÄRZEN — tawny-copper, toasted malt nose, huge hop and toasted malt flavor is short-lived, light body, faint roasted malt finish and aftertaste, very nice but just doesn't last long enough.

AYINGER JAHRHUNDERT BIER — pale gold, faint malt aroma, good hop and malt flavor up front, becomes simple off-dry malt at the finish, long faint hop aftertaste.

AYINGER ALTBAYERISCHE DUNKEL — deep red-brown, rich toasted malt nose, off-dry roasted malt flavor, enough hop backing for good balance, medium body, long pleasant dry malt aftertaste. Also labelled **AYINGER ALTBAIRISCH DUNKEL.**

AYINGER WEIHNACHTSBOCK — dark brown, lovely slightly toasted malt nose, pleasant dry malt flavor, fades a bit at the finish, very little aftertaste.

AYINGER OKTOBER FEST-MÄRZEN — brilliant amber, pleasant malt nose, caramel malt flavor well backed with hops, dry hop finish and aftertaste, very pleasant and drinkable.

Brauerei Isenbeck, A.G.

Brewery in **Hamm**

ISENBECK EXPORT DELUXE — gold, pleasant off-dry malt aroma, off-dry malt and hop flavor, long dry hop aftertaste.

ISENBECK EXTRA DRY — gold, mild beautiful smoky hop nose, big hop flavor, hop finish, long dry hop aftertaste.

ISI 08 SPECIAL BEER — pale gold, faint malt aroma, light malt and hop flavor, light body, cereal grain aftertaste, little length, a very low-alcohol malt beverage.

Kaiser Brauerei

Brewery in **Neuhaus**

KAISER BAVARIA LIGHT BEER — medium gold, light austere hop aroma, dry and well-hopped palate, good body, long dry hop aftertaste.

NEUHAUS KAISER PILS — bright greenish-gold, hop nose and big hop flavor, dry hop finish and medium long dry hop aftertaste.

Privatbrauerei Kaiserbräu

Brewery in **Bamberg**

BAMBERGER KRONEN PREMIUM PILSENER BEER — bright gold, beautiful hop nose, strong hop flavor, long dry hop aftertaste borders on being bitter.

Karlsberg Brauerei

Brewery in **Homberg**

KARLSBRÄU GERMAN LAGER — deep golden amber, faint hop and malt aroma, flavor of yeast and malt, mild hop background, sour hop finish and aftertaste.

WALSHEIM BEER — gold, beautiful malt and hop nose, flavor starts out on the sweet side, finishes dry and slightly sour hops, long dry hop aftertaste.

KARLSBRÄU MANNLICH — bright yellow-gold, nice hop nose, good balance, off-dry malt and hop palate, hop finish, medium long dry hop aftertaste, good tasting satisfying brew.

Notes:

Brauerei Kiesel

Brewery in Traunstein

KIESEL HEFE-WEISSBIER EXPORT — bright amber, pleasant chocolate, almond and toasted wheat-malt aroma, toasted malt and hop flavor, very long on the palate, refreshing, long, and very good of type.

KIESEL PILS — gold, beautiful off-dry malt nose with good hop balance, touch of apple in back, big complex hop flavor well backed with malt, rich and full, long complex dry malt and hop aftertaste.

KIESEL MÄRZEN — medium deep dull gold, lightly carbonated, pleasant malt aroma, light grainy flavor, some hop character but not much, short dry malt aftertaste.

KIESEL EXPORT HELL — pale yellow, pleasant malt and hop aroma, medium body, good-flavored malt and hop palate, well-balanced, long dry hop aftertaste keeps the good flavor in your mouth.

KIESEL FESTBIER — pale yellow, good hop aroma, medium body, bright hop flavor has plenty of malt in support, good balance, good body, long dry malt and hop aftertaste, a tasty brew from start to finish.

KIESEL PERL-BOCK DOPPELBOCK — medium yellow, malt aroma, heavy body, all-malt flavor, big and complex, wine-like with high alcohol, long off-dry malt aftertaste, good but could use more hops.

KIESEL WEISSBIER EXPORT — bright gold, foamy, off-dry malt nose and taste with hops in back, there's a little lactic-like bite on the sides of the tongue, but there is no lactic flavor, pleasant and refreshing, fairly short dry malt aftertaste.

Berliner Kindl Brauerei, A.G.

Brewery in Berlin

BERLINER KINDL PILS GERMAN BEER — pale gold, malt and hop aroma, medium body, some complexity, malt palate until the finish when the hops come in, dry bitter hop aftertaste.

BERLINER KINDL WEISSE — yellow-gold, foamy, very complex yeast-bread-wheat-malt aroma, very aromatic, flavor like the nose at first, but the finish tends toward sour, and the long aftertaste is decidedly sour.

Kloster Brauerei Hamm Gmbh.

Brewery in Hamm

KLOSTER PILSENER — tawny-gold, slighly smoky hop nose, somewhat sour hop and malt flavor, long dry and slightly sour malt aftertaste.

König Brauerei, K.G.

Brewery in Duisberg

KÖNIG PILSENER — brilliant gold, good hop aroma, big hop flavor is smooth and well balanced with malt, finishes malty, long dry hop aftertaste.

Königsbacher Brauerei, A.G.

Brewery in Koblenz

KÖNIGSBACHER PILS — gold, big vegetal malt nose, off-dry vegetal malt flavor, long pleasant off-dry malt aftertaste.

KÖNIGSBACHER ALT — deep copper, heavy roasted malt nose, big malt flavor with plenty of hops, medium body, lots of character, good malt finish, brief malt aftertaste.

KÖNIGSBACHER UR-BOCK — tawny gold, rich roasted malt nose, big beautiful roasted malt flavor, magnificent balance, huge and long, they don't get any better than this, a perfect 90!

KÖNIGSBACHER MALZ — reddish-brown color, sweet malt nose, very sweet malt flavor, only bite is from carbonation, very long sweet malt aftertaste.

Privatbrauerei Krombacher

Brewery in Krombach

KROMBACHER PILS — brilliant deep gold, toasted malt aroma and flavor, creamy but lightly carbonated, good strong flavor with a fine hop finish, complex hop and malt aftertaste is long and fairly dry, good balance, likeable beer.

Kronenbrauhaus Lüneberg

Brewery in Lüneberg

MORAVIA BEER — bright pale gold, good fragrant aromatic hop nose, big hop flavor, medium-length dry hop aftertaste.

MORAVIA DARK BEER — tawny-brown, hop nose, roasted malt flavor with only faint hops, long dry malt aftertaste, some off flavors persist throughout and mar the palate.

Privatbrauerei A. Kropf

Brewery in Kassel

KROPF EDEL PILS — bright medium deep gold, faint malt nose, dull dry hop flavor, fairly light body, weak dull dry hop finish and aftertaste.

MEISTER PILS — pale gold, toasted malt nose, good toasted malt flavor, medium body, long pleasant dry toasted malt aftertaste.

KROPF GENUINE GERMAN DRAFT — bright gold, beautiful roasted malt nose, good hop palate well backed with malt, good tasting, good body, short dry hop aftertaste.

KROPF DARK GERMAN BEER — brown, faint malt aroma, dry malt flavor, burnt finish, good balance but little zest, fair length.

KROPF GENUINE GERMAN LIGHT — pale gold, pleasant malt nose, sour hop flavor, light body, metallic finish, long bitter hop aftertaste.

KROPF MAI-BOCK — deep gold, rich malt nose, big malt flavor, rich and full-bodied, long malt aftertaste.

Kulmbacher Schweizerhofbräu

Brewery in Kulmbach

KULMBACHER SCHWEIZERHOFBRÄU — bright gold, magnificent hop aroma, flavor starts out bitter hops, malt comes in at mid-palate, and it finishes off-dry malt, balance is very good, good body, long dry malt and hop aftertaste.

KULMBACHER SCHWEIZERHOFBRÄU BOCK — brilliant gold, lush hop aroma, good body, rich malt and hop flavor, extremely complex, marvelous balance, long well-hopped aftertaste, a delicious gem of a beer.

KULMBACHER SCHWEIZERHOFBRÄU HELLER — deep golden amber, beautiful hop nose, big body, big rich flavor of hops well backed with malt, good balance, very long on the palate, loaded with flavor.

Brauerei Kaiser (W. Kumpf)

Brewery in Geislingen/Steige

KAISER WEISSBIER — hazy yellow, big head, faintly lactic wheat nose and flavor, fades almost immediately upon swallowing.

GEISLINGER KAISER IMPORTED GERMAN BEER — bright pale gold, nice zesty hop nose, complex and aromatic, bright hop flavor, smooth faint papaya way in back, but it never comes forward, long dry hop aftertaste.

Kuppers Kölsch, A.G.

Brewery in Köln

KUPPERS KÖBES KÖLSCH — deep gold, beautiful aromatic hop nose, off-dry hop flavor, perfumy finish, long delicious aftertaste that ends up bittering hops, a good long complex brew.

Lederer Bräu

Brewery in Nürnberg

LEDERER EXPORT — amber, good hop nose with malt and yeast in back, big flavor of molasses, hops, and salt (each flavor separate and distinct), big body, long dry hop aftertaste.

LEDERER EXPORT LIGHT — pale yellow-gold, low carbonation, faint malt nose, thin body, light dull malt palate, short dry malt aftertaste.

Brauerei Robert Leicht, A.G.

Brewery in Vahingen/Stuttgart

SCHWABEN BRÄU GERMAN PILSNER BEER — yellow-gold, light malt nose with some hops, dull malt flavor, bitter hop aftertaste.

SCHWABEN BRÄU PILSENER — gold, hop nose and taste, long dry hop aftertaste.

SCHWABEN BRÄU MEISTER PILS — bright gold, hop nose, pronounced hop flavor, hop finish, long dry hop aftertaste.

SCHWABEN BRÄU EXPORT — bright tawny-gold, balanced hop and malt nose and flavor, good body, fairly smooth, appetizing, long dry malt and hop aftertaste.

DAS ECHTE SCHWABEN BRÄU — tawny-gold, big hop nose, heavy body, big hop flavor, plenty of malt in support, long dry hop aftertaste.

Notes:

Lindener Gilde-Bräu, A.G.

Gilde brewery in Hannover

GILDE RATSKELLER PILS-BEER — bright gold, well-hopped nose, hops dominate the flavor, some off-dry malt appears at the finish, aftertaste is out-of-balance hops and off-dry malt.

GILDE EDEL EXPORT — deep gold, good hop aroma, big body, big hop flavor, hops fade at the finish but are replaced with malt, excellent balance, a marvelous-tasting brew with a long dry malt and hop aftertaste.

GILDE PILSENER — gold, hop nose, big hop flavor, big body, very long dry hop aftertaste.

BROYHAN PREMIUM BEER — gold, hop aroma and strong hop flavor, long dry and somewhat bitter hop aftertaste.

GERMAN IMPORT
BIERGARTEN, UM 1915, MAX LIEBERMANN
12 fl. oz.
Broyhan
Premium Beer
BREWED AND BOTTLED IN W GERMANY BY LINDENER GILDE BRAU · HANNOVER

Notes:

Brauerei Löwenbräu

Brewery in **Munich**

LÖWENBRÄU MUNICH LIGHT SPECIAL — gold, lovely hop nose, marvelous complex hop and malt flavor, big body, chewy, very well balanced, long dry hop aftertaste.

LÖWENBRÄU MUNICH DARK SPECIAL — deep brown with an amber tinge, very clean malt aroma with some hops, strong flavor starts out malt, finishes hops, long dry hop aftertaste has a little sour malt in back, gives it an earthy quality.

MUNICH OKTOBERFEST BEER — amber, beautiful hop aroma with a touch of caramel, big body, big hop flavor is well equipped with toasted malt, long rich and dry malt aftertaste.

DER LÖWENBRÄU PREMIUM PILS — pale gold, nice thick head, sweet hop nose, big hop flavor with a complex off-dry citrus background, high carbonation is more noticeable to the eye than the palate, creamy texture, delicious complex long dry hop aftertaste.

Privatbrauerei GEBR Maisel

Brewery in **Bayreuth**

HERRENBRÄU GERMAN PILSNER — gold, nice malt aroma with a touch of hops, good malt-hop balance, bitter finish, long strong hop aftertaste.

HERRENBRÄU GERMAN WEIZEN — pale gold, dense head, pleasant smoky wheat aroma, sweet and sour wheat beer flavor (fruity-spicy), clean off-dry long malt aftertaste.

HERRENBRÄU GERMAN LIGHT — deep bright gold, fine hop and roasted malt aroma, very appetizing, sharp hop flavor with the malt in back, hop finish, long bitter hop aftertaste.

MAISEL FEST BIER — bright amber, beautiful well-hopped roasted malt aroma, delicious smooth brew with plenty of hops and malt, excellent balance, clean, good body, long roasted malt aftertaste, a really fine beer.

MAISEL BAYRISCH — deep bright gold, foamy, complex hop nose and flavor, malt finish, brief dry malt aftertaste.

MAISEL DAMPFBIER — bright amber, faint off-dry malt aroma, palate starts out sweet malt, goes a little sour in the middle and dry hops come in for the finish and long aftertaste.

MAISEL'S PILSNER — pale gold, light pleasant malt and hop aroma, bright malt and hop flavor, good balance, good body, off-dry malt finish, long dry hop aftertaste, not complex but very pleasant all the way through.

MAISEL MALT LIQUOR EXPORT — pale gold, light hop aroma, bright hop flavor, good body and balance, long dry hop aftertaste, very much like the Maisel Pilsner.

MAISEL'S KRISTALLKLAR WEIZEN — deep bright gold, big head, tart nose, lactic acid and cloves start the flavor, softens as it goes, smooth light dry malt aftertaste, nicely balanced and very drinkable.

MAISEL'S HEFE-WEISSBIER — pale cloudy amber, light pleasant malt aroma, sour banana flavor, long malt aftertaste retains much of the banana.

MAISEL HEFE WEISSE — hazy amber, big head, light lactic-malt aroma, big clove flavor, zesty and bright, hefty body, refreshing and dry, dry malt finish and aftertaste.

MAISEL BRÄU SPEZIAL — pale copper-gold, malt nose with an artificially sweet quality, palate similar but more noticeable, complex but strange and unbalanced, highly carbonated, pleasant malt and hop aftertaste has good length.

MAISEL TRADITIONAL — pale apricot color, light toasted malt aroma, flavor like the nose, sweet malt in the finish, slightly sour hop aftertaste that loses most of its sourness as you continue to drink the beer.

MAISEL ORIGINAL 1887 HELLES EXPORT BIER — bright gold, pleasant aroma is mostly malt, good refreshing light hop flavor, malt finish, smooth and very drinkable, long dry malt aftertaste.

MAISEL'S WEIZEN BOCK — cloudy brown, has sediment, very foamy, fruity wheat grain and apple peel aroma, initially some lactic acid on the palate, but it didn't last, promises sweetness but stays dry, full but not heavy, high carbonation balances complex flavors rather than intrudes, long on the palate, feel good in your mouth, very good of type.

MAISEL DUNKEL — deep orange-brown, dry malt nose, dull dry malt flavor, long faintly sour malt aftertaste.

FORST HEFE-WEISSBIER — tawny-gold, slightly sharp wheat nose, complex and full bodied, big grainy palate, long complex malt aftertaste.

FORST WEISSBIER — bright gold, huge head, grainy wheat aroma, clean light pleasant grainy palate, medium to long dry malt aftertaste, very good tasting.

JOHANN GOTTFRIED FORST PILS — slightly cloudy yellow-gold, toasted malt aroma and taste, good hop tang but a bit on the sour side, long dry hop aftertaste. Faust Brauerei, Miltenberg.

JOHANN GOTTFRIED FORST DUNKEL — medium deep copper, roasted malt nose, good head, creamy roasted malt flavor, light body, lacks depth and is a bit dull, medium long dry malt aftertaste.

Mönchshof Brauerei Gmbh.

Brewery in Kulmbach

KULMBACHER MONKSHOF KLOSTER SCHWARZ BIER — deep copper-brown, light toasted malt aroma, mellow and smooth, lovely malt flavor, beautiful balance, long dry malt aftertaste, a lovely brew.

KULMBACHER MONKSHOF AMBER LIGHT BEER — gold, fragrant roasted malt and hop aroma, big body, big roasted malt and hop flavor, excellent balance, an excellent beer.

KULMBACHER MÖNCHSHOF FESTBIER — bright gold, subdued malt and hop aroma, smooth malt flavor has good hop backing, good balance, heavy body, long and delicious hop and malt aftertaste.

KULMBACHER MÖNCHSHOF PILSENER — bright pale gold, malt nose and flavor, medium to light body, dry hop finish, and long hop aftertaste which is a tad sour.

GREGORIUS WIESENFESTBIER — bright gold, delicious toasted malt nose is really malty (like malted milk-malty), delicious appetizing palate is first malt, then hops, all stays in balance right into the long complex malt and hop aftertaste, a very, very nice drinkable brew.

MÖNCHSHOF URSTOFF DARK SPEZIAL STARKBIER — reddish brown, malt nose, huge strong smooth malt flavor, enormous body, you can taste the alcohol, very long pleasant strong malt aftertaste, a pleasure to sip.

MÖNCHSHOF URSTOFF SPEZIAL STARKBIER — deep amber, huge malt nose, concentrated malt palate, medium body, long dry malt aftertaste is like dry molasses.

KULMBACHER MONKSHOF DRY LIGHT BEER — pale gold, good malt nose with hops in back, a little toasted malt barely found in the nose is the good flavor, medium body, hops appear at the finish, long dry roasted malt aftertaste.

KULMBACHER MONKSHOF KLOSTERBOCK BEER— rosy-amber, fragrant roasted malt, caramel, and hop aroma, , big body, front palate is off-dry roasted malt, finishes dry malt and hops, long pleasant malt and hop aftertaste leaves your mouth feeling good.

KULMBACHER MONKSHOF DARK BEER — tawny-brown, rich toasted malt aroma with hops in back, rich full toasted malt flavor, good balance, malty-molasses middle and finish, but the long aftertaste is tasty dry malt and the lasting memory is that dry malt rather than the sweeter malt earlier.

KULMBACHER MÖNCHSHOF OKTOBERBIER — brilliant gold, big toasted malt aroma with hops in back, light body, light flavor of hops and toasted malt, long dry hop aftertaste, not big but very drinkable.

KULMBACHER MONKSHOF HELLER BOCK — medium gold, rising toasted malt and hop aroma, big body, rich dark malt flavor has powerful hops in back trying to break through, strong, complex, and excellently balanced, very long complex dry hop and malt aftertaste.

KAPUZINER SCHWARZE HEFE-WEIZEN — amber-brown, big head, malt nose and fresh malt flavor, medium body, smooth rather than zesty, pleasant long dry malt aftertaste.

Notes:

Hofbrauhaus Moy

Brewery in **Freising**

HOFBRAUHAUS MOY JÄGERBIER — bright gold, light off-sweet nose with hops in back, good smooth delicate malt and hop flavor, finely balanced, slightly sweet malt aftertaste, a nice silky smooth brew.

HOFBRAUHAUS MOY REGENT — bright gold, dry complex malt nose with a little ale-like tartness, good smooth delicate taste similar to above but with more hops in front, long dry hop aftertaste.

HOFBRAUHAUS MOY EDELWEIZEN KRISTALLKLAR — bright gold, big head, clean wheat nose, zesty clean wheat and malt flavor, tastes good, good body, slightly sweet finish and aftertaste, medium to short.

Nordbräu Gmbh.

Brewery in **Ingolstadt**

POPPER MALT BEVERAGE — medium deep yellow-gold, grainy malt nose, light grain and hop palate, clean tasting, medium length aftertaste like the flavor.

Osnabrücker Aktien-Brauerei

Brewery in **Osnabrück**

WÖLFBRÄU IMPORTED GERMAN BEER — medium deep gold, dry hop and grainy malt nose with an off-dry malt component in the background, dry hop palate, some sour malt in the finish, brief dry and sour aftertaste.

Parkbrauerei

Breweries in **Pirmasens** and **Zweibrücken**

PARKBRÄU EXPORT — pale gold, light but very good hop aroma well backed with malt, good body, creamy texture, bright tangy hop flavor and long dry hop aftertaste, good-tasting refreshing brew.

Notes:

Paderborner Brauerei Gmbh.

Brewery in **Paderborn**

PADERBORNER LIGHT BEER — pale gold, light malt nose, sour hop flavor, medium long dry hop aftertaste.

PADERBORNER REGULAR BEER — deep gold, hop aroma, yeasty cereal and malt flavor, malt finish and short malt aftertaste.

PADERBORNER GERMAN PILSENER — deep bright gold, mild malt and hop nose, bright hop flavor, sour metallic finish, short dry hop aftertaste keeps some of the metallic nature of the finish.

Patrizier-Bräu, A.G.

Brewery in **Nürnberg**

PATRIZIER EXPORT — deep amber, light hop nose, medium body, good malt flavor with the hops in back, long dry malt aftertaste.

PATRIZIER EDELHELL EXPORT — bright gold, nice complex hop aroma, big hop flavor up front, malt shows through in the finish, good balance, very good taste, complex, softens and gets better as you sip, pleasant long malt aftertaste.

PATRIZIER PILS — bright deep gold, toasted malt and hop aroma, light malt and hop palate, not exciting, brief malt aftertaste.

BAMBERGER HOFBRÄU BEER — tawny-gold, slightly off-dry malt and grain aroma, grainy slightly toasted palate, very light body, virtually no finish or aftertaste.

PATRIZIER ZERO NON-ALCOHOLIC MALT BEVERAGE — amber-gold, grainy malt aroma like Grape-Nuts, lightoff-dry grainy flavor, brief dry malt aftertaste.

Paulaner Salvator Thomasbräu, A.G.

Brewery in Munich

PAULANER SALVATOR — deep brown, complex hop and malt aroma, huge fresh malt flavor, big body, very rich, clean and complex, extremely long dry malt aftertaste, noticeable alcohol, a great double bock.

PAULANER HELL URTYP EXPORT — gold, rich malt aroma, strong hop flavor, sour malt and dry hop finish and aftertaste, good long palate.

PAULANER ALTBAYERISCHES HEFE WEISSBIER — bright gold, clean wheat nose with only the faintest trace of yeast, bright perky dry spicy flavor, big body, fresh, long dry hop aftertaste.

PAULANER OKTOBERFEST BIER — bright deep gold, well-balanced hop and toasted malt aroma, complex toasted malt flavor, hop backing, good balance, good tasting, long pleasing rich and dry malt and hop aftertaste.

PAULANER URTYP 1634 — deep gold, toasted malt aroma, medium body, flavor is mostly malt but there are enough hops for good balance, slightly sour hop finish, medium long dry hop aftertaste, lacks the depth and character normally found with a Paulaner beer.

PAULANER MÜNCHENER MÄRZEN — copper-gold, toasted malt aroma, creamy texture, rich toasted malt flavor, hops are there but well in back, decent balance, good tasting flavor and finish, long refreshing dry malt aftertaste.

PAULANER ALT MÜNCHENER DUNKEL — deep reddish brown, very faint malt aroma, lovely malty flavor is a bit light, full bodied, light malt finish, lighter and brief malt aftertaste.

PAULANER FEST-BIER — bright gold, pleasant hop nose and flavor, good body, good feeling in the mouth, very long pleasant dry hop aftertaste.

PAULANER WIES'N-MÄRZEN — amber, delicate roasted malt aroma, pleasant toasted malt flavor, not much depth or character, but it is pleasant, dry malt finish and aftertaste.

PAULANER GERMAN PILS — yellow-gold, beautiful hop nose, delicious big hop flavor, long slightly sour dry hop aftertaste.

PAULANER MÜNCHENER UR-BOCK HELL — amber-gold, toasted malt and hop aroma, medium body, good-tasting toasted malt and hop flavor, bright and hoppy up front, rich toasted malt at the finish, complex, balanced, long toasted malt aftertaste.

PAULANER MAIBOCK — bright tawny-gold, light roasted malt nose, light body, flavor is mostly hops, but there is malt and carbonation showing as well, bitter and dry hop finish and aftertaste.

PAULANER WEISSBIER ALTBAYERISCHES BRAUART — bright gold, foamy, clove-apple-wheat-citrus aroma, spicy-sweet palate is mostly cloves, malt finish and aftertaste shows little of the spiciness and is quite long.

PAULANER ORIGINAL MÜNCHENER HELL — pale gold, smooth malt and hop nose, hefty flavor has both malt and hops aplenty, very straightforward hop character, good balance, dry hop finish and long aftertaste.

PAULANER HEFE-WEIZEN — hazy gold, big head, off-dry tangy spicy nose with a caramel background, bright zesty flavor has good balance between the spice and the sweetness of the malt, good body, refreshing, good length, the touch of cloves in the nose and taste is just right for the balance.

PAULANER MÜNCHEN NR. 1 EXTRA PREMIUM LAGER — bright gold, hop nose and flavor, good body, long dry hop aftertaste, an excellent well-balanced brew that is most satisfying.

PAULANER OKTOBERFEST — amber, big malt nose, big toasted malt flavor, smooth and dry, long dry hop aftertaste, an excellent beer with food.

Brauerei Pinkus Müller

Brewery in Münster

PINKUS WEIZEN — pale gold, faint wheat nose, clean wheat flavor, brief citrus finish, light wheat-malt aftertaste has little duration, good balance, very pleasant drinking beer.

PINKUS PILS — bright gold, pleasant hop aroma, good hop flavor has plenty of malt and carbonation in back, highly hopped finish and long aftertaste.

PINKUS MALZ BIER — dark brown, roasted malt aroma, light body, off-dry roasted malt flavor, brief sweet malt finish, short malt aftertaste, non-alcoholic.

PINKUS ALT — deep tawny-gold, strong hop and roasted malt flavor with an acidic background, medium body, a high acid and very malty brew.

PINKUS HOME BREW UR PILS — gold, good but austere nose, good body, refreshing well-hopped flavor, very drinkable, slightly bitter dry hop aftertaste.

Radeberger Exportbrauerei

Brewery in Berlin

RADEBERGER PILSENER — bright gold, medium hop nose with some malt in back, bright hop flavor, finish, and aftertaste, fairly long but lacks complexity.

RADEBERGER GERMAN PILSENER — tawny-gold, aromatic ester and soapy nose, hop flavor up front, soapy malt finish, good body, long dry malt and hop aftertaste.

LANDSKRON PILS — pale yellow, light sour hop nose, hop flavor, sour hop finish, medium long dry and slightly sour hop aftertaste, so-so balance as there is little malt showing.

Rauchenfels Steinbrauerei

Brewery in Neustadt

RAUCHENFELS STEINBIERE STONE BREWED BEER — tea color, smoky malt aroma, light body, pleasant smoky malt flavor, good tasting, fine finish, fairly long smoked malt aftertaste.

Reichelbrauerei Kulmbach

Brewery in Kulmbach

KULMBACHER REICHELBRÄU HELL EXPORT DE LUXE — bright tawny-gold, big hop nose does have some malt in back, big hop flavor, malt shows well in the finish and stays through the long dry aftertaste.

KULMBACHER REICHELBRÄU FRANKISCHES URBIER — brilliant amber, pleasant toasted malt and hop nose, big body, big malt flavor has a coffee-like background, good balance, long dry malt and hop aftertaste.

KULMBACHER REICHELBRÄU EDELHERB PILS — bright deep gold, lovely flowery hop nose, bright hop palate, good balance and complexity, malt finish, medium body, long dry hop and malt aftertaste.

KULMBACHER REICHELBRÄU BAVARIAN DARK BEER — deep amber-brown, complex toasted malt aroma, medium body, lightly flavored dry toasted malt and hop taste, long dry malt aftertaste.

Privatbrauerei Heinrich Reissdorf

Brewery in Köln

REISSDORF KÖLSCH — medium to deep gold, faint but very clean malt aroma, palate is zesty hops in front, malt in middle and finish, good balance, long dry malt and hop aftertaste, a very good Kölsch.

EUROPE

Bierbrauerei Wilhelm Remmer

Brewery in **Bremen**

BREMER DOM BRÄU — pale yellow, vegetal malt nose, strong hop palate, long dry hop aftertaste.

Brauerei Franz Josef Sailer

Brewery in **Marktoberdorf**

SAILER PILS — pale gold, complex hop and toasted malt nose, light body, toasted malt front palate, tangy hop finish, long dry hop aftertaste.

SAILER WEISSE WITH YEAST— pale cloudy amber, huge head, good grainy nose, gives the sense of being smoky but isn't, sharp grainy flavor, fairly long grainy aftertaste with a bit of spice in back.

SAILER WEISSE — pale golden amber, foamy, lovely aroma is grainy, slightly sweet, and piquant, complex smoky-malty flavor, slightly sweet malt finish, balance is good, long off-dry malt aftertaste, pleasant and refreshing.

OBERDORFER WEISSE — brilliant gold, foamy, spicy-lactic nose, palate has only the faintest trace of lactic acid and is instead quite malty, pleasant and refreshing, very long malt aftertaste, has good zest.

OBERDORFER WEISSE WITH YEAST — hazy gold, foamy, wheat nose, creamy texture, frothy, pleasant and refreshing dry barley malt and wheat palate, grainy finish and aftertaste, good balance, a finely made wheat beer.

OBERDORFER DUNKLES HEFEWEIZENBIER — hazy deep amber, big head, light lactic and fruity wheat-malt aroma, good body, good complex flavor of cloves, wheat, malt, and hops, rich and satisfying, long pleasant malt aftertaste.

Sandlerbrauerei

Brewery in **Kulmbach**

KULMBACHER SANDLERBRÄU PILS — pale gold, toasted malt aroma, mild hop flavor, sour malt finish and long aftertaste.

Notes:

Privatbrauerei Rudolph Schäff

Brewery in **Treuchtlingen**

SCHÄFF FEUERFEST EDEL BIER — tawny port color, beautiful roasted malt aroma, extremely heavy body, almost syrupy, intense roasted smoked malt flavor, sweet sipping beer, very long smoky roasted malt aftertaste, no carbonation, a very long-lived beer, almost impervious to mishandling.

SCHÄFF PILSENER — pale yellow-gold, light sour hop aroma, highly carbonated, palate starts off as strong hops, softens toward middle where some malt joins in to set the balance, malt finish, long sour malt and hop aftertaste.

SCHÄFFBIER — medium pale yellow-gold, lovely well-hopped aroma with a touch of roasted malt, good body, complex flavor is mostly hops, malt finish, good balance, long pleasant malt and hop aftertaste.

Privatbrauerei Sester

Brewery in **Köln**

SESTER KÖLSCH REIN OBERGÄRIG HELL — yellow-gold, light hop nose, dry hop flavor, bitter hop finish, sour aftertaste.

Spaten Franziskaner-Bräu KgaA

Brewery in **Munich**

SPATEN CLUB WEISS BIER — bright gold, big head, fresh clean fruity malt nose has only the faintest wheat component, very fresh slightly grainy flavor with a pleasant spicy tang, good balance, fairly short malt aftertaste and very little spicy-lactic character, but good and refreshing.

SPATEN OPTIMATOR DOPPELSPATEN — deep orange-brown, dry toast and malt aroma, heavy body, medium dry molasses and roasted malt flavor, good-tasting sour malt finish and long aftertaste, excellent balance, a wonderful dark double bock.

SPATEN MUNICH LIGHT — deep gold, toffee malt aroma, heavy body, big hop and malt flavor, the hops are bitter and the malt is off-dry, the balance is excellent, long bright hop aftertaste, a heavy-handed brew, and a wonderful mouthful of beer.

SPATEN URMÄRZEN OKTOBERFEST BEER — copper-gold, good hop and roasted malt aroma, smooth well-balanced malt and hop flavor, flavorful and complex, long dry hop and malt aftertaste, rich satisfying brew.

SPATEN PILS — deep gold, good hop nose and flavor, sharp hop finish, long good hop aftertaste, a good appetizing brew, goes very well with food.

SPATEN FRANZISKUS HELLER BOCK — tawny-gold, toasted malt and hop aroma is very slightly on the off-dry side, big body, flavor like the nose, complex and balanced, slightly off-dry malt and bright hop finish, long malt and hop aftertaste is drier than the flavor, a very satisfying brew that also goes well with food.

SPATEN GOLD — bright gold, light malt and hop nose, good flavor throughout has both hops and malt, well balanced, good complexity, long dry hop and malt aftertaste.

FRANZISKANER HEFE-WEISSBIER — cloudy gold, light wheat aroma, smooth light grainy palate, a touch of lactic acid is immediately noticeable on the front of the palate and again appears in the finish, otherwise it is not there, medium long aftertaste like the finish.

St. Pauli Brauerei

Brewery in Bremen

ST. PAULI GIRL BEER — pale gold, faint malt and hop aroma, mild pleasant hop flavor with good balance between the malt and the hops, slightly hopped finish, mild dry hop aftertaste, a smooth brew.

ST. PAULI GIRL DARK BEER — deep brown, hops more than malt in the nose, taste is heavy malt and light hops, fairly good balance, appetizing finish and medium long aftertaste like the flavor.

ST. PAULI N.A. BREW — gold, pleasant malt nose with some background hops, light dry hop flavor with some malt in back, long dry hop aftertaste.

Privatbrauerei Jacob Stauder

Brewery in Essen

STAUDER BEER — bright tawny gold, faint roasted malt nose and taste, light body, brief dry malt aftertaste.

Brauerei Stumpf

Brewery in Lohr

ORIGINAL 1878 LOHRER BEER — golden amber, pleasant roasted malt and hop aroma, light off-dry roasted malt flavor, hops show well in the finish, long caramel malt and dry bitter hop aftertaste has good length and complexity.

BAVARIAN ABBEY LAGER — pale amber, light roasted malt nose and taste, very light on the hops, brief malt aftertaste, lacks zest without enough hops to balance.

BAVARIAN ABBEY LIGHT LAGER NON-ALCOHOLIC MALT BEVERAGE — gold, dull malt nose, light grainy very malty flavor, straight malt finish and aftertaste.

Notes:

Privatbrauerei Thier

Brewery in Dortmund

DORTMUNDER IMPERIAL IMPORTED BEER — deep gold, beautiful well-hopped aroma with a touch of roasted malt, nicely balanced, palate starts with the malt but quickly goes to hops, finishes toasted malt with a slightly sour background, lingering pleasant dry hop aftertaste, a good complex appetizing brew.

DORTMUNDER IMPERIAL OKTOBERFEST BIER — orange-brown, very faint roasted malt aroma, toasted malt flavor with little or no hops, pleasant and malty without complexity, fairly long dry malt aftertaste.

DORTMUNDER IMPERIAL ALT BEER — deep copper, soft toasted malt nose, well-hopped flavor, balance seems a bit off, some toasted malt appears at the finish, but it is too little and too late for balancing the flavor, lacks depth as well, short faint dry hop aftertaste.

Tochterfirma Weissbräu Gmbh.

Brewery in Traunstein

AYINGER EXPORT-WEISSBIER — clear bright gold, foamy, pleasant wheat nose, bright grainy flavor with a bit of clove spice in back from the lactic acid, quite tasty and fairly long.

AYINGER HEFE-WEISSBIER — slightly cloudy gold, foamy, slightly sour malt nose, big acidic spicy flavor overwhelms the malt, long spicy aftertaste.

AYINGER UR-WEIZEN — hazy copper, wheaty malt nose, creamy, toasted malt and wheat palate, pleasant and straightforward, short dry toasted malt aftertaste.

Brauerei Treiber

Brewery in Treibe

FESTBRÄU IMPORTED GERMAN PILSENER BEER — brilliant gold, hop and sour malt nose, big hop flavor, sags a bit in the middle, ends in a long soapy hop aftertaste.

Notes:

Tucher Bräu A.G.

Brewery in Nürnberg

TUCHER UBERSEE EXPORT BEER — tawny-gold, malt aroma, medium body, toasted malt and hop flavor, sour hop finish, lightly sour hop and toasted malt aftertaste.

BRAUHAUS ROTHENBURG GERMAN PILSENER — gold, light hop nose, harsh bitter hop flavor, sour metallic finish and aftertaste.

TUCHER GERMAN PILSENER — bright gold, nice hop nose with some malt support, big hop flavor, long dry and bitter hop aftertaste.

TUCHER WEIZEN — bright deep gold, foamy, beautiful malt nose, zesty piquant flavor up front, dry very fresh and crisp wheaty middle, long clean off-dry malt finish and medium long aftertaste, a very fine brew that is a pleasure to drink.

TUCHER HEFE WEIZEN — brilliant deep gold, foamy, good malt aroma with some wheat and yeast in back, picquant spicy flavor starts up front and stays throughout, a bit yeasty in the middle, slightly off-dry raspberry malt finish, medium long dry malt aftertaste keeps much of the piquancy of the flavor, very nicely done.

TUCHER HEFE-WEIZEN DUNKLES — amber, malt nose, high carbonation, hop, spice, and malt flavor (in that order), refreshing and drinkable, fairly light handed, short malt aftertaste.

TUCHER IMPORTED GERMAN BEER LIGHT — medium deep gold, hop and faintly roasted malt aroma, complex palate of hops and dry roasted malt, roasted malt finish, long slightly sour malt aftertaste.

TUCHER IMPORTED GERMAN BEER DARK — pale copper, faint toasted malt nose and flavor, weak body, faintly sweet short malt aftertaste.

TUCHER LORENZI BOCK HELL — bright gold, malt and corn nose, toasted malt and corn flavor, finishes cleaner and better with just the malt, long dry malt aftertaste.

TUCHER ALT FRANKEN EXPORT DUNKEL — deep amber, pleasant malt aroma, good-tasting light malt flavor, light body, almost nothing at the finish, faint brief malt aftertaste.

TUCHER MAIBOCK HELL — deep gold, lovely toasted malt nose, big zesty hop and toasted malt flavor, fairly intense, very long aftertaste like the flavor, an excellent beer.

Brauerei Wagner

Brewery in Kemmern

WAGNER BRÄU MÄRZEN — deep tawny-gold, very faint malt aroma, big hop flavor up front, sour hop finish and aftertaste, not well balanced.

WAGNER BRÄU BOCK — medium deep orange-brown, very faint malt aroma, big creamy head, good texture, smoked coffee flavor, bitter hop finish and long aftertaste, not balanced.

Brauerei Waldschlössen

Brewery in Dresden

EDEL WEISS MALT LIQUOR — deep tawny-gold, faint sweet malt nose, dry hop palate, big body, high extract, long malt aftertaste, noticeable alcohol, not much middle palate.

Notes:

Cramer K.G./Brauerei Warsteiner GEBR

Brewery in Warstein

WARSTEINER PREMIUM VERUM — bright pale gold, very good complex hop aroma, bright complex malt and hop flavor, excellent balance, big hop finish, long dry hop aftertaste, a very fine pilsener.

Brauhaus Weissenbrunn

Brewery in Weissenbrunn

ORIGINAL BAVARIAN OKTOBER BIER — tawny-gold, good malt and hop nose with roasted malt in back, good flavor with plenty of hops, long hop aftertaste.

ADLER BRÄU — gold, beautiful hop nose, pleasant well-balanced hop flavor, pleasant well-balanced hop flavor, plenty of malt backing, malt finish, faintly bitter dry hop aftertaste.

Notes:

Privatbrauerei Heinrich Wenker/ Dortmunder Kronen

Krone am Markt brewery in Dortmund

DORTMUNDER KRONEN CLASSIC — medium deep gold, big hop nose, good hop and grainy malt flavor, slightly off-dry malt finish, medium body, complex and well balanced, long fairly dry hop aftertaste, delightful.

DORTMUNDER KRONEN PILSKRONE — amber, toasted malt aroma, toasted malt flavor has hops in back, sour hop aftertaste detracts from what is otherwise a very nice brew.

DORTMUNDER KRONEN CLASSIC ALT DARK — medium deep copper, nice toasted malt aroma, grainy toasted malt flavor, short dry malt and hop aftertaste.

Privatbrauerei Franz Josef Wicküler

Brewery in Wuppertal

WICKÜLER PILSENER BEER — gold, big hop aroma, finely carbonated, big hop flavor with fine malt backing, excellent example of a pils style from central Germany, good body, malt shows well in the finish and aftertaste, but the hops dominate, good duration.

C. Wiederholt's Brauerei Gmbh.

Brewery in Noerten-Hardenberg

CASSEL SCHLOSS PREMIUM BEER — gold, big hop nose, big hop flavor, plenty of malt backing, finishes hops with the malt showing very well at the end, good balance, refreshing, complex, long complex hop and malt aftertaste.

Brauhaus Winter

Brewery in Köln

RICHMODIS KÖLSCH — cloudy yellow, sweet light ale-like nose, some amyl acetate, unbalanced sour taste, long sour aftertaste.

Notes:

Brauerei Wolters

Brewery in **Brunswick**

WOLTERS PILSENER — deep gold, nice hop nose with good hop backing, flavor starts out as malt but quickly turns hoppy and the hops stay on to give an overall dry and bitter flavor, long hop aftertaste is especially bitter.

Privatbrauerei Burgerbräu Wörner OHG

Brewery in **Bamberg**

KAISERDOM PILSENER — brilliant deep gold, roasted malt aroma with good hops and a touch of caramel, good roasted malt flavor with hops showing up in the middle for a beautiful balance, long roasted malt aftertaste.

KAISERDOM RAUCHBIER — deep copper-brown, rich smoked malt nose, reminds you of smoked cheese, meat, pepperoni, very tasty, smoke overrides the hops and malt flavors, but it is still pleasant, interesting brew, long smoky aftertaste.

BURGERBRÄU BAMBERG PILS — medium gold, off-dry malt and hop nose, big hop flavor with the malt showing in the finish and aftertaste, medium long appetizing malt and hop aftertaste.

SIMPATICO BEER — bright gold, faint sweet hop aroma that turns toward sour shortly, unbalanced sour hop flavor, brief dry and sour hop aftertaste.

DOMFÜRSTEN BIER — medium pale gold, toasted malt and hop aroma, toasted malt up front on the palate, balanced hop and malt middle, long sour aftertaste.

PROSTEL HERBFRISCHES SCHANKBIER — pale gold, stinky grainy aroma, woody-grain flavor, tinny finish and aftertaste.

KAISERDOM UR-BOCK STARKBIER — medium deep amber, mellow toasted malt nose, soft and smooth toasted malt palate, good intensity, no faults, long aftertaste like the flavor.

KAISERDOM HEFE WEISSBIER— hazy amber, faint clove and wheat aroma, refreshing spicy clove, yeast, and wheat flavor, light and smooth, pleasant finish, medium long clean dry aftertaste like the flavor.

KAISERDOM EXTRA DRY — pale gold, rising malt nose, hops in back, sour hop flavor, especially so in the finish, bitter dry hop aftertaste, lots of bite and lots of character.

Würzburger Hofbräu, A.G.

Brewery in **Würzburg**

WÜRZBURGER HOFBRÄU LIGHT BEER — gold, marvelous balanced malty hop aroma, bright sour malt and hop flavor, lingering malt aftertaste, a satisfying bright pilsener beer.

WÜRZBURGER HOFBRÄU BAVARIAN DARK BEER — deep amber-brown, heavy malt nose, hearty rich malt flavor, more mellow than zesty, sour malt finish, long malt aftertaste.

WÜRZBURGER OKTOBERFEST BEER — medium amber-brown color, faint hop aroma, delicious roasted malt flavor with a caramel background, excellent balance, soft and mellow, rich lingering malt aftertaste.

WÜRZBURGER BOCK BEER — deep dark brown, subdued burnt malt nose with plenty of hop support, roasted malt flavor, distinctive and with great character, long roasted malt aftertaste.

WÜRZBURGER HOFBRÄU MAY BOCK — pale copper-gold, hop aroma, tangy big hop flavor, very complex, big body, very long on the palate, really wakes up your tongue.

WÜRZBURGER HOFBRÄU ALCOHOL FREE LIGHT MALT BEVERAGE — amber, slightly sweet grainy aroma, watery, dry grainy flavor and aftertaste, not much length.

WÜRZBURGER HOFBRÄU PILSNER — pale yellow-gold, lovely malt nose, flavor is malt in front, hops at the finish, a little weak in the middle as it makes the transition, sour hop aftertaste.

BOLD GOLD MALT LIQUOR — pale gold, slight grapey-soapy nose, lightly sweet malt flavor, soft and delicate, faint hops appear in the long malt aftertaste.

JULIUS ECHTER HEFE-WEISSBIER — brilliant amber, big head, zesty flowery honeyed malt aroma, bright spicy palate, wheat comes in nicely at the finish, refreshing and well balanced, wheat grain and faint clove aftertaste, good length, lots of character, an excellent beer of the style.

WÜRZBURGER HOFBRÄU BAVARIAN HOLIDAY BEER — deep copper-brown, rich roasted malt aroma, big rich and beautiful toasted toffee-malt flavor, dry finish, excellent balance, long rich malt aftertaste, some sense of alcohol, very drinkable and feels good in your mouth, a great brew.

GREAT BRITAIN

Allied Breweries (U.K.), Ltd.

Breweries include Ind Coope, Tetley-Walker, Lorimer, Beskins, Warrington & Ansells, with locations in Burton-on-Trent and Leeds, England, Edinburgh, Scotland, et al.

DOUBLE DIAMOND ORIGINAL BURTON ALE — deep amber, beautiful rich off-dry roasted malt nose, dry bitter palate up front, off-dry malt finish, long very dry hop aftertaste that borders on bitter, excellent balance, medium body, has a sense of high alcohol, delicious.

DOUBLE DIAMOND PILSENER BEER — amber, big pungent hop aroma, big dry hop flavor, creamy, finely carbonated, long dry hop aftertaste, flavor could use more malt.

TETLEY BITTER — pale amber, nice hop aroma, finely carbonated, tart ale flavor with lots of hop character, fruity malt finish, long dry hop aftertaste. From Joseph Tetley & Son, Leeds.

TETLEY SPECIAL PALE ALE — medium amber, toasted malt aroma, flavor starts out like the nose, but the hop intensity increases across the palate to a sharp bitter hop aftertaste, with the roasted malt sliding into the background.

JOHN BULL BEER — tawny-gold, bright hop and malt aroma, zesty big hop flavor well backed with malt, full bodied, good balance, long dry hop aftertaste.

LORIMER'S TRADITIONAL SCOTCH ALE — golden amber, beautiful roasted malt aroma with good hops and a beneficial touch of sour malt that gives balance, intense roasted malt flavor, lingering dry malt aftertaste, big and powerful brew that has plenty of alcohol (7.2%/vol). From Lorimer's Breweries, Ltd., of Edinburgh.

LORIMER'S SCOTTISH BEER — golden amber, big hop nose, huge mouth-filling malt and hop flavor, good balance, dry hop aftertaste has a touch of sour malt. From Lorimer's Breweries, Ltd., of Edinburgh.

ST. CHRISTOPHER NON-ALCOHOLIC BEER — amber, slightly sweet grainy aroma, watery, dry flavor that shows neither malt nor hops, odd dry aftertaste.

Alpine Ayingerbrau (U.K.), Ltd.

Brewery in Tadcaster

ALPINE AYINGERBRAU LAGER — gold, sour hop nose, flavor, and aftertaste.

Bass Charrington, Ltd.

A conglomerate of breweries comprising the Bass, Worthington, Tennent Caledonian, Mitchells & Butler, and Charrington United. Breweries are in Burton-on-Trent, Birmingham, Sheffield, Tadcaster, and Runcorn, England; Belfast, No. Ireland; and Glasgow and Edinburgh, Scotland.

BASS PALE ALE — brilliant copper color, big malt and hop aroma, full rich malty flavor, excellent balance, marvelous long rich and dry aftertaste. Draft version.

BASS PALE ALE I.P.A. — brilliant copper, pleasant malt aroma, good malt flavor with plenty of hop support, well bodied, excellent balance, long dry hop aftertaste. Bottled version.

WORTHINGTON E BRITISH BEER — pale amber, toasted malt nose, smoky well-hopped roasted malt flavor, complex and long, good flavor but a bit shallow.

WORTHINGTON'S ORIGINAL PALE ALE (WHITE SHIELD) — yellow-gold, yeasty aroma, delicate and complex malt and hop flavor, some yeast in the background, smooth and rich, long dry hop aftertaste.

TENNENT'S LAGER BEER — tawny-gold, creamy, clean malty aroma and malt flavor, faintly soapy backtaste, clean fresh malt finish, long dry malt aftertaste.

TENNENT'S EXTRA — deep gold, mild very good malt and hop aroma, good hop flavor with enough malt for balance, good body, malt finish, long satisfying dry hop aftertaste.

TENNENT'S MILK STOUT — opaque brown, rich malt nose with a smoky-burnt background, rich off-sweet malt flavor, medium body, pleasant long dry malt aftertaste.

PIPER EXPORT ALE — deep amber color, roasted mash aroma, burnt toffee-apple flavor, sour in back, assertive at the beginning with the scorched malt, which mars the pleasant aspects, long dry off aftertaste.

BARBICAN NON-ALCOHOLIC MALT BEVERAGE — deep bright gold, dull toasted grainy nose, very light body, light grainy flavor, tartness in mid-palate, brief dry hop aftertaste.

BASS NO. 1 BARLEY WINE — amber, tart citrus-cherry-licorice nose, palate is sweet malt in front, briny middle, and cuts off quickly at the finish, very complex but surprisingly brief, also the saltiness doesn't go well with the other flavors.

Belhaven Brewery, Ltd.

Brewery in Dunbar, Scotland

BELHAVEN SCOTTISH ALE — copper-amber, toasted malt and hop aroma, sour hop flavor up front, smoother and cleaner toward the finish, but it dies at the end, medium long dry hop aftertaste, good flavor for the most part but the balance is not as good as it might be.

TRAQUAIR HOUSE ALE — bright copper, lovely roasted malt aroma, intense roasted malt and sweet ale flavor, real sipping beer, great finish, long strong medium dry malt aftertaste.

BELHAVEN SCOTTISH PREMIUM LAGER — slightly hazy gold, malt nose that is both sweet and tart, very dry hop flavor with some dull malt in back, dry hop finish and long dry hop aftertaste.

Boddington's Breweries, Ltd.

Brewery in Manchester, England

BODDINGTON'S BITTER BEER — deep bright gold, strong roasted malt aroma, pleasant roasted malt flavor, light body, very light dry hop aftertaste.

S.A. Brain & Co., Ltd.

Brewery in Cardiff, Wales

BRAIN'S RED DRAGON IPA — copper-amber, nice delicate toasted malt nose, tangy complex malt and hop flavor, medium body, excellent balance, long good dry complex malt and hop aftertaste, very drinkable.

Matthew Brown P.L.C.

Lion Brewery in Blackburn, England

JOHN PEEL EXPORT BEER — tawny-gold, off-dry malt nose, big pleasant balanced malt palate, assertive, complex, and very long, a very good brew.

Caledonia Brewery, Ltd.

Brewery in Edinburgh, Scotland

MacANDREW'S SCOTCH ALE — bright copper, strong aromatic hop and toasted malt nose with a spruce-pine resin background, very complex flavor with smoky malt (like Scot's whiskey), licorice, and peat, long rich aftertaste, a very good sipping beer.

Castle St. Brewery, Ltd.

Brewery in Sunderland, England

HERITAGE ENGLISH ALE — bright amber, appetizing toasted malt aroma, complex sharp hop flavor has a sweet malt component as well as licorice, orange peel, etc., sour hop aftertaste, big body, good balance, high alcohol (7.2%/vol), a good barleywine style ale.

Edwin Cheshire Ltd.

Brewery in Stansted, England

KINROSS SCOTCH ALE — bright copper, off-dry caramelized malt nose and taste, not too sweet, consistent across the palate, good balance, long dry malt aftertaste, pleasant sipping beer.

Notes:

Cornish Brewery Co., Ltd.

Brewery in Redruth, England

CHURCHILL AMBER BEER — amber, toasted malt nose and flavor, medium to light body, long scorched malt flavor, toasted malt finish, long toasted malt aftertaste.

CHURCHILL LAGER — hazy gold, damp hay and malt nose, dry malt palate, dry hop finish, long dry hop aftertaste.

CHURCHILL DRY BEER — bright gold, faint malt nose, pleasant malt-hop flavor, hop finish, medium body, faintly sour long dry hop aftertaste.

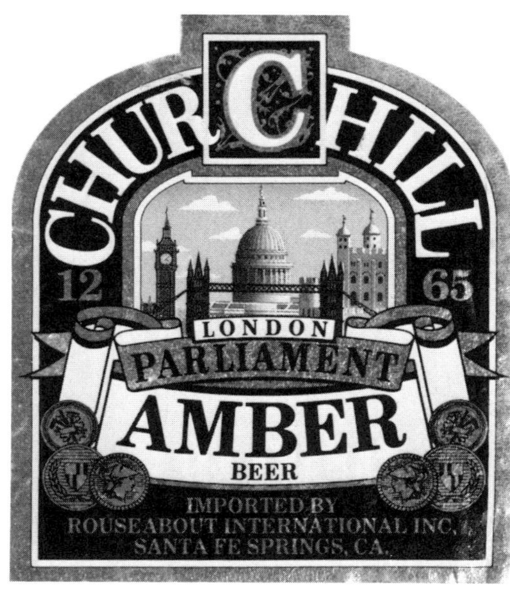

Courage, Ltd.

Breweries in London, Reading, Plymouth, and Bristol, England

COURAGE LAGER EXPORT BEER — yellow-gold, high carbonation, hops dominate the nose and taste, long sour hop aftertaste.

JOHN COURAGE EXPORT — tawny-gold, foamy, off-dry malt nose, bitter hop flavor, doubtful balance, slightly off-dry malt aftertaste.

BULLDOG PALE ALE — pale yellow, hop nose, dull hop flavor up front, light hop finish, very brief dry hop aftertaste, almost none at all.

BULLDOG LAGER BEER — bright pale gold, intense fruity-malt aroma, big body, lots of hops in the flavor all the way through, long dry hop aftertaste, very good brew.

JOHN COURAGE AMBER LAGER — amber, light toasted malt nose, toasted malt flavor, smooth, medium body, long dry malt aftertaste.

Cumbrian Brewery Co., Ltd.

Brewery in Warrington, England

BEAVER EXPORT LAGER BEER — tawny-yellow, off-dry malt aroma, sharp hop flavor, dry hop aftertaste.

BURKE'S IRISH BRIGADE EXPORT STOUT — deep brown, roasted malt nose, good body, mellow flavor, well balanced, pleasant long dry hop aftertaste with a trace of anise in back.

Davenport Brewery, Ltd.

Brewery in Birmingham, England

DAVENPORT'S HARVEST BREW — medium amber, tangy-fruity citrus ale nose, dry malt palate with a faint sour hop component in back, pleasant and very drinkable, some sweet malt appears in the finish, good balance throughout, long complex malt and hop aftertaste, good sipping beer.

Felinfoel Brewing Co., Ltd.

Brewery in Llanelli, Wales

DRAGON ALE — amber, fairly strong hop nose is a little stinky, light body, thin hop flavor, malt finish, light malt and hop aftertaste is medium to long.

DOUBLE DRAGON ALE — very deep amber, zesty hop nose, big sweet hop flavor, good body, zesty hop finish, long spicy hop aftertaste, tastes like a good brew-pub ale.

JOHN BROWN ALE — copper-brown, faint malt aroma and flavor, short dry malt aftertaste.

FELINFOEL BITTER ALE — gold, hop nose, sharp hops up front on the palate, the flavor gradually softens until it is weak sour hops at the finish, thin body, weak watery after-taste, just a quick burst of hops and that's that.

FELINFOEL CREAM STOUT — almost opaque red-brown, faint burnt licorice and malt nose, bitter and dry licorice flavor, finish, and aftertaste.

ST. DAVID'S PORTER — deep red-brown, faint malt aroma, malt flavor with a licorice finish, dry licorice aftertaste.

HERCULES ALE — copper, candy nose, sweet licorice flavor, complex and alcoholic but overwhelmingly sweet right through the aftertaste, 7-8% alc/vol.

WELSH ALE — deep amber, nose a bit off at first, then exotic spicy hops, very strong almost overwhelming malt and hop flavor, sweet then tart then sweet again, finishes sweet leading into a long off-dry aftertaste.

FELINFOEL HERITAGE ALE — deep bright copper, light candy sweet nose, tart candy flavor, sour hop finish, good body, long dry hop aftertaste.

PRINCESS PORTER — deep ruby-amber, chicken coop aroma, dull watery malt flavor, mercifully brief.

FELINFOEL FESTIVE ALE — hazy amber, faintly acetone aroma, noticeable alcohol and big malt flavor, very strong and very long.

Notes:

EUROPE

Fuller, Smith & Turner, Ltd.

Brewery in Chiswick, England

FULLERS PALE ALE — tawny, toasted malt aroma, toasted malt flavor up front, bitter middle and finish, thin and watery, short dry hop aftertaste.

FULLERS LONDON PRIDE TRADITIONAL ENGLISH ALE — pale amber, lightly toasted malt nose, big hop flavor with the malt in back, dry hop finish and aftertaste with a touch of sour malt in back.

FULLERS ESB (EXTRA SPECIAL BITTER) EXPORT ALE —copper-amber, delicate off-dry toasted malt aroma, off-dry front palate, middle is rich hops, big dry hop finish, long dry hop aftertaste, good body, fine carbonation, excellent body, hops dominate but the malt never gets shoved into the background, a super brew. On draft, it is similar but a lot smoother and even more drinkable. This is an excellent beer. I have even had badly mistreated samples that tasted great!

George Gale & Co., Ltd.

Brewery in Horndean, England

ANGEL STEAM BREWED BEER — bright copper, sweet roasted malt aroma, high carbonation, roasted malt and sharp hop flavor, complex but not attractive with the hops and malt clashing at times, long dry hop aftertaste.

ANGEL STEAM BREWED ALE — amber, good roasted malt nose with some background hops, fine hop and roasted malt flavor, light body, pleasant finish, nicely balanced, long pleasing dry hop and malt aftertaste, very tasty and very good with food.

GEORGE GALE & CO. HSB BITTER — deep amber, funky malt nose, huge toasted malt flavor, big body, light hop finish, long dry malt aftertaste.

TUDOR HORNDEAN PALE ALE — deep amber, light malt aroma with good background hops, medium body, good bright malt flavor, malt finish, very drinkable, long off-dry malt aftertaste with hops coming in brightly at the very end.

PRIZE OLD ALE — cloudy deep brown, complex fruity-ale nose, somewhat like a hard cider, but more malty, assertive, strong barleywine style flavor is complex off-dry malt, winey, alcoholic, extremely long malt aftertaste (almost a half hour later you can still taste it), a humongous sipping beer.

Gibbs Mews, PLC.

Brewery in Salisbury, England

OLD THUMPER EXTRA SPECIAL ALE — medium amber, marvelous smooth complex slightly sweet hop aroma, bright smooth complex roasted malt and hop flavor, good body and balance, finishes off-dry malt, extremely long malt aftertaste, very drinkable. Made for Ringwood Brewery, Ringwood.

FORTY-NINER FINEST ALE — pale amber, beautiful hop nose, complex with good malt support, good zesty malt and hop flavor, malt stays through the finish, but mostly the palate is hops, long dry hop aftertaste. Made for Ringwood Brewery.

THE BISHOP'S TIPPLE — deep amber, beautiful complex sweet hop nose, well balanced with malt, good body, big smooth creamy rich malt flavor, off-dry in front, dry at finish, very long dry malt aftertaste, excellent balance, very likeable.

Greenall Whitley Co., Ltd.

Brewery in Cheshire, England

CHESTER GOLDEN ALE — amber, malt nose and flavor, some off-dry malt at the finish, dull dry malt aftertaste.

Notes:

Greene King, Ltd.

Breweries in Bury St. Edmunds and Biggleswade, England

GREENE KING ALE — bright amber, faint sour malt nose, light body, light bitter hop flavor, weak slightly sour malt and hop aftertaste.

ABBOT ALE — pale amber, apple-malt aroma, bitter hop flavor, long dry and bitter hop aftertaste.

ST. EDMUND SPECIAL PALE ALE — fairly deep tawny-gold, candy-like ale nose, sweet with a resiny background, sharp tangy hop-ale flavor, heavy body, big malt finish and aftertaste but there are unlikeable components.

SUFFOLK DARK ENGLISH ALE — deep red-brown, big ale aroma with an off-dry berry-like background, very complex malt and hop flavor with an acidic finish and aftertaste.

Hall & Woodhouse, Ltd.

Brewery in Blandford Forum, England

BROCK LAGER — hazy yellow, malt nose, light body, malt flavor is faintly salty and sour in the finish, medium dry malt aftertaste.

BADGER LIGHT ALE — pale sherry color, faint toffee-like nose, light body, molasses-flavored, pleasant molasses finish and aftertaste, but the weak body is off-putting.

King & Barnes, Ltd.

Brewery in Horsham, England

KING & BARNES SUSSEX BITTER PALE LIGHT ALE — pale amber, light apple-malt nose, watery, light ale palate, little finish and aftertaste, not much to it.

KING & BARNES FESTIVE ALE — deep amber, light faintly soapy malt nose, watery, weak ale flavor, smoky finish, short sour malt aftertaste.

KING & BARNES FINEST OLD BROWN ALE — deep reddish-brown, slightly smoky malt nose, weak malt flavor with light hops in the finish, faint smoky malt aftertaste, questionable balance.

Notes:

Mansfield Brewery, Ltd.

Brewery in Mansfield, England

MARKSMAN IMPORTED ENGLISH LAGER BEER — hazy gold, light hop nose, light body, not much flavor beyond the carbonation, just some faint malt and hops, dry hop finish, very little aftertaste.

KINGPIN ENGLISH LAGER BEER — hazy amber, nice toasted malt nose, good malt flavor but it is a bit too light, faintly sour short malt aftertaste.

OLD BAILY STRONG BITTER — deep amber, flat, well-hopped toasted malt flavor, long dry malt aftertaste, needs some carbonation.

James Paine Brewery, Ltd.

Brewery in St. Noets, England

PAINE'S PALE ALE — tawny-gold, good hop aroma, light body, light watery malt and hop flavor, dull bready aftertaste.

Pitfield Brewery

Brew-pub in London, England

DARK STAR NATURAL BEER — deep amber, off-dry slightly toasted malt nose, toasted malt palate with a slight chocolate background, finishes dry malt but there is only a short aftertaste of dry malt, pleasant but little length.

Eldridge Pope & Co., Ltd.

Brewery in Dorchester, England

THOMAS HARDY'S OLD ALE— bright reddish persimmon color, intense hop nose, very heavy body, robust malty-herbal hop flavor that carries through to a rich finish, long strong malt and hop aftertaste, a concentrated ale, luxuriously flavored. This is the description of the 1979 bottling.

THOMAS HARDY'S ALE 1982 — deep cherry-amber, strong fruity-malt nose with melon, papaya, and acid, heavy body, intensely sweet malt flavor is a little salty at first, extremely long malt and hop aftertaste, quite different from the 1979.

THOMAS HARDY'S ALE 1986 — slightly hazy amber, concentrated off-dry roasted malt aroma, equally concentrated flavor of slightly toasted malt, little or no carbonation, also no ale tang so there is little hop character to offset the concentration of malt, tenacious sweet malt aftertaste. Very much a malt liquor, it could use something to offset the sweetness.

THOMAS HARDY'S ALE 1988 — deep hazy amber, concentrated malt nose, flavor like a malt syrup, very low carbonation, at the finish there is a salty-sweet-salty feeling on the palate as the flavor seems to flip around in confusion (or because the flavors are so strong the palate flips around in confusion), big long malt aftertaste.

THOMAS HARDY'S ALE 1989 — hazy amber, roasted malt nose is light, strong rich malt flavor, very high alcohol, particularly in the finish where it is very volatile, very long dry malt aftertaste.

POPE'S "1880" BEER — bright amber, complex roasted off-dry malt, orange peel, and hop aroma, complex creamy licorice, molasses, and toasted malt flavor, very dry and very long malt aftertaste. This is the bottled POPE'S DORSET INDIA PALE ALE.

ROYAL OAK PALE ALE— brilliant deep amber, complex rich off-dry malt and hop ale nose that favors the malt, big delicious malt flavor, fairly intense but still smooth, big body, finishes gently, long slightly off-dry mild malt aftertaste, not a whole lot of complexity but very well balanced, and a very, very drinkable ale.

THOMAS
HARDY'S ALE
In 'The Trumpet Major' Hardy wrote of Dorchester's famous ale "It was of the most beautiful colour that the eye of an artist in beer could desire; full in body, yet brisk as a volcano; piquant, yet without a twang; luminous as an autumn sunset; . . ."
BOTTLE № B 99990 1987
BREWED AND BOTTLED BY
ELDRIDGE, POPE & Co. PLC ·
DORCHESTER · DORSET · ENGLAND
6.04 FL.OZ.

Notes:

T.D. Ridley & Sons, Ltd.

Brewery in Chelmsford, England

BISHOPS ALE — amber, very big zesty hop and malt aroma, big head, roasted malt flavor, hop finish, long dry aftertaste with plenty of both hops and malt, a good well-balanced beer.

G. Ruddle & Co., Ltd.

Brewery in Oakham, Rutland, England

RUDDLE'S COUNTRY ALE — medium tawny-brown, pungent malt nose, sour malt flavor with a bitter hop finish, long dry bitter hop aftertaste.

RUDDLE'S COUNTY TRADITIONAL ENGLISH BEER — bright medium copper, tea, malt, and hop aroma, complex off-dry malt flavor, medium body, somewhat sweet finish with pine in the back of the tongue, dry hop aftertaste, interesting and fairly likeable.

RUDDLE'S BITTER ENGLISH BEER — brilliant amber, light toasted malt nose, good hop and malt flavor, very light body, short dry hop aftertaste.

Samuel Smith's Old Brewery

Brewery in Tadcaster, England

SAMUEL SMITH'S OLD BREWERY GOLDEN BROWN ALE — medium deep amber, burnt malt aroma with a trace of something like orange oil, smooth fruity-toffee malt flavor, well balanced and mellow, pleasant and appetizing dry malt aftertaste.

SAMUEL SMITH'S OLD BREWERY PALE ALE — pale amber, pale copper head, lovely roasted malt and molasses aroma, big hop flavor with plenty of roasted malt in support, big body, finely carbonated, long dry hop and roasted malt aftertaste, another lovely ale.

SAMUEL SMITH'S NUT BROWN ALE — red-brown, complex off-dry toasted malt nose with an apple backing, medium body, big complex ale flavor, slightly sweet finish, very long dry malt aftertaste.

SAMUEL SMITH'S IMPERIAL STOUT — deep brown, intensely sweet malt nose, big sweet malt flavor but not cloying, good flavor, good body, good balance, dry malt aftertaste, well-made brew.

SAMUEL SMITH'S OATMEAL STOUT — deep ruby-brown, almost opaque, complex fruity-malt aroma, palate is dry malt in fruit, off-dry malt at the finish, rich and full bodied, soft and smooth, no bite whatever, long fairly dry malt aftertaste.

TADDY PORTER — brilliant deep red-brown, generous brown head, complex dry coffee bean aroma, dry rich clean malt and hop flavor has a mocha background, delicious and satisfying, long, long clean dry malt aftertaste, a beautiful brew.

SAMUEL SMITH'S PURE BREWED LAGER BEER — hazy gold, hop nose, dry hop flavor has good malt backing, good balance, high carbonation, medium long dry hop aftertaste.

SAMUEL SMITH'S WINTER WELCOME ALE 1990-1991 — hazy gold, faintly skunky nose, big hop flavor, big body, malt rolls in at mid-palate and is there in quantity, alcoholic finish, long dry malt aftertaste.

SAMUEL SMITH'S WINTER WELCOME ALE 1991-1992 — peach color, strong hop nose is almost skunky, finely carbonated, strong hop flavor, assertive and alcoholic, dull malt and sour hop aftertaste.

Scottish and Newcastle Breweries, Ltd.

Conglomerate comprises MacEwan's, Younger's, and Newcastle Breweries in Edinburgh, Scotland, Newcastle-on-Tyne, England, et al.

MacEWAN'S SCOTCH ALE — deep amber, creamy, big piquant malt nose, big body, distinctive meal and malt flavor with good bittering hops in back, long dry hop and malt aftertaste.

MacEWAN'S TARTAN ALE — dark brown with reddish hues, creamy texture, strong off-dry malt taste, licorice and malt finish and aftertaste, quite long and very good.

MacEWAN'S EDINBURGH ALE — deep brown, creamy, rich very complex malt nose, beautiful rich roasted-smoky malt flavor, long smoky aftertaste, easily the best of the MacEwan ales.

MacEWAN'S STRONG ALE —deep amber-gold, clean delicate malt nose, rich full-flavored off-dry malt taste, very heavy body, long malt aftertaste.

MacEWAN'S MALT LIQUOR — extremely deep brown color, almost opaque, light toffee aroma, heavy body, rich very sweet malt flavor, bitter hop finish, long dry coffee aftertaste, high alcohol (7.8%).

MacEWAN'S STRONG MALT LIQUOR — deep dark brown, slightly sweet roasted malt aroma, sweet caramel and toasted malt flavor with a touch of licorice, big body, balanced, lingering malt aftertaste.

MacEWAN'S EXPORT — amber, off-dry malt nose with some odd background, malt flavor, light body, brief dry malt aftertaste with some sweetness at the end.

NEWCASTLE BROWN ALE — dark amber-brown, nutty malt aroma, smooth and mellow malt flavor, some bitter hops at the finish, long dry hop and malt aftertaste, a delightful brew.

NEWCASTLE LIGHT ALE — medium copper-gold, off-dry malt nose, slightly sweet malt flavor, softens and fades at the finish, very little aftertaste.

YOUNGER'S TARTAN BITTER — amber, strange off nose with malt hidden beneath, sort of like burnt candy, bitter hop flavor, dry bitter hop aftertaste with little length.

YOUNGER'S KESTREL LAGER — bright amber-gold, good hop and malt aroma, strong bitter hop flavor up front, some sour malt in the mid-palate, soft and pleasant malt finish, medium-length dry malt aftertaste, very drinkable.

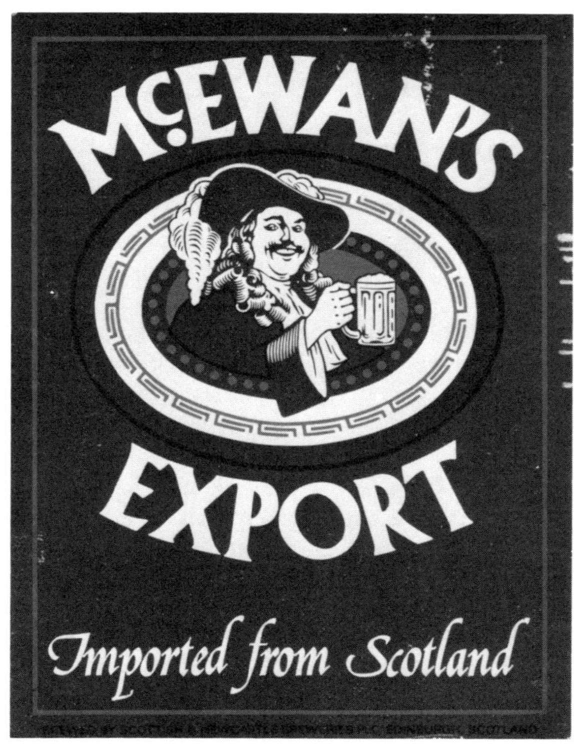

Notes:

T & R Theakston, Ltd.

Breweries at **Masham** and **Carlisle, England**

THEAKSTON OLD PECULIER YORKSHIRE ALE — brown, aroma of canned brown bread, dry malty-molasses flavor, malt finish, light malt aftertaste, tastes a whole lot better than it sounds.

THEAKSTON BEST BITTER ALE — tawny-gold, fragrant hop aroma with a touch of apple cider, light carbonation, good-tasting malt and hop flavor, good balance, bitter hop finish, long dry hop aftertaste.

Daniel Thwaites & Co., Ltd.

Brewery in **Blackburn, England**

BIG BEN ENGLISH BEER — tawny-gold, clean malt and hop aroma with a roasted malt background, pleasant and clean roasted malt flavor, but there is little depth, slightly salty finish, medium long dry roasted malt aftertaste.

Notes:

Tollemache & Cobbold Breweries Ltd.

Brewery in Ipswich, England

TOLLY ORIGINAL PREMIUM ALE — bright pale copper, toasted malt aroma, strong toasted malt flavor, medium body, finish is like the flavor but less intense, long sharp and sour hop aftertaste, overall seems a bit coarse.

Vaux Brewery

Brewery in Sunderland and Sheffield, England

Includes subsidiary S.H. Ward & Co., Ltd.

VAUX DOUBLE MAXIM SUNDERLAND BROWN ALE — amber, mild hop and strong malt nose, flavor starts out as sour malt, but quickly becomes bright hops, sour malt returns for the aftertaste, weak body for a brown ale, and not much duration.

WARD'S ENGLISH ALE — amber, finely carbonated, mild off-dry ale nose, lots of good malt and hop flavor, but light bodied, pleasant flavor is best at the finish, slightly off-dry malt aftertaste has only fair length, and overall the brew lacks depth.

WARD'S GOLDEN ALE — bright amber, faint hop nose with an off-dry malt background, good body, mild slightly sweet malty-ale flavor, very pleasant mild medium long malt aftertaste, no raves but quite pleasant.

Watney-Mann & Truman Brewers, Ltd.

Brewing Co. comprises nine regional companies: Watney, Combe & Reid, Truman, Usher, Bryborough, Wilson, Webster, Phoenix, Norwich, and Mann. Breweries in Norwich, Mortlake, London, Edinburgh, Halifax, Manchester, and Trowbridge.

WATNEY'S RED BARREL — bright amber, tangy malt nose, zesty malt and hop flavor, bright and well balanced, tangy in front, off-dry malt in the middle, dry at the finish, complex and long. This beer has also been labeled **WATNEY'S TRADITIONAL BEER** in the U.S. Widely available on draft.

WATNEY'S STINGO DARK ALE — opaque brown, all-malt treacle nose with a faint sourness in back, taste of heavy malty-molasses, tenacious long sweet malt aftertaste, despite all that sweet malt, the balance is fairly good, an interesting barleywine style with 7% alc/vol.

WATNEY'S STINGO CREAM STOUT — opaque brown, off-dry concentrated malt nose, big smoky (very much burnt) malt flavor, big body, pleasant, decent balance, overall fairly dry, not filling, long dry malt aftertaste.

MANN'S THE ORIGINAL BROWN ALE — brown, good rich coffee aroma with a charcoal background, finely carbonated, full all-malt flavor, no hops noticeable, smooth and mellow, good balance, lightly sweet long malt aftertaste, a delightful "mild."

USHER'S WINTER ALE — medium brown, light malt nose, dry and robust malt flavor, you can really sink your teeth into it, long flavored dry malt aftertaste, marvelous sipping beer.

TRUMAN'S CHRISTMAS ALE — medium deep amber, beautiful complex citrus-ale nose that reminds you of Marguerita mix, malt and hop flavor with an ale-like character, excellent balance, complex, long, and satisfying.

SCOTTISH PRIDE LIGHT BEER — deep tawny-gold, malt nose with a sourness in back, light dry malt flavor, light body, very little aftertaste. From Drybrough & Co., Ltd., Edinburgh.

LONDON LIGHT LAGER BEER — bright gold, malt nose, weak malt flavor, thin body, weak brief malt aftertaste.

WATNEYS LIGHT — deep gold, lovely malt nose with good hop backing, light body, light malt flavor is faintly sour, short dull malt aftertaste. From Watney, Combe, Reid & Co., Ltd.

WATNEY'S LIGHT BEER — hazy gold, slightly stinky soapy hop aroma, strange light sour vegetal malt flavor, reminds you of cabbage, short sour malt aftertaste. From Watney-Truman, Ltd.

Charles Wells, Ltd.

Brewery in Bedford, England

GOLD EAGLE BITTER — tawny-gold, beautiful hop and malt aroma, good balance, bitter hop flavor with a caramel aftertaste.

CHARLES WELLS LIGHT ALE — tawny-gold, hop nose has a pine and barnyard background, hop flavor but there is unpleasantness in behind, long aftertaste like the flavor.

CHARLES WELLS BOMBARDIER ALE — amber, complex elusive nose of flowers and hops, toasted malt flavor with little depth, light body, slightly bitter hop aftertaste with little duration.

OLD BEDFORD ALE — deep brilliant amber, mild toasted malt aroma with a sour background, strong hop flavor has good supporting malt for balance, sweet ale mid-palate, strong finish, long off-dry malt and hop aftertaste, big body, huge flavor, a big bright sipping beer that is not for the weak of spirit.

Whitbread & Co., Ltd.

A large brewing conglomerate with breweries in Cheltenham, Leeds, Liverpool, Luton, Faversham, Durham, Salford, Sheffield, Samlesbury, Marlow, Portsmouth, Tiverton, Wateringbury, and Romsey, England.

WHITBREAD TANKARD LONDON ALE — tawny-brown, caramel and yeast nose, good malty flavor, good balance, short dry malt aftertaste.

WHITBREAD ALE — deep tawny-brown, beautiful rich and smooth caramel-malt aroma, caramel taste, very pleasant and appetizing, finely balanced, long malt aftertaste, a mellow enjoyable brew.

WHITBREAD BREWMASTER — brownish gold, highly carbonated, malt aroma and flavor, dry malt finish and medium aftertaste, not well balanced.

MACKESON STOUT — very deep dark brown, almost opaque, rich malt aroma, heavy body, syrup-like, rich coffee-malt flavor, excellent stout and a worthy rival of Guinness, perhaps not as dry but in some respects a bit richer.

MACKESON TRIPLE STOUT — extremely deep opaque brown, roasted malt aroma, off-dry malt flavor, very rich and very big, long rich off-dry malt aftertaste, quite drinkable for a heavy brew.

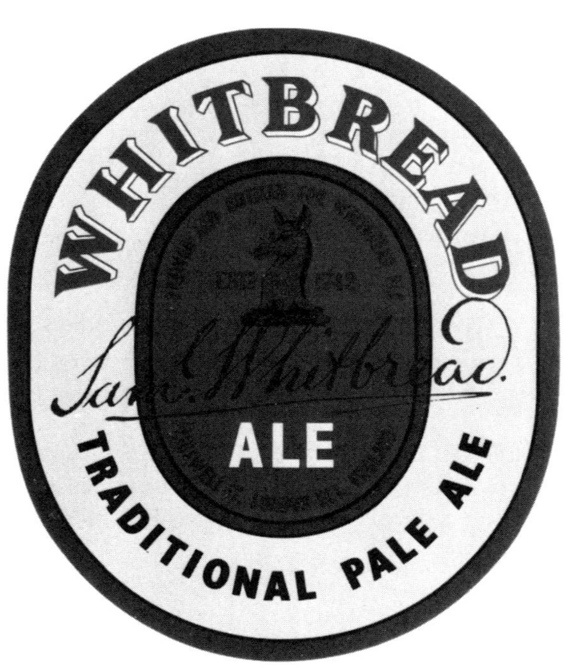

GOLD LABEL NO. 1 SPARKLING BARLEY WINE — rosy-orange, sweet candy-apple nose, assertive aroma and flavor much like some of the strongly flavored fruity cough medicines, but not medicinal, strong hops really bite the corners of your mouth and back of the tongue, long bitter hop aftertaste, a powerfully strong sipping beer.

CAMPBELL'S CHRISTMAS — deep copper, big sweet rising malt nose, rich, complex, intensely flavored malt, big bodied, long off-dry malt aftertaste, an incredible beer made for the Belgian market, a must-try for any serious beer drinker.

CAMPBELL'S SCOTCH — deep reddish-copper, sweet and sharp pineapple nose, intensely bittersweet malt and hop flavor, very insistent, almost overwhelming, not complex, just strong, aftertaste like the flavor but a bit less intense, very long. Also made for the Belgian market.

Wrexham Lager Beer Co., Ltd.

Brewery in **Wrexham, Wales**

WREXHAM LAGER BEER — medium to deep gold, skunky hop nose, high carbonation, complex malt and hop flavor, light body, sour malt finish and aftertaste.

Young & Co. Brewery, PLC.

Brewery in **London, England**

YOUNG'S SPECIAL LONDON ALE — amber, soapy tangy citrus ale nose like hard cider, big tangy zesty strong ale flavor, complex, a real mouthful of ale, good and powerful, extremely long complex dry hop aftertaste, a classy ale with no coarseness.

YOUNG'S RAM ROD SPECIAL ALE — amber, light ale nose, light salty ale flavor, kind of ordinary, light dry hop aftertaste with medium duration.

OLD NICK BARLEY WINE STYLE ALE — deep copper-red, light citrus and fruity malt aroma, tart malt and hop palate, dry hop finish, beautiful flavor transition in the mid-palate, excellent balance, long complex medium dry malt and hop aftertaste.

YOUNG'S WINTER ALE 1988 — very deep amber, faint malt nose, light burnt dry malt flavor, complex dry malt finish, long pleasant dry malt aftertaste, leaves your mouth clean and dry.

YOUNG'S WINTER ALE 1990-1991 — deep amber, light malt aroma, smooth malt flavor, faint buttery background detracts from the enjoyment, sour malt finish, short dry malt aftertaste, lacks zest.

YOUNG'S ORIGINAL LONDON PORTER — deep ruby-amber, very faint dry malt nose, very dry and faintly sour malt flavor, long malt aftertaste ends bitter hops, not really very interesting.

YOUNG'S OATMEAL STOUT — deep ruby-brown, faint malt nose, dry malt flavor, touch of smoke in the finish, dry malt aftertaste has good length.

GREECE

Atalanti Brewery

Brewery in Athens

AEGEAN HELLAS BEER — gold, malt aroma with just a touch of hops, malt flavor with little complexity, light body, sour malt aftertaste.

SPARTAN LAGER EXPORT — bright yellow-gold, pleasant malt nose with good hop background, dull off-dry malt flavor, dry and bitter hop aftertaste.

Notes:

Hellenic Brewery and Winery, S.A.

Brewery in Athens

Also uses names Athenian Brewery, S.A., and Karolos Fix, S.A.

ATLAS GREEK BEER — medium to pale gold, faint malt and hop nose, dull malt flavor and aftertaste.

FIX BEER — gold, malt and hop nose, off-dry malt flavor, finish, and aftertaste.

ATHENIAN GREEK BEER — yellow-gold, creamy head, light pilsener-type nose, slightly bitter hop flavor, very faint and short dry hop aftertaste.

MARATHON GREEK BEER — yellow-gold, faint malt nose, light hop flavor is on the bitter side, very faint dry hop aftertaste.

FIX 1864 SPEZIAL — bright gold, lovely malt and hop aroma, off-dry malt palate up front, sharp hop finish, short dry hop aftertaste, not much character.

HOLLAND

Bavaria Breweries

Brewery in Lieshout

BAVARIA LAGER — pale yellow, vegetal malt nose, malt and hop flavor, dry hop finish and aftertaste.

SWINKEL'S EXPORT BEER — medium gold, highly carbonated, pleasant beery malt and hop aroma, good hop and malt flavor, well balanced, dry hop finish and aftertaste, clean and refreshing.

SWINKEL'S IMPORTED BEER — pale gold, very faint malt nose, light body, light off-dry malt palate, highly carbonated, faint malt aftertaste.

SWINKEL'S LIGHT IMPORTED BEER — bright gold, grainy malt nose, flavor starts as grainy malt and dies out quickly, no finish or aftertaste.

GUILDER IMPORTED BEER — pale gold, grainy barley nose, high carbonation, dull malt flavor, dry malt finish, short dry malt aftertaste.

BAVARIA MALT BIER — bright gold, faint malt nose, weak and watery, pleasant light malt flavor, short malt aftertaste. They claim very low alcohol (<.09%).

Royal Brand Brewery

Brewery in **Wijlre**

Some labels spell the town name Wyrle.

BRAND HOLLAND BEER — pale gold, pleasant hop nose, bright hop well-balanced flavor, good hop finish, long dry hop aftertaste, brisk and refreshing. Also has been labeled **BRAND LAGER BEER**.

BRAND BEER — pale gold, light hop aroma, hop palate is balanced very well with malt, smooth with some complexity, long dry hop aftertaste.

Bierbrowerij de Drie Hoefijzers

Brewery in Breda is affiliated with Skol, International, and owned by Allied Breweries (U.K.), Ltd. Also uses Posthoorn Brewery name.

BREDA ROYAL HOLLAND BEER — gold, strong hop nose, dull malt and hop flavor, dull malt aftertaste.

ROYAL DUTCH — yellow-gold, medium hop nose, dull hop flavor, bitter hop finish and aftertaste.

ROYAL DUTCH KOSHER HOLLAND BEER — deep gold, hop nose with a skunky background, hop palate has some malt in back, dry, almost bitter hop aftertaste.

SKOL LAGER BEER — tawny-gold, finely carbonated, malt and hop nose, light hop flavor, finish, and dry hop aftertaste.

THREE HORSES BRAND PILSENER LAGER BEER — gold, sharp hop nose, flavor is sour malt with a bitter hop background, strong bitter hop aftertaste.

Bierbrowerij St. Christoffel

Brewery in **Roermond, Limburg**

CHRISTOFFEL BIER — hazy gold, big head but light carbonation on the palate, grainy malt nose, very dry hop flavor, big body, solid strong long dry hop aftertaste, a very dry well-hopped beer, but it carries it off very well and is super with food.

Grolsche Bierbrowerij

Brewery in **Enschede**

GROLSCH NATURAL HOLLAND BEER — amber, tart hop nose, rich sour malt flavor with plenty of good hops, long dry hop aftertaste, good complex brew.

GROLSCH LAGER BEER — bright gold, beautiful malt and hop aroma, flavor starts out bright and hoppy but smoothly makes the transition to a dry malt finish, good body, very good balance, long dry aftertaste has both hops and malt, good very drinkable brew.

GROLSCH PREMIUM DRY DRAFT BEER — deep gold, pleasant malt aroma, soapy hop flavor, brief dry hop finish, long faintly dry hop aftertaste comes in quite a while after you swallow.

GROLSCH DARK BEER — deep amber, faintly skunky nose at first but this can be swirled away to be replaced with hops and malt, big hop flavor is too much hops and too little malt for balance, further, the skunk tries to return, long dry hop aftertaste can barely keep the skunk at bay.

B.V. Gulpener Bierbrowerij

Brewery in **Gulpen**

X-PERT HOLLAND BEER — amber-gold, hop nose, thin hop flavor, weak body, watery, bitter hop and sour malt finish, faintly bitter long dry hop aftertaste.

GULPENER HOLLAND PILSENER BEER — tawny-gold, malty-grainy aroma, palate is hops in front, roasted malt in the middle, sour hops at the finish, long dry hop aftertaste, good balance, pleasant drinking beer locally known as Limburg Bitter.

Heineken Brouwerjen

Three breweries at Amsterdam, Rotterdam, and Hertogenbosch

The Rotterdam brewery supplies all the export lager.

HEINEKEN LAGER BEER — medium gold, nose is smooth hops and malt, flavor is dry and well hopped, well balanced, good body, long dry hop aftertaste. On draft it is very similar except that there is less hop intensity in the aftertaste.

HEINEKEN SPECIAL DARK BEER — copper-gold, pleasant rich malt aroma and taste, fine balance, long pleasing medium dry malt aftertaste.

AMSTEL LIGHT — pale gold, faint malt aroma, dull dry malt flavor, brief aftertaste.

BUCKLER NON-ALCOHOLIC BREW — gold, grainy hop nose and taste, light body, thin even, medium-length faint aftertaste like the flavor. The local version (in the Netherlands) is a little better equipped with malt and hops, both in the aroma and flavor, is less grainy and more malty. According to the ratings of my taste panel, about 20% better.

Bierbrowerij dee Leeuw

Brewery in Valkenburg

LEEUW HOLLAND PILSENER — gold, good toasted malt and hop aroma, malt palate shows best at the finish, very tasty, long dry malt and hop aftertaste.

Bierbrowerijen Lindeboom B.V.

Brewery in Meer

LINDEBOOM HOLLAND PILSENER BEER — dull gold, big head, big and bright hop nose, palate starts out off-dry malt, hops come roaring in at mid-palate and stay, malt returns at the finish for balance, aftertaste is long and complex, high carbonation intrudes on the good flavor.

Oranjeboom Breweries

Breweries in Rotterdam

Affiliated with Skol, International, and owned by Allied Breweries (U.K.), Ltd.

ORANJEBOOM HOLLAND PILSENER DE LUXE — yellow-gold, strong vegetal malt and wildflower hop aroma, tart hop flavor with slightly sour malt way in back, weak mid-palate, but finishes well with dry hops, dry hop aftertaste with good duration.

Bierbrouwerij Schinnen

Brewery in Schinnen

Also uses Meens Brewery and Alfa Brewery corporate names.

ALFA FRESH HOLLAND BEER — bright gold, off-dry apple peel and malt aroma, sweet candy apple and caramel flavor, light body, fairly shallow, faint off-dry malt aftertaste.

JOSEPH MEENS HOLLAND PREMIUM BEER — gold, pleasant hop and malt nose, hop palate with the malt in back, a bit coarse and certainly strong flavored, dull sour malt aftertaste.

ALFA EDEL PILS — brilliant gold, finely carbonated, good head, lightly toasted malt aroma, big malt flavor, off-dry malt finish, long dry hop aftertaste.

ALFA SUPER DORTMUNDER — bright gold, beautiful faintly fruity apple nose, marvelous slightly sweet apple-like malt flavor, big body, high alcohol, a big but elegant brew, long dry aftertaste.

United Dutch Breweries

Breweries in **Amsterdam**

Also includes Union Export Brewery, Amersfoort, Holland.

JAEGER BEER — gold, big apple and hop aroma, complex malt and hop flavor, but not balanced, hard bitter hop aftertaste.

PETER'S BRAND HOLLAND PILSENER BEER — pale yellow, nose is a bit skunky briefly at first, then light malt and hops come in like a typical Pils style, hop flavor is also briefly skunky but quickly develops into a good light hops with plenty of complexity and character, long dry hop aftertaste.

IRELAND

Beamish & Crawford, Ltd.

Brewery in **Cork**

BEAMISH IRISH STOUT — deep ruby-brown, big thick head that really stands up, very little nose, only some faint malt, light body, thin bitter coffee flavor, finish, and aftertaste, disappointing.

Dempsey's Brewery, Ltd.

Brewery in **Inchicore, Dublin**

DEMPSEY'S BEER — pale copper, light toasted malt aroma, tangy smoky ale flavor, dry finish, long sour hop aftertaste, starts out good, ends poorly, lacks good balance.

Arthur Guinness Son & Co., Ltd.

St. James's Gate Brewery in **Dublin, Dundalk,** et al.

Also some beers (like Extra Stout) are brewed in Scotland, England, and in many countries throughout the world for local markets.

GUINNESS EXTRA STOUT — opaque red-brown color, creamy tawny head, very full-bodied, dense and thick, complex Worcestershire sauce nose, dry coffee-toffee flavor with a chocolate finish, long dry complex malt aftertaste, excellent stout — the baseline description of the classic stout. On draft, it seems to be darker in color, less carbonated, more spicy, and smoother than the bottled version. It is very mellow, excellently balanced, and the head stays on right to the bottom of the glass.

GUINNESS CREAM STOUT — extremely deep brown, low carbonation, strong scorched malt flavor, bitter and flat, harsh long hop aftertaste.

HARP LAGER — deep gold, pungent hop nose, bitter hop flavor, long bitter hop aftertaste, great for true "hop-heads." Version exported to the U.S.

HARP LAGER BEER — pale gold, lovely well-hopped aroma, finely carbonated, bright strong hop flavor, good balance, more hops than malt but done right. This is the version shipped to Canada; it is higher in alcohol, has better balance, and I find it much tastier than the version above.

GUINNESS GOLD LAGER BEER — pale gold, good well-balanced hop and malt nose, good crisp hop flavor, good balance, clean dry hop finish, long dry hop aftertaste, very drinkable and refreshing.

KALIBER ALL NATURAL NON-ALCOHOLIC BEER — tawny-gold, grainy sweet malt nose, sour grainy palate, slightly roasted character, gets stronger at the finish, very long tenacious dry roasted malt aftertaste.

PUB DRAUGHT GUINNESS — the so-called draft version in a can, deep brown, pleasant hop and malt aroma, very dry mild hop flavor, medium body, dry hop finish, long dry hop aftertaste, seems to be a lot lighter than the bottled or draft versions.

Notes:

James J. Murphy & Co., Ltd.

Lady's Well Brewery in **Cork**

MURPHY EXPORT STOUT — opaque black, red shows when held to strong light, faint sweetness behind a generally sour and dry malt nose, flavor is dry malt up front, sour at the finish, long dry malt aftertaste, balance seems off.

ITALY

Birra Dreher S.p.A.

Breweries in **Milano, Pedavena,** and **Massafra**

DREHER FORTE EXPORT LAGER BEER — deep yellow-amber, dank malt nose, off-dry front palate, middle gets some bitter hops, finish is bitter hops and faintly sour malt which comes off better than it sounds, long dry hop aftertaste, fairly good-tasting brew with a good balance.

DREHER EXPORT BEER — pale gold, faint malt aroma, weak body, dry malt flavor, medium dry malt finish and long malt aftertaste.

DREHER PILSENER — bright gold, high carbonation on the tongue, slightly dank malt aroma, flavor is lightly malt at first and hops show in the middle and finish, there isn't much malt to show, long dry hop aftertaste.

Birra Forst S.p.A.

Brewery in **Merano**

FORST EXPORT — bright gold, perfumy hop aroma, medium body, bitter hop finish and aftertaste, too much carbonation.

Notes:

Birra Messina S.p.A.

Breweries in **Milano** and **Messina**

MESSINA BEER — bright gold, nice beery malt and hop nose, palate is off-dry fruity malt and hops, hops most notable in mid-palate, off-dry malt takes over again in the finish, and stays for the long dry aftertaste.

MESSINA ITALIAN BEER — deep gold, hop nose, big hop flavor, dry hop finish and short dry hop aftertaste.

Birra Moretti S.p.A.

Brewery in **Udine**

Also Castello Brewery in San Giorgio di Nogaro.

MORETTI PILSENER — deep gold, clean malt and hop aroma and taste, excellent balance, light body, long aftertaste like the flavor, very tasty and very drinkable.

SCHLOSS-BIER EXPORT LAGER — gold, creamy, nice hop and malt aroma, faint malt flavor and aftertaste, medium to light body.

MORETTI EXPORT BEER (BIRE FURLANE) RESERVA CASTELLO — brilliant gold, pleasant malt and hop aroma, off-dry apple and malt flavor, palate drops off rapidly after a good start, short faint dry malt aftertaste.

MORETTI BIRRA FRIULANA — bright gold, grainy aroma, grainy malt flavor with a good hop background, long dry malt aftertaste.

MORETTI LA ROSSA DOUBLE MALT BEER — rosy amber, big toasted malt nose, huge rich and complex toasted malt flavor with plenty of hop support, good body, alcoholic, long aftertaste like the flavor, a little clumsy, but there is a lot to it.

CASTELLO BEER — pale bright gold, off-dry fruity malt and apple nose, pleasant light malt flavor, light fruity malt finish, dry malt aftertaste.

SAN SOUCI DOUBLE MALT — pale gold, light beery nose, fresh malt flavor with good hop balance, long dry hop aftertaste, very drinkable.

MORETTI DOUBLE MALT DARK (BIRRA DOPPIO MALTO BRUNA) — deep reddish amber, big sweet malt aroma, buttery brown sugar flavor, light body, long malt aftertaste is a bit flabby.

OLD VENICE ITALIAN PILSENER — yellow-gold, pleasant malt aroma, sour malt and hop palate, bitter hop finish, light body, short dry hop aftertaste.

Birra Peroni S.p.A.

Breweries in **Naples, Rome,** and **Padova**

PERONI PREMIUM BEER — amber-brown, zesty hop and malt nose and taste dominated by the hops, strongly flavored, big bodied, long aftertaste like the flavor.

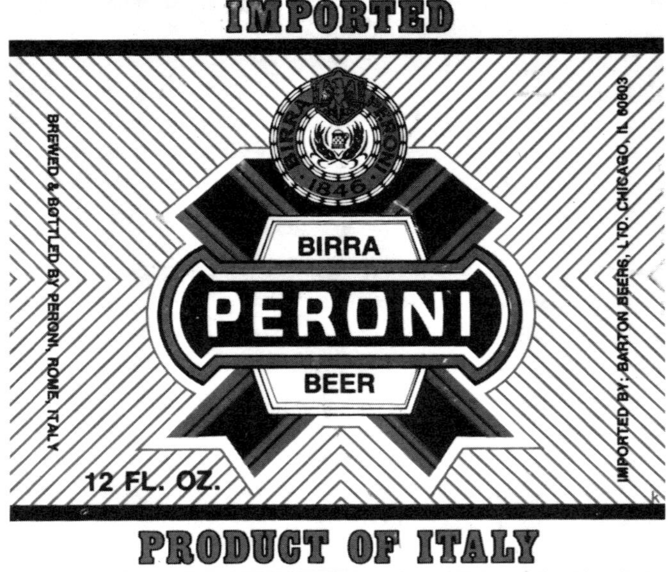

PERONI BEER — bright pale gold, lovely hop and malt aroma, big good-tasting flavor that is more hops up front, malt is there but shows best in the middle, good body, hop finish, malt is most noticeable in the long balanced aftertaste, good brew.

PERONI BIRRA — gold, faint apple peel and malt nose, big body, big hop flavor softens a bit at the finish, pleasant long dry hop aftertaste.

NASTRO AZZURRO EXPORT LAGER — pale gold, faint hop nose with a little malt and yeast, big body, complex flavor is mostly hops, long hop aftertaste has a little sour malt far in back.

ITALA PILSEN — pale gold, hop and malt nose has a skunky component, highly carbonated, good hop and malt flavor, smooth, well balanced, good body, long dry hop aftertaste, very drinkable.

ITALA PILSEN EXPORT BEER — deep amber-gold, big head but not creamy, light hop and malt aroma, big body, complex malt and hop flavor, noticeable alcohol, decent balance, strong dry hop aftertaste, pretty good effort.

RAFFO BEER — brilliant pale tawny-gold, toasted caramel nose, malt and bitter hop flavor, slightly sour malt finish and aftertaste.

Birra Poretti S.p.A.

Breweries in **Induno** and **Olona**

PORETTI ORO BEER — tawny-gold, vegetal malt aroma with some hops in back, flavor is much like the nose, light body, short dry aftertaste.

SPLÜGEN ORO — deep gold, creamy head, faintly sour malt nose, slightly sour malt flavor, big body, aftertaste like the flavor.

SPLÜGEN BOCK — creamy tawny-gold, clean fruit-like malt aroma with the hops in back, complex flavor shows a good balance between the hops and the malt with off-dry malt coming in at the finish, long good dry malt and hop aftertaste, an almost perfect brew.

SPLÜGEN DRY — hazy gold, hop nose, hint of strawberry, front palate is hops, sour malt finish, short dry aftertaste has more metal than merit.

Prinz Bräu Carisio S.p.A.

Brewery in **Carisio**

PRINZ EXPORT — deep gold, beautiful hop aroma with a trace of smoky malt, medium hop flavor has little depth or complexity, dull slightly sour aftertaste.

Notes:

Birra Wührer S.p.A.

Brewery in **Brescia**

CRYSTALL WÜHRER BEER — yellow-brown, lovely malt and hop aroma, bitter hop flavor has a soapy background, clean dry hop finish and aftertaste, actually tastes better than its description.

SIMPLON BRÄU SPECIAL EXPORT — deep gold, beautiful medium hop nose, harsh hop flavor, hops dominate the finish and aftertaste and are a bit softer there, but the flavor is just too much bitter hops.

Wünster S.p.A.

Brewery in **Bergamo**

WÜNSTER EXPORT 14 — gold, beautiful hop nose, big hop flavor with underlying off-dry malt, very good balance, malt rises to the finish, long medium dry malt aftertaste, big-bodied, good-tasting brew.

WÜNSTER SUPER 18 DOPPIO MALTA SCURA — this double malt dark bock is deeply saturated red-brown, has a toasted malt aroma, big body, soft and smooth tasty malt flavor, toffee finish with a touch of licorice, long toffee aftertaste, well-balanced full-flavored brew.

LUXEMBOURG

Brasserie Diekirch Brauerei

Brewery in **Luxembourg City**

DIEKIRCH PILS — gold, good malt aroma, classic Pils flavor, dry hop aftertaste, well-made, well-balanced brew.

DIEKIRCH MALT LIQUOR — deep gold, hop nose with a touch of smoky malt, strong hop and roasted malt flavor, finish is like the flavor but weaker, short faint dry aftertaste.

DIEKIRCH MALT LIQUOR EXCLUSIVE — never found a sample good enough to taste.

Notes:

Brasseries Réunies de Luxembourg S.A.

Breweries at **Mousel** and **Clausen**

MOUSEL BEER — bright gold, dull malt aroma, malt palate has some hops in back, short dry aftertaste.

ALTMUNSTER — medium gold, good malt and hop aroma, flavor is malt at first, hops come in at the middle and stay, good body, long dry hop aftertaste.

NORWAY

Aass Brewery

Brewery in **Drammen**

AASS BOK BEER — very deep copper color, complex yeasty malt aroma, big body, full rich roasted malt flavor, good long rich malt aftertaste, a delicious brew.

AASS NORWEGIAN BEER — light amber-gold, light hop aroma, medium hop flavor with a slightly sour finish, a little unbalanced, medium dry hop aftertaste.

AASS AMBER — medium amber, faintly toasted malt nose, big malt flavor with hops in back, good body, tastes very good, not complex but very drinkable, good balance, hops are in there all the way but never come to the foreground, good balance, dry malt aftertaste.

AASS EXPORT NORWEGIAN BEER — amber-gold, big hop nose, big hop and toasted malt flavor, slightly sour hop finish, good balance, long dry hop aftertaste still retains some of the roasted malt character, a good-tasting beer.

AASS JULE ØL — bright caramel-copper color, lovely light malt and hop aroma, delicious toasted malt flavor, off-dry malt finish with a touch of hops, good appetizing dry malt and hop aftertaste.

AASS PILSNER — amber-gold, flowery complex off-dry melony-malt aroma, very complex malt and hop flavor, fine hop finish, big body, long dry hop aftertaste, malt hangs in there all the way through keeping up an excellent balance.

AASS WINTER — amber, nice straightforward malt and hop nose, honeyed malt front palate, dry middle and finish, very long off-dry malt aftertaste, hops at the very end, some complexity, very drinkable.

E.C. Dahl's Bryggeri A/S

Brewery in Trondheim

DAHL'S PILS — pale gold, good hop and malt nose, smooth, well-balanced hop and malt flavor, medium body, long dry hop aftertaste is also sour and bitter.

DAHL'S EXPORT — tawny-gold, beautiful hop and malt nose is more like a Pils than the Pils above, high carbonation, big hop flavor, good balance, dry hop finish, and brief dry hop aftertaste.

Frydenlund Bryggerie

Brewery in Oslo

FRYDENLUND'S EXPORT III PILSENER BEER — gold, hop nose, bitter hop taste throughout broken only with some off-dry malt in front and a saltiness in the finish, long dry hop aftertaste.

FRYDENLUND NORWEGIAN PILSENER BEER — bright pale gold, skunky nose, thin hop flavor, light body, dry hop finish and short dry hop aftertaste.

NORSK BEER — medium yellow, a briefly skunky nose soon becomes good malt and hops, hoppy flavor up front, sour malt in the back, this sourness becomes the finish and aftertaste, overall poorly balanced.

SKI BEER — medium gold, very light hop and malt aroma, nice well-hopped flavor, thin body, sour malt finish and aftertaste, highly carbonated and not balanced.

Hansa Bryggeri

Brewery in Bergen

HANSA FJORD NORWEGIAN PILSENER BEER — pale hazy yellow-green color, beautiful malt and hop aroma, off-dry malt flavor with excellent hop balance, luscious and full flavored, big body, complex, refreshing, long dry hop aftertaste. Most recently seen labeled HANSA BEER FROM NORWAY.

HANSA EXPORTØL — bright tawny-gold, salty malt cereal aroma, flavor to match, mild salty finish, dry salty hop aftertaste.

HANSA PILSNERØL — pale gold, faint apple-like aroma with hops in back, taste is all up front and is all hops, quick hop finish, virtually no aftertaste.

HANSA PILS — gold, big hop nose, sharp hop flavor, long dry hop aftertaste, a beautiful beer for those who love hops.

HANSA DARK — bright copper color, lovely malt nose with some small amount of hops, pleasant but weak flavor, brief dry malt and hop aftertaste.

Notes:

L. Mack's Ølbryggerie

Brewery in Tromsø

MACK POLAR BEER — hazy amber, dusty malt nose, light body, malt flavor is very slightly papery, dull malt finish and aftertaste.

Ringnes Brewery

Brewery in Oslo

RINGNES SPECIAL BEER — tawny-gold, strong hop nose and big hop flavor, lots of hops and malt and loaded with character, good malt finish and aftertaste, long and delicious.

RINGNES MALT LIQUOR — deep gold, off-dry malt nose, very sweet malty taste and aftertaste, sharp hop bitterness at the very end.

RINGNES EXPORT — gold, aroma of hops and caramel, really good hop and malt flavor up front, but it sags in the middle, and finishes poorly of sour celery, short dry offish aftertaste.

RINGNES SPECIAL BOCK BEER — dark red-brown, strong roasted malt, molasses and prune nose, very heavy body, good molasses-treacle flavor that is really delightful, long rich malt aftertaste, excellent.

RINGNES LOW — bright gold, slightly skunky nose at first, this evolves into hops and tuna salad, very light slightly malty flavor, light body, grainy finish and aftertaste.

RINGNES ZERO PLUS — bright gold, skunky nose at first but the malt soon fights its way through, high carbonation, grainy malt flavor, little body, dry malt finish and aftertaste, medium length.

Net contents 12 fl. oz
R
Ringnes Beer
Special Jubilee
Ringnes Ale
Awarded 24 Honours 17 Gold Medals
PRODUCT OF NORWAY
BREWED AND BOTTLED AT RINGNES BREWERY, OSLO - NORWAY

RINGNES DARK — bright red-brown, sweet malt aroma, light body, pleasant off-dry malt flavor, long off-dry malt aftertaste, nice but could use more heft.

RINGNES SPECIAL CHRISTMAS ALE— deep amber, faintly smoky malt aroma, there is some sweetness in behind, zesty smooth pleasant malt flavor, good balance throughout, medium body, touch of caramel in back, long dry malt aftertaste, didn't find any hops to mention.

NORSK NON-ALCOHOLIC MALT BEVERAGE — pale yellow-gold, faint malt nose, faint grainy malt and CO_2 palate, sour light metallic aftertaste.

RINGNES ALE SPECIAL JUBILEE — bright amber, toasted malt nose, good off-dry malt flavor is like brown sugar, finish and aftertaste are drier malt than the flavor, mellow and long.

Schous Brewery

Brewery in Oslo

SCHOUS NORWEGIAN PILSNER — gold, skunky aroma that really hangs in there, smoked charcoal flavor shows nothing of the skunk, some hops, a little malt, but is unbalanced and watery, a dull brief brew.

POLAND

Okocim Brewery

Brewery in Okocim

OKOCIM FULL LIGHT BEER — yellow-gold, malt aroma and flavor, soapy background, dry hop aftertaste.

OKOCIM PORTER — dark brown, roasted caramel malt nose and flavor, sweet and heavy, long off-dry malt aftertaste, a bit too heavy and sweet.

Zywiec Brewery

Brewery in Zywiec

KRAKUS LIGHT BEER — gold, faint off-dry malt nose, creamy texture, big yeasty barley-malt flavor, fairly long dry malt aftertaste.

KRAKUS PREMIUM BEER — gold, delicate malt aroma with finely balanced hop backing, subtle malt and hop flavor, smooth and light, short dry hop aftertaste.

ZYWIEC FULL LIGHT BEER — deep gold, complex off-dry malt and hop aroma, good body, pleasant flavor has more malt than hops, hop finish, long dry hop aftertaste.

ZYWIEC FULL LIGHT PIAST — very faint malt aroma, sour malt flavor and finish, dry hop aftertaste still has some of the sourness.

ZYWIEC BEER — tawny-gold, malt aroma has a brackish background, good hop flavor but there is still a salty nature, light body, quick dry hop finish and short dry hop aftertaste.

ZYWIEC POLISH LAGER BEER — tawny-gold, good rising malt and hop nose, good body, malt flavor, good hop balance, smooth dry hop finish, pleasant long dry hop aftertaste.

Notes:

PORTUGAL

Sociedad Central de Cervejas

Breweries in **Lisbon, Vialonga,** and **Coimbra**

CERVEJA SAGRES — pale yellow, skunky vegetal nose yields to hops and malt after a few minutes, malt flavor shows some oxidation, bitter hop aftertaste.

SAGRES DARK BEER — very dark brown, strong malt aroma, heavy body, big molasses-like flavor with a bitter background, sweet molasses finish and aftertaste, a very filling beer.

CERVEJA TOPAZIO — medium to deep gold, nose starts out briefly skunky then turns to malt, palate starts as off-dry malt and dries at the finish with the carbonation dominating the middle, sweetness reappears in the long aftertaste.

Companhia União Fabril Portuense, Unicer-União Cervejeria

Breweries in **Oporto** and **Leca do Balio**

CRISTAL BEER — deep yellow-gold, faint malt aroma, very lightly hopped clean dry flavor, medium body, crisp clean finish, tasty dry malt aftertaste.

RUSSIA

Russian Breweries

All beers from Russia were tasted prior to the collapse of the USSR and therefore were from breweries owned and operated by the state. Some, tasted in Europe, bore no identifying brewery of origin.

ALDARA ALUS — hazy gold, sour creamy malt nose, sour malt palate with a hop bite in back, rough hop aftertaste, not a pleasant brew. No brewery cited but a brewery origin date of 1865 given. Alus means ale.

PORTERIS — hazy amber-brown, off-dry roasted malt nose, lovely big roasted malt flavor, rich, delicious, and very long, an excellent porter (porteris). Label says 20%, which I presume to be 20 degrees density. Porteris is labeled almost identically to Aldara, so it is further presumed they are from the same brewery.

RUSSKOYE PREMIUM RUSSIAN LAGER BEER — bright deep gold, soapy malt nose, dry malt flavor, hop finish, soapy malt aftertaste has good length. From Obolon Brewery, Kiev.

MOSCOVA BEER OF RUSSIA— hazy gold, very fruity malt and European hop nose, pleasant fruity malt flavor and finish, lightly hopped, good body, long dry malt aftertaste, bigger in the front than at the finish. Moscow Brewery, Moscow, since 1863.

5 017343 768219
RUSSKOYE
PREMIUM RUSSIAN LAGER BEER
BREWED & BOTTLED AT OBOLON BREWERY, KIEV, U.S.S.R.
IMPORTED BY REITERS BEER DISTRIBUTORS INC.
BROOKLYN, NEW YORK 11208
500ml,
16.9 US Fl. ozs
GOVERNMENT WARNING: (1) ACCORDING TO THE SURGEON GENERAL WOMEN SHOULD NOT DRINK ALCOHOLIC BEVERAGES DURING PREGNANCY BECAUSE OF THE RISK OF BIRTH DEFECTS. (2) CONSUMPTION OF ALCOHOLIC BEVERAGES IMPAIRS YOUR ABILITY TO DRIVE A CAR OR OPERATE MACHINERY AND MAY CAUSE HEALTH PROBLEMS.

Notes:

SPAIN

Sociedad Anonima Damm

Breweries in seven locations including Barcelona

ESTRELLA DORADA CERVEZA ESPECIAL PILSEN — tawny-gold, wine-like aroma with hops and toasted malt, good malt flavor up front, some complexity including nuts and apples, light body, malt aftertaste.

YOLL DAMM EXTRA CERVEZA ESPECIAL — tawny-gold, pleasant malt nose with just a touch of hops, creamy big hop flavor, harsh bitter hop aftertaste.

DAMM BEER — deep gold, faint grainy aroma and taste, front is off-dry, finish is dry, short dry aftertaste.

CERVEZA AGUILA DORADA — tawny-gold, faint malt nose, malt flavor with a nutty background, brief malt aftertaste. Aguila Breweries, S.A.

AGUILA IMPERIAL — bright gold, malt nose, lightly toasted crisp and dry malt flavor, balanced, good body, long malt aftertaste.

Notes:

Cervejeria San Martin

Brewery in **Orense**

SAN MARTIN CERVEJA ESPECIAL — pale amber-gold, faint malt aroma, malt-hop flavor with a salty background, medium length dry malt and hop aftertaste, a little metallic at the end.

San Miguel Fabricas De Cerveja y Malta, S.A.

Breweries in **Lerida, Malaga,** and **Burgos**

SAN MIGUEL LAGER BEER — hazy yellow-gold, sour malt nose and taste, dry malt aftertaste with some hops in back and at very end.

SAN MIGUEL SELECTA — amber-gold, off-dry toasted malt nose and flavor, palate is fairly strong and gets some hops at the finish, good body, a bit winey, long malt aftertaste.

SAN MIGUEL PILSENER — pale gold, faint malt nose with even fainter hops, light body, neutral malt flavor, very light hops, medium-length dry malt aftertaste.

La Zaragozana, S.A.

Brewery in **Zaragoza**

AMBAR SPECIAL BEER — deep gold, big malt nose is off-dry, malt flavor like the nose except there are faint hops at the finish, good balance, fair body, dry hop aftertaste.

SWEDEN

Åbro Brewery

Brewery in **Vimmerby**

VIKING LAGER BEER — brilliant pale gold, floral, spice, and fruit aroma, complex flavor but light, weak malt palate, sour hop finish and aftertaste.

Falcon Brewery

Brewery in **Falkenberg**

FALCON EXPORT III BEER — gold, light malt aroma, bitter hop flavor, light malt finish and aftertaste, some oxidation.

Grängesbergs Breweries, Ltd.

Breweries in **Grängesberg**

GRÄNGES BEER III — light gold, pleasant and balanced malt-hop aroma, flavor mostly hops, bitter hop finish and aftertaste.

GRÄNGES SWEDISH BLONDE BEER — tawny-yellow, dry roasted malt aroma, good dry roasted malt flavor, light body, long roasted malt aftertaste gradually fades without losing any of its character.

Mariestads Bryggerie Aktiebolag

Brewery in **Grängesberg**

MARIESTADS FESTIVAL BEER — deep yellow-gold, faint hop and malt aroma, weak body, almost watery, little flavor beyond the carbonation, bitter hop aftertaste.

Notes:

Pripp Bryggerie

Breweries in **Stockholm** and **Gothenberg**, et al.

PRIPPS EXPORT III SWEDISH BEER — deep tawny-gold, hops dominate the nose and taste, malt shows well in the finish, long malt and apple aftertaste, very good beer.

THREE TOWNS — tawny-gold, beautiful off-dry wine-like malt nose, big hop flavor and hops dominate the palate throughout, long dry hop aftertaste.

PRIPPS 150 JUBILEE EXPORT BEER — deep gold, classical Pilsener aroma of dry slightly vegetal malt and bright hops, big clean hop flavor, good balance, fades at the finish and there is little aftertaste, but it is good while it is there.

DART MÖRKT STARKÖL — copper-red, beautifully balanced hop and malt aroma, mild harmonious hop and malt flavor, long complex dry aftertaste, very good and very drinkable.

KALBACK LAGER — bright pale gold, low carbonation, pungent hop aroma, soft smooth palate shows little of the hops in the nose, light body, dry, clean, but without zest or length.

NORDICK WÖLF LIGHT — medium to pale gold, light hop nose, light body, light hop flavor, brief hop aftertaste, no complexity.

PRIPPS LAGER — bright medium pale yellow-gold, hop nose, high carbonation, hop flavor and finish, brief hop aftertaste, pleasant while it is in your mouth.

Notes:

SWITZERLAND

Cardinal, S.A./ Feldschlossen, S.A.

Breweries in **Fribourg, Sibra, Frankendorf, Rheinfelden,** and **Waedenswil**

CARDINAL LAGER BEER — tawny-gold, smooth malt aroma with good hop backing, finely balanced flavor with good hops and malt, long dry aftertaste, very well-made beer.

FELDSCHLOSSEN HOPENPERLE — amber, malty Tirolean-style aroma, good malt and well-hopped flavor, excellent balance, bright malt finish, long dry hop aftertaste, well-made beer. Previously seen as Feldschlossen Bier Special and Spezial Hell (the latter in Europe).

MOUSSY ALCOHOL-FREE LIGHT MALT BEVERAGE — deep clear bright gold, grainy malt aroma and flavor, medium body, little zest, grainy aftertaste.

EX BIER — bright tawny-gold, malty molasses aroma, flat malt flavor, little zest, but there is a long dry malt aftertaste.

ELAN-THE SWISS BREW — bright gold, grainy nose is off-dry, grainy malt flavor is a tiny bit drier, medium length dry malt aftertaste, not bad for a non-alcoholic brew.

CARDINAL AMBER LIGHT — brassy amber, honeyed malt nose, dull dry malt flavor, medium to short malt aftertaste.

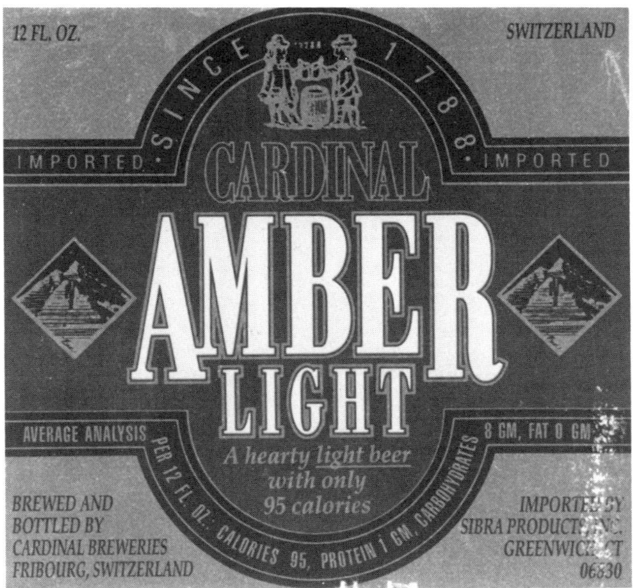

EUROPE

Brauerei Erlen

Brewery in Glarus

GLARNER BEER — bright gold, nice hop nose well backed with malt, good hoppy flavor, pleasant and balanced, very tasty, quick finish, very little aftertaste.

Brauerei A. Hürlimann, A.G.

Brewery in Zurich

HÜRLIMANN STERN BRÄU/SPEZIAL BIER — amber, big off-dry malt aroma with good hops, enormous malt and hop flavor is very assertive, sour hop finish, long dry hop aftertaste, a good-tasting balanced brew with lots of power. This is not the same beer as Hürlimann Export Lager shipped to the U.S. in the 1970s.

BIRELL MALT BEVERAGE — gold, hop and malt nose, light hop flavor, thin body, dry hop finish and aftertaste, seems to get more hops as it goes, very beer-like for a non-alcoholic.

HÜRLIMANN DARK SWISS LAGER — reddish-brown, malt nose, low carbonation, off-dry malt flavor, light body, brief medium dry malt aftertaste.

SAMICHLAUS PALE BEER — brilliant deep amber, complex dry toasted malt nose, huge intensely sweet palate, very complex, powerful sipping beer, long licorice aftertaste, a beauty. Notes are from 1986 brew. The 1987 was very much the same except the alcohol seemed to be a bit more noticeable. This beer has been discontinued, only the Dark is still made.

SAMICHLAUS DARK BIER — very deep bright amber-brown, rich Grape-Nuts and smoky malt nose, very complex, big rich malt flavor is on the sweet side, finishes semi-dry, long dry malt aftertaste, doesn't quite have the complexity of the Samichlaus Pale, but is a good sipping beer for the winter. Notes are for the 1986 brew. The 1987 seemed to be more complex , had a slightly more burnt nature, and was a bit more strongly flavored. The 1988 was not tasted. The 1989 was extremely complex, adding chocolate tones, and at times seemed to have a sherry quality much like Bristol Milk; some tasters thought it overwhelming, a fantastic sipping beer. The 1990 was very alcoholic, winey, much like a sherry, and tasters once again mentioned the Bristol Milk; the aftertaste seemed sweeter than usual. The 1991 was very much like the 1990 except the nose was a bit bready and the aftertaste was a little short and somewhat more dry.

Brauerei Löwenbräu

Brewery in Zurich

LÖWENBRÄU SWISS BEER SPECIAL EXPORT LIGHT — amber, creamy, apple and malt nose, strong malt flavor, bitter hop finish and aftertaste.

LÖWENBRÄU ZURICH EXPORT LIGHT — pale gold, apple peel and malt aroma, good malt and hop flavor, good balance, long dry hop aftertaste has a little unneeded sourness.

LÖWENBRÄU ZURICH EXPORT DARK — deep amber-brown, faint vegetal aroma, dry and dull flavor, sour finish, brief weak malt aftertaste.

LÖWENBRÄU ZURICH LIGHT — pale gold, weak malt aroma, light hop and malt flavor, dry in front, sweet in the finish, light body, brief dry hop aftertaste.

LIBERO NON-ALCOHOLIC MALT BEVERAGE — pale gold, yeasty bready aroma with a faint touch of molasses, watery body, dull malt flavor, quick finish, no aftertaste.

Notes:

Warteck Brewery

Brewery in Basel

WARTECK NON-ALCOHOLIC MALT BEVERAGE — bright deep gold, malty aroma has a skunk for company, sour malt flavor, long dry and sour malt aftertaste.

WARTECK LIGHT BEER — bright gold, faint malt aroma, very light malt flavor, some hop tang in the finish, long dry hop aftertaste.

WARTECK LAGER BEER -- hazy gold, lovely malt and hop nose, good malt flavor backed with hops, good balance, finishes dry hops, long dry hop aftertaste.

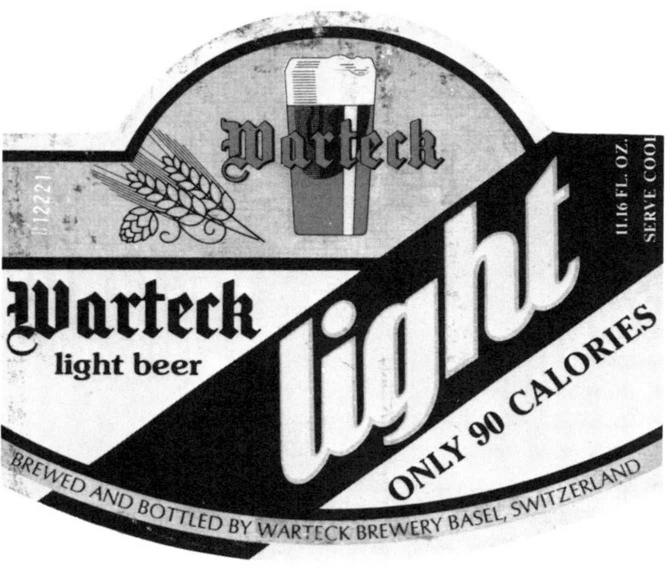

Ziegelhof Brewery

Brewery in Liestal

ALPENSTEIN NON-ALCOHOLIC MALT BEVERAGE — medium gold, lovely well-hopped aroma, good-tasting sour hop flavor, good balance, long dry hop aftertaste.

YUGOSLAVIA

Banjalucka Pivara

Brewery in Banja Luka

NEKTAR BEER — pale amber, malt aroma with an off-dry fruity-apple background, palate like the nose, but there are some hops, long faintly sour dry hop aftertaste.

BIP Pivovare

Brewery in Belgrade

MARCUS BEER — deep yellow, pleasant light malt aroma and flavor, dull malt aftertaste.

BELGRADE GOLD BEER — hazy gold, off-dry malt nose, big malt and hop flavor, expertly balanced, dry malt-hop finish and aftertaste, good body, very much together and very drinkable.

Jadranska Pivovare

Brewery in Split

JADRAN BEER — cloudy yellow, faint fruity malt aroma has some oxidation, highly carbonated, flavor is mostly malt but there are hops in there as well, medium body, hop finish, dry malt aftertaste has little length.

Pivovarna Lasko

Brewery in Lasko, Slovenia

GOLDEN HORN EXPORT SPECIAL — deep golden amber, grainy malt nose, good hop flavor, medium-length grainy aftertaste.

GOLDHORN CLUB — hazy gold, buttery malt nose with sweet hops in back, malt flavor with a hop finish, dry hop aftertaste with return of the buttery malt in the back.

Niksicko Pivovare

Brewery in **Niksic**

NIKSICKO PIVO — gold, malt aroma with a celery-like background, flavor like the nose, salty molasses finish, dry malt aftertaste.

Skopska Pivara

Brewery in **Skopje**

SKOPSKO LAGER BEER — brilliant gold, very strong hop nose and taste, flavor eases off from mid-palate on, good body, finish is hops joined by malt, fairly long dry malt and hop aftertaste.

Notes:

Union Pivovare

Breweries in **Triglav, Ljubijana**

UNION SVETLO PIVO — gold, vegetal malt nose, strong hop flavor, malt well in back, long dry hop aftertaste, very much a German Pils style.

UNION EXPORT BEER — medium gold, apple cider and malt nose, big well-balanced hop flavor, hop finish, brief sour hop aftertaste, highly carbonated, too much so.

UNION EXPORT STOUT — very deep brown color, austere pine needle and celery seed aroma, light body, good roasted-smoky malt flavor, slightly sour brief aftertaste, the flavor is quite pleasing.

Zagrebacke Pivovare

Brewery in **Karlovac**

ZAGREBACKE KARLOVACKO SVIJETLO PIVO LIGHT BEER — pale yellow, sour Pils nose, sour-bitter hop flavor, short aftertaste like the flavor.

KARLOVACKO SPECIAL BEER — amber-yellow, faint winey aroma that is sweet and fruity, watery body, low carbonation, full off-dry malt flavor with a touch of oxidation, slight roasted malt aftertaste.

KARLOVACKO LIGHT BEER — amber-yellow, fruity-malt aroma, fruity sour malt palate, very long sweet-sour aftertaste.

Notes:

UNITED STATES

Abita Brewing Co.

Brewery in **Abita Springs, LA**

ABITA GOLDEN LAGER — hazy gold, malt nose, flavor starts out briefly as malt and immediately dry hops take over, short dry hop aftertaste.

ABITA AMBER LAGER — hazy amber, fruity aroma, fruity malt flavor with a toasted malt background, fades to a brief dry hop aftertaste.

ABITA FALL FEST BEER — amber, rich malt aroma with lots of hops, big hop flavor with plenty of roasted malt in back, very good balance, pleasant hop finish, medium to light body, medium dry hop aftertaste, very drinkable.

ABITA TURBO DOG BEER — deep ruby-amber, light roasted malt aroma, roasted malt flavor, toast finish, finely carbonated, medium body, medium long dry malt aftertaste, very likeable straightforward brew.

Notes:

Alaskan Brewing & Bottling Co.

Brewery in **Juneau, AK**

ALASKAN AMBER BEER — tawny amber, zesty off-dry malty ale aroma, clean and fresh malt, finely carbonated, good- tasting malt and citrus hop flavor with little or no hop bite, good body, very long smooth dry hop aftertaste, excellently balanced, clean, and very drinkable brew.

ALASKAN PALE ALE — gold, bright ale aroma with a citrus background, zesty malt and hop flavor, off-dry malt front, dry hop middle and finish, good body, good balance, long dry hop aftertaste.

ALASKAN SEASONAL SMOKED PORTER 1989 — opaque brown, thick brown head, dry smoked coffee nose, very dry smoked malt flavor, although very smoky it is neither overpowering nor unpleasant, very finely carbonated, very long smoked aftertaste, well-done smoked porter.

ALASKAN 1989 AUTUMN ALE — deep amber, complex toasted malt aroma, big dry toasted malt flavor, finely carbonated, not complex, very long dry malt aftertaste, satisfying and drinkable.

ALASKAN 1990 WINTER STOCK ALE — bright amber-gold, zesty citrus-malt aroma, huge malt and hop flavor, excellent balance, long dry hop aftertaste, all the superlative descriptions apply, an excellent, almost perfect brew. One of the ten best beers on my list.

ALASKAN 1990 WHEAT BEER — hazy-gold, clean fresh light malt aroma, highly carbonated, bright malt flavor on the fruity side, medium body finishes well, but the light short dry malt aftertaste is somewhat disappointing.

Anchor Brewing Co.

Brewery in San Francisco, CA

ANCHOR STEAM BEER — bright copper color, foamy, finely carbonated, rich malt aroma with plenty of hops, creamy malt flavor picks up hops as it crosses the palate, full bodied, complex, long, and very satisfying.

ANCHOR PORTER — deep brown, light malt aroma, big creamy malt flavor, extremely complex with hints of molasses, licorice, and different kinds of malt, big bodied, rich, and very long.

ANCHOR WHEAT — bright gold, pleasant aroma just like freshly milled malt, light malt flavor much like the nose, smooth and pleasant, refreshing and mellow, light dry malt finish and aftertaste, slides down easily. This brew was found on draft as recently as early 1992 and makes occasional brief periodic appearances in bottles.

OLD FOGHORN BARLEYWINE STYLE ALE — reddish-amber, strong roasted malt, caramel, and molasses aroma, rich and intense malt flavor with hops, citrus, and caramel tones, definitely on the sweet side, but complex, well balanced, and very long. A great sipping beer.

LIBERTY ALE — deep amber, lush hop and malt aroma, complex palate with several kinds of malt, hops, spices, citrus, and apricot; very flavorful and very long.

OUR SPECIAL ALE — deep amber, complex and subtle spice aroma, there is both malt and hops, but the spice somewhat overwhelms them, short aftertaste. This is a brew that appears each year as Christmas approaches and which has been spiced since 1987. They are not exactly the same each year, but since they have been spiced, the variation is minor. The 1990 was a bit less spiced, and smoother than the 1989. The 1991 is more subtly spiced and you can taste the malt. Since Anchor started producing a Wassail for Christmas, the 1991 is the most likeable O.S.A. they have offered.

POTRERO COMMONS ALE — cloudy amber, big malt aroma, complex chocolate malt flavor, chewy with an ale bite in back, big bodied, creamy and smooth, balanced and long. A complex brown ale.

ANCHOR SPRUCE BEER — hazy gold, delicate spruce aroma, resiny spruce flavor, aftertaste like spruce gum.

Anderson Valley Brewing Co.

Brewery and brew-pub in Boonville, CA

POLEEKO GOLD LIGHT ALE — hazy gold, pleasant grapefruit nose, grapefruit-ale flavor, long dry hop aftertaste with some of the grapefruit sourness still there.

BOONT AMBER ALE — hazy peachy-amber, fresh citrus ale aroma is a tad soapy, high carbonation, fresh tangy-spicy mildly citrus ale flavor, long off-dry malt and hop aftertaste.

HIGH ROLLERS WHEAT BEER — hazy yellow, peach and melon aroma, finely carbonated, off-dry palate but not malty, pleasant sweetish aftertaste.

DEEP ENDERS DARK PORTER — very deep brown, complex aromatic smoky roasted malt and hop aroma, dry roasted smoked malt flavor, medium body, long dry roasted malt aftertaste with a faint citrus background.

BARNEY FLATS OATMEAL STOUT — deep red-brown color, complex smoky nose, dry smoked malt and coffee flavor, off-dry malt finish, long smoked malt aftertaste, pleasant of type. Another sample had none of the smokiness, but rather a toasted malt aroma, strong off-dry malt flavor, noticeable alcohol, considerable complexity, and a long toasted malt aftertaste.

Angeles Brewing Co.

Brewery in Chatsworth, CA

RHINO CHASERS AMBER ALE — bright amber, big head, light citrus ale aroma and flavor, good body, tasty and complex, medium dry hop finish, and long dry hop aftertaste.

RHINO CHASERS LAGER BEER — hazy gold, fruity malt aroma, tangy malt flavor, medium body, hops are more for bittering than flavor, finishes dry malt, brief dry malt aftertaste.

Notes:

Anheuser-Busch, Inc.

World's largest brewer with breweries in St. Louis, MO; Newark, NJ; Los Angeles, CA; Tampa, FL; Houston, TX; Columbus, OH; Jacksonville, FL; Merrimack, NH; Williamsburg, VA; Fairfield, CA; Baldwinsville, NY; Fort Collins, CO.

BUDWEISER LAGER BEER — pale gold, light but good hop and malt nose, balanced, dry malt and hop finish, and a fairly long aftertaste.

BUDWEISER LIGHT BEER (BUD LIGHT) — brilliant pale gold, pleasant malt aroma, good balance malt and hop flavor, light but tasty, slight malt and hop finish, brief aftertaste.

BUDWEISER DRY BEER (BUD DRY) — bright gold, beautiful malt aroma with hops in back, dry malt flavor is pleasant but brief.

MICHELOB BEER — gold, hop aroma, very good balance between the hops and malt, good body, pleasant fresh and dry malt and hop flavor, medium long aftertaste with slight hop character.

MICHELOB LIGHT — pale gold, fragrant malt aroma, highly carbonated, good but light malt flavor, light hop finish, medium-length aftertaste, good character for a light beer.

MICHELOB DRY — pale bright gold, dry malt nose, dry malt flavor, good balance, but little aftertaste.

MICHELOB GOLDEN DRAFT — bright gold, pleasant hop and malt aroma, mild pleasant flavor showing both hops and malt, medium body, innocuous, nice tasting, with a dry aftertaste.

MICHELOB GOLDEN DRAFT LIGHT — pale gold, hop nose that is almost skunky, light flavor starts out mostly hops, finishes mostly malt, dry malt aftertaste with little duration, light body.

BUSCH PREMIUM BEER — pale yellow, faintly off-dry malt aroma, highly carbonated, smooth malt and hop flavor is all up front, light and refreshing, fades quickly at the finish, slight hop aftertaste.

BUSCH LIGHT DRAFT — pale gold, light malt aroma, good-tasting malt flavor, good body, dry finish and aftertaste.

ANHEUSER NATURAL LIGHT — pale gold, grainy malt aroma, dry and refreshing malt flavor, well balanced, long on the palate and good to drink.

ANHEUSER NATURAL PILSNER — pale gold, faint malt aroma and flavor, noticeable carbonation, hops almost not there at all, brief dry malt aftertaste.

ANHEUSER MAERZEN BEER — amber-gold, terrific malt nose, delicious toasted malt flavor, complex, long hop aftertaste.

KING COBRA PREMIUM MALT LIQUOR — bright gold, appetizing sweet malt aroma, highly carbonated, good malt flavor but definitely on the sweet side, soft and smooth, pleasantly finished and with a good long malt aftertaste.

O'DOULS NON-ALCOHOLIC BREW — bright gold, wet cereal grain aroma, light grainy flavor, dry finish, dull aftertaste of medium duration.

JAGUAR PREMIUM MALT LIQUOR — bright gold, light malt aroma, off-dry malt flavor, sweetest in middle, good body, medium length, dry at very end.

Baltimore Brewing Co.

Brew-pub in Baltimore, MD

BALTIMORE PILS — golden amber, fresh hop nose with lots of malt, big dry hop flavor, long dry hop aftertaste.

BALTIMORE LAGER — bright amber, light hop and malt nose, creamy smooth light hop flavor, plenty of supporting malt, dry hop finish, long dry hop aftertaste.

BALTIMORE AMBER — deep amber, faint malt nose, hop and toasted malt flavor, dry hop finish, medium-length dry hop aftertaste.

Notes:

Bandersnatch Brewing Co.

Brew-pub in Tempe, AZ

BIGHORN PREMIUM ALE — cloudy amber, off-dry fruity malt nose, flavor has bite like a lambic beer, long dry hop aftertaste.

CARDINAL PALE ALE — hazy copper, faint fruity malt nose, creamy, fruity malt flavor, hop finish and aftertaste.

BANDERSNATCH MILK STOUT — opaque brown, huge tan head, beef bouillon aroma, dry malt flavor, long dry malt aftertaste.

Barley's Brewery

Brew-pub in Phoenix, AZ

FAIR DINKUM AMBER — amber, light grapefruit-malt nose, grainy malt flavor with the grapefruit still in back, light malt aftertaste is on the dull side.

Notes:

Belmont Brewing Co.

Brew-pub in Long Beach, CA

MARATHON PALE ALE — gold, big ale nose, hefty hop flavor that drops off abruptly, light dry hop aftertaste.

TOP SAIL AMBER ALE — amber, little nose, dry hop flavor, medium body, dry malt and hop aftertaste with fair duration.

LONG BEACH CRUDE PORTER — deep amber-brown, dry chocolate malt nose, very dry chocolate malt flavor, medium body, long aftertaste like the flavor, more like a stout than a porter.

Berghoff Brewery & Restaurant

Brew-pub and restaurant in Chicago, IL

BERGHOFF LITE — pale gold, pleasant but light malt aroma, weak body, light hop flavor, medium long light hop aftertaste.

BERGHOFF DORTMUNDER REGULAR — pale gold, pleasant malt nose with hops in back, bright hop flavor, excellent balance, long dry hop aftertaste, bright and refreshing.

BERGHOFF WEISSE — hazy gold, faint honeyed malt nose, honeyed malt flavor, light and refreshing, dry malt aftertaste of medium length, no spiciness.

BERGHOFF AMBER ALE — amber, pleasant tangy hop aroma, light hop flavor, long dry hop aftertaste.

BERGHOFF DORTMUNDER DARK — deep amber, zesty hop nose, big flavor is off-dry malt up front, dry hops in the middle, and off-dry malt in the finish and aftertaste, good length. The beer is a bit wine-like in nature, but good.

Gordon Biersch Brewing Co.

Brew-pubs in Palo Alto and San Jose, CA

GORDON BIERSCH PILSENER — deep gold, smooth malt aroma, hops over the malt in the flavor, good body, dry hop finish, long dry hop aftertaste.

GORDON BIERSCH AMBER — medium amber, hop aroma, smooth malt flavor with laid-back hops, good body, richly flavored, long malt aftertaste.

GORDON BIERSCH DOUBLE BOCK — deep amber, rich malt nose, smooth big malt flavor with hops faintly in back, long medium dry malt aftertaste.

Notes:

Black Mountain Brewing Co.

Brewery and restaurant in **Cave Creek, AZ**

CRAZY ED'S BLACK MOUNTAIN GOLD PREMIUM BEER — hazy gold, pronounced hop nose, sharp hop flavor but with plenty of malt for balance, big body, hop finish and long dry hop aftertaste.

DEL RICO — hazy gold, jalapeño pepper nose which comes as no surprise since there is a small jalapeño pepper in the bottle, hot jalapeño pepper and malt taste, strange, hot, and long. Just as a note, the pepper had no flavor or heat left; it was all in the brew by the time I got to it.

CRAZY ED'S ARIZONA PILSNER BEER — gold, bright hop and malt nose, hop flavor is good despite some unbalance in mid-palate, vegetal malt finish, dry hop aftertaste with good length.

Bohannon Brewing Co.

Brewery in **Nashville, TN**

MARKET STREET PILSENER DRAFT BEER — tawny-gold, off-dry malt and carbonated nose, creamy, zesty fruity-malt flavor, medium long malt and hop aftertaste, clean, very pleasant, and very drinkable.

Boston Beer Co.

Brewery in Boston, MA. Facilities of Pittsburgh B.C., F.X. Matt B.C., and G. Heileman B.C. used for regional package production.

SAMUEL ADAMS BOSTON LAGER — golden amber, zesty malt and hop aroma, complex dry hop flavor, plenty of malt in the flavor and in the long aftertaste, good balance throughout, an excellent brew, probably the best of the nationally available brands.

BOSTON LIGHTSHIP — tawny-gold, big luscious off-dry malt nose, big dry malt flavor, dry hop finish, light body, long dry malt aftertaste, good thirst-quencher, one of the most flavorful of the low-calorie beers.

SAMUEL ADAMS DOUBLE BOCK DARK LAGER — deep amber, big fruity toasted malt nose, huge body, big chocolate malt flavor, long and delicious, a chewy lip-smacker.

SAMUEL ADAMS OCTOBERFEST SPECIAL BREW — hazy amber, zesty hop nose, tangy hop palate with good malt backing, very drinkable and very long dry hop aftertaste. Another lip-smacker, but a bit smaller than the double bock, which makes it more drinkable and better with food.

SAMUEL ADAMS BOSTON STOCK ALE — pale amber, complex toasted malt and hop nose, front palate is hops, middle is fruity malt, has dry and off-dry components present at the same time in a complex mix, extremely long malt aftertaste with a background hint of pine. Extremely interesting and pleasant brew that is fair competition to the Boston Lager where they are both available.

SAMUEL ADAMS 1989 WINTER LAGER — amber, rich malt nose, lovely toasted malt and hop flavor, terrific balance, good body, smooth, very tasty, long and delicious, ends surprisingly dry for a big malty brew. This is my favorite from Jim Koch's repertoire.

SAMUEL ADAMS WINTER LAGER 1990-1991 — amber, big toasted malt aroma, bold toasted malt and hop flavor, balanced, complex, very drinkable, and long ending with an extended dry malt aftertaste.

SAMUEL ADAMS WINTER LAGER 1991-1992 — amber, big complex aroma with plenty of malt and hops, huge malt and hop flavor, big body, noticeable alcohol, great complex hop finish and a long dry hop aftertaste. Although different each year, every one is a star!

SAMUEL ADAMS WHEAT BREW — deep gold, zesty spicy clove aroma, medium spicy-lactic flavor, pleasant and refreshing, light body, fairly short aftertaste like the flavor, a German-style Weizen but done with a light hand.

SAMUEL ADAMS CRANBERRY LAMBIC — amber, fruity aroma, fruity-berry tart flavor, long dry tart fruit aftertaste.

Boulder Brewing Co.

Brewery in **Boulder, CO**

BOULDER ENGLISH ALE — pale orange-amber, complex citrus-ale aroma, big well-hopped flavor, complex and full bodied, very long and very good.

BOULDER EXTRA PALE ALE — pale orange-amber, big citrus-ale aroma, strong hop flavor, big body, long and delicious.

BOULDER STOUT — deep amber-brown, big complex malt and tobacco nose, equally complex flavor of roasted (almost burnt) malt with hints of molasses and citrus, good balance, good body, smooth, mellow, and a long dry malt aftertaste with a trace of licorice.

BOULDER PORTER — deep copper, rich roasted malt aroma with a citrus nature and plenty of hops, fine balance, strong and rich off-dry hop and malt ale flavor, with a long dry hop aftertaste.

BOULDER BLACK CHERRY PORTER — opaque brown, attractive smoked cherry nose, smoked flavor is faintly fruity in the finish and aftertaste, light body, not a big number for Boulder.

BOULDER SPORT — bright gold, almost skunky hop aroma, big hop flavor with only a faint hint of malt, fairly brief.

BEST OF SHOW 1988 OKTOBERFEST BEER — bright amber, big toasted malt and hop aroma, smoky-malty dry flavor, medium body, very drinkable but not complex.

BEST OF SHOW 1989 INDIA PALE ALE — golden amber, bright tangy hop nose, big body, big clean and fresh hop flavor well backed with malt, complex dry hop finish, long malt aftertaste, drinkable and refreshing.

BOULDER LIGHT ALE — pale gold, lovely toasted malt nose, off-dry malt palate with hops in back, short watery aftertaste.

TANKER ALE — hazy amber, appetizing delicious toasted malt aroma, almost smoky malt flavor, light body, bit of harshness from the burnt malt at the very end.

BUFFALO GOLD PREMIUM ALE — bright gold, toasted malt aroma, honeyed malt flavor, complex, fairly dry finish and aftertaste with some alcohol noticeable, very drinkable. Made under license from The Walnut Brewery.

BOULDER AMBER ALE — amber color, pleasant toasted malt aroma, medium body, grainy mildly toasted flavor, short aftertaste, lacks complexity and balance.

BOULDER BREWING CO., BOULDER, COLO.
WATER, MALTED BARLEY, HOPS & YEAST
BOULDER
AMBER ALE
12 FL. OZ.
355 ML
GOVERNMENT WARNING: (1) ACCORDING TO THE SURGEON GENERAL, WOMEN SHOULD NOT DRINK ALCOHOLIC BEVERAGES DURING PREGNANCY BECAUSE OF THE RISK OF BIRTH DEFECTS. (2) CONSUMPTION OF ALCOHOLIC BEVERAGES IMPAIRS YOUR ABILITY TO DRIVE A CAR OR OPERATE MACHINERY, AND MAY CAUSE HEALTH PROBLEMS.

Notes:

Breckenridge Brewery

Brew-pub in **Breckenridge, CO**

BRECKENRIDGE INDIA PALE ALE — hazy amber, creamy, soapy citrus malt nose, light malt flavor with a hop and citrus background, dry hop finish, very, very long pleasant complex dry hop and malt aftertaste, well-made brew.

Brewhouse Grill

Brew-pub in **Santa Barbara, CA**

OLD TOWN PALE ALE — deep gold, light hop aroma, tasty hop flavor, slightly sour hop finish, long hop aftertaste, front and mid-palate are excellent.

MISSION CREEK PORTER — dark brown, faint malt aroma, good dry malt flavor, some off-dry malt lingers in back and shows stronger in the finish and aftertaste, a finely carbonated velvety malt brew.

Bridgeport Brewing Co.

Brewery and brew-pub in **Portland, OR**

BRIDGEPORT BLUE HERON PALE ALE — amber, malt and faint citrus nose, off-dry lightly toasted malt flavor, good body, pleasant, good malt finish, long dry slightly smoked malt aftertaste with very dry hops at the end, complex, well-balanced brew.

BRIDGEPORT COHO PACIFIC LIGHT ALE — light amber, complex toasted malt and hop aroma, very dry flavor just like the nose, good body, dry hop finish and long dry hop aftertaste, well made, very drinkable, and very good with food.

British Brewing Co.

Brewery at **Glen Burnie, MD**

OXFORD CLASS AMBER ALE — amber, light malt and hop aroma, low carbonation, light body, dry malt flavor with slight hop backing, light dry malt aftertaste.

Buffalo Bill's Brew-pub

Brew-pub in **Hayward, CA**

BUFFALO BILL'S BREW-PUB BEER — cloudy orange-amber, faint citrus nose, light body, light citrus flavor, medium dry hop aftertaste, interesting but lacks depth.

PUNKIN ALE — hazy pale orange, clean light off-dry fruity tangerine nose, palate is fruity malt first, then hoppy in middle and finish, fruity malt and bright hop aftertaste, medium body, good balance, interesting and very drinkable.

BUFFALO BILL'S DOUBLE CREAM ALE — hazy gold, light fruity aroma (like melon and peaches), creamy texture, hops on front of the palate, fruity malt in the middle, dry hop finish and aftertaste, medium length.

RAUCH BEER SMOKED PORTER — amber, smoked sausage aroma, a bit peppery, harsh smoked flavor, dry smoked aftertaste with considerable length.

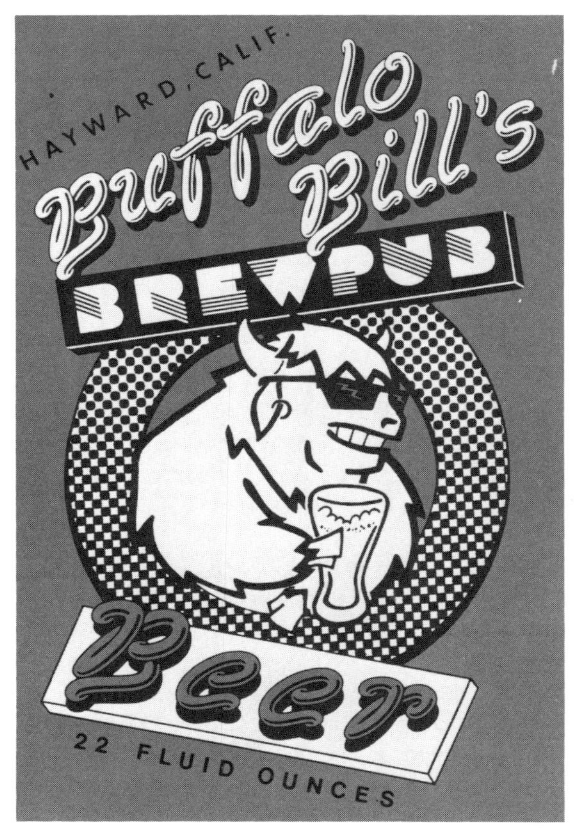

Buffalo Brewing Co.

Microbrewery and brew-pub in **Lackawanna/Buffalo, NY**

BUFFALO LAGER — tawny-gold, malt-hop nose, dry hop flavor and aftertaste, medium length.

BUFFALO PILS — tawny-gold, bright and pleasant hop and off-dry malt nose, front palate is off-dry malt, thence dry hops, good body, good complexity, long and very drinkable.

LIMERICK'S IRISH STYLE RED ALE — hazy amber, hoppy ale nose, bright and balanced malt and hop flavor, good body, long dry hop aftertaste with honeyed malt in support of and balancing the hops, extremely drinkable.

BLIZZARD BOCK BEER — hazy amber, bright hop aroma, tasty dry hop flavor, good body, smooth, long dry hop aftertaste.

Notes:

Callahan's Pub & Brewery

Brew-pub in San Diego, CA

MESA PALE ALE — tawny-gold, big dry hop nose and taste, very long dry hop aftertaste.

Cambridge Brewing Co.

Brew-pub in Cambridge, MA

REGATTA GOLDEN — hazy gold, big malt and hop nose and flavor, complex, good body, good balance, dry hop finish, long dry hop and malt aftertaste.

CAMBRIDGE AMBER — medium pale amber, light malt and hop nose, good body, touch of soap in the finish, long complex dry malt and hop aftertaste.

CHARLES RIVER PORTER — deep mahogany, big malt and hop nose, smooth malt and hop flavor, good balance, good body, long dry hop aftertaste.

TALL TALE PALE ALE — slightly hazy golden amber, rising hop aroma, big complex hop flavor, a little hop bite especially in the finish, very long dry hop aftertaste.

WINTER WARMER — mahogany color, spicy over the malt in the nose, cinnamon-nutmeg off-dry malt flavor, medium body, long spicy aftertaste, enough malt to be tasted but for the most part the spices take center stage.

Capital Brewing Co.

Brewery in **Middleton, WI**

Uses bottling facilities of Stevens Point B.C. in Stevens Point, WI, for packaging.

CAPITAL GARTEN BRAU SPECIAL — amber, well-balanced malt and hop nose, fine malt palate with a light hop finish, medium body, good balance, long dry hop aftertaste.

CAPITAL GARTEN BRAU WILD RICE — amber-gold, malty aroma, fresh off-dry fruity malt flavor, heavy body, medium dry malt finish and aftertaste.

CAPITAL GARTEN BRAU DARK — deep amber, malty-molasses nose, dry malty flavor with the molasses still in back, dry malt aftertaste of medium length.

CAPITAL MAIBOCK — amber-gold, huge complex malt aroma, rich and strong malt flavor, dry malt aftertaste, very tasty, very complex, and very long.

CAPITAL GARTEN BRAU OKTOBERFEST — medium amber-gold color, complex fragrant hop aroma, well-balanced dry hop and malt flavor that continues into a long dry aftertaste, smooth and tasty throughout.

Notes:

Catamount Brewing Co.

Brewery in **White River Junction, VT**

CATAMOUNT GOLD — deep gold, big nose with lots of fruity malt and hops, bright hop palate, good body, long hop aftertaste supported with plenty of malt. A hefty, well-made brew.

CATAMOUNT AMBER — medium deep amber, subdued malt aroma, good-tasting malt flavor, good body, good balance, long malt aftertaste, a satisfying, pleasant, very drinkable brew.

CATAMOUNT PORTER — deep mahogany, rich rising straightforward malt nose, big rich dry malt flavor with a lightly scorched backtaste that doesn't mar the effect, long dry malt aftertaste.

CATAMOUNT CHRISTMAS ALE 1990 — hazy amber, roasted malt aroma, big dry roasted malt flavor, big hop finish, noticeable alcohol, very long dry malt and hop aftertaste. A very good Christmas ale.

CATAMOUNT CHRISTMAS ALE 1991 — amber, beautiful big hop aroma with plenty of malt in back, big strong flavor much like the nose, delicious, appetizing, expertly balanced, very long hop aftertaste. This is the best effort from Catamount to date.

ETHAN ALLEN ALE — hazy gold, melony malt nose, carbonation sting is quite noticeable, malt dominates the flavor but the balance between the malt and hops is so-so, medium to light body, medium-length dry malt aftertaste.

POST ROAD REAL ALE — amber, bright zesty hop nose with good malt, big complex hop flavor, big body, long dry hop aftertaste well supported with malt, very tasty ale, indeed! Made for Old Marlborough B.C., Marlboro, MA.

NEWMAN'S SARATOGA BRAND LAGER BEER — hazy gold, bright fruity hop nose, flavor like the nose, good body, good balance, long dry hop aftertaste.

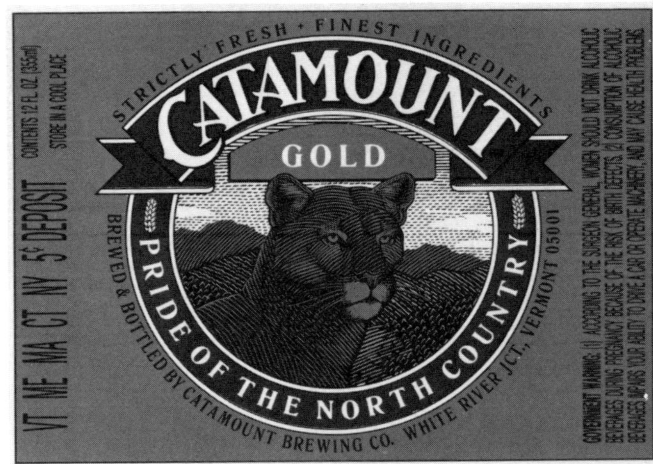

Charter Oak Brewing Co.

Brewery in Bristol, CT

CHARTER OAK LAGER — hazy amber, big bright malt aroma, a bit of a tang appears only in the nose, pleasant malt flavor with no hops showing, light body, lacks zest, medium-length light malt aftertaste.

OLD LEATHER MAN ALE — hazy deep gold, hop aroma, dry metallic hop flavor, dry hop finish, brief dry hop aftertaste.

CHRISTMAS ALE 1991 — deep amber, malt nose, strong malt flavor, light body, weak malt finish, very short malt aftertaste.

BREWED AND BOTTLED BY
CHARTER OAK BREWERS, BRISTOL, CT 06010
Charter Oak
Brewed in Bristol Connecticut
LAGER
GOVERNMENT WARNING: (1) ACCORDING TO THE SURGEON GENERAL, WOMEN SHOULD NOT DRINK ALCOHOLIC BEVERAGES DURING PREGNANCY BECAUSE OF THE RISK OF BIRTH DEFECTS. (2) CONSUMPTION OF ALCOHOLIC BEVERAGES IMPAIRS YOUR ABILITY TO DRIVE A CAR OR OPERATE MACHINERY, AND MAY CAUSE HEALTH PROBLEMS.
CT. 5¢ DEPOSIT
12 FL. OZ.

Notes:

Chicago Brewing Co.

Brewery in Chicago, IL

LEGACY LAGER — an amber brew with an appetizing hop and malt aroma, finely carbonated, good well-hopped flavor, good body, balanced and long.

LEGACY RED ALE — amber color, tangy malt and hop aroma, big and clean well-hopped flavor, complex and tasty, dry hop finish, plenty of malt throughout, long dry aftertaste.

HEARTLAND WEISS — hazy gold, spicy malt aroma with a light lactic touch, light spicy malt flavor, very refreshing, smooth, good body, lightly spiced and dry malt aftertaste, a good German Weissbier style.

CHICAGO'S
THE BEER BREWED ONLY WITH PREMIUM NATURAL INGREDIENTS
Heartland
Weiss
BEER
CHICAGO BREWING CO.
HANDCRAFTED

Clement's Brewing Co.

Brewery in Vernon, NJ, and brew-pub in Ithaca, NY

CLEMENT'S PILSENER SUPER PREMIUM LAGER — gold, hop nose and taste a little on the sour side, medium body, dry hop finish and lengthy aftertaste, good Germanic style beer.

CLEMENT'S DARK DOUBLE BOCK — deep amber, big malt and hop nose, flavor like the nose, excellent balance, long dry hop finish and aftertaste, again very German.

CLEMENT'S BLOND DOUBLE BOCK — hazy gold, big off-dry malt nose, big malt and hop flavor, richly flavored, heavy body, long off-dry malt and hop aftertaste that goes very dry hops at the end.

CLEMENT'S AMBER — amber, good malt and hop aroma, creamy smooth complex malt flavor, dry malt finish, long dry malt aftertaste. Served as **OLD BAY SPECIAL AMBER** in a New Brunswick, NJ, pub.

CLEMENT'S OKTOBERFEST — amber, faint off-dry malt nose, big malt flavor is drier than the nose but not dry, good tasting, finely balanced, creamy texture, good body, very drinkable brew that kicks sweet but stays dry.

CLEMENT'S PORTER — deep ruby-brown, tan head, light dry malt aroma becomes roasted chocolate malt once it warms up, light dry roasted malt flavor, medium body, light dry roasted malt aftertaste with good length, good with food. Named **COLE PORTER** in the brew-pub.

Cold Spring Brewing Co.

Brewery in Cold Spring, MN

COLD SPRING BEER — pale gold, fragrant malt aroma, good clean malt and hop flavor, medium-dry long aftertaste.

KEGLE BRAU — tawny-gold, lovely malt and hop aroma, good malt and hop flavor, very tasty, bright hop finish and long hop aftertaste.

COLD SPRING EXPORT — medium gold, complex hop aroma and flavor, dry hop finish, and long dry hop aftertaste, a well-made and complex brew.

NORTH STAR BEER — medium gold, clean rich malt nose, lightly hopped flavor, light body, clean light malt and hop finish, weak short aftertaste.

GEMEINDE BRAU — gold, malt aroma, malt and hop flavor, dry hop finish and aftertaste with only medium duration. Made for Gemeinde Brau, Inc., Amana, IA.

WESTERN PREMIUM BEER — pale gold, bright malt aroma, pleasant malt flavor, finish, and aftertaste, good length.

FOX DELUXE BEER — pale gold, pleasant malt nose, high carbonation, off-dry malt finish and aftertaste, medium length.

WHITE LABEL LIGHT BEER — medium gold, faint malt aroma, clean refreshing malt aroma, off-dry malt finish and aftertaste.

COLD BRAU PREMIUM BEER — pale gold, light fresh malt aroma, refreshing clean malt flavor, very light in hop character, pleasant malt finish and aftertaste, fair length.

KARLSBRAU OLD TIME BEER — bright gold, sour malt nose, vegetal malt flavor and finish, long slightly sour malt aftertaste.

KOLONIE BRAU — pale gold, lovely complex malt and hop aroma, equally complex malt and hop flavor, good balance, more malt than hops, but the hops do show well in the finish and long aftertaste. Made for Gemeinde Brau, Inc., Amana, IA.

Columbus Brewing Co.

Brew-pub and attached restaurant in Columbus, OH

GIBBY'S GOLD — light gold, nice hop nose, light soapy malt flavor, dry hop aftertaste.

PALE ALE — deep gold, light hop nose, big malt flavor with good hops, long flavor like the aroma, long malt aftertaste, a delicious brew.

NUT BROWN ALE — deep amber-brown, roasted malt aroma, big malt flavor with an acidic background, long rich malt aftertaste also has the acidic bite.

BLACK FOREST PORTER — deep brown, malt nose, sweet malt palate, big body, almost viscous, long malt finish and aftertaste with an acidic tang in back.

Commonwealth Brewing Co.

Brew-pub in Boston, MA

Bottled beers are made under contract by F.X. Matt in Utica, NY. See Matt for descriptions.

STANLEY CUP STRONG ALE — hazy amber, spicy faint clove off-dry nose, medium body, soft, low carbonation, tangy off-dry spicy clove flavor, buttery finish, hop aftertaste.

GOLDEN ALE — pale gold, light hop aroma, medium body, light hop and malt flavor, low carbonation, dry hop aftertaste.

AMBER ALE — amber, light malt aroma, light body, light malt and hop flavor, dry hop finish.

COLD DRAUGHT BLOND ALE — tawny-gold, clean crisp hop nose, light clean dry malt flavor, dry malt finish and medium aftertaste, the 20% wheat malt wouldn't be noticed unless you knew.

BOSTON'S BEST BURTON BITTER — copper color, dry hop nose, flavor, finish, and very dry and long hop aftertaste.

CLASSIC STOUT — very deep brown, light smooth malt aroma with a touch of hops, classic stout nose, , not big but pleasant, good dry malt and hop flavor, smooth finish and long aftertaste like the flavor, very drinkable.

Adolph Coors Co.

Breweries in Golden, CO; Memphis, TN; and Elkton, VA

COORS BEER — pale gold, lovely fresh clean malt aroma, hops barely noticeable, light body, slightly off-dry malt taste, very light, very refreshing, very quaffable, medium to short duration.

COORS LIGHT — very pale yellow-gold, very clean malt aroma, perky clean malt flavor, light and brief.

GEORGE KILLIAN'S IRISH RED LAGER — pale copper-red, light toasted malt aroma, light body, clean fresh and balanced hop and malt flavor, light but lingering malt aftertaste.

COORS GOLDEN LAGER — yellow-gold, clean malt nose, very light malt flavor, a little hop bite in back, light and short malt aftertaste.

COORS EXTRA GOLD — bright yellow-gold, pleasant malt aroma, pleasant off-dry malt and hop flavor, long off-dry malt aftertaste.

COORS WINTERFEST 1991-1992 — brilliant amber, plain malt nose, big malt flavor, especially at the finish, very tasty brew, long hop aftertaste, best of the Winterfests to date.

COORS WINTERFEST 1990-1991 — amber, fruity-malt aroma, malt flavor, an estery quality to both the nose and taste, ends up with an off-dry malt aftertaste, still with that estery quality in back.

COORS WINTERFEST 1989-1990 — tawny-gold, faint fruity malt aroma, off-dry malt flavor, soft and light with low carbonation, medium dry finish, light short malt aftertaste, a wimpy brew. First tasted XMAS 1987 at which time it was similar to the '89-'90, but had more hops.

COORS EXTRA GOLD DRAFT — bright gold, beautiful malt and hop aroma, slightly off-dry malt palate, very drinkable, medium body, long off-dry malt aftertaste.

KEYSTONE — light gold, light malt nose, malt flavor with a touch of apple, medium body, malt aftertaste of medium length.

KEYSTONE LIGHT — light gold, very faint malt nose with a trace of apple, off-dry malt flavor, weak body, dry malt aftertaste, short to medium length.

COORS CUTTER NON-ALCOHOLIC BEER — pale gold, grainy malt nose, thin body, wet paper and malt flavor, dry malt finish, short malt aftertaste.

COORS PREMIUM DRY BEER — gold, pleasant fruity-malt nose, high carbonation, off-dry fruity malt front palate, middle and finish are dry malt, brief light dry malt aftertaste, light body.

Notes:

Crown City Brewery

Brew-pub in Pasadena, CA

MT. WILSON WHEAT BEER — gold, malty-wheat nose, refreshing malt flavor with light hops, long dry malt aftertaste.

ARROYO AMBER ALE — amber, very little aroma (nothing specific to describe), bright smooth hop and malt flavor with a nice little bite, very tasty, light dry malt aftertaste with medium duration.

BLACK CLOUD OATMEAL STOUT — very dark brown, brown head, dry coffee-malt aroma and flavor, tart dry finish, long dry malt aftertaste, quite flavorful.

Note: *They also serve a HALF & HALF, a mix of the WHEAT and STOUT.*

Dallas Brewing Co.

Brewery in Dallas, TX

WEST END LAGER — brilliant gold, pleasant malt nose, fruity malt and light hop flavor, hop finish, dry hop aftertaste.

Notes:

Dead Cat Alley Brewing Co.

Brewery and brew-pub in Woodland, CA

CAT TAIL ALE — amber, pleasant malt nose on the sweet side has hops in back, big malt and hop flavor with a citrus background, light body, long dry malt and hop aftertaste.

FAT CAT PORTER — deep brown, huge malt nose, delicious very dry malt palate, touch of toasted malt and a light salty nature in back, dry malt finish and aftertaste, quite drinkable, tastes like more.

DEAD CAT LAGER — hazy gold, big tangy hop aroma, off-dry complex citrus-pepper-malt-carbonation flavor, very interesting character, very long dry malt aftertaste.

Devil Mountain Brewery

Brewery, brew-pub, and restaurant in Walnut Creek, CA

Recent labels say brewed and bottled by Bay B.C., Benicia, CA, under the trade name Devil Mountain Brewery. Furthermore, I have heard that the Devil Mountain brew-pub has closed. Bay B.C. is likely a corporate name for Huttenhain's Benicia Brewing Co., a brew-pub in Benicia, CA, north of San Francisco.

RAILROAD ALE — hazy amber, pleasant citrus hop ale nose, zesty citrus hop flavor with hop strength growing across the palate and strongest at the finish, delicious and balanced, medium dry malt aftertaste.

IRON HORSE ALE — hazy deep amber, highly carbonated, foamy, tangy citrus nose, good malt and hop flavor with the citrus background, medium body, light malt aftertaste, medium length.

GAYLE'S PALE ALE — hazy gold, bright citrus nose (grapefruit this time), lemon and grapefruit background to the malt flavor, medium body, refreshing but not much like an ale.

DEVIL'S BREW PORTER — deep brown, effervescent, smoky chocolate malt aroma, very dry smoky malt flavor, full-flavored big body, good balance, long strong malt aftertaste, very drinkable, very good of type.

MEDAL WINNER — Great American Beer Festival
Made from only the finest malted barley, hops and yeast
Rich, creamy and full bodied with no aftertaste
DEVIL MOUNTAIN BREWERY
DEVIL'S BREW
BREWED AND BOTTLED BY BAY BREWING CO. INC., BENICIA, CA. UNDER THE TRADE NAME DEVIL MOUNTAIN BREWERY

Dixie Brewing Co.

Brewery in New Orleans, LA

DIXIE LAGER — gold with a touch of amber, lightly hopped slightly sour malt aroma, light body, refreshing hop flavor, medium dry finish and aftertaste.

DIXIE LIGHT BEER — deep golden color, slightly sweet malt and apple aroma, light bodied, light "beery" (pleasant malt and hops) taste, malt finish, and brief aftertaste.

DIXIE AMBER LIGHT — amber color, good malt and hop aroma, light malt flavor, too much carbonation, short aftertaste.

NEW ORLEANS BEST — pale gold, pleasant hop nose, palate is malt with a slight hop bite, light body, medium length. (Royal B.C.)

NEW ORLEANS BEST LIGHT — yellow-gold, light malt aroma, good carbonation level, pleasant malt flavor, medium length. (Royal B.C.)

COY INTERNATIONAL PRIVATE RESERVE CASK 36 — gold, zesty ale-like aroma, clean tangy hop flavor, good body, malt aftertaste. (Royal B.C.)

DIXIE BLACKENED VOO DOO LAGER — deep amber-rose color, pleasant malt and hop aroma, big dry toasted malt flavor with some hops in back but could use more, good body, more hops arrive in the finish but a bit late, dry hop aftertaste.

RATTLESNAKE BEER — pale gold, malt and hop aroma, malt flavor, light body, light hop and malt aftertaste. Made for Kershenstine Enterprises, Eupora, MS. Previously made by Spoetzl B.C.

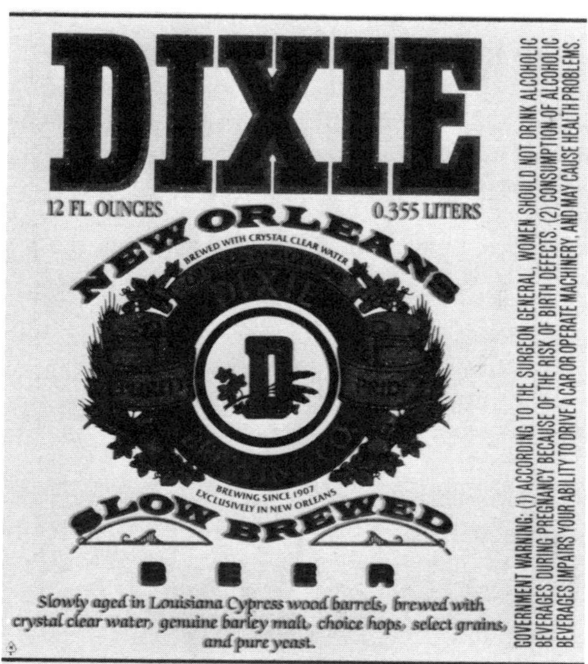

BREWED WITH CRYSTAL CLEAR WATER

SLOW BREWED

Slowly aged in Louisiana Cypress wood barrels, brewed with crystal clear water, genuine barley malt, choice hops, select grains, and pure yeast.

Dock Street Brewing Co.

Brew-pub and restaurant in Philadelphia, PA

DOCK STREET WEISS BIER — hazy gold, light fresh malt aroma, bright malt flavor with plenty of hops, a lot of hops for a wheat beer but the balance is good, dry mostly hop finish, long dry hop aftertaste. Mix is 50% wheat.

DOCK STREET HELLES — deep gold, bright hop nose and taste, hop finish and aftertaste, very long, very German, malt is there but barely noticeable.

DOCK STREET PALE ALE — tawny-gold, faint hop nose, bright hop flavor with plenty of malt, good body, dry hop finish, long dry hop aftertaste, excellent balance, complex, feels good in your mouth.

DOCK STREET IMPERIAL STOUT — opaque brown, tan head, malt aroma, concentrated malt flavor, burnt nature of the malt is most noticeable in the finish, long tapering malt aftertaste.

DOCK STREET BARLEY WINE — deep brown, big dry chocolate malt nose and taste, strong hops back the malt but can barely compete and stay in back except at the finish and aftertaste; big, complex, and very long, feels great in your mouth; have this at the end of your beer drinking, because if you have it first it is almost overwhelming, and, for certain, you won't be able to taste anything else afterwards.

Etna Brewing Co.

Brewery in Etna, CA

ETNA EXPORT LAGER BEER — hazy gold, fresh fruity malt nose, bright hop and malt flavor, light body, tasty, drinkable, short dry aftertaste.

ETNA ALE — hazy amber, malt aroma, light malt and hop flavor, light body, brief light dry malt aftertaste.

ETNA DARK LAGER BEER — deep amber-brown, big dark malt nose with a slightly smoked background, light body, flavor like the nose but not as strong nor as smoked, medium long dry malt aftertaste.

Evansville Brewing Co.

Brewery in Evansville, IN

FALLS CITY LIGHT BEER — pale gold, light malt aroma, light grainy-malt flavor, weak malt finish, short malt aftertaste.

THE EAGLE PREMIUM MALT LIQUOR — gold, grainy malt nose with some background hops, clean refreshing bright off-dry malt and hop flavor, good body, medium long off-dry malt aftertaste.

WIEDEMANN LIGHT — pale gold, light dry hop and malt nose and flavor, medium long dry hop aftertaste, very drinkable and refreshing.

WIEDEMANN BEER — gold, light hop nose, good malt and hop flavor, fairly dry, drinkable, and refreshing, fairly long dry hop aftertaste.

Note: *Evansville acquired several labels from G. Heileman (Drewry's Beer, Drewry's Light 'n Dry Beer, Drummond Bros., Drummond Bros. Light, Cook's Goldblume Beer, Cook's Goldblume Premium Light Beer, Falls City Beer, Sterling Beer, and Sterling Light Beer) and the rights to sell Wiedemann Bohemian Special Beer and Wiedemann Bohemian Special Light Beer in five states. Wiedemann labels sold elsewhere are still produced by G. Heileman.*

Firestone & Fletcher Brewing Co.

Brewery in Los Olivos, CA

FIRESTONE PREMIUM NON-ALCOHOLIC MALT BEVERAGE — brilliant deep gold, malt nose, light malt flavor, light body, dull malt aftertaste.

The Florida Brewery, Inc.

Brewery in Auburndale, FL

GROWLIN GATOR LAGER — pale yellow-gold, pleasant malt nose, refreshing malt flavor is good while it lasts (which is not for long), light body, fine for hot-weather drinking.

Notes:

Frankenmuth Brewery, Inc.

Brewery in Frankenmuth, MI

FRANKENMUTH GERMAN STYLE PILSENER — gold, good malt and hop nose, rich hop flavor, has plenty of malt, good body, long dry hop aftertaste.

FRANKENMUTH GERMAN STYLE DARK — deep rosy-amber, off-dry malt aroma, straightforward dry malt flavor, long dry malt aftertaste, smooth and very drinkable.

Frankenmuth
EXTRA
light
12 FL. OZ. (355 ML.)
Average Analysis Per Bottle:
Calories 97, Carbohydrates 6.1 grams, Protein 1 gram, Fat 0.0 grams
GOVERNMENT WARNING: (1) ACCORDING TO THE SURGEON GENERAL, WOMEN SHOULD NOT DRINK ALCOHOLIC BEVERAGES DURING PREGNANCY BECAUSE OF THE RISK OF BIRTH DEFECTS. (2) CONSUMPTION OF ALCOHOLIC BEVERAGES IMPAIRS YOUR ABILITY TO DRIVE A CAR OR OPERATE MACHINERY, AND MAY CAUSE HEALTH PROBLEMS.

FRANKENMUTH OLD GERMAN STYLE BOCK — brown, big malt nose with a hint of banana and sense of alcohol, smooth complex roasted malt flavor, big body, balanced, richly flavored, long dry malt aftertaste.

FRANKENMUTH WEISSE — bright gold, melon-mango fruit nose, finely carbonated, faint fruity-malt flavor, brief malt finish, medium long spicy malt aftertaste.

FRANKENMUTH EXTRA LIGHT — pale gold, faint malt nose with a hop background that makes you suspect that it will go skunky when it gets over the hill, light body, weak malt flavor is mostly carbonation, light malt finish, brief malt aftertaste with a sour touch at the very end.

OLD DETROIT AMBER ALE — light amber, malt aroma, zesty dry hop flavor, creamy texture, dry hop finish, dry malt aftertaste.

ISLAND GOLD BEER — deep gold, fruity malt aroma, dull malt flavor, thin body, weak short malt aftertaste. Contract brew for Bay B.C., Put-in-Bay, Ohio.

Fullerton Hofbrau

Brew-pub in Fullerton, CA

PRINCE'S PILSENER — hazy gold, hop nose, bright hop and dry malt flavor, crisp and complex, good body, long dry hop aftertaste, an excellent brew.

KING'S LAGER — gold, light hop nose, big dry malt and light hop flavor, good body, smooth, but lacks the complexity of the Pils, long dry malt and hop aftertaste.

EARL'S ALE — amber, big hop nose and taste, good body, smooth, plenty of malt for good balance, long hop aftertaste.

DUKE'S BOCK — deep amber, chocolate malt aroma, huge malt flavor with the hops in behind, big body, smooth and rich, long rich malt and hop aftertaste.

D.L. Geary Brewing Co.

Brewery in Portland, ME

GEARY'S PALE ALE — deep bright golden amber, big citrus hop and fruity-malt nose, complex dry hop palate borders on bitter but comes off very good, dry hop finish, long dry hop aftertaste that is a bit tart at the end, a very well-made and likeable brew.

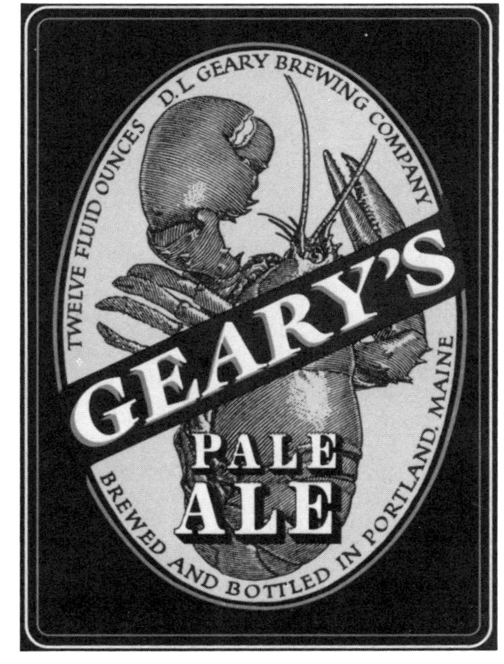
D.L. GEARY BREWING COMPANY
TWELVE FLUID OUNCES
GEARY'S
PALE
ALE
BREWED AND BOTTLED IN PORTLAND, MAINE

HAMPSHIRE WINTER ALE 1989-1990 — cloudy amber, tart complex fruity-hop aroma, huge dry hop flavor with loads of malt in back, big body, extremely long dry hop aftertaste, a big sipping beer with very good balance.

HAMPSHIRE SPECIAL ALE 1990-1991 — bright amber, big toasted malt aroma, huge malt and hop flavor, rich and delicious, long dry hop aftertaste, great balance, good sipping beer.

HAMPSHIRE SPECIAL ALE 1991-1992 — hazy amber, citrus hop and malt aroma, big zesty complex hop ale flavor, rich malt backing, big long hop aftertaste, another delicious sipping beer.

Genesee Brewing Co.

Brewery in Rochester, NY

GENESEE BEER — gold, good malt aroma, pleasant malt flavor with a slight hop taste, good balance, good body, short dry hop aftertaste.

GENESEE CREAM ALE — gold, big malt nose with a slight hop backing, good balanced malt and hop flavor, finishes a bit weakly, medium-length aftertaste, what is there is pleasant.

GENESEE BOCK BEER — deep amber, malt aroma with lightly roasted malt character, fair body, good balance, pleasant long malt aftertaste.

GENESEE OKTOBERFEST BEER — deep amber, nice malt aroma, very smooth malt flavor, lightly hopped, dry malt finish and aftertaste, medium duration.

GENESEE LIGHT — pale color, mild malt aroma with some yeast in back, light body, dry and light hop flavor, light finish and brief aftertaste.

GENESEE NA NON-ALCOHOLIC BREW — pale gold, dull malt nose, thin body, weak malt flavor, almost watery, high carbonation, little aftertaste, light but refreshing when you are very thirsty.

GENESEE CREAM LIGHT CREAM ALE — yellow-gold, light fruity malt and talcum powder nose, medium dry malt and hop flavor, hop finish, off-dry malt aftertaste has good length.

TWELVE HORSE ALE — bright gold, fresh malt aroma, bright malt flavor with the hops gradually coming in as it crosses the palate, dry hop finish and aftertaste, lighter than I remember it from some years back, but still pleasant and refreshing.

KOCH'S GOLDEN ANNIVERSARY BEER — bright gold, light malt aroma, malt flavor, medium body, fairly long malt aftertaste. Uses corporate name of Fred Koch Brewery from which brewery in Dunkirk, NY, originated the brand.

KOCH'S GOLDEN ANNIVERSARY LIGHT BEER — pale gold, pleasant hop and malt aroma, light body, weak malt flavor, thin body, brief aftertaste.

BLACK HORSE PREMIUM ALE — bright gold, nice hop and malt aroma, rich flavor with a malt front and hop middle and finish, good balance, quite zesty, long aftertaste shows both hops and malt.

Notes:

Golden Pacific Brewing Co.

Brewery in Emeryville, CA

GOLDEN PACIFIC BITTERSWEET ALE — deep amber, light off-dry citrus-ale nose with a spiciness in back, zesty well-hopped palate with some smoked malt in back, dry hop finish and long smoky aftertaste.

PACIFIC CASCADE WHOLE MALT BEER — pale hazy-gold, grapefruit nose, big hop flavor with the grapefruit in back, dry hop finish and long aftertaste retains some of the grapefruit.

Golden Bear
DARK
MALT LIQUOR
TWELVE FLUID OUNCES / KEEP REFRIGERATED

Goose Island Brewing Co./Lincoln Park Brewery, Inc.

Brew-pub in Chicago, IL

GOLDEN GOOSE PILSNER — gold, mild hop aroma, very dry hop palate, good balance, very dry hop finish, long dry hop aftertaste.

TANZEN GANS KOLSCH — gold, light hop aroma, zesty hop flavor, medium body, dry hop finish and aftertaste. Very good brew.

HONKER'S ALE — amber-gold, faintly sour hop nose, big hop flavor, especially good on back and sides of tongue, real bittering hops used, dry hop finish, long very dry hop aftertaste showing good malt at the end. Another very good brew.

PMD MILD ALE — amber brown, malt nose, good dry malt flavor, finishes dry hops but the malt is still there, excellent with food.

OLD CLYBOURN PORTER — deep brown, dry malt aroma, very dry malt flavor, medium to long dry malt aftertaste.

DUNKELWEIZENBOCK — hazy amber, some malty sweetness in the nose, big malt lightly spiced flavor, long off-dry malt aftertaste, a lovely sipping beer.

VICE WEIZEN — hazy gold, malt nose, smooth refreshing malt flavor, lightly spiced, finish and aftertaste is dry malt.

RAF BETTER BITTER ALE — deep amber-gold, bright hop aroma, has plenty of malt in back, zesty hop flavor still with plenty of supporting malt, dry hop finish, long very dry hop aftertaste.

Gorky's Cafe & Russian Brewery

Brew-pubs in Los Angeles and Hollywood, CA

IMPERIAL STOUT — deep amber, fruity malt aroma, very dry smoky malt flavor, long dry roasted malt aftertaste.

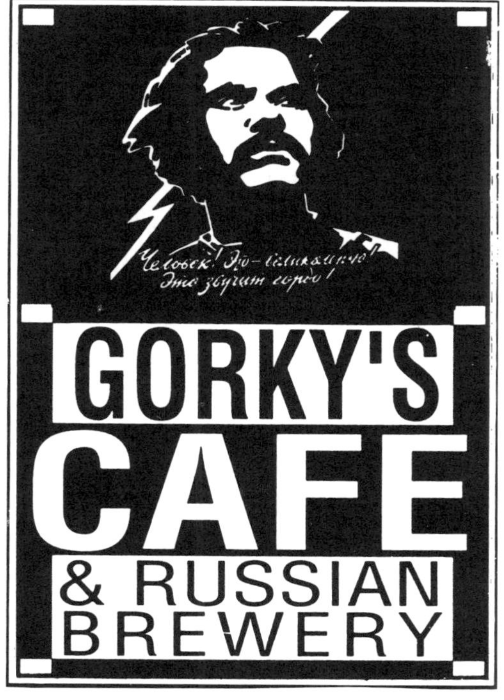

Great Lakes Brewing Co.

Brew-pub in Cleveland, OH

GREAT LAKES DORTMUNDER STYLE — pale golden-amber, good malt aroma is almost ale-like, very pleasant big toasted malt flavor, dry malt finish, long rich malt aftertaste, hop presence is from start to finish but keeps in the back well surrounded by the richness of the malt, pleasant and satisfying. At the brew-pub this is called **HEISMAN** and is brilliant gold, has a bright hop aroma and taste, with a dry malt finish and aftertaste.

GREAT LAKES VIENNA STYLE — deep amber, very faint malt and hop aroma, rich but dry roasted malt flavor, medium long dry malt aftertaste, good body, excellent example of a Vienna style lager. At the brew-pub this brew is called **ELIOT NESS** and is amber, has a malt nose, a very smooth and balanced malt-hop flavor, and a dry malt aftertaste.

BURNING RIVER PALE ALE STYLE — brilliant deep amber, delicious malt aroma, big hop ale flavor, dry hop finish, long dry hop aftertaste.

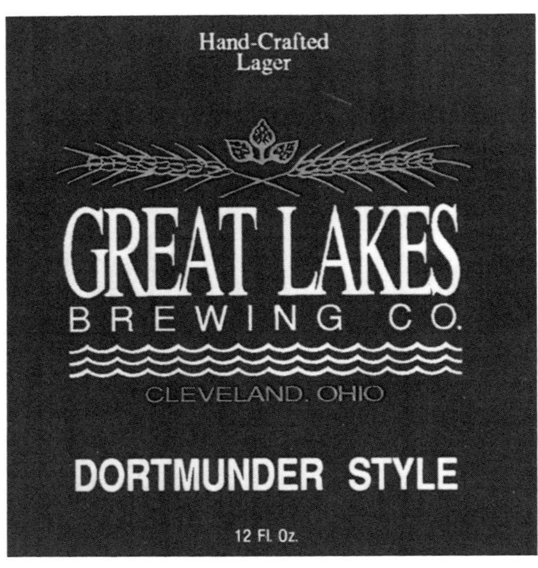

Notes:

Happy Valley Brewing Co.

Brew-pub in State College, PA

GOLDEN LION PALE ALE — gold, hop nose, dry well-hopped smooth flavor, dry hop finish, long dry aftertaste has both hops and malt, very drinkable and very good.

SCOTCH ALE — deep amber-brown, caramel malt aroma, rich malt and smooth hop flavor, long dry malt and hop aftertaste.

PENN PORTER — deep amber-brown, smooth dry hop and malt flavor, dry and long well-hopped aftertaste, very drinkable, good with food.

WEIZEN BIER — amber, fresh malt aroma, bright big hop flavor, excellent balance, dry hop finish, long dry hop aftertaste with plenty of malt showing.

NITTANY LAGER — gold, hop nose, smooth dry hop flavor, excellent balance, long dry hop aftertaste, light, smooth, and drinkable.

Hart Brewing Co.

Brewery in Kalama, WA

PACIFIC CREST ALE — medium pale hazy amber, fruity toasted malt nose, big tangy ale flavor, lots of hops and toasted malt, good balance, fairly complex, big body, good dry hop finish and long hop and malt aftertaste.

PYRAMID WHEATEN ALE — hazy amber-gold, pleasant malt and citrus hop aroma, light dry tangy flavor with a light citrus background, medium body, short dry hop aftertaste, what is there is good, but there just isn't enough of it.

SPHINX STOUT — opaque brown, brown head, smoky burnt malt aroma, some vegetal malt in back, dry burnt caramel palate, a sweet-sour finish that doesn't come off well, smoky aftertaste.

SNOW CAP ALE 1990 — deep reddish amber, big complex malt and hop nose, huge flavor, malt dominates at first, the hops vie for the lead in mid-palate, they don't clash in the contest and it comes off very well, big body, long dry hop aftertaste with plenty of malt support. This is a winner! It is as good as or better than any other seasonal winter beer offered.

The Hartford Brewery Ltd.

Brew-pub in Hartford, CT

PITTBULL GOLDEN — hazy gold, aroma is malt at first, then hops, hop flavor, long rich dry hop aftertaste, feels good in your mouth.

ARCH AMBER — hazy amber, hop aroma and flavor, very dry hop finish and aftertaste, almost too bitter.

MAD LUDWIG'S OKTOBERFEST ALE — deep hazy amber, hop nose, big body, complex hop and malt flavor, dry hop finish and aftertaste, smooth brew.

PITBULL
GOLDEN
BREWED IN CONNECTICUT BY
The Hartford Brewery Limited

G. Heileman Brewing Co.

Breweries in La Crosse, WI; Seattle, WA; Baltimore, MD; Portland, OR; and San Antonio, TX. Owned by Bond Corp. of Australia.

CHAMPALE MALT LIQUOR — pale gold, grapelike aroma that makes you think of Champagne, light body, good carbonation, slightly sweet grapey flavor. Certainly tries to be Champagne-like and does so fairly successfully.

GOLDEN CHAMPALE FLAVORED MALT LIQUOR — bright gold, fruit gum aroma, flavor much like a Scottish soda called Irn-Bru (Iron Brew in eastern Canada), fairly sweet and clean tasting, interesting for a flavored malt liquor.

PINK CHAMPALE FLAVORED MALT LIQUOR — pale pink, nose like Cold Duck, which I presume it is intended to emulate, mildly flavored sweet taste (grenadine?), very drinkable and pleasant.

BLACK HORSE ALE — tawny-gold, bright hop aroma with plenty of supporting malt, caramel-malt flavor, good balance, long rich malt aftertaste.

METBRAU NEAR BEER — pale gold, faintly salty malt aroma, highly carbonated, flavor is light malt and carbonated, little finish and aftertaste.

HEILEMAN'S SPECIAL EXPORT BEER — tawny-gold, lusty hop aroma, flavor starts out hops but slightly off-dry, then gets bigger and more hoppy at mid-palate and into the finish, stays smooth, is complex and very much European in style, has plenty of character, finishes dry hops and has good length.

HEILEMAN'S SPECIAL EXPORT LIGHT BEER — pale bright gold, pleasant malt aroma, thin body, light malt flavor with some sour hop background in mid-palate, fleeting off-dry malt finish, very little aftertaste.

HEILEMAN'S SPECIAL EXPORT DARK — deep copper color, very little nose, only a faint sense of sweetness, faint hop flavor, low carbonation, light body, dull and uninteresting.

HEILEMAN'S OLD STYLE LIGHT LAGER BEER — gold color, fragrant malt and hop nose, bright hop flavor, balanced and fairly long.

OLD STYLE SPECIAL DRY — pale gold, sweet malt aroma, highly carbonated, off-dry malt front palate, dry middle and finish, faint brief malt aftertaste.

OLD STYLE PREMIUM DRY BEER — pale gold, apple-malt nose, fairly dry and smooth hop flavor, plenty of malt in support, finishes dry, not much aftertaste.

OLD STYLE CLASSIC DRAFT — gold, pleasant malt and hop aroma, high carbonation, flavor is malt, hops, and carbonation, light but clean, melony finish, dry aftertaste.

OLD STYLE CLASSIC DRAFT LIGHT — gold, light malt and faint hop aroma, high carbonation, light flavor like the nose but the carbonation is a major part, light bodied, light dry finish, little aftertaste.

HEILEMAN'S LIGHT BEER — bright pale gold, faint malt aroma, light hop flavor that is less dry in front than it is in middle and finish, good balance and fairly long.

WIEDEMANN BOHEMIAN SPECIAL FINE BEER — pale gold, fresh malt aroma with some hops, light malt flavor with a hop background, good fresh-tasting pilsener-type beer, fairly long dry hop aftertaste.

WIEDEMANN LIGHT — gold, grainy aroma with a soapy background, light body, weak malt flavor, seltzer-like finish and aftertaste, clean but uninteresting.

RED WHITE AND BLUE SPECIAL LAGER BEER — pale gold, light clean malt aroma and flavor, light body, dry malt finish and short aftertaste, quaffable hot-weather beer.

BURGERMEISTER BEER — pale gold, pleasant light hop nose, light hop and malt flavor, dry hop finish and aftertaste, medium duration.

BLATZ BEER — gold, light malt nose, light malt flavor, light body, finishes dry and has a short malt aftertaste, what hops there are well in back, another hot-weather quaffing beer.

BLATZ LIGHT BEER — pale gold, lovely malt nose, malt flavor but you can taste the carbonation, hops come in with a bitter touch in the finish leading to a dry, brief, and slightly bitter hop aftertaste

BLATZ LIGHT CREAM ALE — medium yellow-gold color, off-dry fruity malt aroma, tangy hop flavor, some off flavors in the backtaste which take a more dominant position in the aftertaste.

BLATZ LA BEER — gold, pleasant fragrant aroma with both malt and hops, watery body, very little flavor, what's there is pleasant but too weak.

BLITZ-WEINHARD BEER — tawny-gold, malt and hop nose, high carbonation, malt flavor that has a salty component, dry malt finish with some hops in aftertaste.

HENRY WEINHARD PRIVATE RESERVE — light to medium gold, good hop aroma, very appetizing, a zesty flavor that features both malt and hops, good balance, medium to good body, light hop aftertaste with good length. Each bottling is numerically identified on the neck label.

HENRY WEINHARD'S PRIVATE RESERVE DARK BEER — medium tawny-brown, slightly smoky malt aroma, light body, flavor starts dry but becomes less so toward the middle, some complexity but not much, pleasant and refreshing. It is more like a colored light beer than a dark beer.

HENRY WEINHARD PRIVATE RESERVE LIGHT BEER — bright gold, dull hop nose, light malt and hop flavor, not interesting and not long.

WEINHARD'S IRELAND STYLE PREMIUM LIGHT ALE — deep gold, tangy hop aroma, light hop flavor, light body, pleasant and drinkable, medium to long aftertaste, malt is there but well in back.

ST. IDES PREMIUM MALT LIQUOR — deep gold, malt nose, off-dry malt flavor, smooth and mellow, refreshing, finishes medium dry, long malt aftertaste.

HAUENSTEIN NEW ULM BEER — pale gold, clean malt aroma with some hops, clean bright malt flavor, light body, light hop finish and aftertaste.

GRAIN BELT BEER — pale gold, off-dry malt nose, light malt flavor, high carbonation, short malt aftertaste.

GRAIN BELT PREMIUM — pale gold, light malt aroma, malt flavor is lightly hopped and off-dry, light malt aftertaste shows a little more hopping but not much.

SCHMIDT BEER — pale gold, light fragrant hop aroma, medium body, malt and hop flavor on the light side, weak bodied and brief.

SCHMIDT EXTRA SPECIAL BEER — pale gold, fruity malt aroma, off-dry malt flavor, only lightly hopped, medium aftertaste like the flavor.

SCHMIDT LIGHT BEER — pale gold, pleasant light malt and hop aroma, light but complex hop flavor, dry hop finish and aftertaste.

THE NATIONAL BEER OF TEXAS
GOVERNMENT WARNING: (1) ACCORDING TO THE SURGEON GENERAL, WOMEN SHOULD NOT DRINK ALCOHOLIC BEVERAGES DURING PREGNANCY BECAUSE OF THE RISK OF BIRTH DEFECTS. (2) CONSUMPTION OF ALCOHOLIC BEVERAGES IMPAIRS YOUR ABILITY TO DRIVE A CAR OR OPERATE MACHINERY, AND MAY CAUSE HEALTH PROBLEMS.
LONE STAR
BEER
©G. HEILEMAN BREWING CO., LA CROSSE, WISCONSIN
12 FL. OZ.
(355ml)

SCHMIDT SELECT NEAR BEER — pale gold, faint malt aroma, weak watery body, dry dusty malt flavor, brief aftertaste.

KINGSBURY BREW NEAR BEER — very pale golden color, faint malt nose, watery body, grainy flavor, faint grainy aftertaste has little length.

LONE STAR BEER — gold, light malt and hop aroma, flavor to match, light body, medium dry finish, little aftertaste.

LONE STAR LIGHT BEER — pale gold, light malt aroma, weak body, light malt flavor, fairly short light malt aftertaste.

LONE STAR DRAFT BEER — pale yellow-gold, full malt aroma, good malt flavor, medium dry malt aftertaste with good duration.

STAG LIGHT BEER — pale gold, light malt aroma and flavor, little finish and aftertaste save some faint hops.

STAG BEER — gold, clean fresh malt aroma, good body, flavor starts off good malt and hops but does not sustain, becoming more faint as it crosses the palate, light hop aftertaste.

MICKEY'S FINE MALT LIQUOR — bright gold, malt nose, fruity malt flavor that is on the sweet side, finishes sweet but the malt in the aftertaste dries a bit, medium duration.

RAINIER ALE — amber, good well-hopped nose, big body, tangy hop and malt flavor, the malt is off-dry but the bite of the hops keeps it all in balance, good length.

RAINIER MOUNTAIN FRESH BEER — pale gold, hoppy nose, but the flavor is more malt and even more carbonation, finish and aftertaste seem highly influenced by the carbonation and ends brackish.

RAINIER LIGHT — pale gold, pleasant malt and hop nose, low carbonation, malt palate with very little hops, fairly brief.

CARLING'S BLACK LABEL BEER — pale yellow-gold, palate is off-dry malt at first, then some hops come in for the finish and aftertaste, medium body, fair length.

CARLING'S BLACK LABEL 11-11 EXTRA SPECIAL MALT LIQUOR — light gold, sweet malt aroma with a hop tang in back, highly carbonated, sweet malt flavor with a fruit background, complex, but it will be a matter of taste to like it.

CARLING'S BLACK LABEL L.A. — yellow-gold, stinky hop nose that faded, watery body, slightly sweet malt flavor, little left at the finish, only a faint sweetness for an aftertaste.

CARLING'S BLACK LABEL LIGHT BEER — gold, faint malt aroma, light and dry malt flavor with a trace of hops, little aftertaste.

CARLING'S BLACK LABEL NA MALT BEVERAGE — deep gold, grainy nose, grainy watery palate, thin and short.

CARLING'S ORIGINAL RED CAP ALE — tawny gold, big hop aroma, strong hop flavor, good body, long hop aftertaste that has too much malt to be called dry, but well balanced.

COY INTERNATIONAL — pale yellow, good malt nose, off-dry malt flavor that continues into a long aftertaste.

HEIDELBERG BEER — pale gold, faint malt aroma, light malt and hop flavor, light body, little finish and aftertaste.

HEIDELBERG LIGHT — very pale gold, malt nose, light clean malt flavor, off-dry, medium body, dry malt aftertaste.

NATIONAL BOHEMIAN LIGHT BEER — gold, good clean malt aroma, sprightly clean malt and hop flavor, off-dry at first then good balanced dry malt and hops, finishes well and has a long crisp aftertaste.

NATIONAL PREMIUM PALE DRY BEER — medium deep gold, good malt aroma, pleasant light hop flavor, good balance, smooth and long.

NATIONAL PREMIUM LIGHT BEER — pale yellow, pleasant light malt aroma, fresh light hop flavor, light body, touch of sour malt in the brief aftertaste.

COLT .45 MALT LIQUOR — deep gold, lovely malt aroma, smooth and soft, off-dry malt flavor and long aftertaste.

COLT .45 SILVER DELUXE MALT LIQUOR — pale yellow, malt nose, malt flavor, fairly heavy body, long malt aftertaste with some imbalance in back.

COLT .45 DRY — bright gold, dry malt nose, dry malt palate with a sweetness in back that stays into a long aftertaste.

COLT .45 POWERMASTER MALT LIQUOR — gold, light malt aroma, big alcoholic malt flavor, sweet and smooth with sweet hops in back of the malt, good balance, quite long. Very good of type.

TUBORG GOLD EXPORT QUALITY BEER — medium gold, well-hopped malt aroma, off-dry malt palate up front, but the hops soon come in for a clean, complex, and well-balanced flavor, long and pleasant throughout.

TUBORG DELUXE DARK EXPORT QUALITY BEER — copper-brown color, malty molasses nose, light body, mild malt flavor with the hops present but in back, malt finish and aftertaste.

FISCHER'S OLD STYLE GERMAN BEER — pale yellow-gold, pleasant off-dry malt and hop nose, light malt flavor, light body, pleasant, off-dry, and short aftertaste.

FISCHER'S OLD STYLE ENGLISH ALE — pale yellow-gold, pleasant malt and hop aroma, dry malt flavor, faint hops in back, short dry aftertaste.

FISCHER'S LIGHT BEER — deep bright gold, fresh malt nose with a yeasty background, light body, light hop flavor that finishes dry and a bit sour, fairly short.

SCHMIDT'S — pale gold, pleasant hop and malt nose, off-dry malt flavor with hops in back, medium body, dry finish, pleasant but short aftertaste, good summer quaffing beer.

SCHMIDT'S BAVARIAN BEER — pale gold, faint malt aroma, slightly sour malt flavor, bitter hop finish, dry hop aftertaste.

READING LIGHT PREMIUM BEER — pale gold, light malt aroma, pleasant malt flavor with some light hop background, light bodied, clean, refreshing, light dry hop aftertaste.

KOEHLER QUALITY BEER — pale gold, good malt aroma, pleasant light malt flavor, hop finish, long pleasant dry malt and hop aftertaste.

RHEINGOLD EXTRA DRY LAGER BEER — pale gold, fresh malt aroma with some hops in back, light body, light malt flavor with some bittering hops in back, these hops come forward in the finish and aftertaste, but more to make the effect of being dry rather than bitter.

RHEINGOLD EXTRA LIGHT — pale gold, light malt aroma, off-dry flavor takes on some sour malt character in the finish and aftertaste.

KNICKERBOCKER NATURAL — pale gold, malt nose, smooth, soft malty flavor with good hop balance, light body, long dry aftertaste.

COQUI 900 MALT LIQUOR — bright deep gold, malt aroma, sweet malt flavor, clean malt finish and aftertaste.

McSORLEY'S CREAM ALE — tawny brown, tangy malt and hop aroma, full flavored with plenty of both malt and hops, good balance, well-hopped but not overly bitter for the malt, long aftertaste, very good with food.

BLATZ MILWAUKEE 1851 — bright gold, sweet malt nose, sort of a fruity-apple, palate is off-dry with a bite in the middle, quick finish, and little aftertaste. A bit too sweet up front, but improves across the palate as it gets drier. Overall reasonably drinkable.

BLATZ MILWAUKEE 1851 LIGHT — brilliant pale gold, lovely beery malt aroma, light body, pleasant malt flavor, some hops in aftertaste, pleasant but too watery and too brief.

ABC BEER — gold, big head, lovely hop and malt nose, very fragrant, clean malt flavor, light but pleasant, medium length.

ABC ALE — gold, big head, dry hop nose, dry hop flavor, pleasant, medium body, brief aftertaste.

ABC LIGHT — pale gold, pleasant malt and hop nose, almost perfumy, light malt flavor, highly carbonated, short malt finish and aftertaste.

MIDNIGHT DRAGON SPECIAL RESERVE MALT LIQUOR — gold, slightly stinky malt nose, high carbonation, big malt and hop flavor, very drinkable and very good, backs off a bit in the finish and aftertaste, but still a big flavorful brew. Contract brew for Ferolito & Vultaggio & Sons of Brooklyn, NY, along with the three following brews. The three Midnight Dragon brews were likely made at Pittsburgh prior to the split, and, at present, details of production haven't been revealed.

MIDNIGHT DRAGON ROYAL RESERVE LAGER — gold, flowery hop aroma, light dry hop flavor and finish, short aftertaste.

MIDNIGHT DRAGON GOLD RESERVE ALE — golden amber, slightly stinky malt nose, highly carbonated, big malt and hop flavor, finishes strong with big hops well-backed with malt, long, very drinkable, and very good.

CRAZY HORSE MALT LIQUOR — deep gold, slightly sour malt nose, big malt palate, noticeable alcohol, long off-dry malt aftertaste. Made for Dakota Hills Ltd. by Hornell Brewing Co., Inc. of Baltimore, but Ferolito & Vultaggio & Sons is embossed on the shoulder of the bottle.

Heritage Brewing Co.

Brew-pub in Dana Point, CA

LANTERN BAY BLONDE — hazy gold, faint citrus nose, light citrus flavor, light body, very short aftertaste but refreshing while it is there.

SAIL ALE — amber, fruity melon and malt nose that is very pleasant, flavor starts grapefruit and quickly turns to malt, creamy, lightly toasted malt finish, medium long dry malt aftertaste.

DANA PORTER — deep ruby-brown, big chocolate malt nose, chocolate malt flavor stays right through into a long aftertaste.

Notes:

Honolulu Brewing Co.

Brewery in Honolulu, Oahu, HI

KOOLAU LAGER — beautiful deep gold, big hop nose, strong dry hop palate, slightly sour hop finish, dry hop aftertaste, medium length.

DIAMOND HEAD DRY BEER — brilliant gold, dry malt aroma with citrus hops in back, bright hop flavor with a citrus background, good body, dry hop finish, medium-length dry hop aftertaste.

PALI HAWAIIAN BEER — bright pale gold, chocolate malt aroma, honeyed malt flavor, good body, some hops appear in the finish but it is mostly malt, good long malt aftertaste.

Hood River Brewing Co.

Brewery and brew-pub in Hood River, OR

FULL SAIL GOLDEN ALE — faintly hazy amber-gold, pleasant and clean malt aroma, tasty malt and hop flavor, good balance, good body, lovely malt finish, long dry malt aftertaste, very, very drinkable.

FULL SAIL AMBER ALE — amber, beautiful zesty hop aroma, big hop flavor with plenty of malt for support, medium body, very tasty, long dry hop aftertaste. Very good-tasting brew.

Hoster Brewing Co.

Brew-pub in Columbus, OH

EAGLE LIGHT — pale gold, almost no discernible aroma, clean light and dry hop flavor, light body, dry hop finish and brief aftertaste.

GOLD TOP — deep gold, hop nose, pleasant dry hop flavor, good body, long dry hop aftertaste.

AMBER — amber, light roasted malt aroma, flavor like the nose but with some hops, pleasant and tasty, good body, fairly long aftertaste much like the flavor, a Vienna-style lager,

BUCKEYE BOCK — deep amber, big hop and malt aroma, big hop flavor, plenty of malt backing, long dry hop aftertaste.

EAGLE DARK-SON OF BLACKTOP — dark brown, complex malt and hop aroma on the dry side, big body, dry stout-like flavor but not heavy like a stout, long dry malt aftertaste.

Huber-Berghoff Brewing Co.

Brewery in Monroe, WI

Several corporate names used on labels, including Jos. Huber B.C.

REGAL BRAU BAVARIAN STYLE BEER — gold, fresh clean malt aroma, good malt and hop balanced flavor, off-dry finish, sour malt aftertaste.

WISCONSIN CLUB PREMIUM BEER — medium gold, pleasant malt nose, malt palate, light body, off-dry malt finish and aftertaste.

HUBER PREMIUM BEER — bright gold, good hop and malt aroma, fresh and clean off-dry malt and hop flavor, nicely balanced, pleasant malt finish, long malt aftertaste.

HUBER PREMIUM BOCK BEER — deep amber-brown, malt nose, malt flavor up front becomes more and more hoppy as it proceeds to a dry, almost bitter hop finish and aftertaste.

RHINELANDER EXPORT PREMIUM BEER — bright gold, clean malt aroma, off-dry malt flavor up front, but this dries toward the finish and ends in a fairly dry hop aftertaste of little length. It is good with food.

ED DEBEVIC'S BEER — tawny-gold, good big hop aroma, off-dry hop front palate, drier at the finish, and ends with a short dry hop aftertaste. Made for a Chicago restaurant, but available elsewhere.

ROUGHRIDER PREMIUM BEER — hazy pale gold, light malt nose, high carbonation, light malt flavor and finish, short dry hop aftertaste, light bodied. Contract brew for Dakota B.C.

OLD CHICAGO LAGER BEER — gold, sour hop nose, hop flavor that is a little sour in front, dry hop finish and aftertaste.

BERGHOFF BEER — bright amber, hop nose, bright hop and malt flavor, good body, tasty, light hop finish, long dry hop aftertaste, complex and likeable brew.

BERGHOFF DARK BEER — amber-brown, rich hop aroma, light body, fairly rich malt flavor that is a tad burnt, fairly pleasant, light body, long dry malt aftertaste, a little hop bitterness at the very end. You could drink a lot of it.

BERGHOFF BOCK BEER — deep mahogany, dry slightly roasted malt nose, roasted malt flavor, medium body, medium dry malt aftertaste, straightforward dry and light beer with little complexity.

BERGHOFF LIGHT BEER — deep gold, flowery malt aroma, light malt and hop flavor, balanced but light, medium to short dry hop aftertaste.

A. FITGER & CO.'s EXPORT BEER — pale amber, light hop nose, good body, good dry hop and malt flavor, long dry hop aftertaste.

VIENNA LAGER BEER — amber, complex off-dry malt and hop aroma, bright hop flavor, finish, and long aftertaste, an interesting and appetizing beer.

AMBIER VIENNA STYLE BEER — brilliant amber, very light toasted malt aroma, front palate is malt, dry hop middle and finish, complex long candy-malt aftertaste that slowly dries as it goes on. This brew is very much a Vienna-style lager. Made for Ambier (Vienna) B.C. of Milwaukee, WI.

LEMON & LAGER — light gold, lemon aroma, zesty lemony flavor but very little resemblance to a beer, as there is very little malt showing through the lemon except in the long aftertaste, it is supposed to be like a lemon shandy by the style.

VAN MERRITT LIGHT BEER — bright gold, light hop nose, very light hop flavor, almost nothing at the finish and no aftertaste.

DEMPSEY'S ALE — pale amber, beautifully balanced hop and lightly roasted malt nose, zesty ale taste with good hops and some toasted malt, high carbonation, light body, dry malt finish, medium-length dry malt aftertaste.

HARLEY DAVIDSON HEAVY BEER 1988 — hazy-gold, malt nose is a touch sour, big malt and hop palate, heavy body, good balance, long malt aftertaste. Made annually for a Harley-Davidson motorcycle meet held each year in the vicinity.

HARLEY DAVIDSON HEAVY BEER 1989 — pale amber, malt aroma, good malt flavor, big body, long pleasant malt aftertaste.

HARLEY DAVIDSON HEAVY BEER 1990 — gold, clean fruity malt nose and taste, big body, long dry malt aftertaste.

BOXER PREMIUM MALT LIQUOR — deep gold, god fruity malt nose, pleasant straightforward malt flavor, finishes as it starts, long malt aftertaste.

BRAUMEISTER LIGHT BEER — deep gold, pleasant malt and hop aroma, light malt-hop flavor, very thin, very short.

TELLURIDE BEER — tawny-gold, pleasant soft malt aroma, pleasant off-dry malt front palate, dry hops come in the middle, finishes dry malt, long dry malt and hop aftertaste, medium body, overall dry and well balanced and very drinkable. Made for Telluride B.C., Moab, UT.

SNAKE BITE BEER — gold, faint melony malt nose, light malt flavor, carbonation bite pretty much overwhelms anything subtle, short dry malt aftertaste. Made for Snake Bite Beer Co., Muskego, WI.

FOECKING PREMIUM BEER — pale gold, light malt aroma, high carbonation, good malt flavor with the hops in back, balanced and very drinkable, dry aftertaste drops off very fast. Made for Foecking Alcohol Beverage Co. of Illinois, Rock Island, IL.

FOECKING PREMIUM LIGHT — gold, pleasant malt and hop nose, high carbonation, light dry malt and hop flavor, light body, short dry finish and aftertaste. Contract brew as above.

CERVEZA VICTORIA — deep gold, good fragrant hop and malt nose, dry malt palate, good body, dry malt aftertaste with a hop background, touch of bitter hops at the end of the long aftertaste. Made under licence of Compañhia Cerveceria de Nicaragua, a contract brew for distribution in Nicaragua.

CERVEZA VICTORIA LIGHT BEER — pale gold, flowery hop and malt aroma, big malt flavor, very refreshing, medium body, medium long dry hop aftertaste.

CERVEZA VICTORIA MORENA BEER — deep amber-brown, fragrant rich malt nose, good malt flavor, pleasant and straightforward, light body, long rich and dry malt aftertaste.

Privatbrauerei Hubsch

Brew-pub in Davis, CA

HUBSCH BRAU GERMAN STYLE BEER — gold, finely carbonated, pleasant fruity malt aroma, big hop flavor, big body, dry hop finish, long dry hop aftertaste.

Hudepohl-Schoenling Brewing Co.

Brewery in Cincinnati, OH

Company is results of the merger of Hudepohl and Schoenling breweries.

BOHEMIAN TAP LAGER BEER — bright gold, slightly sweet malt aroma, highly carbonated, light sweet malt flavor, off-dry malt finish and aftertaste.

HOFBRAU BIER — deep gold, clean malt and hop nose, light body, bright hop flavor up front, malt comes in middle and adds a little sweetness to the finish and aftertaste.

HUDEPOHL GOLD — bright gold, big fruity malt aroma, good dry malt flavor, light but pleasant, refreshing, and wellbalanced.

HUDEPOHL 14K PREMIUM BEER — pale gold, vegetal malt nose, grainy off-dry malt flavor, somewhat straw-like in back and in the finish and aftertaste.

HUDY DELIGHT BEER — pale yellow-gold, faint roasted character to the malt, but there is a little straw in back that seems to dull the taste, light body, light malt aftertaste with little length.

HUDEPOHL PURE GRAIN BEER — pale gold, light hop aroma followed by a hop palate well backed with malt, good body, lightly spicy hop and malt finish and aftertaste.

BURGER BEER — very pale gold, pleasant light malt aroma and taste, which continues into the medium-length aftertaste.

LUDWIG HUDEPOHL ORIGINAL BOCK BEER — deep amber, lovely roasted malt nose, smooth dry roasted malt flavor, long malt aftertaste, medium body, very drinkable.

LUDWIG HUDEPOHL SPECIAL OKTOBERFEST BEER — pale amber-orange, dry malt aroma, good dry malt flavor, good body, well balanced, long refreshing malt aftertaste.

CHRISTIAN MOERLEIN CINCINNATI SELECT BEER — amber-gold, big malt aroma with plenty of hops in back, big malty flavor with good support from hops in back, hint of smokiness in the middle, finish cuts off quickly but there is a long dry malt aftertaste.

CHRISTIAN MOERLEIN DOPPEL DARK BEER — amber color, sweet rich malt nose, dry toasted malt flavor, medium body, off-dry malt at finish, slightly off-dry malt aftertaste of medium length.

CHRISTIAN MOERLEIN BOCK BEER — dark amber, malt nose that is slightly smoky, malt flavor with a touch of potato peel at the finish, medium body, little finish and aftertaste, overall on the dull side.

LITTLE KINGS CREAM ALE (SCHOENLING CREAM ALE) — gold, fragrant aroma has both hops and malt, flavor starts out briskly with fresh bright hops, sweetens out a bit at the finish, and ends that way, long aftertaste. A bright, good-tasting little brew.

TOP HAT BEER — pale gold, faint malt aroma with even fainter hops in back, very light malt and hop flavor, medium body, short dry malt and hop aftertaste.

SCHOENLING DRAFT BEER — gold, beautiful malt nose, high carbonation, pleasant malt and hop flavor, brief but clean and refreshing. Also labelled BIG JUG BEER.

SCHOENLING OLD TIME BOCK BEER — deep ruby-amber, malt aroma, thin body, high carbonation, malt and cherry-pit taste, off-dry malt finish and medium aftertaste.

WILLIAM PENN COLONIAL LAGER — deep amber, rich malt aroma, good body, a good malt and hop flavor but it is quite light, dry malt aftertaste, very drinkable. Contract brew for Wm. Penn B.C. of Langhorne, PA.

BRUCKS JUBILEE BEER — pale gold, good malt aroma and flavor, decent body, good long malt aftertaste. Contract brew for C.J. Brockman Brewery, Cincinnati, OH.

FEHR'S XL — bright gold, big rich malt aroma, hops in back, clean dry malt flavor, very dry malt finish, fairly short dry malt aftertaste, a little charcoal/smoke in the background, very drinkable, nice while it is in your mouth. Made for Frank Fehr B.C., Cincinnati, Ohio.

Humboldt Brewery

Brew-pub in Arcata, CA

RED NECTAR ALE — hazy amber, strong hop nose, big smoky dry malt and hop flavor, medium body, strong and long dry malt aftertaste with hops breaking through at the end. I have also tasted this brew where it is big dry hops throughout without much malt at all, and certainly no smoky malt.

GOLD NECTAR ALE — pale gold, fruity malt nose, soft dry malt flavor, dry malt finish and aftertaste, dry malt all the way through.

GOLD RUSH EXTRA PALE ALE — gold, pleasant fruity-malt nose, dry hop and malt flavor with a citrus background, medium body, brief aftertaste is just a memory of the flavor.

Notes:

Indianapolis Brewing Co.

Brewery in Indianapolis, IN

MAIN STREET GOLDEN PILSENER — pale gold, hop aroma, hop flavor, dry hop finish and aftertaste.

DUESSELDORFER DRAFT ALE — hazy amber, melony malt nose, fruity malt flavor with the hops in back, dry hop finish and aftertaste.

J & L Brewing Co.

Brewery in San Rafael, CA

SAN RAFAEL GOLDEN ALE — hazy gold, fruity malt aroma with an ale-like tang, faintly lemony, tangy dry hop and fruity malt flavor, dry finish and long dry malt aftertaste, good body.

SAN RAFAEL AMBER ALE — amber, pleasant fruity malt aroma that is citrus-orange, dry toasted malt flavor has the citrus nature as well, pleasant and dry, dry chocolate malt aftertaste is lightly hopped and still has the touch of orange, smooth and drinkable.

SAN RAFAEL TRADITIONAL ALE — gold, clean malty ale-like nose, tangy light citrus hop flavor, may be a faint trace of lactic acid developing in back, hop finish and aftertaste, refreshing but short.

SAN RAFAEL ALE — deep amber, zesty hop nose, bright malt background, sharp hop flavor, good body, long dry hop aftertaste.

Jones Brewing Co.

Brewery in **Smithton, PA,** subsidiary of Ft. Pitt B.C., Pittsburgh, PA

STONEY'S PILSENER BEER — bright yellow gold, appetizing malt aroma, good malt and hop flavor with a salty nature, malt finish with hops returning in the aftertaste.

STONEY'S LIGHT — bright golden color, pleasant fruity malt and hop aroma, highly carbonated, light and dry malt flavor, very lightly hopped, medium to light body, brief aftertaste.

PREMIUM PILSNER BEER
JONES
Stoney's
BEER
A SMOOTH, REFRESHING ALL GRAIN BEER.
This beer is brewed and aged the natural, costlier way. Using the finest barley malt, selected grains and hops to produce a smooth and refreshing Stoney's Beer.
NO SUGAR OR PRESERVATIVES ADDED.
GOVERNMENT WARNING: (1) ACCORDING TO THE SURGEON GENERAL, WOMEN SHOULD NOT DRINK ALCOHOLIC BEVERAGES DURING PREGNANCY BECAUSE OF THE RISK OF BIRTH DEFECTS. (2) CONSUMPTION OF ALCOHOLIC BEVERAGES IMPAIRS YOUR ABILITY TO DRIVE A CAR OR OPERATE MACHINERY, AND MAY CAUSE HEALTH PROBLEMS.
Contents 12 Fl. Oz.
Brewed and Bottled by Jones Brewing Co., Smithton, Pa.

ESQUIRE PREMIUM PALE BEER — pale straw color, pleasant grainy hop nose, light hop flavor and finish, brief dry hop aftertaste.

ESQUIRE EXTRA DRY BEER — deep gold, rich malt aroma with plenty of hop backing, big malt flavor with hops well in back, fairly long malt aftertaste with hops arriving at very end.

ESQUIRE DRY LIGHT — pale gold, dry malt aroma, light malt flavor, light body, highly carbonated such that much of the flavor is masked, brief aftertaste of malt and faint hops.

OLDE TOWNE OCEAN CITY BEER — bright gold, faint malt aroma, very light body, dry malt flavor, dry malt aftertaste with medium length. Made for Ocean City B.C.

BUBBA'S BREW — bright gold, malt aroma and flavor, light to medium body, dry malt aftertaste. Made for Alabama B.C.

NASHVILLE BEER — gold color, light malt aroma, dry malt palate and aftertaste, fairly short. Made for Alabama B.C.

HINKY DINK KENNA'S BEER — pale amber, good malt aroma with hops in back, good malt and hop flavor, fairly long aftertaste. Brewed for Alabama B.C. for distribution by Marshall Field's in Chicago.

GOLD CROWN PREMIUM BEER — gold color, good malt aroma, malt flavor, dry hop background, medium body, finishes dry hops, but is not long. A good popular priced beer.

FT. PITT SUPER PREMIUM BEER — hazy gold, pleasant malt aroma and flavor, more or less dry especially at the finish, short dry hop aftertaste.

PENNSYLVANIA PILSENER — deep bright amber, zesty off-dry malt and hop nose, plenty of both malt and hops on the palate, beautiful balance, good body, solid finish, long and lovely aftertaste. A contract brew for the Pennsylvania B.C./ Allegheny Brewery & Pub of Pittsburgh, PA.

BIRELL — gold, hop aroma, good hop and malt flavor, good body, fairly long dry hop and malt aftertaste, good for a non-alcoholic brew.

Notes:

Kalamazoo Brewing Co.

Brewery in Kalamazoo, MI

BELL'S BEER — hazy gold, faint malt nose with melon, pineapple, and kumquat in back, fruity malt flavor, dry hop finish and aftertaste, medium length, doubtful balance.

BELL'S AMBER ALE — faintly hazy amber, hop nose, big hop flavor well backed with malt, malt moves forward at the finish, long dry aftertaste has plenty of both malt and hops.

THIRD COAST BEER — hazy amber, lychee nut aroma that takes on a citrus character in time, flat fruity malt palate, very dry malt aftertaste.

THIRD COAST OLD ALE — hazy deep amber, coconut chocolate malt nose, huge off-dry malt taste, complex and interesting, dried apple finish, heavy body, extremely tenacious complex dry aftertaste with candy, coconut, chocolate, malt, and hops.

GREAT LAKES AMBER ALE — hazy amber, light lychee nut nose, light citrus malt flavor, pleasant, fairly long hop aftertaste that is drier than the flavor, tastes a lot like a toned-down Sierra Nevada Pale Ale.

KALAMAZOO STOUT — opaque brown, coffee-colored head, delightful appetizing malt aroma, pleasant dry roasted malt flavor, dry malt finish and aftertaste, not complex, not big, not long, but quite pleasant.

BELL'S KALAMAZOO STOUT — opaque brown, brown head, smooth smoky nose, very dry smooth malt flavor, good balance, good body, dry malt finish and long dry malt aftertaste, good sipping beer.

GREAT LAKES CHERRY STOUT 1988 — opaque brown, coffee-colored head, fruity malt aroma, black cherry flavor with a tart artificial quality, medium body, medium long malt aftertaste that is dry on the tongue but sour in the corners of the mouth.

EXPEDITION STOUT — deep opaque brown, lovely sweet malt aroma is very strong at the outset, softens slightly with time, first seems to be off-dry malt on the palate but becomes more dry as it goes, high density, huge body, almost viscous, long strong complex off-dry malt aftertaste.

BELL'S SPECIAL DOUBLE CREAM STOUT — deep brown, pleasant light malt nose, very pleasant smooth and mellow big straightforward malt flavor, satisfying and very long. The brew is on the off-dry side, but can't be called overly sweet for the type, in fact it is very good of type.

BELL'S PORTER — deep amber, rich chocolate malt nose with a little fruitiness in back, straightforward dry malt taste, big body, touch of sourness behind the malt in the finish, long dry malt aftertaste, well-done drinkable brew.

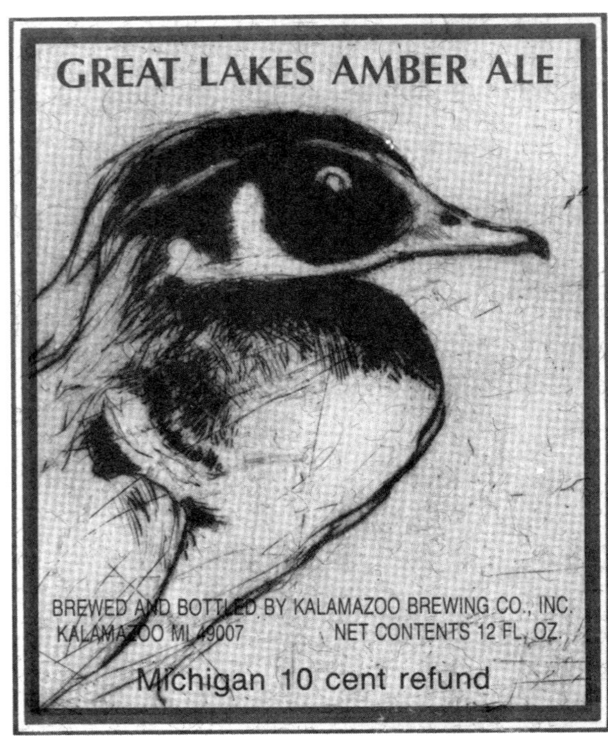

GREAT LAKES AMBER ALE
BREWED AND BOTTLED BY KALAMAZOO BREWING CO., INC.
KALAMAZOO MI 49007
NET CONTENTS 12 FL. OZ.
Michigan 10 cent refund

Kelmer's Brewhouse

Brew-pub in Santa Rosa, CA

KRYSTAL FRESH WHEAT BEER — hazy gold, wheat nose, touch of lactic in back, creamy texture, dry slightly lactic grapefruit-like flavor, fairly short aftertaste like the flavor.

KRIS KRINGLE SPECIAL CHRISTMAS ALE 1990 — amber, big head, zesty soapy hop nose, big hop flavor, big and alcoholic, finishes dry hops, long dry hop aftertaste, very good full-flavored brew.

KELMER'S KLASSIC FINE ALE — hazy amber, clean zesty hop nose much like a pils, complex flavor is smoky malt and hops, smoky finish, long very dry malt aftertaste without any smokiness whatever.

Notes:

Kemper Brewing Co.

Brewery in Poulsbro, WA

THOMAS KEMPER ROLLING BAY BOCK — hazy gold, malt aroma, finely carbonated, malt and hop flavor seems to have a citrus background, long and strong dry hop finish and aftertaste.

THOMAS KEMPER PILSENER BEER — hazy yellow-gold, hop aroma has citrus tones, hop flavor has a lemony background but there is plenty of malt, good body, medium dry hop aftertaste.

Montana Beverages, Ltd./Kessler B.C.

Brewery in Helena, MT

KESSLER BEER — pale gold, complex malt nose with a lightly toasted nature, medium body, good complex rich malt flavor, feels good in your mouth, excellent balance, ever so slightly off-dry, but aftertaste is drier, full-flavored long aftertaste.

KESSLER BOCK BEER — deep copper-red, citrus hop aroma, big body, big sweet and sharp citrus flavor, a bit too sharp, long malt aftertaste on the sour side.

KESSLER WHEAT BEER — medium to deep copper-brown color, sweet fruity malt aroma that is quite attractive, there is a brief sweet foretaste, then it turns sort of burnt vegetal that tastes much better than it reads, a faint spicy-lactic touch appears at the end and in the brief aftertaste. Actually, it is a very good try at making a Weizen.

BACH'S BOCK — deep brown, light malt aroma with a fruitiness, malt palate that is dry, well balanced, and quite long. There certainly is plenty of alcohol, but otherwise it is not a big brew. It is very tasty and very drinkable. Made for Eugene City B.C. of Eugene, OR.

SUN VALLEY WHITE CLOUD ALE — amber, complex aromatic malt and hop nose, a fruity citrus well-hopped flavor, medium body, dry hop aftertaste, pleasant, complex, and very drinkable. Made for Sun Valley B.C., Bellevue, ID.

SUN VALLEY SAWTOOTH GOLD LAGER — hazy amber-gold, big malt nose with a hop background, malt flavor, finish, and long aftertaste. Made for Sun Valley B.C. Latest label (Feb '92) calls this brew **SUN VALLEY GOLD LAGER**.

SUN VALLEY OUR HOLIDAY ALE 1989 — amber, slightly toasted malt nose, big roasted rich malt flavor slightly on the sweet side, dry in the middle, good body, very tasty, finishes strongly, stays smooth, mostly malt but plenty of hops in back, very long malt aftertaste. Made for Sun Valley B.C.

SUN VALLEY OUR HOLIDAY ALE 1990 — bright amber, malt and pineapple juice aroma at first, thence roasted malt, off-dry strong malt flavor with noticeable alcohol, complex, hops arrive at the finish and add dryness to the long aftertaste. Made for Sun Valley B.C.

SUN VALLEY OUR HOLIDAY ALE 1991 — deep amber, laid-back malt aroma, strong malt flavor, finish and aftertaste even strong, as that is where the hops come in with a bang, very, very long hop and malt aftertaste, a blockbuster brew. Made for Sun Valley B.C.

EUGENE CELEBRATION LAGER — hazy gold, fruity apple and malt nose with some background hops, pleasant malt flavor has a light tangerine background, zesty citrus nature adds to the character of the long aftertaste, which is more complex than the flavor. Made for Eugene City B.C.

EUGENE ALE — deep amber, lovely toasted malt (Ovaltine) nose, very tasty and drinkable complex malt front palate, the zest sags a bit in mid-palate, but finishes with that pleasant fruity-Ovaltine flavor, and ends dry. Made for Eugene City B.C.

EUGENER WEIZEN WHEAT BEER — slightly hazy-amber, delicious sweet malt aroma, light and bright clean fresh flavor, medium body, pleasant dry malt finish and aftertaste, very refreshing. Made for Eugene City B.C.

KESSLER LORELEI EXTRA PALE BEER — tawny-gold, big complex malt aroma and flavor with good hop support, medium body, good balance, dry malt finish and aftertaste, fairly short.

KESSLER WINTER BEER — amber, grainy roasted malt aroma, flavor like the nose but the hops appear in back, off-dry flavor starts to dry at finish, and aftertaste is very long, very dry, and very grainy. The hops never come out of the background.

FRONTIER TOWN SELECT BEER — gold, lovely malt and hop aroma, refreshing off-dry malt flavor, finish shows a bit drier, and aftertaste is dry hops and has good length, good-tasting balanced brew.

PACIFIC COAST PREMIUM LAGER — hazy yellow-gold, canned corn nose, malt palate, medium body, dry malt finish and aftertaste. Made for Pacific Coast Beer Co., Newport Beach, CA.

PACIFIC COAST LAGER — gold, light fruity-lemony nose, dry malt flavor, medium body, pleasant creamy texture, feels good in your mouth, finishes dry with a trace of grapefruit in the long aftertaste. Contract brew as above.

OREGON STATE FAIR GOLDEN ALE — gold, appetizing malt-Ovaltine nose, pleasant very malty flavor, light to medium body, very drinkable, pleasant malt finish, fairly long dry malt aftertaste.

ST. NICK'S DARK ALE — deep amber, rich sweet slightly roasted malt aroma, rich smooth off-dry malt flavor benefits from some chocolate malt, very pleasant and very drinkable, quite long. Made for Eugene City B.C.

BONE DRY WET DRY BEER — gold, lovely malt aroma (lots of malt), very dry malt flavor, light body, light hops, dry right to the end.

Notes:

La Jolla Brewing Co.

Brew-pub in La Jolla, CA

SEALANE STEAM BEER — very dark amber, malt nose, very dry smooth malt flavor, long dry malt aftertaste.

LITTLE POINT PALE ALE — gold, hop nose, huge hop flavor, very brightly flavored, long dry hop-ale aftertaste.

Latrobe Brewing Co.

Brewery in Latrobe, PA, owned and operated by Labatt's USA, Darien, CT

ROLLING ROCK PREMIUM BEER — pale gold, very pleasant light malt aroma with light hops in back, fairly big malt flavor is strongest in front, bittering hops in back make for balance and a dry finish and aftertaste. A good beer for the bowling alley.

ROLLING ROCK LIGHT BEER — pale gold, faint malt aroma, light body, malt flavor with hops in back, finish and aftertaste a bit weak and a tad sour.

ROLLING
ROCK
Extra Pale
PREMIUM
BEER
©1939
BREWED FROM MOUNTAIN SPRINGS
LATROBE BREWING CO., LATROBE, PA. 12 FL. OZ.
CONTAINS NO ADDITIVES OR PRESERVATIVES BREWED FROM WATER, MALT, RICE, CORN, HOPS, BREWERS YEAST
GOVERNMENT WARNING: (1) ACCORDING TO THE SURGEON GENERAL, WOMEN SHOULD NOT DRINK ALCOHOLIC BEVERAGES DURING PREGNANCY BECAUSE OF THE RISK OF BIRTH DEFECTS. (2) CONSUMPTION OF ALCOHOLIC BEVERAGES IMPAIRS YOUR ABILITY TO DRIVE A CAR OR OPERATE MACHINERY, AND MAY CAUSE HEALTH PROBLEMS.

Notes:

Jacob Leinenkugel Brewing Co.

Brewery in Chippewa Falls, WI, is a subsidiary of the Miller B.C.

LEINENKUGEL'S BEER — pale gold, light malt aroma, slightly grainy malt flavor, very light hops well in the back, light body, light dry malt aftertaste.

LEINENKUGEL'S GENUINE BOCK BEER — copper-amber, faint malt aroma, weak malt flavor, brief malt aftertaste.

LEINENKUGEL'S LIMITED BEER — deep gold, light malt aroma and flavor, good body, pleasant malt finish and aftertaste, good tasting and very drinkable, slides down easily, a quality beer.

LEINIE'S LIGHT NATURAL LIGHT PREMIUM BEER — tawny-gold, appetizing malt and hop aroma, light body, light malt flavor with some hops in back and more toward the finish, medium long malt aftertaste.

CHIPPEWA PRIDE LIGHT PREMIUM BEER — bright gold, clean malt aroma, flavor is more malt than hops but still has good character and balance, good long dry malt aftertaste.

TAHOE BEER — pale gold, malt aroma has a sour component, palate starts out off-dry malt and finishes dry hops, long dry hop aftertaste. Contract brew for Carson B.C., Carson City, NV.

BOSCH PREMIUM BEER — pale gold, fragrant malt aroma, malt flavor, dry malt finish and aftertaste of medium length.

FAMOUS
SINCE 1867
Leinenkugel's
Limited
American
Beer

The Lion, Inc.

Brewery in Wilkes-Barre, PA

A number of corporate names are used, e.g., Pocono Brewing Co.

GIBBONS FAMOUS LAGER BEER — gold, clean light malt nose, fresh malt flavor, medium dry finish, short dry malt and hop aftertaste.

Famous Lager Beer
GIBBONS

THE LION INC.
WILKES-BARRE, PA. 18703
NET CONTENTS ONE PINT
Pocono Mountain Water
Makes the Difference
GOVERNMENT WARNING: (1) ACCORDING TO THE SURGEON GENERAL, WOMEN SHOULD NOT DRINK ALCOHOLIC BEVERAGES DURING PREGNANCY BECAUSE OF THE RISK OF BIRTH DEFECTS. (2) CONSUMPTION OF ALCOHOLIC BEVERAGES IMPAIRS YOUR ABILITY TO DRIVE A CAR OR OPERATE MACHINERY, AND MAY CAUSE HEALTH PROBLEMS.

LIEBOTSCHANER CREAM ALE — pale gold, fresh and clean slightly sweet malt aroma, off-dry malt flavor, light bodied, quick finish, little aftertaste, pleasant and refreshing, good hot-weather beer.

LIEBOTSCHANER BOCK BEER — copper colored, light malt aroma, lightly scorched malt flavor, light body, dry finish, brief aftertaste.

ESSLINGER PREMIUM BEER — light yellow, light malt aroma, pleasant malt and hop flavor, good balance, some character, light body, dry finish, medium-length dry aftertaste.

LIONSHEAD DELUXE PILSENER BEER — tawny-gold, malt aroma, light body, high carbonation, good bright clean flavor with both malt and hops, off-dry malt finish and aftertaste.

STEGMAIER GOLD MEDAL BEER — pale gold, light malt aroma, light malt flavor, light body, finish drops off to nothing, little aftertaste.

STEGMAIER 1857 LAGER BEER — pale amber, pleasant malt nose, palate starts out malt, finishes hops, just hop bitterness for an aftertaste, medium body.

STEGMAIER PORTER — ruby-toned brown color, fresh clean malt aroma, dry malt flavor cuts off abruptly, little or no aftertaste, thin body.

STEGMAIER 1857 LIGHT BEER — golden amber, malt aroma, light hop flavor is mostly carbonation, light body, aftertaste is hops with a touch of malt but is not long.

STEGMAIER LIGHT BEER — pale gold, light malt aroma and very light malt flavor, little hops, plenty of carbonation (maybe too much), not much finish or aftertaste.

STEGMAIER 1857 DRY BEER — very deep gold, pleasant malt and hop nose, bright malt flavor, high carbonation, quick finish, no aftertaste. It is good while it is in your mouth.

MALTA INDIA — opaque brown, big grainy malt nose, big malt flavor, light to medium body, long malt aftertaste is not dry, but is drier than the flavor. Made for Cerveceria India, Mayaguez, Puerto Rico.

MIDNIGHT DRAGON MALTA ESPECIAL — deep brown, concentrated Ovaltine malt nose and flavor with some hops for balance, heavy body, short palate is sweet but not cloying.

BARTELS PURE BEER — medium gold, faint malt aroma and flavor, some hops but not much, malt finish, brief malt aftertaste.

NEUWEILER'S TRADITIONAL LAGER BEER — pale gold, malt nose, palate is mostly malt in front, hops come in middle and make their contribution at the finish and in the aftertaste, bright and refreshing, medium body, medium length.

CRYSTAL PREMIUM BEER — bright pale gold, light malt aroma and flavor, high carbonation, light body, fairly short, a refreshing hot-weather beer that a beer drinker would like better than Perrier.

KAPPY'S PREMIUM QUALITY BEER — gold, pleasant malt and hop aroma, light dry malt flavor, fairly short dry malt aftertaste. Store label for Kappy's liquor stores in the Boston area.

TRUPERT AMERICAN PILSENER BEER — golden amber, toasted malt aroma and flavor, good balance, dry malt finish and aftertaste, not long but very drinkable. Contract brew made for Braumeister Ltd., Drexel Hill, PA.

BLUE HEN BEER — bright tawny gold, pleasant fruity-malty nose with some hops in back, off-dry malt front palate, hop middle, dry malt finish and aftertaste, medium long, flavors seem a bit separated. Contract brew for Blue Hen Brewery, Ltd., of Newark, DE.

JERSEY LAGER BEER — deep gold, beautiful malt and hop aroma, dull malt flavor, light body, little finish and no aftertaste. It's all in the nose. Contract brew for Jersey Lager Beer Co. of Bordentown, NJ.

SKIPJACK LAGER — pale amber, toasted malt aroma, pleasant roasted malt flavor, has zest, long toasted malt aftertaste. Contract brew for Skipjack B.C. of Secaucus, NJ.

HOPE LAGER BEER — golden amber, very pleasant dry malt aroma with a European hop background, finely carbonated, malt flavor, medium-length malt aftertaste, medium body, pleasant and drinkable. Contract beer made for Hope B.C. of Providence, RI.

HOPE BOCK BEER — medium deep amber, light toasted malt nose, medium body, dry toasted malt flavor, has a touch of smoked malt in back, finish and aftertaste are more smoky, dry, refreshing, and very drinkable. Contract brew as above.

HOPE LIGHT LAGER — gold, vegetal malt nose, off-dry but fruity malt flavor, finishes quite dry and has good length, excellent balance, a very good light beer. Contract brew as above.

HOPE RED ROOSTER ALE — bright amber, faintly soapy hop aroma, complex bright and dry hop palate, very long dry hop aftertaste, excellent beer. Contract brew as above.

NATHAN HALE GOLDEN LAGER — deep gold, soapy malt and hop nose, fairly dry malt flavor, medium body, clean light dry malt aftertaste with medium duration. Contract brew for Connecticut B.C., Hartford, CT.

ATLANTIC CITY DIVING HORSE LAGER BEER — light amber, lovely hop aroma, dry hop flavor, very drinkable but brief on the palate. Made for Atlantic City B.C. of Atlantic City, NJ.

BUNKERHILL LAGER BEER — pale amber, hop nose, sour hop flavor, dull hop aftertaste that retains some of the sourness of the flavor.

STOUDT'S OKTOBERFEST DARK — deep amber, off-dry malt nose, big hop flavor, quite dry, medium to light body, dry hop aftertaste of medium duration. A contract beer for Stoudt B.C. of Adamstown, PA, which allowed the release of the beer in 12-oz. bottles.

QUEEN CITY LAGER — gold, very pleasant clean malt nose, bright clean crisp off-dry malt flavor, very refreshing, good body, medium long dry malt aftertaste with good hop support. Contract brew for Queen City Brewing Co., Buffalo, NY.

Notes:

Los Angeles Brewing Co.

Brew-pub and restaurant in **Los Angeles, CA**

EUREKA CALIFORNIA LAGER — deep gold, bright hop aroma, German-style hop flavor, dry hop finish, brief dry hop aftertaste. This description is for the bottled version.

EUREKA CALIFORNIA LAGER (FILTERED DRAFT) — tawny-gold, hop aroma, tasty flavor shows plenty of malt and hops, dry hop finish and very long dry hop aftertaste, a very tasty brew. It is more dry and longer on the palate than the bottled version (from the same batch, I should add) above.

EUREKA CALIFORNIA LAGER (UNFILTERED DRAFT) — hazy gold, a great deal of malt joins the hops in the nose, very balanced smooth malt and hop flavor, the better balance means the hops don't hit so hard when they roll in on the palate, dry finish but not so obviously dry as in the two versions above, a very long-lasting good flavor.

EUREKA AMBER LAGER (FILTERED DRAFT) — amber, smooth malt aroma and flavor, dry malt finish and aftertaste, good but doesn't have the character or the length of the CALIFORNIA LAGER.

EUREKA AMBER LAGER (UNFILTERED DRAFT) — hazy amber, malt nose, smooth malt flavor with some hops in back, dry malt finish and aftertaste with mild hop support, very good tasting, very well-balanced, a noticeably better-tasting brew than the filtered version.

EUREKA DARK LAGER — deep amber, dry malt nose, light chocolate malt in back, big dry malt flavor, long and strong malt aftertaste, sort of a big brother to the amber.

PROSPECTOR JOE'S SPECIAL DARK BEER — golden amber, huge hop and malt aroma with the emphasis on the hops, big hop palate, plenty of malt in support, long big dry hop aftertaste.

Lost Coast Brewery

Microbrewery and brew-pub in **Eureka, CA**

LOST COAST BREWERY PALE ALE — hazy gold, fruity malt aroma has a pineapple background, fruity flavor (again the pineapple), pleasant tasting, good body, dry malt finish and aftertaste, nice but not much depth.

LOST COAST BREWERY DOWNTOWN BROWN — hazy amber, slightly toasted malt nose, mild chocolate roasted malt flavor, medium body, pleasant, very drinkable, light malt aftertaste, good with food.

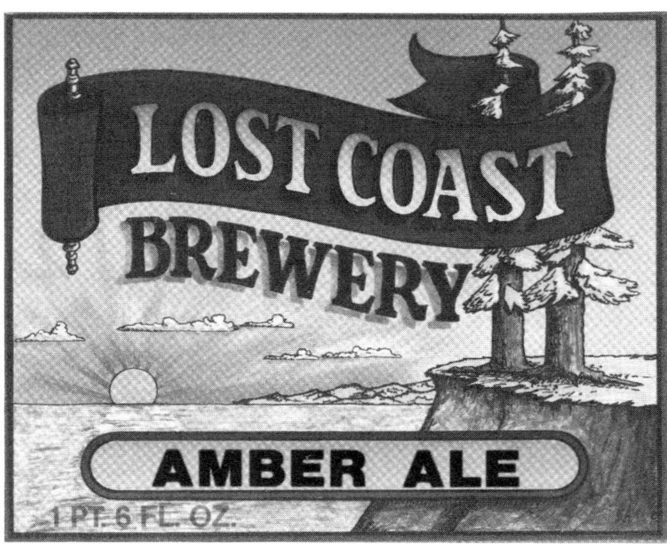

Mad River Brewing Co.

Brewery in **Blue Lake, CA**

STEELHEAD EXTRA PALE ALE — hazy gold, beautiful appetizing fruity hop aroma, big delicious hop flavor, good body, extremely long dry hop aftertaste, marvelous!

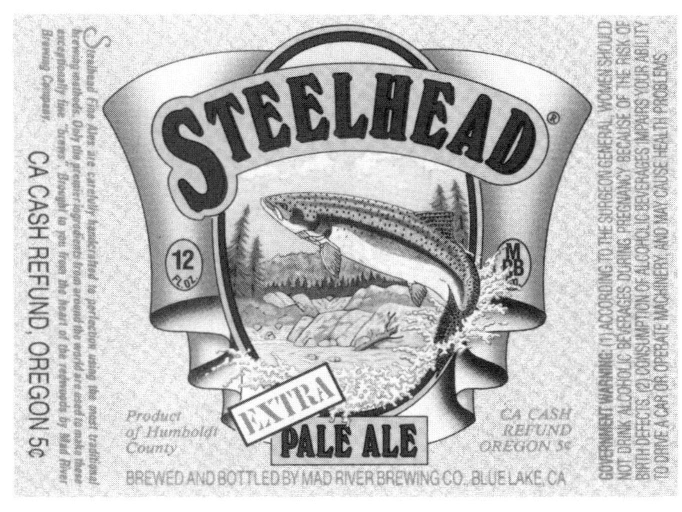

Manhattan Brewing Co.

Brew-pub in New York City, NY

Draft beer made on premises and bottled beer made under contract by F.X. Matt in Utica, NY.

MANHATTAN GOLDEN LIGHT ALE — tawny amber, sweet hop aroma, light body, tangy off-dry hop palate well backed with malt, smooth and pleasant, hop finish, fairly long malt aftertaste.

MANHATTAN ROYAL AMBER — amber, good ale-like nose, plenty of hops and malt, smooth palate has more malt than hops, long slightly sweet malt finish and aftertaste.

MANHATTAN PREMIUM AMBER — deep amber, full rich malt aroma, big malt flavor that is off-dry, smooth and long with a very good balance.

MANHATTAN SPECIAL PORTER — deep brown, roasted malt and licorice nose, very good balance, rich yet dry malt flavor, complex and appetizing, very long aftertaste.

MANHATTAN STOUT — almost opaque brown, foamy brown head, roasted malt aroma backed with plenty of hops, big body, off-dry malt palate up front, but the eventual effect is overall dry.

MANHATTAN SPECIAL PALE ALE — amber, light malt aroma, light smooth ale flavor, touch of malty sweetness in front, good hop bite in the middle, dry hop finish, long dry hop aftertaste, decent balance.

MANHATTAN SPECIAL DRY IRISH STOUT — deep brown, tan head, light malt aroma, toasted (almost burnt) malt flavor, dry malt finish, long dry hop aftertaste.

Manhattan Beach Brewing Co.

Brew-pub in Manhattan Beach, CA

DOMINATOR WHEAT BEER — gold, light malt nose and flavor, light body, short light malt aftertaste.

SOUTH BAY BITTER — tawny-gold, virtually no aroma, light malt and hop flavor, dry malt finish and aftertaste, little complexity.

PACIFICA PALE ALE — gold, good malt and hop aroma, bright but light malt and hop flavor, dry malt finish, long dry malt aftertaste.

LIVE OAK GOLD — amber-gold, no aroma I could find, weak malt flavor, long dry malt aftertaste is a little grassy.

STRAND AMBER — amber, light malt nose, hop flavor, good body, long dry hop aftertaste.

Marin Brewing Co.

Brew-pub in Larkspur, CA

MT. TAM PALE ALE — cloudy amber-gold, citrus and kumquat malt nose, flavor is a bit like the nose at first but subsequent sips are better and the malt develops, kumquat and malt aftertaste with good length, interesting brew despite the description and not bad at all.

POINT REYES PORTER — deep brown, zesty hop nose, big bright toasted malt and hop flavor, long dry malt aftertaste, very drinkable.

SAN QUENTIN'S BREAKOUT STOUT — opaque, almost black, burnt malt nose, high alcohol, medium dry scorched malt and hop flavor, finishes drier than it starts, very long dry malt and hop aftertaste, good balance, very good.

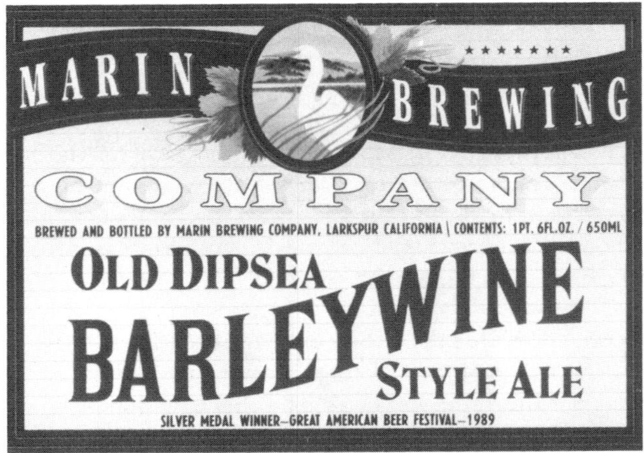

MARIN BREWING
COMPANY
BREWED AND BOTTLED BY MARIN BREWING COMPANY, LARKSPUR CALIFORNIA | CONTENTS: 1PT. 6FL.OZ. / 650ML
OLD DIPSEA
BARLEYWINE
STYLE ALE
SILVER MEDAL WINNER–GREAT AMERICAN BEER FESTIVAL–1989

Massachusetts Bay Brewing Co.

Brewery in Boston, MA

Most (and perhaps all) bottled products are made by F.X. Matt of Utica, NY, under contract. Very early bottlings were made at the brewing facility in Boston.

HARPOON WINTER WARMER (1988) — medium to deep amber, complex aroma of nutmeg, chocolate, peppermint, spices, malt, and rye bread, equally complex palate of chocolate, malt, alcohol, spices, and citrus, big body, long complex aftertaste like the flavor. This one was produced in Boston. Subsequent WW's were made in Utica and, although good, have never measured up to this one.

F.X. Matt Brewing Co.

Brewery at Utica, NY

Several corporate names used, including Old New York Beer Co., formerly of New York City.

UTICA CLUB PILSENER BEER — gold, smooth malt and hop aroma a bit on the sweet perfumy side, flavor is mostly malt, soft and somewhat dull.

UTICA CLUB CREAM ALE — yellow-gold, zesty malt and hop aroma, highly carbonated, dry balanced malt flavor, fair length.

UTICA CLUB NON-ALCOHOLIC — deep gold, attractive off-dry aroma mostly malt but backed with good hops, off-dry malt flavor, medium body, good malt finish and medium dry malt aftertaste.

UTICA CLUB LIGHT BEER — bright golden color, aroma is mainly malt but there are hops in back, flavor is like the nose, little finish and no aftertaste to speak of.

MATT'S LIGHT PREMIUM BEER — pale gold, light dry malt and hop nose, pleasant malt flavor not quite so dry as the nose, finishes dry malt but the aftertaste is brief.

MATT'S PREMIUM LAGER — golden color, aroma of malt with hops in back, malt flavor, light body, malt finish and aftertaste, medium length.

MATT'S SPECIAL DRY — pale gold, melony off-dry malt aroma, flavor is off-dry malt at first, then is tart hops in the middle and finish, ending up in a long not-so-dry malt aftertaste.

F.X. MATT'S TRADITIONAL SEASON'S BEST PREMIUM AMBER BEER 1991 — amber, faint malt aroma, highly carbonated, flavor is malt with faint hops, medium length, overall light and not interesting for a Christmas brew. The 1990 was less carbonated and had a malt flavor with an apple-like background. It was only slightly more interesting.

SARANAC ADIRONDACK LAGER — golden amber, bright hop and malt aroma, zesty big hop flavor, dry hop finish and aftertaste, well balanced and very drinkable. Seems to be the new label for SARANAC 1888 ALL MALT LAGER.

MAXIMUS SUPER MALT LIQUOR — golden amber, flowery malt nose, high carbonation, big flavor is mostly malt but there are some hops, off-dry malt finish and aftertaste, quite long and very good of the type.

EL PASO LIGHT BEER — very pale golden color, faint malt aroma, very watery, faint and short malt palate.

STALLION X EXTRA MALT LIQUOR — pale gold, dusty malt nose, big vegetal malt flavor, bittering hops in back, noticeable alcohol, doesn't quite come together. Made for Tighe, International.

MONTAUK LIGHT — pale gold, pleasant but fleeting malt nose, light malt flavor, low calorie (105), short aftertaste. Made for Long Island Brewery Co., Huntington, NY.

SPORTS LIGHT BEER — medium to deep gold color, malt and light hop aroma, light malt flavor, medium to light malt aftertaste with short duration. Made for Manhattan B.C. of New York.

M.W. BRENNER'S AMBER LIGHT BEER — amber, tangy hop nose, dry lightly hopped malt palate, light body, short dry finish and aftertaste. Made for Monarch B.C. of Brooklyn, NY.

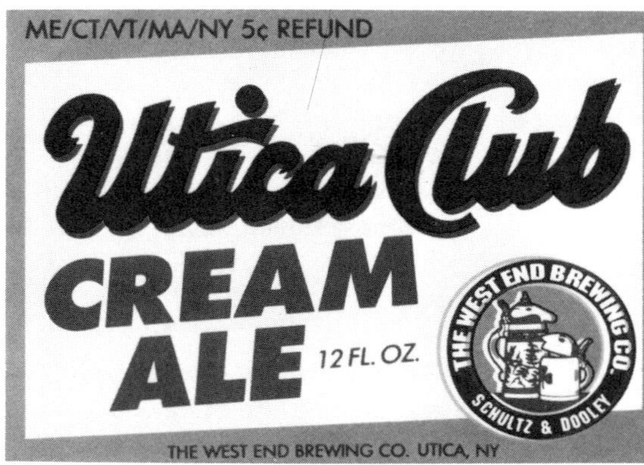

INDEPENDENCE ALE — deep amber, well-hopped ale-like aroma, strongly flavored with a good ale tang, zesty, tasty, and long. Made for Manhattan B.C.

NEWMAN'S ALBANY AMBER — amber, big malt aroma, bright malt and hop flavor, high carbonation, good long malt finish and aftertaste. Made for William S. Newman B.C., Albany, NY.

OLDE HEURICH MAERZEN BIER — hazy amber, light malt and hop aroma, good bright malt and hop flavor, tasty, balanced, well bodied, pleasant long mild hop aftertaste, very drinkable and refreshing. Made for Olde Heurich B.C., Washington, D.C.

PORTLAND LAGER — amber, good malt aroma, big balanced malt and hop flavor, good body, tasty and complex, aftertaste is long extension of the flavor. Made for Maine Coast B.C., Portland, ME.

HARPOON ALE — hazy tawny-amber, complex hop aroma, big hop flavor well backed with malt, good body, complex, balanced, and long. Made for Massachusetts Bay B.C., Boston, MA.

HARPOON OCTOBERFEST BEER — amber, pleasant malt and hop nose, good hop flavor, but thin and brief. Made for Mass Bay B.C.

HARPOON WINTER WARMER 1991 — amber, spicy malt nose much like a pumpkin pie, flavor like the nose but with the addition of hops, medium body, medium length. The 1990 was similar and also made by Matt for Mass Bay B.C. of Boston, MA.

GOLDEN HARPOON LAGER — deep gold, light fruity hop aroma, malt appears first on the palate, then hops through the finish and into the long aftertaste, finely carbonated and well balanced. Made for Mass Bay B.C.

SPECIAL OLD ALE — hazy amber, fruity malt aroma, an off-dry malt flavor with strawberry tones, some chocolate malt as well, big body, dry hop aftertaste, pleasant, long, and interesting. Made for Commonwealth B.C. of Boston, MA.

GOLDEN EXPORT SELECT BEER — deep gold, bright clean malt nose, finely carbonated, zesty fresh hop flavor, straightforward, tasty, well bodied, medium duration, very drinkable. Made for Commonwealth B.C. of Boston.

FAMOUS PORTER — nearly opaque ruby-brown, big head, fairly dry malt aroma, dry roasted malt flavor, medium body, bite in the aftertaste which is dry but not very long, very drinkable. Made for Commonwealth B.C.

DOCK STREET AMBER BEER — amber, beautiful malt nose, bright flavor with good malt and hops, good body, long and delicious. Made for Dock Street B.C. of Bala Cynwyd, PA.

D'AGOSTINO FRESH REAL PUB BEER — hazy tawny-gold, sweet malt nose, balanced hop and malt palate, low carbonation, good body, dry hop finish, long hop aftertaste, very tasty. Made for Manhattan B.C. of New York City for sale at D'Agostino Markets.

BROOKLYN BRAND LAGER — pale amber, pleasant malt and hop aroma, bright malt and hop flavor, well balanced, clean and pleasant, dry malt finish and aftertaste of medium length. Made for Brooklyn Brewery, Brooklyn, NY.

BROOKLYN BROWN DARK ALE — amber-brown, lovely malt and hop aroma, pleasant balanced dry malt and hop flavor, not complex but very likeable, medium to long dry malt aftertaste. Made for Brooklyn Brewery.

NEW AMSTERDAM AMBER BEER — pale copper-amber, toasted malt aroma, bright well-hopped flavor with plenty of lightly toasted malt in support, good balance, long and very drinkable. Original brew of Old New York Beer Co., now part of Matt.

NEW AMSTERDAM NEW YORK ALE — amber, ale-like aroma, tangy citrus-hop flavor that tails off into a dry hop aftertaste, medium body, starts out strong, but doesn't develop. Old New York Beer Co. brand that was originally scheduled to be released as Whyte's Pale Ale.

OLD BUCKEYE DRAFT STYLE — gold color, malty aroma with fruity hops in back, high carbonation, light malt flavor, dry malt finish, short malt aftertaste. Made for Old Buckeye B.C., Toledo, OH.

OLD BUCKEYE DRAFT STYLE LIGHT — very pale gold, Concord grape aroma, light malt flavor that is faintly grapey, dry finish, short aftertaste, 89 calories. Made for Olde Buckeye B.C.

PRIOR DOUBLE DARK — dark amber-brown, good malt aroma, medium body, pleasant bright hop and malt flavor, long dry malt and hop aftertaste. Not the old brew from a decade back, but still enjoyable to drink. It's on draft only.

SHAN SUI YEN SUM BEER — gold, bright hop nose with plenty of malt in back, flowery malt and light hop flavor lacks the sparkle of the nose, light body, made with ginseng extract which doesn't show up until the finish and is blended with the hops, since both are bitter, long flowery dry hop and ginseng aftertaste. The ginseng is the most remarkable thing about it, and that is barely noticeable; perhaps it is good for you. Made for Shan Sui Brewing Co. of Hong Kong.

Gritty McDuff's Brew Pub

Brew-pub in **Portland, ME**

SEBAGO LIGHT ALE — very pale gold, good malt aroma, light body, pleasant dry hop flavor and finish, long dry hop aftertaste.

PORTLAND HEAD LIGHT PALE ALE — pale gold, light fruity-malt aroma, medium body, good hop flavor, dry hop finish and aftertaste, medium length.

McDUFF'S BEST BITTER — gold, light malt nose, medium body, bright hop flavor, dry hop finish and aftertaste.

LION'S PRIDE — brown-amber, light caramel-malt nose, very light malt flavor, medium dry malt aftertaste, fair length.

BLACK FLY STOUT — deep brown, very faint malt nose, dry hop flavor, soft, smooth, drinkable, dry hop finish and aftertaste.

Melbourne Brewing Co.

Brew-pub and Restaurant in **Strongsville, OH**

WOMBAT WHEAT BEER — deep gold, fresh fruity aroma, fresh clean pilsener style flavor, refreshing light and dry, dry hop finish and aftertaste. Uses mix of one-third wheat.

BONDI BEACH BLONDE — amber-gold, nice hop aroma, light hop flavor, good body, plenty of malt, dry hop finish and aftertaste.

DOWN UNDER BEER — deep brown, clean malt nose, rich roasted chocolate malt flavor, stays dry despite richness, long dry malt aftertaste.

IRISH RED ALE — amber, dusty hop nose, big malt and well-hopped flavor, balanced, long hop and malt aftertaste like the flavor, very drinkable.

Mendocino Brewing Co.

Brewery and brew-pub in **Hopland, CA**

RED TAIL ALE — hazy copper, fruity citrus aroma that reminds you somewhat of a California Johannisberg Riesling wine, good body, dry hop finish and aftertaste.

BLUE HERON PALE ALE — cloudy amber, pleasant aroma shows both hops and malt, flavor like the nose, good body and good balance, highly carbonated but the flavor is big enough to handle it, good long aftertaste, considerable complexity.

BLACK HAWK STOUT — opaque brown, rich off-dry malt aroma, dry palate with plenty of malt and hops, good body, good length.

YULETIDE PORTER — deep amber-brown, lovely fragrant malt aroma with a touch of citrus, big malt flavor, finishes quite dry but there is noticeable alcohol, long dry malt aftertaste.

Mill Bakery, Eatery & Brewery

Brew-pub in **Winter Park, FL**

HARVEST GOLD LIGHT — pale yellow-gold, light malt and hop nose and flavor, light body, clean and pleasant, light short malt aftertaste.

KNIGHT LIGHT — pale gold, aromatic hop nose, light hop flavor, light body, light medium long clean dry hop aftertaste.

MAGIC BREW — deep ruby-amber, big hop nose, good hop and malt flavor shows the hops to good advantage, light body, good long dry malt aftertaste.

Miller Brewing Co.

Breweries in Milwaukee, WI; Azusa and Irwindale, CA; Eden, NC; South Volney, NY; Trenton, OH; Albany, GA; and Fort Worth, TX.

MILLER HIGH LIFE — bright gold, pleasant aromatic hop nose, clean flavorful malt and hop palate, refreshing and fairly complex, good body, long dry hop aftertaste.

LITE PILSENER BEER — pale gold, good malt aroma, light body, pleasant malt flavor, dry finish and aftertaste, has good length.

LITE ULTRA — gold, very pleasant malt and hop aroma, front palate is pleasant dry malt with a substantial carbonation component, flavor cuts off suddenly without much finish and no aftertaste, but it is very good while it is there. This is a test brew for Miller in a very low-calorie beer (77 calories) and, for the type, is excellent.

LOWENBRAU LIGHT SPECIAL — light gold, clean malt aroma, hops dominate the flavor, good balance, good body, long dry hop aftertaste.

LOWENBRAU DARK SPECIAL — deep amber, appetizing malt and hop aroma is very Bavarian, big hop flavor, surprisingly light body, very little aftertaste.

SHARP'S NA BEER — gold, off-dry malt aroma and flavor, light body, short aftertaste.

MEISTER BRAU — bright gold, dry malt nose, off-dry malt and tangy hop flavor, hops develop nicely at finish and in aftertaste; the malt, however, doesn't and tends toward sour, long aftertaste.

MEISTER BRAU LIGHT — bright gold, pleasant malt and hop nose, light malt flavor, light body, good but brief.

MAGNUM MALT LIQUOR — pale yellow, fruity sweet malt aroma, slightly sweet malt flavor, light bodied for a malt liquor, slightly sweet malt finish and aftertaste with medium duration.

MILLER SPECIAL RESERVE BEER — bright gold, big aromatic hop nose, weak flabby flavor, hops show only as a hint, and that comes in the aftertaste.

MILLER SPECIAL RESERVE LIGHT — gold, dusty light malt nose, light dry malt flavor, light body, only a brief malt faint aftertaste.

MILWAUKEE'S BEST BEER — pale gold, pleasant malt aroma, highly carbonated, light body, slightly sweet malt flavor, good finish and long aftertaste feature both malt and hops.

MILWAUKEE'S BEST LIGHT — pale gold, malt aroma, light slightly sweet malt flavor, high carbonation, hops appear at the finish and carry into the aftertaste, which is light and short.

MILLER GENUINE DRAFT — medium deep gold, faint malt aroma, wonderfully dry malt flavor without being bitter, dry finish and aftertaste, good length.

MILLER GENUINE DRAFT LIGHT — very pale gold, very faint malt aroma and flavor, very little finish and almost no aftertaste.

DAKOTA WHEAT BREWED BEER — pale gold, slightly off-dry malt and hop aroma, pleasant dry malt flavor, good body, ends abruptly, very clean and refreshing, very good except for the lack of an aftertaste. Miller has tried this several times in test markets and, despite it being one of the best efforts in the genre, has decided not to follow through with regular production.

Millstream Brewing Co.

Brewery in Amana, IA

MILLSTREAM LAGER BEER — hazy gold, good malt and hop aroma, lots of both malt and hops for the palate but the balance is not as good as it could be, comes off as being off-dry malt and sour hops right into the aftertaste.

SCHILD BRAU — amber, beautiful roasted malt nose, has a fruity component as well, delicious complex roasted malt flavor, great balance, zesty hops in support, fresh fruity malt finish and long aftertaste, an excellent brew.

MILLSTREAM WHEAT LAGER BEER — bright gold, perky malt aroma, low carbonation even to the eye, light malt flavor, dull malt aftertaste of medium length.

Monterey Brewing Co.

Brew-pub in Monterey, CA

SEA LION STOUT — deep opaque brown, dark-brown head, huge roasted malt nose, big complex coffee hop and dry malt flavor, very dry long coffee and roasted malt aftertaste, great complexity.

KILLER WHALE AMBER ALE — cloudy amber, big head, citrus ale nose, huge citrus-ale flavor, long assertive citrus hop aftertaste, big and complex.

Mountain Brewers, Inc.

Brewery in Bridgewater, VT

LONG TRAIL ALE — amber, big toasted malt aroma, dry malt and bright hop flavor, very dry hop finish and aftertaste.

VERMONT BICENTENNIAL ALE — hazy gold, light citrus-ale aroma, bright hop flavor with a good ale character, good-tasting bitter hop finish and long dry hop aftertaste, medium body, good balance.

Napa Valley Brewing Co.

Brew-pub and restaurant in Calistoga, CA

CALISTOGA RED ALE — amber, dry oxidized nose, taste of dry madeira/nebbiolo wine, a dank short palate, obviously damaged although supposedly from a fresh keg.

Nevada City Brewing Co.

Brewery in Nevada City, CA

NEVADA CITY CALIFORNIA LAGER GOLD — deep gold, bright hop nose, big hop flavor with plenty of malt backing, good body, long dry hop aftertaste, smooth and very well-balanced.

Notes:

New England Brewing Co.

Brewery in Norwalk, CT

NEW ENGLAND ATLANTIC AMBER ALE — amber, good hop aroma, complex hop palate with plenty of malt in back, medium dry hop finish, long dry hop aftertaste, lots of character and excellent balance.

NEW ENGLAND GOLD STOCK ALE — deep golden color, great complex hop and malt nose with faint citrus in the background, big body, big hops but also plenty of malt for a great balanced brew, complex and very long rich hop and malt aftertaste, a fine big brew worth trying.

NEW ENGLAND HOLIDAY ALE — deep amber, spicy gingerbread nose, big ginger and malt flavor, off-dry, the good ale flavor comes out from behind the spices at the finish and holds well through a long aftertaste.

NEW ENGLAND OATMEAL STOUT — deep brown, beautiful nose of roasted barley, big dry roasted malt flavor like a coffee, richly flavored, long smooth dry malt aftertaste, very drinkable.

Notes:

New Haven Brewing Co.

Brewery in **New Haven, CT**

BLACKWELL STOUT — deep amber, rich chocolate malt nose, light toasted chocolate malt flavor, light body, very drinkable, malt finish, medium length malt aftertaste.

ELM CITY GOLDEN ALE — clear gold, pleasant malt and hop aroma, flavor is malt with hops in back, dry hop finish, long dry hop aftertaste.

ELM CITY CONNECTICUT ALE — pale amber, fragrant malt and hop aroma, light dry malt flavor with some caramel hiding in back, dry malt finish, medium long dry hop and malt aftertaste.

HOBOKEN SPECIAL RESERVE ALE — gold, clean and big malt nose, big malt flavor, good body, hops show well in the finish, long dry hop aftertaste, tasty brew.

MR. MIKE'S LIGHT ALE — gold, fresh malt nose, light body, light malt flavor, you can feel the high carbonation, brief malt aftertaste, very quaffable.

Notes:

North Coast Brewing Co.

Brewery and brew-pub in **Fort Bragg, CA**

RUEDRICH'S RED SEAL ALE — hazy amber, good malt nose, lightly smoked zesty malt palate, medium body, dry hop finish, long dry hop aftertaste. Later samples were more highly hopped and had more of a citrus back taste.

CHRISTMAS ALE 1989 — hazy deep amber, light toasted malt aroma, light toasted smoky malt flavor, dry finish and aftertaste like the flavor, seems like there is just too much toast and it masks the rest of the flavors.

CHRISTMAS ALE 1990 — hazy amber, lovely huge toasted malt nose with a fruity-ale tang, big taste just like the nose, big malt finish, long aftertaste like you had been chewing on malt, very flavorful, and there is a subtle hop presence throughout.

CHRISTMAS ALE 1991 — deep amber, rich chocolate roasted malt nose, dry malt flavor, light body, good complexity, long dry malt aftertaste.

SCRIMSHAW PILSENER STYLE BEER — hazy gold, complex aroma with malt, chocolate, tobacco, etc., off-dry complex malt flavor with grapefruit, cherry pits, tobacco, and chocolate, smooth and mellow, good long dry malt aftertaste.

NORTH COAST BREWING Co TM
MENDOCINO COUNTY
Oktoberfest
ALE
WATER · MALTED BARLEY · HOPS · YEAST & THAT'S ALL
1 PINT 6 FL.OZ.

SUMMER ALE 1990 — hazy amber-gold, fruity malt aroma, big hop and fruity-malt palate, very good balance, touch of sour hops at the finish, long malt aftertaste.

OKTOBERFEST ALE — hazy amber, complex fruity hop California ale nose, big toasted malt flavor, hop finish, long hop and malt aftertaste, complex, balanced, and drinkable.

OLD No. 38 STOUT — deep ruby color, chocolate malt nose, roasted chocolate malt flavor is slightly burnt, good body, long burnt malt/smoky aftertaste, still very palatable despite the over-roasting of the malt.

TRADITIONAL BOCK — hazy amber, big malt nose, flavor starts out big and malty, finishes with dry hops, long dry malt aftertaste, has complexity, balance, and body.

CENTENNIAL 100 ALE — amber-gold, chocolate-Ovaltine malt nose, big malt flavor, big body, smooth, dry malt finish and long dry malt aftertaste.

Northampton Brewery

Brew-pub in Northampton, MA

Affiliated with and shares a brewmaster with The Portsmouth Brewery of New Hampshire.

GOLDEN — gold, malt aroma at first, then hops, palate is sweet malt in front, hop middle, dry malt and hop finish, off-dry hop aftertaste, complex, good body, good length, interesting.

AMBER — amber, bright hop nose, hop palate with a hop background, medium dry hop finish and aftertaste.

DANIEL SHAY'S BEST BITTER — hazy amber, big hop nose, zesty spicy hop flavor, dry hop finish, long dry spicy hop aftertaste.

BROWN DOG — deep amber-brown, hop nose, dry hop flavor with plenty of malt in the middle, smooth dry hop finish, long dry aftertaste, a porter-style brew.

Okie Girl Brewery

Brew-pub in Lebec, CA

CALIFORNIA CONDOR PALE ALE — copper-amber, hop nose well backed with malt, flavor like the aroma, good body, long dry hop aftertaste.

CHEROKEE CHOICE AMERICAN STYLE LAGER — gold, light fresh hop nose, complex hop flavor with plenty of malt for balance, dry hop finish, dry hop aftertaste with some duration.

RIVER BOTTOM STOUT — deep brown, smoky malt nose has some coffee-like aspects, light body, hefty flavor of both hops and malt, dry malt finish, long dry malt aftertaste. Hops are in the foreground only on the front of the palate, otherwise it is malt.

WINTERFEST — deep amber, hop aroma, big roasted malt flavor with good hop backing, long dry malt aftertaste.

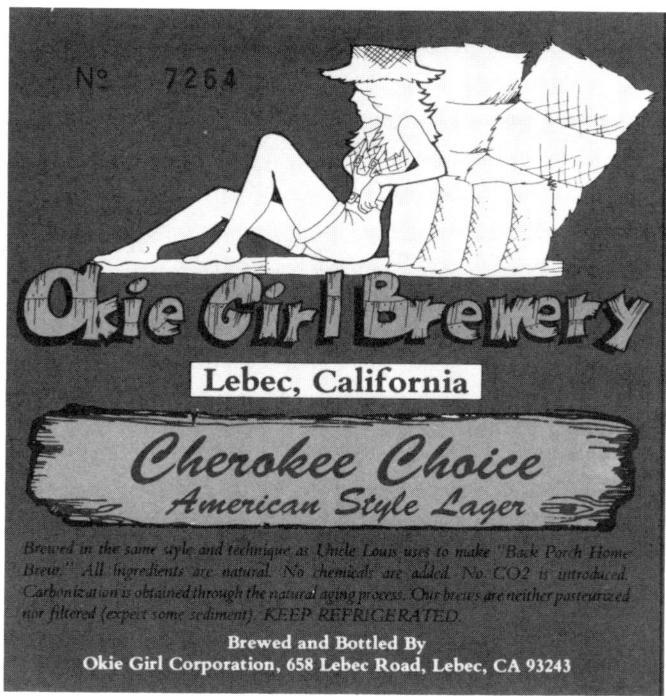

No 7264
Okie Girl Brewery
Lebec, California
Cherokee Choice
American Style Lager
Brewed in the same style and technique as Uncle Louis uses to make "Back Porch Home Brew." All ingredients are natural. No chemicals are added. No CO2 is introduced. Carbonization is obtained through the natural aging process. Our brews are neither pasteurized nor filtered (expect some sediment). KEEP REFRIGERATED.
Brewed and Bottled By
Okie Girl Corporation, 658 Lebec Road, Lebec, CA 93243

Notes:

Oldenberg Brewing Co.

Brewery, restaurants, hotel, shops, entertainment and convention center in **Ft. Mitchell, KY**

OLDENBERG PREMIUM VERUM — tawny-gold, good dry hop and malt aroma, dry malt and hop flavor has some zest, good balance, some malty sweetness in the middle, has some complexity, pleasant malt finish with hops in back, medium dry long malt and hop aftertaste, a good beer by itself or with food.

VAIL ALE — brilliant amber, citrus hop and malt aroma, good body, big malt flavor well backed with citrus and hop character, malt is first encountered with the hops coming in at the middle and staying on, smooth, good body, off-dry malt and hop finish and long aftertaste. Made for Vail B.C., Vail, CO.

OLDENBERG BLONDE DRY LIGHT PILS — deep gold, bright malt aroma, complex dry malt flavor, off-dry malt in finish, medium length off-dry malt aftertaste.

NORTH AMERICA

OLDENBERG STOUT — opaque brown, dry hop aroma and flavor, good body, dry, almost coffee-like finish, long dry hop aftertaste, satisfying substantial brew.

McGUIRES IRISH ALE — amber, malt aroma, light dry malt flavor with light hops in back, medium body, dry malt finish and medium-length aftertaste. Made for McGuires B.C., Pensacola, FL.

LAS BRISAS CARIBBEAN STYLE BEER — hazy gold, sour malt aroma, light body, zesty hop and malt flavor, malt is a bit on the sour side but there is a balance of sorts achieved through the bitterness of the hops, good length.

OLDENBERG WEISS WHEAT BEER — gold, light but bright fruity wheat-malt nose with a very faint toastiness in back, pleasant light wheaty-malt flavor, light body, medium long malt aftertaste, pleasant but a bit too light flavored.

PITTS ALL AMERICAN BEER — golden-amber, faint fruity malt nose, dry malt flavor, hop finish, long dry hop aftertaste. Made for Burbank's Bar-B-Q, a local restaurant.

Pacific Brewing Co.

Brewery at **Wailuku, Maui, HI**

MAUI LAGER BEER — bright tawny-gold, toasted malt aroma and flavor, appetizing and very tasty, dry hop finish and long dry hop aftertaste, a scrumptious little beer.

Pacific Beach Brewhouse

Brew-pub in **Pacific Beach, CA**

OVER THE LINE STOUT — deep amber, smooth dry malt nose and taste, light body, very drinkable, hops don't show until the aftertaste, more like a porter than a stout.

Notes:

Pacific Coast Brewing Co.

Brew-pub in Oakland, CA

HOLIDAY ALE 1988 — hazy amber, huge head, effervescent citrus-soapy malt and hop nose, huge flavor of hops and malt, high alcohol, chewy body, hop finish, long hop aftertaste, another really good Christmas beer.

HOLIDAY BARLEYWINE ALE 1990 — cloudy amber, tangy citrus ale nose has a wininess about it, big spicy complex hop and malt flavor, both sweet and sharp at the same time, very complicated palate with all different kinds of malt showing, big body, huge and extremely long. This is another fine Christmas brew.

HOLIDAY STRONG ALE 1991 — hazy amber, fruity kumquat-malt nose, interesting odd malt flavor that is fruity sweet and dry at the same time, very complex and very drinkable, long off-dry malt and hop aftertaste.

Notes:

James Page Brewing Co.

Brewery in Minneapolis, MN

JAMES PAGE PRIVATE STOCK — amber, malty nose with a trace of fruit, good dry malt flavor with hops in back, medium body, dry malt finish, long dry malt aftertaste, pleasant dry beer.

BOUNDARY WATERS BOCK — hazy amber, malt nose, dry malt flavor, briefly a touch of something metallic in the finish, dry malt aftertaste. I never would guess that it was made with wild rice.

BOUNDARY WATERS BEER — hazy amber-gold, faint hop nose, dry hop flavor, mellow and smooth, light body, dry hop finish, medium-long dry hop aftertaste, a pleasant dry beer.

A. FITGER & CO. FLAGSHIP BEER — bright tawny-gold, light pleasant malt and hop aroma, light hop flavor well backed with malt, medium body, dry hop finish, very long dry hop aftertaste.

Notes:

Paso Robles Brewing Co.

Brewery in Paso Robles, CA

DRY LAND LAGER — hazy amber, big head, creamy texture all the way through to the end, fruity malt nose and taste reminds me of a spruce beer but is not spruce-like, extremely long malt aftertaste.

Pavichevich Brewing Co.

Brewery located in Elmhurst, IL

BADERBRAU PILSENER BEER — amber, appetizing malt and hop aroma, somewhat smoky roasted malt flavor, good body, dry smoky finish, long roasted malt aftertaste, has a European style and is well made.

Pittsburgh Brewing Co.

Brewery in Pittsburgh, PA

Until quite recently was owned by the Bond Corp. of Australia and, through that ownership, affiliated with G. Heileman, producing many Heileman labels for distribution on the East Coast. At time of this writing, there is no information available on what future affiliation might result.

IRON CITY PREMIUM BEER — gold, light malt aroma with a faint hop background, light malt and hop flavor, medium body, light malt finish, dry hop aftertaste of medium length.

IRON CITY DARK — almost opaque brown, light smoky-toasted malt aroma, similar flavor but with hops in back, medium body, good coffee-like finish and aftertaste, good length.

IRON CITY DRAFT BEER — gold, light off-dry malt aroma, off-dry malt flavor, medium-length aftertaste is still malty but is a little drier.

IRON CITY LIGHT — pale gold, malt aroma has a slight sour backing, light malt flavor has that sourness as well, dry malt finish and brief aftertaste.

I.C. SPECIAL DRY BEER — bright gold, bright malt nose, light dry malt palate does have some zest, thin body, light malt aftertaste of medium duration.

I.C. GOLDEN LAGER — pale gold, off-dry malt aroma, soft malt flavor, low carbonation, only a faint hop background, medium length.

PITTSBURGH BREWING CO. CLASSIC DRAFT LIGHT — pale gold, fruity light malt nose, dull dry malt flavor, short malt aftertaste.

PITTSBURGH BREWING CO. CLASSIC DRAFT — gold, herbal aroma, grapey malt flavor, soapy malt aftertaste.

OLD FROTHINGSLOSH PALE STALE ALE — gold, light grainy nose, light malt flavor, light body, short dry aftertaste.

AMERICAN BEER — gold, malt aroma with a very slight hop character, a lot of the flavor is carbonation, light body, off-dry malt finish, short off-dry malt aftertaste.

AMERICAN LIGHT BEER — pale gold, malt nose, light body, off-dry malt finish and aftertaste, light and short.

TECH LIGHT BEER — gold, grainy malt nose, light body, light malt palate, brief malt aftertaste.

OLD EXPORT PREMIUM BEER — gold, malt aroma and flavor, faint hops in back, medium-length malt aftertaste.

MUSTANG PREMIUM MALT LIQUOR — deep gold, light sweet malt aroma, big body, smooth malt flavor, finishes clean, long malt aftertaste.

ST. MICHAEL'S NON-ALCOHOLIC MALT BEVERAGE — pale gold, light hop aroma has some skunkiness hiding in back, low carbonation, light grainy malt flavor, very weak body, very brief. Made for St. Michaels B.C., Lancaster, PA.

OLDE HEURICH AMBER LAGER — pale amber, pleasant malt and hop nose with a faint citrus-like tang in back, big hop palate backed with sufficient malt for excellent balance, long dry hop aftertaste. A very good brew made under contract for Olde Heurich B.C. of Washington, DC. Now believed to be replaced by Olde Heurich Maerzen Bier (see F.X. Matt).

ERIN BREW — amber, lightly toasted malt aroma, clean fresh off-dry malt flavor, dry hop middle and finish, long dry hop aftertaste, well made and well balanced, very drinkable. Made for Cleveland B.C., Cleveland, OH. Now understood to be made by F.X. Matt, but this product has not yet been tasted.

HARD ROCK CAFE BEER — hazy gold, light grainy malt and carbonation flavor, light dry hop finish and aftertaste, not much there, but it is refreshing.

Note: Pittsburgh B.C. has made contract brews for Boston Beer Co. for some time, but since these brews are not made exclusively by Pittsburgh, they are listed under Boston Beer Co. They include BOSTON LIGHTSHIP, SAMUEL ADAMS BOSTON LAGER, SAMUEL ADAMS BOCK, SAMUEL ADAMS DOUBLE BOCK, SAMUEL ADAMS WINTER LAGER, SAMUEL ADAMS OKTOBERFEST, SAMUEL ADAMS BOSTON STOCK ALE, and SAMUEL ADAMS WHEAT BEER.

Portland Brewing Co.

Brew-pub in **Portland, OR**

PORTLAND DRY HONEY BEER — deep gold, honeyed (really!) malt aroma, off-dry malt flavor has a touch of honeyed sweetness, medium dry finish, long malt aftertaste is reasonably dry.

WINTER ALE WITH SPICES — deep ruby-brown, spice aroma, nutmeg, cinnamon, etc., spice flavor with malt and alcohol showing, medium length spicy-malt aftertaste.

PORTLAND ALE — tawny-gold, big hop and malt nose, very smooth malt flavor, medium body, dry hop finish and aftertaste, fairly long, well hopped throughout.

Notes:

Portsmouth Brewery

Brew-pub in **Portsmouth, NH**

It is affiliated with and shares the brewmaster of the Northampton Brewery of Massachusetts.

GOLDEN LAGER — gold, fruity malt and hop nose, mild fairly dry hop flavor, long dry hop aftertaste.

AMBER LAGER — amber, faint caramel and hop nose, complex hop and caramel malt flavor, fairly dry, smooth and refreshing, flavor tails off at the finish, light dry hop aftertaste.

BLONDE ALE — light gold, mild malt and hop nose, very light malt flavor, light dry hop finish, dry malt aftertaste, medium length.

PALE ALE — deep amber, clean light malt and hop aroma, zesty, almost spicy, hop-ale flavor, dry hop finish, long dry hop aftertaste.

OLD BROWN DOG — deep amber, faint hop nose, fairly rich but dry malt and hop flavor, malt shows well in mid-palate, dry hop finish, long dry hop aftertaste.

Red Hook Ale Brewery, Inc.

Brewery and brew-pub in **Seattle, WA**

RED HOOK ESB ALE — amber, light malt aroma, very flavorful big malt and hop flavor, dry hop finish, long dry hop aftertaste complex and long.

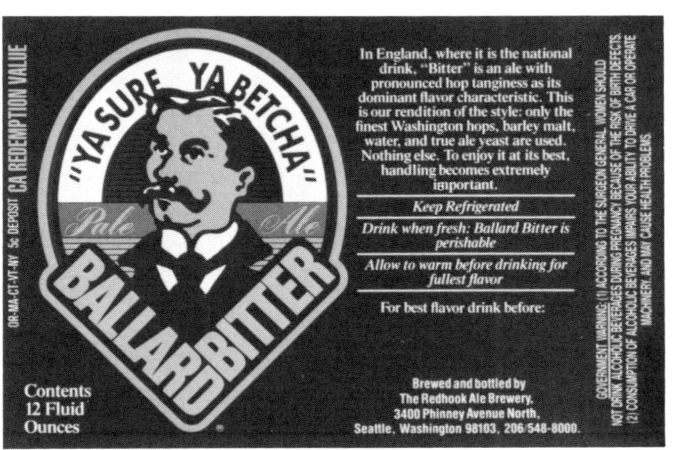

BLACKHOOK PORTER — deep ruby-amber, big bright and dry malt nose, dry malt palate, medium body, malt finish with a touch of fruity-citrus-spice-smoke, dry malt aftertaste, good length, pleasant, very drinkable.

BALLARD BITTER PALE ALE — deep gold, slightly buttery toffee-malt aroma, light body, buttery malt flavor, dry hop aftertaste.

WHEAT HOOK WHEATEN ALE — hazy gold, fruity complex malt nose with a hint of butterscotch, very complex dry flavor that shows some hops, malt, fruitiness, butterscotch, and tartness, long dry hop aftertaste.

WINTERHOOK CHRISTMAS ALE 1990 — hazy amber, light malt aroma, good toasted malt flavor, good body, dry malt finish, nicely balanced, long malt aftertaste, noticeable alcohol, very drinkable.

WINTERHOOK CHRISTMAS ALE 1991 — amber color, malt nose with a light citrus background, complex ale flavor, dry hop finish and long dry hop aftertaste, very good brew.

Rogue Brewing Co.

Brewery in Newport, OR; bottling facility in Tigard, OR; brew-pubs in Newport and Ashland, OR

ROGUE GOLDEN ALE — hazy gold, bright flowery hop and malt nose, pleasant big hop flavor, lots of fruity malt balanced with big tangy hops, big hop finish, extremely long fruity malt and bright dry hop aftertaste, well-made brew.

ROGUE NEW-PORTER — deep ruby-brown, brown head, smooth toasted malt nose, very dry malt flavor with a smoky-toasty character, rich yet dry, good malt finish, long dry toasted malt aftertaste, balanced, smooth, and flavorful.

ROGUE SHAKESPEARE STOUT — near opaque ruby-brown, brown head, chocolate malt nose with a fruity background, also some faint smoke in back, fairly dry and faintly smoky malt palate, medium body, dry finish and long dry malt aftertaste, very drinkable.

ST. ROGUE RED — deep reddish-amber, fresh roasted malt and hop nose has a little citric tang in back that blends in nicely, big rich hop and roasted malt flavor is very well balanced, medium body, dry hop and malt finish, long dry hop aftertaste, a super brew with enough hops and malt for anyone.

ROGUE SPRINGBOCK — hazy amber, off-dry flowery malt nose, strong fruity malt flavor, medium body, very drinkable, long dry malt aftertaste, good brew.

ROGUE OLD CRUSTACEAN BARLEY WINE — hazy amber, strong good malt nose, lovely with a touch of citrus fruit, huge body, high alcohol, concentrated hop and malt flavor, big and strong, good fruity finish, very long malt aftertaste, excellent sipping beer.

ROGUE WELCOMMEN RAUCH BIER — deep amber, smoked meat nose, smooth smoked malt flavor, medium body, extremely long dry smoked malt aftertaste, done with a delicate hand.

Rubicon Brewing Co.

Brew-pub in Sacramento, CA

RUBICON INDIA PALE ALE — hazy gold, light dry hop flavor, brief dry hop aftertaste.

S & P Co.

Group of brewing companies including Falstaff, Pearl, General, and Pabst with brewing plants listed as being in Tumwater, WA (Olympia); Milwaukee, WI; San Antonio, TX; and Ft. Wayne, IN. There are additional corporate names used including San Antonio Beverage Co. Corporate HQ is in Corte Madera, CA.

FALSTAFF BEER — pale yellow, rich malt nose, clean fresh flavor is mostly malt but there are hops in support, pleasant average American pilsener-style beer that sometimes is overcarbonated.

FALSTAFF FINE LIGHT BEER — pale gold, light fresh malt nose, light malt aroma, flavor is light malt but the contribution of the carbonation is significant, light bodied, and little aftertaste.

LUCKY LAGER BEER — bright clear gold, interesting and somewhat complex malt and hop nose, off-dry flavor that doesn't dry out, still pleasant and refreshing, good length.

LUCKY BOCK BEER — dark brown but not deeply colored, sweet malt nose that doesn't really change across the palate, high carbonation tries to balance off the sweetness, but the end result is a bit dull.

LUCKY 50 EXTRA LIGHT BEER — bright pale gold, faint grainy aroma, light grainy palate, little aftertaste, the major flavor component is carbonation.

LUCKY ORIGINAL DRAFT BEER — gold, big hop aroma, malt and hop flavor, good body, fair duration with both the malt and hops showing in the aftertaste.

BREW 102 PALE DRY BEER — pale yellow-gold, clean fresh malt aroma on the sweet side, pleasant slightly sweet malt flavor, good length, would be better if less sweet but still is pleasant and refreshing in hot weather.

HAMM'S SPECIAL LIGHT — medium to deep gold, light malt and hop aroma, weak and watery, faint malt flavor, little finish and aftertaste.

HAMM'S BEER — bright gold, pleasant malt nose, off-dry malt flavor, short malt aftertaste with some hops in back, pleasant hot-weather quaffing beer.

HAMM'S GENUINE DRAFT BEER — pale gold, faint malt nose, light off-dry malt flavor, very short on the palate.

HAMM'S NON-ALCOHOLIC MALT BEVERAGE — gold, malt aroma, sour malt flavor, very weak and grainy, fairly brief.

HAMM'S BIG BEAR MALT LIQUOR — pale gold, light malt nose, malt palate, sense of high alcohol, winey finish, long malt aftertaste.

BALLANTINE PREMIUM LAGER BEER — light gold, clean fresh malt aroma, clean fresh light flavor is more malt than hops, medium body, pleasant and refreshing, medium length.

BALLANTINE XXX ALE — deep gold, big well-hopped and malt nose, big taste with plenty of hop bite, good body, good length.

BALLANTINE INDIA PALE ALE — tawny-gold, pungent hop aroma, big well-hopped nose, big hop flavor, good body, good balance, lingering full-flavored aftertaste. It's not as big as it used to be, but it is still a mouthful.

NARRAGANSETT LAGER BEER — bright gold, off-dry malt nose, flavor mostly malt as the hops are very light, medium body, light dry aftertaste.

NARRAGANSETT PORTER — deep brown with a red-orange tinge, clean light malt nose, clean light malt flavor, slightly sweet at the finish, hops show only in the aftertaste.

PABST BLUE RIBBON BEER — pale gold, light malt and hop nose, clean malt and hop flavor, pleasant, light, and refreshing, light body, fairly dry, medium length.

PABST BLUE RIBBON LIGHT BEER — pale bright gold, pleasant malt aroma, light dry mostly malt flavor, tasty, very drinkable, light and refreshing, and with good length.

PABST LIGHT BEER — pale gold, faint hop and malt aroma, weak off-dry malt flavor, faint hops in back, short malt aftertaste is drier than the flavor.

PABST BLUE RIBBON DRY BEER — pale yellow-gold, refreshing malt and hop nose, light body, good carbonation level, pleasant light off-dry malt flavor, refreshing, medium length.

PABST BLUE RIBBON DRAFT BEER — deep gold, malt nose, pleasant malt flavor, off-dry palate, medium dry finish and aftertaste, tastes better well chilled.

ANDEKER LAGER BEER — bright gold, hop aroma seems to be off-dry but is more fragrant than it is sweet, pleasant hoppy flavor finishes off-dry, nicely balanced, and fairly long, would be better if more dry.

HAFFENREFFER PRIVATE STOCK MALT LIQUOR — medium deep gold color, malt aroma, light malt flavor, medium body is light for a malt liquor, soft light malt flavor, medium-length aftertaste.

PEARL FINE LAGER BEER — bright gold, good malt nose, good flavor, plenty of hops to support the malt, clean and refreshing, good balance, good length.

PEARL XXX LIGHT LAGER BEER — pale gold, good malt and hop aroma, light body, light malt and hop flavor finishes off-dry, short aftertaste.

PEARL CREAM ALE — bright clear gold, off-dry malt nose, off-dry malt flavor but there are hops in back for balance, finishes clean and has a long pleasant dry aftertaste.

PEARL NA NON-ALCOHOLIC BEER — brilliant gold, grainy malt nose, light dull malt flavor, light body, little aftertaste.

BUCKHORN BEER — pale gold, pleasant off-dry malt aroma, malt flavor has very little hop support until the finish, little aftertaste, pleasant but very light.

JAX BEER — yellow-gold, pleasant malt nose has to compete with high carbonation, pleasant mild flavor has a good hop and malt balance, off-dry aftertaste, refreshing for hot-weather drinking.

OLYMPIA BEER — pale gold, light malt aroma, clean light flavor with the hops apparent only in the finish, medium dry hop aftertaste, a light pleasant-tasting beer that is very drinkable.

OLYMPIA GENUINE DRAFT BEER — pale gold, dusty dry malt nose, off-dry malt palate that is fairly pleasant, high carbonation, good balance, faint fruity malt and dry hop finish and aftertaste.

OLYMPIA DRY BEER — pale gold, malt aroma, light dry grainy malt flavor, short.

OLYMPIA LIGHT — pale gold, good hop aroma that is a bit grainy, thin hop flavor that has sour malt tones, finishes dull and doesn't last.

ST. BART'S NON-ALCOHOLIC MALT BEVERAGE — bright gold, pleasant grainy aroma with a touch of fruitiness, dry palate that is pleasant malt in front, but there is little or no finish or aftertaste.

OLYMPIA GOLD LIGHT BEER — pale gold, light fresh malt aroma, light malt flavor that picks up quite a bit of hops in mid-palate, dry well-hopped finish and brief aftertaste.

COUNTRY CLUB MALT LIQUOR — tawny-gold, winey malt aroma, light malt flavor, off-dry finish and aftertaste is only malt.

GOETZ PALE NEAR BEER — brilliant deep gold, light cereal grain aroma, flavor is grain and carbonation, light body, grainy malt aftertaste with little length.

TEXAS PRIDE EXTRA LIGHT LAGER BEER — bright gold, light malt aroma, light malt flavor only faintly hopped, little finish and aftertaste.

TEXAS SELECT — bright yellow, faint grainy nose, light grainy malt flavor, somewhat unbalanced hop and malt aftertaste.

TEXAS LIGHT NON-ALCOHOLIC MALT BEVERAGE — bright yellow, light grainy malt nose and flavor, little finish and aftertaste.

TEXAS LIGHT DARK NON-ALCOHOLIC MALT BEVERAGE — red-brown, light malt aroma, watery malt flavor has little depth, finish is even weaker and there is virtually no aftertaste.

LODI BEER — bright gold, good rising malt and hop aroma, zesty malt and hop flavor, hop finish and aftertaste that has good length and hop balance.

JOLIE BLONDE BEER — hazy amber, big complex malt aroma, heavy body, a lot of malt extract, soft and wine-like in style, faint hops in the finish, but is a predominantly malty brew. Contract brew for Bayou Brew Bros. Inc. Louisiana.

ORIGINAL CAJUN FLAVORED BEER — amber, fruity malt aroma, flavor starts out fruity malt, but quickly there is hot Cajun spice that dominates by the finish and extends through the long dry aftertaste.

SMITH & REILLY HONEST BEER — faintly hazy gold, good hop nose, bright zesty hop flavor, dry hop finish, hop aftertaste of medium duration, a refreshing all-barley malt beer. Contract brew for Smith & Reilly, Vancouver, WA.

CHEERS NON-ALCOHOLIC MALT BEVERAGE — tawny-gold, dank malt and hop nose, flavor is thin malt and hops, light dry hop finish, brief aftertaste has faint hops.

BEER — gold, light malt and hop aroma, light malt and hop flavor, medium body, short hop aftertaste. Generic supermarket beer on West Coast.

LITE BEER — pale gold, light slightly grainy malt nose and taste, light body, little aftertaste. Generic brew for supermarkets on West Coast.

NA NON-ALCOHOLIC BEER — deep gold, malt nose, grainy malt flavor, weak body, light and short malt aftertaste.

OLD ENGLISH 800 MALT LIQUOR — gold, strong malt aroma, big aromatic malt flavor, big body, very long malt aftertaste that is quite sweet like the flavor.

BEACH BREW NA MALT BEVERAGE — pale gold, grainy malt nose, slight hops in back, malty water flavor, sour finish, short, overall dank and weak. Contract brew for Beach Beer Brewing Co. of California.

ORIGINAL BEACH BEER — pale gold, hop aroma, sour malt and hop flavor, light and dry, somewhat sour finish and aftertaste. Contract brew as above.

STEAMER LANE LAGER BEER — tawny-gold, pleasant malt aroma, palate is slightly sour malt at first, then is dry toasted malt and hops, hops are bigger at finish leading into a long dry hop aftertaste. Contract brew as above.

BEACH BEER NATURAL DRAFT — gold, aroma starts out hops and then the malt comes in, the flavor is big malt but with the hops sufficient for balance, soft textured, big bodied, dry finish, short aftertaste. Contract brew as above.

BROWN DERBY LAGER BEER — pale gold, light hop nose, big malt flavor, medium dry malt aftertaste, not long. Made for Safeway markets.

Note: *Many of the S&P brews distributed on the East Coast are made and packaged in Stroh breweries.*

Samuel Adams Brewhouse/ Philadelphia Brewing Co.

Brew-pub in **Philadelphia, PA**

All beers are made from extracts.

BEN FRANKLIN'S GOLDEN — gold, big hop nose, slightly soapy malt palate, hops in finish, long dry hop aftertaste.

POOR RICHARD'S AMBER — golden amber, light smooth hop nose, smooth very hoppy flavor, long hop aftertaste.

GEORGE WASHINGTON'S PORTER — deep amber, chocolate malt nose with some hops, very dry hop and malt flavor, dry hop finish and aftertaste.

San Andreas Brewing Co.

Brewery and brew-pub in **Hollister, CA**

KIT FOX AMBER RICHTER SCALE ALE — hazy amber, zesty tangy ale nose and flavor, bright citrus character, sour cherries in the finish, tangy dry malt aftertaste.

EARTHQUAKE PALE ALE — hazy gold, nice citrus-hop aroma, big grapefruit-hop flavor goes dry hops at the finish, long dry hop aftertaste.

EARTHQUAKE PORTER — deep brown, almost totally opaque, brown head, complex fruity roasted malt aroma, big smoky dry malt flavor, light body, dry malt finish, long dry malt aftertaste has a faint citrus component.

OKTOBER QUAKE ALE — hazy amber, big sharp hop nose, assertive hop flavor, light body, sharp hop finish, long harsh hop aftertaste, a bit too sharp.

SEISMIC ALE — hazy amber, fruity malt nose, low carbonation, big malt flavor, not complex, ale-like hop bite at the finish, short to medium malt aftertaste, questionable balance.

GREEN LEPRECHAUN ALE — lime green, malt aroma, flavor is mostly hops but there is malt in back, light bodied, dry bitter hop aftertaste, a very dry beer.

CRANBERRY NOEL — pinkish orange-amber, fruity-berry (cranberry) fruit flavor, not tart or sour or sweet, good malt background, good balance with the fruit and malt, long dry malt aftertaste.

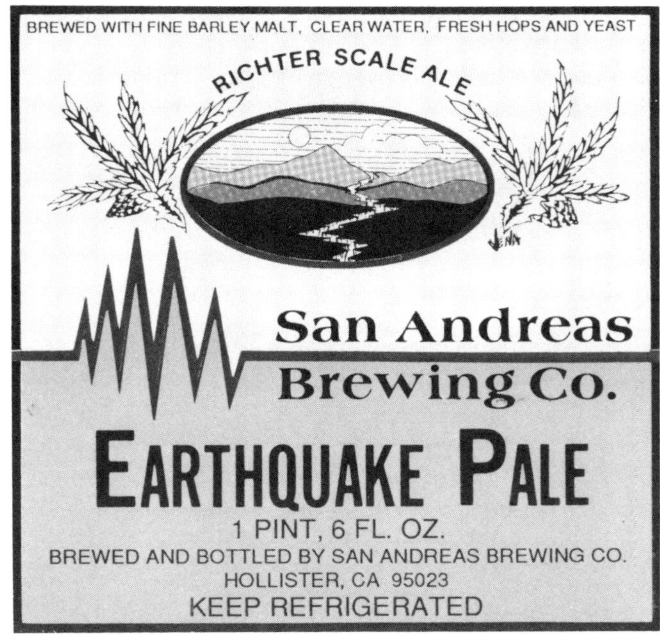

BREWED WITH FINE BARLEY MALT, CLEAR WATER, FRESH HOPS AND YEAST
RICHTER SCALE ALE
San Andreas
Brewing Co.
EARTHQUAKE PALE
1 PINT, 6 FL. OZ.
BREWED AND BOTTLED BY SAN ANDREAS BREWING CO.
HOLLISTER, CA 95023
KEEP REFRIGERATED

Notes:

San Francisco Brewing Co.

Brew-pub in San Francisco, CA

ALBATROSS LAGER — deep tawny-gold, light hop nose, big hop flavor, medium body, very long dry hop aftertaste.

ALBATROSS LAGER (DRAFT) — hazy gold, light malt and hop nose, bright hop flavor but a bit austere, good body, long dry hop aftertaste.

EMPEROR NORTON LAGER — amber, malt aroma, hop and malt flavor has a sour background, hop finish, medium long dry hop aftertaste.

EMPEROR NORTON LAGER (DRAFT) — hazy tawny-amber, good malt and hop nose, bright hop flavor is similar to Albatross but less austere, having much more malt, very good body, long dry hop aftertaste has good malt in behind, very enjoyable.

GRIPMAN'S PORTER — cloudy-brown, citrus hop and malt nose, citrus overshadows the malt in the flavor, finishes like the flavor, medium long aftertaste.

BONZO'S BROWN ALE — dark brown, very light malt nose, light dry malt flavor with some roasted malt and celery seed in back, medium body, long dry malt aftertaste. Special Chinese New Year draft beer for Year of the Monkey.

Notes:

Santa Cruz Brewing Co.

Brewery and brew-pub located in Santa Cruz, CA

LIGHTHOUSE LAGER — gold, light citrus nose, refreshing and bright malt and citrus hop flavor, complex, good body, hop finish, long hop aftertaste, good balance.

LIGHTHOUSE AMBER — hazy amber, faint grapefruit and malt aroma, very dry malt palate, so dry you are reminded of a tannic wine, complex dry hop finish, good body, short dry hop aftertaste.

PACIFIC PORTER — deep, almost opaque brown, off-dry malt nose, dry malt flavor, short dry malt aftertaste, medium body, little complexity.

Santa Fe Brewing Co.

Brewery in Galisteo, NM

SANTA FE PALE ALE — hazy amber, luscious off-dry citrus hop and malt nose, very appetizing, big malt flavor with a light citrus background, dry hop finish and aftertaste, good length.

August Schell Brewing Co.

Brewery at New Ulm, MN

AUGUST SCHELL PILS BEER — deep amber-gold, beautiful flowery hop nose, big hop flavor with plenty of malt, good body, long dry hop aftertaste. This is a classic German-style pilsener, a great recipe and excellent execution.

AUGUST SCHELL EXPORT BEER — bright gold, faint malt aroma, light malt flavor, light body, faintly sweet malt finish and brief malt aftertaste.

AUGUST SCHELL LIGHT BEER — pale gold, light malt aroma, light body, dry hop finish, short dry hop aftertaste.

SCHELL DEER BRAND BEER — very pale gold, pleasant malt aroma with a faint trace of apple, high carbonation, off-dry malt flavor with some esters in back, dry malt finish, short aftertaste.

AUGUST SCHELL WEISS BEER — brilliant pale amber, grainy nose, spicy malt palate that stays throughout and into a long aftertaste.

AUGUST SCHELL WEIZEN BEER — bright gold, clean fresh fruity-malt nose is a bit on the sweet side, light body, tangy background to the malt flavor much like many German Weizens, clean and refreshing, finishes dry, medium length aftertaste, refreshing hot-weather beer.

AUGUST SCHELL OKTOBERFEST 1991 — rosy-amber, pleasant complex malt aroma, good body, big strong hop and malt flavor, complex and balanced, smooth and delicious, dry hop finish, long dry hop aftertaste.

GOVERNMENT WARNING: (1) ACCORDING TO THE SURGEON GENERAL, WOMEN SHOULD NOT DRINK ALCOHOLIC BEVERAGES DURING PREGNANCY BECAUSE OF THE RISK OF BIRTH DEFECTS. (2) CONSUMPTION OF ALCOHOLIC BEVERAGES IMPAIRS YOUR ABILITY TO DRIVE A CAR OR OPERATE MACHINERY AND MAY CAUSE HEALTH PROBLEMS
August
Schell
Since 1860
Oktoberfest
BEER
Contents
1 Pint, 6 Fl. Oz.
CT ME VT DE MA NY IA OR 5¢ / MI 10¢ REFUND
August Schell Brewing Co.
NEW ULM MINN.
0 880675 8

AUGUST SCHELL OKTOBERFEST 1990 — amber, bright tangy hop aroma, big ale-like flavor with lots of hop bite and plenty of malt, good body, dry hop finish and aftertaste, an assertive brew.

SCHELL BOCK BEER — bright amber, dry caramel malt nose, dry caramel flavor, light body, could use more hops, light medium dry malt finish, off-dry short malt aftertaste.

GEMEINDE BRAU — medium pale gold, malt nose, good body, good flavor with plenty of malt and light hops, off-dry malt finish and aftertaste. Contract brew for Gemeinde Brau, Inc., Amana, IA.

ULMER BRAUN BEER — deep amber-brown, dry malt nose and taste, almost soapy, but that feature doesn't develop enough to mar the flavor, dry malt finish and medium-length aftertaste. Ulmer B.C., New Ulm, MN.

PETE'S WICKED ALE — brilliant deep amber, slightly toasted malt and hop aroma, big complex and zesty malt flavor with hops rolling in from mid-palate on, a touch of scorched malt among the hops at the finish and in the long dry aftertaste, an excellent, balanced, satisfying, drinkable brew. Contract brew for Pete's B.C., Palo Alto, CA.

PETE'S GOLD COAST LAGER — hazy amber, bright hop aroma, big hop flavor that lasts and lasts, big body, complex, balanced, delicious, feels good in your mouth, long dry hop aftertaste. Contract brew as above.

PETE'S PACIFIC DRY BEER — amber-gold, lovely malt aroma with a bit of toasted malt in back, good body, dry malt flavor, nice while it lasts, but it is brief. Contract brew as above.

HELENBOCH BEER — clear deep gold, appetizing hop nose, dry hop flavor, long dry hop aftertaste. Contract brew for Friends B.C., Helen, GA.

JEFFERSON BLUE RIDGE MOUNTAIN BRAND LAGER — sherry color, lovely toasted malt aroma, full rich malt flavor, good hop balance, malt and hop finish, long malt aftertaste. Contract brew for Federal Hill B.C., Forest, VA.

SUMMER PALE LAGER — bright gold, fresh clean bright malt nose, dry hop palate, highly carbonated, dry hop aftertaste is a bit dull. Contract brew for Saloon B.C., Sweeny's Saloon in St. Paul, MN.

SALOON LIGHT LAGER — brilliant pale gold, dry malt nose, very little flavor, just a hint of banana behind some malt, dull short malt aftertaste. Contract brew as above.

AUBURN DARK LAGER — deep amber-brown, malt nose, thin malt flavor, light body, thin malt aftertaste that lasts a short time. Contract brew as above.

PECAN ST. LAGER — amber-gold, very pleasant toasted malt and hop nose, hefty toasted malt flavor with hops coming in well at the finish, long dry aftertaste, smooth, pleasant, and drinkable. Made for The Old City B.C., Austin, TX.

Notes:

Schirf Brewing Co.

Brewery and brew-pub located in **Park City, UT**

WASATCH CHRISTMAS ALE — hazy tawny-gold, fragrant hop aroma, flowery hops and good malt, , complex palate, dry hops in front, then it takes on a stronger hop-ale character, could use more malt for better balance, dry hop finish, bitter and dry hop aftertaste with good duration.

WASATCH SLICKROCK LAGER — hazy gold, fresh fruity malt aroma, big malt up front, hops join in at mid-palate and give the flavor some complexity, finish is still malty, and the aftertaste is faintly roasted malt.

WASATCH PREMIUM ALE — medium deep amber, big toasted malt nose, roasted malt flavor, long off-dry malt aftertaste, very drinkable.

WASATCH IRISH STOUT — deep brown, dry chocolate malt nose, creamy very dry roasted malt flavor, medium body, long dry malt aftertaste, nicely done and very drinkable.

WASATCH
WEIZENBIER
NO ADDITIVES
NO PRESERVATIVES
12 FLUID OUNCES
KEEP REFRIGERATED

Notes:

Seabright Brewery

Brew-pub in **Santa Cruz, CA**

SEABRIGHT AMBER — amber, beautiful light hop aroma, smooth and mellow malt flavor with light hops in back, dry malt finish, medium-length dry malt aftertaste.

PELICAN PALE — gold, hop nose, delicious malt-hop flavor, excellent balance, dry hop finish and aftertaste with good length, a beautiful brew — Seabright's best!

EXTRA SPECIAL BITTER — amber, faint hop nose, light hop flavor, smooth, well-balanced, dry hop finish, short dry hop aftertaste, very drinkable.

BANTY ROOSTER — gold, light hop nose and taste, good body, dry hop finish and aftertaste, hops light at first in the malt, but they come on strong in mid-palate.

TRI-CENTURY PORTER — deep dark amber-brown, coffee-like malt aroma, smooth, dry malt flavor, finish, and aftertaste, very long and very drinkable.

CENTURY RED — amber, very attractive fresh and lively malt and hop aroma, bright hop flavor with good malt, very refreshing, long dry hop aftertaste.

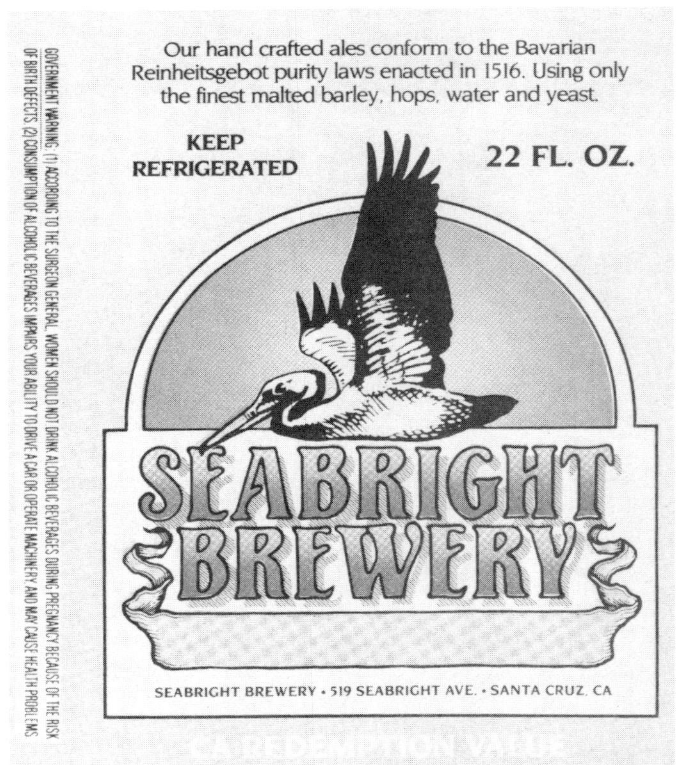
Our hand crafted ales conform to the Bavarian Reinheitsgebot purity laws enacted in 1516. Using only the finest malted barley, hops, water and yeast.
KEEP REFRIGERATED
22 FL. OZ.
GOVERNMENT WARNING: (1) ACCORDING TO THE SURGEON GENERAL, WOMEN SHOULD NOT DRINK ALCOHOLIC BEVERAGES DURING PREGNANCY BECAUSE OF THE RISK OF BIRTH DEFECTS. (2) CONSUMPTION OF ALCOHOLIC BEVERAGES IMPAIRS YOUR ABILITY TO DRIVE A CAR OR OPERATE MACHINERY AND MAY CAUSE HEALTH PROBLEMS.
SEABRIGHT BREWERY
SEABRIGHT BREWERY • 519 SEABRIGHT AVE. • SANTA CRUZ, CA
CA REDEMPTION VALUE

Notes:

Shield's Brewing Co.

Brew-pub in Ventura, CA

GOLD COAST BEER — hazy deep gold, malt aroma and flavor, good body, long malt aftertaste, very drinkable.

CHANNEL ISLANDS ALE — amber, light hop aroma with good malt in back, flavor is like the aroma but with more malt, good body, hops show more in the finish, and the long aftertaste is dry hops.

SHIELD'S STOUT — dark brown, light malt aroma, smooth off-dry malt flavor, dry malt finish, medium body, short dry malt aftertaste, good balance, but very brief.

Sierra Nevada Brewing Co.

Brewery at Chico, CA

SIERRA NEVADA PALE ALE — deep amber, complex tangy hop and malt aroma that seems off-dry, smooth rich malt and hop flavor, hops strongest at the finish, very long hop aftertaste, a big delicious brew.

SIERRA NEVADA PORTER — deep red-brown, complex tangy off-dry malt and hop nose smooth rich malt flavor with strong hops coming in for the finish, very long and very delicious, a big satisfying brew.

SIERRA NEVADA STOUT — opaque brown, big rich clean and sweet nose, complex herbal flavor in front, good hops and roasted malt at the finish, very long off-dry and roasted malt aftertaste, another big-bodied full-flavored brew.

SIERRA NEVADA PALE BOCK — bright pale gold, great nose with lots of hops and malt, big body, big hop flavor, extremely long bright hop aftertaste, a big and beautiful brew with incredible balance.

BIG FOOT BARLEYWINE STYLE ALE 1987 — hazy amber, complex citrus and licorice nose, huge citrus ale flavor, enormous body, great complexity, more malt and hops than you've had in a mouthful before; almost too powerful, but it is balanced so you can enjoy its quality; extremely long on the palate.

BIG FOOT BARLEYWINE STYLE ALE 1988 — cloudy amber, toasted malt nose, huge, almost overwhelming toasted malt flavor with incredible duration.

BIG FOOT BARLEYWINE STYLE ALE 1990 — deep amber, complex malt aroma, strong alcoholic rich malt flavor, excellent balance, richness stays right through the long, long toasted malt aftertaste. Note that these Big Foot brews can handle quite a bit of bottle aging. Try keeping them for a year or so.

SIERRA NEVADA CELEBRATION ALE 1987 — brilliant deep amber, roasted malt aroma, big strong beautifully balanced roasted malt and hop flavor, delicious and very long.

SIERRA NEVADA CELEBRATION ALE 1988 — orange-amber, a citrus and pine aroma, intense malt flavor with a big hop finish and long hop aftertaste. A big delicious brew.

SIERRA NEVADA CELEBRATION ALE 1989 — medium amber, complex tangy citrus-ale nose, big zesty ale flavor, lots of both malt and hops, complex sipping beer, not overwhelming, just big and good, excellent balance, very long hop aftertaste.

SIERRA NEVADA CELEBRATION ALE 1989 — batch made October 25, 1989, golden amber, big fruity-citrus nose, strong malt and hop flavor, high alcohol, very dry finish and aftertaste, huge and long.

SIERRA NEVADA CELEBRATION ALE 1989 — batch made November 27, 1989, golden amber, faint malt aroma, same flavor as above but lighter, excellent balance, long dry malt and hop aftertaste, much like brew above but a more subtle version.

SIERRA NEVADA CELEBRATION ALE 1990 — medium to deep amber, huge citrus ale nose, enormous but smooth malt and hop flavor, excellent balance, extremely long aftertaste.

SIERRA NEVADA CELEBRATION ALE 1991 — pale amber, fruity citrus and apricot aroma, big citrus ale flavor, very good balance, plenty of both malt and hops, smooth, rich, and a great-tasting long, long aftertaste .

SIERRA NEVADA SUMMERFEST BEER 1991 — gold, clean malt and hop aroma, big flavor is mostly hops but there is malt aplenty in support, malt kicks in at the finish, and it ends refreshingly dry and quite long.

Sisson's South Baltimore Brewing Co.

Brew-pub in **Baltimore, MD**

MARBLE PILSENER — hazy gold, very faint hop aroma, austere dry hop flavor, medium body, long sour and dry hop aftertaste.

STOCKADE AMBER — hazy amber, very faint hop aroma, dry hop flavor, finish, and aftertaste. There is a bit more malt in the aftertaste, but the overall effect is very dry hops. Despite the austerity, the balance is good, there is a creamy texture to it, good body, good length, and complexity.

Notes:

SLO Brewing Co.

Brew-pub in **San Luis Obispo, CA**

SLO PALE ALE — gold, nice hop nose, bright hop flavor, faint bite in back, bright and smooth, well balanced, long medium dry hop aftertaste.

SLO AMBER ALE — amber, light hop aroma, malt flavor is smooth, medium body, hops are light and in back, medium dry malt finish, long dry malt aftertaste.

SLO PORTER — deep brown, light coffee-malt nose, light malt flavor, medium body, more dry than rich, dry malt finish, medium length, dry malt aftertaste.

SLO NUT BROWN ALE — deep amber, hop nose, smooth dry nutty flavor, very dry finish, long dry nutty aftertaste.

Spenard Brewing Co.

Brewery in **Seattle, WA**

CHILKOOT CHARLIE'S SOURDOUGH WHEAT ALE — hazy golden-amber, dry malt and hop aroma has a sausage background (like bologna), light body, off-dry dull malt flavor, dry hop finish and aftertaste.

Notes:

Spoetzl Brewing Co.

Brewery in Shiner, TX

SHINER PREMIUM BEER — pale gold, well-hopped malt aroma, well-balanced slightly hoppy flavor, hops better in the finish and aftertaste, pleasant and refreshing.

SHINER PREMIUM BOCK BEER — brilliant amber color, strong hop and roasted (almost burnt) malt aroma, weak body, pleasant malt flavor is sometimes too burned, finish has little zest.

RATTLESNAKE BEER — pale yellow, hop nose, pleasant malt flavor, little body, little aftertaste.

DEVIL BEER — pale gold, light grainy malt aroma, flavor dominated by the carbonation, faint malt finish and aftertaste.

Notes:

Sprecher Brewing Co.

Brewery in Milwaukee, WI

SPRECHER MAI BOCK — hazy gold, great appetizing hop and malt aroma, big malty flavor, well backed with hops, long malt aftertaste with a hop bite in back, a real honest Mai Bock.

SPRECHER MILWAUKEE WEISS — hazy gold, lovely fresh malt nose with hints of grapefruit and lemon, tart citrus flavor, light body, tart malt finish, long dry and slightly tart malt aftertaste.

SPRECHER DUNKEL WEIZEN — deep amber, off-dry roasted malt nose, slightly burnt roasted malt flavor, light body, well made, long dry roasted malt aftertaste.

SPRECHER OKTOBERFEST — hazy amber, dusty malt aroma, lightly toasted malt flavor, light body, some complexity, dry malt finish and aftertaste.

SPRECHER BLACK BAVARIAN STYLE — deep ruby-brown, rich malt aroma, faint licorice background, dry malt flavor, dry malt aftertaste, uniform flavor throughout.

SPRECHER SPECIAL AMBER — amber, malt and hop aroma, hop flavor with a citrus background, bright and crisp, low carbonation, clean refreshing hop aftertaste with a trace of yeast at the end, a zesty brew.

SPRECHER WINTER BREW — ruby-brown, toasted malt aroma with a hop tang in back, slightly scorched malt flavor, off-dry malt finish, long aftertaste starts as off-dry malt and goes to dry malt at the end.

Stanislaus Brewing Co.

Brewery in Modesto, CA

ST. STAN'S AMBER ALT — hazy amber, big citrus hop aroma, zesty hop flavor with plenty of malt backing, fair balance, complex and flavorful, medium to long hop aftertaste.

ST. STAN'S DARK ALT — deep amber-brown, very complex aroma with blueberries, raspberries, currants, and melon, malt palate is dull compared to the very interesting nose, finishes with roasted malt, aftertaste is roasted malt with some scorching, good length.

ST. STAN'S FEST ALT BIER — hazy amber-gold, complex zesty big citrus hop and fruity malt aroma, big malt flavor with plenty of hops to support the balance and to provide a bright zesty quality, medium to good body, high alcohol, good drinking beer, long alcoholic aftertaste, really good and really long. This brew actually improves with bottle aging. If you think it is good at Christmas time, try it again about May or June.

ST. STAN'S GRAFFITI ALT 1990 — light hazy amber, complex fruity malt aroma with all kinds of interesting components, a regular fruit cocktail, smooth hop flavor, light body, fairly short aftertaste, but a good effort nonetheless. This brew is made annually but is available only briefly each time.

CHAU TIEN EMPEROR ALE — hazy gold, pleasant off-dry malt nose, pleasant clean malt flavor, hops appear in the finish, light body, long malt aftertaste, quite pleasant.

Stevens Point Beverage Co.

Brewery at Stevens Point, WI

POINT SPECIAL PREMIUM BEER — pale gold, light malt aroma with just a trace of hops, pleasant clean light malt flavor, light body, medium-length dry malt aftertaste, smooth and very drinkable.

POINT LIGHT — gold, very pleasant fragrant malt and hop nose, medium body, good-tasting dry malt flavor, light dry hop aftertaste, highly carbonated.

POINT GENUINE BOCK BEER — brilliant amber, big malt aroma, big dry malt flavor, very smooth, light body, long fairly dry malt aftertaste, very much like a May bock.

POINT SPECIAL EDITION — bright deep gold, good hop and malt nose, good body, satisfying malt flavor, balanced, dry hop finish and aftertaste, not long but good.

EAGLE PREMIUM PILSNER — pale yellow-gold, good malt and hop nose, bright hop flavor, medium body, good long aftertaste with both malt and hops, a good little beer.

CHIEF OSHKOSH RED LAGER BEER — amber, sweet malt nose, sweet malt flavor up front, alcoholic middle, hop finish and long hop aftertaste.

NEW YORK HARBOR ALE — bright deep gold, good hop aroma, lusty hop flavor with some complexity stays fairly dry, good body and some complexity, long dry hop aftertaste, in general the malt stays in the background. Made for Old World Brewing Co., Staten Island, NY.

SPUD PREMIUM BEER — gold, vegetal malt aroma, earthy dry malt palate, medium long dry malt aftertaste with some hops showing.

Stoudt Brewing Co.

Brewery, brew-pub, restaurant, antique center in **Adamstown, PA**

STOUDT'S GOLDEN LAGER — gold, good malt nose, dry malt flavor with good hop support, touch of off-dry malt at the finish, then a long dry malt and hop aftertaste, very good balance, very drinkable.

STOUDT'S ADAMSTOWN AMBER — bright amber, hop nose, hop taste with plenty of malt in support, very good balance, good body, malt comes to the fore at the finish, long dry malt and hop aftertaste, another very drinkable brew.

STOUDT'S HOLIDAY BOCK — ruby-amber, light toasted malt aroma, toasted malt flavor that might have a little smokiness way way back, long dry malt aftertaste, good brew but somewhat unidimensional.

STOUDT'S OKTOBERFEST DARK — see Lion, Inc.

STOUDT'S MARDI GRAS (FASCHING) — beautiful ruby-amber color, low carbonation, off-dry fruity-grapey malt aroma, dull malt flavor, short malt aftertaste.

STOUDT'S OKTOBERFEST — deep amber, good roasted malt and hop nose, big hop and well-roasted malt flavor, finishes as it starts, extremely dry brief roasted malt aftertaste.

STOUDT'S PILSENER STYLE — gold, lovely European (Saaz) hop nose, big dry hop flavor, big body, complex, dry hop finish and long aftertaste.

STOUDT'S BOCK BIER — deep mahogany color, toasted malt nose and taste, some complexity, creamy texture with a big solid head that lasts to the bottom of the glass, fairly dry malt finish and aftertaste, good length.

STOUDT'S BOCK — mahogany color, light roasted malt nose and taste, some hops in the finish, medium-length dry hop aftertaste.

STOUDT'S BULL ALE — amber, faintly soapy malt nose, light malt flavor feels good in your mouth, off-dry malt finish and aftertaste, good length.

STOUDT'S SOUR MASH ALE — deep amber, slightly buttery malt nose, off-dry malt flavor, slightly sour finish, long dry aftertaste.

STOUDT STOUT — opaque brown, light malt nose, dry malt palate, some malty sweetness appears at the finish, long dry malt aftertaste, very drinkable, medium body.

STOUDT'S OKTOBERFEST BOCK — deep ruby-amber, very faint malt aroma, dry lightly scorched malt flavor, pleasant, long dry aftertaste like the flavor.

STOUDT'S RASPBERRY WEIZEN — reddish color, dry raspberry nose is a little sour, very dry malt and faint raspberry in the flavor, maintains a fruity malt character, finishes dry malt, fairly long dry malt aftertaste.

STOUDT'S OKTOBERFEST MAERZEN — medium deep amber, dry malt nose, thin body, odd sort of vegetal malt flavor, not appetizing, short malt aftertaste.

STOUDT'S HOLIDAY ALE — amber, big hop and big malt aroma, flavor starts out with big hops and plenty of bite, malt comes in the middle and stays, excellent balance, big body, luscious and long, a real lip-smacker.

STOUDT'S GOLD MEDAL HEFE-WEIZEN — cloudy gold, fresh clean lightly spiced malt nose, light dry spicy malt flavor, hops come in at the finish, moderately dry hop aftertaste with good duration.

STOUDT'S ANNIVERSARY ALE — amber, hop nose with some caramel, dry malt flavor, long dry malt aftertaste.

STOUDT'S BEERFEST BOCK — very deep amber, dry malt nose with a hint of caramel, very dry malt flavor, long dry malt aftertaste with hops faintly in back.

STOUDT'S DOPPELBOCK — amber, buttery malt nose, malt and hop flavor with the butter still there but far in back, dry malt finish and long aftertaste.

STOUDT'S RED ALE — reddish-amber, faint hop-ale aroma, big tangy hop palate, good malt backing, good body, long dry hop aftertaste.

STOUDT'S WINTERFEST — amber, light malt and hop nose, off-dry malt and bitter hop palate, balanced, somewhat winy in nature, dry malt finish, medium-length dry malt aftertaste, very nice drinkable brew. Labeled Oktoberfest, but released in January, and, according to the Stoudts, it's their winterfest beer.

STOUDT'S DOUBLE BOCK — deep amber, sour malt nose, sharp sour malt flavor with a candy-like background, long dry malt aftertaste, seems to be mishandled.

STOUDT'S FESTIVAL RESERVE FEST BEER — hazy amber, sour malt nose and taste, dry off-sour malt aftertaste, another mishandled sample.

Straub Brewery, Inc.

Brewery in **St. Mary's, PA**

STRAUB ALL GRAIN BEER — light tawny gold, big malt nose with plenty of hops, big body, full malt and hop flavor, a hefty mouthful of beer, long dry aftertaste with plenty of malt and hops.

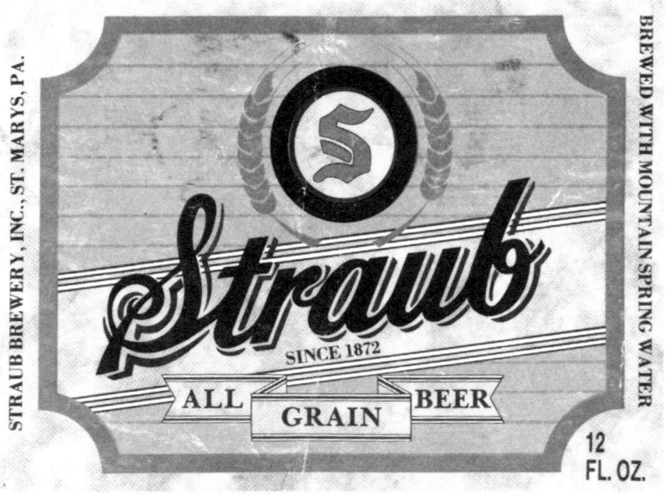

Notes:

Stroh Brewing Co.

Headquarters in Detroit, MI; breweries in Lehigh Valley, PA; Longview, TX; St.Paul, MN; Los Angeles, CA; Memhis, TN; Winston-Salem, NC.

STROH'S PREMIUM QUALITY AMERICAN BEER — bright gold, fresh malt aroma, bright hop flavor with malt supporting and in balance, good hop-malt finish and aftertaste.

STROH'S OWN BOCK BEER — copper-amber, good malt aroma and caramel-malt flavor, flavorful, smooth, balanced, and long.

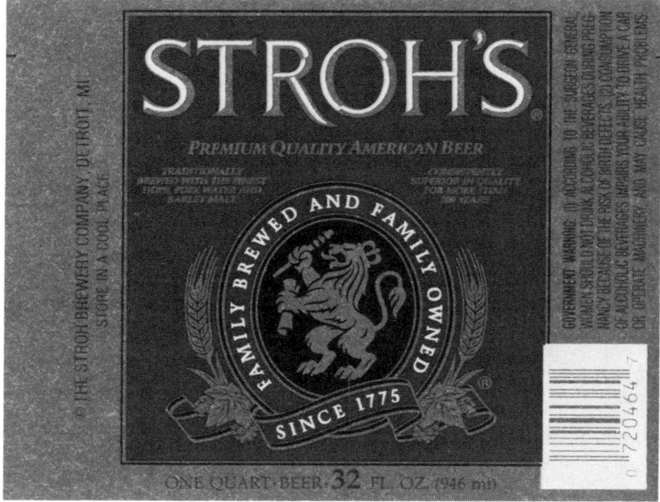

STROH LIGHT BEER — pale gold, light malt aroma, refreshing light malt flavor, pleasant and with better-than-average length for a light beer.

STROH SIGNATURE — brilliant gold, very good hop aroma with complexity and character, dry well-balanced malt and hop flavor, good and long, a true super-premium beer.

GOEBEL GOLDEN LIGHT LAGER — pale gold, faint malt aroma, light but balanced and clean tasting, highly carbonated but refreshing.

SILVER THUNDER MALT LIQUOR — bright pale gold, pleasant malt aroma, sweetish malt flavor (but not flabby), has complexity and interest, fairly long and balanced.

SCHLITZ BEER — pale gold, light malt aroma with hops faintly in back, light malt flavor lightly hopped, pleasant and inoffensive and dry overall.

SCHLITZ LIGHT BEER — pale gold, light malty-vanilla nose and taste, pleasant, fairly dry and brief.

SCHLITZ MALT LIQUOR — deep gold, hearty malt aroma and flavor, medium body, off-dry malt finish and aftertaste.

SCHLITZ RED BULL MALT LIQUOR — pale gold, heady aromatic malt nose, off-dry and faintly salty malt flavor, heavy body, sweet malt finish and aftertaste.

OLD MILWAUKEE BEER — bright pale gold, faint hop aroma with malt, good malt flavor, finishes pleasantly malted and has a good aftertaste.

OLD MILWAUKEE PREMIUM LIGHT BEER — pale yellow, faint but clean malt aroma, carbonation dominates the palate, wiping out what malt there is, slight malt finish, little aftertaste.

OLD MILWAUKEE NON-ALCOHOL — very pale gold, faint grainy aroma, very light grainy flavor, short.

OLD MILWAUKEE GENUINE DRAFT LIGHT — pale gold, light hop nose and flavor, high carbonation, light dry hop aftertaste, decent light-bodied summertime quaffing beer.

OLD MILWAUKEE GENUINE DRAFT — gold, hop nose and flavor, high carbonation, medium body, fairly long dry hop aftertaste.

SCHAEFER BEER — bright gold, good malt and hop aroma, zesty hop flavor, good body, good balance, overall dry, well-hopped long aftertaste.

SCHAEFER LIGHT LAGER BEER — bright gold, faint malt aroma, faint hops and slightly sour malt palate, little flavor, less aftertaste.

SCHAEFER LOW ALCOHOL BEER — medium deep gold, grainy off-dry malt aroma, dry sour malt flavor, watery, no follow-through.

PIELS LIGHT BEER — pale gold, light malt aroma, light malt flavor, lightly hopped, long and pleasant aftertaste, thirst quenching.

PIELS REAL DRAFT PREMIUM BEER — bright gold, clean malt aroma, high carbonation pretty well wipes out the light malt and hop flavor.

PRIMO BEER — pale yellow-gold, vegetal malt aroma and flavor, bit of sweet malt in front and in finish, light bodied. Primo Brewing & Malting Co., Ltd., made from wort brewed on mainland.

AUGSBURGER BEER — gold, very bright hop nose, zesty hop flavor, great character and excellent balance, bitter hop finish with a nice touch of malt underneath, long fairly dry hop aftertaste, one of America's best beers.

AUGSBURGER DARK — reddish-brown, slightly off-dry roasted malt aroma, malt palate, finish, and aftertaste, very good balance, and quite satisfying.

AUGSBURGER BOCK — deep amber-brown, faint malt aroma, big smooth dry malt palate, there are hops in there, but it is mostly malt, dry finish, good body, long dry malt and hop aftertaste, an excellent bock, and probably one of the top ten dark domestic brews.

AUGSBURGER LIGHT — bright gold, clean appetizing hop aroma, medium body, bright crisp hop flavor, dry finish, and fairly long dry hop aftertaste.

Note: *Many of the S&P Co. brews are made in eastern Stroh breweries for distribution on the East Coast. They are listed under S&P.*

Summit Brewing Co.

Brewery in St, Paul, MN

SUMMIT EXTRA PALE ALE — amber, melony malt aroma, clean fruity malt front palate, dry malt finish and aftertaste, medium body, medium length.

SUMMIT SPARKLING ALE — deep gold, malt nose, off-dry malt flavor, dry hop finish, medium body, weak brief hop aftertaste.

GOVERNMENT WARNING: (1) ACCORDING TO THE SURGEON GENERAL, WOMEN SHOULD NOT DRINK ALCOHOLIC BEVERAGES DURING PREGNANCY BECAUSE OF THE RISK OF BIRTH DEFECTS. (2) CONSUMPTION OF ALCOHOLIC BEVERAGES IMPAIRS YOUR ABILITY TO DRIVE A CAR OR OPERATE MACHINERY, AND MAY CAUSE HEALTH PROBLEMS.
SUMMIT
BREWING COMPANY
EXTRA PALE ALE
12 Fluid Ounces
Brewed & Bottled by Summit Brewing Co. St. Paul, MN
Ingredients: Water, Malt, Hops and Yeast.
For best flavor, drink before:
JAN FEB MAR APR MAY JUN JUL AUG SEP OCT NOV DEC

Notes:

Tied House Cafe & Brewery

Brew-pubs in **San Jose, Alameda,** and **Mountain View, CA**

TIED HOUSE AMBER — deep tawny-gold, bright hop and malt nose and taste, very long dry complex aftertaste much like the flavor, a good lusty brew.

Triple Rock Brewery & Alehouse

Brew-pub in **Berkeley, CA**

SWHEATHEART HEFE-WEIZEN — cloudy gold, lovely big malt nose, bright malt flavor, long and dry, as nice a Weizen as I've found in the U.S.

20 Tank Brewery

Brew-pub in **San Francisco, CA**

MARTIN'S MELLOW-GLOW PALE ALE — pale gold, good hop nose, bright hop flavor, creamy, good body, long dry hop aftertaste.

MOODY'S HI-TOP ALE — deep gold, sweet malt nose, big off-dry malt flavor, creamy, good body, medium-length dry hop aftertaste.

DOUBLE BOCK HEFEWEIZEN — light hazy amber, off-dry malt aroma at first, dries as it goes, flavor a lot like the nose (first off-dry malt, dries toward finish), good long dry malt aftertaste, 40% wheat not really noticeable, decent American-style Hefeweizen (no clove spice).

INDICATOR DOPPELBOCK — deep amber, big malt nose, hefty body, alcohol noticeable (6.5%), big off-dry malt and hop flavor, dry malt aftertaste, a good doublebock.

KINNIKINICK IMPERIAL STOUT — opaque brown, fresh malt nose, big strong and complex malt flavor, big body, long aftertaste is reasonably dry malt, alcohol is present throughout (8%), good brew for the strong of spirit.

Notes:

NORTH AMERICA

The Vermont Pub & Brewery

Brew-pub in **Burlington, VT**

BLACK BEAR LAGER — amber, malt nose, rich malt flavor, long dry malt aftertaste, pleasant and drinkable.

AULD BARLEY BREE WEE HEAVY — very dark brown, fairly strong malt nose, big strong and rich malt flavor, noticeable alcohol, long rich medium dry malt aftertaste.

Notes:

Virginia Brewing Co.

Brewery in **Clark's Gap, VA** (Virginia Beach)

GOLD CUP PREMIUM PILSENER — yellow-gold, malt nose, malt flavor, dry malt finish with the hops making their appearance, faintly sour malt aftertaste, creamy texture, nice complexity, and good balance.

GOLD CUP EXPORT BEER — bright deep gold, nice flowery malt aroma, beautifully balanced malt and hop flavor, hops move into prominence at the finish, medium long dry hop aftertaste.

DARK HORSE AMBER BEER — peach-amber color, malt nose, rich complex toasted malt flavor, good body, long malt aftertaste, satisfying and drinkable.

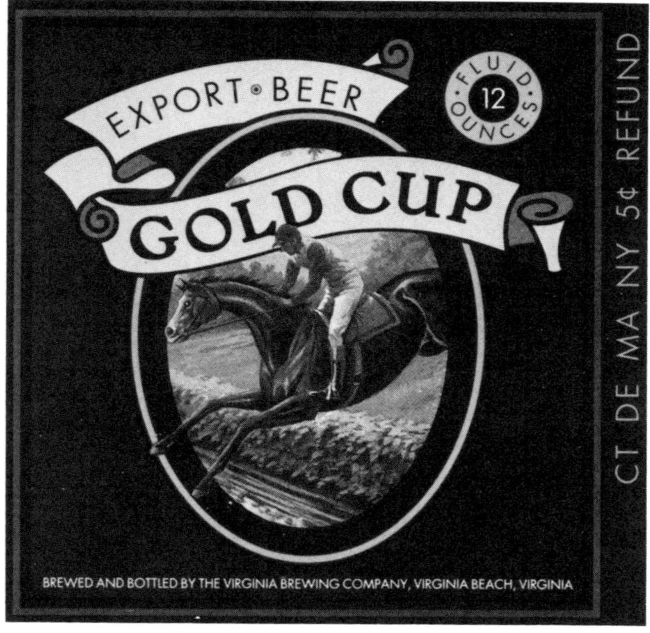
EXPORT • BEER
FLUID 12 OUNCES
GOLD CUP
CT DE MA NY 5¢ REFUND
BREWED AND BOTTLED BY THE VIRGINIA BREWING COMPANY, VIRGINIA BEACH, VIRGINIA

Weinkeller Brewery

Brew-pub in **Berwyn, IL**

ABERDEEN AMBER ALE — amber, dry coffee-like malt nose, dry malt flavor, light body, fairly smooth and balanced, short dry malt aftertaste with hops in back.

Notes:

Widmer Brewing Co.

Brewery in **Portland, OR,** situated adjacent to a restaurant giving the effect of a brew-pub.

WIDMER HEFE-WEIZEN — cloudy gold, malt and faint smoked-sausage nose, malt flavor is neutral (neither dry nor sweet), long dry malt aftertaste, there are faint off flavors that get in the way of the goodness.

Wild Goose Brewery

Brewery in **Cambridge, MD**

WILD GOOSE AMBER BEER — bright amber, very nice smooth hop aroma, big rich malt and hop flavor, aromatic and bitter hop finish and long aftertaste, a good English-style beer.

THOMAS POINT LIGHT GOLDEN ALE — hazy gold, appetizing malt aroma, good dry malt and hop flavor, light body, refreshing and drinkable, dry malt finish, medium-length dry malt and hop aftertaste.

SAMUEL MIDDLETON'S PALE ALE — hazy tawny-gold, dull malt nose, slightly buttery, flavor is faintly sour malt, but dry and also faintly buttery, long dry malt aftertaste.

WILD GOOSE
Amber
BEER
12 fl. oz.
BREWED & BOTTLED BY WILD GOOSE BREWERY, CAMBRIDGE, MARYLAND
GOVERNMENT WARNING: (1) ACCORDING TO THE SURGEON GENERAL, WOMEN SHOULD NOT DRINK ALCOHOLIC BEVERAGES DURING PREGNANCY BECAUSE OF THE RISK OF BIRTH DEFECTS. (2) CONSUMPTION OF ALCOHOLIC BEVERAGES IMPAIRS YOUR ABILITY TO DRIVE A CAR OR OPERATE MACHINERY, AND MAY CAUSE HEALTH PROBLEMS.

Winchester Brewing Co.

Brew-pub in San Jose, CA

WINCHESTER RED ALE — hazy red-amber, big head, dry malt nose, big smoky malt flavor, medium body, soapy finish, and long dry malt aftertaste.

LA-VE CON COP BEER — faintly hazy gold, malt aroma, very, very dry malt flavor, long dry malt aftertaste.

WINCHESTER CHRISTMAS ALE — hazy amber, fruity-spicy apricot nose, light body, palate starts sweet malt, finishes drier with some spice and smoke, very dry malt finish and aftertaste, doubtful balance.

WINCHESTER PALE ALE — hazy gold, malt aroma, big dry malt flavor, medium body, dry malt finish and aftertaste.

Yakima Brewing & Malting Co.

Brewery and brew-pub in Yakima, WA. First brew-pub in U.S. in modern era.

GRANT'S IMPERIAL STOUT — deep brown color, toasted dry caramel malt aroma, big dry malt flavor with good hop backing, medium body, good balance, smooth, clean,pleasant long dry finish and aftertaste.

GRANT'S WEIS BEER — amber-gold, pleasant citrus-malt aroma, refreshing tangy palate like the nose, medium body, zesty citrus tang balances the sweetness of the malt, likeable and long.

GRANT'S INDIA PALE ALE — tawny-gold, complex citrus ale aroma, big hop flavor well balanced with malt, malty sourness in middle, big body, long hop aftertaste.

GRANT'S CELTIC ALE — very deep amber-rose, off-dry malt aroma and flavor, dry finish and aftertaste, delicate and brief.

GRANT'S SCOTTISH ALE — amber, mild malty-citrus aroma, big but well-mannered fruity malt and citrus ale palate, very flavorful but smooth and balanced, long dry aftertaste.

GRANT'S SPICED ALE — amber, spicy malt (pumpkin pie) aroma, strong pleasant spicy flavor, a wassail, light body, aftertaste is only the spice.

Notes:

D.G. Yuengling & Son, Inc.

Brewery in Pottsville, PA

YUENGLING PREMIUM BEER — light gold, good malt aroma with subtle hop background, clean and bright hop flavor, fine malt finish and aftertaste.

YUENGLING'S PREMIUM LAGER — amber, balanced hop and malt aroma, medium body, smooth balanced hop and malt flavor, long fresh and clean aftertaste.

YUENGLING DARK BREW PORTER — deep red-brown, dry malt aroma has a richness, roasted malt flavor has a coffee-like background which you then notice in the aroma, good body, dry hops come in for the finish and fairly long aftertaste.

YUENGLING TRADITIONAL AMERICAN LAGER — amber color, complex malt aroma, good dry malt flavor, finish cuts off quickly.

Notes:

YUENGLING PREMIUM LIGHT BEER — pale yellow-gold, malt and light hop aroma, flavor is carbonation and light malt, medium to light body, short light dry malt and hop finish and aftertaste.

OLD GERMAN BRAND BEER — pale gold, malt nose and flavor, dry hop finish and aftertaste, medium length.

LORD CHESTERFIELD ALE — yellow-gold, good off-dry malt aroma, bright clean hop flavor, good body, good balance, lingering hop aftertaste.

BAVARIAN TYPE PREMIUM BEER — medium gold, off-dry malt aroma with some hops in back, hop flavor up front, malt comes in middle, but the finish and aftertaste are a forceful return of the bittering hops.

Zele Brewing Co.

Brewery in **Dubuque, IA**

This was the old Dubuque Star brewery and seems to operate under a variety of corporate names, mostly Zele B.C., but also Dubuque Star B.C., Rhomberg B.C., and Simpatico Breweries. Further complicating the situation is the large number of contract beers made in Dubuque under and for a variety of corporate names.

ERLANGER MAERZEN BIER — amber, soapy malt aroma, clean malt flavor, good body, fairly long malt aftertaste with hops at the very end.

DARRYL'S ORIGINAL PREMIUM LAGER BEER — hazy gold, light malt aroma, touch of hops first then light malt for the palate, fresh malt finish and aftertaste, little depth or duration.

RHOMBERG ALL MALT BEER — bright amber, zesty malt-hop nose and flavor, smooth, balanced, tasty, medium body, long dry hop aftertaste.

RHOMBERG ALL MALT CLASSIC PALE BEER — bright deep gold, big malt aroma, heavy body, almost too much malt on the palate, but it is balanced off not by hops but with carbonation, soft malt finish and long malt aftertaste, nicely done and very drinkable.

DUBUQUE STAR BEER — pale gold, pleasant off-dry malt and hop aroma, light hop flavor, medium body, clean and refreshing, brief malt aftertaste.

CHAU TIEN EMPEROR BEER — gold, hop nose with good malt backing, fruity hop flavor has good hops and malt in the middle, high carbonation, good body, dry finish and long dry hop aftertaste, complex, clean, and long.

BULL SHOOTERS BEER — brilliant pale gold, malt aroma, highly carbonated, big rich malt flavor, hefty body, long pleasant medium dry malt aftertaste. Contract brew for Sporting Chance, Inc., Kirkland, WA.

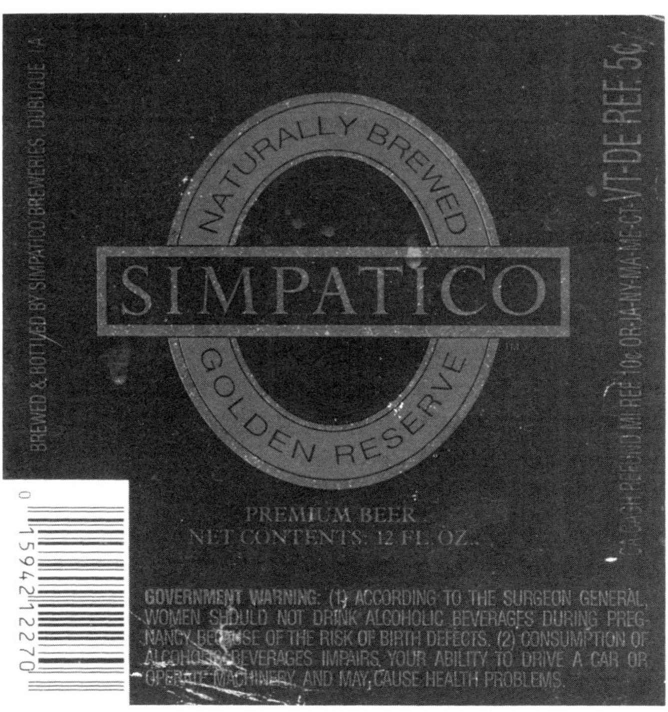

WILD BOAR SPECIAL AMBER — golden amber, clean fruity-malt aroma, big fleshy malt flavor, hops appear at finish, balanced hop and malt aftertaste, big body, excellent balance.

BEERGUY AT THE TOP — bright gold, dry malt aroma, creamy good medium dry malt flavor, hops come in the middle but stay far back, good malt finish, medium-long dry malt aftertaste, good balance, very drinkable. Contract brew for American Beerguy, Berkeley, CA.

TRESTLES LAGER BEER — hazy gold, big hop nose leaps out at you (hops-malt-hops), flavor is malt-hops-malt, finishes dry malt, long dry malt aftertaste, good body, good balance, very drinkable brew. Contract brew for Beach Beer Inc., Newport Beach, CA.

SIMPATICO AMBER — hazy amber, malt nose, good malt and hop flavor, good body, creamy finish, long malt aftertaste, a very well-made beer.

SIMPATICO GOLDEN RESERVE — gold, malt aroma, off-dry malt flavor, tart hop finish, malt finish and aftertaste has a buttery background.

Notes:

Zip City Brewing Co.

Brew-pub in New York City, NY

ZIP CITY CZECH STYLE PILSENER — hazy gold, aroma of hops and malt, big dry hop flavor well-backed with malt, quite tasty and very well hopped, finishes like it starts, medium to long dry hop aftertaste.

ZIP CITY VIENNA AMBER — slightly hazy amber, rising hop aroma with a dry malt background, rich malt and hop flavor, good hop support, very long dry aftertaste shows both the malt and hops, good balance.

ZIP CITY DUNKEL — brown, fairly dry malt aroma and taste, very mild and smooth, soft dry malt finish and aftertaste.

Notes:

Notes:

CANADA

Algonquin Brewing Co.

Brewery in Formosa Springs, Ontario

Some labels say Northern Algonquin B.C.

FORMOSA SPRINGS LIGHT — gold, faint malt and hop aroma, flavor is mostly carbonation with faint hops in back, faint malt finish, short dry aftertaste.

FORMOSA SPRINGS COLD-FILTERED DRAFT — gold, faint malt and hop nose, estery malt flavor is grape-like, finish and aftertaste like the flavor but more grainy, short dry aftertaste.

ALGONQUIN LIGHT BEER — pale gold, malt and hop aroma, good body, creamy, malt palate with some hops, pleasant finish and aftertaste.

ALGONQUIN COUNTRY LAGER — gold, malt nose, weak malt flavor, light body, dull dry malt aftertaste.

ALGONQUIN SPECIAL RESERVE ALE — pale amber, faint malt nose, high carbonation, tart hop and buttery malt flavor, medium body, short dry malt aftertaste.

ALGONQUIN CANADIAN LIGHT — pale gold, clean malt and hop nose, light body, hop finish, metallic flavors in the aftertaste.

NORTHERN GOOSE SUPER LIGHT BREW NON-ALCOHOLIC MALT BEVERAGE — gold, off-dry grainy nose, carbonation and grainy malt flavor, little follow-through except for a sour grainy sensation.

Amstel Brewery of Canada, Ltd.

Brewery in E. Hamilton, Ontario

HENNINGER EXPORT BEER — bright gold, beautiful hop aroma, finely carbonated, bright hop flavor, good balance, finish is both hops and malt, as is the long aftertaste, good German-style brew.

HENNINGER MEISTER PILS PREMIUM PILSENER — pale gold, perfumy hop nose, finely carbonated, well-balanced hop and malt flavor, hops stronger than the malt, light hop finish, dry hop aftertaste with good length.

AMSTEL BEER — pale gold, light hop and malt aroma and flavor, good body, hop finish, short hop aftertaste.

AMSTEL LIGHT BEER — very pale gold, faint grainy sour hop nose, thin sour hop flavor, brief aftertaste.

GRIZZLY BEER CANADIAN LAGER — bright gold, lovely hop nose, zesty hop flavor, good character, medium dry hop finish, long aftertaste; while the hops stay in the foreground throughout, there is a background of off-dry malt in back that comes in early and stays, all is harmoniously done, good brew of its type.

LAKER LAGER — gold, malt and hop aroma, light hop flavor with good malt backing, medium body, hop finish, long dry hop aftertaste.

LAKER LIGHT — pale gold, faint malt nose, light hop flavor, light body, brief aftertaste, like a little brother of Laker Lager.

STEELER LAGER — bright gold, malt aroma, malt palate with hops coming in at the finish, medium long dry hop aftertaste.

BIRRA PERONI — brilliant deep gold, fragrant hop aroma, pleasant dry hop flavor, long dry hop aftertaste, a good reproduction of the well-known Italian beer.

Notes:

Bavarian Specialties Ltd.

Hans Haus Brewery in
Moncton, New Brunswick

WESTNER'S CANADIAN CLASSIC — yellow, straightforward malt and hop aroma, sour hop flavor and finish, medium to short hop aftertaste a bit sour like the palate.

HANSHAUS LAGER — tawny-gold, toasted malt nose, off-dry malt flavor backed with hops, hop finish, nicely balanced, medium to long hop aftertaste, good German-style brew.

HANSHAUS O'BRUNSWICK MALT LIQUOR — pale amber, lovely malt aroma has noticeable alcohol, big malt flavor, a real mouthful, very big body, smooth and rich, very long malt aftertaste, the more you sip it, the maltier it becomes, one of Canada's best brews.

Big Rock Brewery

Brewery in **Calgary, Alberta**

ROYAL COACHMAN DRY ALE — gold, toasted malt aroma reminds you of Grape-Nuts cereal, tasty toasted malt flavor, light body, toasted malt aftertaste with medium length.

BUZZARD BREATH ALE — tawny-gold, light dry toasted malt aroma, dry malt flavor is slightly toasted, medium body, dry malt finish and aftertaste, medium length.

COLD COCK WINTER PORTER — very deep amber-brown, complex rich malt aroma, dry malt palate but there are complex hop flavors, light hop background shows best in the finish and aftertaste, interesting and fairly long dry malt aftertaste.

TRADITIONAL
ale
produced by:
Big Rock Brewery Calgary, Alberta, Canada
341 ml
5% alc/vol.

COCK O' THE ROCK PORTER — deep ruby-brown, complex chocolate malt and hop nose, surprisingly dry palate, flavor is big, lots of hops and malt but the malt dominates, very long, a big pushy brew.

TRADITIONAL ALE — light copper-amber, malt nose, pleasant malt flavor, medium long malt aftertaste.

BIG ROCK PALE ALE — deep gold, toasted chocolate malt nose, delicious light malt flavor, pleasant but brief.

BIG ROCK BITTER PALE ALE — pale amber, bright citrus-ale nose, zesty well-hopped flavor, good body, very flavorful, nice balance, big but not overdone, some complexity, good hop finish, long hop aftertaste.

McNALLY'S EXTRA PURE MALT IRISH STYLE ALE — deep bright amber, good toasted malt nose really comes at you, rich malt flavor is delicious, faint hop finish, long malt aftertaste with hints of caramel and butter.

Brick Brewing Co., Ltd.

Brewery in **Waterloo, Ontario**

BRICK PREMIUM LAGER BEER — gold, off-dry malty aroma, dry malt flavor, dry hop finish, long dry malt and hop aftertaste, good balance.

RED BARON BEER — pale gold, light malt and hop nose, light malt flavor with good hop backing, dry hop finish and aftertaste.

BRICK AMBER DRY BEER — deep gold, malt nose, slightly buttery malt palate, creamy, smooth, pleasant, dry malt finish and aftertaste.

Canadian Heritage Brewing Co.

Brewery in **Richmond, British Columbia**

STEVESTON HERITAGE OLD COUNTRY PREMIUM PILSNER — amber-gold, off-dry fruity melon and citrus nose, fruity malt flavor, dry hop finish and aftertaste.

Creemore Springs Brewery, Ltd.

Brewery in Creemore, Ontario

CREEMORE SPRINGS PREMIUM LAGER — pale amber, faint caramel nose, big malt flavor, touch of bitter hops at the finish, good body, dry hop aftertaste, flavors don't quite come together and the effect is fairly dull.

Notes:

Don Valley Brewing Co./The Conners B.C.

Conners Brewing Enterprises, Ltd. Brewery on earlier labels listed as being in Mississauga, Ontario; now listed as Toronto, Ontario; brewery is in St. Catherines, Ontario.

CONNERS BREWERY BEST BITTER — hazy amber-gold, toasted malt nose with a hop tang in back, tart hop and malt flavor, hops in front and end, malt in the middle, a definite ale-like tang, good balance, complex and interesting, hop finish, lemony aftertaste, a fine well-hopped brew.

CONNERS BREWERY ALE — amber, light malt aroma, hops dominate the flavor but there is still plenty of malt, big body, hop finish, short dry hop aftertaste.

Notes:

Drummond Brewing Co. Ltd.

Brewery in Red Deer, Alberta

Calgary and Edmonton mentioned on early labels.

DRUMMOND DRY — hazy gold, very nice hop and malt aroma and flavor, medium body, good balance, finishes just like the flavor and this stays into a medium-length aftertaste.

DRUMMOND BEER — pale gold, dry malt nose, dry hop and malt flavor, balanced, hop finish and aftertaste.

DRUMMOND LIGHT — pale gold, slightly stinky sour hop nose, dull sour malt and hop palate has little length.

Granville Island Brewing Co.

Brewery in Vancouver, British Columbia

ISLAND LAGER TRADITIONAL BEER — bright gold, toasted malt aroma, big body, complex well-hopped flavor, bitter hop finish, long complex dry hop and toasted malt aftertaste.

ISLAND BOCK — amber, rich malt nose, big toasted malt and bright hop flavor, perfect balance, delicious and very long aftertaste like the flavor. Can't think of a thing to improve on this brew; one of Canada's finest.

Notes:

Great Lakes Brewing Co.

Brewery in Brampton, Ontario

GREAT LAKES LAGER — pale amber, slightly scorched fruity malt nose with a little tang, lightly scorched hard candy malt flavor, light body, malt aftertaste with medium duration.

UNICORN ALE — deep amber, pleasant malt nose is a bit sweet, caramel malt front palate, hops come in at the finish and clash, light body, complex, long, but there is an imbalance.

YORK PILSNER LAGER BEER — gold, Ovaltine malt nose, big malt flavor, hop finish, long malt aftertaste. York B.C., Brampton.

Great Western Brewing Co.

Brewery listed as being in Saskatoon, Saskatchewan

GREAT WESTERN LAGER BEER — hazy gold, very foamy, faint hop and malt nose, malt flavor, big body, long off-dry malt aftertaste. Made for Connoisseur Beverage International Inc. of Minneapolis, MN.

GREAT WESTERN LIGHT BEER — gold, hop nose, light hop flavor, light body, faint dry hop finish and aftertaste, very little aftertaste, and no complexity. Contract brew as above.

Heuther Hotel/The Lion Brewery & Museum

Brew-pub and hotel in **Waterloo, Ontario**

LION LIGHT LAGER — gold, light dry malt nose and flavor, hop finish, medium to short dry hop aftertaste, clean and refreshing.

LION DRY — pale bright gold, little aroma, bright malt flavor, dry malt-hop finish and aftertaste.

HEUTHER'S PREMIUM LAGER — medium deep gold, good big malt aroma and taste, good body, long clean malt and hop aftertaste, excellent balance, noticeable alcohol, Heuther's best brew.

LION LAGER — gold, light malt aroma, good malt flavor with hops in back, similar to the LION LIGHT but bigger, bright refreshing malt flavor, dry hop finish and aftertaste, good and long.

ENGLISH ALE — deep dark amber, malt aroma, very dry strong malt flavor, a touch winey from the alcohol, austere dry malt finish and aftertaste, almost like a stout but with a good rather than heavy body, nicely made and enjoyable.

ADLY'S ALE — amber, malt nose, strong dry malt flavor, big body, a bit winey from the alcohol, dry malt finish, short dry aftertaste, very drinkable.

Notes:

Labatt Brewing Co., Ltd.

Breweries in St. John's, Newfoundland; Halifax, Nova Scotia; St. John, New Brunswick; Quebec City, Quebec; Waterloo, London, and Weston, Ontario; Winnipeg, Manitoba; Saskatoon, Saskatchewan; Edmonton, Alberta; Creston and New Westminster, British Columbia. Corporate HQ is in London, Ontario.

LABATT'S 50 ALE — medium deep bright gold, light hop nose, medium body, bright zesty hop flavor, quite tasty, long hop aftertaste with some slightly sour malt background. Export to the U.S. labeled LABATT'S 50 CANADIAN ALE.

LABATT'S PILSENER BEER — bright gold, dry hop nose, dry malt and hop flavor, medium body, finish and long aftertaste like the flavor, good clean serviceable pilsener. Long known as LABATT'S BLUE in Canada and more recently labeled as such.

GOLD KEG BEER — deep tawny-gold, big malt and hop aroma, good hop flavor, tasty, pleasant sour hop aftertaste is long.

COOL SPRING LIGHT BEER — bright gold, virtually no nose, light body, faint off-dry malt flavor fades as it crosses the palate, brief dull malt aftertaste.

CERVOISE ALE — pale gold, good malt aroma, bright malt flavor that fades across the palate, short dull malt aftertaste.

LABATT'S CRYSTAL LAGER BEER — gold, malt and hop nose, high carbonation, complex malt and hop flavor, long dry hop aftertaste, a pleasant, very drinkable beer.

LABATT'S DRY LIGHT BEER — pale yellow, faint malt nose, palate is faint malt and carbonation, very short dry malt aftertaste.

LABATT'S DRY — bright gold, light malt and hop aroma, smooth, light bodied, well balanced, very faint brief malt aftertaste.

LABATT'S IPA — gold, malt nose, big off-dry malt flavor, high carbonation but it is needed to balance the malt, dry malt finish and short aftertaste, better than average malty brew.

LABATT'S VELVET CREAM PORTER — brown, light malt nose, light malt flavor is off-dry up front, medium body, dry malt finish, long dry malt aftertaste, very drinkable.

JOHN LABATT'S EXTRA STOCK MALT LIQUOR — deep bright gold, fragrant complex malt and hop aroma, big body, huge complex malt flavor, excellent hop balance, dry malt finish and long aftertaste, a big beautiful brew!

LABATT'S EXTRA STOCK MALT LIQUOR — gold, straightforward malt flavor, good body, hefty malt flavor, finish and aftertaste like the flavor. I thought this would be the same as above exported to the U.S., but it doesn't have the heft or the complexity.

KOOTENAY PALE ALE — medium to deep gold, lovely zesty hop nose, clean and bright at the start, flattens out at the finish, and has a slightly dull malt aftertaste, still a pleasant beer.

KOKANEE PILSENER BEER — medium gold, light hop nose, pleasant and smooth malt and hop flavor, dry malt aftertaste, pleasant but a bit light.

JOCKEY CLUB BEER — deep gold, pleasant malt-hop aroma, tasty malt and hop flavor, long dry hop aftertaste.

BLUE STAR — tawny gold, hop nose, flavor briefly is malt, quickly turns hop bitter, bitter finish, and long dry bitter hop aftertaste, very good of type.

GUINNESS EXTRA STOUT — opaque brown, roasted malt nose, heavy body, complex coffee-malt flavor, long dry malt aftertaste retains much of the richness of the flavor.

LABATT BLUE LIGHT — pale gold, malt nose, light nondescript malt flavor, light body, little aftertaste.

JOHN LABATT CLASSIC BEER — bright deep gold color, off-dry hop nose, big dry malt and bitter hop flavor, dry hop finish and aftertaste, medium length.

JOHN LABATT'S CLASSIC LIGHT — bright gold, light hop nose, dull malt and hop flavor, mostly carbonation, brief malt-hop aftertaste.

OLAND EXPORT ALE — pale gold, pleasant malt aroma, good clean taste, medium to light body, good balance, a little hop zest at the finish, dry clean hop aftertaste. Oland Breweries, Halifax, Nova Scotia, is the originating brewery and brewery of record.

OLAND'S OLD SCOTIA ALE — bright gold, light tangy ale nose with good hops, big ale flavor with plenty of hops and slightly off-dry malt, good body, sags a little at the middle to finish, but rebounds well in the long hop aftertaste, good brew.

OLAND'S LIGHT BEER — bright gold, nice hop nose, fairly complex lightly hopped flavor, light body, hop and faintly sour malt aftertaste.

OLAND'S SCHOONER BEER — pale bright gold, good fresh malt and hop aroma, high carbonation, balanced malt and hop flavor, lovely malt finish, lingering dry hop aftertaste.

OLAND EXTRA STOUT — dark brown, light molasses aroma, light body, medium sweet malt flavor, likeable although light.

ALEXANDER KEITH'S INDIA PALE ALE — tawny-gold, fine malt aroma with good hop character, pleasant malt flavor that finishes with good hops, long dry hop aftertaste, good balance, and very drinkable. Oland Breweries, Ltd.

ALEXANDER KEITH'S LIGHT BEER — light tawny-gold, pleasant malt-hop aroma and flavor, light body, quick hop finish, light short dry hop aftertaste.

BUDWEISER LAGER BEER — pale gold, light malt and hop aroma, good balanced hop and malt flavor, very good body, good balance, dry hop finish, long dry hop aftertaste. A good Budweiser indeed, and one with 5% alcohol, which you don't find in the U.S.

BUD LIGHT — pale gold, pleasant light malt aroma, very light malt flavor, faint off-dry malt aftertaste with little length.

Notes:

The Master's Brasserie & Brew-pub

Brew-pub and restaurant in **Ottawa, Ontario**

MASTER'S LAGER — amber, bright malt and hop nose, dry hop flavor, finish, and aftertaste, balanced and bright.

MASTER'S ALE — amber, malt and hop nose, well-hopped flavor, dry hop finish and aftertaste, good length, similar to the MASTER'S LAGER but more complex.

McAusland Brewing Inc.

Brewery in **Montreal, Quebec**

ST. AMBROISE PALE ALE — amber, zesty ale nose with plenty of hops, strong hop flavor well backed with malt, smooth, balanced, long, and very drinkable.

Molson Breweries of Canada, Ltd.

Breweries in St. John's, Newfoundland; Montreal, Quebec; Toronto and Barrie, Ontario; Edmonton and Calgary, Alberta; Winnipeg, Manitoba; Regina, Saskatchewan; and Vancouver, British Columbia. Molson recently merged with Carling O'Keefe, one of the two other large national Canadian brewers.

MOLSON CANADIAN LAGER BEER — pale gold, off-dry malt aroma with hops in back, good malt flavor well balanced with hops, good long dry malt and hop aftertaste, very smooth drinkable brew.

MOLSON CANADIAN LIGHT — gold, slightly skunk hop nose, hop flavor, high carbonation, dull malt finish and aftertaste.

MOLSON EXPORT ALE — brilliant tawny-gold, clean malt and distinctive hop nose, good flavor with balanced hops and malt, a bright beer with good body, and a long and pleasant malt-hop aftertaste.

MOLSON GOLDEN — pale gold, light malt and hop aroma, light body, light off-dry malt flavor, hops way in back, light malt and hop finish, medium dry hop aftertaste with little length.

OLD STYLE PILSNER BEER — bright gold, aromatic hop and malt nose, highly carbonated, big well-balanced hop and malt flavor, finishes well and the aftertaste is pleasant and long.

MOLSON STOCK ALE — gold, off-dry malt nose, good malt and hop flavor, smooth, balanced, long dry hop aftertaste.

INDIA BEER — bright yellow-gold, off-dry malt aroma with a good hop backing, pleasant mild hop flavor, very good balance, dry malt finish, long dry hop aftertaste.

LAURENTIDE ALE — pale gold, fresh beery malt and hop nose, refreshing fruity malt flavor, medium dry malt finish, hop aftertaste that works at going dry as it goes.

MOLSON LIGHT — pale gold, pleasant well-hopped malt aroma, light body, faint malt flavor, light hop finish, short hop aftertaste.

MOLSON PORTER — deep copper-brown, lovely roasted malt nose, roasted malt flavor, just enough hops to balance and retain the porter character, smooth, slightly dry hop aftertaste with good length.

MOLSON BRADOR MALT LIQUOR — bright gold, light off-dry malt aroma, heavy body, noticeable alcohol, pleasant sweet malt flavor, medium dry hop finish, dry hop aftertaste, nicely made beer, very good of type.

MOLSON SPECIALE — bright gold, pleasant malt and hop nose, light malt flavor, light body, slight hop finish drops off quickly, short dry hop aftertaste.

MOLSON EXPORT LIGHT — medium gold, good malt and hop aroma, good malt flavor up front, hops come in nicely in the middle and finish, short dry hop aftertaste.

MOLSON LITE — pale gold, slightly vegetal malt nose, light malt and hop flavor, light body, short slight hop aftertaste.

MOLSON DIAMOND LAGER BEER — bright pale gold, austere malt nose, highly carbonated, bright well-hopped flavor, malt and hop finish, dull malt aftertaste.

MOLSON SPECIAL DRY — pale yellow-gold, hop nose, some noticeable alcohol, dry hop flavor, medium body, medium-length dry hop aftertaste.

MOLSON DRY — pale gold, touch of skunk in a hop nose, good hop and malt flavor, good body, long dry hop aftertaste.

LOWENBRAU SPECIAL BEER — pale gold, light hop and malt aroma, mild hop and off-dry malt palate, more malty in the front, more dry hops in the middle and finish, pleasant long dry hop aftertaste.

MOLSON EXEL — pale gold, grainy nose reminds you of Grape-Nuts, grainy grapefruit flavor, dry hop finish, short dry aftertaste.

MOLSON CLUB ALE — bright gold, fruity malt aroma with off tones in back (like a sweaty sock), hop flavor is a bit sour, dry hop aftertaste.

BENNETT'S DOMINION ALE — bright gold, hop aroma and flavor, finishes a bit sour, very long bitter hop aftertaste.

CARLING BLACK LABEL BEER — medium gold, tangy hop and malt aroma, good dry hop flavor, pleasant dry hop aftertaste.

BLACK HORSE BEER PREMIUM STOCK — yellow-gold, hop nose, big bitter hop flavor, full bodied, good complex aftertaste that is on the bitter side.

MAGNUM ALE — deep gold, hop aroma with good malt background, malt and hops both vie for the lead on the palate, hop finish and aftertaste.

RALLYE ALE — gold, malt aroma and flavor, light body, light malt finish, little aftertaste.

O'KEEFE'S OLD VIENNA LAGER BEER — gold, malt and hop aroma and flavor, medium dry hop finish, dry hop aftertaste.

CALGARY AMBER LAGER BEER — amber, light toasted malt nose and taste, good balance, good body, smooth, dry malt finish, malt aftertaste has medium duration.

CINCI LAGER BEER — gold, appetizing well-hopped malt aroma, dry balanced malt and hop flavor, dry hop finish and aftertaste, good length.

CINCI CREAM LAGER BEER — pale bright gold, beautiful beery nose with plenty of hops and malt, off-dry pleasant malt flavor, light body, short dry hop finish and aftertaste, pleasant tasty brew.

DOW CREAM PORTER — deep red brown, creamy, very faint malt aroma, slightly sweet malt flavor, but still pleasant, fair balance, smooth, dry light malt finish and aftertaste, tasty and drinkable.

TRILIGHT EXTRA LIGHT BEER — pale gold, very faint flowery hop nose, light very dry hop and malt flavor, very light body, very short dull aftertaste.

COLT .45 BEER — medium bright gold, light malt aroma with faint hops, creamy inoffensive malt flavor, light grainy finish and short aftertaste.

CHAMPLAIN PORTER — deep red brown, faintly smoky and roasted malt aroma, overall malt is off-dry, perhaps a little too sweet, but still quite smooth and mellow, sweet finish and aftertaste.

O'KEEFE'S EXTRA OLD STOCK MALT LIQUOR — brilliant deep gold, beautiful clean sweet malt aroma, good off-dry hop and malt flavor, excellent balance, very long pleasant malt aftertaste.

O'KEEFE ALE — gold, clean malt and bright hop nose, good balanced malt-hop flavor, pleasant hop finish and lingering aftertaste. Version shipped to the U.S. is called CANADIAN O'KEEFE ALE and is identical to the domestic Canadian product.

O'KEEFE LIGHT — pale gold, light malt nose, light off-dry malt flavor, dry malt and hop aftertaste, medium length.

O'KEEFE GOLDEN LIGHT CANADIAN BEER — medium yellow, sour malt aroma with some hops, complex flavor is sour malt in front and dry hops in the middle and finish, short dry hop aftertaste.

MONTREAL EXPORT — deep gold, hop nose, off-dry front palate, dry hop middle and finish, dry hop aftertaste, medium length. Contract brew for Montreal Brewery, Inc.

TOBY ALE — amber-orange color, off-dry hoppy malt aroma, front palate is balanced hops and malt, flattens out a bit in the middle, finishes bitter hops and malt, balance is off.

BROWN'S ORIGINAL CANADIAN BEER — gold, faint apple-malt nose, dull malt and hop flavor, little aftertaste. Contract brew using Yukon B.C. corporate name, made for F&A Importers, Louisville, KY.

F&A IMPORTED CANADIAN BEER — bright gold, big head, pleasant malt-hop nose and flavor, good balance, short dry hop aftertaste. Contract brew for F&A Importers, Ltd., Louisville, KY.

HEIDELBERG FINE QUALITY BEER — medium gold, faint hop nose, light body, light malt flavor, faint malt finish, dry aftertaste.

CANADIAN RED CAP CREAM ALE — deep yellow-gold, light hop nose with a fruity-malt background, off-dry and sharp ale-like flavor, plenty of malt and hops, dry hop finish, long dry hop aftertaste.

CARLSBERG BEER — bright pale gold, off-dry malt nose, balanced hops and malt flavor, dry hop and sour malt aftertaste, medium length.

CARLSBERG LIGHT BEER — tawny gold, light hop and malt aroma, carbonation dominates the flavor, which is faint off-dry malt and hops, aftertaste like the flavor, medium length.

MILLER HIGH LIFE — pale yellow gold, pleasant fragrant hop nose, dull malt and hop palate, pleasant dry hop finish, fairly dry hop aftertaste with good duration.

COORS LIGHT — pale gold, fresh beery nose, light off-dry malt flavor, very light hop finish, brief hop aftertaste.

MILLER LITE — pale gold, malt and faint hop nose, very light body, faint malt and hop finish, no aftertaste.

COORS BEER — very pale gold, light malt and hop nose, pleasant flavor is mostly off-dry malt, pleasant fairly long aftertaste shows both malt and hops.

FOSTER'S LAGER — deep gold, light off-dry malt nose, off-dry malt and hop palate, good body, dry hop finish, dry hop aftertaste fades quickly.

DUFFY'S ALE — amber, smooth malt and hop nose and taste, very good balance, long dry malt aftertaste.

Notes:

Moosehead Breweries, Ltd.

Brewery in St. John, New Brunswick

MOOSEHEAD CANADIAN LAGER BEER — pale gold, very good malt and hop nose, balanced slightly off-dry malt and hop flavor, smooth, very pleasant and quite drinkable, long malt aftertaste.

MOOSEHEAD LIGHT — pale gold, light malt nose, light off-dry malt flavor at first, then dry at the finish, brief malt aftertaste, on the dull side.

MOOSEHEAD PALE ALE — pale gold, light off-dry aroma shows malt, yeast, and hops, off-dry malt and well-hopped flavor, dry hop-malt finish, medium dry hop-malt aftertaste.

MOOSEHEAD PREMIUM DRY — bright gold, light malt nose, zesty dry hop flavor, good body, excellent balance, crisp and refreshing, medium length dry hop aftertaste.

TEN-PENNY ALE — pale amber, light hop aroma and flavor, dry hop finish and aftertaste, a decent little Canadian ale.

MOOSEHEAD EXPORT ALE — pale amber-gold, off-dry malt and bitter hop nose, flavor like the nose, great complexity, good hop finish, long hop aftertaste, one of Moosehead's better efforts.

ALPINE LAGER BEER — pale gold, malt aroma and taste with hops in back, pleasant tasting and very drinkable, light body, light malt finish and aftertaste, the carbonation is high and the hops stay in back.

ALPINE LITE BEER — pale yellow-gold, malt and hop aroma, pleasant light malt and hop flavor, finely carbonated, medium long light malt and hop aftertaste.

MOOSEHEAD'S GOLDEN LIGHT BEER — pale gold, lovely fragrant hop nose, pleasant malt flavor, light body, medium long malt aftertaste, well made and good for a low-calorie beer.

MOOSEHEAD LONDON STOUT — very deep brown, almost opaque, molasses and malt flavor, quite sweet, very long aftertaste like the flavor, definitely a dessert beer.

JAMES READY ORIGINAL LAGER BEER — bright gold, light aromatic off-dry clover, hop, and grain nose, light hop and malt flavor, faint malt finish, light body, short malt aftertaste.

Notes:

Niagara Falls Brewing Co., Ltd.

Brewery in Niagara Falls, Ontario

GRITSTONE PREMIUM ALE — deep amber, faint sour malt nose, ephemeral malt flavor, long dry malt aftertaste, there are hops but is not a good balance between those hops and the malt.

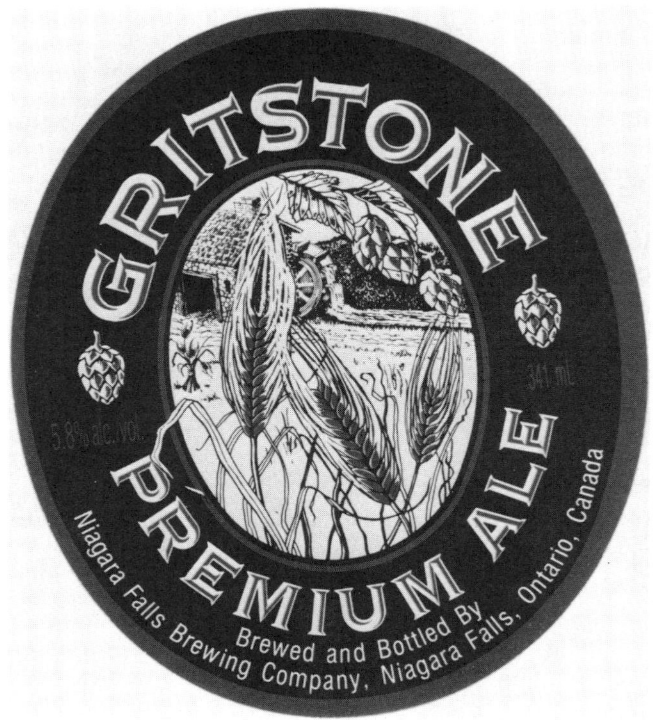

Northern Breweries Ltd.

Breweries in Sudbury, Sault Ste. Marie, Timmins, and Thunder Bay, Ontario

NORTHERN LIGHT BEER — gold, faint sour hop nose, hop flavor, light body, faint malt finish, short dry hop aftertaste.

NORTHERN ALE — bright yellow, light hop nose, sour hop flavor, medium body, light malt finish and aftertaste.

NORTHERN SUPERIOR LAGER BEER — hazy gold, light hop nose, high carbonation, light body, flavor has light hops and malt but is mostly carbonation, brief aftertaste with little or no flavors.

NORTHERN EXTRA LIGHT BEER — pale gold, very faint malt aroma, light malt flavor, brief malt aftertaste, light flavored and light bodied.

EDELBRAU BEER — hazy gold, light hop nose, high carbonation, very light malt and hop flavor, brief malt aftertaste.

Okanagan Spring Brewery Ltd.

Brewery in Vernon, British Columbia

SPRING PREMIUM LAGER — gold, malt nose, dry malt flavor, dry slightly buttery malt aftertaste.

OKANAGAN SPRING OLD MUNICH WHEAT BEER — cloudy brown, like old-time cider, dry malt aroma with a brown sugar background, off-dry roasted malt flavor with a tart finish, roasted malt aftertaste.

OLD ENGLISH PORTER STYLE MALT LIQUOR — deep ruby brown, huge malt Ovaltine nose, big funky malt flavor, sort of earthy, big body, dry malt finish, short dry malt aftertaste.

SPRING EXTRA SPECIAL PALE ALE — hazy golden amber, malty Postum/Ovaltine nose, medium body, dry malt flavor offers little of interest, brief malt aftertaste, fine while it is in your mouth, but there is no real character.

Old Heidelberg House

Old Heidelberg Brewery and Restaurant in Heidelberg, Ontario

It is a malt extract brewery.

HEIDELBERG O-B BREW — amber, dry malt and hop nose, very dry hop flavor, light body, dry short bitter hop aftertaste.

Pacific Western Brewing Co., Ltd.

Brewery in Prince George, British Columbia. Some early labels also include a Vancouver origin. Zélé beers carry corporate identifier of Zélé Brewing Co., Prince George, BC.

YUKON CANADIAN CREAM ALE — pale gold, hop nose, off-dry malt and hop flavor, off-dry malt finish and aftertaste, a bit dull overall.

PACIFIC REAL DRAFT — gold, fruity malt nose, fruity malt and carbonation palate, medium body, off-dry malt finish and short aftertaste.

BULLDOG CANADIAN LAGER BEER — tawny-gold, pleasant malt aroma, good hop flavor, light body, well balanced, dry hop finish, virtually no aftertaste.

IRON HORSE MALT LIQUOR — bright gold, good malt and hop aroma, off-dry malt flavor, good balance, pleasant and long malt aftertaste.

YUKON GOLD PREMIUM PILSNER — yellow, appetizing hop nose, off-dry malt and hop flavor, good balance, very tasty, long aftertaste like the flavor.

ROYAL CANADIAN PREMIUM BEER — tawny-gold, big malt and hop aroma, bright hop flavor, dry hop finish, medium body, long off-dry malt and hop aftertaste.

ZÉLÉ DRY LIGHT BEER — pale gold, persistent skunky nose; that the flavor is pleasant malt with a subtle hop background comes as a surprise; light body, short malt aftertaste.

ZÉLÉ DRY BEER — bright gold, pleasant malt aroma is not really dry, but the malt flavor goes dry quite suddenly, ending up very dry in the finish and aftertaste.

Sleeman Brewing & Malting Co., Ltd.

Silver Creek Brewery in Guelph, Ontario

TORONTO LIGHT — pale yellow-gold, fruity soda pop nose, light body, low carbonation, soft and flabby, light dry slightly sour hop flavor, dull hop finish and aftertaste.

SLEEMAN SILVER CREEK LAGER — hazy gold, off-dry malt nose, fruity-malt front palate, balanced middle, hop finish, medium dry hop aftertaste.

SLEEMAN CREAM ALE — tawny-gold, off-dry malt aroma, zesty hop flavor, fruity malt and citrus backing, fruity malt finish, long malt aftertaste.

STROH'S FIRE BREWED BEER — pale gold, light fruity malt aroma, malt flavor, very little hops, malt finish, brief malt aftertaste.

Notes:

Thornbury Brewing Co.

Brewery in Thornbury, Ontario

BEAVER VALLEY AMBER — amber, malt aroma with a sour background, very light flavor like the nose, dull off-dry malt finish and aftertaste.

Notes:

Upper Canada Brewing Co., Ltd.

Brewery in Toronto, Ontario

UPPER CANADA ALE — amber, complex hop aroma with smoky slightly off-dry malt in back, flavor is like the aroma, smoky hop finish, off-dry malt aftertaste, doesn't quite come together.

UPPER CANADA DARK ALE — deep amber, complex aromatic hop and malt aroma with a trace of lactic acid in back, flavor is much like the aroma except the acid is more noticeable, big hop finish and aftertaste has plenty of malt in back, but the effect is harmed by the acidity.

UPPER CANADA TRUE LIGHT — bright gold, light malt nose, very light malt flavor, weak body, very dry brief malt aftertaste.

UPPER CANADA LAGER — bright gold, faint malt and hop aroma, dry hop flavor is too bitter for the amount of malt, bitter finish and aftertaste, poorly balanced.

UPPER CANADA REBELLION MALT LIQUOR — bright deep gold, nice malt aroma, big fresh malt flavor, big body, hop finish, very long hop aftertaste, balanced, excellent-tasting brew.

UPPER CANADA NATURAL LIGHT LAGER — deep gold, fruity hop nose, sour hop flavor, light body, minty finish, short hop aftertaste.

UPPER CANADA WHEAT BEER — tawny-gold, very nice complex but faint malt aroma, tangy sour malt flavor, light body, refreshing dry wheat finish, medium to short dry wheat and malt aftertaste.

PUBLICAN'S SPECIAL BITTER ALE — amber, malt nose, hop flavor, short dry hop aftertaste, questionable balance.

Wellington County Brewery Ltd.

Brewery in Guelph, Ontario

WELLINGTON SPECIAL PALE ALE — amber, nice toasted malt aroma, zesty toasted malt and hop flavor, good body, excellent balance, pleasant, but only a brief aftertaste with a little smokiness.

WELLINGTON ARKELL BEST BITTER — pale amber, toasted malt aroma, good toasted malt start, fades out at the finish, little aftertaste.

WELLINGTON IRON DUKE — deep amber, faint malt nose, big malt flavor, balanced, plenty of hops in back and in the finish, long malt and hop aftertaste.

WELLINGTON COUNTY LAGER BEER — tawny-gold, pleasant off-dry malt and hop aroma, off-dry malt palate up front, dry malt and hop middle, dry hop finish, good balance, dry hop aftertaste.

WELLINGTON COUNTY ORIGINAL ALE — copper-amber, pleasant off-dry malt nose, dry malt flavor, dry hop finish, long dry hop aftertaste, a very flavorful brew.

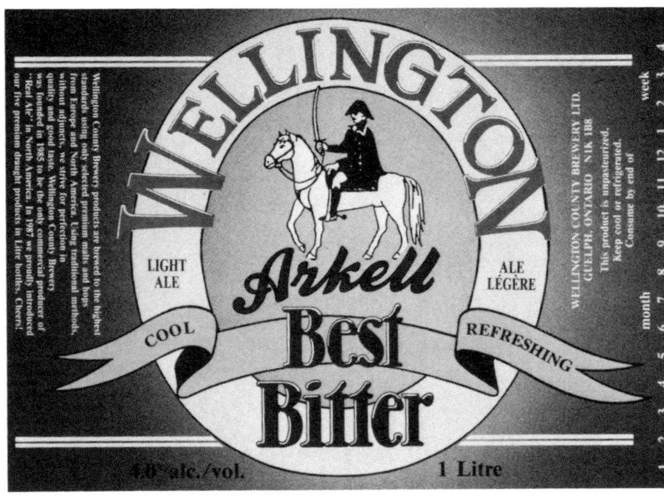

Notes:

York Brewing Co.

Brewery in Brampton, Ontario

I have heard that York B.C. has recently ceased operations.

YORK PILSNER LAGER BEER — gold malty-Ovaltine nose, big malt flavor, hops at finish, long dry hop and malt aftertaste.

Notes:

MEXICO

Cerveceria Cruz Blanca, S.A.

Brewery in **Ciudad Juarez**

CRUZ BLANCA CERVEZA FINA — pale gold, pleasant malt aroma with a touch of hops, bitter hops greet the palate, softening slightly and changing to malt by the finish, somewhat dull dry malt and hop aftertaste.

CHIHUAHUA MEXICAN BEER — pale gold, hop nose, light hop flavor, short dry hop aftertaste.

CERVEZA HOMBRE — gold, slightly sweet fresh clean malt nose, light malt flavor, almost no aftertaste.

NUDE BEER — pale gold, sweet grapey and grainy aroma, highly carbonated, malt flavor is sort of sweet in front, dull in the middle, and dry in the aftertaste, more of a label novelty than a quality beer.

SIMPATICO BEER — pale gold, sour hop aroma, little flavor on the front of the palate, sour hop finish and aftertaste, weak and dull. There is also a Simpatico beer made in Germany and several versions made in the U.S.

Cerveceria Cuauhtemoc, S.A.

Breweries in **Monterrey, Toluca, Guadalajara, Tecate, Mexico City, Nogales, Culican,** and **Ciudad Juarez**

BOHEMIA ALE — pale gold, off-dry malt aroma, fresh malt flavor, dry malt and hop finish and aftertaste, good body, has complexity, length, and interest, very pleasant and refreshing.

TECATE CERVEZA — pale gold, very nice malt and hop aroma, very light and pleasant malt and hop flavor, light body, good balance, light aftertaste is a continuation of the flavor, very nice but just too light.

CERVEZA CARTA BLANCA — pale gold, malt aroma and light malt flavor, medium body, very light dry hop aftertaste, good hot-weather quaffing beer.

CARTA BLANCA DARK SPECIAL — bright rosy-amber, sour hop nose, malt starts out the flavor but only briefly, little mid-palate and finish, light malt aftertaste.

INDIO CERVEZA OSCURA — copper color, very faint caramel malt nose, full faintly sweet malt flavor, off-dry malt aftertaste, no complexity.

BRISA CERVEZA LIGERA — very pale gold, faint sour malt aroma, weak body, very faint malt flavor, no aftertaste.

NAVIDAD CERVEZA COMMERATIVA — red-brown color, very faint dull malt aroma, mealy flavor with a tart-sweet background, weak body, off-dry malt aftertaste. A Christmas beer not seen recently.

Cerveceria Moctezuma, S.A.

Breweries in **Orizaba, Guadalajara, Mexico City, Monterrey**

SUPERIOR LIGHT BEER — pale gold, light malt aroma, light body, light malt flavor has only a trace of hops, fairly long dry malt aftertaste.

DOS EQUIS XX AMBER BEER — deep mahogany, clean off-dry malt nose, big malty-molasses flavor with a fine hop finish, stays reasonably dry throughout, medium body, good balance, long dry malt aftertaste.

DOS EQUIS XX LIGHT BEER — bright gold, faint malt aroma and flavor, clean malt finish, long dry malt aftertaste.

DOS EQUIS SPECIAL LAGER — bright gold, high carbonation, flowery malt aroma, off-dry malt palate, finishes sour malt, dry malt aftertaste.

SOL ESPECIAL — bright gold, perfumy hop nose, light body, dry hop flavor, pleasant dry hop and malt aftertaste.

TRES EQUIS XXX LIGHT BEER — very pale color, almost colorless, light malt aroma, very mild malt flavor and aftertaste.

TRES EQUIS XXX CERVEZA OSCURA — deep copper color, slightly sour malt nose, hop flavor with some herbal character, dry hop aftertaste still has the herbal nature.

NOCHE BUENA CERVEZA ESPECIAL — brilliant pretty red-brown color, soft malt nose with light background hops, big hop flavor up front, roasted malt finish, good balance, long dry malt aftertaste, good flavorful Christmas beer.

HUSSONG'S CERVEZA CLARA — bright pale gold, light hop nose, light grainy malt flavor, thin body, watery and weak, doesn't develop much and fades quickly.

Cerveceria Modelo, S.A.

Breweries in Mexico City, Torreon, Guadalajara, Ciudad Obregon, and Mazatlan

MODELO ESPECIAL — tawny-gold, malt aroma, faint malt flavor that gains in strength at the finish, fairly long dry malt aftertaste.

HATUEY BEER — tawny-gold, candy malt aroma, sweet malt flavor at first, dull middle, faint hop finish behind the malt, short dry malt and hop aftertaste. Label says Modelo Brewing Co., Auburndale, FL, bottled under authority and supervision of Bacardi & Co., Nassau, Bahamas.

CORONA EXTRA — bright gold, pleasant malt and hop nose, bright hop flavor, light body, dry hop finish and aftertaste, little strength and little length.

CORONA LIGHT — bright gold, light pleasant fruity-honey-malt nose, light dry hop flavor, light body, short sour hop aftertaste.

NEGRA MODELO DARK BEER — medium brown, malt aroma, dry malt flavor, dry malt finish and aftertaste, good balance, good length.

Notes:

Cerveceria del Pacifico, S.A.

Brewery at Mazatlan

CERVEZA PACIFICO CLARA — brilliant pale gold, complex and interesting off-dry flowery hop aroma, very dry hop and malt flavor, short dry aftertaste.

Cerveceria Yucateca, S.A.

Brewery in Merida

MONTEJO PREMIUM BEER — yellow-gold, clean malt aroma with a light hop background, slightly soapy hop flavor, dry sort of salty finish, short sour hop and malt aftertaste.

MONTEJO DARK BEER — deep copper, creamy, faint malt nose and taste, light body, short malt aftertaste.

ARGENTINA

Cerveceria Bieckert, S.A.

Breweries in **Buenos Aires, Rio Segundo** and **Cochobamba**

BIECKERT ETIQUETA AZUL PILSEN ESPECIAL CERVEZA BLANCA GENUINA — yellow-gold with a greenish cast, fruity-malt aroma that is almost wine-like, heavy body, complex sour malt flavor with a touch of anise in back, long malt aftertaste, an interesting brew.

BIECKERT ESPECIAL LIVIANA — deep amber, toasted malt and prune aroma, scorched malt flavor that finishes a bit sour, long malt aftertaste, unusual brew, very interesting.

LEON de ORO CERVEZA GENUINA — deep gold, delicate malt and hop aroma, pleasant flavor like the nose only much bigger, lots of hops across the palate, good malt finish, complex, good bodied, long dry malt and hop after-taste, a well-made, well-balanced, likeable brew.

BIECKERT PREMIUM IMPORTED BEER — pale gold, sweet malt and cardboard nose, fruity malt flavor with a papery background, faint sweet malt aftertaste.

Cerveceria Cordoba, S.A.

Brewery in **Cordoba**

CORDOBA DORADA — brilliant pale gold, clean fruity malt nose, zesty hop and fruity malt palate with some melon and papaya, flattens out at the finish leading into a brief dull malt aftertaste.

Cerveceria y Malteria Quilmes

Brewery in **Buenos Aires**

QUILMES EXPORT — very pale yellow, highly carbonated, so much so that it dominates the nose and taste, what isn't carbonation is like fresh-cut alfalfa, short dry aftertaste.

QUILMES IMPERIAL — pale yellow-gold, slightly papery malt nose, good body, pleasant light malt flavor, good balance, hops appear in the finish and stay through the long dry aftertaste.

Cerveceria Santa Fe, S.A.

Breweries in **Santa Fe** and **Buenos Aires**

SANTA FE PREMIUM LAGER BEER — tawny-gold, a touch of skunk started the nose, but this quickly yielded to green hay, the flavor was off-dry malt with a slightly oxidized finish, short dry malt aftertaste with tones of the oxidation.

BAHAMAS

Commonwealth Brewery, Ltd.

Brewery in **Nassau**

KALIK — pale gold, light hop aroma, light hop flavor, light hop finish and aftertaste.

Notes:

BARBADOS

Banks Barbados Breweries, Ltd.

Breweries in **Bridgetown, St. Michael** and **Wildey**

BANKS LAGER BEER — pale gold, delicate sweet malt nose, flavor like the nose fades across the palate, weak malt finish, short malt aftertaste.

EBONY SUPER STRENGTH — deep brown, strong caramel, molasses, and roasted malt aroma, strong alcoholic component to the roasted malt flavor giving it a port-like quality, long and strong off-dry roast malt aftertaste.

BELIZE

Belize Brewing Co.

Brewery in **Ladyville**

BELIKIN BEER — bright gold, large bubble carbonation, good malt aroma with light hops, dry malt flavor, straightforward without complexity, dry malt aftertaste with fair duration, pleasant.

BELIKIN STOUT — deep brown, sweet malt nose, sweet complex wine-like palate, heavy body, high alcohol, faintly bitter dry hop aftertaste.

BOLIVIA

Cerveceria Boliviana Nacional, S.A.

Brewery in **La Paz**

PACENA CENTENARIO BEER — slightly hazy gold, fruity malt nose, malt palate has a sour middle, sour-bitter finish, and a long dry hop aftertaste.

Cerveceria Taquiña, S.A.

Brewery in **Cochabamba** and **Santa Cruz**

TAQUINA EXPORT CERVEZA — pale yellow, pleasant off-dry malt aroma with good hop balance, flavor is pleasant off-dry malt up front, finish is slightly sour malt and hops, dry aftertaste similar to the flavor, very good when fresh.

Notes:

BRAZIL

Companhia Antarctica Paulista, S.A.

Brewery in Sao Paulo

ANTARCTICA BRAZILIAN BEER — gold, faint sour malt nose, high carbonation, sour hop flavor has a papery finish, long dry hop aftertaste.

Companhia Cervejaria Brahma

Breweries in Rio de Janeiro, Sao Paulo, Porto Alegro, et al.

BRAHMA CHOPP EXPORT BEER — yellow-gold with a green cast, vanilla malt cookie dough nose and taste, sour malt finish, dry malt aftertaste with little length.

BRAHMA BRAZILIAN PILSENER BEER — gold, fruity malt nose, malt flavor has some roasted malt backing that appears a little bit stronger in the finish and aftertaste, medium dry malt flavor throughout.

BRAHMA BEER — medium gold, pleasant malt and hop aroma, medium body, pleasant hop flavor has decent off-dry malt backing and a little apple is in there too, long dry hop aftertaste.

Cervejaria Cacador, S.A.

Brewery in Cacador

XINGU BLACK BEER — opaque brown, dry malt aroma is faintly coffee-like, clean off-sweet roasted malt palate, a trifle less sweet would be better, but not bad, long medium dry malt aftertaste, very drinkable.

Cervejaria Mogiana, Ltd.

Brewery in Mogi Mirim

INGLESINHA STOUT — opaque brown, foam is deep brown, very faint roasted malt nose, very sweet roasted malt flavor, soapy treacle finish and aftertaste, very sweet and lacks balance.

Cervejaria Paraense, S.A.

Breweries in Belem and Cerpasa

TIJUCA EXTRA PREMIUM BEER — brilliant gold, faint malt nose, good body, malt flavor has some licorice and fruit, dry malt finish, brief dry malt aftertaste, flavor is good but ephemeral.

Cervejarias Reunidas Skol Caracu, S.A.

Breweries in Rio Clara, Nova Lima, Guarulhos, Bonsucesso, et al.

SKOL LAGER BEER — yellow-gold, faintly sweet malt nose, clean grainy malt flavor, austere finish and very little aftertaste.

CARACU CERVEJA FORTE STOUT — opaque brown, roasted malt nose, low carbonation, sweet palate with roasted/smoky malt, big body, almost too sweet, long clean off-dry malt aftertaste.

CHILE

Compañia Cervecerias Unidas, S.A.

Brewery in Santiago

ESCUDO CHILEAN PILSENER — pale gold, fairly decent malt and hop nose, flavor like the nose except for a sour component, long very dry hop aftertaste.

CRISTAL PILSENER — gold, off-dry malt nose, palate is malt up front, hops in the middle, has a dry hop finish and a long dry hop aftertaste, good balance throughout.

ANDES CHILEAN PILSENER — gold, faintly skunky nose at first, then good hops, flavor has a touch of barley at first, then hops, malt returns in the aftertaste, pretty good except for that skunk.

COLOMBIA

Bavaria, S.A.

Breweries in Bogota and Santa Marta

CLUB COLOMBIA PILSENER-TYPE BEER — pale yellow-gold with a greenish cast, malty pineapple aroma, malt flavor is sweet in front, dries to middle and finishes bitter hops, dry very bitter hop aftertaste, balance is off.

CERVEZA CLAUSEN EXPORT — medium yellow-gold, interesting appetizing hop aroma, big hop flavor, good balance up to the finish which gets too bitter, long dry and bitter hop aftertaste.

COLOMBIAN GOLD BEER — gold, malt nose, sour malt palate with a slightly sweeter finish, very little aftertaste.

COSTA RICA

Cerveceria Costa Rica, S.A.

Brewery in San José

BAVARIA GOLD BEER — medium deep gold, faint off-dry fruity malt aroma with a cardboard background, light sour malt flavor, hop finish and aftertaste, not well balanced and some off flavors in back.

DOMINICAN REPUBLIC

Cerveceria Bohemia, S.A.

Brewery in Ciudad Trujillo

BOHEMIA CERVEZA — hazy pale amber-gold, light malt nose and flavor with some hops in back, cuts off quickly, brief aftertaste.

Cerveceria Nacional Dominicana, C.X.A.

Brewery in Santo Domingo

PRESIDENTE CERVEZA PILSENER TYPE BEER — bright gold, hop aroma, grainy flavor, dry malt and hop finish, short dry aftertaste, smooth but brief. Export version.

PRESIDENTE CERVEZA TIPO PILSENER — hazy gold, hop nose, dry malt flavor with hops coming in at the finish, good balance, dry malt aftertaste has a bit of oxidation.

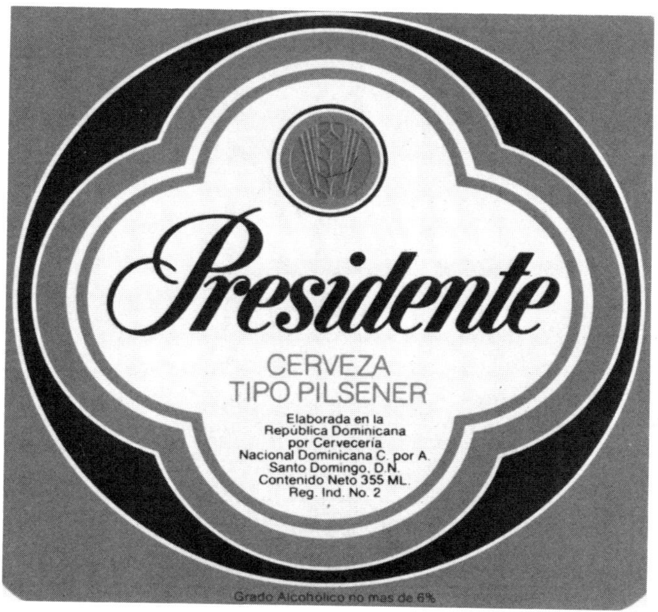

Cerveceria Vegana, S.A.

Brewery in Ciudad Trujillo

CERVEZA QUISQUEYA — bright gold, off-dry buttery nose, off-dry fruity-malt palate, high carbonation tends to balance the sweetness, buttery finish and aftertaste. Export version.

CERVEZA QUISQUEYA TIPO PILSENER — hazy gold, pleasant malt aroma, good-tasting malt flavor with good hop support, creamy, balanced, long dry malt and hop aftertaste. Domestic version.

Notes:

ECUADOR

Cerveceria Club, S.A.

Brewery in Quito

CERVEZA CLUB PREMIUM — pale tawny-gold, mushroom nose, palate is hops first, then sweet malt in the middle, and sour hops at the finish and aftertaste, poorly balanced.

EL SALVADOR

Cerveceria la Constancia, S.A.

Brewery in San Salvador

PILSENER OF EL SALVADOR EXPORT BEER — pale tawny-gold, light off-dry hop aroma, light body, off-dry straightforward malt and hop flavor, dry hop finish and aftertaste, not much length, but pleasant and refreshing.

GUATEMALA

Cerveceria Centroamericana, S.A.

Brewery in Guatemala City

MONTE CARLO LAGER BEER — pale yellow, slightly skunky hop nose, bright hop flavor, nice hop finish, light body, short dry hop aftertaste, refreshing but very short.

MEDALLA DE ORO — pale gold, skunky hop nose, high carbonation, big hop flavor, dull malt finish and aftertaste.

MOZA BOCK BEER — amber, faint fruity nose, light off-dry malt palate, faint hops way in the back, long off-dry malt aftertaste.

FAMOSA IMPORTED LAGER BEER — gold, nose is more malt than hops but there is plenty of both, dry hop flavor, very dry hop aftertaste, medium length.

CABRO EXTRA — pale gold, light malt and hop nose, gassy, medium body, flavor almost completely masked by the carbonation until the finish which is hops and malt, medium long dry malt and hop aftertaste, probably pretty good if there were less carbonation. Cerveceria Nacional, S.A., Guatemala City.

GUYANA

Banks DIH, Ltd.

Brewery in Georgetown

BANKS BEER — bright gold, fruity malt nose with a touch of oxidation, faint fruity malt flavor has a butterscotch background, weak body, very brief dry malt aftertaste.

HONDURAS

Cerveceria Hondureña, S.A.

Brewery in San Pedro Sala

PORT ROYAL EXPORT — medium gold, faintly skunky hop nose, elusive malt and hop palate that is slightly fruity at the finish, high carbonation, light body, soapy aftertaste.

JAMAICA

Desnoes & Geddes, Ltd.

Brewery in Kingston

RED STRIPE LAGER BEER — pale tawny-gold, good bright hop and malt nose, full-flavored dry malt and hop palate, hops dominate, pleasant and very drinkable, long dry hop aftertaste.

DRAGON STOUT — opaque, brown head, faintly sweet malt nose, medium body, lightly sweet malt and dry coffee palate, long dry malt aftertaste.

DRAGON
STOUT
12 fl. ozs.
355 ml.
Brewed & Bottled by
DESNOES & GEDDES LTD. KINGSTON, JAMAICA W.I.
GOVERNMENT WARNING: (1) According to the Surgeon General, women should not drink alcoholic beverages during pregnancy because of the risk of birth defects. (2) Consumption of alcoholic beverages impairs your ability to drive a car or operate machinery, and may cause health problems.

PANAMA

Cerveceria del Baru, S.A.

Brewery in David and Chiriqui

CERVEZA CRISTAL — pale gold, fruity off-dry malt nose with some cardboard in back, light body, cardboard reflects into the flavor, fairly long neutral malt aftertaste.

CERVEZA PANAMA LAGER ALEMANIA STYLE — bright gold, light malt nose, slightly sweet malt flavor, medium-length dry malt aftertaste, lightly done but pleasant and refreshing.

PERU

Cerveceria Backus y Johnston, S.A.

Brewery in Lima

CRISTAL — pale gold, faint malt nose and flavor, clean, but weak and short.

CERVEZA MALTINA — deep brown, sweet smoky malt nose, sweet slightly smoked malt flavor, big long dry malt aftertaste.

Compañia Nacional de Cerveza, S.A.

Brewery in Callao

CALLAO PERUVIAN PILSEN BEER — pale yellow-gold, off-dry malt nose, good tasting hop flavor, well-balanced, has complexity and zest, very drinkable, long dry hop aftertaste.

CALLAO EXPORT DARK BEER — opaque brown, faint burnt toast and caramel nose, unusual chocolate-smoky-BBQ sauce flavor, heavy body, neither dry nor sweet, sort of in-between, complex and interesting, long dry malt aftertaste, flavors are sort of compartmented and don't come together, needs food to be at its best.

DURANGO IMPORTED BEER — pale yellow, slightly skunky hop nose, hop flavor, dry and sour hop aftertaste with considerable length.

BREWED & BOTTLED BY CIA. NACIONAL DE CERVEZA S.A. AV. SAENZ PEÑA Nº 471 CALLAO PERU
Since 1863
CERVEZA
Pilsen
CALLAO
¡Calidad!
12 FL. OZ.
PERUVIAN LAGER BEER
GOVERNMENT WARNING: (1) ACCORDING TO THE SURGEON GENERAL, WOMEN SHOULD NOT DRINK ALCOHOLIC BEVERAGES DURING PREGNANCY BECAUSE OF THE RISK OF BIRTH DEFECTS. (2) CONSUMPTION OF ALCOHOLIC BEVERAGES IMPAIRS YOUR ABILITY TO DRIVE A CAR OR OPERATE MACHINERY, AND MAY CAUSE HEALTH PROBLEMS.

Companhia Cerveceria del sur del Peru, S.A.

Brewery in Cuzco

CUZCO PREMIUM PERUVIAN BEER — brilliant gold, clean malt aroma, highly carbonated, bright zesty flavor, light body, clean and refreshing, long dry hop aftertaste.

PUERTO RICO

Brew Master's Corp.

Brewery in San Juan

BREW MASTER'S LAGER BEER — medium deep gold, off-dry malt aroma, off-dry fruity malt and cardboard flavor, dry malt finish and aftertaste.

Cerveceria Corona, Inc.

Breweries in San Juan and Santurce

CORONA BEER — pale golden yellow, good hop nose, malt flavor is mostly carbonation, light dry malt aftertaste. Export version.

CORONA CERVEZA — pale gold, hop nose, light body, light dry malt flavor, light dry malt aftertaste.

MEDALLA LIGHT CERVEZA — gold, light off-dry malt aroma, high carbonation, light dry malt flavor, light body, short faint dry malt aftertaste. Packed for Medalla Co., San Juan.

Cerveceria India, Inc.

Brewery in Mayaguez

INDIA BEER — pale yellow, fresh malt aroma, clean malt flavor but a little dull, lacking balance and complexity, short uninteresting aftertaste. Export version.

INDIA LA CERVEZA DE PUERTO RICO — pale gold, pleasant malt nose, creamy texture, off-dry grainy malt flavor, light dry malt aftertaste has good length, light but pleasant. Domestic version.

TRINIDAD

Caribe Development Co.

Brewery in Port-of-Spain

CARIBE LAGER — pale yellow-gold, lovely hop and fruity malt aroma, light body, light fairly dry malt flavor, short off-dry malt aftertaste.

CARIBE — pale gold, lovely hop aroma, dry light flavor doesn't show much of either hops or malt, no aftertaste beyond a faint sensation of dryness.

URUGUAY

Fabricas Nacionales de Cerveza, S.A.

Brewery in Montevideo

DOBLE URUGUAYA — bright pale amber, off-dry fruity malt nose with an estery background, smoked malt flavor with a sour backing, bitter hops with the malt in the finish, and a long dull smoky faintly chemical aftertaste.

PILSEN — hazy gold, malt aroma, watery body, faint fruity malt and butterscotch flavor and aftertaste, not likeable.

VENEZUELA

Cerveceria Nacional

Brewery in Caracas

CERVEZA ANDES — pale gold, nice malt and hop nose, crisp malt flavor, dry and refreshing, touch of sour malt in the aftertaste does little to mar a nice effect.

CARDENAL TIPO MUNICH — medium pale gold, faint sour citrus nose, light off-dry malt flavor with that same citrus component, more noticeable in the finish and long aftertaste, but the beer remains quite drinkable despite the flaw.

Cerveceria Polar, S.A.

Brewery in Caracas

POLAR CERVEZA TIPO PILSEN — gold, light malt nose, smooth, well-balanced good flavor of hops and malt, long dry hop aftertaste. Domestic version.

POLAR BEER — gold, fresh malt nose, well-balanced hop and malt flavor, very tasty, long dry hop aftertaste. Export version.

POLAR DARK BEER — deep ruby-brown, faint sweet malt nose and flavor, long off-dry malt aftertaste, very malty much like a malta.

Notes:

Notes:

Taster's Notes

BEER NAME ____________

Type (Ale, Stout, etc.) ____________

Country of Origin ____________

Bottled by ____________

Container (can, bottle, etc.) ____________

Serving Temperature ________ Cold ________ Room ________

Where Purchased ____________ Date ________

Quantity Purchased ____________ Price ________

PERSONAL EVALUATION

Appearance ________ Clear ________ Cloudy ________

Visible Sediment ________ Yes ________ No ________

Color ____ Pale ____ Amber ____ Brown ____ Dk. Brown ____

Head ____ None ____ Little ____ Full ____ Too Much ____

Aroma ________ Good ________ Bad ________ None ________

Other ____________

Flavor ________ Good ________ Too Much Body ________

Too Little Body ________ Flat ________

Does Flavor Taste ________ Sweet ________ Sour ________

Bitter ________ Malty ________ Yeasty ________

Metallic ________ Salty ________ Other ________

After Taste ________ None ________ Mild ________ Strong ________

Would you purchase more? ____________

Would you recommend it to others? ____________

____

Taster's Notes

BEER NAME ____________

Type (Ale, Stout, etc.) ____________

Country of Origin ____________

Bottled by ____________

Container (can, bottle, etc.) ____________

Serving Temperature ________ Cold ________ Room ________

Where Purchased ____________ Date ________

Quantity Purchased ____________ Price ________

PERSONAL EVALUATION

Appearance ________ Clear ________ Cloudy ________

Visible Sediment ________ Yes ________ No ________

Color ____ Pale ____ Amber ____ Brown ____ Dk. Brown ____

Head ____ None ____ Little ____ Full ____ Too Much ____

Aroma ________ Good ________ Bad ________ None ________

Other ____________

Flavor ________ Good ________ Too Much Body ________

Too Little Body ________ Flat ________

Does Flavor Taste ________ Sweet ________ Sour ________

Bitter ________ Malty ________ Yeasty ________

Metallic ________ Salty ________ Other ________

After Taste ________ None ________ Mild ________ Strong ________

Would you purchase more? ____________

Would you recommend it to others? ____________

____

Notes: ____________

____

____

____

____

____

Taster's Notes

BEER NAME ____________________

Type (Ale, Stout, etc.) ____________________

Country of Origin ____________________

Bottled by ____________________

Container (can, bottle, etc.) ____________________

Serving Temperature ________ Cold ________ Room ________

Where Purchased ____________ Date ________

Quantity Purchased ____________ Price ________

PERSONAL EVALUATION

Appearance ________ Clear ________ Cloudy ________

Visible Sediment ________ Yes ________ No ________

Color ____ Pale ____ Amber ____ Brown ____ Dk. Brown ____

Head ____ None ____ Little ____ Full ____ Too Much ____

Aroma ______ Good ______ Bad ______ None ______

Other ____________________

Flavor ______ Good ______ Too Much Body ______

Too Little Body ______ Flat ______

Does Flavor Taste ______ Sweet ______ Sour ______

Bitter ______ Malty ______ Yeasty ______

Metallic ______ Salty ______ Other ______

After Taste ______ None ______ Mild ______ Strong ______

Would you purchase more? ____________________

Would you recommend it to others? ____________________

____

Taster's Notes

BEER NAME ____________________

Type (Ale, Stout, etc.) ____________________

Country of Origin ____________________

Bottled by ____________________

Container (can, bottle, etc.) ____________________

Serving Temperature ________ Cold ________ Room ________

Where Purchased ____________ Date ________

Quantity Purchased ____________ Price ________

PERSONAL EVALUATION

Appearance ________ Clear ________ Cloudy ________

Visible Sediment ________ Yes ________ No ________

Color ____ Pale ____ Amber ____ Brown ____ Dk. Brown ____

Head ____ None ____ Little ____ Full ____ Too Much ____

Aroma ______ Good ______ Bad ______ None ______

Other ____________________

Flavor ______ Good ______ Too Much Body ______

Too Little Body ______ Flat ______

Does Flavor Taste ______ Sweet ______ Sour ______

Bitter ______ Malty ______ Yeasty ______

Metallic ______ Salty ______ Other ______

After Taste ______ None ______ Mild ______ Strong ______

Would you purchase more? ____________________

Would you recommend it to others? ____________________

____

Notes: ____

____

____

____

____

____

Taster's Notes

BEER NAME ______________________

Type (Ale, Stout, etc.) ______________________

Country of Origin ______________________

Bottled by ______________________

Container (can, bottle, etc.) ______________________

Serving Temperature ________ Cold ________ Room ________

Where Purchased ________________ Date ________

Quantity Purchased ________________ Price ________

PERSONAL EVALUATION

Appearance ________ Clear ________ Cloudy ________

Visible Sediment ________ Yes ________ No ________

Color _____ Pale _____ Amber _____ Brown _____ Dk. Brown _____

Head _____ None _____ Little _____ Full _____ Too Much _____

Aroma ________ Good ________ Bad ________ None ________

Other ______________________

Flavor ________ Good ________ Too Much Body ________

Too Little Body ________ Flat ________

Does Flavor Taste ________ Sweet ________ Sour ________

Bitter ________ Malty ________ Yeasty ________

Metallic ________ Salty ________ Other ________

After Taste ________ None ________ Mild ________ Strong ________

Would you purchase more? ______________________

Would you recommend it to others? ______________________

____

Taster's Notes

BEER NAME ______________________

Type (Ale, Stout, etc.) ______________________

Country of Origin ______________________

Bottled by ______________________

Container (can, bottle, etc.) ______________________

Serving Temperature ________ Cold ________ Room ________

Where Purchased ________________ Date ________

Quantity Purchased ________________ Price ________

PERSONAL EVALUATION

Appearance ________ Clear ________ Cloudy ________

Visible Sediment ________ Yes ________ No ________

Color _____ Pale _____ Amber _____ Brown _____ Dk. Brown _____

Head _____ None _____ Little _____ Full _____ Too Much _____

Aroma ________ Good ________ Bad ________ None ________

Other ______________________

Flavor ________ Good ________ Too Much Body ________

Too Little Body ________ Flat ________

Does Flavor Taste ________ Sweet ________ Sour ________

Bitter ________ Malty ________ Yeasty ________

Metallic ________ Salty ________ Other ________

After Taste ________ None ________ Mild ________ Strong ________

Would you purchase more? ______________________

Would you recommend it to others? ______________________

____

Notes: ____

____

____

____

____

____

1993 UPDATE

North America

the BEER log

BY JAMES D. ROBERTSON

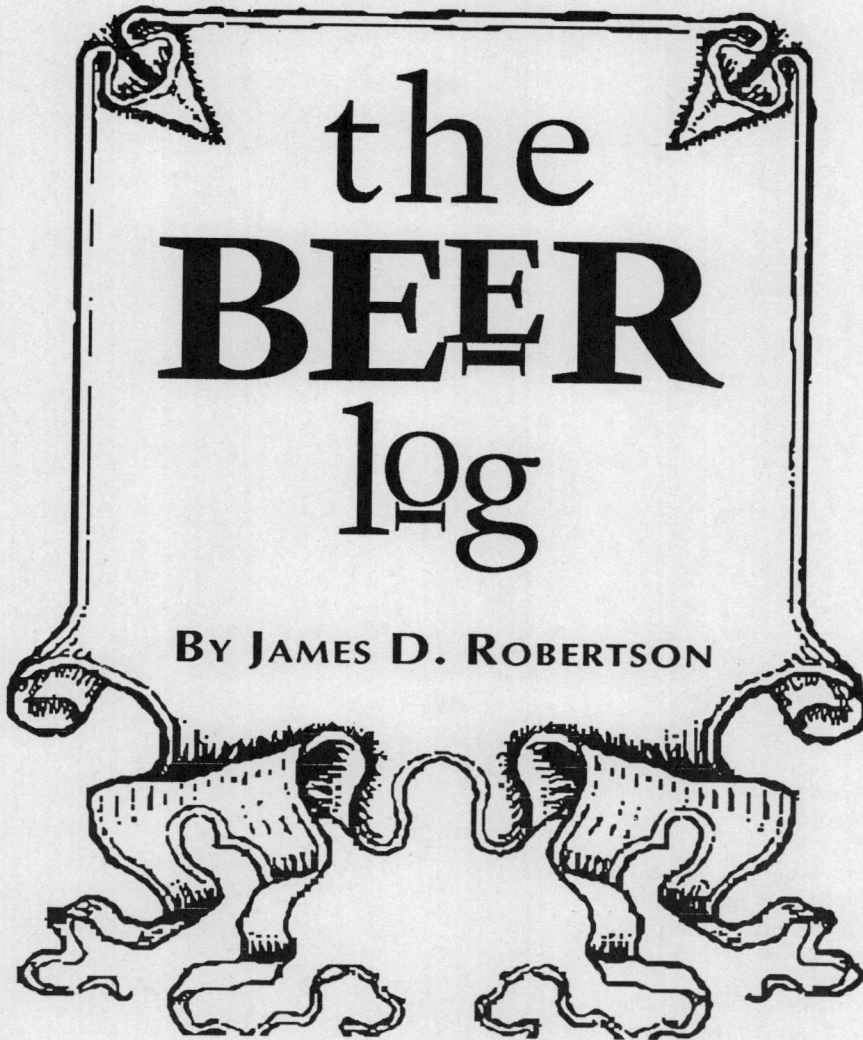

The Beer Log Update: North America

All inquiries should be addressed to Bosak Publishing Company, 4764 Galicia Way, Oceanside, CA 92056, (619) 724-4447.

ISBN: 0-9635332-1-5

Printed in the United States of America

INTRODUCTION

When *The Beer Log* was assembled in draft, with its 2,300+ descriptions, we were concerned that we might be hard pressed to add enough new brews to make the promised update worth doing. We should not have worried. We came up with enough new items to necessitate this first update to be in two sections, together totalling over 1,150 reports on new brands, in addition to a number of revised descriptions.

Section I consists entirely of beers made in North America. The bulk of these were tasted at The Great American Beer Festival in Denver in October 1992 with many follow-up tastings on location as I wandered about the country checking out new beers and retasting old ones.

Section II covers beers made abroad.

This 1993 update is printed on colored paper so that it remains recognizable as 1993 update material, even if it is incorporated into *The Beer Log* in alphabetical position (or any other way the owner prefers to do it). Subsequent update issues will be printed in different colors so the owner can always identify the year of issue. All updates will contain a complete, fully revised appendix listing all brews and their ratings.

Each year, the update will have some additional information we feel is of value to the log. This year it is the description of The Classic Beer Styles, as printed in the program for the 1992 Great American Beer Festival by The Association of Brewers. We gratefully acknowledge their cooperation in allowing us to print this very valuable material. In the 1994 update, we plan to print a complete listing of American breweries and brewpubs, with addresses and telephone numbers.

As we go, we are listening to owners of *The Beer Log* and will respond to their desires insofar as is practical. One of the things we will do is to expand on the descriptions of beers from craft breweries to discuss the malts and hops used. This is potentially misleading, since brewmasters move on and recipes can be changed (and frequently are), but we will take more chances in the future.

To help users to create more flexibility in employment of *The Beer Log* and its updates, we will make copies of the loose-leaf binder available at cost plus shipping and handling. This will allow for any configuration required. I could see a logical choice where one binder holds American breweries and a second holds only foreign breweries. In time, a single binder certainly will not be able to accommodate all the pages that will be available, but by then users should have an idea of how they would prefer to use the data and be able to make the proper arrangement with a second binder. These binders can be ordered using the card provided in the back of this section, along with cards for ordering additional copies of *The Beer Log* and for reserving the 1994 update. With about eight months to go before I have to wrap up the text on that effort, I have well over 500 new items and it could hit close to 1000 again.

The 1994 update will feature everything American, most of the new Canadian beers, virtually all of Australia and New Zealand, all of the many new imports, and a scattering of beers from around the world as we head for the 5,000 mark. Stay with us and we promise some fine guidance of beer drinking pleasure.

THE CLASSIC BEER STYLES

There are four basic families of beer: lagers, ales, hybrid and specialty beers. Americans are most familiar with the lager style brewed by every major North American brewery. Travelers to England have experienced the ale family of beers. The hybrid styles are often bred of necessity where conditions or tastes suggest mixing the brewing techniques of ales and lagers. Specialty beers hark back to older times when brewers tried any ingredient for the pleasure of it. National and individual peculiarities often bend a beer style away from its original design into something distinct and beautiful in its own right.

Brown Ale

English Mild Ale

English Milds range from deep copper to dark brown in color. Malty sweet tones dominate the flavor profile with very little hop flavor or aroma. Slight diacetyl flavors are not appropriate in this low alcohol beer.

English Brown Ale

English Brown Ales range from deep copper to brown in color. A dry to sweet maltiness dominates with very little hop flavor or aroma. Fruity and/or buttery flavors are appropriate.

American Brown Ale

American Brown Ales look like their English counterparts but have an evident hop aroma. Estery and fruity characters should be subdued; diacetyl should not be present. Strong hop aroma.

Classic English Pale Ale

Classic English Pale Ales are pale to copper-colored. This medium bodied beer characteristically displays English variety high hop bitterness, flavor and aroma with low to medium maltiness. Fruity estery flavors are evident.

India Pale Ale

India Pale Ale has a high alcohol content and a high hopping rate. This pale to deep copper-colored ale has a full, flowery hop aroma. The use of water high in mineral content contributes to the dry flavor of the beer. IPA's are characterized by a medium maltiness.

American Pale Ale/American Amber Ale

American Pale Ales range from pale to light copper-colored. The style is characterized by American style hopping and low to medium maltiness. The style also has a fruity-ester character; however, diacetyl should be absent or present only in small quantities.

Traditional Bitter

English Bitters range from pale to copper in color, are well-attenuated with good hop character and mild carbonation. Diacetyl and fruity characters are acceptable in all forms of bitter. Bitters are often prepared with hard water.

English Ordinary Bitter

Ordinary Bitter is gold to copper-colored with medium bitterness, light to medium body and low to medium residual malt character. Diacetyl and fruity properties should be minimized in this form of bitter. Very low carbonation is a must with CO_2 volumes between 0.75 and 1.3.

English Special Biter

Special Bitter is more robust than ordinary bitter, has increased hop character and more residual maltiness.

English Extra Special Bitter

Extra Special Bitter is full-bodied and possesses assertive hop qualities. The residual maltiness of this bitter is more pronounced than in other bitters.

Scottish Ales

Scottish Ales are characterized by a rounded flavor profile. These ales are malty, soft, and chewy. Hop rates are low. Yeast characters such as diacetyl and sulfuriness are possible. Scottish Ales range from pale to deep brown in color. Faint smoky character acceptable.

Scottish Light Ale

Scottish Light represents the mildest form of this ale.

Scottish Heavy Ale

Heavy Ale is moderate in strength and dominated by maltiness.

Scottish Export Ale

Export Ale is malty, slightly more bitter and has more carbonation than the other Scottish Ales.

Blonde Ale

Golden Ale/Canadian Style Ale

Golden Ales are a pale blond variation of the classic pale ale. However, golden ale more closely approximates a lager in its crisp, dry palate, noticeable floral aroma and light body.

Kölsch

Kölsch is warm fermented and aged at cold temperatures (Alt-style beer), very pale in color, with a slightly dry, winey and subtly sweet palate. This beer has low hop flavor and aroma with medium bitterness. Wheat can be used in brewing this beer which is fermented using ale or lager yeasts.

Porter

Porters range in flavor from bitter to sweet and are dark brown in color. The darkness in color comes from the use of black malt rather than the roasted barley featured in stouts. This medium bodied beer attains a light mouthfeel and quick finish through bitter hopping.

Stouts

Dry Classic Irish Stout

Dry Stouts have an initial malt and caramel flavor profile with a distinctive dry-roasted bitterness in the finish. Dry Stouts achieve a dry roasted character by use of roasted barley. Some slight acidity and a light to medium mouthfeel are appropriate. Hop aroma and flavor not present.

Foreign Style Stout

As with classic dry stouts, Foreign Style Stouts have an initial malt and caramel flavor profile with a distinctive dry-roasted bitterness in the finish. Some slight acidity and a medium to full mouthfeel are appropriate. Hop aroma and flavor not present.

Sweet Stout

Sweet Stouts, or Cream Stouts, have less roasted bitter flavor and more mouthfeel than Dry Stouts. The style can be given more body with "milk," or lactose sugar, before bottling. Malt, chocolate and caramel should dominate the flavor profile. Hops should balance sweetness without contributing apparent flavor or aroma.

Oatmeal Stout
Oatmeal Stouts typically include oatmeal in their grist, resulting in a pleasant, full flavor, and smooth profile that is rich without being grainy.

Strong Ale

English Old/Strong Ale
English Strong Ales are full-bodied with a grainy, malty sweetness. Fermentation characters, such as fruity-estery flavors, should contribute to the flavor profile.

Strong "Scotch" Ale
Scotch Ales are overwhelmingly malty and full-bodied. Color ranges from deep copper to brown. The clean alcohol flavor balances the rich and dominant maltiness. Buttery flavors are acceptable.

Imperial Stout
Imperial Stouts, dark copper to very black and highly hopped ales, typically have alcohol contents exceeding 8%. The extremely rich malty flavor is balanced with assertive hopping and fruity characteristics. This style has a strong bouquet.

Barley Wine
Barley Wines range from copper, tawny to dark brown in color and usually have a high residual malty sweetness. Estery and fruity characters are counterbalanced by medium to assertive bitterness and extraordinary alcohol content.

Fruit, Vegetable Beers
Fruit Beers are any beers using fruit as an adjunct in either primary or secondary fermentation, providing obvious yet harmonious fruit qualities. Fruit qualities should not be overpowered by hop character.

Herb, Spice Beers
Herb Beers use herbs or spices other than hops to create a distinct character. Under hopping allows the spice or herb to contribute to the flavor profile.

Specialty
These beers are brewed using fermentables other than, or in addition to, malted barley.

Smoke-Flavored Beers

Bamberg-Style Rauchbier
Rauchbier should have a smoky characteristic prevalent in the aroma and flavor. The beer is generally sweet and malty with thick body and low to medium bitterness. The aroma should strike a balance between malt, hop and smoke.

Smoke-Flavored Beer
Any style of beer can be smoked; the trick is to reach a balance between the style's character and the smoky properties. See brewer's specifics for style being smoked.

Bock

Traditional Bock
Traditional Bock — a strong, malty, bottom fermented beer with moderate hop bitterness that should increase proportionately with the starting gravity. Bocks can range in color from deep copper to dark brown (generally brown in the U.S.). Esters may be present, but not to the extent that they are in top fermented beers.

Heller Bock
The German word 'hell' means light or pale, and as such, a Heller Bock is pale in color. This German style beer should be made exclusively with pale malted barley and perhaps a small percentage of pale or medium colored dextrin malt. The malty character should come through in the aroma and flavor, but bitterness/hop aroma should also be present. Bitterness increases with gravity. Esters should be minimal.

Doppelbock
Malty sweetness is dominant, but should not be cloying. The deep amber to dark brown color of a Doppelbock comes from the use of dark, Munich style malts and dark dextrin malts. Alcoholic strength is high and esters are commonly present. Bitterness should again be moderate, and hop rates increase with gravity.

Amber Lager

Vienna
Beers in this category are reddish brown or copper-colored, which comes from the use of medium colored malts and perhaps a small percentage of light or dark dextrin malt. Malty aroma is distinct and hop bitterness is clean; lightly sweet and with no esters present.

Märzen/Oktoberfest
Similar to the Vienna style, only usually stronger and the range of color is broader. Traditional Märzens were deep brown, but today their hue is lighter. Oktoberfests can range from deep golden to reddish brown, and technically, the starting gravity of an Oktoberfest should be between 1054-1056 (13.5-14). In any case, maltiness should dominate slightly over a clean, hop bitterness. Esters are minimal, if present.

Dark Lager

European Dark/Münchener Dunkel
These beers have a pronounced malty aroma and flavor that dominates over the clean, crisp hop bitterness. A classic Münchener Dunkel should have a bread-like aroma that comes from the use of Munich dark malt. Chocolate or roast malts can be used, but the percentage used should be minimal.

American Dark Lager
This beer style is similar to the European version, but the maltiness is less pronounced, and the gravity is somewhat lower. Adjuncts are sometimes used and hop rates are generally low. Carbonation is higher than a European Dark Lager, but standard for an American Lager.

Münchener Helles and Export

Münchener Helles
This is the everyday beer of Southern Germany, and it has a relatively low alcohol content and bitterness. This is a malt-emphasized beer; however, certain versions can approach a balance of maltiness to hop character. Color is pale and esters should not be present. In a Dortmunder/Export Style, both starting gravity and bitterness are somewhat higher than a Münchener Helles. The color of this style may be slightly darker, and body will be fuller. Alcohol content is also higher.

European Pilsner

German Style Pilsner

Popular throughout Germany, this style serves as an example for pale lagers the world over. A classic German Pils is very pale and well hopped. It is a well-attenuated, medium bodied beer, but a malty accent can be present. Esters should not be present.

Bohemian Style Pilsner

Having originated in the Bohemian town of Pilzen, this style was responsible for the lager revolution of the 19th Century. Pilsners in this style are essentially similar to German Pilsners. However, they are slightly more full bodied and darker. This style balances bitterness and noble hop aroma with a malty, slightly sweet character. Diacetyl may be present.

American Lager

Very light in body and color, American Lagers are very clean and crisp and aggressively carbonated. Adjuncts such as corn or rice are often used. Hop bitterness is slight and flavor is mild.

American Light Lager

When used in reference to caloric content, "light" beers must have at least 25% fewer calories than the "regular" version of that beer, according to FDA regulations. Such beers must have certain analysis data printed on the package label. These beers are extremely pale, low in body and high in carbonation. Flavor is mild and bitterness is very low.

American Premium Lager

Similar to the American Lager, this style is an attempt at a more flavorful, full bodied beer, that may contain little or no adjuncts at all. Color may be deeper than the American Lager, and alcohol content and bitterness may also be greater.

American Dry Lager

This one is a hybrid between American Lager and American Light Lager. The lack of sweetness is reminiscent of a light, but in terms of starting gravity and alcoholic strength, it approaches the characteristics of a standard lager. As is the case with all American Lagers, hop rates are low and carbonation is high.

American Malt Liquor

This is the strongest of the American style beers. High in starting gravity and alcoholic strength, this style is somewhat diverse. Some American Malt Liquors are just slightly stronger than American Lagers, while others approach Bock strength. Some residual sweetness is present and hop rates are low.

Düsseldorf–Style Altbier

Brown in color, this German ale is highly hopped and has a malty body and flavor. A variety of malts, including wheat, are used, and the color is adjusted using dark caramel malts, colored beer or even by simply using 100% dark malt. The overall impression is clean, crisp and flavorful, which results in part from low fermentation temperatures.

American Lager/Ale or Cream Ale

A uniquely American term for a mild, pale light-bodied ale, these beers can be made using a warm bottom or top fermentation and cold lagering or by blending top and bottom fermented beers. Sometimes referred to as Cream Ales, these beers are crisp and refreshing. A fruity or estery aroma may be present.

German Wheat

Berliner Weisse

This is the lightest of all the German Wheat beers. The unique combination of a yeast and lactic acid bacteria fermentation yields a beer that is acidic and highly attenuated. The carbonation of a Berliner Weisse is high and hop rates are very low. Some esters may be present, and in Berlin this beer is served in large schooners with a dash of raspberry or woodruff syrup.

Weizen/Weissbier

The most popular of all the German Wheat beers, this distinctive ale is bottle or keg conditioned, and it is customarily served with the yeast sediment. In Germany, Weizen beer served with the yeast sediment is named Hefe-Weizen (hefe is the German word for yeast). When the yeast is filtered out, it is called Kristall-Klar (crystal clear). The aroma and flavor of a Weissbier is decidedly fruity and phenolic. The phenolic characteristics are often clove- or nutmeg-like, and can be smokey or even vanilla-like. It is made with at least 50% malted wheat, and hop rates are quite low.

Weissbier is well-attenuated and very highly carbonated, yet its relatively high starting gravity and alcohol content make it a full bodied beer.

Dunkelweizen

Gaining in popularity throughout Germany, this beer style is characterized by a distinct maltiness, but the estery and phenolic elements of a pale weissbier still prevail. Color can range from rusty brown to dark brown. Carbonation and hop bitterness are similar to a pale weissbier. Usually dark barley malts are used in conjunction with dark caramel or color malts, and the percentage of wheat malt is at least 50%.

Weizenbock

Commonly brewed for the holiday season, this style can be either pale or dark and, like a bottom fermented bock, has a high starting gravity and alcohol content. The malty sweetness of a Weizenbock is balanced with the phenolic, estery element to produce a well rounded aroma and flavor. As is true with all German Wheat beers, hop rates are low and carbonation is high.

American Wheat

Perhaps the newest, bona fide beer style in America, this beer can be made using either an ale or lager yeast. Brewed with 30-50% wheat, hop rates are higher and carbonation is lower compared to German Wheat beers. Like the German Wheat beers, a fruity aroma and flavor is typical, however, phenolic characteristics should not be present. Color is usually pale.

Abita Brewing Co.

Brewery in Abita Springs, LA

ABITA GOLDEN LAGER — gold, malt nose, flavor starts out briefly as malt and immediately dry hops take over, good body, medium dry hop aftertaste, good refreshing beer.

ABITA AMBER LAGER — amber, fruity aroma, fruity malt flavor with a toasted malt background, fades to a brief dry hop aftertaste, pleasant and very good with food.

ABITA FALL FEST BEER — brilliant amber, rich malt aroma with lots of hops, big hop flavor with plenty of roasted malt in back, very good balance and mouth feel, pleasant hop finish, medium to light body, medium dry hop aftertaste, very drinkable, a good well-made beer.

ABITA TURBO DOG BEER — deep ruby-amber, light roasted malt aroma, roasted malt flavor, toast finish, finely carbonated, medium body, medium long dry malt aftertaste, very likeable straightforward brew.

ABITA ANDYGATOR — amber, great malty nose, big bright malt flavor backed with an abundance of hops, strongly flavored(with both the malt and hops), big body, plenty of hop bite, complex, sense of alcohol, long big dry hop aftertaste. This is Abita's Christmas beer, made with several malts, Golding and Kent hops and a German alt yeast. It's a dandy.

ABITA BOCK BEER — amber, big hop aroma shows malt as well, big complex flavor is mostly hops but there is enough malt to provide balance, big body, some sense of alcohol, finishes dry hops, but the very long aftertaste keeps the complexity and has an abundance of both hops and malt. This is Abita's Mardi Gras beer available from late January to May.

Acadia Brewing Co.

Micro-brewery and The Lompoc Cafe & Brewery (brewpub) in Bar Harbor, ME

BAR HARBOR REAL ALE — cloudy amber, very light aroma is mostly yeast, yeast dominates the palate as well, masking the malt and the hops. Brewmaster Roger Normand advised me that they had been having trouble with this recipe and has recently reported that they have licked the problem.

ACADIA PALE ALE — deep gold, pleasant malt and hop aroma, zesty hop flavor, good body, very drinkable, long dry hop aftertaste with plenty of malt in back.

ACADIA AMBER ALE — dark amber, light malt and hop nose, good body, very smooth malt flavor, long dry aftertaste.

COAL PORTER — brown, hop nose, smooth malt and hop flavor, dry malt finish and aftertaste.

MICRO-FILTERED • KEEP REFRIGERATED
BAR HARBOR
REAL ALE
Brewed and Bottled by
Acadia Brewing Company
Bar Harbor, Maine
Net Contents 12 Fl. Oz.
ME — 5¢ DEPOSIT
GOVERNMENT WARNING: (1) ACCORDING TO THE SURGEON GENERAL, WOMEN SHOULD NOT DRINK ALCOHOLIC BEVERAGES DURING PREGNANCY BECAUSE OF THE RISK OF BIRTH DEFECTS. (2) CONSUMPTION OF ALCOHOLIC BEVERAGES IMPAIRS YOUR ABILITY TO DRIVE A CAR OR OPERATE MACHINERY, AND MAY CAUSE HEALTH PROBLEMS.

Alaskan Brewing & Bottling Co.

Brewery in Juneau, AK

ALASKAN AMBER BEER — tawny amber, zesty off-dry malty ale aroma, clean and fresh malt, finely carbonated, good tasting malt and citrus hop flavor with little or no hop bite, good body, very long smooth dry hop aftertaste, excellently balanced, clean and very drinkable brew.

ALASKAN PALE ALE — gold, bright ale aroma with a citrus background, zesty malt and hop flavor, off-dry malt front, dry hop middle and finish, good body, good balance, smooth and mellow, long dry hop aftertaste.

ALASKAN SEASONAL SMOKED PORTER 1989 — opaque brown, thick brown head, dry smoked coffee nose, very dry smoked malt flavor, although very smoky, it is neither overpowering or unpleasant, very finely carbonated, very long smoked aftertaste, well done smoked porter.

ALASKAN 1989 AUTUMN ALE — deep amber, complex toasted malt aroma, big dry toasted malt flavor, finely carbonated, not complex, very long dry malt aftertaste, satisfying and drinkable.

ALASKAN 1990 WINTER STOCK ALE — bright amber-gold, zesty citrus-malt aroma, huge malt and hop flavor, excellent balance, long dry hop aftertaste, all the superlative descriptions apply, an excellent almost perfect brew. One of the ten best beers on my list.

ALASKAN 1990 WHEAT BEER — hazy-gold, clean fresh light malt aroma, highly carbonated, bright malt flavor on the fruity side, medium body, finishes well but the light short dry malt aftertaste is somewhat disappointing.

ALASKAN SPRING WHEAT — gold, wheaty malt aroma, off-dry malt palate has a wheat-like background, finishes like the flavor leading into a fairly clean but brief malt aftertaste that is a little drier than the flavor.

ALASKAN SEASONAL BREAKUP BOCK — amber, big malt nose, rich and dry malt flavor, very smooth, creamy, high alcohol, drinkable, long dry malt aftertaste.

ALASKAN ARCTIC ALE — brown, big malt and hop aroma, complex and big malt-hop flavor, very smooth, big bodied, dry finish and aftertaste.

Anchor Brewing Co.

Brewery in **San Francisco, CA**

ANCHOR STEAM BEER — bright copper color, foamy, finely carbonated, rich malt aroma with plenty of hops, creamy malt flavor picks up hops as it crosses the palate, full bodied, complex, long and very satisfying.

ANCHOR PORTER — deep brown, light malt aroma, big creamy malt flavor, extremely complex with hints of molasses, licorice and different kinds of malt, big bodied, rich and very long.

ANCHOR WHEAT — bright gold, pleasant aroma just like freshly milled malt, light malt flavor much like the nose, smooth and pleasant, refreshing and mellow, light dry malt finish and aftertaste, slides down easily. This brew was found on draft as recently as early 1992 and makes brief periodic appearances in bottles.

OLD FOGHORN BARLEYWINE STYLE ALE — reddish-amber, strong roasted malt, caramel and molasses aroma, rich and intense malt flavor with hops, citrus and caramel tones, definitely on the sweet side, but complex, well-balanced and very long. A great sipping beer.

LIBERTY ALE — deep amber, lush hop and malt aroma, complex palate with several kinds of malt, hops, spices, citrus and apricot; very flavorful and very long.

OUR SPECIAL ALE — deep amber, complex and subtle spice aroma, there is both malt and hops, but the spice somewhat overwhelms them, short aftertaste. This is a brew that appears each year as Christmas approaches and which has been spiced since 1987. They are not exactly the same each year, but since they have been spiced, the variation is minor. The 1990 was a bit less spiced and smoother than the 1989. The 1991 is more subtly spiced and you can taste the malt. Since Anchor started producing a Wassail for Christmas, the 1991 is the most likeable O.S.A. they have offered. The 1992 also ranks well as it has a very complex spicy aroma and a good dry spicy flavor with a lot of cinnamon.

POTRERO COMMONS ALE — cloudy amber, big malt aroma, complex chocolate malt flavor, chewy with an ale bite in back, big bodied, creamy and smooth, balanced and long. A complex brown ale.

ANCHOR SPRUCE BEER — hazy gold, delicate spruce aroma, resiny spruce flavor, aftertaste like spruce gum.

Appleton Brewing Co.

Microbrewery in **Appleton, WI**, adjacent to two restaurants to which the beer is piped directly, giving it the additional status as a brewpub.

ADLER BRAU LIGHT — gold, hop nose, light malt flavor, very light body, not much of an aftertaste.

ADLER BRAU LAGER — gold, light hop aroma and flavor, medium body, dry hop finish and aftertaste.

ADLER BRAU AMBER — amber, dry malt and hop aroma, smooth dry malt and hop flavor, medium to good body, long dry malt and hop aftertaste.

ADLER BRAU OKTOBERFEST — gold, hop nose, big malty taste with the hops in back, good body, medium dry malt finish and aftertaste.

ADLER BRAU PILSNER — gold, big hop nose (Saaz hops, it seems), medium body, dry hop flavor, finish and aftertaste.

ADLER BRAU WEISS — gold, malt aroma, smooth wheat and barley malt flavor, no spice, soft, smooth and refreshing, light body, medium dry malt aftertaste.

ADLER BRAU PUMPKIN SPICE — gold, spicy nose and taste, an appetizing pumpkin pie flavor, good body, long aftertaste like the flavor.

ADLER BRAU BOCK — golden amber, pleasant hop and malt aroma, taste to match, pleasant, dry, appetizing, light body, light hop and malt aftertaste.

ADLER BRAU PORTER — brown, dry malt aroma and flavor, good body, dry malt aftertaste.

ADLER BRAU OATMEAL STOUT — brown, dry roasted barley and chocolate malt nose, flavor is like the nose but a bit more dry, good body, dry malt finish and aftertaste.

Arrowhead Brewing Co.

Brewery in Chambersburg, PA

RED FEATHER PALE ALE — pale amber, big ale-like hop and malt aroma with some citrus, zesty hop flavor, malt in back, full body, big and balanced, long dry hop aftertaste has a subtle malt component in back, an excellent beer.

Bandersnatch Brewing Co.

Brewpub in Tempe, AZ

BIGHORN PREMIUM ALE — brilliant clear amber, light hop nose, complex hop flavor shows plenty of malt, medium body, good Northwest hop character, stays hoppy throughout but doesn't lack for malt, long dry hop aftertaste, a good English bitter style ale.

CARDINAL PALE ALE — bright gold, light hop nose, creamy, light and bright dry hop flavor, light to medium body, dry hop finish and long dry hop aftertaste, again the Northwest hop character but lighter and refreshing.

BANDERSNATCH MILK STOUT — opaque brown, huge tan head, beef bouillon aroma, dry malt flavor, long dry malt aftertaste. This sample was bottled by the brewpub and shipped to me on the East Coast. It was slightly harmed by the journey, but this showed up only in the aroma. A recent change in recipe has resulted in more of an Australian style stout, much less dry than reported here.

EDINBREW — deep amber, aroma of dry hops and malt, a big flavor with plenty of both malt and hops, good balance, good body, long dry malt aftertaste, done like a Scottish ale, but with a Northwest hop twist.

Bar Harbor Brewing Co.

Microbrewery in Bar Harbor, ME

HARBOR LIGHT ALE — deep hazy amber, light malt and hop nose, bright tangy ale taste, hop front and malt back, good body, long dry malt and hop aftertaste is much like the flavor, some complexity as the malt and hops vie for dominance and never clash.

CADILLAC MTN. STOUT — opaque brown, brown head, malt nose with a complex citrus-yeast background, big dry malt palate, hops come in at the finish, long dry malt and hop aftertaste, definitely a dry stout style and although your first thought is homebrew, it really grows on you.

Notes:

Beach Brewing Co.- T/A Mill Bakery, Eatery & Brewery

Brewpub and microbrewery in **Orlando, FL**

Brews for itself and for Tallahassee and Gainesville Mill Bakery, Eatery & Brewery establishments. Affiliated with other Mills in Winter Park, FL, Baton Rouge, LA, Charlotte, NC and others as planned.

KNIGHT LIGHT — gold, grainy malt aroma and flavor, light body, little length.

RED ROCK — amber, good malt and faint hop aroma, malt comes through much stronger on the palate with a caramel background, good body, creamy, balanced, finishes fairly dry leading into a long dry malt and hop aftertaste.

MAGIC BREW — ruby amber, malt aroma, creamy caramel flavor, good mouth feel, decent balance, hops slowly come in at the finish, long dry malt and hop aftertaste.

HORNET'S TAIL — amber, big hop nose, big bright hop flavor has plenty of malt, big body, sense of alcohol, long strong hop and malt aftertaste, a real mouthful of taste, huge and good.

Belmont Brewing Co.

Brewpub in **Long Beach, CA**

MARATHON PALE ALE — gold, big ale nose, hefty hop flavor that drops off abruptly, light dry hop aftertaste.

TOP SAIL AMBER ALE — amber, little nose, dry hop flavor, medium body, dry malt and hop aftertaste with fair duration.

LONG BEACH CRUDE PORTER — deep amber-brown, dry chocolate malt nose, very dry chocolate malt flavor, medium body, long aftertaste like the flavor, more like a stout than a porter.

WHALE ALE — hazy gold, faint malt nose, dry soapy malt flavor, finishes very dry, short dry malt aftertaste.

Note: The brewpub offers mixtures of some brews: PENNY FOGGER — a mix of the porter and amber that comes out malty and dry and BLACK AND TAN — a mix of the pale and porter which also comes out malty like the Penny Fogger, but lighter.

H.C. Berger Brewing Co.

Microbrewery in **Fort Collins, CO**

INDIGO ALE — amber, complex hop aroma and taste, smooth and balanced, very drinkable, long dry hop aftertaste.

INDIA PALE ALE — amber, light hop aroma, very dry hop flavor, smooth, balanced, very long dry hop aftertaste.

WHEAT BEER — golden amber, big foamy head, fresh malt aroma and flavor, smooth, balanced, tasty, long dry malt aftertaste, a nice American style wheat.

GOVERNMENT WARNING: (1) ACCORDING TO THE SURGEON GENERAL, WOMEN SHOULD NOT DRINK ALCOHOLIC BEVERAGES DURING PREGNANCY BECAUSE OF THE RISK OF BIRTH DEFECTS. (2) CONSUMPTION OF ALCOHOLIC BEVERAGES IMPAIRS YOUR ABILITY TO DRIVE A CAR OR OPERATE MACHINERY, AND MAY CAUSE HEALTH PROBLEMS.
H.C. Berger Brewing Co.
FRESH
ALES
FORT COLLINS
COLORADO
PLEASE KEEP REFRIGERATED
Indego Pale Ale
12 FL.OZ.
Fresh Brewed & Bottled in Ft. Collins, Colorado
355 ML
CONTAINS: PURE COLORADO WATER, MALTED GRAINS, HOPS, SPECIAL GERMAN YEAST

Big Time Brewing Co.

Brewpub in **Seattle, WA**

HEFERYZEN — hazy gold, rye bread aroma, hop and malt flavor, dry hop finish, long dry hop and malt aftertaste, very nicely done.

ATLAS AMBER — hazy amber, hop nose with a hint of caramel, hop and malt flavor to the finish, thereafter just dry hops.

OLD RIP OATMEAL STOUT — deep brown, roast barley aroma and flavor, medium body, medium dry malt finish, dry malt aftertaste.

OLD WOOLY PORTER — dark brown, chocolate nose, chocolate malt flavor, dry malt aftertaste with some dry hops.

PRIME TIME — gold, big off-dry malt nose, flavor is malt also but a bit drier, good body, dry malt finish and aftertaste.

BHAGWANS BEST IPA — amber, hop nose, big hop flavor, good body, long dry hop aftertaste.

Bird Creek Brewery

Microbrewery in **Anchorage, AK**

OLD 55 PALE ALE — amber gold, big hop aroma, big hop flavor, heavy body, long dry hop aftertaste, a good well-hopped brew.

Birmingham Brewing Co.

Microbrewery in **Birmingham, AL**

RED MOUNTAIN GOLDEN LAGER — gold, big hop-malt aroma and flavor, good body, dry hop finish and aftertaste.

RED MOUNTAIN GOLDEN ALE — gold, malt aroma and flavor, good body, dry malt finish and aftertaste.

Black Mountain Brewing Co.

Brewery and restaurant in **Cave Creek, AZ**

CRAZY ED'S BLACK MOUNTAIN GOLD PREMIUM BEER — hazy gold, pronounced hop nose, sharp hop flavor but there is plenty of malt for balance, big body, hop finish and long dry hop aftertaste.

DEL RICO — hazy gold, jalapeño pepper nose which comes as no surprise since there is a small jalapeño pepper in the bottle, hot jalapeño pepper and malt taste, strange, hot and long. Just as a note, the pepper had no flavor or heat left; it was all in the brew by the time I got to it.

CRAZY ED'S ARIZONA PILSNER BEER — gold, bright hop and malt nose, hop flavor is good despite some unbalance in mid-palate, vegetal malt finish, dry hop aftertaste with good length.

CRAZY ED'S CAVE CREEK CHILI BEER — gold, bright jalapeño pepper nose, hot jalapeño pepper taste, finish and aftertaste. Made in bottles at Cave Creek and by Minnesota B.C. of St. Paul under contract for distribution in various major metropolitan areas (like Washington, DC, for instance). Some early samples were found without the chili pepper in the bottle, but recent ('92-'93) ones do have the pepper.

Bohannon Brewing Co.

Brewery in Nashville, TN

MARKET STREET PILSENER DRAFT BEER — tawny-gold, off-dry malt and CO_2 nose, creamy, zesty fruity-malt flavor, medium long malt and hop aftertaste, clean, very pleasant and very drinkable.

MARKET STREET OKTOBERFEST — amber,hop nose, big malt flavor has plenty of supporting hops, big body, balanced, long dry malt aftertaste.

MARKET STREET WHEAT BEER — gold, malt nose, dry malt flavor, clean American style wheat, light bodied, finishes dry malt, very quaffable.

MARKET STREET GOLDEN — gold, nice hop aroma, bright hop flavor, good balance, malt and hop finish, dry malt and hop aftertaste.

Boston Beer Co.

Brewery in **Boston, MA**

Facilities of Pittsburgh B.C., F.X. Matt B.C. and G. Heileman B.C. used for regional package production.

SAMUEL ADAMS BOSTON LAGER — golden amber, zesty malt and hop aroma, complex dry hop flavor, plenty of malt in the flavor and in the long aftertaste, good balance throughout, an excellent brew, probably the best of the nationally available brands.

BOSTON LIGHTSHIP — tawny-gold, big luscious off-dry malt nose, big dry malt flavor, dry hop finish, light body, long dry malt aftertaste, good thirst quencher, one of the most flavorful of the low-calorie beers.

SAMUEL ADAMS DOUBLE BOCK DARK LAGER — deep amber, big fruity toasted malt nose, huge body, big chocolate malt flavor, long and delicious, a chewy lip-smacker.

SAMUEL ADAMS 1989 WINTER LAGER — amber, rich malt nose, lovely toasted malt and hop flavor, terrific balance, good body, smooth, very tasty, long and delicious, ends surprisingly dry for a big malty brew. This is my favorite from Jim Koch's repertoire.

SAMUEL ADAMS WINTER LAGER 1990-1991 — amber, big toasted malt aroma, bold toasted malt and hop flavor, balanced, complex, very drinkable and long ending with an extended dry malt aftertaste.

SAMUEL ADAMS WINTER LAGER 1991-1992 — amber, big complex aroma with plenty of malt and hops, huge malt and hop flavor, big body, noticeable alcohol, great complex hop finish and a long dry hop aftertaste. Although different each year, every one is a star!

SAMUEL ADAMS WINTER LAGER 1992-1993 — amber, interesting complex malt and hop aroma, very smooth, good body, easy to drink, dry hop finish, long dry hop aftertaste, excellent balance throughout.

SAMUEL ADAMS OCTOBERFEST SPECIAL BREW — hazy amber, zesty hop nose, tangy hop palate with good malt backing, very drinkable and very long dry hop aftertaste. Another lip-smacker, but a bit smaller than the double bock which makes it more drinkable and better with food.

SAMUEL ADAMS CREAM STOUT — brown, dry roasted malt nose and taste, faint chocolate malt in back, medium body,dry malt finish, short dry malt aftertaste.

SAMUEL ADAMS BOSTON STOCK ALE — pale amber, complex toasted malt and hop nose, front palate is hops, middle is fruity malt, has dry and off-dry components present at the same time in a complex mix, extremely long malt aftertaste with a background hint of pine. Extremely interesting and pleasant brew that is fair competition to the Boston Lager where they are both available.

SAMUEL ADAMS WHEAT BREW — deep gold, zesty spicy clove aroma, medium spicy-lactic flavor, pleasant and refreshing, light body, fairly short aftertaste like the flavor, a German-style weizen but done with a light hand.

SAMUEL ADAMS CRANBERRY LAMBIC — amber, fruity aroma, fruity-berry tart flavor, long dry tart fruit aftertaste.

SAMUEL ADAMS DUNKELWEIZEN — brown, tangy hop aroma, zesty spicy flavor, spicy finish and long well-spiced aftertaste, a real European style weizenbier.

Boston Beer Works

Brewpub in **Boston, MA**

BOSTON RED — amber, good dry well-hopped aroma, big hop and malt flavor is extremely complex, four malts (Vienna, wheat, black and crystal) and Hallertau hops all contribute to that complexity, long dry malt aftertaste.

KENMORE KÖLSCH — medium gold, light malt nose, bright malt flavor shows some of the wheat (10% wheat malt), good body, very smooth, light long medium dry malt aftertaste.

ACME LIGHT — pale gold, clean malt nose, very dry hoppy flavor (Tettnanger), medium body, long dry hop aftertaste.

RASPBERRY ALE — deep gold, light malt flavor with just a hint of raspberry, bright fruity malt flavor (would have trouble recognizing the raspberry on the palate), light body, finish is more fruity than raspberry, light dry malt aftertaste, very refreshing pleasant easy-to-drink beer.

HERCULES STRONG ALE — deep amber-gold, honeyed fruity malt aroma, some apricot in back, low carbonation, huge body, very complex enormous malt flavor, noticeable alcohol,almost viscous, extremely long and strong chocolate malt and hop aftertaste, great sipping brew, a blockbuster beer that I could get stuck on very easily.

BUCKEYE OATMEAL STOUT — opaque brown, rich complex malt nose, dry malt flavor (very dry), medium body, fairly short dry malt aftertaste.

BEANTOWN BROWN ALE — ruby-brown, big malt nose and taste, similar to the stout, but not so dry, good body, fairly long dry malt aftertaste.

BLUEBERRY ALE — deep gold, very much a berry nose, somewhat candy-like, flavor like the nose, finishes dry, very long dry malt aftertaste, but the berry is in behind all the way through.

Boulder Brewing Co.

Brewery in Boulder, CO

BOULDER ENGLISH ALE — pale orange-amber, complex citrus-ale aroma, big well-hopped flavor, complex and full-bodied, very long and very good.

BOULDER EXTRA PALE ALE — pale orange-amber, big citrus-ale aroma, strong hop flavor, big body, long and delicious.

BOULDER BEER CO., BOULDER, COLORADO
CA REDEMPTION VALUE
WATER, MALTED BARLEY, HOPS & YEAST
MI REF. 10¢, OR. IA. NY. MA. ME. CT. VT. DE REF. 5¢
BOULDER
EXTRA PALE ALE
12 FL. OZ.
355 ML
GOVERNMENT WARNING: (1) ACCORDING TO THE SURGEON GENERAL, WOMEN SHOULD NOT DRINK ALCOHOLIC BEVERAGES DURING PREGNANCY BECAUSE OF THE RISK OF BIRTH DEFECTS. (2) CONSUMPTION OF ALCOHOLIC BEVERAGES IMPAIRS YOUR ABILITY TO DRIVE A CAR OR OPERATE MACHINERY, AND MAY CAUSE HEALTH PROBLEMS.

BOULDER STOUT — deep amber-brown, big complex malt and tobacco nose, equally complex flavor of roasted (almost burnt) malt with hints of molasses and citrus, good balance, good body, smooth, mellow and a long dry malt aftertaste with a trace of licorice.

BOULDER PORTER — deep copper, rich roasted malt aroma with a citrus nature and plenty of hops, fine balance, strong and rich off-dry hop and malt ale flavor, with a long dry hop aftertaste.

BOULDER BLACK CHERRY PORTER — opaque brown, attractive smoked cherry nose, smoked flavor is faintly fruity in the finish and aftertaste, light body, not a big number for Boulder.

BOULDER SPORT — bright gold, almost skunky hop aroma, big hop flavor with only a faint hint of malt, fairly brief.

BEST OF SHOW 1988 OKTOBERFEST BEER — bright amber, big toasted malt and hop aroma, smoky-malty dry flavor, medium body, very drinkable but not complex.

BEST OF SHOW 1989 INDIA PALE ALE — golden amber, bright tangy hop nose, big body, big clean and fresh hop flavor well-backed with malt, complex dry hop finish, long malt aftertaste, drinkable and refreshing.

BOULDER LIGHT ALE — pale gold, lovely toasted malt nose, off-dry malt palate with hops in back, short watery aftertaste.

TANKER ALE — hazy amber, appetizing delicious toasted malt aroma, almost smoky malt flavor, light body, bit of harshness from the burnt malt at the very end.

BUFFALO GOLD PREMIUM ALE — bright gold, toasted malt aroma, honeyed malt flavor, complex, fairly dry finish and aftertaste with some alcohol noticeable, very drinkable. Made under license from The Walnut Brewery.

BOULDER AMBER ALE — amber color, pleasant toasted malt aroma, medium body, grainy mildly toasted flavor, short aftertaste, lacks complexity and balance. Bottled version.

WRIGLEY RED — amber, weak dull malt nose, malt flavor, hop finish, a bit sudsy, dry hop aftertaste, very drinkable. Made for affiliate Old Chicago Pasta &Pizza chain of restaurants in Colorado.

ROCKIES PREMIUM DRAFT — gold, malt aroma and flavor, light but balanced, dry hop finish and aftertaste.

BUFFALO GOLD PREMIUM ALE — gold, hop aroma and palate, balanced off well with good malt, long dry hop finish and aftertaste. This is the draft version served at the brewery.

BOULDER SUMMER ALE — amber, faint hop nose, fairly bright hop flavor, medium body, smooth, drinkable, slightly dry malt aftertaste.

BOULDER SUMMER ALE CASK CONDITIONED — amber, light hop nose, light dry hop flavor, light body, smooth, light dry hop finish and aftertaste.

BOULDER OKTOBERFEST — gold, hop nose with a faint grainy background, bright hop palate, good body, long aftertaste just like the flavor, a very good brew.

BOULDER OKTOBERFEST CASK CONDITIONED — gold, hop nose, very smooth hop flavor well backed with malt, very good and drinkable, but not quite as bright as above, long dry hop aftertaste.

BOULDER AMBER ALE— amber, hop and faint caramel aroma, flavor like the nose, good balance, good body, dry hop finish and aftertaste. This is the draft version served at the brewery.

BOULDER PORTER — brown, roasted malt nose and flavor, good body, dry malt finish and long dry malt aftertaste. Draft version at brewery.

ASPEN SILVER CITY ALE — hazy gold, fruity malt aroma, interesting complex citrus fruit malt flavor, a little off-dry but there is plenty of hop bitterness in there as well, a hint of spiciness but not lactic, stays clean and has great length. Made for Aspen Beer Co.

Boulder Creek Brewing Co./ Boulder Creek Grill & Cafe

Microbrewery and Brewpub in **Boulder Creek, CA**

ST. SEVERINS KÖLSCH — pale gold, nice malt nose, dry hop flavor, finish and aftertaste, pretty good kölsch style beer.

OLD MACLUNKS SCOTTISH ALE — amber, hop nose and flavor, plenty of malt but only in support of the hops, malt more noticeable in the finish and aftertaste where it provides a good balance with the dry hops, good length.

Breckenridge Brewery

Brewpub in **Breckenridge, CO**

BRECKENRIDGE INDIA PALE ALE — hazy amber, creamy, soapy citrus malt nose, light malt flavor with a hop and citrus background, dry hop finish, very long pleasant complex dry hop and malt aftertaste, well-made brew.

BRECKENRIDGE MOUNTAIN WHEAT — pale hazy gold, lemony spicy malt aroma, spicy malt flavor, finish and aftertaste.

AVALANCHE ALE — gold, fruity malt nose and flavor, hops stay in back, dry malt finish and aftertaste. Bottled versions had an acidic backtaste.

OATMEAL STOUT — deep brown, classic roasted barley and chocolate malt nose, good tasting flavor like the aroma, very dry and very long, a good stout.

BLUE RIVER BOCK — amber, hop and off-dry malt aroma, flavor is big bright hops well backed with an off-dry malt, finishes dry malt and has more of a dry hop aftertaste, a very bright refreshing beer.

MÄRZEN OKTOBERFEST — deep gold, big malt nose and taste, clean, fresh and long.

Brewed and Baked in Telluride

Brewpub in **Telluride, CO**

SNOW WHEAT — amber, big spicy nose, tangy well-spiced palate, a hefe-weizen style, good body, well-spiced into the finish and the long aftertaste.

RUNNER'S HIGH — amber-brown, hop nose and palate, good body, medium dry malt and hop finish and aftertaste.

PANDORA PORTER — brown, malt nose has a sour lactic background, flavor even more lactic, too sour, bad sample.

Brewhouse Grill

Brewpub in Manhattan Beach, CA

Same ownership as the Brewhouse Grill of Santa Barbara, but different beers are offered.

HEAD LIGHT — pale gold, light hop aroma, light dry hop flavor, light body, pleasant tasting, short dry hop aftertaste.

HIGHLAND AMBER — deep gold, no noticeable aroma, mild hop flavor, dry hop finish and aftertaste, short.

NUT BROWN ALE — deep amber, faint malt aroma, malt flavor is on the dry side, good body, tasty and satisfying, long dry malt aftertaste.

OATMEAL STOUT — brown, chocolate malt and roasted barley aroma and flavor, medium body, pleasant and easy to drink, long dry roasted malt aftertaste.

Brewmasters Pub Restaurant & Brewery

Brewpub in Kenosha, WI

KENOSHA GOLD — gold, hop aroma and taste, good body, very dry hop finish and aftertaste.

JOHNSON'S HONEY LAGER — gold, honeyed malt aroma and flavor, good body, dry malt finish and aftertaste.

AMBER VIENNA STYLE — amber, complex malt and hop aroma, sharp malty flavor, malt finish goes very dry in the aftertaste.

OKTOBERFEST ALT — brown, big fruity malt aroma and taste, very complex, off-dry malt finish, dry malt aftertaste.

Brewski's Gaslamp Pub, Inc.

Brewpub in San Diego, CA

RED SAILS ALE — amber, hop aroma, bright hop flavor, good body, long dry hop aftertaste.

AZTEC AMBER ALE — golden amber, ale-like hop and fruity malt aroma, hop and fruity malt flavor, good body, nicely balanced, dry hop finish, long dry hop aftertaste has plenty of supporting malt.

PIONEER PORTER — brown, medium dry malt aroma and flavor, good body, decent balance, dry malt finish and aftertaste.

CHARGER GOLD — golden amber, big hop aroma, very flavorful hop palate, good body, long slightly dry hop aftertaste.

TWO BERRY ALE — a weizen with a blackberry/raspberry aroma, more berry flavor than weizen, on the sweet side, more like a cooler than a fruit-weizen, long off-dry berry aftertaste.

DOWNTOWN CHESTNUT BROWN — dark amber, mild ale aroma, light malt and hop flavor has only a light ale tang, medium body, long dry malt aftertaste.

DUNKELWEIZEN — dark amber, very little aroma, just some faint malt, mild malt flavor, light body, brief malt aftertaste.

WEIZEN ALE — gold, light hop aroma, lemony flavor, medium body, light lemony malt aftertaste with not much duration.

Broad Ripple Brewing Co.

Brewpub in Indianapolis, IN

BROAD RIPPLE ESB — tawny gold, hop nose and taste, very dry, good body, dry hop finish, long dry hop aftertaste, smoothly hopped all across the palate.

BROAD RIPPLE IPA — gold, strong hop nose, big hop flavor, quite highly hopped, good body, dry hop finish and long dry hop aftertaste.

BROAD RIPPLE PORTER — brown, caramel malt aroma, dull malt flavor, short dry malt aftertaste.

BROAD RIPPLE KÖLSCH — tawny-gold, big malt and hop nose, huge dry hop flavor, good body, long dry hop aftertaste retains much of the strength of the flavor.

Buffalo Bill's Brewpub

Brew-pub in Hayward, CA

BUFFALO BILL'S BREWPUB BEER — cloudy orange-amber, faint citrus nose, light body, light citrus flavor, medium dry hop aftertaste, interesting but lacks depth.

PUMPKIN ALE — hazy pale orange, clean, light, off-dry fruity tangerine nose, palate is fruity malt first, then hoppy in middle and finish, fruity malt and bright hop aftertaste, medium body, good balance, interesting and very drinkable.

BUFFALO BILL'S PUMPKIN ALE 1992 — gold, pumpkin spice and eucalyptus aroma, big spicy cinnamon, nutmeg, etc. flavor, good body, long spicy aftertaste like the flavor, very good of the type.

BUFFALO BILL'S DOUBLE CREAM ALE — hazy gold, light fruity aroma (like melon and peaches), creamy texture, hops on front of the palate, fruity malt in the middle, dry hop finish and aftertaste, medium length.

RAUCH BEER SMOKED PORTER — amber, smoked sausage aroma, a bit peppery, harsh smoked flavor, dry smoked aftertaste with considerable length.

Butterfield Brewing Co.

Brewpub and restaurant in Fresno, CA

SAN JOAQUIN ALE — gold, light hop aroma and flavor, fairly dry, medium body, dry hop finish, not much of an aftertaste.

WILLAMETTE ALE — amber-gold, hop aroma, light hop flavor, dry hop finish and aftertaste.

BRIDALVEIL ALE — amber, light hop nose, big malt flavor, hefty body, soft and smooth, good balance, medium dry finish and aftertaste shows both the malt and the hops.

TOWER DARK ALE — brown, overdone roast malt aroma, a bit burnt as well, roasted malt flavor lacks complexity and interest, dull malt aftertaste.

MAIBOCK — gold, hop nose, smooth malt and hop flavor, has balance, malt shows best in the finish, dry malt and hop aftertaste.

IMPERIAL STOUT — brown, faint roasted malt aroma, light roast barley malt flavor, finishes dry malt, long dry malt aftertaste.

Cambridge Brewing Co.

Brewpub in Cambridge, MA

REGATTA GOLDEN — hazy gold, big malt and hop nose and flavor, complex, good body, good balance, dry hop finish, long dry hop and malt aftertaste.

CAMBRIDGE AMBER — medium pale amber, light malt and hop nose, good body, touch of soap in the finish, long complex dry malt and hop aftertaste.

CHARLES RIVER PORTER — deep mahogany, big malt and hop nose, smooth malt and hop flavor, good balance, good body, long dry hop aftertaste.

TALL TALE PALE ALE — slightly hazy golden amber, rising hop aroma, big complex hop flavor, a little hop bite especially in the finish, very long dry hop aftertaste.

WINTER WARMER — mahogany color, spicy over the malt in the nose, cinnamon-nutmeg off-dry malt flavor, medium body, long spicy aftertaste, enough malt to be tasted but for the most part the spices take center stage.

TRIPEL THREAT — gold, fruity nose, strong sweet peach fruity flavor, good body, long medium dry hop aftertaste, interesting, done in the Belgian style.

Capital Brewing Co.

Brewery in Middleton, WI

Uses bottling facilities of Stevens Point B.C., Stevens Point, WI, for packaging.

CAPITAL GARTEN BRÄU SPECIAL — amber, well-balanced malt and hop nose, fine malt palate with a light hop finish, medium body, good balance, long dry hop aftertaste.

CAPITAL GARTEN BRÄU WILD RICE — amber-gold, malty aroma, fresh off-dry fruity malt flavor, heavy body, medium dry malt finish and aftertaste.

CAPITAL GARTEN BRÄU DARK — deep amber, malty-molasses nose, dry malty flavor with the molasses still in back, dry malt aftertaste of medium length.

CAPITAL MAIBOCK — amber-gold, huge complex malt aroma, rich and strong malt flavor, dry malt aftertaste, very tasty, very complex and very long.

CAPITAL GARTEN BRÄU OKTOBERFEST — medium amber-gold color, complex fragrant hop aroma, well-balanced dry hop and malt flavor that continues into a long dry aftertaste, smooth and tasty throughout.

CAPITAL GARTEN BRÄU BOCK — amber-brown, big malt nose, almost molasses-like, big slightly toasted malt flavor and finish, excellent long dry malt aftertaste, very drinkable.

CAPITAL GARTEN BRÄU LAGER — pale amber, big hop and malt nose, big rich malt and hop flavor, good body and balance, long dry malt and hop aftertaste.

WISCONSIN AMBER — amber, hop aroma, good balanced hop and malt flavor, medium to good body, dry hop finish and aftertaste still has some malt.

Carver's Bakery Cafe Brewery

Brewpub in Durango, CO

RASPBERRY WHEAT ALE — deep gold, malt aroma with no apparent berry, big malt and bitter hop flavor (again no raspberry), dry malt finish and aftertaste.

Catamount Brewing Co.

Brewery in White River Junction, VT

CATAMOUNT GOLD — deep gold, big nose with lots of fruity malt and hops, bright hop palate, good body, long hop aftertaste supported with plenty of malt. A hefty well-made brew.

CATAMOUNT AMBER — medium deep amber, subdued malt aroma, good tasting malt flavor, good body, good balance, long malt aftertaste, a satisfying, pleasant, very drinkable brew.

CATAMOUNT PORTER — deep mahogany, rich rising straightforward malt nose, big rich dry malt flavor with a lightly scorched backtaste that doesn't mar the effect, long dry malt aftertaste.

CATAMOUNT CHRISTMAS ALE 1990 — hazy amber, roasted malt aroma, big dry roasted malt flavor, big hop finish, noticeable alcohol, very long dry malt and hop aftertaste. A very good Christmas ale.

CATAMOUNT CHRISTMAS ALE 1991 — amber, beautiful big hop aroma with plenty of malt in back, big strong flavor much like the nose, delicious, appetizing, expertly balanced, very long hop aftertaste. This is the best effort from Catamount to date.

CATAMOUNT CHRISTMAS ALE 1992 — deep amber, great spicy malt-hop aroma, big complex spicy palate loaded with both malt and hops, richly flavored, excellent balance, very long dry hop aftertaste, like the '91— why change a good thing?

ETHAN ALLEN ALE — hazy gold, melony malt nose, carbonation sting is quite noticeable, malt dominates the flavor but the balance between the malt and hops is so-so, medium to light body, medium length dry malt aftertaste.

POST ROAD REAL ALE — amber, bright zesty hop nose with good malt, big complex hop flavor, big body, long dry hop aftertaste well supported with malt, very tasty ale, indeed! Made for Old Marlborough B.C., Marlboro, MA.

NEWMAN'S SARATOGA BRAND LAGER BEER — hazy gold, bright fruity hop nose, flavor like the nose, good body, good balance, long dry hop aftertaste. Made for William S. Newman B.C., Albany, NY.

COMMONWEALTH BURTON ALE — amber, dank nose, dull malt flavor, short dry malt aftertaste. Made for Commonwealth B.C. of Boston.

CATAMOUNT OCTOBERFEST — amber-gold, spicy hop nose, nice dry hop and malt flavor, medium body, dry malt aftertaste has some length.

PIKE PLACE PALE ALE — hazy amber, light malt nose, light toasted nutty malt flavor, burnt malt finish, long aftertaste shows faintly of the burnt malt. Made for Pike Place Brewery and Merchant du Vin for national distribution.

Celis Brewery

Microbrewery in Austin, TX

CELIS WHITE — very pale cloudy yellow-gold, almost white, attractive spicy aroma and flavor, dry with plenty of hops and malt, medium body, dry malt aftertaste, a very nice typical Belgian white ale style wheat brew.

CELIS GOLDEN — pale gold, malt and flowery hop nose, big malt flavor, big body, malt finish and aftertaste, long with hops showing well at the end.

CELIS PALE BOCK — gold, complex fruity malt aroma that has peach and melon tones, malt flavor has the fruitiness in back, medium body, dry malt finish and aftertaste, not much length.

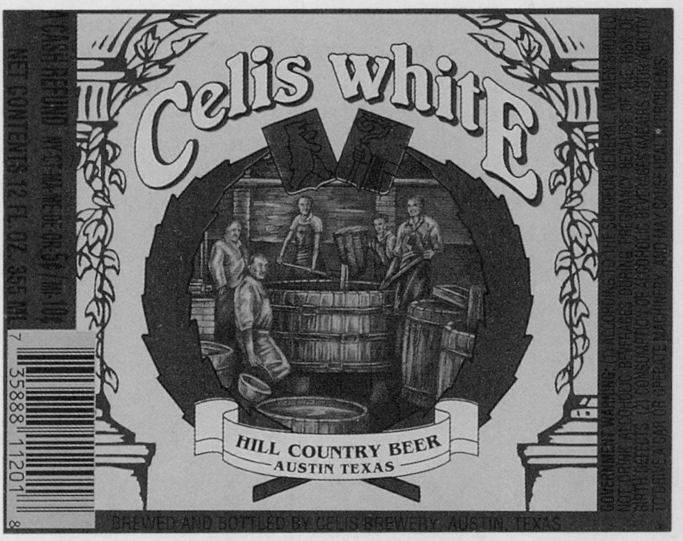

Champion Brewing Co.

Brewpub in Denver, CO

RED LIGHT — reddish amber, hop aroma and flavor, medium body, dry hop finish and aftertaste.

HOME RUN ALE — deep amber, no discernible aroma, lightly roasted barley malt flavor, medium body, very dry malt finish and aftertaste, long duration.

STOUT STREET STOUT — dark brown, light roasted barley and chocolate malt aroma, bright flavor but the body is a bit weak, medium to long dry malt aftertaste.

BLACK FOREST — deep amber, black cherry nose, big black cherry flavor, like a tart maraschino, very long dry malt aftertaste with the cherry remaining faintly to the end.

Cherryland Brewery

Microbrewery in **Sturgeon Bay, WI**

GOLDEN RAIL — amber-gold, malt and hop nose and taste, medium body, dry malt and hop finish and aftertaste.

SILVER RAIL — gold, hop aroma and flavor, medium body, fairly dry hop finish and aftertaste.

Coeur D'Alene Brewing Co./ T.W. Fischer's Brewpub

Microbrewery and brewpub in **Coeur D'Alene, ID**

T.W. FISHER'S LIGHT — gold, dank nose, malt flavor has a cooked corn background, light body, brief light and dry malt aftertaste.

T.W. FISHER'S CENTENNIAL PALE ALE — gold, off-dry malt aroma, dry malt and light hop flavor, medium body, short dry malt aftertaste.

T.W. FISHER'S FESTIVAL DARK — deep amber, cooked corn nose, grainy cooked corn flavor, same for finish and aftertaste.

T.W. FISHER'S FULL MOON STOUT — dark brown, roasted malt nose with a cooked corn and grain background, same for the flavor, dull grainy aftertaste.

Cold Spring Brewing Co.

Brewery in **Cold Spring, MN**

COLD SPRING BEER — pale gold, fragrant malt aroma, good clean malt and hop flavor, medium dry long aftertaste.

KEGLE BRAU — tawny-gold, lovely malt and hop aroma, good malt and hop flavor, very tasty, bright hop finish and long hop aftertaste.

COLD SPRING EXPORT — medium gold, complex hop aroma and flavor, dry hop finish and long dry hop aftertaste, a well-made and complex brew.

NORTH STAR BEER — medium gold, clean rich malt nose, lightly hopped flavor, light body, clean light malt and hop finish, weak short aftertaste.

GEMEINDE BRAU — gold, malt aroma, malt and hop flavor, dry hop finish and aftertaste with only medium duration. Made for Gemeinde Brau, Inc., Amana, IA.

WESTERN PREMIUM BEER — pale gold, bright malt aroma, pleasant malt flavor, finish and aftertaste, good length.

FOX DELUXE BEER — pale gold, pleasant malt nose, high carbonation, off-dry malt finish and aftertaste, medium length.

WHITE LABEL LIGHT BEER — medium gold, faint malt aroma, off-dry malt finish and aftertaste.

COLD BRAU PREMIUM BEER — pale gold, light fresh malt aroma, refreshing clean malt flavor, very light in hop character, pleasant malt finish and aftertaste, fair length.

KARLSBRAU OLD TIME BEER — bright gold, sour malt nose, vegetal malt flavor and finish, long slightly sour malt aftertaste.

KOLONIE BRAU — pale gold, lovely complex malt and hop aroma, equally complex malt and hop flavor, good balance, more malt than hops, but the hops do show well in the finish and long aftertaste. Made for Gemeinde Brau, Inc., Amana, IA.

COLD SPRING SELECT STOCK PREMIUM BEER — gold, clean dry malt aroma, medium body, light dry malt flavor, brief dry malt aftertaste.

Columbus Brewing Co.

Brewpub and attached restaurant in **Columbus, OH**

Has bottled beers made by F.X. Matt in Utica, NY.

GIBBY'S GOLD — light gold, nice hop nose, light soapy malt flavor, dry hop aftertaste.

PALE ALE — deep gold, light hop nose, big malt flavor with good hops, long flavor like the aroma, long malt aftertaste, a delicious brew.

NUT BROWN ALE — deep amber-brown, roasted malt aroma, big malt flavor with an acidic background, long rich malt aftertaste also has the acidic bite.

BLACK FOREST PORTER — deep brown, malt nose, sweet malt palate, big body, almost viscous, long malt finish and aftertaste with an acidic tang in back.

COLUMBUS PALE ALE — amber, pleasant malt and hop aroma and flavor, balanced, good body, dull dry malt finish and aftertaste.

COLUMBUS NUT BROWN ALE — brown, malt nose, off-dry malt flavor dries a bit at the finish, thin body, dry malt aftertaste.

Commonwealth Brewing Co.

Brewpub in Boston, MA

Bottled beers are made under contract by F.X. Matt, Utica, NY and Catamount B.C., White River Junction, VT.

STANLEY CUP STRONG ALE — hazy amber, spicy faint clove off-dry nose, medium body, soft, low carbonation, tangy off-dry spicy clove flavor, buttery finish, hop aftertaste.

GOLDEN ALE — pale gold, light hop aroma, medium body, light hop and malt flavor, low carbonation, dry hop aftertaste.

AMBER ALE — amber, light malt aroma, light body, light malt and hop flavor, dry hop finish.

COLD DRAUGHT BLOND ALE — tawny-gold, clean crisp hop nose, light clean dry malt flavor, dry malt finish and medium aftertaste, the 20% wheat malt wouldn't be noticed unless you knew.

BOSTON'S BEST BURTON BITTER — copper color, dry hop nose, flavor and finish, and very dry and long hop aftertaste.

CLASSIC STOUT — very deep brown, light smooth malt aroma with a touch of hops, classic stout nose, not big but pleasant, good dry malt and hop flavor, smooth finish and long aftertaste like the flavor, very drinkable.

INDIA PALE ALE — amber, big hop nose has a buttery background, malt flavor doesn't show as much of the buttery nature, good body, long dry malt aftertaste.

CooperSmith's Pub & Brewing

Brewpub in Fort Collins, CO

MOUNTAIN AVENUE WHEAT — hazy gold, fresh malt aroma, big spicy flavor, smooth, bright and tasty, finishes dry, a very well-made brew.

PEACH WHEAT — tawny-gold, clean fruity nose, very big spicy palate is excellent except that there is little follow-thru, weak finish, dry aftertaste.

DUNKEL WEIZEN — brown, malt nose, light lactic flavor could use a bit more malt for balance, good body, smooth long dry malt aftertaste shows more malt and less spice than the flavor.

PUNJABI PALE ALE — amber, malt aroma with some orange peel, flavor is all malt to mid-palate and thence hops, doesn't quite come together, big body, sour hop finish, dry sour hop aftertaste.

ALBERT DAMM BITTER — amber, faint malt nose, thin body, low carbonation, light malt flavor, finish and aftertaste, dry and dull.

NUT BROWN ALE — reddish-amber-brown, light chocolate malt aroma, light chocolate and black malt flavor, light body, pleasant, smooth and short.

HORSETOOTH STOUT — very dark brown, coffee and chocolate nose, light malt flavor, low carbonation, light body, short dry malt aftertaste.

DUNRAVIN ALE — amber, appetizing malt nose, tasty malt and hop flavor, light body, very smooth and drinkable, dry aftertaste doesn't give enough follow-thru to the flavor.

SIGDA'S GREEN CHILI BEER — gold, light chili pepper nose, almost like green bell peppers, flavor like the aroma, dry and hot and very long.

Adolph Coors Co.

Breweries in Golden, CO, Memphis, TN and Elkton, VA

COORS BEER — pale gold, lovely fresh clean malt aroma, hops barely noticeable, light body, slightly off-dry malt taste, very light, very refreshing, very quaffable, medium to short duration.

COORS LIGHT — very pale yellow-gold, very clean malt aroma, perky clean malt flavor, light and brief.

GEORGE KILLIAN'S IRISH RED LAGER — pale copper-red, light toasted malt aroma, light body, clean, fresh and balanced hop and malt flavor, light but lingering malt aftertaste.

COORS GOLDEN LAGER — yellow-gold, clean malt nose, very light malt flavor, a little hop bite in back, light and short malt aftertaste.

COORS EXTRA GOLD — bright yellow-gold, pleasant malt aroma, pleasant off-dry malt and hop flavor, long off-dry malt aftertaste.

HERMAN JOSEPH'S ORIGINAL LIGHT DRAFT BEER — pale gold, nice beery malt nose, highly carbonated, light body, pleasant malt and hop flavor, good balance, brief aftertaste.

HERMAN JOSEPH'S ORIGINAL DRAFT BEER — gold, pleasant, light, fresh malt and hop nose, clean flavor like the nose, zesty hop finish, short hop aftertaste, a very pleasant little brew.

COORS WINTERFEST 1992-1993 — deep gold, light dry hop nose, malt and dry hop flavor is a bit rough but there is a lot of it, fair to good balance, good body, light short dry malt aftertaste.

COORS WINTERFEST 1991-1992 — brilliant amber, plain malt nose, big malt flavor, especially at the finish, very tasty brew, long hop aftertaste, best of the Winterfests to date.

COORS WINTERFEST 1990-1991 — amber, fruity-malt aroma, malt flavor, an estery quality to both the nose and taste, ends up with an off-dry malt aftertaste, still with that estery quality in back.

COORS WINTERFEST 1989-1990 — tawny-gold, faint fruity malt aroma, off-dry malt flavor, soft and light with low carbonation, medium dry finish, light short malt aftertaste, a wimpy brew. Similar to the 1987, which had more hops than the '89-'90.

COORS EXTRA GOLD DRAFT — bright gold, beautiful malt and hop aroma, slightly off-dry malt palate, very drinkable, medium body, long off-dry malt aftertaste.

KEYSTONE — light gold, light malt nose, malt flavor with a touch of apple, medium body, malt aftertaste of medium length.

KEYSTONE LIGHT — light gold, very faint malt nose with a trace of apple, off-dry malt flavor, weak body, dry malt aftertaste, short to medium length.

KEYSTONE DRY — pale hazy gold, fruity malt nose, faint fruity malt flavor, light body, dull faintly fruity malt aftertaste.

COORS CUTTER NON-ALCOHOLIC BEER — pale gold, grainy malt nose, thin body, wet paper and malt flavor, dry malt finish, short malt aftertaste.

COORS PREMIUM DRY BEER — gold, pleasant fruity-malt nose, high carbonation, off-dry fruity malt front palate, middle and finish are dry malt, brief light dry malt aftertaste, light body.

Coyote Springs Brewing Co. & Cafe

Brewpub in Phoenix, AZ

Formerly named Barley's Brewpub.

KOYOTE KÖLSCH — gold, malt nose, very bright malt and hop flavor, good body, dry malt and hop finish and aftertaste, a very tasty zesty brew.

NUTS TO YOU NUT BROWN ALE — brown, hoppy fruity aroma, a sense of lactic in back, flavor has even more (and clearly) lactic acid in behind the hops, good body, acidity mars the flavor and aftertaste. Tasted at Great America Beer Festival (GABF) in Denver; apparently a victim of some mistreatment on its journey.

TRICK PALE ALE — gold, big bright hop aroma with lactic acid behind the hops; lactic acid is more pronounced on the palate but behind the hops, staying well into the aftertaste. This was also tasted at GABF and had suffered from mishandling.

PROSPECTOR PALE ALE — amber-gold, aroma shows both malt and hops, big hop flavor with plenty of malt for good balance, overall it is a dry flavor, especially at the finish, long dry hop aftertaste.

COYOTE GOLD — gold, dry hop nose with some malt showing, very dry hop flavor, finish and aftertaste, not much malt showing past the aroma, but enough for balance.

DRY GULCH STOUT — very deep brown color, roasted barley nose, dry roasted malt flavor makes you think of coffee, finish shows that it was dry hopped, long dry hop aftertaste, very pleasant and drinkable.

FRONTIER BROWN — very deep amber-brown, light malt aroma, roasted barley malt flavor, very smooth, good body, malty and drinkable, light dry roasted malt finish and aftertaste, short duration.

COYOTE CHRISTMAS ALE — deep amber-gold, spicy nose made me think of ginger, but it is nutmeg, cloves, coriander and cinnamon, spicy flavor (still made me think of ginger, but I had a head cold), long dry spicy aftertaste, a good wassail.

COYOTE LAGER — pale gold, bright hop aroma and flavor, light to medium body, dry hop finish and aftertaste. Tasted while still in second fermentation, so it was not finished. It does show good promise for a bright refreshing pilsener style beer.

VIENNA LAGER — amber, good malt nose and taste, good body, hops stay in back as they should for the style. Tasted while in second fermentation; showing good characteristics of the intended style, but tasted too early for complete comment.

OATMEAL STOUT — very dark brown, roasted barley and chocolate malt aroma, dry roasted malt flavor, complex, showing some chocolate and coffee, good balance, finishes very well leading into a long aftertaste like the flavor, but drier. This, too, was tasted while still fermenting, but it was very near to being ready for release.

Crescent City Brewhouse

Brewpub in New Orleans, LA

CRESCENT CITY PILSNER — gold, fresh and crisp hop nose, bright hop flavor, good body, dry hop finish and aftertaste, good length, very nice European style pils.

CRESCENT CITY
BREWHOUSE

RED STALLION — amber-gold, malt aroma immediately makes you think of a Vienna style lager, slightly off-dry malt flavor has the hops in back, malt finish and long malt aftertaste.

BLACK FOREST — dark mahogany, complex chocolate malt nose, dry chocolate malt flavor is very attractive, good body, long aftertaste is an extension of the taste, very drinkable and satisfying.

CRESCENT CITY MARDI GRAS — dark amber, malt nose, light dry malt flavor, medium body, medium length.

Crested Butte Brewery & Pub, Idlespur, Inc.

Brewpub in Crested Butte, CO

RED LADY ALE — reddish amber, bright malt and hop nose, mild malt and hop flavor, very drinkable, balanced, pleasant, long dry hop aftertaste.

BUCKS WHEAT— hazy gold, malt nose, malt flavor with good hop balance, medium body, dry hop finish and aftertaste.

3-PIN GRIN PORTER — brown, no nose, dull malt flavor and aftertaste.

RASPBERRY-OATMEAL STOUT — deep brown, great tart raspberry-malt nose, thin body, dull malt flavor shows little of the aroma, dull aftertaste.

Crested Butte Brewery & Pub, Crested Butte, Colorado
BREWED & BOTTLED BY HAND AT THE CRESTED BUTTE BREWERY & PUB
CRESTED BUTTE, CO. CONTENTS 650 ML.
RED LADY ALE
Made from the finest Malted Barley, Hops, Yeast and Purest Mountain Water Only
CB
"Quaff the Fresh"
GOVERNMENT WARNING: (1) ACCORDING TO THE SURGEON GENERAL, WOMEN SHOULD NOT DRINK ALCOHOLIC BEVERAGES DURING PREGNANCY BECAUSE OF THE RISK OF BIRTH DEFECTS. (2) CONSUMPTION OF ALCOHOLIC BEVERAGES IMPAIRS YOUR ABILITY TO DRIVE A CAR OR OPERATE MACHINERY, AND MAY CAUSE HEALTH PROBLEMS.

Dallas Brewing Co.

Brewery in Dallas, TX

WEST END LAGER — brilliant pale gold, pleasant fruity malt nose reminds me of lychee nuts, fruity malt and light sour hop flavor, medium body, hop finish, very short dry malt and hop aftertaste.

OUTBACK LAGER — bright pale gold, malt aroma has a fruity nature like lychee nuts and citrus, dry malt and hop flavor, medium body, long dry malt and hop aftertaste.

DALLAS GOLD — gold, strong malt nose has a mandarin orange-lychee nut style, good body, big hop and malt flavor, dry hop aftertaste.

COWBOY PREMIUM — amber, big fruity malt nose has a faintly vegetal background, bright malt flavor, medium body, dry malt aftertaste.

BLUEBONNET — pale gold, faintly vegetal malt aroma and taste, dry malt finish and aftertaste.

Note: *The following brews were labels of the Reinheitsgebot B.C. of Plano, TX. Mary and Donald Thompson owned and operated Reinheitsgebot until it closed a few years back. Mary is now Brewery Manager of Dallas B.C. and Donald is the new brewmaster. They plan to begin production of the Collin County brands soon, so I am including two of them here.*

COLLIN COUNTY BLACK GOLD BEER — deep amber, perfumy and tangy malt aroma, a touch of citrus lays in back, light body, mild malt flavor has a slightly burnt backtaste, malt finish, medium long malt aftertaste is a touch sour.

COLLIN COUNTY EMERALD BEER — brilliant green, nice hop aroma, bright hop flavor, clean and refreshing, medium body, long dry hop aftertaste.

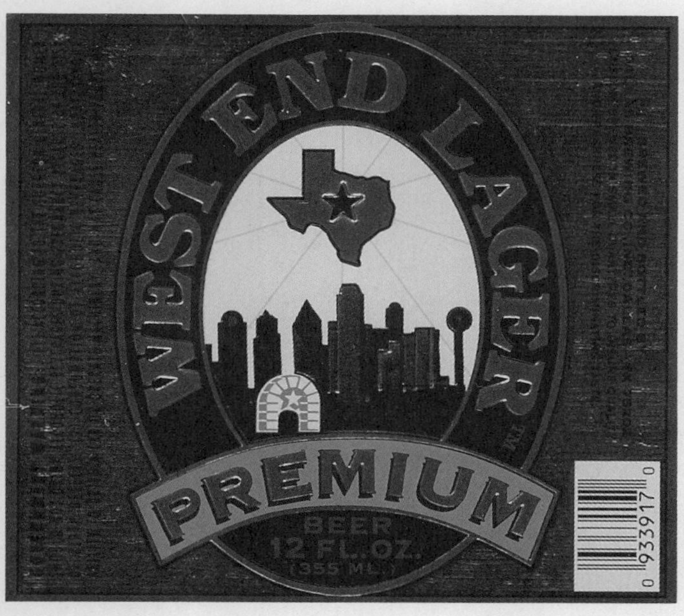

Deschutes Brewery & Public House

Brewpub in Bend, OR

DESCHUTES BREWERY JUBEL ALE 1991 — deep amber, gorgeous rich malt nose, rich malt flavor, medium long, big bodied, fairly dry malt aftertaste.

DESCHUTES DUNKELWEIZEN — brown, complex malt and hop aroma, good body, off-dry malt flavor backed with hops, slightly drier malt aftertaste has more hop character.

CASCADE GOLDEN ALE — gold, malt aroma, light malt flavor, dry malt aftertaste.

BACHELOR BITTER — cloudy amber, good big hop flavor, good body, fairly dry flavor and long dry hop aftertaste.

BLACK BUTTE PORTER — brown, lightly fruity sweet malt aroma and flavor, has good balance despite being sort of sweet because there are good hops in there as well as several kinds of malt, hops do stay in back throughout, dry malt finish and aftertaste.

MIRROR POND PALE ALE — amber-gold, fruity malt aroma, good body, dry hop finish and aftertaste.

FESTIVAL PILS — gold, big hop aroma, big bright hoppy flavor, very dry through to the long dry hop aftertaste.

BOND STREET BROWN ALE — brown, roasted malt aroma and flavor, touch of chocolate also, good body, dry malt finish and aftertaste.

OBSIDIAN STOUT — dark brown, roasted barley and chocolate malt aroma and flavor, good balance, good body, dry malt finish and aftertaste, a very drinkable brew.

WYCHICK WEIZEN —cloudy amber, malt aroma, off-dry malt flavor, no spice.

SOUTH SISTER SCOTCH ALE — dark brown, sweet caramel malt aroma, dry malt flavor, off-dry malt finish and aftertaste, goes dry malt at the very end.

Detroit & Mackinac Brewery

Microbrewery in **Detroit, MI**

WEST CANFIELD ALE — gold, buttery nose, thin malt and hop flavor, short dry hop aftertaste.

DETROIT & MACKINAC IPA — gold, malt nose, flavor has more hops than malt but is light to point of seeming thin, light body, light dry hop and malt aftertaste.

DETROIT & MACKINAC RED ALE — amber, malt aroma, caramel malt and faint hop flavor, creamy, good body, dry malt aftertaste.

Dilworth Brewing Co.

Brewpub in **Charlotte, NC**

REED'S GOLD — gold, hop aroma, sweet malt in back, cardboard and malt flavor, dry malt aftertaste.

ALBEMARLE ALE — dark amber, faint malt aroma and flavor, fairly brief dry malt aftertaste.

DILWORTH PORTER — dark brown, roasted barley aroma and flavor, good body, harsh malt and hop flavor, lacks balance.

Dock Street Brewing Co.

Brewpub/restaurant in **Philadelphia, PA**

DOCK STREET WEISS BIER — hazy gold, light fresh malt aroma, bright malt flavor with plenty of hops, a lot of hops for a wheat beer but the balance is good, dry mostly hop finish, long dry hop aftertaste. Mix is 50% wheat.

DOCK STREET HELLES — deep gold, bright hop nose and taste, hop finish and aftertaste, very long, very German, malt is there but barely noticeable.

DOCK STREET PALE ALE — tawny-gold, faint hop nose, bright hop flavor with plenty of malt, good body, dry hop finish, long dry hop aftertaste, excellent balance, complex, feels good in your mouth.

DOCK STREET IMPERIAL STOUT — opaque brown, tan head, malt aroma, concentrated malt flavor, burnt nature of the malt is most noticeable in the finish, long tapering malt aftertaste.

DOCK STREET BARLEY WINE — deep brown, big dry chocolate malt nose and taste, strong hops back the malt but can barely compete and stay in back except at the finish and aftertaste, big, complex and very long, feels great in your mouth. Have this at the end of your beer drinking, because if you have it first, it is almost overwhelming and, for certain, you won't be able to taste anything else afterwards.

DOCK STREET AMBER — pale amber, light malt nose, dry malt and hop flavor, long aftertaste has dry hops and malt with a touch of malt sweetness at the end.

DOCK STREET BOHEMIAN PILSNER — golden amber, beautiful hop nose and taste, very well balanced with malt, some complexity, dry hop finish and aftertaste, good duration.

DOCK STREET CREAM ALE — gold, appetizing malt aroma, smooth and soft malt flavor, dry malt finish, aftertaste is soft dry malt but lacks length.

DOCK STREET DORTMUNDER — amber-gold, hop nose, good dry hop flavor, well bodied, long dry hop aftertaste, made to style.

DOCK STREET OLD ALE — gold, spicy hop aroma, big off-dry malt flavor, good body, dry finish, but very little aftertaste.

Durango Brewing Co.

Microbrewery in **Durango, CO**

DURANGO DARK — deep amber, malt aroma, light malt flavor, not much follow-thru.

COLORFEST — pale gold, malt nose and taste, thin body, no follow-thru.

Electric Dave Brewing Co.

Microbrewery in South Bisbee, AZ

ELECTRIC BEER — amber-gold, dry hop nose and flavor, good balance, malt shows best in the finish, long dry after-taste, good length, quite dry throughout, very drinkable.

CACTUS LAGER — cloudy amber, dry hop nose, extremely dry hop flavor, not strong, but very very dry, short dry hop aftertaste. Made for the San Francisco Bar & Grill of Tuscon.

Etna Brewing Co.

Brewery in Etna, CA

ETNA EXPORT LAGER BEER — hazy gold, fresh fruity malt nose, bright hop and malt flavor, light body, tasty, drinkable, short dry aftertaste.

ETNA ALE — hazy amber, malt aroma, light malt and hop flavor, light body, brief light dry malt aftertaste.

ETNA DARK LAGER BEER — deep amber-brown, big dark malt nose with a slightly smoked background, light body, flavor like the nose but not as strong nor as smoked, medium long dry malt aftertaste.

ETNA WEIZEN — pale gold, malt aroma, slightly spicy malt flavor, light wheaty finish and aftertaste.

Etna Ale
ETNA BREWERY
NET CONTENTS 1 PINT 6 FLUID OZ.

Firehouse Brewing Co.

Brewpub in Rapid City, SD

BUFFALO BITTER — amber, buttery caramel malt aroma, tastes very much like the aroma, this continues thru the finish into the long aftertaste.

RUSHMORE STOUT — brown, dark malt and alcoholic nose, big roasted barley flavor, not much follow-thru.

BROWN COW ALE — brown, fruity malt nose and taste, off-dry malt finish, medium long dry malt aftertaste.

The Florida Brewery, Inc.

Brewery in Auburndale, FL

GROWLIN GATOR LAGER — pale yellow-gold, pleasant malt nose, refreshing malt flavor is good while it lasts (which is not for long), light body, fine for hot weather drinking.

ABC BEER — gold, malt and light hop nose, flavor like the aroma, light hop finish, medium long aftertaste has some hops and malt, overall fairly dry. Made for ABC Liquor chain of Florida.

ABC ALE — deep gold, dry hop nose, tangy hop flavor, has some malt in back, dry hop finish and aftertaste, medium length. Also made for ABC Liquors.

ABC LIGHT — gold, attractive malt and hop nose, light malt flavor, light body, very faint and brief malt aftertaste. Another made for ABC Liquors.

ABC MALT LIQUOR — deep gold, malt and hop nose, flavor is mostly malt but there are some hops in back, long off-dry malt aftertaste. Also made for ABC Liquors.

Flying Dog Brew Pub

Brewpub in Aspen, CO

RIN TIN TAN BROWN ALE— brown, very appetizing hop aroma, big bright hop flavor with plenty of malt, very drinkable, good body, finishes dry hops, long dry hop after-taste.

BULLMASTIFF BROWN ALE — brown, malty nose and taste, good body but on the dull side.

AIREDALE PALE ALE — deep gold, lovely nose shows hops and malt, flavor nicely balanced between the malt and the hops, good body, long dry malt and hop aftertaste, a very pleasant easy to drink brew.

DOGGIE STYLE PALE ALE — amber, peachy fruit malt aroma, big hop flavor, big body, complex and interesting, long dry hop aftertaste, another winner from the Dog.

ENGLISH SETTER BITTER — amber-gold, hops dominate the nose and the flavor, taste is very big hops, yet the brew is complex and well-balanced, finishes dry hops leading into a long dry hop aftertaste, one of the better English bitter style ales made on this continent.

SCOTTIE SCOTTISH EXPORT ALE — deep amber, big hop nose, big and bright hop palate, very zesty, medium long dry hop aftertaste.

OL' YELLER GOLDEN ALE — gold, hop nose and taste, medium body, dry hop finish and aftertaste.

HAIR OF THE DOG PORTER — brown, dry malt nose and flavor, good body, smooth, dry and balanced, but short.

WOLFHOUND IRISH STOUT — brown, roasted barley and chocolate malt nose and taste, very smooth and dry, good body, long dry aftertaste like the flavor.

IRISH SETTER STOUT — dark brown, malt nose and taste, medium body, fairly long dry malt aftertaste.

SHEEPDOG STOUT — dark brown, soapy nose and taste, one taster felt it was like detergent.

FLYING McDOG SCOTCH ALE — ruby-brown, buttery malt nose, caramel malt flavor has an alcohol and medicinal background, dry malt finish and aftertaste.

BULLDOG IMPERIAL STOUT — dark brown, malt aroma and flavor, big body, seems a bit duller than other stouts from Flying Dog.

BLITZEN'S GNARLY BARLEY WINE — amber, hop nose, huge hop flavor, big body, faint lactic bite in back, long hop aftertaste.

RED WARLOCK RASPBERRY COOLER — pink, spicy nose and taste, dry finish and aftertaste, somewhat short.

BLOODHOUND RASPBERRY STOUT — almost black, certainly opaque, big raspberry nose, medium strength raspberry-malt flavor, finishes very dry, fairly long dry malt aftertaste.

RED DOG GINGER BEER — pale gold, ginger nose like a ginger snap cookie, light ginger flavor, dry finish and aftertaste is malt and hops, no ginger. This is not a soft drink, but rather a beer made with grated ginger root in the brew kettle.

GREYHOUND HONEY ALE — pale gold, honey malt nose and taste, very light finish and less aftertaste.

K-9 CLASSIC PALE ALE — gold, malt nose and taste, very light flavor, light body, dry finish and aftertaste without much character.

DOG HOUSE WHEAT — gold, cereal nose and grainy taste, stays a little off-dry and is only faintly spicy.

Frankenmuth Brewery, Inc.

Brewery in **Frankenmuth, MI**

FRANKENMUTH GERMAN STYLE PILSENER — gold, good malt and hop nose, rich hop flavor, has plenty of malt, good body, long dry hop aftertaste.

FRANKENMUTH GERMAN STYLE DARK — deep rosy-amber, off-dry malt aroma, straight forward dry malt flavor, long dry malt aftertaste, smooth and very drinkable.

FRANKENMUTH GERMAN STYLE BOCK — brown, big malt nose, smooth complex roasted malt flavor, big body, balanced, richly flavored, long dry malt aftertaste.

FRANKENMUTH WEISSE — bright gold, melon-mango fruit and malt nose, finely carbonated, faint fruity-malt-wheat flavor, light body, faint spice joins malt in the finish, medium long spicy malt aftertaste.

FRANKENMUTH EXTRA LIGHT — pale gold, faint malt nose with a hop background that makes you suspect that it will go skunky when it gets over-the-hill, light body, weak malt flavor is mostly carbonation, light malt finish, brief malt aftertaste with a sour touch at the very end.

OLD DETROIT AMBER ALE — light amber, malt aroma, zesty dry hop flavor, creamy texture, dry hop finish, dry malt aftertaste.

ISLAND GOLD BEER — deep gold, fruity malt aroma, dull malt flavor, thin body, weak short malt aftertaste. Contract brew for Bay B.C., Put-in-Bay, OH.

D.L. Geary Brewing Co.

Brewery in **Portland, ME**

GEARY'S PALE ALE — deep bright golden amber, big citrus hop and fruity-malt nose, complex dry hop palate borders on bitter but comes off very well, dry hop finish, long dry hop aftertaste that is a bit tart at the end, a very well-made and likeable brew.

HAMPSHIRE WINTER ALE 1989-1990 — cloudy amber, tart complex fruity-hop aroma, huge dry hop flavor with loads of malt in back, big body, extremely long dry hop aftertaste, a big sipping beer with very good balance.

HAMPSHIRE SPECIAL ALE 1990-1991 — bright amber, big toasted malt aroma, huge malt and hop flavor, rich and delicious, long dry hop aftertaste, great balance, good sipping beer.

HAMPSHIRE SPECIAL ALE 1991-1992 — hazy amber, citrus hop and malt aroma, big zesty complex hop ale flavor, rich malt backing, big long hop aftertaste, another delicious sipping beer.

HAMPSHIRE SPECIAL ALE 1992-1993 — hazy amber, smooth light citrus hop nose (some samples were faintly buttery), complex malt, hop and alcohol palate, very rich and distinctive, an abundance of hops, malt and alcohol throughout, big body, long tart hop aftertaste, perhaps a bit too much bite, but still good.

Genesee Brewing Co.

Brewery in **Rochester, NY**

GENESEE BEER — gold, good malt aroma, pleasant malt flavor with a slight hop taste, good balance, good body, short dry hop aftertaste.

GENESEE CREAM ALE — gold, big malt nose with a slight hop backing, good balanced malt and hop flavor, finishes a bit weakly, medium length aftertaste, what is there is pleasant.

GENESEE BOCK BEER — deep amber, malt aroma with lightly roasted malt character, fair body, good balance, pleasant long malt aftertaste.

GENESEE OKTOBERFEST BEER — deep amber, nice malt aroma, very smooth malt flavor, lightly hopped, dry malt finish and aftertaste, medium duration.

GENESEE LIGHT — pale color, mild malt aroma with some yeast in back, light body, dry and light hop flavor, light finish and brief aftertaste.

GENESEE NA NON-ALCOHOLIC BREW — pale gold, dull malt nose, thin body, weak malt flavor, almost watery, high carbonation, little aftertaste, light but refreshing when you are very thirsty.

GENESEE CREAM LIGHT CREAM ALE — medium yellow-gold, light fruity malt and talcum powder nose, medium dry malt and hop flavor, hop finish, off-dry malt aftertaste has good length.

TWELVE HORSE ALE — bright gold, fresh malt aroma, bright malt flavor with the hops gradually coming in as it crosses the palate, dry hop finish and aftertaste, lighter than I remember it from some years back, but still pleasant and refreshing.

KOCH'S GOLDEN ANNIVERSARY BEER — bright gold, light malt aroma, malt flavor, medium body, fairly long malt aftertaste. Uses corporate name of Fred Koch Brewery, the Dunkirk, NY brewery that originated the brand.

KOCH'S GOLDEN ANNIVERSARY LIGHT BEER — pale gold, pleasant hop and malt aroma, light body, weak malt flavor, thin body, brief aftertaste.

BLACK HORSE PREMIUM ALE — bright gold, nice hop and malt aroma, rich flavor with a malt front and hop middle and finish, good balance, quite zesty, long aftertaste shows both hops and malt.

MICHAEL O'SHEA'S IRISH AMBER PUB STYLE LAGER — amber, cooked malt aroma, vapid dull flavor like the nose, dull dry malt aftertaste.

Gentle Ben's Brewing Co.

Brewpub in **Tuscon, AZ**

BEAR DOWN BROWN — amber-brown, hop aroma, malt flavor with a noticeable lactic acid background, lactic impaired finish and aftertaste.

HARVEST MOON LIGHT — pale gold, bright spicy hop aroma, lemony malt flavor, dry malt finish and aftertaste.

CATALINA ALE — pale gold, light malt aroma, very bright and very dry hop flavor, refreshing, long dry hop aftertaste.

COPPERHEAD ALE — deep gold, rich hop and malt aroma, complex and interesting, flavor is both rich malt and strong dry hops, a big flavor, big body, long, dry and delicious.

TAYLOR JANE RASPBERRY — deep gold, sprightly raspberry aroma, very much a raspberry taste, dry berry finish and medium length aftertaste. I'm told it is made with some percentage of wheat malt.

RED CAT AMBER ALE — amber, hop aroma and big hop flavor, seems faintly soapy but it is not obtrusive, malt comes in at the finish, long dry malt and hop aftertaste.

OATMEAL STOUT — dark amber, spicy malt nose, ginger-malt flavor, good body, not heavy, long dry and spicy malt aftertaste.

Goose Island Brewing Co./Lincoln Park Brewery, Inc.

Brew-pub in Chicago, IL

GOLDEN GOOSE PILSNER — gold, mild hop aroma, very dry hop palate, good balance, very dry hop finish, long dry hop aftertaste.

TANZEN GANS KÖLSCH — gold, light hop aroma, zesty hop flavor, medium body, dry hop finish and aftertaste. Very good brew.

HONKER'S ALE — amber-gold, faintly sour hop nose, big hop flavor, especially good in back and sides of tongue, real bittering hops used, dry hop finish, long very dry hop aftertaste showing good malt at the end. Another very good brew.

PMD MILD ALE — amber brown, malt nose, good dry malt flavor, finishes dry hops but the malt is still there, excellent with food.

OLD CLYBOURN PORTER — deep brown, dry malt aroma, very dry malt flavor, medium to long dry malt aftertaste.

DUNKELWEIZENBOCK — hazy amber, some malty sweetness in the nose, big malt lightly spiced flavor, long off-dry malt aftertaste, a lovely sipping beer.

VICE WEIZEN — hazy gold, malt nose, smooth refreshing malt flavor, lightly spiced, finish and aftertaste is dry malt.

RAF BETTER BITTER ALE — deep amber-gold, bright hop aroma, has plenty of malt in back, zesty hop flavor still with plenty of supporting malt, dry hop finish, long very dry hop aftertaste.

WINTER WARMER BARLEY WINE — amber, big malt and hop nose and taste, big body, off-dry malt and hop finish and aftertaste.

OATMEAL STOUT — brown, dry roasted barley and chocolate malt aroma, flavor like the nose but not strong, rather it is smooth and light, medium body, fairly short dry malt aftertaste.

RUSSIAN IMPERIAL STOUT — black, tan head, dry roasted barley nose, medium strength dry roast malt flavor, medium body, fairly short dry roast malt aftertaste.

Great Lakes Brewing Co.

Brewpub in Cleveland, OH

GREAT LAKES DORTMUNDER STYLE — pale golden-amber, good malt aroma is almost ale-like, very pleasant big toasted malt flavor, dry malt finish, long rich malt aftertaste, hop presence is from start to finish but keeps in the back well surrounded by the richness of the malt, pleasant and satisfying. At the brewpub this is called HEISMAN and is brilliant gold, has a bright hop aroma and taste, with a dry malt finish and aftertaste.

GREAT LAKES VIENNA STYLE — deep amber, very faint malt and hop aroma, rich but dry roasted malt flavor, medium long dry malt aftertaste, good body, excellent example of a Vienna style lager. At the brewpub this brew is called ELIOT NESS and is amber, has a malt nose, a very smooth and balanced malt-hop flavor and a dry malt aftertaste.

BURNING RIVER PALE ALE STYLE — brilliant deep amber, delicious malt aroma, big hop ale flavor, dry hop finish, long dry hop aftertaste.

THE EDMUND FITZGERALD PORTER — dark brown, roasted black malt nose, good hop and malt flavor, good body, finishes dry malt.

THE COMMODORE PERRY INDIA PALE ALE — deep gold, bright hop nose, big bright spicy complex malt and hop flavor, long dry hop aftertaste.

MOON DOG ALE — amber, nice hop aroma, smooth and balanced hop-malt flavor, finishes smoothly, long aftertaste shows both the hops and malt in harmony, a very pleasant brew.

HOLY MOSES ALE — amber, very nice fruity hop aroma, creamy malt flavor, balanced, smooth, long dry malt and hop aftertaste.

Hart Brewing Co.

Brewery in Kalama, WA

PACIFIC CREST ALE — medium pale hazy amber, fruity toasted malt nose, big tangy ale flavor, lots of hops and toasted malt, good balance, fairly complex, big body, good dry hop finish and long hop and malt aftertaste.

PYRAMID WHEATEN ALE — hazy amber-gold, pleasant malt and citrus hop aroma, light dry tangy flavor with a light citrus background, medium body, short dry hop aftertaste, what is there is good, but there just isn't enough of it.

PYRAMID AMBER WHEATEN — amber, faint caramel nose, sort of spritzy dry hop flavor with caramel malt in back, finishes dry hops, malt and hop aftertaste.

PYRAMID SPHINX STOUT — opaque brown, brown head, smoky slightly burnt roasted malt aroma, dry burnt caramel palate, dry smoky malt finish, very dry slightly smoky malt aftertaste.

SNOW CAP ALE 1990 — deep reddish amber, big complex malt and hop nose, huge flavor, malt dominates at first, the hops vie for the lead in mid-palate, they don't clash in the contest and it comes off very well, big body, long, dry hop aftertaste with plenty of malt support. This is a winner! It is as good or better than any other seasonal winter beer offered.

G. Heileman Brewing Co.

Breweries in La Crosse, WI; Seattle, WA; Baltimore, MD; Portland, OR; and San Antonio, TX. Owned by Bond Corp. of Australia.

CHAMPALE MALT LIQUOR — pale gold, grapelike aroma that makes you think of champagne, light body, good carbonation, slightly sweet grapey flavor. Certainly tries to be champagne-like and does so fairly successfully.

GOLDEN CHAMPALE FLAVORED MALT LIQUOR — bright gold, fruit gum aroma, flavor much like a Scottish soda called Irn-Bru (Iron Brew in eastern Canada), fairly sweet and clean tasting, interesting for a flavored malt liquor.

PINK CHAMPALE FLAVORED MALT LIQUOR — pale pink, nose like Cold Duck which I presume it is intended to emulate, mildly flavored sweet taste (grenadine?), very drinkable and pleasant.

BLACK HORSE ALE — tawny-gold, bright hop aroma with plenty of supporting malt, caramel-malt flavor, good balance, long rich malt aftertaste.

METBRAU NEAR BEER — pale gold, faintly salty malt aroma, highly carbonated, flavor is light malt and carbonation, little finish and aftertaste.

HEILEMAN'S SPECIAL EXPORT BEER — tawny-gold, lusty hop aroma, flavor starts out hops but slightly off-dry, then gets bigger and more hoppy at mid-palate and into the finish, stays smooth, is complex and very much European in style, has plenty of character, finishes dry hops and has good length.

HEILEMAN'S SPECIAL EXPORT LIGHT BEER — pale bright gold, pleasant malt aroma, thin body, light malt flavor with some sour hop background in mid-palate, fleeting off-dry malt finish, very little aftertaste.

HEILEMAN'S SPECIAL EXPORT DARK — deep copper color, very little nose, only a faint sense of sweetness, faint hop flavor, low carbonation, light body, dull and uninteresting.

HEILEMAN'S OLD STYLE LIGHT LAGER BEER — gold color, fragrant malt and hop nose, bright hop flavor, balanced and fairly long.

OLD STYLE SPECIAL DRY — pale gold, sweet malt aroma, highly carbonated, off-dry malt front palate, dry middle and finish, faint brief malt aftertaste.

OLD STYLE PREMIUM DRY BEER — pale gold, apple-malt nose, fairly dry and smooth hop flavor, plenty of malt in support, finishes dry, not much aftertaste.

OLD STYLE CLASSIC DRAFT — gold, pleasant malt and hop aroma, high carbonation, flavor is malt, hops and carbonation, light but clean, melony finish, dry aftertaste.

OLD STYLE CLASSIC DRAFT LIGHT — gold, light malt and faint hop aroma, high carbonation, light flavor like the nose but the carbonation is a major part, light bodied, light dry finish, little aftertaste.

HEILEMAN'S LIGHT BEER — bright pale gold, faint malt aroma, light hop flavor that is less dry in front than it is in middle and finish, good balance and fairly long.

WIEDEMANN BOHEMIAN SPECIAL FINE BEER — pale gold, fresh malt aroma with some hops, light malt flavor with a hop background, good fresh tasting pilsener-type beer, fairly long dry hop aftertaste.

WIEDEMANN LIGHT — gold, grainy aroma with a soapy background, light body, weak malt flavor, seltzer-like finish and aftertaste, clean but uninteresting.

RED WHITE AND BLUE SPECIAL LAGER BEER — pale gold, light clean malt aroma and flavor, light body, dry malt finish and short aftertaste, quaffable hot weather beer.

BURGERMEISTER BEER — pale gold, pleasant light hop nose, light hop and malt flavor, dry hop finish and aftertaste, medium duration.

BLATZ BEER — gold, light malt nose, light malt flavor, light body, finishes dry and has a short malt aftertaste, what hops there are are well in back, another hot weather quaffing beer.

BLATZ LIGHT BEER — pale gold, lovely malt nose, malt flavor but you can taste the carbonation, hops come in with a bitter touch in the finish leading to a dry, brief and slightly bitter hop aftertaste

BLATZ LIGHT CREAM ALE — medium yellow-gold color, off-dry fruity malt aroma, tangy hop flavor, some off flavors in the backtaste which take a more dominant position in the aftertaste.

BLATZ LA BEER — gold, pleasant fragrant aroma with both malt and hops, watery body, very little flavor, what there is is pleasant but it is too weak.

BLITZ-WEINHARD BEER — tawny-gold, malt and hop nose, high carbonation, malt flavor that has a salty component, dry malt finish with some hops in aftertaste.

HENRY WEINHARD PRIVATE RESERVE — light to medium gold, good hop aroma, very appetizing, a zesty flavor that features both malt and hops, good balance, medium to good body, light hop aftertaste with good length. Each bottling is numerically identified on the neck label.

HENRY WEINHARD'S PRIVATE RESERVE DARK BEER — medium tawny-brown, slightly smoky malt aroma, light body, flavor starts dry but becomes less so toward the middle, some complexity but not much, pleasant and refreshing. It is more like a colored light beer than a dark beer.

HENRY WEINHARD PRIVATE RESERVE LIGHT BEER — bright gold, dull hop nose, light malt and hop flavor, not interesting and not long.

WEINHARD'S IRELAND STYLE PREMIUM LIGHT ALE — deep gold, tangy hop aroma, light hop flavor, light body, pleasant and drinkable, medium to long aftertaste, malt is there but well in back.

ST. IDES PREMIUM MALT LIQUOR — deep gold, malt nose, off-dry malt flavor, smooth and mellow, refreshing, finishes medium dry, long malt aftertaste.

HAUENSTEIN NEW ULM BEER — pale gold, clean malt aroma with some hops, clean bright malt flavor, light body, light hop finish and aftertaste.

GRAIN BELT BEER — pale gold, off-dry malt nose, light malt flavor, high carbonation, short malt aftertaste.

GRAIN BELT PREMIUM — pale gold, light malt aroma, malt flavor is lightly hopped and off-dry, light malt aftertaste shows a little more hopping but not much.

SCHMIDT BEER — pale gold, light fragrant hop aroma, medium body, malt and hop flavor on the light side, weak bodied and brief.

SCHMIDT EXTRA SPECIAL BEER — pale gold, fruity malt aroma, off-dry malt flavor, only lightly hopped, medium aftertaste like the flavor.

SCHMIDT LIGHT BEER — pale gold, pleasant light malt and hop aroma, light but complex hop flavor, dry hop finish and aftertaste.

SCHMIDT SELECT NEAR BEER — pale gold, faint malt aroma, weak watery body, dry dusty malt flavor, brief aftertaste.

KINGSBURY BREW NEAR BEER — very pale golden color, faint malt nose, watery body, grainy flavor, faint grainy aftertaste has little length.

LONE STAR BEER — gold, light malt and hop aroma, flavor to match, light body, medium dry finish, little aftertaste.

LONE STAR LIGHT BEER — pale gold, light malt aroma, weak body, light malt flavor, fairly short light malt aftertaste.

LONE STAR DRAFT BEER — pale yellow-gold, full malt aroma, good malt flavor, medium dry malt aftertaste with good duration.

LONE STAR NATURAL BOCK BEER — amber, thick head (showing what 100% barley malt can do), rich malt aroma and flavor is off-dry and a little alcoholic, finishes off-dry malt, medium long off-dry malt aftertaste, very little hop appearance.

STAG LIGHT BEER — pale gold, light malt aroma and flavor, little finish and aftertaste save some faint hops.

STAG BEER — gold, clean fresh malt aroma, good body, flavor starts off good malt and hops but does not sustain, becoming fainter as it crosses the palate, light hop aftertaste.

MICKEY'S FINE MALT LIQUOR — bright gold, malt nose, fruity malt flavor that is on the sweet side, finishes sweet but the malt in the aftertaste dries a bit, medium duration.

RAINIER ALE — amber, good well-hopped nose, big body, tangy hop and malt flavor, the malt is off-dry but the bite of the hops keeps it all in balance, good length.

RAINIER DRY — pale amber, big hop nose, very little flavor, finish, or aftertaste.

RAINIER MOUNTAIN FRESH BEER — pale gold,

hoppy nose, but the flavor is more malt and even more carbonation, finish and aftertaste seem highly influenced by the CO_2 and ends brackish.

RAINIER LIGHT — pale gold, pleasant malt and hop nose, low carbonation, malt palate with very little hops, fairly brief.

RAINIER DRAFT BEER — tawny-gold, hop and malt nose, dry malt flavor, not much flavor though, medium body, short dry malt aftertaste.

CARLING'S BLACK LABEL BEER — pale yellow-gold, palate is off-dry malt at first, then some hops come in for the finish and aftertaste, medium body, fair length.

CARLING'S BLACK LABEL 11-11 EXTRA SPECIAL MALT LIQUOR — light gold, sweet malt aroma with a hop tang in back, highly carbonated, sweet malt flavor with a fruit background, complex, but it is a matter of taste to like it.

CARLING'S BLACK LABEL L.A. — yellow-gold, stinky hop nose that faded, watery body, slightly sweet malt flavor, little left at the finish, only a faint sweetness for an aftertaste.

CARLING'S BLACK LABEL LIGHT BEER — gold, faint malt aroma, light and dry malt flavor with a trace of hops, little aftertaste.

CARLING'S BLACK LABEL NA MALT BEVERAGE — deep gold, grainy nose, grainy watery palate, thin and short.

CARLING'S ORIGINAL RED CAP ALE — tawny gold, big hop aroma, strong hop flavor, good body, long hop aftertaste that has too much malt to be called dry, but well-balanced.

COY INTERNATIONAL — pale yellow, good malt nose, off-dry malt flavor that continues into a long aftertaste.

HEIDELBERG BEER — pale gold, faint malt aroma, light malt and hop flavor, light body, little finish and aftertaste.

HEIDELBERG LIGHT — very pale gold, malt nose, light clean malt flavor, off-dry, medium body, dry malt aftertaste.

NATIONAL BOHEMIAN LIGHT BEER — gold, good clean malt aroma, sprightly clean malt and hop flavor, off-dry at first then good balanced dry malt and hops, finishes well and has a long crisp aftertaste.

NATIONAL PREMIUM PALE DRY BEER — medium deep gold, good malt aroma, pleasant light hop flavor, good balance, smooth and long.

NATIONAL PREMIUM LIGHT BEER — pale yellow, pleasant light malt aroma, fresh light hop flavor, light body, touch of sour malt in the brief aftertaste.

COLT .45 MALT LIQUOR — deep gold, lovely malt aroma, smooth and soft, off-dry malt flavor and long aftertaste.

COLT .45 SILVER DELUXE MALT LIQUOR — pale yellow, malt nose, malt flavor, fairly heavy body, long malt aftertaste with some imbalance in back.

COLT .45 DRY — bright gold, dry malt nose, dry malt palate with a sweetness in back that stays into a very long aftertaste.

COLT .45 POWERMASTER MALT LIQUOR — gold, light malt aroma, big alcoholic malt flavor, sweet and smooth with sweet hops in back of the malt, good balance, quite long. Very good of type.

TUBORG GOLD EXPORT QUALITY BEER — medium gold, well-hopped malt aroma, off-dry malt palate up front, but the hops soon come in for a clean, complex and well-balanced flavor, long and pleasant throughout.

TUBORG DELUXE DARK EXPORT QUALITY BEER — copper-brown color, malty molasses nose, light body, mild malt flavor with the hops present but in back, malt finish and aftertaste.

FISCHER'S OLD STYLE GERMAN BEER — pale yellow-gold, pleasant off-dry malt and hop nose, light malt flavor, light body, pleasant, off-dry and short aftertaste.

FISCHER'S OLD STYLE ENGLISH ALE — pale yellow-gold, pleasant malt and hop aroma, dry malt flavor, faint hops in back, short dry aftertaste.

FISCHER'S LIGHT BEER — deep bright gold, fresh malt nose with a yeasty background, light body, light hop flavor that finishes dry and a bit sour, fairly short.

SCHMIDT'S — pale gold, pleasant hop and malt nose, off-dry malt flavor with hops in back, medium body, dry finish, pleasant but short aftertaste, good summer quaffing beer.

SCHMIDT'S BAVARIAN BEER — pale gold, faint malt aroma, slightly sour malt flavor, bitter hop finish, dry hop aftertaste.

READING LIGHT PREMIUM BEER — pale gold, light malt aroma, pleasant malt flavor with some light hop background, light bodied, clean, refreshing, light dry hop aftertaste.

KOEHLER QUALITY BEER — pale gold, good malt aroma, pleasant light malt flavor, hop finish, long pleasant dry malt and hop aftertaste.

RHEINGOLD EXTRA DRY LAGER BEER — pale gold, fresh malt aroma with some hops in back, light body, light malt flavor with some bittering hops in back, these hops come forward in the finish and aftertaste, but more to make the effect of being dry rather than bitter.

RHEINGOLD EXTRA LIGHT — pale gold, light malt aroma, off-dry flavor takes on some sour malt character in the finish and aftertaste.

KNICKERBOCKER NATURAL — pale gold, malt nose, smooth, soft malty flavor with good hop balance, light body, long dry aftertaste.

COQUI 900 MALT LIQUOR — bright deep gold, malt aroma, sweet malt flavor, clean malt finish and aftertaste.

McSORLEY'S CREAM ALE — tawny brown, tangy malt and hop aroma, full flavored with plenty of both malt and hops, good balance, well-hopped but not overly bitter for the malt, long aftertaste, very good with food.

BLATZ MILWAUKEE 1851 — bright gold, sweet malt nose, sort of a fruity-apple, palate is off-dry with a bite in the middle, quick finish and little aftertaste. A bit too sweet up front, but improves across the palate as it gets drier. Overall, reasonably drinkable.

BLATZ MILWAUKEE 1851 LIGHT — brilliant pale gold, lovely beery malt aroma, light body, pleasant malt flavor, some hops in aftertaste, pleasant but too watery and too brief.

CRAZY HORSE MALT LIQUOR — deep gold, slightly sour malt nose, big malt palate, noticeable alcohol, long off-dry malt aftertaste. Made for Dakota Hills Ltd. by Hornell Brewing Co., Inc. of Baltimore, but Ferolito & Vultaggio & Sons is embossed on the shoulder of the large painted bottle that makes you think it is a whiskey.

JAMES BOWIE PILSNER BEER — deep gold, basically a malt nose but there are some hops, big malt flavor, big body, medium long off-dry malt aftertaste. Apparently a successor or companion product to Crazy Horse as it is produced in a large painted bottle that looks like it is a whiskey bottle. Embossed on the bottle is Ferolito & Vultaggio & Sons.

MIDNIGHT DRAGON SPECIAL RESERVE MALT LIQUOR — gold, slightly stinky malt nose, high carbonation, big malt and hop flavor, very drinkable and very good, backs off a bit in the finish and aftertaste, but still a big flavorful brew. Contract brew for Ferolito & Vultaggio & Sons of Brooklyn, NY. along with the two following brews. The three Midnight Dragon brews were likely made at Pittsburgh prior to the split and, at present, details of production haven't been revealed.

MIDNIGHT DRAGON ROYAL RESERVE LAGER — gold, flowery hop aroma, light dry hop flavor and finish, short aftertaste.

MIDNIGHT DRAGON GOLD RESERVE ALE — golden amber, slightly stinky malt nose, highly carbonated, big malt and hop flavor, finishes strong with big hops well-backed with malt, long, very drinkable and very good.

Hood River Brewing Co./ Full Sail Brewing Co.

Brewery and brewpub in Hood River, OR

FULL SAIL GOLDEN ALE — faintly hazy amber-gold, pleasant and clean malt aroma, tasty malt and hop flavor, good balance, good body, lovely malt finish, long dry malt aftertaste, very, very drinkable.

FULL SAIL AMBER ALE — amber, beautiful zesty hop aroma, big hop flavor with plenty of malt for support, medium body, very tasty, long dry hop aftertaste. Very good tasting brew.

WASSAIL WINTER ALE — deep brown, chocolate aroma, bright malt flavor, good body, off-dry malt aftertaste, few hops to be found.

5¢ OREGON DEPOSIT
FULL SAIL
12 FLUID OZ.
GOLDEN ALE
0.355 LITRES
GOVERNMENT WARNING: (1) ACCORDING TO THE SURGEON GENERAL, WOMEN SHOULD NOT DRINK ALCOHOLIC BEVERAGES DURING PREGNANCY BECAUSE OF THE RISK OF BIRTH DEFECTS. (2) CONSUMPTION OF ALCOHOLIC BEVERAGES IMPAIRS YOUR ABILITY TO DRIVE A CAR OR OPERATE MACHINERY, AND MAY CAUSE HEALTH PROBLEMS.

Notes:

Hops! Bistro & Brewery

Brewpub in Scottsdale, AZ

HOPS! PILSNER — gold, light malt and hop nose, flavor starts out initially as malt but the hops don't take long to arrive and dominate the taste thereafter, medium to good body, crisp and clean, dry finish and aftertaste stays hoppy but the malt also peeks through again, good length, a very different kind of pils, complex and tasty.

HOPS! AMBER ALE — amber, faint malt and dry English hop aroma, bright dry hop flavor, finish and aftertaste similar to the flavor but drier, good body.

HOPS! HEFE-WEIZEN — gold, bright and spicy clove aroma, spicy clove and fruity malt flavor, plenty of both malt and cloves, aftertaste is long and shows more of the malt than the spice.

PETER'S PORTER — brown, dry malt aroma and flavor, could use even more malt, light body, dry malt aftertaste.

HOPS! RASPBERRY — reddish-amber, raspberry aroma, dry berry flavor, brief dry malt aftertaste.

HOPS! BARLEY WINE — amber gold, huge malt aroma, hefty malt flavor, huge body, syrupy, long off-dry malt aftertaste.

THE DICTATOR'S LITTLE SISTER BOCK — brown, very dry hop and malt aroma and taste, finishes even drier, too dry, it misses out on much of the flavor of the malt and hops.

HOPS! OCTOBERFEST — amber brown, big hop and malt aroma, dry hop and malt flavor, good body, long dry hop finish and aftertaste.

HOPS! CHRISTMAS ALE — deep amber, aroma of ginger, cinnamon, nutmeg, hops and fruity malt, very complex, good flavor like the nose, good body, long dry spicy aftertaste, one of the better wassails.

OATMEAL STOUT — opaque brown, toasted barley and caramel aroma, complex and aromatic, extremely complex flavor that is sometimes not dry (I can't really call it being sweet) and sometimes dry as it crosses your palate, when it is being not dry it takes on a candy caramel nature, when it is dry it still has the caramel but shows the hops and grains, big body, good balance, the finish and aftertaste actually show oats. A unique and excellent brew.

Hoster Brewing Co.

Brewpub in Columbus, OH

EAGLE LIGHT — pale gold, almost no discernable aroma, clean light and dry hop flavor, light body, dry hop finish and brief aftertaste.

GOLD TOP BEER — deep gold, hop nose, pleasant dry hop flavor, good body, long dry hop aftertaste. This is the draft version served at the brewpub.

GOLD TOP BEER — deep gold, malt nose, malt and hop flavor, medium body, dry malt aftertaste, some nuttiness at the end, refreshing, very good with food. Bottled version.

AMBER — amber, light roasted malt aroma, flavor like the nose but with some hops, pleasant and tasty, good body, fairly long aftertaste much like the flavor, a Vienna-style lager,

EAGLE DARK-SON OF BLACKTOP — dark brown, complex malt and hop aroma on the dry side, big body, dry stout-like flavor but not heavy like a stout, long dry malt aftertaste.

BUCKEYE BOCK — deep amber, big hop and malt aroma, big hop flavor, plenty of malt backing, long dry hop aftertaste.

Hubcap Brewery & Kitchen

Brewpub in Vail, CO

WHITE RIVER WHEAT — pale amber-gold, malt nose and taste, medium body, dry malt finish and aftertaste. Bottled samples were marred with a butterscotch nose and taste.

CAMP HALE GOLDEN ALE — gold, dry malt and hop nose, malt flavor had a light hop background, dry hop finish and aftertaste. Bottled samples had a buttery background to the predominantly malt flavor which tended to make the palate slightly dull.

ACE AMBER ALE — gold, dry hop nose, smooth malt flavor, medium body, somewhat dry hop finish and aftertaste. Bottled samples had a buttery background to the flavor and a sourness in the aftertaste.

BEAVER TAIL BROWN ALE — deep amber, malt aroma and flavor with solid hop support, medium body, well-balanced, but fairly short. Again, bottled versions were overlaid with a butterscotch flavor.

RAINBOW TROUT STOUT — deep brown, chocolate malt and roasted barley nose, medium body, big flavor like the nose, dry hop aftertaste is a little sour at the end.

SOLSTICE ALE — gold, hoppy aroma and flavor, good body, dry hop finish and aftertaste.

BOCK N' ROLL — gold, dry aroma has both malt and hops, smooth flavor is good malt well supported by hops, well-balanced, good body, long dry malt and hop aftertaste.

Notes:

Huber-Berghoff Brewing Co.

Brewery in **Monroe, WI**

Several corporate names used on labels, including Jos. Huber B.C.

REGAL BRAU BAVARIAN STYLE BEER — gold, fresh clean malt aroma, good malt and hop balanced flavor, off-dry finish, sour malt aftertaste.

WISCONSIN CLUB PREMIUM BEER — medium gold, pleasant malt nose, malt palate, light body, off-dry malt finish and aftertaste.

HUBER PREMIUM BEER — bright gold, good hop and malt aroma, fresh and clean off-dry malt and hop flavor, nicely balanced, pleasant malt finish, long malt aftertaste.

HUBER PREMIUM BOCK BEER — deep amber-brown, malt nose, malt flavor up front becomes more and more hoppy as it proceeds to a dry almost bitter hop finish and aftertaste.

RHINELANDER EXPORT PREMIUM BEER — bright gold, clean malt aroma, off-dry malt flavor up front, but this dries toward the finish and ends in a fairly dry hop aftertaste of little length. It is good with food.

ED DEBEVIC'S BEER — tawny-gold, good big hop aroma, off-dry hop front palate, drier at the finish and ends with a short dry hop aftertaste. Made for a Chicago restaurant, but available elsewhere.

ROUGHRIDER PREMIUM BEER — hazy pale gold, light malt nose, high carbonation, light malt flavor and finish, short dry hop aftertaste, light bodied. Contract brew for Dakota B.C.

OLD CHICAGO LAGER BEER — gold, sour hop nose, hop flavor that is a little sour in front, dry hop finish and aftertaste.

BERGHOFF BEER — bright amber, hop nose, bright hop and malt flavor, good body, tasty, light hop finish, long dry hop aftertaste, complex and likeable brew.

BERGHOFF DARK BEER-amber-brown, rich hop aroma, light body, fairly rich malt flavor that is a tad burnt, fairly pleasant, light body, long dry malt aftertaste, a little hop bitterness at the very end. You could drink a lot of it.

BERGHOFF BOCK BEER — deep mahogany, dry slightly roasted malt nose, roasted malt flavor, medium body, medium dry malt aftertaste, straightforward dry and light beer with little complexity.

BERGHOFF LIGHT BEER — deep gold, flowery malt aroma, light malt and hop flavor, balanced but light, medium to short dry hop aftertaste.

A. FITGER & CO.'s EXPORT BEER — pale amber, light hop nose, good body, good dry hop and malt flavor, long dry hop aftertaste.

VIENNA LAGER BEER — amber, complex off-dry malt and hop aroma, bright hop flavor, finish and long aftertaste, an interesting and appetizing beer.

AMBIER VIENNA STYLE BEER — brilliant amber, very light toasted malt aroma, front palate is malt, dry hop middle and finish, complex long candy-malt aftertaste that slowly dries as it goes on. This brew is very much a Vienna style lager. Made for Ambier (Vienna) B.C. of Milwaukee, WI.

LEMON & LAGER — light gold, lemon aroma, zesty lemony flavor but very little resemblance to a beer as there is very little malt showing through the lemon except in the long aftertaste. It is supposed to be like a lemon shandy by the style.

VAN MERRITT LIGHT BEER — bright gold, light hop nose, very light hop flavor, almost nothing at the finish and there is no aftertaste.

DEMPSEY'S ALE — pale amber, beautifully balanced hop and lightly roasted malt nose, zesty ale taste with good hops and some toasted malt, high carbonation, light body, dry malt finish, medium length dry malt aftertaste.

HARLEY DAVIDSON HEAVY BEER 1988 — hazy-gold, malt nose is a touch sour, big malt and hop palate, heavy body, good balance, long malt aftertaste. Made annually for a Harley-Davidson motorcycle meet held each year in the vicinity.

HARLEY DAVIDSON HEAVY BEER 1989 — pale amber, malt aroma, good malt flavor, big body, long pleasant malt aftertaste.

HARLEY DAVIDSON HEAVY BEER 1990 — gold, clean fruity malt nose and taste, big body, long dry malt aftertaste.

BOXER PREMIUM MALT LIQUOR — deep gold, good fruity malt nose, pleasant straightforward malt flavor, finishes as it starts, long malt aftertaste.

BRAUMEISTER LIGHT BEER — deep gold, pleasant malt and hop aroma, light malt-hop flavor, very thin, very short.

TELLURIDE BEER — tawny-gold, pleasant soft malt aroma, pleasant off-dry malt front palate, dry hops come in the middle, finishes dry malt, long dry malt and hop aftertaste, medium body, overall dry and well-balanced and very drinkable. Made for Telluride B.C., Moab, UT.

SNAKE BITE BEER — gold, faint melony malt nose, light malt flavor, carbonation bite pretty much overwhelms anything subtle, short dry malt aftertaste. Made for Snake Bite Beer Co., Muskego, WI.

FOECKING PREMIUM BEER — pale gold, light malt aroma, high carbonation, good malt flavor with the hops in back, balanced and very drinkable, dry aftertaste drops off very fast. Made for Foecking Alcohol Beverage Co. of Illinois, Rock Island, IL.

FOECKING PREMIUM LIGHT — gold, pleasant malt and hop nose, high carbonation, light dry malt and hop flavor, light body, short dry finish and aftertaste. Contract brew as above.

CERVEZA VICTORIA —deep gold, good fragrant hop and malt nose, dry malt palate, good body, dry malt aftertaste with a hop background, touch of bitter hops at the end of the long aftertaste. Made under license of Compañhia Cerveceria de Nicaragua, a contract brew for distribution in Nicaragua.

CERVEZA VICTORIA LIGHT BEER — pale gold, flowery hop and malt aroma, big malt flavor, very refreshing, medium body, medium long dry hop aftertaste. Contract brew as above.

CERVEZA VICTORIA MORENA BEER — deep amber-brown, fragrant rich malt nose, good malt flavor, pleasant and straightforward, light body, long rich and dry malt aftertaste. Contract brew as above.

LIQUOR MART BOCK BEER — deep amber, buttery malt aroma, malt and butterscotch flavor, medium body, burnt buttery malt aftertaste. Made for Liquor Mart of Boulder, CO.

Privatbrauerei Hübsch

Brewpub in Davis, CA

HÜBSCH BRÄU GERMAN STYLE BEER — gold, finely carbonated, pleasant fruity malt aroma, big hop flavor, big body, dry hop finish, long dry hop aftertaste.

HÜBSCH BRÄU LAGER — amber, low carbonation, pleasant malt nose, smooth slightly off-dry malt flavor, good balance, very drinkable, fairly long dry malt aftertaste.

HÜBSCH BRÄU PILS — gold, faint hop aroma, pleasant smooth light hop flavor, low carbonation, dry hop finish and aftertaste, medium duration.

HÜBSCH BRÄU WEIZEN — gold, low carbonation, bright malt and light lactic spice nose, bright wheat and malt flavor, very smooth, hops come in at the middle, faint spiciness stays in back behind the hops, nicely balanced, fairly complex, interesting, a nice beer somewhere between American and German styles.

HÜBSCH BRÄU MÄRZEN — amber, low carbonation, light roasted barley nose, dry malt flavor, light on the hops, smooth, dry malt aftertaste.

HÜBSCH BRÄU DARK — brown, roasted malt nose and taste, very smooth and balanced, dry malt finish and aftertaste, very drinkable.

Hudepohl-Schoenling Brewing Co.

Brewery in **Cincinnati, OH**

Company is result of the merger of the two Cincinnati, OH breweries.

BOHEMIAN TAP LAGER BEER — bright gold, slightly sweet malt aroma, highly carbonated, light sweet malt flavor, off-dry malt finish and aftertaste.

HOFBRAU BIER — deep gold, clean malt and hop nose, light body, bright hop flavor up front, malt comes in middle and adds a little sweetness to the finish and aftertaste.

HUDEPOHL GOLD — bright gold, big fruity malt aroma, good dry malt flavor, light but pleasant, refreshing and well-balanced.

HUDEPOHL 14K PREMIUM BEER — pale gold, vegetal malt nose, grainy off-dry malt flavor, somewhat straw-like in back and in the finish and aftertaste.

HUDY DELIGHT BEER — pale yellow-gold, faint roasted character to the malt but there is a little straw in back that seems to dull the taste, light body, light malt aftertaste with little length.

HUDEPOHL PURE GRAIN BEER — pale gold, light hop aroma followed by a hop palate well backed with malt, good body, lightly spicy hop and malt finish and aftertaste.

BURGER BEER — very pale gold, pleasant light malt aroma and taste, this continues into the medium length aftertaste.

LUDWIG HUDEPOHL ORIGINAL BOCK BEER — deep amber, lovely roasted malt nose, smooth dry roasted malt flavor, long malt aftertaste, medium body, very drinkable.

LUDWIG HUDEPOHL SPECIAL OKTOBERFEST BEER — pale amber-orange, dry malt aroma, good dry malt flavor, good body, well-balanced, long refreshing malt aftertaste.

CHRISTIAN MOERLEIN CINCINNATI SELECT BEER — amber-gold, big malt aroma with plenty of hops in back, big malty flavor with good support from hops in back, hint of smokiness in the middle, finish cuts off quickly but there is a long dry malt aftertaste.

CHRISTIAN MOERLEIN DOPPEL DARK BEER — amber color, sweet rich malt nose, dry toasted malt flavor, medium body, off-dry malt at finish, slightly off-dry malt aftertaste of medium length.

CHRISTIAN MOERLEIN BOCK BEER — dark amber, malt nose that is slightly smoky, malt flavor with a touch of potato peel at the finish, medium body, little finish and aftertaste, overall on the dull side.

MOERLEIN'S CINCINNATI BOCK BEER — deep amber, toasted off-dry perfumy malt aroma, dry malt flavor that fades away fast, medium body, aftertaste is only a roasted dry quality.

LITTLE KINGS CREAM ALE (SCHOENLING CREAM ALE) — gold, fragrant aroma has both hops and malt, flavor starts out briskly with fresh bright hops, it sweetens out a bit at the finish and ends that way, long aftertaste. A bright, good tasting little brew.

TOP HAT BEER — pale gold, faint malt aroma with even fainter hops in back, very light malt and hop flavor, medium body, short dry malt and hop aftertaste.

SCHOENLING DRAFT BEER — gold, beautiful malt nose, high carbonation, pleasant malt and hop flavor, brief but clean and refreshing. Also labelled **BIG JUG BEER.**

SCHOENLING OLD TIME BOCK BEER — deep ruby-amber, malt aroma, thin body, high carbonation, malt and cherry pit taste, off-dry malt finish and medium aftertaste.

WILLIAM PENN COLONIAL LAGER — deep amber, rich malt aroma, good body, a good malt and hop flavor but it is quite light, dry malt aftertaste, very drinkable. Contract brew for Wm. Penn B.C. of Langhorne, PA.

BRUCKS JUBILEE BEER — pale gold, good malt aroma and flavor, decent body, good long malt aftertaste. Contract brew for C.J. Brockman Brewery, Cincinnati, OH.

FEHR'S XL — bright gold, big rich malt aroma, hops in back, clean dry malt flavor, very dry malt finish, fairly short dry malt aftertaste, a little charcoal/smoke in the background, very drinkable, nice while it is in your mouth. Made for Frank Fehr B.C., Cincinnati, OH.

GOVERNMENT WARNING: (1) ACCORDING TO THE SURGEON GENERAL, WOMEN SHOULD NOT DRINK ALCOHOLIC BEVERAGES DURING PREGNANCY BECAUSE OF THE RISK OF BIRTH DEFECTS. (2) CONSUMPTION OF ALCOHOLIC BEVERAGES IMPAIRS YOUR ABILITY TO DRIVE A CAR OR OPERATE MACHINERY, AND MAY CAUSE HEALTH PROBLEMS.
MOERLEIN'S
Cincinnati
BOCK
BEER
REINHEITSGEBOT PURE
CONTENTS: 12 FL. OZ. (355 ML)
Brewed and packaged by and under the authority of the Hudepohl Brewing Co., Cincinnati, Oh 45214

MT. EVEREST MALT LIQUOR — gold, soapy malt nose like a perfumed apple scent bath soap or shampoo, soapy apple flavor, good body, dry malt aftertaste.

BANKS BEER — gold, lychee nut nose, dull fruity-vegetal malt flavor, good body, vegetal malt aftertaste is sour at the end. This is the U.S. domestic version of the Banks beer of the Bahamas.

Humboldt Brewery

Brewpub in Arcata, CA

RED NECTAR ALE — hazy amber, strong hop nose, big smoky dry malt and hop flavor, medium body, strong and long dry malt aftertaste with hops breaking through at the end. I have also tasted this brew where it is big dry hops throughout without much malt at all and certainly no smoky malt.

GOLD NECTAR ALE — pale gold, fruity malt nose, soft dry malt flavor, dry malt finish and aftertaste, dry malt all the way through.

GOLD RUSH EXTRA PALE ALE — gold, pleasant fruity-malt nose, dry hop and malt flavor with a citrus background, medium body, brief aftertaste is just a memory of the flavor.

STORMCELLAR PORTER — brown, rich malt nose and flavor, good body, dry malt finish and aftertaste.

OATMEAL STOUT — deep brown, rich roasted cherry malt nose, dry roasted malt flavor, medium body, dry malt aftertaste.

Irons Brewing Co.

Microbrewery in Lakewood, CO

IRONS ALE — gold, malt nose, malt flavor with hops supporting, light body, short medium dry malt aftertaste.

IRONS AMBER LAGER — cloudy gold, hop aroma, tangy hop flavor, medium body, brief dry hop aftertaste cuts off abruptly.

Frank Jones Brewing Co.

Microbrewery in Portsmouth, NH

PORTSMOUTH ALE — amber, hop and malt aroma, malt flavor with hops in back, dry hop finish and aftertaste.

GRANITE STATE GOLDEN ALE — gold, light hop aroma, hop flavor, dry hop finish shows some faint lactic acid, dry hop aftertaste.

PORTSMOUTH ALE
Frank Jones
FRANK JONES
INDIA PALE
ALE
12 FLUID OUNCES
BREWED AND BOTTLED BY THE FRANK JONES BREWING COMPANY, PORTSMOUTH, NEW HAMPSHIRE.
GOVERNMENT WARNING: (1) ACCORDING TO THE SURGEON GENERAL, WOMEN SHOULD NOT DRINK ALCOHOLIC BEVERAGES DURING PREGNANCY BECAUSE OF THE RISK OF BIRTH DEFECTS. (2) CONSUMPTION OF ALCOHOLIC BEVERAGES IMPAIRS YOUR ABILITY TO DRIVE A CAR OR OPERATE MACHINERY, AND MAY CAUSE HEALTH PROBLEMS.

Judge Baldwin's Brewing Co.

Brewpub in Colorado Springs, CO

AMBER — pale gold, malt aroma, smooth malt flavor, light body, fairly dry malt finish and aftertaste.

PORTER — brown, roasted barley nose, flavor is roasted malt with a chocolatey background, light body, smooth flavor, very pleasant, medium long malt aftertaste.

WHEAT — gold, nice malt nose, good malty flavor, light body, light to medium dry malt aftertaste.

PALE — pale gold, pleasant malt aroma, good malt flavor, very lightly hopped, finishes dry malt, light dry malt aftertaste.

BREWING
Judge Baldwin's
COMPANY

Kalamazoo Brewing Co.

Brewery in **Kalamazoo, MI**

BELL'S BEER — hazy gold, faint malt nose with melon, pineapple and kumquat in back, fruity malt flavor, dry hop finish and aftertaste, medium length, doubtful balance.

BELL'S AMBER ALE — golden amber, spicy malt and hop nose, big hop flavor well backed with malt, complex, dry, tart, malt moves forward at the finish but still can't match the hops, long dry aftertaste has plenty of both malt and hops, a very good drinking beer.

THIRD COAST BEER — hazy amber, lychee nut aroma that takes on a citrus character in time, flat fruity malt palate, very dry malt aftertaste.

THIRD COAST OLD ALE — hazy deep amber, coconut chocolate malt nose, huge off-dry malt taste, complex and interesting, dried apple finish, heavy body, extremely tenacious, complex, dry aftertaste with candy, coconut, chocolate, malt and hops.

GOVERNMENT WARNING: (1) ACCORDING TO THE SURGEON GENERAL, WOMEN SHOULD NOT DRINK ALCOHOLIC BEVERAGES DURING PREGNANCY BECAUSE OF THE RISK OF BIRTH DEFECTS. (2) CONSUMPTION OF ALCOHOLIC BEVERAGES IMPAIRS YOUR ABILITY TO DRIVE A CAR OR OPERATE MACHINERY, AND MAY CAUSE HEALTH PROBLEMS.
BELL'S
EXPEDITION
STOUT
BREWED AND BOTTLED BY KALAMAZOO BREWING CO. INC., KALAMAZOO, MI 49007
NET CONTENTS 12 FL. OZ. (355 ML) • MICHIGAN 10¢ REFUND

GREAT LAKES AMBER ALE — hazy amber, light lychee nut nose, light citrus malt flavor, pleasant, fairly long hop aftertaste that is drier than the flavor, tastes a lot like a toned down Sierra Nevada Pale Ale.

BELL'S KALAMAZOO STOUT — opaque brown, coffee colored head, delightful appetizing malt aroma with plenty of smoky chocolate malt, strong but pleasant dry roasted malt flavor, dry malt finish and aftertaste, smoke enhances rather than diminishes, long and good.

GREAT LAKES CHERRY STOUT 1988 — opaque brown, coffee colored head, fruity malt aroma, black cherry flavor with a tart artificial quality, medium body, medium long malt aftertaste that is dry on the tongue but sour in the corners of the mouth.

EXPEDITION STOUT — deep opaque brown, lovely sweet malt aroma is very strong at the outset, softens slightly with time, first seems to be off-dry malt on the palate but becomes more dry as it goes, high density, huge body, almost viscous, long, strong, complex, off-dry malt aftertaste.

BELL'S SPECIAL DOUBLE CREAM STOUT — deep brown, pleasant light malt nose, very pleasant smooth and mellow big straightforward malt flavor, satisfying and very long. The brew is on the off-dry side, but can't be called overly sweet for the type; in fact it is very good of type.

BELL'S PORTER — deep amber, rich chocolate malt nose with a little fruitiness in back, straightforward dry malt taste, big body, touch of sourness behind the malt in the finish, long dry malt aftertaste, well-done drinkable brew.

Kelmer's Brewhouse

Brewpub in **Santa Rosa, CA**

KRYSTAL FRESH WHEAT BEER — hazy gold, wheat nose, touch of lactic in back, creamy texture, dry slightly lactic grapefruit-like flavor, fairly short aftertaste like the flavor.

KRIS KRINGLE SPECIAL CHRISTMAS ALE 1990 — amber, big head, zesty soapy hop nose, big hop flavor, big and alcoholic, finishes dry hops, long dry hop aftertaste, very good full flavored brew.

KELMER'S KLASSIC FINE ALE — hazy amber, clean zesty hop nose much like a pils, complex flavor is smoky malt and hops, smoky finish, long very dry malt aftertaste without any smokiness whatever.

ST. PATS STOUT — very dark brown, big roasted barley nose and taste, not big bodied, finishes dry malt, medium long dry malt aftertaste.

KRYSTAL WHEAT — gold, faint malt nose, light malt flavor, light body, brief light malt aftertaste.

INDEPENDENCE ALE — amber, fragrant fruity hop nose, very sweet malt flavor, good body, off-dry malt finish, long slightly sweet malt aftertaste.

KELMER'S KLASSIC AMBER — amber, very dry hop nose and flavor, dry hop finish and aftertaste, thin body and flavor, short length.

Thomas Kemper Brewing Co.

Brewery in Poulsbro, WA

THOMAS KEMPER ROLLING BAY BOCK — hazy gold, malt aroma, finely carbonated, malt and hop flavor seems to have a citrus background, long and strong dry hop finish and aftertaste.

THOMAS KEMPER PILSENER BEER — hazy yellow-gold, hop aroma has citrus tones, hop flavor has a lemony background but there is plenty of malt, good body, medium dry hop aftertaste.

THOMAS KEMPER MAIBOCK — deep gold, malt nose, big malty flavor has plenty of hops, high density (17.5%), good balance between the hops and malt, smooth, tasty, dry finish and aftertaste.

VIKINGFEST VIENNA-STYLE AMBER — amber, hop nose, hop palate with malt in back, good body, dry hop finish and aftertaste, medium duration.

Montana Beverages, Ltd./ Kessler Brewing Co.

Brewery in Helena, MT

KESSLER BEER — pale gold, complex malt nose with a lightly toasted nature, medium body, good complex rich malt flavor, feels good in your mouth, excellent balance, ever so slightly off-dry, but aftertaste is drier, full flavored long aftertaste.

KESSLER BOCK BEER — deep copper-red, citrus hop aroma, big body, big sweet and sharp citrus flavor, a bit too sharp, long malt aftertaste on the sour side.

KESSLER WHEAT BEER — medium to deep copper-brown color, sweet fruity malt aroma that is quite attractive, there is a brief sweet foretaste, then it turns sort of burnt vegetal that tastes much better than it reads, a faint spicy-lactic touch appears at the end and in the brief aftertaste. Actually, it is a very good try at making a weizen.

BACH'S BOCK — deep brown, light malt aroma with a fruitiness, malt palate that is dry, well-balanced and quite long. There certainly is plenty of alcohol, but otherwise it is not a big brew. It is very tasty and very drinkable. Made for Eugene City B.C. of Eugene, OR.

SUN VALLEY WHITE CLOUD ALE — amber, complex aromatic malt and hop nose, a fruity citrus well-hopped flavor, medium body, dry hop aftertaste, pleasant, complex and very drinkable. Made for Sun Valley B.C., Bellevue, ID.

SUN VALLEY SAWTOOTH GOLD LAGER — hazy amber-gold, big malt nose with a hop background, malt flavor, finish and long aftertaste. Made for Sun Valley B.C. Latest label (Feb '92) calls this brew SUN VALLEY GOLD LAGER.

SUN VALLEY OUR HOLIDAY ALE 1989 — amber, slightly toasted malt nose, big roasted rich malt flavor slightly on the sweet side, dry in the middle, good body, very tasty, finishes strongly, stays smooth, mostly malt but plenty of hops in back, very long malt aftertaste. Made for Sun Valley B.C.

SUN VALLEY OUR HOLIDAY ALE 1990 — bright amber, malt and pineapple juice aroma at first, thence roasted malt, off-dry strong malt flavor with noticeable alcohol, complex, hops arrive at the finish and add dryness to the long aftertaste. Made for Sun Valley B.C.

SUN VALLEY OUR HOLIDAY ALE 1991 — deep amber, laid back malt aroma, strong malt flavor, finish and aftertaste even stronger as that is where the hops come in with a bang, very very long hop and malt aftertaste, a blockbuster brew. Made for Sun Valley B.C.

SUN VALLEY OUR HOLIDAY ALE 1992 — deep amber, malt aroma, strong malt flavor with good hop backing, big body, finishes strongly, great balance, marvelous to sip, very long hop and malt aftertaste, another treasure.

EUGENE CELEBRATION LAGER — hazy gold, fruity apple and malt nose with some background hops, pleasant malt flavor has a light tangerine background, zesty citrus nature adds to the character of the long aftertaste which is more complex than the flavor. Made for Eugene City B.C.

EUGENE ALE — deep amber, lovely toasted malt (Ovaltine) nose, very tasty and drinkable, complex malt up front, the zest sags a bit in mid-palate, but finishes with that pleasant fruity-Ovaltine flavor and ends dry. Made for Eugene City B.C.

EUGENER WEIZEN WHEAT BEER — slightly hazy-amber, delicious sweet malt aroma, light and bright clean fresh flavor, medium body, pleasant dry malt finish and aftertaste, very refreshing. Made for Eugene City B.C.

KESSLER LORELEI EXTRA PALE BEER — tawny- gold, big complex flowery hop and malt aroma, smooth rich malt flavor with good hop support, a little molasses in back, medium body, good balance, dry hop finish and aftertaste, fairly short.

KESSLER WINTER BEER — amber, grainy roasted malt aroma, flavor like the nose but the hops appear in back, off-dry flavor starts to dry at finish, and aftertaste is very long, very dry and very grainy. The hops never come out of the background.

FRONTIER TOWN SELECT BEER — gold, lovely malt and hop aroma, refreshing off-dry malt flavor, finish shows a bit drier and aftertaste is dry hops and has good length, good tasting balanced brew.

PACIFIC COAST PREMIUM LAGER — hazy yellow-gold, canned corn nose, malt palate, medium body, dry malt finish and aftertaste. Made for Pacific Coast Beer Co., Newport Beach, CA.

PACIFIC COAST LAGER — gold, light fruity-lemony nose, dry malt flavor, medium body, pleasant creamy texture, feels good in your mouth, finishes dry with a trace of grapefruit in the long aftertaste. Contract brew as above.

OREGON STATE FAIR GOLDEN ALE — gold, appetizing malt-Ovaltine nose, pleasant very malty flavor, light to medium body, very drinkable, pleasant malt finish, fairly long dry malt aftertaste.

ST. NICK'S DARK ALE — deep amber, rich sweet slightly roasted malt aroma, rich smooth off-dry malt flavor benefits from some chocolate malt, very pleasant and very drinkable, quite long. Made for Eugene City B.C.

BONE DRY WET DRY BEER — gold, lovely malt aroma (lots of malt), very dry malt flavor, light body, light hops, dry right to the end.

Kidder's Brewery & Eatery

Brewpub in **Ft. Myers, FL**

KIDDER'S PALE ALE — amber, hop aroma, dry hop flavor, a bright hoppy brew, good body, dry hop finish and long aftertaste.

KIDDER'S SCOTTISH ALE — amber, hop nose, dry hop flavor, good balance and body, dry hop finish, long dry hop aftertaste.

Lakefront Brewery, Inc.

Microbrewery in **Milwaukee, WI**

EAST SIDE DARK — dark amber, malt nose and flavor, medium body, light dry malt aftertaste.

Latrobe Brewing Co.

Brewery in **Latrobe, PA**

Owned and operated by Labatt's U.S., Darien, CT

ROLLING ROCK PREMIUM BEER — pale gold, very pleasant light malt aroma with light hops in back, fairly big malt flavor is strongest in front, bittering hops in back make for balance and a dry finish and aftertaste. A good beer for the bowling alley.

ROLLING ROCK LIGHT BEER — pale gold, faint malt aroma, light body, malt flavor with hops in back, dry faintly hopped finish and aftertaste.

Lind Brewing Co.

Microbrewery in **San Leandro, CA**

DRAKE'S GOLD — gold, bitter hop and fruity malt aroma and flavor, good body, quite complex, very dry and well-hopped finish and aftertaste, good length.

DRAKE'S ALE — amber, strange aroma is fruity yet hoppy, this strangeness is reflected on the palate, dry hop and malt aftertaste.

SIR FRANCIS STOUT — brown, faint roasted barley malt nose, very very dry roast malt flavor, finish and aftertaste.

The Lion, Inc.

Brewery in Wilkes-Barre, PA

A number of corporate names are used, e.g. Pocono Brewing Co.

GIBBONS FAMOUS LAGER BEER — gold, clean light malt nose, fresh malt flavor, medium dry finish, short dry malt and hop aftertaste.

LIEBOTSCHANER CREAM ALE — pale gold, fresh and clean slightly sweet malt aroma, off-dry malt flavor, light bodied, quick finish, little aftertaste, pleasant and refreshing, good hot weather beer.

LIEBOTSCHANER BOCK BEER — copper colored, light malt aroma, lightly scorched malt flavor, light body, dry finish, brief aftertaste.

ESSLINGER PREMIUM BEER — light yellow, light malt aroma, pleasant malt and hop flavor, good balance, some character, light body, dry finish, medium length dry aftertaste.

LIONSHEAD DELUXE PILSENER BEER — tawny-gold, malt aroma, light body, high carbonation, good bright clean flavor with both malt and hops, off-dry malt finish and aftertaste.

STEGMAIER GOLD MEDAL BEER — pale gold, light malt aroma, light malt flavor, light body, finish drops off to nothing, little aftertaste.

STEGMAIER 1857 LAGER BEER — pale amber, pleasant malt nose, palate starts out malt, finishes hops, just hop bitterness for an aftertaste, medium body.

STEGMAIER PORTER — ruby-toned brown color, fresh clean malt aroma, dry malt flavor cuts off abruptly, little or no aftertaste, thin body.

STEGMAIER 1857 LIGHT BEER — golden amber, malt aroma, light hop flavor is mostly CO_2, light body, aftertaste is hops with a touch of malt but is not long.

STEGMAIER LIGHT BEER — pale gold, light malt aroma and very light malt flavor, little hops, plenty of carbonation (maybe too much), not much finish or aftertaste.

STEGMAIER 1857 DRY BEER — very deep gold, pleasant malt and hop nose, bright malt flavor, high carbonation, quick finish, no aftertaste. It is good while it is in your mouth.

MALTA INDIA — opaque brown, big grainy malt nose, big malt flavor, light to medium body, long malt aftertaste is not dry, but is drier than the flavor. Made for Cerveceria India, Mayaguez, Puerto Rico.

BARTELS PURE BEER — medium gold, faint malt aroma and flavor, some hops but not much, malt finish, brief malt aftertaste.

MIDNIGHT DRAGON MALTA ESPECIAL — deep brown, concentrated Ovaltine malt nose and flavor with some hops for balance, heavy body, short palate is sweet but not cloying.

NEUWEILER'S TRADITIONAL LAGER BEER — pale gold, malt nose, palate is mostly malt in front, hops come in middle and make their contribuion at the finish and in the aftertaste, bright and refreshing, medium body, medium length. Contract brew for Neuweiler B.C. of Allentown, PA.

NEUWEILER'S BREWED PORTER — brown, malt nose and flavor, somewhat light body, dry malt flavor and finish, brief aftertaste. Contract brew as above.

NEUWEILER BLACK AND TAN — light brown, malt aroma and flavor, medium body, hops come in at mid-palate and help to balance malt which stays dominant, flavor is medium dry, finish and aftertaste are drier, medium length. Contract brew as above. A blend of the porter and lager and perhaps better than either.

CRYSTAL PREMIUM BEER — bright pale gold, light malt aroma and flavor, high carbonation, light body, fairly short, a refreshing hot weather beer that a beer drinker would like better than Perrier.

KAPPY'S PREMIUM QUALITY BEER — gold, pleasant malt and hop aroma, light dry malt flavor, fairly short dry malt aftertaste. Store label for Kappy's liquor stores in the Boston area.

TRUPERT AMERICAN PILSENER BEER — golden amber, toasted malt aroma and flavor, good balance, dry malt finish and aftertaste, not long but very drinkable. Contract brew made for Braumeister Ltd., Drexel Hill, PA.

BLUE HEN BEER — bright tawny gold, pleasant fruity-malty nose with some hops in back, off-dry malt front palate, hop middle, dry malt finish and aftertaste, medium long, flavors seem a bit separated. Contract brew for Blue Hen Brewery, Ltd. of Newark, DE.

JERSEY LAGER BEER — deep gold, beautiful malt and hop aroma, dull malt flavor, light body, little finish and no aftertaste. It's all in the nose. Contract brew for Jersey Lager Beer Co. of Bordentown, NJ.

SKIPJACK LAGER — pale amber, toasted malt aroma, pleasant roasted malt flavor, has zest, long toasted malt aftertaste. Contract brew for Skipjack B.C. of Secaucus, NJ.

HOPE BOCK BEER — medium deep amber, light toasted malt nose, medium body, dry toasted malt flavor, has a touch of smoked malt in back, finish and aftertaste are smokier, dry, refreshing and very drinkable. Contract brew as above.

HOPE LAGER BEER — golden amber, very pleasant dry malt aroma with a European hop background, finely carbonated, malt flavor, medium length malt aftertaste, medium body, pleasant and drinkable. Contract beer made for Hope B.C. of Providence, RI.

HOPE LIGHT LAGER — gold, vegetal malt nose, off-dry but fruity malt flavor, finishes quite dry and has good length, excellent balance, a very good light beer. Contract brew as above.

HOPE RED ROOSTER ALE — bright amber, faintly soapy hop aroma, complex bright and dry hop palate, very long dry hop aftertaste, excellent beer. Contract brew as above.

NATHAN HALE GOLDEN LAGER — deep gold, soapy malt and hop nose, fairly dry malt flavor, medium body, clean light dry malt aftertaste with medium duration. Contract brew for Connecticut B.C., Hartford, CT.

ATLANTIC CITY DIVING HORSE LAGER BEER — light amber, lovely hop aroma, dry hop flavor, very drinkable but brief on the palate. Made for Atlantic City B.C. of Atlantic City, NJ.

BUNKERHILL LAGER BEER — pale amber, hop nose, sour hop flavor, dull hop aftertaste that retains some of the sourness of the flavor.

STOUDT'S OKTOBERFEST DARK — deep amber, off-dry malt nose, big hop flavor, quite dry, medium to light body, dry hop aftertaste of medium duration. A contract beer for Stoudt B.C. of Adamstown, PA which allowed the release of the beer in 12-oz bottles.

QUEEN CITY LAGER — gold, very pleasant clean malt nose, bright clean crisp off-dry malt flavor, very refreshing, good body, medium long dry malt aftertaste with good hop support. Contract brew for Queen City Brewing Co., Buffalo, New York.

GOLDFINCH AMBER BEER — deep amber, finely carbonated, clean mild hop aroma, medium body, pleasant light hop and malt flavor, good balance, long dry spicy hop and malt aftertaste, very drinkable. Contract brew for Goldfinch B.C., Mt. Laurel, NJ.

Los Angeles Brewing Co.

Brewpub and restaurant in Los Angeles, CA

EUREKA CALIFORNIA LAGER — deep gold, bright hop aroma, German-style hop flavor, dry hop finish, brief dry hop aftertaste. This description is for the bottled version.

EUREKA CALIFORNIA LAGER (FILTERED DRAFT) — tawny-gold, hop aroma, tasty flavor shows plenty of malt and hops, dry hop finish and very long dry hop aftertaste, a very tasty brew. It is drier and longer on the palate than the bottled version (from the same batch, I should add) above.

EUREKA CALIFORNIA LAGER (UNFILTERED DRAFT) — hazy gold, a great deal of malt joins the hops in the nose, very balanced smooth malt and hop flavor, the better balance means the hops don't hit so hard when they roll in on the palate, dry finish but not so obviously dry as in the two versions above, a very long lasting good flavor.

EUREKA AMBER LAGER (FILTERED DRAFT) — amber, smooth malt aroma and flavor, dry malt finish and aftertaste, good but doesn't have the character or the length of the California Lager.

EUREKA AMBER LAGER (UNFILTERED DRAFT) — hazy amber, malt nose, smooth malt flavor with some hops in back, dry malt finish and aftertaste with mild hop support, very good tasting, very well-balanced, a noticeably better tasting brew than the filtered version.

EUREKA DARK LAGER — deep amber, dry malt nose, light chocolate malt in back, big dry malt flavor, long and strong malt aftertaste, sort of a big brother to the amber.

PROSPECTOR JOE'S SPECIAL GOLDEN BEER — brilliant bright amber, rich complex roasted malt and hop nose, delicious roasted malt flavor, big body, hops roll in at the finish and stay into the long long dry hop aftertaste, a very well-made brew.

PROSPECTOR JOE'S SPECIAL DARK GOLDEN BEER — golden amber, huge hop and malt aroma with the emphasis on the hops, big hop palate, complex and rich, plenty of malt in support, long big dry hop aftertaste.

Lost Coast Brewery & Cafe

Microbrewery and brewpub in Eureka, CA

LOST COAST BREWERY PALE ALE — hazy gold, fruity malt aroma has a pineapple background, fruity flavor (again the pineapple), pleasant tasting, good body, dry malt finish and aftertaste, nice but not much depth.

LOST COAST BREWERY DOWNTOWN BROWN — hazy amber, slightly toasted malt nose, mild chocolate roasted malt flavor, medium body, pleasant, very drinkable, light malt aftertaste, good with food.

LOST COAST BREWERY AMBER ALE — hazy deep amber, big nose is rich roasted malt backed with citrus hops, bright and luscious hop and roasted malt flavor, good body, very flavorful, balanced, long, dry and rich malt aftertaste shows some hops at the end. Feels very good in your mouth; an excellent amber ale type brew. Some production runs tend to be more hoppy; others decidedly feature the malt. It is always good.

LOST COAST BREWERY STOUT — opaque brown, brown head, light dry malt aroma, faintly roasted and faintly chocolate, smooth chocolate malt flavor with a slightly roasted barley background, fair body, hops show a bit at the finish, medium long dry malt aftertaste.

LOST COAST SUMMERTIME WHEAT — hazy amber, big dry malt nose and very dry flavor, good body, finishes dry malt like it starts, a hefe-weizen but done American style.

M.J. Barleyhoppers, Brewery and Public House

Brewpub in **Moscow, ID**

PALOUSE WEIZEN — gold, malt aroma, uninteresting malt flavor, finish and aftertaste, somewhat dull overall.

PARADISE PALE ALE — gold, hop aroma, good English style pale ale hop palate, good body, dry hop finish and aftertaste, fairly long.

BARLEYHOPPER BROWN — brown, malt and hop nose and taste, medium body, dry light hop finish and aftertaste.

McGINTY'S OLD IRISH STOUT — deep brown, hop aroma, roasted malt flavor, dry roasted malt and hop finish and aftertaste.

Mad River Brewing Co.

Brewery in **Blue Lake, CA**

STEELHEAD EXTRA PALE ALE — gold, beautiful appetizing fruity hop aroma, big delicious hop flavor, zesty and smooth, good body, extremely long, dry hop aftertaste, marvelous!

STEELHEAD EXTRA STOUT — dark brown, brown thick head, aroma is roasted barley and chocolate malt, flavor like the nose, finishes dry roasted malt, long roased dry malt aftertaste.

Three people came from Kent to plough
for wheat and rye. And these three made

CA CASH REFUND

JOHN BARLEYCORN BARLEYWINE STYLE ALE — amber, ginger and coriander aroma, big gingery taste, dry ginger aftertaste, light body and fairly brief, not what I think of as a barleywine.

Marin Brewing Co.

Brewpub in **Larkspur, CA**

MT. TAM PALE ALE — cloudy amber-gold, citrus-hop and kumquat malt nose, flavor is a bit hoppy like the nose at first but subsequent sips develop the malt, kumquat and malt aftertaste with good length, interesting brew, not bad at all.

MARIN
BREWING
COMPANY
BREWED AND BOTTLED BY MARIN BREWING COMPANY, LARKSPUR CALIFORNIA | CONTENTS: 1PT. 6FL.OZ. / 650ML
POINT REYES
PORTER

POINT REYES PORTER — deep brown, zesty hop nose, big bright toasted malt and hop flavor, long dry malt aftertaste, very drinkable.

SAN QUENTIN'S BREAKOUT STOUT — opaque almost black, smoky malt nose, high alcohol, medium dry scorched barley malt and hop flavor, finishes drier than it starts, very long dry malt and hop aftertaste, good balance, very good.

RASPBERRY TRAIL ALE — tawny-gold, fruity raspberry nose, big bright raspberry-malt flavor, tart raspberry is best at the finish and stays in a long dry tart raspberry malt aftertaste, very nicely done.

OLD DIPSEA BARLEY WINE — deep amber, very big malt and hop flavor, all kinds of malt and very hoppy, strong and long, a monster.

BLUEBEERY ALE — gold, blueberry pie nose, tart blueberry flavor, balanced, very interesting and very good, the best blueberry effort I've tasted.

STINSON BEACH PEACH — gold, clean fresh peach nose, fresh peach flavor, good body, peach and malt get a bit drier at the finish, even drier and less peachy aftertaste, really captures the peach quality in a very nice way.

HOPPY HOLIDAZE ALE — golden amber, vanilla and pumpkin pie spice nose and flavor, finishes dry, aftertaste is a bit maltier but retains the vanilla and allspice like it started.

MIWOK WEIZENBOCK — amber, alcoholic malt nose, dry malt palate, dry malt finish quickly fades to nothing.

ST. BRENDAN'S IRISH ALE — amber, faint malt nose and taste, no follow-through on the flavor.

Market Street Pub

Brewpub in **Gainesville, FL**

HONEY WHEAT BEER — amber, light malt aroma, clean refreshing off-dry malt flavor, finishes dry, medium length dry malt aftertaste.

F.X. Matt Brewing Co.

Brewery at **Utica, NY**

Several corporate names used including Old New York Beer Co., formerly of New York City.

UTICA CLUB PILSENER BEER — gold, smooth malt and hop aroma a bit on the sweet perfumy side, flavor is mostly malt, soft and somewhat dull.

UTICA CLUB CREAM ALE — yellow-gold, zesty malt and hop aroma, highly carbonated, dry balanced malt flavor, fair length.

UTICA CLUB NON-ALCOHOLIC — deep gold, attractive off-dry aroma mostly malt but backed with good hops, off-dry malt flavor, medium body, good malt finish and medium dry malt aftertaste.

UTICA CLUB LIGHT BEER — bright golden color, aroma is mainly malt but there are hops in back, flavor is like the nose, little finish and no aftertaste to speak of.

MATT'S LIGHT PREMIUM BEER — pale gold, light dry malt and hop nose, pleasant malt flavor not quite so dry as the nose, finishes dry malt but the aftertaste is brief.

MATT'S PREMIUM LAGER — golden color, aroma of malt with hops in back, malt flavor, light body, malt finish and aftertaste, medium length.

MATT'S SPECIAL DRY — pale gold, melony off-dry malt aroma, flavor is off-dry malt at first, then is tart hops in the middle and finish, ending up in a long not-so-dry malt aftertaste.

F.X. MATT'S TRADITIONAL SEASON'S BEST PREMIUM AMBER BEER 1991 — amber, faint malt aroma, highly carbonated, flavor is malt with faint hops, medium length, overall light and not interesting for a Christmas brew. The 1990 was less carbonated and had a malt flavor with an apple-like background. It was only slightly more interesting.

F.X. MATT'S TRADITIONAL SEASON'S BEST PREMIUM AMBER BEER 1992 — golden amber, piney-waxy malt nose, odd spicy flavor sort of like bayberry, medium body, dry soapy hop finish and aftertaste.

SARANAC ADIRONDACK LAGER — golden amber, bright hop and malt aroma, zesty big hop flavor, dry hop finish and aftertaste, well-balanced and very drinkable. Seems to be the new label for SARANAC 1888 ALL MALT LAGER.

MAXIMUS SUPER MALT LIQUOR — golden amber, flowery malt nose, high carbonation, big flavor is mostly malt but there are some hops, off-dry malt finish and aftertaste, quite long and very good of the type.

EL PASO LIGHT BEER — very pale golden color, faint malt aroma, very watery, faint and short malt palate.

STALLION X EXTRA MALT LIQUOR — pale gold, dusty malt nose, big vegetal malt flavor, bittering hops in back, noticeable alcohol, doesn't quite come together. Made for Tighe, International.

MONTAUK LIGHT — pale gold, pleasant but fleeting malt nose, light malt flavor, low calorie (105), short aftertaste. Made for Long Island Brewery Co., Huntington, NY.

SPORTS LIGHT BEER — medium to deep gold color, malt and light hop aroma, light malt flavor, medium to light malt aftertaste with short duration. Made for Manhattan B.C. of New York.

M.W.BRENNER'S AMBER LIGHT BEER — amber, tangy hop nose, dry lightly hopped malt palate, light body, short dry finish and aftertaste. Made for Monarch B.C. of Brooklyn, NY.

INDEPENDENCE ALE — deep amber, well-hopped ale-like aroma, strongly flavored with a good ale tang, zesty, tasty and long. Made for Manhattan B.C.

NEWMAN'S ALBANY AMBER — amber, big malt aroma, bright malt and hop flavor, high carbonation, good long malt finish and aftertaste. Made for William S. Newman B.C., Albany, NY.

OLDE HEURICH MAERZEN BIER — hazy amber, light malt and hop aroma, good bright malt and hop flavor, tasty, balanced, well-bodied, pleasant long mild hop aftertaste, very drinkable and refreshing. Made for Olde Heurich B.C., Washington, DC.

PORTLAND LAGER — amber, good malt aroma, big balanced malt and hop flavor, good body, tasty and complex, aftertaste is long extension of the flavor. Made for Maine Coast B.C., Portland, ME.

HARPOON ALE — hazy tawny-amber, complex hop aroma, big hop flavor well backed with malt, good body, complex, balanced and long. Made for Massachusetts Bay B.C., Boston, MA.

HARPOON WINTER WARMER 1991 — amber, spicy malt nose much like a pumpkin pie, flavor like the nose but with the addition of hops, medium body, medium length. The 1990 was similar and also made by Matt for Mass Bay B.C. of Boston, MA.

HARPOON OCTOBERFEST BEER — amber, pleasant malt and hop nose, good hop flavor, but thin and brief. Made for Mass Bay B.C.

GOLDEN HARPOON LAGER — deep gold, light fruity hop aroma, malt appears first on the palate thence hops through the finish and into the long aftertaste, finely carbonated and well-balanced. Made for Mass Bay B.C.

SPECIAL OLD ALE — hazy amber, fruity malt aroma, an off-dry malt flavor with strawberry tones, some chocolate malt as well, big body, dry hop aftertaste, pleasant, long and interesting. Made for Commonwealth B.C. of Boston, MA.

GOLDEN EXPORT SELECT BEER — deep gold, bright clean malt nose, finely carbonated, zesty fresh hop flavor, straightforward, tasty, well-bodied, medium duration, very drinkable. Made for Commonwealth B.C. of Boston.

FAMOUS PORTER — nearly opaque ruby-brown, big head, fairly dry malt aroma, dry roasted malt flavor, medium body, bite in the aftertaste which is dry but not very long, very drinkable. Made for Commonwealth B.C.

DOCK STREET AMBER BEER — amber, beautiful malt nose, bright flavor with good malt and hops, good body, long and delicious. Made for Dock Street B.C., Bala Cynwyd, PA.

D'AGOSTINO FRESH REAL PUB BEER — hazy tawny-gold, sweet malt nose, balanced hop and malt palate, low carbonation, good body, dry hop finish, long hop aftertaste, very tasty. Made for Manhattan B.C. of New York City for sale at D'Agostino Markets.

BROOKLYN BRAND LAGER — pale amber, pleasant malt and hop aroma, bright malt and hop flavor, well-balanced, clean and pleasant, dry malt finish and aftertaste of medium length. Made for Brooklyn Brewery, Brooklyn, NY.

BROOKLYN BROWN DARK ALE — amber-brown, lovely malt and hop aroma, pleasant balanced dry malt and hop flavor, not complex but very likeable, medium to long dry malt aftertaste. Made for Brooklyn Brewery.

NEW AMSTERDAM AMBER BEER — pale copper-amber, toasted malt aroma, bright well-hopped flavor with plenty of lightly toasted malt in support, good balance, long and very drinkable. Original brew of Old New York Beer Co., now part of Matt.

NEW AMSTERDAM NEW YORK ALE — amber, ale-like aroma, tangy citrus-hop flavor that tails off into a dry hop aftertaste, medium body, starts out strong, but doesn't develop. Old New York Beer Co. brand that was originally scheduled to be released as Whyte's Pale Ale.

NEW AMSTERDAM WINTER ANNIVERSARY NEW YORK BEER — deep amber, nice roasted malt aroma, pleasant dry roasted malt flavor, good body, brief light dry roasted malt aftertaste.

OLD BUCKEYE DRAFT STYLE — gold color, malty aroma with fruity hops in back, high carbonation, light malt flavor, dry malt finish, short malt aftertaste. Made for Old Buckeye B.C., Toledo, Ohio.

OLD BUCKEYE DRAFT STYLE LIGHT — very pale gold, Concord grape aroma, light malt flavor that is faintly grapey, dry finish, short aftertaste, 89 calories. Made for Olde Buckeye B.C.

PRIOR DOUBLE DARK — dark amber-brown, good malt aroma, medium body, pleasant bright hop and malt flavor, long dry malt and hop aftertaste. Not the old brew from a decade back, but still enjoyable to drink. It's on draft only.

SHAN SUI YEN SUM BEER — gold, bright hop nose with plenty of malt in back, flowery malt and light hop flavor lacks the sparkle of the nose, light body, made with ginseng extract which doesn't show up until the finish and it is blended with the hops since both are bitter, long flowery dry hop and ginseng aftertaste. The ginseng is the most remarkable thing about it and that is barely noticeable; perhaps it is good for you. Made for Shan Sui Brewing Co. of Hong Kong.

MANHATTAN GOLD LAGER BEER — hazy pale amber, pleasant fruity-malt aroma, complex rich and dry malt flavor carries into the long aftertaste where it is joined by some hops, good body, good tasting satisfying brew. Made for Manhattan B.C. of New York City.

COLUMBUS 1492 LAGER — amber-gold, big hop nose well-backed with malt, bright and zesty, big hop and malt flavor, some caramel comes through at the finish, good long dry hop aftertaste. Contract brew made for the Columbus B.C., Columbus, OH.

FREEPORT USA — pale gold, grainy cardboard nose and taste, no aftertaste beyond the oxidation. Matt's new non-alcoholic (0%) brew; newly bottled and apparently quite fragile.

McGuire's Irish Pub & Brewery

Brewpub in **Pensacola, FL**

McGUIRE'S LITE — gold, good malt aroma, pleasant bright brew with good fruity malt and hop character, long dry malt and Tettnanger hop aftertaste, a light ale that is more like a "regular" beer. Some malted wheat gives it the fruity character, but it is not like a weizen. Very nicely done.

GOVERNMENT WARNING: (1) ACCORDING TO THE SURGEON GENERAL, WOMEN SHOULD NOT DRINK ALCOHOLIC BEVERAGES DURING PREGNANCY BECAUSE OF THE RISKS OF BIRTH DEFECTS. (2) CONSUMPTION OF ALCOHOLIC BEVERAGES IMPAIRS YOUR ABILITY TO DRIVE A CAR OR OPERATE MACHINERY, AND MAY CAUSE HEALTH PROBLEMS.
McGUIRE'S
SINCE 1988
IRISH·ALE
BOTTLED BY McGUIRE'S BREWING COMPANY
ABITA SPRINGS, LA., & PENSACOLA, FL.
TO ENSURE BREWING EXCELLENCE, McGUIRE'S IRISH ALE USES ONLY THE FINEST BARLEY, HOPS, YEAST, AND PURE SPRING WATER IN THE BREWING PROCESS. NO ADDITIVES OR PRESERVATIVES ARE PRESENT. NET CONTENTS: 12 FL. OZ. 0.355 LITERS. KEEP REFRIGERATED.

McGUIRE'S RED ALE — amber, dry well-hopped aroma, smooth but tangy ale flavor, plenty of northwest (Willamette and Chinook) hops and good malt support, very good balance, plenty of character, long dry hop aftertaste.

McGUIRE'S PORTER — dark brown, chocolate malt aroma, flavor is complex malt from a mix of pale, chocolate and caramel malts, big and bright, stays malty throughout and finishes off-dry. Chinook hops provide a good balance.

McGUIRE'S STOUT — deep opaque brown color, faint roasted barley aroma, light smooth malt flavor, pleasant dry malt aftertaste shows plenty of hop character which has stayed in back under the roasted barley all the way through.

McNeill's Brewery

Microbrewery in **Brattleboro, VT**

DUCK'S BREATH BITTER — gold, bright hop aroma, sharp hop flavor, a real bitter style, there is malt, however, giving a fruity background to the finish and aftertaste and an additional degree of balance, works out well.

FIREHOUSE PALE — gold, dry malt aroma, very dry malt flavor, this continues on unchanged into the long aftertaste.

McNEILL'S SPECIAL BITTER — gold, hop nose and taste, good complexity, good body, dry hop finish and aftertaste. The Duck's Breath is a more classical style.

SLOPBUCKET BROWN — brown, hop aroma, dry malt flavor, dry hop finish and aftertaste, medium body, fair length.

DEAD HORSE IPA — gold, bright malt and hop aroma, flavor like the nose, very good balance, very long dry malt and hop aftertaste, more malt than hop in this IPA.

PALE BOCK — gold, hop aroma and taste, big body, balanced, dry hop finish, long dry hop aftertaste, good effort.

Eddie McStiff's

Brewpub in **Moab, UT**

AMBER ALE — amber, light hop nose and flavor, dry hop finish and aftertaste, very brief.

RASPBERRY WHEAT — gold, raspberry nose, nice berry flavor, off-dry malt and fruit finish and aftertaste.

Mendocino Brewing Co.

Brewery and brewpub in **Hopland, CA**

RED TAIL ALE — hazy copper, fruity citrus aroma that reminds you somewhat of a California Johannisberg Riesling wine, good body, dry hop finish and aftertaste.

BLUE HERON PALE ALE — cloudy amber, pleasant aroma shows both hops and malt, flavor like the nose, good body and good balance, highly carbonated but the flavor is big enough to handle it, good long aftertaste, considerable complexity.

BLACK HAWK STOUT — opaque brown, rich off-dry malt aroma, dry palate with plenty of malt and hops, good body, good length.

YULETIDE PORTER — deep amber-brown, lovely fragrant malt aroma with a touch of citrus, big malt flavor, finishes quite dry but there is noticeable alcohol, long dry malt aftertaste.

EYE OF THE HAWK — amber, very big hop nose, strong hop flavor, alcoholic, long dry hop aftertaste has plenty of malt in support, a big lusty brew.

Mill Bakery, Eatery & Brewery

Brewpub in Winter Park, FL

HARVEST GOLD LIGHT — gold, faint malt and hop nose, light malt and hop flavor, light body, clean and pleasant, light dry short malt aftertaste.

KNIGHT LIGHT — pale gold, aromatic hop nose, light hop flavor, light body, light medium long clean dry hop aftertaste.

MAGIC BREW — deep ruby-amber, big hop nose, good hop and malt flavor shows the hops to good advantage, light body, good long dry malt aftertaste.

PALE ALE — golden amber, clean flowery hop and malt aroma, big hop palate, malt comes in at the middle, good body, long dry hop aftertaste, lots of character, an excellent bright and refreshing well-hopped brew.

The Mill Bakery, Eatery & Brewery

Brewpub in Charlotte, NC

COPPER CREEK ALE — gold, big bright hop aroma and flavor, good body, off-dry malt finish and aftertaste.

RED OKTOBER — gold, big hop aroma and flavor, good body, dry hop finish and aftertaste.

49ER GOLD — gold, hop and malt aroma and flavor, good body, dry hop finish and aftertaste.

NUT BROWN ALE — amber, light malt aroma, very light malt flavor on the dry side, no discernible aftertaste.

Miller Brewing Co.

Breweries in Milwaukee, WI; Azusa and Irwindale, CA; Eden, NC; South Volney, NY; Trenton, OH; Albany, GA; and Fort Worth, TX.

MILLER HIGH LIFE — bright gold, pleasant aromatic hop nose, clean flavorful malt and hop palate, refreshing and fairly complex, good body, long dry hop aftertaste.

LITE PILSENER BEER — pale gold, good malt aroma, light body, pleasant malt flavor, dry finish and aftertaste, has good length.

LITE ULTRA — gold, very pleasant malt and hop aroma, front palate is pleasant dry malt with a substantial CO_2 component, flavor cuts off suddenly without much finish and no aftertaste, but it is very good while it is there. This is a test brew for Miller in a very low calorie beer (77) and, for the type, is excellent.

LOWENBRAU LIGHT SPECIAL — light gold, clean malt aroma, hops dominate the flavor, good balance, good body, long dry hop aftertaste.

LOWENBRAU DARK SPECIAL — deep amber, appetizing malt and hop aroma is very Bavarian, big hop flavor, surprisingly light body, very little aftertaste.

SHARP'S NA BEER — gold, off-dry malt aroma and flavor, light body, short aftertaste.

MEISTER BRAU — bright gold, dry malt nose, off-dry malt and tangy hop flavor, hops develop nicely at finish and in aftertaste, the malt, however, doesn't and tends toward sour, long aftertaste.

MEISTER BRAU LIGHT — bright gold, pleasant malt and hop nose, light malt flavor, light body, good but brief.

MAGNUM MALT LIQUOR — pale yellow, fruity sweet malt aroma, slightly sweet malt flavor, light bodied for a malt liquor, slightly sweet malt finish and aftertaste with medium duration.

MILLER SPECIAL RESERVE BEER — bright deep gold, rich malt nose, smooth malt flavor has a richness but stays on the dry side, hops show only as a hint and that comes in the aftertaste.

MILLER SPECIAL RESERVE LIGHT — gold, dusty light malt nose, light dry malt flavor, light body, only a brief and faint malt aftertaste.

MILWAUKEE'S BEST BEER — pale gold, pleasant malt aroma, highly carbonated, light body, slightly sweet malt flavor, good finish and long aftertaste feature both malt and hops.

MILWAUKEE'S BEST LIGHT — pale gold, malt aroma, light slightly sweet malt flavor, high carbonation, hops appear at the finish and carry into the aftertaste which is light and short.

MILLER GENUINE DRAFT — medium deep gold, faint malt aroma, wonderfully dry malt flavor without being bitter, dry finish and aftertaste, good length.

MILLER GENUINE DRAFT LIGHT — very pale gold, very faint malt aroma and flavor, very little finish and almost no aftertaste.

DAKOTA WHEAT BREWED BEER — pale gold, slightly off-dry malt and hop aroma, pleasant dry malt flavor, good body, ends abruptly, very clean and refreshing, very good except for the lack of an aftertaste. Miller has tried this several times in test markets and, despite it being one of the best efforts in the genre, decides not to follow through with regular production.

COLDERS 29 LIGHT —pale gold, light very pleasant off-dry malt nose, light malt flavor, light body, refreshing like a dry malty club soda, short faint dry malt aftertaste.

COLDERS 29 — pale gold, light fruity malt nose, smooth balanced light malt and hop flavor, light body, brief dry malt aftertaste.

Millstream Brewing Co.

Brewery in Amana, IA

MILLSTREAM LAGER BEER — hazy gold, good malt and hop aroma, lots of both malt and hops for the palate but the balance is not as good as it could be, comes off as being off-dry malt and sour hops right into the aftertaste.

SCHILD BRAU — amber, beautiful roasted malt nose, has a fruity component as well, delicious complex roasted malt flavor, great balance, zesty hops in support, fresh fruity malt finish and long aftertaste, an excellent brew.

MILLSTREAM WHEAT LAGER BEER — bright gold, perky malt aroma, low carbonation, even to the eye, light malt flavor, dull malt aftertaste of medium length.

MILLSTREAM OKTOBERFEST — amber-gold, big malt nose, big malt and hop flavor, good body, long dry malt aftertaste.

Minnesota Brewing Co.

Brewery in St. Paul, MN

(The old Jacob Schmidt Brewery.)

PIG'S EYE PILSNER — gold, hop and vegetal aroma, hop flavor with some sour malt in back, medium body, dry malt and hop finish and long aftertaste.

LANDMARK OCTOBERFEST — amber, malt nose, dry malt flavor, dry malt finish and aftertaste.

LANDMARK LIGHT— gold, pleasant malt aroma and flavor, hops are in back, good tasting, good body, short dry hop finish and aftertaste.

LANDMARK — gold, dry hop nose, dry hop flavor, thin body, light finish, short dry aftertaste.

LANDMARK BOCK — amber, malt nose, spicy roasted malt and dry hop flavor, medium body, fair to good balance, dry malt aftertaste has good duration.

GRAIN BELT BEER — gold, vegetal malt aroma, vegetal malt and light hop flavor, light body, short dry malt aftertaste.

GRAIN BELT LIGHT — pale gold, malt aroma, grainy fruity-grapey malt flavor at first, then goes a bit drier (but stays malty), medium body, dull malt finish and aftertaste.

GRAIN BELT PREMIUM LIGHT — pale gold, malt nose, light dry hop and malt flavor, light body, light dry hop and malt aftertaste, medium length.

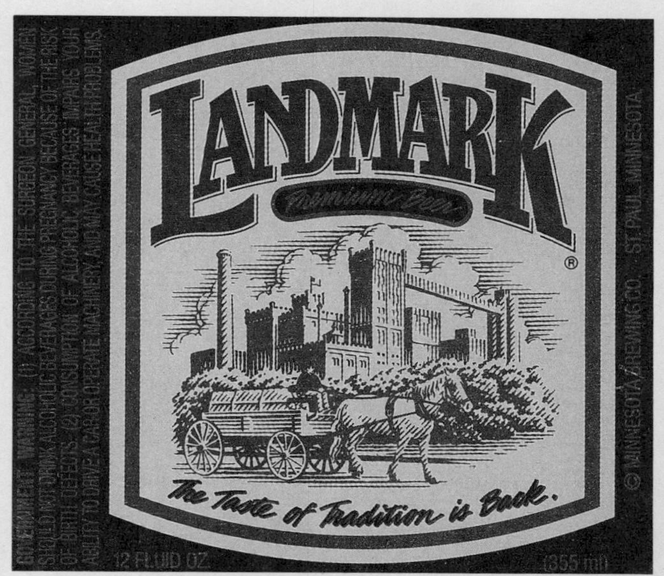
GOVERNMENT WARNING: (1) ACCORDING TO THE SURGEON GENERAL, WOMEN SHOULD NOT DRINK ALCOHOLIC BEVERAGES DURING PREGNANCY BECAUSE OF THE RISK OF BIRTH DEFECTS. (2) CONSUMPTION OF ALCOHOLIC BEVERAGES IMPAIRS YOUR ABILITY TO DRIVE A CAR OR OPERATE MACHINERY, AND MAY CAUSE HEALTH PROBLEMS.
LANDMARK
Premium Beer
®
The Taste of Tradition is Back.
12 FLUID OZ
(355 ml)
© MINNESOTA BREWING CO. · ST. PAUL, MINNESOTA

PETE'S WICKED ALE — brilliant deep amber, slightly toasted malt and hop aroma, zesty malt flavor with hops rolling in from mid-palate on, malt and hops balanced throughout, good hop and malt finish and a long dry aftertaste, an excellent, balanced, satisfying, drinkable brew.

PETE'S GOLD COAST LAGER — hazy amber, bright hop aroma, big hop flavor, big body, complex, balanced, delicious, feels good in your mouth, long dry hop aftertaste. Contract brew as above.

CRAZY ED'S CAVE CREEK CHILI BEER — gold, bright jalapeño pepper nose, hot jalapeño taste (pepper first then the heat), finish and aftertaste. Lots of real jalapeño character. Made for Black Mountain Brewery, Cave Creek, AZ.

CERVEZA CALIENTE — gold, light honeyed malt nose, light malt at first (for an instant) on the tongue, then dry hot pepper for flavor, finish and aftertaste. Made for Cerveza Caliente Ltd.

Mountain Brewers, Inc.

Brewery in **Bridgewater, VT**

LONG TRAIL ALE — amber, big toasted malt aroma, dry malt and bright hop flavor, very dry hop finish and aftertaste.

VERMONT BICENTENNIAL ALE — hazy gold, light citrus-ale aroma, bright hop flavor with a good ale character, good tasting bitter hop finish and long, dry hop aftertaste, medium body, good balance.

LONG TRAIL LIGHT — gold, dry malt nose and taste, light body, short, dry malt aftertaste.

VERNMENT WARNING: (1) ACCORDING TO THE SURGEON GENERAL, WOMEN SHOULD NOT DRINK ALCOHOLIC BEVERAGES DURING PREGNANCY BECAUSE OF THE RISK OF BIRTH DEFECTS. (2) CONSUMPTION OF ALCOHOLIC BEVERAGES IMPAIRS YOUR ABILITY TO DRIVE A CAR OR OPERATE MACHINERY, AND MAY CAUSE HEALTH PROBLEMS.
VERMONT
1791
1991
BICENTENNIAL
ALE
BREWED AND BOTTLED BY
MOUNTAIN
VERMONT'S
BREWERS
LIMITED EDITION
VT, MA
5¢ REFUND
PRODUCT OF THE UNITED STATES
12 FL OZ. (355 ml.)
BREWED AND BOTTLED BY THE MOUNTAIN BREWERS, INC.,
THE MARKETPLACE AT BRIDGEWATER MILL, BRIDGEWATER, VT 05034

LONG TRAIL IPA — amber-gold, bright hoppy aroma and flavor, strong and complex, lots of ale bite, alcohol shows a bit, good body, extremely long, dry hop aftertaste.

O'BRIEN'S LONG TRAIL STOUT — dark, roasted barley and chocolate malt aroma and taste, somewhat light on flavor and body, good aftertaste like the flavor, but again light and a bit short. Draft version.

LONG TRAIL STOUT — opaque brown, nose like ashes and roasted barley, smoky, burnt malt flavor, low carbonation, overhopped, unbalanced, rough to drink. Bottled version.

MULLIGAN'S BREW — gold, malt aroma, dry hop and malt flavor, smooth and balanced, long dry hop aftertaste.

Napa Valley Brewing Co.

Brewpub and restaurant in **Calistoga, CA**

CALISTOGA RED ALE — amber, dry malt nose, dry hop flavor, good balance, smooth, dry hop finish and aftertaste.

CALISTOGA GOLDEN LAGER — gold, hop aroma, malt flavor, smooth, light but balanced, dry hop and malt finish and aftertaste, a bit short.

CALISTOGA WHEAT ALE — gold, malt nose, American style malt and wheat flavor (no spiciness), brief aftertaste.

New Belgium Brewing Co.

Microbrewery in **Fort Collins, CO**

SUNSHINE WHEAT BEER — hazy gold, complex nose has ginger, nutmeg and spruce, light body, very complex ginger-allspice flavor, light body, long dry spicy aftertaste retains the complexity, not especially dry.

FAT TIRE AMBER ALE — amber, lovely appetizing hop nose (Cascade hops), flavor is nutty malt but is very light and it finishes weakly.

OLD CHERRY ALE — peachy-amber, aroma is faintly of cherries, front of the palate is tart cherries, middle is bright malt, finish is again the cherry tartness, there is some hint of cinnamon in there as well, body is good, balance is shaky. The cherry tartness builds as you continue to sip. A very interesting beer.

ABBEY TRAPPISTE STYLE ALE — brown, complex alcoholic malt aroma, big rich alcoholic malt flavor with a lactic background, huge mouth-filling brew, hops jump out at the finish and balance the malt in the long dry aftertaste, a superior brew that is absolutely true to style.

TRIPPEL TRAPPISTE STYLE ALE — pale amber-gold, big hop nose and bigger hop flavor, smooth despite the hoppiness because there is more than enough malt for good balance, dry finish and aftertaste.

New England Brewing Co.

Brewery in Norwalk, CT

NEW ENGLAND ATLANTIC AMBER ALE — amber, good hop aroma, complex hop palate with plenty of malt in back, medium dry hop finish, long dry hop aftertaste, lots of character and excellent balance.

NEW ENGLAND GOLD STOCK ALE — deep golden color, great complex hop and malt nose with faint citrus in the background, big body, big hops but also plenty of malt for a great balanced brew, complex and very long rich hop and malt aftertaste, a fine big brew worth trying.

NEW ENGLAND HOLIDAY ALE '91— deep amber, spicy gingerbread nose, big ginger and malt flavor, off-dry, the good ale flavor comes out from behind the spices at the finish and holds well through a long aftertaste.

NEW ENGLAND HOLIDAY ALE '92 — deep amber, complex pumpkin pie spice nose, dry pumpkin spice flavor, stays on the sweet side, the malt character does not come out from behind the spices in this year's effort.

NEW ENGLAND OATMEAL STOUT — deep brown, beautiful nose of roasted barley, big dry roasted malt flavor, like a coffee, richly flavored, long smooth dry malt aftertaste, very drinkable.

North Coast Brewing Co.

Brewery and brewpub in Fort Bragg, CA

RUEDRICH'S RED SEAL ALE — hazy amber, good malt nose, lightly smoked zesty malt palate, medium body, dry hop finish, long dry hop aftertaste. Later samples were more highly hopped and had more of a citrus back taste.

CHRISTMAS ALE 1989 — hazy deep amber, light toasted malt aroma, light toasted smoky malt flavor, dry finish and aftertaste like the flavor, seems like there is just too much toast and it masks the rest of the flavors.

CHRISTMAS ALE 1990 — hazy amber, lovely huge toasted malt nose, with a fruity-ale tang, big taste just like the nose, big malt finish, long aftertaste like you had been chewing on malt, very flavorful and there is a subtle hop presence throughout.

CHRISTMAS ALE 1991 — deep amber, rich roasted chocolate malt nose, creamy dry chocolate malt flavor, good body, chewey, good complexity, long dry malt aftertaste has hops in back.

CHRISTMAS ALE 1992 — amber, light dry hop aroma with some faint chocolate malt background, dry hop flavor shows none of the malt promised by the aroma, lacks the mouth feel of the '91, some faint off-dry malt in back in the aftertaste.

SCRIMSHAW PILSENER STYLE BEER — hazy gold, complex aroma with malt, chocolate, tobacco, etc., off-dry complex malt flavor with grapefruit, cherry pits, tobacco and chocolate, smooth and mellow, good long dry malt aftertaste.

SUMMER ALE 1990 — hazy amber-gold, fruity malt aroma, big hop and fruity-malt palate, very good balance, touch of sour hops at the finish, long malt aftertaste.

OKTOBERFEST ALE — hazy amber, complex fruity hop California ale nose, big toasted malt flavor, hop finish, long hop and malt aftertaste, complex, balanced and drinkable.

OLD No. 38 STOUT — deep ruby color, chocolate malt nose, roasted chocolate malt flavor is slightly burnt, good body, long burnt malt/smoky aftertaste, still very palatable despite the over roasting of the malt.

TRADITIONAL BOCK — hazy amber, big malt nose, flavor starts out big and malty, finishes with dry hops, long dry malt aftertaste, has complexity, balance and body.

CENTENNIAL 100 ALE — amber-gold, chocolate-Ovaltine malt nose, big malt flavor, big body, smooth, dry malt finish and long dry malt aftertaste.

O'Dell Brewing Co.

Microbrewery in **Fort Collins, CO**

90 SHILLING ALE — amber, bright complex hop aroma, big malt flavor stays dry and is well backed with hops, nicely balanced, very pleasant drinkable beer, long dry malt and hop aftertaste, excellent with food.

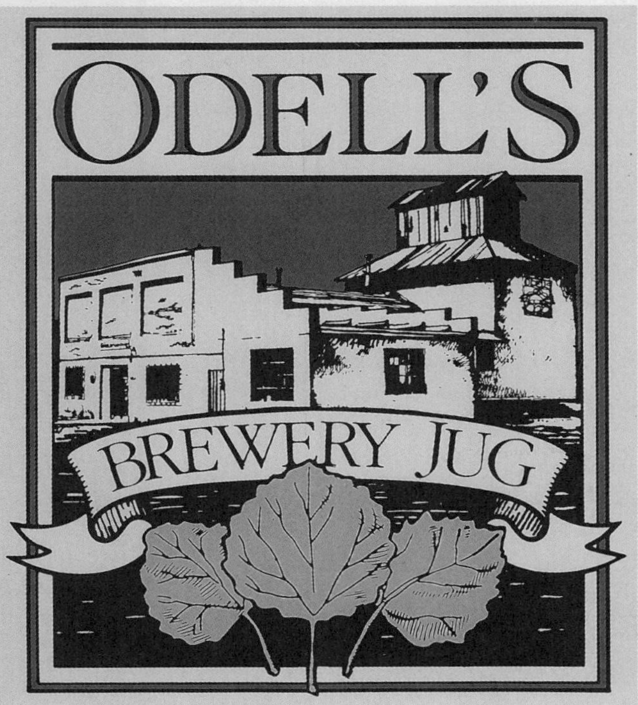

HEARTLAND WHEAT — gold, bright fresh malt nose and flavor, lightly hopped, long dry malt aftertaste, an American-style wheat beer. This brew was called **WHEATLAND WHEAT** at the brewery.

OLD TOWN ALE — amber, bright complex malt and hop nose, smooth, balanced, mostly malty flavor, good hop backing, long dry aftertaste.

O'DELL'S GOLDEN ALE — amber-gold, bright dry malt flavor, lightly hopped, medium to light body, cuts off quickly, dry malt finish and aftertaste.

O'DELL SPECIAL BITTER — gold, hop aroma and dry hop flavor, medium body, short dry hop aftertaste.

O'Fallon Brewing Co.

Brewpub in **O'Fallon, IL**

NUMBSKULL AMBER LAGER — golden amber, malt aroma, malt flavor has some faint lactic acid in back behind the hops, dry malt and hop finish and aftertaste.

HORST'S OKTOBERFEST — amber, hop nose and flavor has a lactic background, dry hop finish and aftertaste follow from the flavor.

Oasis Brewery

Brewpub in **Boulder, CO**

TUT BROWN ALE — deep amber-brown, strange weak aroma, chocolate malt flavor, somewhat nutty, good body, finish and aftertaste are a continuation of the flavor.

ZOSER OATMEAL STOUT — black, roasted barley and chocolate malt nose, big body, rich flavor like the aroma, plenty of both malt and hops, quite zesty, good balance, dry malt finish and aftertaste, enjoyable stout.

CAPSTONE ESB — amber, hop nose, big hop flavor (there is plenty of malt but even more bittering hops), very assertive, dry hop finish and aftertaste.

OASIS PALE ALE — deep gold, light hop aroma with a citrus background, sour malt and hop flavor, slightly sour and very dry hop aftertaste.

OASIS OKTOBERFEST — deep amber, no discernible nose, touch of malty sweetness on the front and middle of the palate, finish is dry malt, lightly hopped dry malt aftertaste and it disappears abruptly.

Old Dominion Brewing Co.

Microbrewery in **Ashburn, VA**

DOMINION LAGER — gold, malt aroma and flavor, good body, malt finish and dry malt aftertaste.

DOMINION STOUT — brown, dry hop aroma and flavor with faint roasted barley and chocolate malt, the roasted character is more developed on the palate but stays light, light body, light dry malt finish and aftertaste.

DOMINION ALE — gold, dry hop aroma and flavor, good body, dry hop finish and aftertaste, pleasant, medium intensity brew.

HARD TIMES SELECT — gold, malt nose and taste, has some complexity, the hops stay in the background but provide enough character for interest and balance, long fairly dry malt and hop aftertaste.

Oldenberg Brewing Co.

Brewery, restaurants, hotel, shops, entertainment and convention center in **Ft. Mitchell, KY**

OLDENBERG PREMIUM VERUM — tawny-gold, good dry hop and malt aroma, dry malt and hop flavor has some zest, good balance, some malty sweetness in the middle, has some complexity, pleasant malt finish with hops in back, medium dry long malt and hop aftertaste, a good beer by itself or with food.

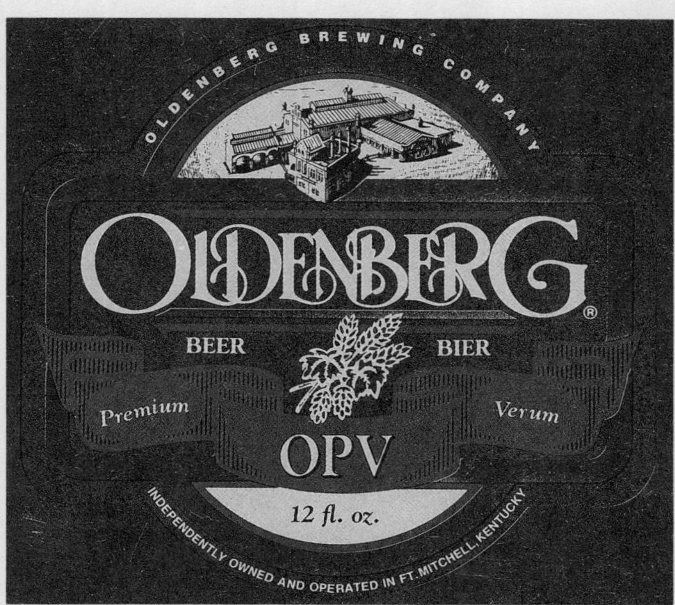

VAIL ALE — brilliant amber, citrus hop and malt aroma, good body, big malt flavor well-backed with citrus and hop character, malt is first encountered with the hops coming in at the middle and staying on, smooth, good body, off-dry malt and hop finish and long aftertaste. Made for Vail B.C., Vail, CO.

OLDENBERG BLONDE DRY LIGHT PILS — deep gold, bright malt aroma, complex dry malt flavor, off-dry malt in finish, medium length off-dry malt aftertaste.

OLDENBERG STOUT — opaque brown, dry hop aroma and flavor, good body, dry almost coffee-like finish, long dry hop aftertaste, satisfying substantial brew.

OLDENBERG WINTER ALE — amber-gold, tangy bright hop nose and taste, plenty of both hops and malt, zesty up front, smooth in the middle, big right to the end, long dry hop aftertaste.

McGUIRE'S IRISH ALE — amber, malt aroma, light dry malt flavor with light hops in back, medium body, dry malt finish and medium length aftertaste. Made for McGuire's B.C., Pensacola, FL.

LAS BRISAS CARIBBEAN STYLE BEER — hazy gold, sour malt aroma, light body, zesty hop and malt flavor, malt is a bit on the sour side but there is a balance of sorts achieved through the bitterness of the hops, good length.

OLDENBERG WEISS WHEAT BEER — gold, light but bright fruity wheat-malt nose with a very faint toastiness in back, pleasant light wheaty-malt flavor, light body, medium long malt aftertaste, pleasant but a bit too light flavored.

PITTS ALL AMERICAN BEER — golden-amber, faint fruity malt nose, dry malt flavor, hop finish, long dry hop aftertaste. Made for Burbank's Bar-B-Q, a local restaurant.

IRONSIDE ALE — amber, appetizing hop and malt nose, some caramel in back, light tasty smooth malt palate, light body, evenly balanced, long dry malt aftertaste. Contract brew for Olde Time Brewers Inc., Boston, MA.

RAY'S CLASSIC LAGER — hazy pale amber, fresh malt and hop nose, good hop flavor, quite tasty, balanced and full bodied, some complexity, long dry hop aftertaste.

OLDENBERG CELEBRATION ALE — amber, bright hop nose and flavor, good dry malt and hop finish and aftertaste, good body, balanced, drinkable and fairly long.

Otto Brothers' Brewing Co.

Microbrewery in Jackson, WY

TETON ALE — amber, English style hop aroma, very dry and strong hop flavor, good body, very dry hop finish and long dry hop aftertaste, a lusty well-hopped brew.

OLD FAITHFUL STOUT — gold, dry hop aroma and flavor, good body, dry hop finish and aftertaste.

MOOSE JUICE STOUT — amber-brown, very big dry malt and hop aroma and flavor, not roasted or chocolate malt, just huge malt and hops, great complexity, big body, very dry finish, long dry malt and hop aftertaste.

Pacific Coast Brewing Co.

Brewpub in Oakland, CA

HOLIDAY ALE 1988 — hazy amber, huge head, effervescent citrus-soapy malt and hop nose, huge flavor of hops and malt, high alcohol, chewy body, hop finish, long hop aftertaste, another really good Xmas beer.

HOLIDAY BARLEYWINE ALE 1990 — cloudy amber, tangy citrus ale nose has a wineyness about it, big spicy complex hop and malt flavor, both sweet and sharp at the same time, very complicated palate with all different kinds of malt showing, big body, huge and extremely long. This is another fine Xmas brew.

HOLIDAY STRONG ALE 1991 — hazy amber, fruity kumquat-malt nose, interesting odd malt flavor that is fruity sweet and dry at the same time, very complex and very drinkable, long off-dry malt and hop aftertaste.

GRAY WHALE ALE — hazy amber, malt nose, dull malty flavor, good body, dry malt aftertaste.

BLUE WHALE ALE — deep amber, fruity hop nose and taste, good body, dry hop aftertaste has length, a good tasting ale.

KILLER WHALE STOUT — deep brown, pleasant roasted barley nose, very light roasted malt flavor, medium body, dry and light roasted malt aftertaste, not much length.

IMPERIAL STOUT — deep brown, alcohol in the nose dominates the roasted malt, big body, alcohol and roasted malt flavor, dry malt finish and aftertaste, considerable length.

TRADITIONAL IPA — amber, hop nose and taste, good body, dry hop finish, long dry hop aftertaste.

PEARL WHEAT — hazy golden amber, faint malt and butterscotch nose and taste, brief buttery aftertaste.

EMERALD ALE — amber, beautiful malt and hop nose, flavor to match, balanced, short dry hop aftertaste, except for the brevity of the aftertaste a very well made brew.

James Page Brewing Co.

Brewery in Minneapolis, MN

JAMES PAGE PRIVATE STOCK — amber, malty nose with a trace of fruit, good dry malt flavor with hops in back, medium body, dry malt finish, long dry malt aftertaste, pleasant dry beer.

BOUNDARY WATERS BOCK — hazy amber, malt nose, dry malt flavor, briefly a touch of something metallic in the finish, dry malt aftertaste. I never would guess that it was made with wild rice.

BOUNDARY WATERS BEER — hazy amber-gold, faint hop nose, dry hop flavor, mellow and smooth, light body, dry hop finish, medium long dry hop aftertaste, a pleasant dry beer.

BOUNDARY WATERS WILD RICE BEER — deep gold, off-dry malt aroma and flavor, medium body, light off-dry malt aftertaste has medium length, quite refreshing while it is in your mouth.

A. FITGER & CO. FLAGSHIP BEER — bright tawny-gold, light pleasant malt and hop aroma, light hop flavor well-backed with malt, medium body, dry hop finish, very long dry hop aftertaste.

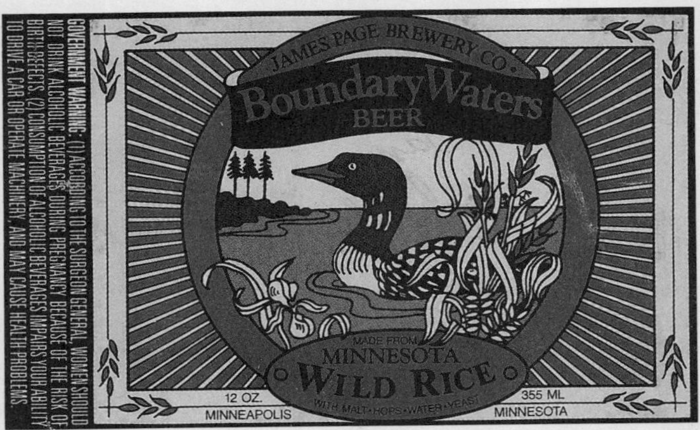

Pennsylvania Brewing Co./Allegheny Brewery & Pub

Microbrewery and brewpub in Pittsburgh, PA

PENN LIGHT LAGER — gold, light malt and hop aroma and flavor, medium to light body, dry malt and hop finish and aftertaste.

OKTOBERFEST — golden amber, grainy grassy aroma, dull grainy malt flavor, light to medium body, not well knit, dry malt finish and aftertaste.

PENN DARK — brown, faint malt aroma, uninteresting malt flavor is off-dry, dull malt finish and aftertaste.

Pike Place Brewery

Microbrewery in Seattle, WA

PIKE PLACE PALE ALE — amber, hop aroma, big hop flavor is balanced well with background malt, very tasty and drinkable, good body, dry hop finish and aftertaste.

EAST INDIA PALE ALE — amber, hop aroma, big hop flavor, good balance, good body, long dry hop aftertaste.

PIKE PLACE XXXX STOUT — deep brown, roasted barley and chocolate malt aroma, flavor like the nose, excellent balance, smooth, dry and long.

OLD BAWDY BARLEY WINE — gold, big hop and malt aroma, huge flavor is balanced hops and malt, very big and bold, long long complex hop and malt aftertaste, the hops tend to dry and the malt tends toward sweetness so they never get either place but the balance stays, very enjoyable.

Pizza Deli & Brewery

Brewpubs in Cave Junction and Brookings Harbor, OR

HARBOR LIGHTS KÖLSCH — hazy gold, clean fruity malt aroma and flavor, medium body, hop finish and aftertaste, pleasant and easy to drink.

CAVE BEAR WHEAT WINE — hazy amber, big complex malt aroma, big body, high alcohol, off-dry malt flavor, low carbonation, long malt aftertaste, it really grows on you.

PIZZA DELI HEFE-WEIZEN — hazy pale amber, wheaty malt aroma, light malt flavor, hops appear softly in the finish, very drinkable, medium long dry malt aftertaste.

SNUG HARBOR OLD ALE — deep mahogany, big malt aroma, huge rich alcoholic malt flavor, straightforward malt, stays rich throughout, a long delicious sipping beer.

ENGLISH BROWN NUT BROWN ALE — hazy amber-brown, fruity malt aroma, smooth roasted malt flavor, dry but not pushing it, medium body, excellent with food and very drinkable.

PIZZA DELI EXTRA SPECIAL BITTER ALE — deep amber, lovely toasted malt aroma reminds you of fine rich English bacon, malt flavor is not as good as the nose, malt gradually fades and is replaced with hops, malt reappears at the finish and stays for the aftertaste with the hops in back.

Portland Brewing Co.

Brewpub in Portland, OR

PORTLAND DRY HONEY BEER — deep gold, honeyed (really!) malt aroma, off-dry malt flavor has a touch of honeyed sweetness, medium dry finish, long malt aftertaste is reasonably dry.

WINTER ALE WITH SPICES — deep ruby-brown, spice aroma, nutmeg, cinnamon, etc., spice flavor with malt and alcohol showing, medium length spicy-malt aftertaste.

MT. HOOD BEER — gold, faint off-dry malt nose, dry CO_2 and malt flavor, long dry malt aftertaste turns to hops at the very end.

PORTLAND ALE — tawny-gold, big hop and malt nose, very smooth malt flavor, medium body, dry hop finish and aftertaste, fairly long, well-hopped throughout.

PORTLAND PORTER — opaque brown, dry chocolate malt and roasted barley nose, sort of coffee-like, big soft chocolate malt and roasted barley flavor, very pleasant and drinkable, medium to light body, long medium dry malt aftertaste.

McTARNAHAN'S ALE — amber, citrus-ale nose, bright hop flavor, good body, smooth and bright, finely carbonated, pleasant drinking, very dry hop aftertaste.

Red Hook Ale Brewery, Inc.

Brewery and brewpub in Seattle, WA

RED HOOK ESB ALE — amber, light malt aroma, very flavorful big malt and hop flavor, dry hop finish, long dry hop aftertaste, complex and long.

BLACKHOOK PORTER — deep ruby-amber, big bright and dry malt nose, dry malt palate, medium body, malt finish with a touch of fruity-citrus-spice-smoke, dry malt aftertaste, good length, pleasant, very drinkable.

BALLARD BITTER PALE ALE — deep gold, malt aroma, light body, malt flavor, dry hop aftertaste.

WHEAT HOOK WHEATEN ALE — hazy gold, fruity complex malt nose with a hint of butterscotch, very complex dry flavor that shows some hops, malt, fruitiness, butterscotch and tartness, long dry hop aftertaste.

WINTERHOOK CHRISTMAS ALE 1990 — hazy amber, light malt aroma, good toasted malt flavor, good body, dry malt finish, nicely balanced, long malt aftertaste, noticeable alcohol, very drinkable.

WINTERHOOK CHRISTMAS ALE 1991 — amber color, malt nose with a light citrus background, complex ale flavor, dry hop finish and long dry hop aftertaste, very good brew.

WINTERHOOK CHRISTMAS ALE 1992 — deep amber, fragrant malt nose, strong malt flavor has a faintly sour hop background, rich malt finish, somewhat drier in the aftertaste but keeps its strength, very long on the palate, hops more noticeable at the end and the last impression is slightly sour hops. Several samples that were tasted on the East Coast had been mishandled.

Rock Bottom Brewery

Brewpub in Denver, CO

Affiliated with the Boulder Brewing Co.

AZTEC ALE — very deep amber, faint malt nose, caramel malt flavor, dull malt finish and aftertaste.

FALCON PALE ALE — deep amber, faint hop and malt aroma, flavor has plenty of both hops and malt but the balance is not good, medium body, dry hop finish and aftertaste.

RED ROCKS RED — amber, light hop nose, bright hoppy flavor, quite zesty, good body, long dry hop aftertaste has plenty of malt for balance.

ROCKIES PREMIUM DRAFT — pale gold, lovely hop aroma, bright hop and malt flavor is very tasty, excellent balance, light dry hop finish and aftertaste, a delicious and very drinkable brew.

ARAPAHOE AMBER — deep amber, faint malt nose, bright hop flavor, good body, plenty of malt, at the finish it abruptly goes dry as if the hops and malt disappear.

RED HAWK ALE CASK CONDITIONED — gold, malt nose, weak malt flavor, slightly oxidized, dull malt finish and aftertaste.

MOLLY'S TITANIC BROWN ALE — deep amber-brown, malt nose, big malt and hop flavor, just doesn't quite come together.

BLACK DIAMOND STOUT — deep ruby-brown, faint malt nose, bright malt and roasted barley flavor, good body, good carbonation level, very tasty, quite drinkable and long.

JAZZBERRY — amber, very fruity raspberry aroma, raspberry flavor, good body, medium dry raspberry aftertaste.

LAGERHEAD — gold, malt and hop nose, slightly sour malt flavor with hops in back, dry hop aftertaste.

SCHWARZ HACKER — brown, big hop nose well-backed with malt, flavor like the aroma, good body, light dry malt finish and aftertaste, good length.

Rogue Brewing Co.

Brewery in Newport, OR

Bottling facility in Tigard, OR. Brewpubs in Newport and Ashland, OR.

ROGUE GOLDEN ALE — hazy gold, bright flowery hop and malt nose, pleasant big hop flavor, lots of fruity malt balanced with big tangy hops, big hop finish, extremely long fruity malt and bright dry hop aftertaste, well-made brew.

ROGUE NEW-PORTER — deep ruby-brown, brown head, smooth toasted malt nose, very dry malt flavor with a smoky-toasty character, rich yet dry, good malt finish, long dry toasted malt aftertaste, balanced, smooth and flavorful.

ROGUE SHAKESPEARE STOUT — near opaque ruby-brown, brown head, chocolate malt nose with a fruity background, also some faint smoke in back, fairly dry and faintly smoky malt palate, medium body, dry finish and long dry malt aftertaste, very drinkable.

ST. ROGUE RED — deep reddish-amber, fresh roasted malt and hop nose has a little citric tang in back that blends in nicely, big rich hop and roasted malt flavor is very well balanced, medium body, dry hop and malt finish, long dry hop aftertaste, a super brew with enough hops and malt for anyone.

ROGUE SPRINGBOCK — hazy amber, off-dry flowery malt nose, strong fruity malt flavor, medium body, very drinkable, long dry malt aftertaste, good brew.

ROGUE OLD CRUSTACEAN BARLEY WINE — hazy amber, strong good malt nose, lovely with a touch of citrus fruit, huge body, high alcohol, concentrated hop and malt flavor, big and strong, good fruity finish, very long malt aftertaste, excellent sipping beer.

ROGUE WELCOMMEN RAUCH BIER — deep amber, smoked meat nose, smooth smoked malt flavor, medium body, extremely long dry smoked malt aftertaste, done with a delicate hand.

MEXICALI ROGUE — gold, light hop nose, light jalapeño flavor, dry spicy finish and aftertaste, very lightly done with the peppers and very pleasant, the first one of the chili beers I actually enjoyed.

ROGUE IMPERIAL STOUT — brown, huge nose of alcohol, hops and malt, enormous flavor almost overwhelms the senses, high octane brew, very strongly flavored and very long.

ROGUE MOGUL ALE — deep amber, appetizing northwest hop aroma, complex flavor is first citrus hops, then dry hops with a good malt backing, medium to good body, long dry malt aftertaste seems to be a blend of chocolate and black patent malt.

Rubicon Brewing Co.

Brewpub in Sacramento, CA

RUBICON INDIA PALE ALE — hazy gold, bright hop nose, light dry hop flavor, good balance provided by some malt in mid-palate, long dry hop aftertaste.

RUBICON WHEAT — gold, malt nose, bright malt flavor, clean fresh malt aftertaste, no spiciness.

RUBICON STOUT — dark brown, roasted barley nose, smooth roasted barley and chocolate malt flavor, good body, long dry aftertaste like the flavor.

RUBICON HEFE WEIZEN — gold, mild malt aroma, smooth malt flavor, medium to good body, long clean malt aftertaste.

RUBICON AMBER ALE — amber, clean malt nose, smooth malt flavor, good balance with the hops of the background, long dry malt and hop aftertaste.

S & P Co.

Group of brewing companies including Falstaff, Pearl, General and Pabst with brewing plants listed as being in Tumwater, WA (Olympia); Milwaukee, WI; San Antonio, TX; and Ft. Wayne, IN. There are additional corporate names used including San Antonio Beverage Co. Corporate HQ is in Corte Madera, CA.

FALSTAFF BEER — pale yellow, rich malt nose, clean fresh flavor is mostly malt but there are hops in support, pleasant average American pilsener style beer that sometimes is overcarbonated.

FALSTAFF FINE LIGHT BEER — pale gold, light fresh malt nose, light malt aroma, flavor is light malt but the contribution of the carbonation is significant, light bodied and little aftertaste.

LUCKY LAGER BEER — bright clear gold, interesting and somewhat complex malt and hop nose, off-dry flavor that doesn't dry out, still pleasant and refreshing, good length.

LUCKY BOCK BEER — dark brown but not deeply colored, sweet malt nose that doesn't really change across the palate, high carbonation tries to balance off the sweetness but the end result is a bit dull.

LUCKY 50 EXTRA LIGHT BEER — bright pale gold, faint grainy aroma, light grainy palate, little aftertaste, the major flavor component is carbonation.

LUCKY ORIGINAL DRAFT BEER — gold, big hop aroma, malt and hop flavor, good body, fair duration with both the malt and hops showing in the aftertaste.

BREW 102 PALE DRY BEER — pale yellow-gold, clean fresh malt aroma on the sweet side, pleasant slightly sweet malt flavor, good length, would be better if less sweet but still is pleasant and refreshing in hot weather.

HAMM'S SPECIAL LIGHT — medium to deep gold, light malt and hop aroma, weak and watery, faint malt flavor, little finish and aftertaste.

HAMM'S BEER — bright gold, pleasant malt nose, off-dry malt flavor, short malt aftertaste with some hops in back, pleasant hot weather quaffing beer.

HAMM'S GENUINE DRAFT BEER — pale gold, faint malt nose, light off-dry malt flavor, very short on the palate.

HAMM'S NON-ALCOHOLIC MALT BEVERAGE — gold, malt aroma, sour malt flavor, very weak and grainy, fairly brief.

HAMM'S BIG BEAR MALT LIQUOR — pale gold, light malt nose, malt palate, sense of high alcohol, winey finish, long malt aftertaste.

BALLANTINE PREMIUM LAGER BEER — light gold, clean fresh malt aroma, clean fresh light flavor is more malt than hops, medium body, pleasant and refreshing, medium length.

BALLANTINE XXX ALE — deep gold, big well-hopped and malt nose, big taste with plenty of hop bite, good body, good length.

BALLANTINE INDIA PALE ALE — tawny-gold, pungent hop aroma, big well-hopped nose, big hop flavor, good body, good balance, lingering full flavored aftertaste. It's not as big as it used to be, but it is still a mouthful.

NARRAGANSETT LAGER BEER — bright gold, off-dry malt nose, flavor mostly malt as the hops are very light, medium body, light dry aftertaste.

NARRAGANSETT PORTER — deep brown with a red-orange tinge, clean light malt nose, clean light malt flavor, slightly sweet at the finish, hops show only in the aftertaste.

PABST BLUE RIBBON BEER — pale gold, light malt and hop nose, clean malt and hop flavor, pleasant, light and refreshing, light body, fairly dry, medium length.

PABST BLUE RIBBON LIGHT BEER — pale bright gold, pleasant malt aroma, light dry mostly malt flavor, tasty, very drinkable, light and refreshing and with good length.

PABST LIGHT BEER — pale gold, faint hop and malt aroma, weak off-dry malt flavor, faint hops in back, short malt aftertaste is drier than the flavor.

PABST BLUE RIBBON DRY BEER — pale yellow-gold, refreshing malt and hop nose, light body, good carbonation level, pleasant light off-dry malt flavor, refreshing, medium length.

PABST BLUE RIBBON DRAFT BEER — deep gold, malt nose, pleasant malt flavor, off-dry palate, medium dry finish and aftertaste, tastes better well-chilled.

PABST GENUINE DRAFT — pale hazy gold, dusty sour malt nose, faint off-dry malt flavor, weak and watery, brief hop finish and faint malt aftertaste.

ANDEKER LAGER BEER — bright gold, hop aroma seems too off-dry but is more fragrant than it is sweet, pleasant hoppy flavor finishes off-dry, nicely balanced and fairly long, would be better if drier.

HAFFENREFFER PRIVATE STOCK MALT LIQUOR — medium deep gold color, malt aroma, light malt flavor, medium body is light for a malt liquor, soft light malt flavor, medium length aftertaste.

PEARL FINE LAGER BEER — bright gold, good malt nose, good flavor, plenty of hops to support the malt, clean and refreshing, good balance, good length.

PEARL XXX LIGHT LAGER BEER — pale gold, good malt and hop aroma, light body, light malt and hop flavor finishes off-dry, short aftertaste.

PEARL CREAM ALE — bright clear gold, off-dry malt nose, off-dry malt flavor but there are hops in back for balance, finishes clean and has a long pleasant dry aftertaste.

PEARL NA NON-ALCOHOLIC BEER — brilliant gold, grainy malt nose, light dull malt flavor, light body, little aftertaste.

BUCKHORN BEER — pale gold, pleasant off-dry malt aroma, malt flavor has very little hop support until the finish, little aftertaste, pleasant but very light.

JAX BEER — yellow-gold, pleasant malt nose has to compete with high carbonation, pleasant mild flavor has a good hop and malt balance, off-dry aftertaste, refreshing for hot weather drinking.

OLYMPIA BEER — pale gold, light malt aroma, clean light flavor with the hops apparent only in the finish, medium dry hop aftertaste, a light pleasant tasting beer that is very drinkable.

OLYMPIA DARK BEER — deep amber, pleasant light malt and hop aroma, with a metallic (tinny) background, dull malt flavor, dry malt finish and aftertaste.

OLYMPIA GENUINE DRAFT BEER — pale gold, dusty dry malt nose, off-dry malt palate that is fairly pleasant, high carbonation, good balance, faint fruity malt and dry hop finish and aftertaste.

OLYMPIA DRY BEER — pale gold, malt aroma, light dry grainy malt flavor, short.

OLYMPIA LIGHT — pale gold, good hop aroma that is a bit grainy, thin hop flavor that has sour malt tones, finishes dull and doesn't last.

ST. BART'S NON-ALCOHOLIC MALT BEVERAGE — bright gold, pleasant grainy aroma with a touch of fruitiness, dry palate that is pleasant malt in front but there is little or no finish and aftertaste.

OLYMPIA GOLD LIGHT BEER — pale gold, light fresh malt aroma, light malt flavor that picks up quite a bit of hops in mid-palate, dry well-hopped finish and brief aftertaste.

COUNTRY CLUB MALT LIQUOR — tawny-gold, winey malt aroma, light malt flavor, off-dry finish and aftertaste is only malt.

GOETZ PALE NEAR BEER — brilliant deep gold, light cereal grain aroma, flavor is grain and carbonation, light body, grainy malt aftertaste with little length.

TEXAS PRIDE EXTRA LIGHT LAGER BEER — bright gold, light malt aroma, light malt flavor only faintly hopped, little finish and aftertaste.

TEXAS SELECT — bright yellow, faint grainy nose, light grainy malt flavor, somewhat unbalanced hop and malt aftertaste.

TEXAS LIGHT NON-ALCOHOLIC MALT BEVERAGE — bright yellow, light grainy malt nose and flavor, little finish and aftertaste.

TEXAS LIGHT DARK NON-ALCOHOLIC MALT BEVERAGE — red-brown, light malt aroma, watery malt flavor has little depth, finish is even weaker and there is virtually no aftertaste.

LODI BEER — bright gold, good rising malt and hop aroma, zesty malt and hop flavor, hop finish and aftertaste that has good length and hop balance.

JOLIE BLONDE BEER — hazy amber, big complex malt aroma, heavy body, a lot of malt extract, soft and wine-like in style, faint hops in the finish, but this is a predominantly malty brew. Contract brew for Bayou Brew Bros. Inc of Louisiana.

ORIGINAL CAJUN FLAVORED BEER — amber, fruity malt aroma, flavor starts out fruity malt but quickly there is hot Cajun spice that dominates by the finish and extends through the long long dry aftertaste.

SMITH & REILLY HONEST BEER — faintly hazy gold, good hop nose, bright zesty hop flavor, dry hop finish, hop aftertaste of medium duration, a refreshing all malt (no adjuncts) beer. Contract brew for Smith & Reilly, Vancouver,WA.

CHEERS NON-ALCOHOLIC MALT BEVERAGE — tawny-gold, slightly dank malt and hop nose, flavor is thin malt and hops, light dry hop finish, brief aftertaste has faint hops.

BEER — gold, light malt and hop aroma, light malt and hop flavor, medium body, short hop aftertaste. Generic supermarket beer on West Coast.

LITE BEER — pale gold, light slightly grainy malt nose and taste, light body, little aftertaste. Generic brew for supermarkets on West Coast.

NA NON-ALCOHOLIC BEER — deep gold, malt nose, grainy malt flavor, weak body, light and short malt aftertaste.

OLDE ENGLISH 800 MALT LIQUOR — gold, strong malt aroma, big aromatic malt flavor, big body, very long malt aftertaste that is quite sweet like the flavor.

OLDE ENGLISH 800 GENUINE DRAFT MALT LIQUOR — gold, fruity malt aroma, dry sharp fruity malt flavor, not balanced, finish is malt but drier, short dull malt aftertaste.

BEACH BREW NA MALT BEVERAGE — pale gold, grainy malt nose, slight hops in back, malty water flavor, sour finish, short, overall dank and weak. Contract brew for Beach Beer B.C., CA.

ORIGINAL BEACH BEER — pale gold, hop aroma, sour malt and hop flavor, light and dry, somewhat sour finish and aftertaste. Contract brew as above.

STEAMER LANE LAGER BEER — tawny-gold, pleasant malt aroma, palate is slightly sour malt at first, then is dry toasted malt and hops, hops are bigger at finish leading into a long dry hop aftertaste. Contract brew as above.

BEACH BEER NATURAL DRAFT — gold, aroma starts out hops and then the malt comes in, the flavor is big malt but with the hops sufficient for balance, soft textured, big bodied, dry finish, short aftertaste. Contract brew as above.

BROWN DERBY LAGER BEER — pale gold, light hop nose, big malt flavor, medium dry malt aftertaste, not long. Made for Safeway markets.

OLD TANKARD ALE — amber, zesty malt nose, very ale-like, big hop flavor, hops well balanced with malt, quite tangy, very long dry well-hopped aftertaste, a pleasant surprise. Made for Specialty B.C. of Milwaukee, WI.

MILWAUKEE GERMANFEST BIER — gold, faint hop nose, hop and malt flavor, dry hop finish and aftertaste, medium length. Also made for Specialty B.C.

COUNTRY CLUB ALE — very pale gold, nose is stinky at first with a lemon oil background, this turns to a candy sweetness, dull malt flavor, faintly sweet dull malt aftertaste.

Note: *Many of the S&P brews distributed on the East Coast are made and packaged in Stroh breweries.*

Salt Lake Brewing Co./ Squatter's Pub Brewery

Microbrewery and brewpub in Salt Lake City, UT

EMIGRATION AMBER ALE — amber-gold, hop nose and taste, dry hop finish, short dry hop aftertaste, just hops.

PARLEY'S PORTER — brown, hop nose, dry hop flavor and finish; short aftertaste.

ROCKY MOUNTAIN WHEAT —gold, light hop nose, light malt flavor, light body, very light and dry malt aftertaste.

COLE'S SPECIAL BITTER — gold, hop nose, light hop flavor, medium body, dry hop finish and aftertaste.

Samuel Adams Brewhouse/Philadelphia Brewing Co.

Brewpub in **Philadelphia, PA**

All beers are made from extracts.

BEN FRANKLIN'S GOLDEN — gold, big hop nose, slightly soapy malt palate, hops in finish, long dry hop aftertaste.

POOR RICHARD'S AMBER — golden amber, light smooth hop nose, smooth very hoppy flavor, long hop aftertaste.

GEORGE WASHINGTON'S PORTER — deep amber, chocolate malt nose with some hops, very dry hop and malt flavor, dry hop finish and aftertaste.

BREWHOUSE BROWN ALE — brown, malt nose and taste, light body, dry malt finish and aftertaste.

BREWHOUSE CRANBERRY WHEAT — amber-gold, malt nose, tart cranberry malt flavor that is very tasty, long off-dry fruity aftertaste.

San Andreas Brewing Co.

Brewery and brewpub in **Hollister, CA**

KIT FOX AMBER RICHTER SCALE ALE — hazy amber, zesty tangy ale nose and flavor, bright citrus character, sour cherries in the finish, tangy dry malt aftertaste.

EARTHQUAKE PALE ALE — hazy gold, nice citrus-hop aroma, big grapefruit-hop flavor goes dry hops at the finish, long dry hop aftertaste.

EARTHQUAKE PORTER — deep brown, almost totally opaque, brown head, complex fruity roasted malt aroma, big smoky dry malt flavor, light body, dry malt finish, long dry malt aftertaste has a faint citrus component.

OKTOBER QUAKE ALE — hazy amber, big sharp hop nose, assertive hop flavor, light body, sharp hop finish, long harsh hop aftertaste, a bit too sharp.

SEISMIC ALE — hazy amber, fruity malt nose, low carbonation, big malt flavor, not complex, ale-like hop bite at the finish, short to medium malt aftertaste, questionable balance.

GREEN LEPRECHAUN ALE — lime green, malt aroma, flavor is mostly hops but there is malt in back, light bodied, dry bitter hop aftertaste, a very dry beer.

CRANBERRY NOEL — pinkish orange-amber, fruity-berry (cranberry) fruit flavor, not tart or sour or sweet, good malt background, good balance with the fruit and malt, long dry malt aftertaste.

WOODRUFF ALE — amber, raspberry-woodruff nose, interesting spicy flavor, quite drinkable, very dry finish and spicy dry aftertaste.

APRICOT ALE — gold, hop nose, dry malt flavor with faint apricot, dry fruity finish shows the apricot a little better, but the long dry aftertaste is just hops.

San Francisco Bar & Grill

Brewpub in **Tuscon, AZ**

CACTUS LAGER — cloudy amber, dry hop aroma, extremely dry hop flavor, short dry hop aftertaste. Sometimes made by Electric Dave B.C. of Bisbee, AZ, when demand exceeds brewery capacity.

San Juan Brewing Co.

Brewpub in **Telluride, CO**

BLACK BEAR PORTER — brown, chocolate malt and roasted barley nose, taste like the aroma but very light, medium body, dry malt finish and aftertaste.

BOOMERANG BROWN — brown, hop nose, hop flavor with good malt backing, good body, very drinkable, fairly complex as well, dry hop finish and aftertaste.

TOMBOY BITTER — amber, hop aroma and flavor, medium body, dry hop finish and aftertaste, somewhat unidimensional.

GALLOPING GOOSE GOLDEN ALE — gold, hop nose, balanced hop and malt flavor, a bright taste that is very drinkable, fairly dry finish and aftertaste, but short in length.

Santa Fe Brewing Co.

Brewery in Galisteo, NM

SANTA FE PALE ALE — hazy amber, luscious off-dry citrus hop and malt nose, very appetizing, big malt flavor with a light citrus background, dry hop finish and aftertaste, good length. Original gravity is 1052.

FIESTA INDIA PALE ALE — amber-gold, big Northwest hop nose and flavor (Cluster and Cascade), bright hop finish, long dry hop aftertaste, excellent balance, well put together thanks to three months aging. Original gravity is 1060.

SANTA FE NUT BROWN ALE — pretty amber-brown, dry chocolate malt and hop aroma and taste, aroma is more chocolate malt than is the flavor, very complex with a fine balance, good body, smooth, dry aftertaste like the flavor is plenty long. Original gravity is 1052.

OLD POJOAQUE PORTER — deep amber-ruby brown, big complex nutty malt nose and taste, good body, excellent balance, dry malt finish and aftertaste, a classical porter. Original gravity is 1056.

GALISTEO WEISS — amber, malt nose and flavor, no spiciness, medium dry malt finish and aftertaste, pleasant American style wheat beer.

CHICKEN KILLER BARLEY WINE — deep amber, dry malt nose and taste, not big like most barley wines, but rather nicely smooth and deliciously malty, long malt aftertaste.

SANGRE DE FRAMBUESA — reddish gold, pink foam, raspberry nose, big tart raspberry flavor is fruity but not really sweet, good body, dry raspberry finish and aftertaste, quite pleasant and very nice of the style.

SANTA FE IMPERIAL STOUT — deep brown, big malt aroma and flavor shows a touch of chocolate, big body, plenty of alcohol (original gravity of 1080), hefty malt finish and long malt aftertaste shows alcohol.

August Schell Brewing Co.

Brewery at New Ulm, MN

AUGUST SCHELL PILS BEER — deep amber-gold, beautiful flowery hop nose, big hop flavor with plenty of malt, good body, long dry hop aftertaste. This is a classic German-style pilsener, a great recipe and excellent execution.

AUGUST SCHELL EXPORT BEER — bright gold, faint malt aroma, light malt flavor, light body, faintly sweet malt finish and brief malt aftertaste.

AUGUST SCHELL LIGHT BEER — pale gold, light malt aroma, light body, dry hop finish, short dry hop aftertaste.

SCHELL DEER BRAND BEER — very pale gold, pleasant malt aroma with a faint trace of apple, high carbonation, off-dry malt flavor with some esters in back, dry malt finish, short aftertaste.

AUGUST SCHELL WEISS BEER — brilliant pale amber, grainy nose, spicy malt palate that stays throughout and into a long aftertaste.

AUGUST SCHELL WEIZEN BEER — bright gold, clean fresh fruity-malt nose is a bit on the sweet side, light body, tangy background to the malt flavor much like many German weizens, clean and refreshing, finishes dry, medium length aftertaste, refreshing hot weather beer.

AUGUST SCHELL OKTOBERFEST 1992 — amber, bright citrus hop aroma, flavor starts off bright hops with a citrus nature, malt joins in at the middle and stays, strong hop finish and long aftertaste, interesting, balanced, finely carbonated, good brew.

AUGUST SCHELL OKTOBERFEST 1991 — rosy-amber, pleasant complex malt aroma, good body, big strong hop and malt flavor, complex and balanced, smooth and delicious, dry hop finish, long dry hop aftertaste.

AUGUST SCHELL OKTOBERFEST 1990 — amber, bright tangy hop aroma, big ale-like flavor with lots of hop bite and plenty of malt, good body, dry hop finish and aftertaste, an assertive brew.

SCHELL BOCK BEER — bright amber, dry caramel malt nose, dry caramel flavor, light body, could use more hops, light medium -dry malt finish, off-dry short malt aftertaste.

GEMEINDE BRAU — medium pale gold, malt nose, good body, good flavor with plenty of malt and light hops, off-dry malt finish and aftertaste. Contract brew for Gemeinde Brau, Inc., Amana, IA.

Schell
GOVERNMENT WARNING: (1) ACCORDING TO THE SURGEON GENERAL, WOMEN SHOULD NOT DRINK ALCOHOLIC BEVERAGES DURING PREGNANCY BECAUSE OF THE RISK OF BIRTH DEFECTS. (2) CONSUMPTION OF ALCOHOLIC BEVERAGES IMPAIRS YOUR ABILITY TO DRIVE A CAR OR OPERATE MACHINERY, AND MAY CAUSE HEALTH PROBLEMS.
CT-ME-VT-DE-MA-NY-IA-OR 5¢/MI 10¢ REFUND
August Schell Brewing Co.
NEW ULM, MINN.
BOCK
BEER
CONTENTS 12 FL.OZ.

ULMER BRAUN BEER — deep amber-brown, dry malt nose and taste, almost soapy, but that feature doesn't develop enough to mar the flavor, dry malt finish and medium length aftertaste. Ulmer B.C., New Ulm, MN.

PETE'S WICKED ALE — brilliant deep amber, slightly toasted malt and hop aroma, big complex and zesty malt flavor with hops rolling in from mid-palate on, a touch of scorched malt among the hops at the finish and in the long dry aftertaste, an excellent, balanced, satisfying, drinkable brew. Contract brew for Pete's B.C., Palo Alto, CA. In late 1992, contract terminated and brewing shifted to Minnesota B.C.

PETE'S GOLD COAST LAGER — hazy amber, bright hop aroma, big hop flavor that lasts and lasts, big body, complex, balanced, delicious, feels good in your mouth, long dry hop aftertaste. Contract brew as above. In late 1992, contract terminated as above.

PETE'S PACIFIC DRY BEER — amber-gold, lovely malt aroma with a bit of toasted malt in back, good body, dry malt flavor, nice while it lasts, but it is brief. Contract brew as above. Discontinued in 1992.

HELENBOCH BEER — clear deep gold, appetizing hop nose, dry hop flavor, long dry hop aftertaste. Contract brew for Friends B.C., Helen, GA.

1992 HELENBOCH OKTOBERFEST — deep amber, big malty nose and taste, long off-dry malt aftertaste.

JEFFERSON BLUE RIDGE MOUNTAIN BRAND LAGER — sherry color, lovely toasted malt aroma, full rich malt flavor, good hop balance, malt and hop finish, long malt aftertaste. Contract brew for Federal Hill B.C., Forest, VA.

SUMMER PALE LAGER — bright gold, fresh clean bright malt nose, dry hop palate, highly carbonated, dry hop aftertaste is a bit dull. Contract brew for Saloon B.C., Sweeny's Saloon in St. Paul, MN.

SALOON LIGHT LAGER — brilliant pale gold, dry malt nose, very little flavor, just a hint of banana behind some malt, dull short malt aftertaste. Contract brew as above.

AUBURN DARK LAGER — deep amber-brown, malt nose, thin malt flavor, light body, thin malt aftertaste that lasts a short time. Contract brew as above.

PECAN ST. LAGER — amber-gold, very pleasant toasted malt and hop nose, hefty toasted malt flavor with hops coming in well at the finish, long dry aftertaste, smooth, pleasant and drinkable. Made for The Old City B.C., Austin, TX.

Schirf Brewing Co.

Brewery and brewpub located in Park City, UT

WASATCH CHRISTMAS ALE — hazy tawny-gold, fragrant hop aroma, flowery hops and good malt, complex palate, dry hops in front, then it takes on a stronger hop-ale character, could use more malt for better balance, dry hop finish, bitter and dry hop aftertaste with good duration.

WASATCH SLICKROCK LAGER — hazy gold, fresh fruity malt aroma, big malt up front, hops join in at mid-palate and give the flavor some complexity, light body, finish is still malty and the aftertaste is faintly roasted malt.

WASATCH PREMIUM ALE — medium deep amber, big toasted malt nose, roasted malt flavor, long off-dry malt aftertaste, very drinkable.

WASATCH IRISH STOUT — deep brown, dry chocolate malt nose, roasted barley in back, creamy very dry roasted malt flavor, medium body, long dry malt aftertaste, nicely done and very drinkable.

WASATCH STOUT — opaque brown, dry chocolate malt aroma with some roasted barley in back, smooth and dry, seems to have less bite than the Irish stout, but they are very similar, medium length.

WASATCH WEIZENBIER — hazy gold, dry slightly toasted malt nose, good dry malt flavor like the nose, medium body, very long malt aftertaste, not much hops to find.

WASATCH WHEAT BEER — hazy light amber, very fruity aroma, medium dry palate, finishes dry malt, short dry malt aftertaste.

SNOWBIRD TRAM ALE — amber, toasted malt nose, dry toasted malt flavor, low carbonation, medium body, finishes pleasantly malty and has a long dry malt aftertaste, not much hops evident.

Seabright Brewery

Brewpub in Santa Cruz, CA

SEABRIGHT AMBER ALE— amber, beautiful light hop aroma, smooth and mellow malt flavor with light hops in back, dry malt finish, medium length dry malt aftertaste.

PELICAN PALE — gold, hop nose, delicious malt-hop flavor, excellent balance, dry hop finish and aftertaste with good length, a beautful brew-Seabright's best!

BANTY ROOSTER IPA— gold, light hop nose and taste, good body, dry hop finish and aftertaste, hops light at first in the malt, but they come on strong in mid-palate.

TRI-CENTURY PORTER — deep dark amber-brown, coffee-like malt aroma, smooth, dry malt flavor, finish and aftertaste, very long and very drinkable.

CENTURY RED — amber, very attractive fresh and lively malt and hop aroma, bright hop flavor with good malt, very refreshing, long dry hop aftertaste.

EXTRA SPECIAL BITTER — bright gold, zesty fresh malt and hop aroma and flavor, balanced, very true to style with plenty of hop character, long dry hop aftertaste.

ACE'S STRONG ALE — deep gold, big hop aroma, huge hop flavor also is well stocked with malt, big body, feels great in your mouth, high density (16), long dry hop aftertaste.

SEABRIGHT OATMEAL STOUT — deep brown, roasted barley and chocolate malt aroma, dry malt flavor, smooth, well-balanced, good body, very drinkable, long dry malt aftertaste shows some of the roasted quality.

SEABRIGHT WEIZEN — hazy gold, 50-50 wheat and malt nose, very lightly hopped malt palate, good body, smooth and clean, refreshing, long off-dry malt aftertaste.

PLEASURE POINT PORTER — deep amber-brown, malt aroma, dry malt flavor, smooth and very drinkable, finish and aftertaste show some hops but mostly malt, very long and enjoyable.

Sierra Nevada Brewing Co.

Brewery at Chico, CA

SIERRA NEVADA PALE ALE — deep amber, complex tangy hop and malt aroma that seems off-dry, smooth rich malt and hop flavor, hops strongest at the finish, very long hop aftertaste, a big delicious brew.

SIERRA NEVADA PORTER — deep red-brown, complex tangy off-dry malt and hop nose, smooth rich malt flavor with strong hops coming in for the finish, very long and very delicious, a big satisfying brew.

SIERRA NEVADA STOUT — opaque brown, big rich clean and sweet nose, complex herbal flavor in front, good hops and roasted malt at the finish, very long off-dry and roasted malt aftertaste, another big bodied full-flavored brew.

SIERRA NEVADA
Finest Quality
Purest Ingredients
BOTTOM FERMENTED
Summerfest
BEER
OREGON 5¢ CA CASH REFUND
ALC. 3.9% —WT.
NET 12 FL.OZ.
© 1991 S.N.BR. CO.
BREWED AND BOTTLED BY SIERRA NEVADA BREWING CO., CHICO, CA
GOVERNMENT WARNING: (1) ACCORDING TO THE SURGEON GENERAL, WOMEN SHOULD NOT DRINK ALCOHOLIC BEVERAGES DURING PREGNANCY BECAUSE OF THE RISK OF BIRTH DEFECTS. (2) CONSUMPTION OF ALCOHOLIC BEVERAGES IMPAIRS YOUR ABILITY TO DRIVE A CAR OR OPERATE MACHINERY, AND MAY CAUSE HEALTH PROBLEMS.

SIERRA NEVADA PALE BOCK — bright pale gold, great nose with lots of hops and malt, big body, big hop flavor, extremely long bright hop aftertaste, a big and beautiful brew with incredible balance.

BIG FOOT BARLEYWINE STYLE ALE 1987 — hazy amber, complex citrus and licorice nose, huge citrus ale flavor, enormous body, great complexity, more malt and hops than you've had in a mouthful before, almost too powerful but it is balanced so you can enjoy its quality, extremely long on the palate.

BIG FOOT BARLEYWINE STYLE ALE 1988 — cloudy amber, toasted malt nose, huge almost overwhelming toasted malt flavor with incredible duration.

BIG FOOT BARLEYWINE STYLE ALE 1990 — deep amber, complex malt aroma, strong alcoholic rich malt flavor, excellent balance, richness stays right through the long long toasted malt aftertaste. Note that these Big Foot brews can handle quite a bit of bottle aging. Try keeping them for a year or so.

SIERRA NEVADA CELEBRATION ALE 1987 — brilliant deep amber, roasted malt aroma, big strong beautifully balanced roasted malt and hop flavor, delicious and very long.

SIERRA NEVADA CELEBRATION ALE 1988 — orange-amber, a citrus and pine aroma, intense malt flavor with a big hop finish and long hop aftertaste. A big delicious brew.

SIERRA NEVADA CELEBRATION ALE 1989 — medium amber, complex tangy citrus-ale nose, big zesty ale flavor, lots of both malt and hops, complex sipping beer, not overwhelming, just big and good, excellent balance, very long hop aftertaste.

SIERRA NEVADA CELEBRATION ALE 1989 — batch made October 25, 1989, golden amber, big fruity-citrus nose, strong malt and hop flavor, high alcohol, very dry finish and aftertaste, huge and long.

SIERRA NEVADA CELEBRATION ALE 1989 — batch made November 27, 1989, golden amber, faint malt aroma, same flavor as above but lighter, excellent balance, long dry malt and hop aftertaste, much like brew above but a more subtle version.

SIERRA NEVADA CELEBRATION ALE 1990 — medium to deep amber, huge citrus ale nose, enormous but smooth malt and hop flavor, excellent balance, extremely long aftertaste.

SIERRA NEVADA CELEBRATION ALE 1991 — pale amber, fruity citrus and apricot aroma, big citrus ale flavor, very good balance, plenty of both malt and hops, smooth, rich and a great, very long aftertaste.

SIERRA NEVADA SUMMERFEST BEER 1991 — gold, clean malt and hop aroma, big flavor is mostly hops but there is malt aplenty in support, malt kicks in at the finish and it ends refreshingly dry and quite long.

SIERRA NEVADA PALE BOCK 1992 — gold, big hop aroma, big rich malt and hop flavor, beautiful balance, great taste, big body, long and good.

SIERRA NEVADA SUMMERFEST BEER 1992 — gold, hop and melon aroma, pleasant hop and malt flavor is both fruity and spicy, finishes dry, long fruity malt aftertaste with a dry hop background.

SIERRA NEVADA CELEBRATION ALE 1992 — golden amber, beautiful citrus hop nose, big and luscious flavor, simply wonderful, big and bold, bitter hop finish and long bitter hop aftertaste.

Signature Beer Co.

Microbrewery in St. Louis, MO

SPIRIT OF ST. LOUIS ALE — gold, hop aroma, light malt and hop flavor, dry hop finish and aftertaste.

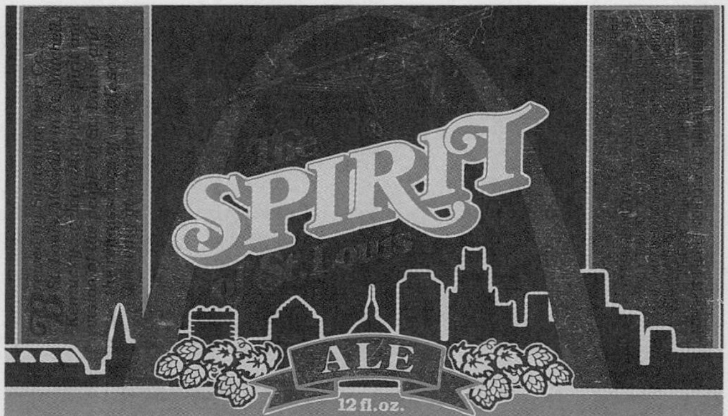

Southern California Brewery

Brewery in Torrance, CA

Formerly known as the Alpine Village Brewery, Inc. The brewery is attached to a restaurant which gives effect of a brewpub. Part of the Alpine Village complex of shops, hotel, restaurant, etc. All bottling has been done accomplished at the Angeles B.C. in Chatsworth, CA.

ALPINE VILLAGE HOFBRAU SPECIAL RESERVE LAGER — deep gold, malt and hop aroma, smooth dry malt and hop flavor, good body, dry malt finish, long dry malt and hop aftertaste.

ALPINE VILLAGE HOFBRAU SUPERIOR PILSNER — pale gold, bright pilsener style hop and malt nose, bright dry hop flavor, good body, great balance, long dry hop aftertaste, good German style.

ALPINE VILLAGE HOFBRAU BOCK — copper-brown, big dry malt nose, big dry roasted chocolate malt flavor, smooth, dry and well-hopped, long hop and malt aftertaste, big bodied and delicious.

ALPINE VILLAGE HOFBRAU PREMIUM LIGHT — gold, light hop nose has a faint strawberry background, light dry hop flavor, dry hop finish and medium dry hop aftertaste with fair length.

ALPINE VILLAGE HOFBRAU RED ALE — amber, light malt nose, bright hop flavor with great malt backing, off-dry malt finish, long dry malt aftertaste with a sense of nutmeg in there somewhere, a big bright delicious brew.

ALPINE VILLAGE HOFBRAU WHEAT BEER — gold, faint dry malt and wheat aroma, light wheat and malt flavor, faintly off-dry, dry finish, long dry malt aftertaste, refreshing and interesting. Malt mix contains 40% wheat.

ALPINE VILLAGE HOFBRAU HEFE-WEIZEN —hazy gold, a nice citrus background adds to the malt and wheat nose, also gives zest to the flavor, finish and aftertaste, like the above but a little brighter, more refreshing and more satisfying.

ALPINE VILLAGE HOFBRAU FESTBIER — bright amber, dry malt and hop nose, dry malt flavor well backed with hops, dry hop finish, smooth long dry hop aftertaste, a zesty highly malted and well-hopped brew.

Spanish Peaks Brewing Co., Ltd.

Brewpub and cafe in Bozeman, MT

SPANISH PEAKS PORTER — brown, malt aroma, bright hop and malt flavor, good balance, good body, smooth, dry malt and hop finish and aftertaste, nicely done classical porter.

YELLOWSTONE PALE ALE — bright gold, hop aroma, balanced hop flavor with good supporting malt, bright dry hop finish and aftertaste.

BLACK DOG BITTER — gold, no nose, hoppy palate, long dry hop aftertaste.

EYE OF THE ROCKIES WHEAT — gold, malt nose and clean malt flavor, medium body, dry malt finish and brief dry malt aftertaste.

AUTUMN FEST ALE — amber, hop aroma, balanced hop and malt flavor, smooth, light, light dry hop finish, short dry hop aftertaste.

St. Stan's Brewing Co.

Brewery in Modesto, CA

Previously known as the Stanislaus Brewing Co.

ST. STAN'S AMBER ALT — hazy amber, big citrus hop aroma, zesty hop flavor with plenty of malt backing, fair balance, complex and flavorful, medium to long hop aftertaste.

ST. STAN'S DARK ALT — deep amber-brown, very complex aroma with blueberries, raspberries, currants and melon, malt palate is dull compared to the very interesting nose, finishes with roasted malt, aftertaste is roasted malt with some scorching, good length.

ST. STAN'S FEST ALT BIER — hazy amber-gold, complex zesty big citrus hop and fruity malt aroma, big malt flavor with plenty of hops to support the balance and to provide a bright zesty quality, medium to good body, high alcohol, good drinking beer, long alcoholic aftertaste, really good and really long. This brew actually improves with bottle aging. If you think it is good at Christmastime, try it again about May or June.

ST. STAN'S GRAFFITI ALT 1990 — light hazy amber, complex fruity malt aroma with all kinds of interesting components, a regular fruit cocktail, smooth hop flavor, light body, fairly short aftertaste, but a good effort nonetheless. This brew is made annually, but available only briefly each time.

ST. STAN'S GRAFFITI '92 — gold, light dull malt aroma with some off tones, big hop flavor well-backed with malt, big body, long hop and malt aftertaste, a good tasting brew, but the aroma hurts it.

CHAU TIEN EMPEROR ALE — hazy gold, pleasant off-dry malt nose, pleasant clean malt flavor, hops appear in the finish, light body, long malt aftertaste, quite pleasant.

Steelhead Brewery and Cafe

Brewpub in Eugene, OR

STEELHEAD AMBER — amber, malt and hop aroma, balanced malt and hop flavor, very smooth, drinkable, medium body, dry finish and aftertaste.

OATMEAL STOUT — brown, dry malt and hop aroma and flavor, heavy body, dry malt finish and aftertaste, good length.

FRENCH PETE'S PORTER — brown, dry malt aroma and flavor, medium body, short dry malt aftertaste.

GINGER BELLS — amber, light gingery aroma like a ginger snap cookie, flavor the same, ditto the finish and aftertaste, not bad, but I'd like it better if it were less gingery and more beerlike.

RILEY'S RYE —amber, hop nose, hop flavor, dry malt aftertaste, where's the rye?

TIME WARP WEIZENBOCK — amber, malt aroma, malt and hop flavor, fair balance, good body, medium dry malt finish and aftertaste with the hops in back.

STEELHEAD CREAM ALE — gold, hop nose, light hop and malt flavor, medium body, medium dry finish and aftertaste.

Stevens Point Beverage Co.

Brewery at Stevens Point, WI

POINT SPECIAL PREMIUM BEER — pale gold, light malt aroma with just a trace of hops, pleasant clean light malt flavor, light body, medium length dry malt aftertaste, smooth and very drinkable.

POINT LIGHT — gold, very pleasant fragrant malt and hop nose, medium body, good tasting dry malt flavor, light dry hop aftertaste, highly carbonated.

POINT GENUINE BOCK BEER — brilliant amber, big malt aroma, big dry malt flavor, very smooth, light body, long fairly dry malt aftertaste, very much like a May bock.

POINT SPECIAL EDITION — bright deep gold, good hop and malt nose, good body, satisfying malt flavor, balanced, dry hop finish and aftertaste, not long but good.

EAGLE PREMIUM PILSNER — pale yellow-gold, good malt and hop nose, bright hop flavor, medium body, good long aftertaste with both malt and hops, a good little beer.

CHIEF OSHKOSH RED LAGER BEER — amber, mostly malt in the aroma and on the front of the palate, hops come in at the finish and stay through the long dry aftertaste. Despite the initial malty character, the overall impression is dry hops. Contract brew for Mid-Coast B.C.

NEW YORK HARBOR ALE — bright deep gold, good hop aroma, lusty hop flavor with some complexity stays fairly dry, good body and some complexity, long dry hop aftertaste, in general the malt stays in the background. Made for Old World Brewing Co., Staten Island, NY.

SPUD PREMIUM BEER — gold, vegetal malt aroma, earthy dry malt palate, medium long dry malt aftertaste with some hops showing.

RJ'S GINSENG BEER — bright gold, intriguing spicy aroma, flavor is even spicier, good body, dry but zesty spiced finish and aftertaste, good length, the most interesting of the ginseng beers. Made for R.J.'s Ginseng Co. Inc. of Chicago, IL (R. J. Corr Natural Beverages, Posen, IL).

Stoudt Brewing Co.

Brewery, brewpub, restaurant, antique center in **Adamstown, PA**

STOUDT'S GOLDEN LAGER — gold, good malt nose, dry malt flavor with good hop support, touch of off-dry malt at the finish, then a long dry malt and hop aftertaste, very good balance, very drinkable.

STOUDT'S ADAMSTOWN AMBER — bright amber, hop nose, hop taste with plenty of malt in support, very good balance, good body, malt comes to the fore at the finish, long dry malt and hop aftertaste, another very drinkable brew.

STOUDT'S HOLIDAY BOCK — ruby-amber, light toasted malt aroma, toasted malt flavor that might have a little smokiness way way back, long dry malt aftertaste, good brew but somewhat unidimensional.

STOUDT'S OKTOBERFEST DARK — see Lion, Inc.

STOUDT'S MARDI GRAS (FASCHING) — beautiful deep ruby-amber color, light malt aroma, dry malt and hop flavor, mild and smooth, long dry malt aftertaste.

STOUDT'S OKTOBERFEST — deep amber, good roasted malt and hop nose, big hop and well-roasted malt flavor, finishes as it starts, extremely dry brief roasted malt aftertaste.

STOUDT'S PILSENER STYLE — gold, lovely European (Saaz) hop nose, big dry hop flavor, big body, complex, dry hop finish and long aftertaste.

STOUDT'S BOCK BIER — deep mahogany color, toasted malt nose and taste, some complexity, creamy texture with a big solid head that lasts to the bottom of the glass, fairly dry malt finish and aftertaste, good length.

STOUDT'S BOCK — mahogany color, light roasted malt nose and taste, some hops in the finish, medium length dry hop aftertaste.

STOUDT'S BULL ALE — amber, faintly soapy malt nose, light malt flavor feels good in your mouth, off-dry malt finish and aftertaste, good length.

STOUDT'S SOUR MASH ALE — deep amber, slightly buttery malt nose, off-dry malt flavor, slightly sour finish, long dry aftertaste.

STOUDT'S RASPBERRY WEIZEN — reddish color, dry raspberry nose is a little sour, very dry malt and faint raspberry in the flavor, maintains a fruity malt character, finishes dry malt, fairly long dry malt aftertaste.

STOUDT'S OKTOBERFEST BOCK — deep ruby-amber, very faint malt aroma, dry lightly scorched malt flavor, pleasant, long dry aftertaste like the flavor.

STOUDT'S OKTOBERFEST MAERZEN — medium deep amber, dry malt nose, thin body, odd sort of vegetal malt flavor, not appetizing, short malt aftertaste.

STOUDT'S STOUT — opaque brown, light malt nose, dry malt palate, some malty sweetness appears at the finish, long dry malt aftertaste, very drinkable, medium body.

STOUDT'S HOLIDAY ALE — amber, big hop and big malt aroma, flavor starts out with big hops and plenty of bite, malt comes in the middle and stays, excellent balance, big body, luscious and long, a real lip-smacker.

STOUDT'S GOLD MEDAL HEFE-WEIZEN — cloudy gold, fresh clean lightly spiced malt nose, light dry spicy malt flavor, hops come in at the finish, moderately dry hop aftertaste with good duration.

STOUDT'S ANNIVERSARY ALE — amber, hop nose with some caramel, dry malt flavor, long dry malt aftertaste.

STOUDT'S BEERFEST BOCK — very deep amber, dry malt nose with a hint of caramel, very dry malt flavor, long dry malt aftertaste with hops faintly in back.

STOUDT'S DOPPELBOCK — amber, buttery malt nose, malt and hop flavor with the butter still there but far in back, dry malt finish and long aftertaste.

STOUDT'S RED ALE — reddish-amber, faint hop-ale aroma, big tangy hop palate, good malt backing, good body, long dry hop aftertaste.

STOUDT'S WINTERFEST — amber, light malt and hop nose, off-dry malt and bitter hop palate, balanced, somewhat winey in nature, dry malt finish, medium length dry malt aftertaste, very nice drinkable brew. Labelled Oktoberfest, but released in January and, according to the Stoudts, it's their winterfest beer.

STOUDT'S DOUBLE BOCK — deep amber, sour malt nose, sharp sour malt flavor with a candy-like background, long dry malt aftertaste, seems to be mishandled.

STOUDT'S FESTIVAL RESERVE FEST BEER — amber, light malt nose, light dry malt and hop flavor, dry malt and hop aftertaste, medium duration.

STOUDT'S HONEY DOUBLE BOCK — tawny-gold, mellow off-dry malt and hop aroma, big body, big bright malt flavor, honey shows best in the middle, hops come in at the finish to stay for the aftertaste, the aftertaste is balanced off-dry malt and dry hops, very complex and interesting brew.

Karl Strauss' Old Columbia Brewery & Grill

Brewpub in San Diego, CA

KARL STRAUSS AMBER LAGER — amber-gold, light malt nose has a faint roasted background, good body, dry hop and malt flavor, lightly dry hop finish and aftertaste.

PT. LOMA LIGHTHOUSE STOUT — gold, malt aroma and palate, dry malt finish and aftertaste has some hops but they are faint.

GASLAMP GOLD ALE — amber, faint malt and hop aroma, carbonation tang mars the malty flavor, some hops in back, very dry malt and hop finish and aftertaste, good length.

HORTON'S HOOTCH — pale amber, malt nose and taste, off-dry malt flavor, finish and aftertaste.

AMERICA'S FINEST PILSENER — gold, light hop aroma, well-balanced hop and malt flavor, lightly hopped finish, malt aftertaste has good length.

CYNIC'S ELECTION LAGER — golden amber, faint malt aroma, light malt flavor with just a hint of hops, brief malty aftertaste.

RED TROLLEY ALE — ruby-amber, faint roasted barley aroma and flavor, hops are in back, fair to good balance, you taste the malt and feel the hops, dry malt and hop aftertaste is quite long.

Tied House Cafe & Brewery

Brewpubs in San Jose, Alameda and Mountain View, CA

TIED HOUSE AMBER — deep tawny-gold, bright hop and malt nose and taste, very long dry complex aftertaste much like the flavor, a good lusty brew.

ALPINE PEARL PALE — gold, light malt nose and taste, medium body, light dry malt finish and aftertaste. From Alameda.

CASCADE AMBER — deep amber, faint hop aroma, good hop flavor, dry hop finish, not much aftertaste. From Alameda.

WHEAT BOCK — brown, hoppy nose and taste, dry sharp hop finish, long dry hop aftertaste. From Alameda.

PASSION PALE — gold, fruity malt aroma, flavor like the nose, good body, off-dry malt finish and aftertaste, has length. From Alameda.

Triple Rock Brewery & Alehouse

Brewpub in Berkeley, CA

SWHEATHEART HEFE-WEIZEN — cloudy gold, lovely big malt nose, bright malt flavor, long and dry, as nice a weizen as I've found in the U.S.

HOP OF THE ROCK IPA — deep gold, big hop aroma, big bright hop flavor, very long dry hop aftertaste, a very pleasant enjoyable beer.

RED ROCK STRONG ALE — amber, hop aroma, dull hop flavor, dull and short dry hop aftertaste.

TREE FROG STRONG ALT — dark amber, light hop nose, dry hop palate, very long dry hop aftertaste.

PINNACLE PALE — gold, hop and malt aroma, bright hop flavor, very tasty and interesting, good body, dry hop finish and aftertaste, quite long.

Umpqua Brewing Co.

Brewpub in Roseburg, OR

NO DOUBT STOUT — dark brown, roasted barley and chocolate malt nose, flavor like the aroma but very light, medium body, dry roasted malt aftertaste, has medium length.

DOWNTOWN BROWN — brown, lactic malt aroma and flavor, spoiled sample.

SUMMER WHEAT — gold, vegetal malt nose, lightly lactic malt flavor, light body, dry malt aftertaste still has the acid background, not unexpected in a wheat beer, but this comes off as being somewhere between a German style and an American style and isn't quite either.

The Vermont Pub & Brewery

Brewpub in Burlington, VT

BLACK BEAR LAGER — amber, malt nose, rich malt flavor, long dry malt aftertaste, pleasant and drinkable.

AULD BARLEY BREE WEE HEAVY — very dark brown, fairly strong malt nose, big strong and rich malt flavor, noticeable alcohol, long rich medium dry malt aftertaste.

GLEN WALTER WEE HEAVY — amber, big malt nose, big rich caramel malt and molasses flavor, big body, long off-dry malt aftertaste.

FARMALL WHEAT BEER — gold, clean malt aroma with a wheaty background, bright spicy flavor, finish and aftertaste, very nice zesty European style wheat beer.

ZATEC RED — gold, malt aroma, lactic backing to a malt palate, dry spicy finish and aftertaste.

O'FEST — amber, malt aroma, dry malt flavor, no aftertaste.

VERMONT SMOKED PORTER — brown, dry malt aroma, smoky dry malt flavor, long smoked malt aftertaste.

GRAND SLAM BASEBALL BEER — gold, winey fruity malt nose, fruity hop flavor, reminds one of a Reisling grape wine, off-dry malt aftertaste.

The Walnut Brewery

Brewpub in Boulder, CO; affiliated with Boulder B.C.

INDIAN PEAKS PALE ALE — pale gold, faint malt and hop nose, light malt flavor is slightly soapy with very little hops at all, light body, finishes dry and has a brief aftertaste.

OLD ELK BROWN ALE — amber, malt aroma, flavor like a home brew, not well knit, malt and hops are coming at you and not blending, dry finish and short dry aftertaste.

BIG HORN BITTER — amber, no nose, flavor is mostly hops with a caramel background, dry hop aftertaste.

BUFFALO GOLD PREMIUM ALE — gold, no nose, faint butterscotch in behind light malt and hops on the palate, just some faint dry malt for an aftertaste.

THE JAMES IRISH RED ALE — reddish-amber, soapy malt nose and taste, medium body, just a very faint malt aftertaste.

DEVIL'S THUMB STOUT — deep brown, light dry chocolate malt and coffee nose and taste, finished quite well and the aftertaste was good and like the flavor, dry but not overly so, the best beer tasted at The Walnut.

BLUE NOTE AMBER — amber, light hop nose and taste, dry hop finish and aftertaste.

SWISS TRAIL WHEAT — hazy gold, malt and wheat nose, bright refreshing flavor, but not lactic or spicy in any way, light dry malt aftertaste.

Water Street Brewery

Brewpub in Milwaukee, WI

OLD WORLD OKTOBERFEST — deep gold, big malt and hop aroma and flavor, very alcoholic, big bodied, long dry malt and hop aftertaste, a hearty brew.

BAVARIAN WEISS — deep gold, cloudy like a hefe-weizen, clove nose, bright zesty well spiced flavor, good body, long spicy malt aftertaste, well-made in a Germanic style.

CALLAN'S ENGLISH RED ALE — medium to deep amber, malt aroma, smooth hop flavor, good body, dry hop aftertaste.

WATER STREET PALE ALE — amber, hop aroma, zesty hop flavor, good malt backing, complex, big body, dry malt finish and aftertaste, a very good ale.

Weeping Radish Restaurant & Brewery

Brewpub and restaurant in **Manteo, NC**

WEEPING RADISH BREWERY HELLES BEER — hazy gold, fresh malt aroma, creamy, dry malt flavor with the hops far in back, light body, off-dry malt flavor, slides down easily, light malt aftertaste, an easy-going brew.

WEEPING RADISH BREWERY FEST BEER — hazy amber, fruity-melony malt nose and taste, light body, a little malty sweetness in the finish carries into the aftertaste, medium long.

Weinkeller Brewery

Brewpub in **Berwyn, IL**

ABERDEEN AMBER ALE — amber, dry coffee-like malt nose, dry malt flavor, light body, fairly smooth and balanced, short dry malt aftertaste with hops in back.

DÜSSELDORFER DOPPELBOCK — gold, malt aroma, off-dry malt flavor, finishes dry as some hops come in for the ending, but the hops are very light and don't stretch the aftertaste enough.

DOUBLIN STOUT — brown, roasted barley and chocolate malt nose and flavor, light flavored, but well-balanced, medium body, long good tasting aftertaste reflects the flavor, nicely made.

BAVARIAN WEISS — gold, very fruity off-dry malt-wheat nose, only the faintest suggestion of spice, medium body, light off-dry malt aftertaste.

OKTOBERFEST — gold, malt aroma, off-dry malt flavor, finish and aftertaste.

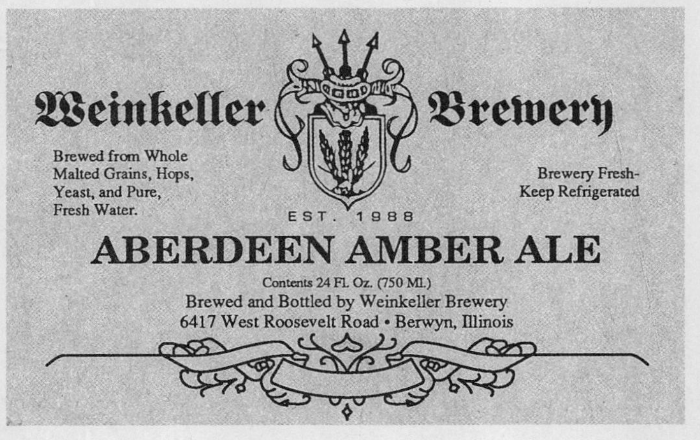

Weinkeller Brewery
Brewed from Whole Malted Grains, Hops, Yeast, and Pure, Fresh Water.
Brewery Fresh-Keep Refrigerated
EST. 1988
ABERDEEN AMBER ALE
Contents 24 Fl. Oz. (750 ML)
Brewed and Bottled by Weinkeller Brewery
6417 West Roosevelt Road • Berwyn, Illinois

Widmer Brewing Co.

Brewery in **Portland, OR**

Situated adjacent to a restaurant giving the effect of a brewpub.

WIDMER HEFE-WEIZEN — cloudy gold, malt and faint smoked sausage nose, malt flavor is neutral (neither dry nor sweet), long dry malt aftertaste, there are faint off flavors that get in the way of the goodness.

WIDMER OKTOBERFEST — deep amber, no discernible aroma, flavor starts out tangy hops, quickly turns to malt with some chocolate malt noticeable, stays malty thereafter, much like a porter.

Wild Goose Brewery

Brewery in **Cambridge, MD**

WILD GOOSE AMBER BEER — bright amber, very nice smooth hop aroma, big rich malt and hop flavor, aromatic and bitter hop finish and long aftertaste, a good English style beer.

THOMAS POINT LIGHT GOLDEN ALE — hazy gold, appetizing malt aroma, good dry malt and hop flavor, light body, refreshing and drinkable, dry malt finish, medium length dry malt and hop aftertaste.

SAMUEL MIDDLETON'S PALE ALE — hazy tawny-gold, dull malt nose, slightly buttery, flavor is faintly sour malt, but dry and also faintly buttery, long dry malt aftertaste.

SNOW GOOSE WINTER ALE — reddish-orange-amber, beautiful dry toasted malt aroma, big hop and toasted malt flavor, long and complex, big bodied, really well made brew, dry hop finish and aftertaste, excellent.

Windham Brewery

Brewpub and Grille in **Brattleboro, VT**

MOONBEAM PALE ALE — golden amber, beautiful hop aroma, bright hop flavor, good malt backing, complex, balanced, long dry hop aftertaste.

WHETSTONE GOLDEN LAGER — gold, honeyed malt aroma, smooth off-dry malt palate, light body, low hops, medium dry long malt aftertaste.

WINDHAM PORTER — brown, roasted barley and chocolate malt aroma, flavor like the nose, body on the light side, good long dry malt aftertaste. This may also be named **OLD GUILFORD PORTER.**

Woodstock Brewing Co.

Microbrewery in **Kingston, NY**

HUDSON LAGER — gold, hop aroma, hop palate, good balance with the supporting malt, good body, medium dry hop aftertaste, a very smooth and drinkable beer.

Wynkoop Brewing

Brewpub in **Denver, CO**

WILDERNESS WHEAT — pale gold, light malt nose, light fresh malt flavor, no spice, dry malt finish, sort of peters out right after the finish so there is little aftertaste.

ELVIS BRAU — gold, faint hop nose, good hop flavor, malt finish, medium body, dry hop aftertaste, very long on the palate, a good brew.

INDIA PALE ALE — pale amber, light hop nose, light fruity malt flavor, hop finish, medium dry hop aftertaste, a soft and smooth beer.

ST. CHARLES ESB — amber, hop nose and bitter hop flavor, some caramel comes in at the middle and mitigates the bitterness, caramel finish, fair to good balance, good body, after initial big hoppy character, the caramel balances it off and it becomes soft and smooth, unfortunately it is too much so and ends up rather bland, light dry hop aftertaste.

SAGEBRUSH STOUT — dark brown, roasted barley and chocolate malt nose and taste, light body, finishes medium dry malt, aftertaste is more dry and shows some hops.

MONTEZUMA CHILI BEER — gold, chili pepper nose, hot chili flavor especially gets you in the throat and wipes out everything else.

KYLE'S LIGHT BROWN ALE — amber-brown, faint malt aroma, very light hop and malt flavor, medium body, low carbonation, light dry hop aftertaste, sort of dull.

SPLATZ PORTER — dark brown, big malt nose followed by a big malt flavor with plenty of hops in back, good body, long dry malt aftertaste.

IRISH CREAM STOUT — very dark brown, black malt nose, big malt flavor like the aroma, good body, long dry malt aftertaste.

CHURCHYARD ALE — brown, big hop nose, sharp hop flavor, long dry hop aftertaste with something faintly in back that may be lactic acid.

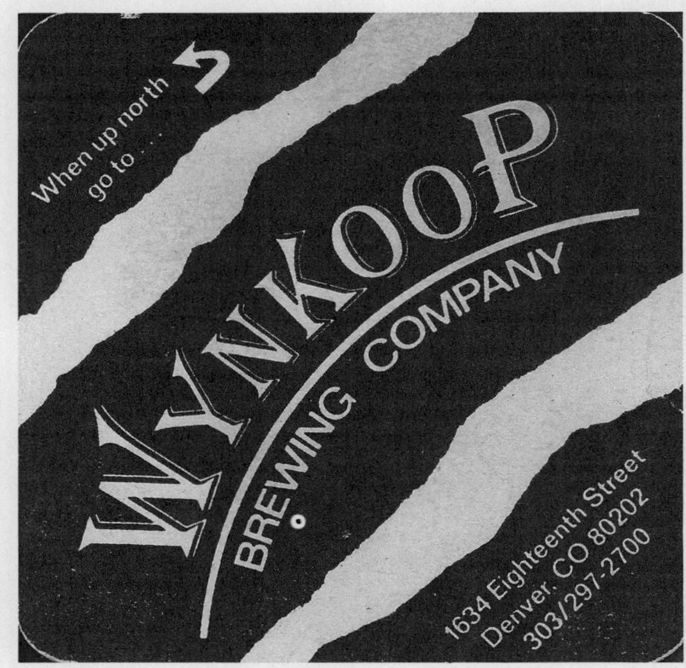

When up north go to . . .
WYNKOOP
BREWING COMPANY
1634 Eighteenth Street
Denver, CO 80202
303/297-2700

Zip City Brewing Co.

Brewpub in New York City, NY

ZIP CITY CZECH STYLE PILSENER — hazy gold, aroma of hops and malt, big dry hop flavor well-backed with malt, quite tasty and very well-hopped, finishes like it starts, medium to long dry hop aftertaste.

ZIP CITY HELLES — pale hazy gold, light malt aroma, light body, light malt flavor, some hops in back, light dry malt aftertaste.

ZIP CITY VIENNA AMBER — slightly hazy amber, rising hop aroma with a dry malt background, rich malt and hop flavor, good hop support, very long dry aftertaste shows both the malt and hops, good balance.

ZIP CITY DUNKEL — brown, fairly dry malt aroma and taste, very mild and smooth, soft dry malt finish and aftertaste.

ZIP CITY MÄRZEN — amber-gold, malt nose and flavor have a little lactic acid way in back, off-dry malt finish and aftertaste still have that faint acidity.

ZIP CITY OKTOBERFEST — hazy amber, dry hop and malt aroma features the malt, pleasant dry hop and malt flavor, long dry malt aftertaste, a very good smooth malty brew.

ZIP CITY MAIBOCK — hazy amber, mild malt aroma and flavor, hops are in back but do provide balance, dry malt finish and aftertaste, a light, smooth, pleasant tasting beer, very drinkable.

CANADA

Algonquin Brewing Co.

Brewery in Formosa Springs, Ontario

Some labels say Northern Algonquin B.C.

FORMOSA SPRINGS LIGHT — gold, faint malt and hop aroma, flavor is mostly carbonation with faint hops in back, faint malt finish, short dry aftertaste.

FORMOSA SPRINGS COLD-FILTERED DRAFT — gold, faint malt and hop nose, estery malt flavor is grape-like, finish and aftertaste like the flavor but more grainy, short dry aftertaste.

Algonquin
Formosa
Springs
Famous for Beer since 1870
Cold Filtered
Bière Draft Beer
341ml 5% alc./vol.
Algonquin Brewing Company Limited, Formosa, Ontario, Canada

ALGONQUIN LIGHT BEER — pale gold, malt and hop aroma, good body, creamy, malt palate with some hops, pleasant finish and aftertaste.

ALGONQUIN COUNTRY LAGER — gold, malt nose, weak malt flavor, light body, dull dry malt aftertaste.

ALGONQUIN SPECIAL RESERVE ALE — pale amber, faint malt nose, high carbonation, tart hop and buttery malt flavor, medium body, short dry malt aftertaste.

ALGONQUIN CANADIAN LIGHT — pale gold, clean malt and hop nose, light body, hop finish, metallic flavors in the aftertaste.

NORTHERN GOOSE SUPER LIGHT BREW NON-ALCOHOLIC MALT BEVERAGE — gold, off-dry grainy nose, carbonation and grainy malt flavor, little follow-through except for a sour grainy sensation.

MARCONI EUROPEAN LAGER — gold, faint solvent smell behind dull malt, sour weak grainy flavor, good body, dull soapy malt aftertaste ends sour.

Big Rock Brewery

Brewery in Calgary, Alberta

ROYAL COACHMAN DRY ALE — gold, toasted malt aroma reminds you of grape-nuts cereal, tasty toasted malt flavor, light body, toasted malt aftertaste with medium length.

BUZZARD BREATH ALE — tawny-gold, light dry toasted malt aroma, dry malt flavor is slightly toasted, medium body, dry malt finish and aftertaste, medium length.

COLD COCK WINTER PORTER — very deep amber-brown, complex rich malt aroma, dry malt palate but there are complex hop flavors, light hop background shows best in the finish and aftertaste, interesting and fairly long dry malt aftertaste.

COCK O' THE ROCK PORTER — deep ruby-brown, complex chocolate malt and hop nose, surprisingly dry palate, flavor is big, lots of hops and malt but the malt dominates, very long, a big pushy brew.

Cold Cock
Winter Porter
341 ml.
11.51 fl. oz.
Big Rock Brewery produced by Calgary Alta. Canada
"Government warning: (1) According to the Surgeon General, women should not drink alcoholic beverages during pregnancy because of the risk of birth defects. (2) Consumption of alcoholic beverages impairs your ability to drive a car or operate machinery, and may cause health problems."

TRADITIONAL ALE — light copper-amber, malt nose, pleasant malt flavor, medium long malt aftertaste.

BIG ROCK PALE ALE — deep gold, toasted chocolate malt nose, delicious light malt flavor, pleasant but brief.

BIG ROCK BITTER PALE ALE — pale amber, bright citrus-ale nose, zesty well-hopped flavor, good body, very flavorful, nice balance, big but not overdone, some complexity, good hop finish, long hop aftertaste.

McNALLY'S EXTRA PURE MALT IRISH STYLE ALE — deep bright amber, good toasted malt nose really comes at you, rich malt flavor is delicious, faint hop finish, long malt aftertaste with hints of caramel and butter.

SPRINGBOK ALE — deep gold, light chocolate malt aroma, big bright creamy malt and hop flavor, smooth, balanced, tasty, good body, long dry malt aftertaste.

ZEB O'BREENS IRISH ALE — amber, dry malt and hop nose, flavor, finish and aftertaste, very well-balanced, smooth and dry, medium body, fairly long. Contract brew for the Goat Hill Tavern of Costa Mesa, CA.

ALBINO RHINO — amber-gold, dry malt and hop aroma, very dry hop flavor, driest at finish, long dry hop aftertaste goes more bitter at the end. Contract brew for Goat Hill Tavern of Costa Mesa, CA and Whistler Brewing Co. of Whistler, BC (so I have been told).

Canadian National Breweries

Brewery in **Markham, Ontario**

CANADIAN GOLD — gold, very beautiful malt and hop aroma, very light fresh malt and hop flavor, good balance, light body, brief light dry malt and hop aftertaste.

Don Valley Brewing Co./ The Conners B.C.

Conners Brewing Enterprises, Ltd. Brewery on earlier labels listed as being in Mississauga, Ontario; now listed as Toronto, Ontario; brewery is in St. Catherines, Ontario.

CONNERS BREWERY BEST BITTER — hazy amber-gold, toasted malt nose with a hop tang in back, tart hop and malt flavor, hops in front and end, malt in the middle, a definite ale-like tang, good balance, complex and interesting, hop finish, lemony aftertaste, a fine well-hopped brew.

CONNERS BREWERY ALE — amber, light malt aroma, hops dominate the flavor but there is still plenty of malt, big body, hop finish, short dry hop aftertaste.

CONNERS SPECIAL DRAFT — amber-gold, faint malt aroma, bitter and dry hop flavor, high carbonation, long dry bitter aftertaste, a straight plain bitter brew.

Great Western Brewing Co., Ltd.

Brewery in **Saskatoon, Saskatchewan**

GREAT WESTERN LAGER BEER — hazy gold, very foamy, faint hop and malt nose, malt flavor, big body, long off-dry malt aftertaste. Made for Connoisseur Beverage International Inc. of Minneapolis, MN.

GREAT WESTERN LIGHT BEER — gold, hop nose, light hop flavor, light body, faint dry hop finish and aftertaste, very little aftertaste and no complexity. Contract brew as above.

LISTWIN'S KODIAK MILD DRAFT LAGER BEER — deep gold, hop aroma, very malty flavor with good hop support, sour hop finish, very end is dry hops, overall appearance (package is a large plastic bottle) cries out to malt liquor fans.

Horseshoe Bay Brewing Co.

Microbrewery in **Horseshoe Bay, Vancouver, BC**

BAY ALE — amber, malt nose, very little carbonation, slightly sour malt flavor, dry finish and aftertaste, very brief.

Labatt Brewing Co., Ltd.

Breweries in St. John's, Newfoundland; Halifax, Nova Scotia; St. John, New Brunswick; Quebec City, Quebec; Waterloo, London and Weston Ontario; Winnipeg, Manitoba; Saskatoon, Saskatchewan; Edmonton, Alberta; Creston and New Westminster, British Columbia. Corporate HQ is in London, Ontario.

LABATT'S 50 ALE — medium deep bright gold, light hop nose, medium body, bright zesty hop flavor, quite tasty, long hop aftertaste with some slightly sour malt background. Export to the U.S. labelled LABATT'S 50 CANADIAN ALE.

LABATT'S PILSENER BEER — bright gold, dry hop nose, dry malt and hop flavor, medium body, finish and long aftertaste like the flavor, good clean serviceable pilsener. Long known as LABATT'S BLUE in Canada and more recently labelled as such.

GOLD KEG BEER — deep tawny-gold, big malt and hop aroma, good hop flavor, tasty, pleasant sour hop aftertaste is long.

COOL SPRING LIGHT BEER — bright gold, virtually no nose, light body, faint off-dry malt flavor fades as it crosses the palate, brief dull malt aftertaste.

CERVOISE ALE — pale gold, good malt aroma, bright malt flavor that fades across the palate, short dull malt aftertaste.

LABATT'S CRYSTAL LAGER BEER — gold, malt and hop nose, high carbonation, complex malt and hop flavor, long dry hop aftertaste, a pleasant very drinkable beer.

LABATT'S DRY LIGHT BEER — pale yellow, faint malt nose, palate is faint malt and carbonation, very short dry malt aftertaste.

LABATT'S DRY — bright gold, light malt and hop aroma, smooth, light bodied, well-balanced, very faint brief malt aftertaste.

LABATT EXTRA DRY BEER — pale gold, faint malt nose, malt palate, dry hop finish and aftertaste.

LABATT'S IPA — gold, malt nose, big off-dry malt flavor, high carbonation but it is needed to balance the malt, dry malt finish, short aftertaste. Better than average malty brew.

LABATT'S VELVET CREAM PORTER — brown, light malt nose, light malt flavor is off-dry up front, medium body, dry malt finish, long dry malt aftertaste, very drinkable.

JOHN LABATT'S EXTRA STOCK MALT LIQUOR — deep bright gold, fragrant complex malt and hop aroma, big body, huge complex malt flavor, excellent hop balance, dry malt finish and long aftertaste, a big beautiful brew!

LABATT'S EXTRA STOCK MALT LIQUOR — gold, straightforward malt flavor, good body, hefty malt flavor, finish and aftertaste like the flavor. I thought this would be the same as above exported to the U.S., but it doesn't have the heft or the complexity.

KOOTENAY PALE ALE — medium to deep gold, lovely zesty hop nose, clean and bright at the start, flattens out at the finish and has a slightly dull malt aftertaste, still a pleasant beer.

KOKANEE PILSENER BEER — medium gold, light hop nose, pleasant and smooth malt and hop flavor, dry malt aftertaste, pleasant but a bit light.

JOCKEY CLUB BEER — deep gold, pleasant malt-hop aroma, tasty malt and hop flavor, long dry hop aftertaste.

BLUE STAR — tawny gold, hop nose, flavor briefly is malt, quickly turns hop bitter, bitter finish and long dry bitter hop aftertaste, very good of type.

GUINNESS EXTRA STOUT — opaque brown, roasted malt nose, heavy body, complex coffee-malt flavor, long dry malt aftertaste retains much of the richness of the flavor.

LABATT BLUE LIGHT — medium deep gold, bright hop and malt nose, light non-descript malt and hop flavor, light body, little aftertaste.

JOHN LABATT CLASSIC BEER — bright deep gold color, off-dry hop nose, big dry malt and bitter hop flavor, dry hop finish and aftertaste, medium length.

JOHN LABATT'S CLASSIC LIGHT — bright gold, light hop nose, dull malt and hop flavor, mostly carbonation, brief malt-hop aftertaste.

LABATT GENUINE COLD FILTERED DRAFT — gold, malt nose, malt and hop flavor, a touch of citrus in back, high carbonation, short dry malt and hop aftertaste.

LABATT .5 — pale gold, grainy malt and hop nose, also a trace of corn comes through, light body, dull malt flavor, weak grainy aftertaste, another uninteresting non-alcoholic malt beverage.

OLAND EXPORT ALE — pale gold, pleasant malt aroma, good clean taste, medium to light body, good balance, a little hop zest at the finish, dry clean hop aftertaste. Oland Breweries, Halifax, Nova Scotia is the originating brewery and brewery of record.

OLAND'S OLD SCOTIA ALE — bright gold, light tangy ale nose with good hops, big ale flavor with plenty of hops and slightly off-dry malt, good body, sags a little at the middle to finish, but rebounds well in the long hop aftertaste, good brew.

OLAND'S LIGHT BEER — bright gold, nice hop nose, fairly complex lightly hopped flavor, light body, hop and faintly sour malt aftertaste.

OLAND'S SCHOONER BEER — pale bright gold, good fresh malt and hop aroma, high carbonation, balanced malt and hop flavor, lovely malt finish, lingering dry hop aftertaste.

OLAND EXTRA STOUT — dark brown, light molasses aroma, light body, medium sweet malt flavor, likeable although light.

ALEXANDER KEITH'S INDIA PALE ALE — tawny-gold, fine malt aroma with good hop character, pleasant malt flavor that finishes with good hops, long dry hop aftertaste, good balance and very drinkable. Oland Breweries, Ltd.

ALEXANDER KEITH'S LIGHT BEER — light tawny-gold, pleasant malt-hop aroma and flavor, light body, quick hop finish, light, short, dry hop aftertaste.

KEITH'S SPECIAL DRY — pale gold, rising malt and hop nose, good body, big malt and light hop flavor, good balance, fairly long dry malt aftertaste, one of the better dry beers.

BUDWEISER LAGER BEER — pale gold, light malt and hop aroma, good balanced hop and malt flavor, very good body, good balance, dry hop finish, long dry hop aftertaste. A good Budweiser indeed and one with 5% alcohol, which you don't find in the U.S.

BUD LIGHT — pale gold, pleasant light malt aroma, very light malt flavor, faint off-dry malt aftertaste with little length.

Molson Breweries of Canada, Ltd.

Breweries in St. John's, Newfoundland; Montreal, Quebec; Toronto and Barrie, Ontario; Edmonton and Calgary, Alberta; Winnipeg, Manitoba; Regina, Saskatchewan; and Vancouver, British Columbia. Molson recently merged with Carling O'Keefe, one of the two other large national Canadian brewers.

MOLSON CANADIAN LAGER BEER — pale gold, off-dry malt aroma with hops in back, good malt flavor well-balanced with hops, good long dry malt and hop aftertaste, very smooth drinkable brew.

MOLSON CANADIAN LIGHT — gold, slightly skunk hop nose, hop flavor, high carbonation, dull malt finish and aftertaste.

MOLSON EXPORT ALE — brilliant tawny-gold, clean malt and distinctive hop nose, good flavor with balanced hops and malt, a bright beer with good body and a long and pleasant malt-hop aftertaste.

MOLSON GOLDEN — pale gold, light malt and hop aroma, light body, light off-dry malt flavor, hops way in back, light malt and hop finish, medium dry hop aftertaste with little length.

OLD STYLE PILSNER BEER — bright gold, aromatic hop and malt nose, highly carbonated, big well-balanced hop and malt flavor, finishes well and the aftertaste is pleasant and long.

MOLSON STOCK ALE — gold, off-dry malt nose, good malt and hop flavor, smooth, balanced, long dry hop aftertaste.

INDIA BEER — bright yellow-gold, off-dry malt aroma with a good hop backing, pleasant mild hop flavor, very good balance, dry malt finish, long dry hop aftertaste.

LAURENTIDE ALE — pale gold, fresh beery malt and hop nose, refreshing fruity malt flavor, medium dry malt finish, hop aftertaste that works at going dry as it goes.

MOLSON LIGHT — pale gold, pleasant well-hopped malt aroma, light body, faint malt flavor, light hop finish, short hop aftertaste.

MOLSON PORTER — deep copper-brown, lovely roasted malt nose, roasted malt flavor, just enough hops to balance and retain the porter character, smooth, slightly dry hop aftertaste with good length.

MOLSON BRADOR MALT LIQUOR — bright gold, light off-dry malt aroma, heavy body, noticeable alcohol, pleasant sweet malt flavor, medium dry hop finish, dry hop aftertaste, nicely made beer, very good of type.

MOLSON SPECIALE — bright gold, pleasant malt and hop nose, light malt flavor, light body, slight hop finish drops off quickly, short dry hop aftertaste.

MOLSON EXPORT LIGHT — medium gold, good malt and hop aroma, good malt flavor up front, hops come in nicely in the middle and finish, short dry hop aftertaste.

MOLSON LITE — pale gold, slightly vegetal malt nose, light malt and hop flavor, light body, short slight hop aftertaste.

MOLSON DIAMOND LAGER BEER — bright pale gold, austere malt nose, highly carbonated, bright well-hopped flavor, malt and hop finish, dull malt aftertaste.

MOLSON SPECIAL DRY — pale yellow-gold, hop nose, some noticeable alcohol, dry hop flavor, medium body, medium length dry hop aftertaste.

MOLSON EXEL — pale gold, grainy hop nose reminds you of grape-nuts, grainy flavor, dry hop finish, short dry grain and sour hop aftertaste.

MOLSON DRY — pale gold, touch of skunk in a hop nose, good hop and malt flavor, good body, long dry hop aftertaste.

MOLSON CLUB ALE — bright gold, fruity malt aroma with off tones in back (like a sweaty sock), hop flavor is a bit sour, dry hop aftertaste.

LOWENBRAU SPECIAL BEER — pale gold, light hop and malt aroma, mild hop and off-dry malt palate, more malty in the front, more dry hops in the middle and finish, pleasant long, dry hop aftertaste.

BENNETT'S DOMINION ALE — bright gold, hop aroma and flavor, finishes a bit sour, very long, bitter hop aftertaste.

CARLING BLACK LABEL BEER — medium gold, tangy hop and malt aroma, good dry hop flavor, pleasant dry hop aftertaste.

BLACK HORSE BEER PREMIUM STOCK — yellow-gold, hop nose, big bitter hop flavor, full-bodied, good complex aftertaste that is on the bitter side.

MAGNUM ALE — deep gold, hop aroma with good malt background, malt and hops both vie for the lead on the palate, hop finish and aftertaste.

RALLYE ALE — gold, malt aroma and flavor, light body, light malt finish, little aftertaste.

O'KEEFE'S OLD VIENNA LAGER BEER — gold, malt and hop aroma and flavor, medium dry hop finish, dry hop aftertaste.

CALGARY AMBER LAGER BEER — amber, light toasted malt nose and taste, good balance, good body, smooth, dry malt finish, malt aftertaste has medium duration.

CINCI LAGER BEER — gold, appetizing well-hopped malt aroma, dry balanced malt and hop flavor, dry hop finish and aftertaste, good length.

CINCI CREAM LAGER BEER — pale bright gold, beautiful beery nose with plenty of hops and malt, off-dry pleasant malt flavor, light body, short dry hop finish and aftertaste, pleasant tasty brew.

DOW CREAM PORTER — deep red brown, creamy, very faint malt aroma, slightly sweet malt flavor, but still pleasant, fair balance, smooth, dry light malt finish and aftertaste, tasty and drinkable.

TRILIGHT EXTRA LIGHT BEER — pale gold, very faint flowery hop nose, light very dry hop and malt flavor, very light body, very short dull aftertaste.

COLT .45 BEER — medium bright gold, light malt aroma with faint hops, creamy inoffensive malt flavor, light grainy finish and short aftertaste.

CHAMPLAIN PORTER — deep red brown, faintly smoky and roasted malt aroma, overall malt is off-dry, perhaps a little too sweet, but still quite smooth and mellow, sweet finish and aftertaste.

O'KEEFE'S EXTRA OLD STOCK MALT LIQUOR — brilliant deep gold, beautiful clean sweet malt aroma, good off-dry hop and malt flavor, excellent balance, very long pleasant malt aftertaste.

O'KEEFE ALE — gold, clean malt and bright hop nose, good balanced malt-hop flavor, pleasant hop finish and lingering aftertaste. Version shipped to the U.S. is called CANADIAN O'KEEFE ALE and is identical to the domestic Canadian product.

O'KEEFE LIGHT — pale gold, light malt nose, light off-dry malt flavor, dry malt and hop aftertaste, medium length.

O'KEEFE GOLDEN LIGHT CANADIAN BEER — medium yellow, sour malt aroma with some hops, complex flavor is sour malt in front and dry hops in the middle and finish, short dry hop aftertaste.

MONTREAL EXPORT — deep gold, hop nose, off-dry front palate, dry hop middle and finish, dry hop aftertaste, medium length. Contract brew for Montreal Brewery, Inc.

TOBY ALE — amber-orange color, off-dry hoppy malt aroma, front palate is balanced hops and malt, flattens out a bit in the middle, finishes bitter hops and malt, balance is off.

BROWN'S ORIGINAL CANADIAN BEER — gold, faint apple-malt nose, dull malt and hop flavor, little aftertaste. Contract brew using Yukon B.C. corporate name, made for F&A Importers, Louisville, KY.

F&A IMPORTED CANADIAN BEER — bright gold, big head, pleasant malt-hop nose and flavor, good balance, short dry hop aftertaste. Contract brew for F&A Importers, Ltd., Louisville, KY.

HEIDELBERG FINE QUALITY BEER — medium gold, faint hop nose, light body, light malt flavor, faint malt finish, dry aftertaste.

CANADIAN RED CAP CREAM ALE — deep yellow-gold, light hop nose with a fruity-malt background, off-dry and sharp ale-like flavor, plenty of malt and hops, dry hop finish, long dry hop aftertaste.

CARLSBERG BEER — bright pale gold, off-dry malt nose, balanced hops and malt flavor, dry hop and sour malt aftertaste, medium length.

CARLSBERG LIGHT BEER — tawny gold, light hop and malt aroma, carbonation dominates the flavor which is faint off-dry malt and hops, aftertaste like the flavor, medium length.

MILLER HIGH LIFE — pale yellow gold, pleasant fragrant hop nose, dull malt and hop palate, pleasant dry hop finish, fairly dry hop aftertaste with good duration.

COORS LIGHT — pale gold, fresh beery nose, light off-dry malt flavor, very light hop finish, brief hop aftertaste.

MILLER LITE — pale gold, malt and faint hop nose, very light body, faint malt and hop finish, no aftertaste.

COORS BEER — very pale gold, light malt and hop nose, pleasant flavor is mostly off-dry malt, pleasant fairly long aftertaste shows both malt and hops.

FOSTER'S LAGER — deep gold, light off-dry malt nose, off-dry malt and hop palate, good body, dry hop finish, dry hop aftertaste fades quickly.

DUFFY'S ALE — amber, smooth malt and hop nose and taste, very good balance, long dry malt aftertaste.

OV BOCK BIER 1992 — golden amber, rich fruity malt aroma, good balanced malt and hop flavor, an abundance of malt, big body, sense of alcohol, long malt aftertaste, a full-flavored brew.

Moosehead Breweries, Ltd.

Brewery in St. John, New Brunswick

MOOSEHEAD CANADIAN LAGER BEER — pale gold, very good malt and hop nose, balanced slightly off-dry malt and hop flavor, smooth, very pleasant and quite drinkable, long malt aftertaste.

MOOSEHEAD LIGHT — pale gold, light malt nose, light off-dry malt flavor at first, then dry at the finish, brief malt aftertaste, on the dull side.

MOOSEHEAD PALE ALE — pale gold, light off-dry aroma shows malt, yeast and hops, off-dry malt and well-hopped flavor, dry hop-malt finish, medium dry hop-malt aftertaste.

MOOSEHEAD PREMIUM DRY — bright gold, light malt nose, zesty dry hop flavor, good body, excellent balance, crisp and refreshing, medium length dry hop aftertaste.

TEN-PENNY ALE — pale amber, light hop aroma and flavor, dry hop finish and aftertaste, a decent little Canadian ale.

MOOSEHEAD EXPORT ALE — pale amber-gold, off-dry malt and bitter hop nose, flavor like the nose, great complexity, good hop finish, long hop aftertaste, one of Moosehead's better efforts.

ALPINE LAGER BEER — pale gold, malt aroma and taste with hops in back, pleasant tasting and very drinkable, light body, light malt finish and aftertaste, the carbonation is high and the hops stay in back.

ALPINE LITE BEER — pale yellow-gold, malt and hop aroma, pleasant light malt and hop flavor, finely carbonated, medium long light malt and hop aftertaste.

ALPINE GENUINE COLD FILTERED BEER — gold, faint malt nose, malt flavor has a faint citrus background, highly carbonated, medium body, short and light dry malt and hop aftertaste.

MOOSEHEAD'S GOLDEN LIGHT BEER — pale gold, lovely fragrant hop nose, pleasant malt flavor, light body, medium long malt aftertaste, well-made and good for a low-calorie beer.

MOOSEHEAD LONDON STOUT — very deep brown, almost opaque, molasses and malt flavor, quite sweet, very long aftertaste like the flavor, definitely a dessert beer.

JAMES READY ORIGINAL LAGER BEER — bright gold, light aromatic off-dry clover, hop and grain nose, light hop and malt flavor, faint malt finish, light body, short malt aftertaste.

Niagara Falls Brewing Co., Ltd.

Brewery in Niagara Falls, Ontario

GRITSTONE PREMIUM ALE — deep amber, faint sour malt nose, ephemeral malt flavor, long dry malt aftertaste, there are hops but there is not a good balance between those hops and the malt.

OLDE JACK BITTER STRONG ALE — amber, very malty aroma and flavor, straightforward malt, medium body, medium dry malt finish and short light malt aftertaste, 7.2% alc/vol.

Saxon Brewery

Brewery in Montreal, Canada

KEELE'S CANADIAN BEER — pale gold, very faint malt aroma, low carbonation, light body, light malt flavor, brief aftertaste.

Summit Brewery

Brewery at Prince George, British Columbia and St. Catherines, Ontario, Canada

W J MACKAY CLASSIC CANADIAN PILSNER — pale gold, faint malt aroma, light body, slightly off-dry malt flavor, malt finish and brief malt aftertaste.

Upper Canada Brewing Co., Ltd.

Brewery in Toronto, Ontario

UPPER CANADA ALE — amber, complex hop aroma with smoky slightly off-dry malt in back, flavor is like the aroma, smoky hop finish, off-dry malt aftertaste, doesn't quite come together.

UPPER CANADA DARK ALE — deep amber, complex aromatic hop and malt aroma with a trace of lactic acid in back, flavor is much like the aroma except the acid is more noticeable, big hop finish and aftertaste has plenty of malt in back, but the effect is harmed by the acidity.

UPPER CANADA TRUE LIGHT — bright gold, light malt nose, very light malt flavor, weak body, very dry brief malt aftertaste.

UPPER CANADA LAGER — bright gold, faint malt and hop aroma, dry hop flavor is too bitter for the amount of malt, bitter finish and aftertaste, poorly balanced.

UPPER CANADA REBELLION MALT LIQUOR — bright deep gold, nice malt aroma, big fresh malt flavor, big body, hop finish, very long hop aftertaste, balanced, excellent tasting brew.

UPPER CANADA NATURAL LIGHT LAGER — deep gold, fruity hop nose, sour hop flavor, light body, minty finish, short hop aftertaste.

UPPER CANADA WHEAT BEER — tawny-gold, very nice complex but faint malt aroma, tangy sour malt flavor, light body, refreshing dry wheat finish, medium to short dry wheat and malt aftertaste.

PUBLICAN'S SPECIAL BITTER ALE — amber, malt nose, hop flavor, short dry hop aftertaste, questionable balance.

NATURAL POINT NINE — gold, fruity malt nose, dull malt flavor, thins out greatly at the finish, disappears to a metallic aftertaste, 0.9% alc/vol.

Vancouver Island Brewing Co.

Microbrewery in Victoria, British Columbia

PIPER'S PALE ALE — amber, malt flavor has a faint lactic component, finely carbonated, very drinkable, pleasant and interesting, long dry malt aftertaste.

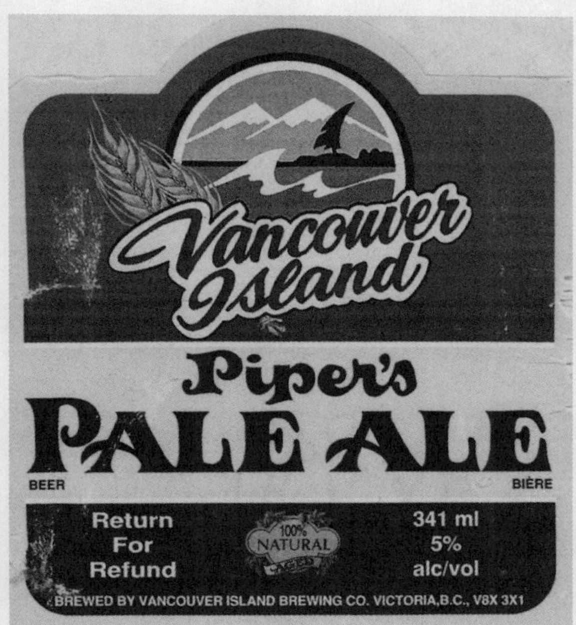

Whistler Brewing Co., Ltd.

Microbrewery in Whistler, British Columbia

WHISTLER BLACK TUSK ALE — deep amber-brown, light chocolate malt nose, flavor to match, light body, short dry malt aftertaste.

Notes:

Notes:

1993 UPDATE

Foreign

the BEER log

By James D. Robertson

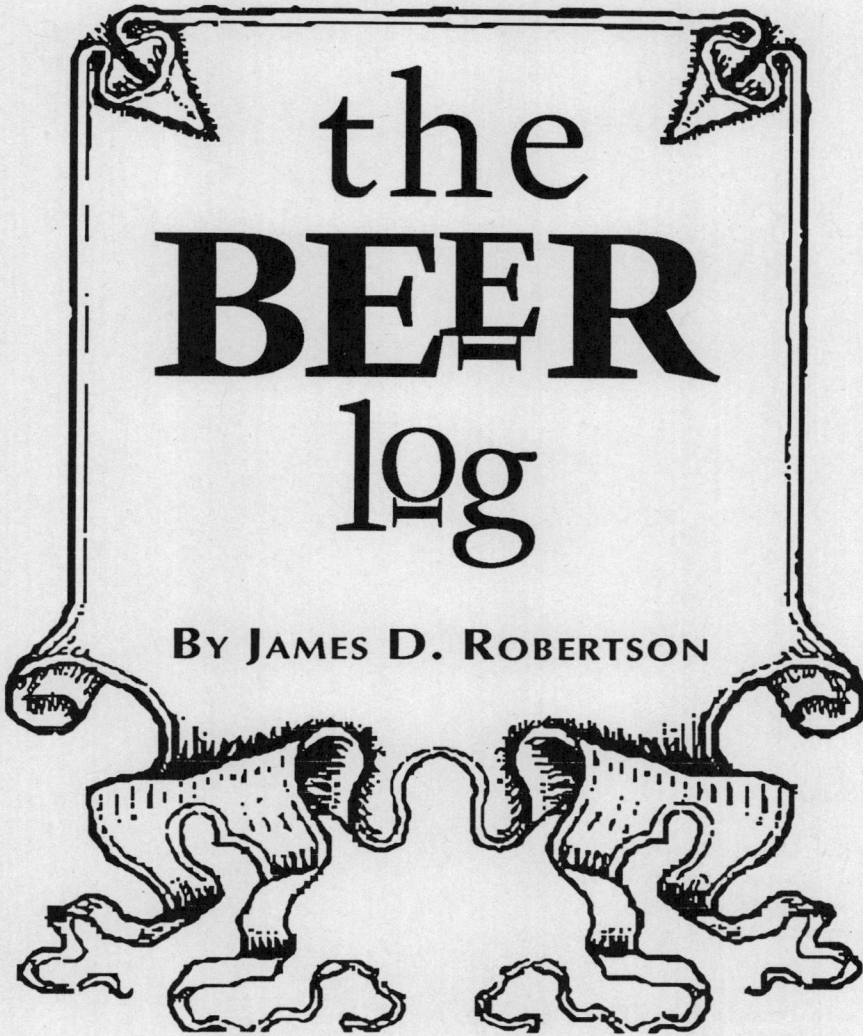

The Beer Log Update: Foreign

All inquiries should be addressed to Bosak Publishing Company, 4764 Galicia Way, Oceanside, CA 92056, (619) 724-4447.

ISBN: 0-9635332-2-3

Printed in the United States of America

AUSTRIA

Brauerei Fohrenburg

Brewery in Bludenz

FOHRENBURGER JUBILÄUM — gold, toasted malt nose and taste, off-dry malt finish, malt aftertaste is a bit drier, good body.

FOHRENBURGER BLONDES — gold, hop nose does have some malt in back, flavor is slightly sour malt, malt finish and aftertaste with hops at the end.

Brauerei Hofstetten

Brewery at St. Martin

STEINBOCK 17º — tawny-gold, huge toasted malt nose, intense malt flavor like the nose, chewy big body, long malt aftertaste, 7.7% alcohol.

Notes:

Burgerbräu Kaiser

Brewery in Innsbrück

KAISER MÄRZEN FASSTYP — gold, big malt nose, malt flavor is on the dry side, dry malt aftertaste, lacks richness but otherwise is good.

KAISER KUR PILS — gold, hop nose and flavor, dry hop aftertaste.

KAISER PREMIUM — gold, bright hop aroma, picquant spicy malt flavor, smooth and balanced, good body, long dry hop aftertaste, an interesting complex beer.

Brauerei Stiegl

Brewery in Salzburg

STIEGL GOLDBRAU — deep golden amber, big malt nose, big malt front palate, vanishes in the middle, dull malt finish and long dull malt aftertaste.

STIEGL WEIHNACHTSBOCK — deep gold, faint off-dry malt nose, huge malt flavor, heavy body, rich and full flavored, complex, rich malt finish, feels good in your mouth, long malt aftertaste holds the richness of the flavor, very satisfying, a marvelous brew.

COLUMBUS MÄRZEN — amber-gold, light clean hop and malt nose, flavor is strong hops at first, smooths out a bit, malt comes in at the middle and stays through the finish and into the aftertaste, good complexity, good balance.

COLUMBUS GOLDEN BOCK — bright deep gold, toasted malt and hop nose, hops dominate front palate, lacks a middle, malt at the finish and aftertaste, not much complexity, so-so balance.

COLUMBUS FESTIVAL DARK — deep ruby color, roast malt aroma and flavor, off-dry malt finish, medium body, long sweet malt aftertaste. It is luscious but heavy and filling; one would probably be enough.

STIEGL PILSNER — gold, good hop nose, bright hop flavor, long dry hop aftertaste.

Notes:

Brauerei Wurmhöringer

Brewery in **Altheim**

WURMHÖRINGER SPEZIAL BIER — gold, roasted malt aroma with good balancing hops (a very appetizing nose), smooth roasted malt and hop flavor, excellent balance, good body, long dry hop aftertaste, a marvelous beer.

WURMHÖRINGER MÄRZEN BIER — gold, big malt and hop nose and taste, good balance, good body, very tasty, long malt and hop aftertaste, a delectable brew.

SEIT
1652
BRAUEREI WURMHÖRINGER ALTHEIM O.Ö.
Märzen
Bier
9015 3501
12° Stammwürze,
4,8 Vol. % Alkohol.
Bitte kühl und
dunkel lagern.

BELGIUM

S.A. Bass Sales N.V.

Brewery in **Mechelen**

MAC EWANS SCOTCH ALE — almost opaque red-brown, tan head, sweet malt and hop palate, very pleasant, high alcohol (7.2%), less sweet at the finish, good balance, off-dry malt and hop aftertaste is quite long. Brewed under licence by Scottish and Newcastle Breweries of Edinburgh, Scotland.

BASS OLD BARLEY STOUT — opaque brown, brown head, off-dry malt nose, rich malt palate, nicely balanced, dry malt finish and aftertaste.

LAMOT PILSOR BEER — yellow-gold, more hops than malt in the nose, strong hop flavor with a sour malt background, aftertaste like the flavor.

Bry de Block

Brewery in **Merchtem/Peizegem**

SATAN ALE — hazy amber, big head, lemony nose, strong sweet and sour palate, lots of lemony-lactic bite, long aftertaste.

KAASTAR — hazy amber, rich malt nose, very rich malt flavor, hop finish, big body, long malt and hop aftertaste, a powerful brew.

Brie du BOCQ

Brewery in **Purnode-Yvoir**

SAISON REGAL CHRISTMAS CUVEE 1982 — medium amber, light malt nose, full body, sweet malt palate, overly so from front to the middle, finish is slightly drier, excellent fresh malt aftertaste, high alcohol (8%).

SAISON REGAL — medium amber, slightly hazy, beautiful long lasting fluffy white head, clean perfumy malt aroma, malt flavor with some acid at mid-palate, good balance, malt finish with acid in back, acidic hop aftertaste with surprisingly little malt showing, fairly high density (13º).

LA GAULOISE — medium to deep amber, beautiful fluffy white head, perfumy malt and faint acid nose, much like the Saison Regal above but sweeter, less acidic and maltier, big winey malt flavor, big body, some acid comes in at the finish and stays behind the malt through the long aftertaste, the acid never dominates like it did in the Saison Regal, a very high density brew rated at 20º.

Bernardijner Bier/ Abbaye de Bornem

Abbey brewery at **Bornem**

ABBAYE DE BORNEM DOUBLE — rosy brown, malt aroma with a faint wintergreen background and a trace of acid, fresh picquant malt flavor, acid is more noticeable in the long complex malt aftertaste, but never becomes obtrusive; in fact, it grows on you. A very complex brew.

Abbaye de Brogne

Abbey brewery at **Defosse St. Gerard**

ABBAYE DE BROGNE CHRISTMAS — brilliant red, rich sweet malt nose, rich winey malt palate is not quite so sweet as the nose, picquant finish, wine-like aftertaste.

De Smedt Brewery

Brewery in Opwijk

AFFLIGEM TRIPLE ABBEY BEER — deep amber, tangy hop nose, big fruity hop flavor, huge and complex, very long and very good.

ABBAYE d'AULNE 8% — deep amber, toasted malt aroma, strong toasted malt flavor with a carbonation bite, high alcohol, smooth, wine-like, finishes big, very long malt and alcohol aftertaste.

ABBAYE d'AULNE 10% — deep amber, big toasted malt aroma, very strong toasted malt flavor, no carbonation bite, very high alcohol component on the palate, also very smooth, winey, finishes lighter and drier, but then the alcohol is more noticeable, long and alcoholic.

S.A. Brasserie Demarche

Brewery at Ciney

CUVEE DE CINEY SPECIALE DE CHEVTOGNE — deep amber, beautiful malty-soapy nose, palate starts off light malt but quickly gains intensity to a big complex off-sweet malt middle and finish, long rich off-sweet malt aftertaste.

CUVEE DE CINEY BLONDE — amber, malt aroma, acidic malt palate, very acidic finish and aftertaste, the malt fades but the acid lingers.

CINEY 10 SPECIALE — amber, very faint fruity malt nose, big malt and alcohol flavor, lacks balancing hops, long malt aftertaste.

Brasserie Lefebvre/ Abbaye de Floreffe

Abbey Brewery at Quenast

ABBBAYE DE FLOREFFE LA MEILLEURE — deep rosy amber, sweet malt nose and flavor, good body, good clean malt finish and aftertaste, quite long and tasty.

Gouden Carolus

Brewery in Mechelen

GOUDEN CAROLUS BELGIAN ALE —deep amber, faint off-dry malt nose, complex malt flavor is strong and off-dry in the middle and finish, dry malt aftertaste.

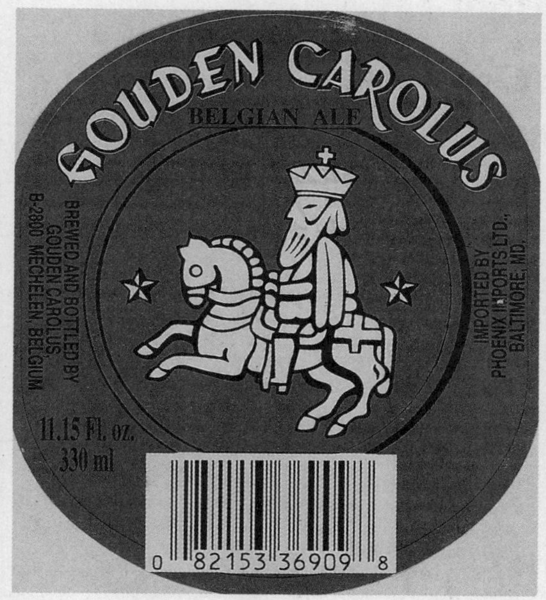

N.V. Br. Haacht, S.A.

Brewery in Boortmeerbeek

ADLER PREMIUM LUXUS BIER — pale tawny-gold, fairly good head, malt aroma, light malt and hop palate, faint off-dry malt aftertaste, overall light and brief.

PRIMUS HAACHT PILS — bright yellow, big head, but short lived, light malt and hop nose, dry hop flavor, little aftertaste.

HAACHT DRAFT — bright gold, low head, smooth light hop and malt nose, off-dry malt palate, light hop aftertaste. Also called STAR PILS EXCELSIOR.

VERY DIEST — medium deep rosy-brown, grainy malt nose, weak body, watery, off-dry clean malt flavor, short malt aftertaste, low-alcohol beer.

ADLER BIER — bright gold, good creamy head, clean pilsener aroma with plenty of malt and hops, front palate is all hops, malt joins the hops in the middle and stays to the finish, mild hop aftertaste is fairly long.

Brasserie Halle

Brewery in **Halle**

FRAMBOISE VANDER LINDEN — reddish-amber, fine creamy head, raspberry nose, raspberry-malt flavor, off-sweet but tending toward sour at the finish, long long raspberry aftertaste.

Brasserie de Abbaye de Leffe

Abbey brewery in **Dinant**

Other Abbaye de Leffe brews are made by Brasserie St. Guibert. Also label may say S.A. Abbaye de Leffe, Leffe, BG.

ABBEY DE LEFFE BIERE LUXE — deep reddish orange-brown, good malt nose, off-dry malt flavor, clean and bright, not flabby or cloying, long sour malt aftertaste.

ABBEY OF LEFFE BLOND — pale amber, faint malt aroma, thin malt flavor, a bit weak, medium body, dry malt finish, some off-dry malt in the aftertaste.

N.V. Br. Martinas S.A.

Brewery in **Merchtem**

GINDER ALE — deep tawny-gold, huge thick head, small bubbles and long lasting, toasted malt nose, good body, toasted malt flavor, a little background acid, soft malt aftertaste with good duration.

Brasserie Neve

Brewery in **Schepdaal**

GUEZE DE NEVE — amber, big head, aroma of sardines in olive oil with an acidic background, palate is briefly malt thence acid, little aftertaste.

S.A. Brasserie Piedboeuf N.V.

Brewery in **Jupile**

PIEDBOEUF BLONDE — pale tawny-gold, pleasant hop nose, light body, low carbonation, light malt flavor, dry brief malt and hop aftertaste. This is labelled a "table beer". In Belgium, it costs about 23-25 cents.

PIEDBOEUF TRIPLE — pale gold, dry malt and hop aroma, slightly off-dry malt flavor, hop and malt middle and finish, hop aftertaste, fairly long and also fairly dry, light body, but pretty good for under 30 cents.

JUPILER — bright gold, medium head, malt and hop aroma, off-dry malt palate, hop finish, dry malt aftertaste.

HORSE ALE — amber, faint malt and hop nose, big flavor has both hops and malt, very complex, malt finish, aftertaste starts out malt but there is considerable hop character at the very end.

Brewery Riva

Brewery in **Dentergem**

RIVA 2000 LAGER BEER — brilliant gold, well-carbonated, off-dry malt aroma with hops and toasted malt in back, complex flavor, bitter hop finish, long malt and dry hop aftertaste.

WITTEKOP BIERE BLANCHE — cloudy yellow, delicate fruity aroma with an acidic backtaste, lemony palate is forthright but delicate, interesting, pleasant, well-balanced, wine-like and very long.

VONDEL TRIPLE — copper, picquant candy-citrus aroma, intense off-dry malt and tangy hop palate, long aftertaste like the flavor.

LUCIFER ALE — gold, big foamy head, perfumy winey fruity aroma, big strong zesty hop palate, good tasting, big body, lots of alcohol, off-dry malt finish with a mild licorice background, extremely long malt aftertaste, big and very good.

DENTERGEMS WHITE ALE — hazy yellow, huge head, soapy nose, wheaty-malt flavor, smooth, medium body, cuts off abruptly, little or no aftertaste.

RIVA CHRISTMAS 1983 — medium deep amber, big tan head, clean malt aroma, big refreshing clean malt flavor, full body, very satisfying, long straightforward rich malt aftertaste.

RIVA BLANCHE DENTERGEMS BELGIAN ALE — cloudy yellow, tart spicy complex malt aroma, low carbonation, light body, flavor is first faintly sweet for a brief moment, thence light dry malt with a faint lactic acid bite, medium long dry malt aftertaste has a spicy component, but overall comes off as being surprisingly bland and light for a white beer.

Abbaye St. Remy

Abbey brewery at Rochefort

BIERE DES TRAPPISTES ROCHEFORT 10° — deep red-brown, fairly clear, tan head, sweet clean malt nose with some cherry fruit tones, big sweet clean malt flavor, a very big strong flavor with lots of hops and malt and complexities like anise, coffee and various fruits, big body, highly carbonated, the first thing you notice is the carbonation, then the hops and lastly the malt, but the overall impression is more malt than anything else, a very long complex aftertaste. This is a beautiful beer. Balanced, strong but smooth and very long.

BIERE DES TRAPPISTES ROCHEFORT 8° — deep red-brown, a bit hazy, fluffy tan head, zesty malt aroma, good body, big malt and hop flavor, excellent balance, very big and very tasty, medium long complex aftertaste, crisp and bright throughout, real sipping beer.

BIERE DES TRAPPISTES ROCHEFORT 6° — deep amber, slightly hazy, big eggshell colored head, light malt nose, good tasting light malt and hop flavor, medium body, fine balance, refreshing and drinkable, good drinking beer, especially with food.

Brasserie Friart/ Abbaye Le Roeulx

Abbey brewery at Le Roeulx

ST. FEUILLIEN CHRISTMAS — deep rosy-amber, off-sweet malt nose, semi-dry malt palate, brief finish, very little aftertaste.

Roman N.V.

Brewery at Oudenaard

ROMAN SPECIALE MATER — red, lovely malt aroma, smooth off-sweet malt flavor, lovely long malt aftertaste, a very very drinkable beer.

S.A. Interbrew N.V.

Brewery in Brussels

CAMPBELL'S CHRISTMAS 1992 — very deep dark amber, smooth rich malt aroma, big malt flavor, high alcohol,very classy brew, finely carbonated, very long and smooth, wants for nothing. Made under the supervision of Whitbread PLC London, England.

CAMPBELL'S CHRISTMAS 1991 — deep rosy-amber, huge nose of alcohol, hops and malt, flavor is mostly malt on the sweet side, more rich than sweet, very big in flavor and body, long rich malt aftertaste, alcohol shows all the way through (8.1%). This could be either made by Whitbread in England or made in Belgium under licence frrom Whitbread.

Notes:

Brasserie St. Guibert S.A. NV

Abbey brewery in **Mont St. Guibert**

VIEUX TEMPS — medium to deep amber, dense amber head, malt aroma and palate, touch of acid in back, malt finish and aftertaste, the acid background is there all the way through.

TONGERLO NORBERTIJNERBIER — nearly opaque reddish-brown, fine creamy head, malt nose, slightly acidic malt palate, the acid fades as you go, medium body, long malt aftertaste has only the faintest trace of the acid.

ABBAYE DE LEFFE BLONDE ALE — deep gold, highly carbonated, light hop aroma, good hoppy ale-like flavor, long hop aftertaste.

LEFFE RADIEUSE BELGIAN ALE — deep copper, hop nose, complex hop palate with bitter and off-dry tones, very long hop aftertaste.

LEFFE BELGIAN DARK ALE — dark copper, good malt and hop aroma, fine malt flavor with hops in back, well-balanced, long aftertaste, pleasant to drink.

Brasserie/ Brouwerijen Dilbeek

Brewery in **Itterbeek**

Export labels say Timmerman's Breweries.

TIMMERMAN'S PECHE LAMBIC — hazy gold, sour peach nose, complex peach flavor with a lambic tang, very tasty, fairly dry medium long aftertaste, nicely done.

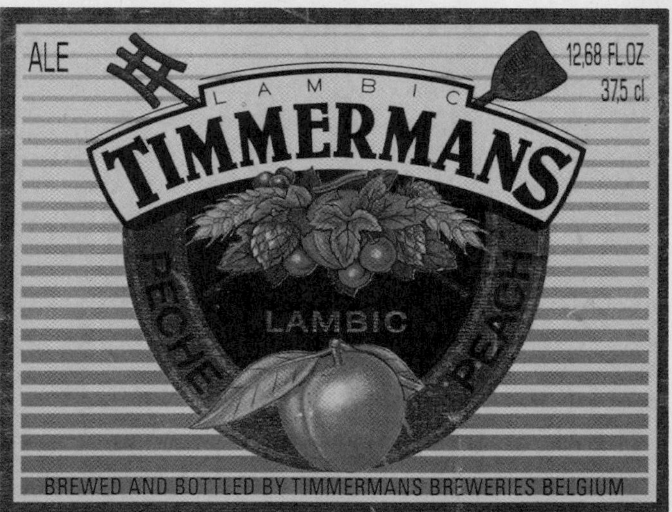

TIMMERMAN'S FRAMBOISE LAMBIC — hazy red-brown, raspberry nose, raspberry-lambic flavor, tasty, medium length aftertaste like the flavor, nicely done as well.

TIMMERMAN'S KRIEK LAMBIC — cloudy orange-brown, sharp citrus-sweet cherry nose, intense sharp acidic and sweet cherry flavor, off-sweet finish, faint malt aftertaste.

Brasserie Union S.A.

Brewery in **Jumet**

CUVEE DE L'HERMITAGE — tawny-amber, rich malt aroma, off dry toasted malt and bitter hop flavor, big wine-like body, strong malt flavor, big hop finish, smooth hop aftertaste with plenty of malt, a fine sipping beer with 8% alcohol/vol.

CUVEE DE L'HERMITAGE CHRISTMAS — deep amber, big complex rich tangy candy caramel malt aroma, concentrated malt and hop flavor, long hop and malt aftertaste, big body, fairly strong flavor, high alcohol (7.5%), strong stuff. This was the 1987 issue.

GRIMBERGEN DOUBLE — deep ruby-amber, big malt aroma, big malt and hop flavor, very complex, off-dry roasted malt finish, drops off fast to a surprisingly weak aftertaste.

GRIMBERGEN TRIPLE — deep gold, light fruity lychee nut nose, big strong malt and hop flavor, lots of alcohol, particularly at the finish and in the aftertaste, very long rich malt aftertaste has a touch of sweetness, a huge delicious beer.

Notes:

Van Steenberge Brewery

Brewery in Ertvelde

The corporate name Brasserie Bios is still used on some labels.

AUGUSTIJN — amber, tangy-soapy aroma, grain and bitter hop flavor, tangy sweet finish, long off-dry hop aftertaste, very complex, very big and assertive, very long.

BIOS COPPER ALE — medium deep cloudy red-brown, sharp yeasty sweet spicy nose, sweet and sour lactic palate, tenacious long hop aftertaste.

GULDEN DRAAK — hazy amber, hefty malt aroma shows lots of the 11.5% alcohol, huge alcoholic malt flavor is off-dry in the mouth, really fills your mouth and senses, long dry malt aftertaste.

Westmalle Abbey

Cistercian Trappiste Abbey Brewery in Westmalle

WESTMALLE TRIPLE ABBEY BEER 8% — bright gold, fine bitter hop aroma and bright hop flavor, full-bodied, good balance, dry hop and malt finish, long dry hop aftertaste, high alcohol (8%), delicious brew.

WESTMALLE TRIPLE 9% — hazy amber, honeyed fruity malt nose, big sweet malt flavor, very smooth and very long.

WESTMALLE DUBBEL ABBEY BEER — fairly deep cloudy orange-brown, delicious complex off-dry malt nose, rich and full bodied, big roasted malt flavor is quite complex and seems to change as it goes, very long aftertaste like the flavor, a truly great Trappiste brew.

Brasserie Wiel

Brewery just outside Bruxelles

WIEL'S — pale tawny-gold, fine head, beautifully hopped nose (Saaz hops), medium body, good hop flavor well-backed with malt, fairly dry, smooth long dry hop aftertaste.

Brouwerij Van Zulte

Brewery in Zulte

ZULTE — medium deep red-brown, rich malt aroma and palate, medium body, touch of sourness in back of the palate develops and comes forward in the long malt aftertaste. (Note: I have seen this brew labelled as having been made by NV Alken-Maes S.A.)

Miscellaneous Belgian Beers

While travelling in the Flemish areas of Belgium, I found a number of beers not labelled sufficiently for me to identify the brewer or location. Even when I could find people willing to tolerate my French or German (which sometimes can carry one through a Flemish conversation), they were unable to shed light on the problem. Rather than leave them out, I have grouped them together in this section with whatever information I was able to obtain.

SILVER PILS — pale gold, fine head, toasted malt and hop aroma, slightly sweet malt and hop taste, malt in front, malt and hops in the middle, hop finish, long aftertaste starts out malty but ends up mostly hops, plenty of body, quite complex and has character throughout. Beer bottled in Belgium for Delhaize Le Lion supermarkets.

DB URTYP — pale gold, fine head, lightly hopped malt nose, well-hopped flavor, sour hop finish and aftertaste. This was a much advertised brew, supposedly made in Germany for Belgian tastes.

KETJE PALE ALE — pretty tawny-gold, huge fluffy long lasting head, very faint malt aroma, zesty pale ale style well-hopped flavor, malt finish, long slightly sour hop aftertaste. Locals thought this to be either made by Whitbread in England, or made in Belgium under license by Whitbread.

ENGHEIN SAISON DOUBLE — light amber, big head, light toasted barley and wheat malt nose with an acidic background, light body, cereal-like brief palate, faintly sour malt aftertaste, like a light saison. Naturally fermented in the bottle according to the label and made by R.C.M. 12313 H.R.B. ***Note:** A Saison is a top-fermented, naturally conditioned Belgian summer ale indigenous to Walloon, Belgium.*

PETRUS OUD BRUIN — deep rosy-brown, tight tan head, rich heavy malt aroma that is sort of bready, palate starts out sweet malt, then goes to neutral at the middle, takes on a bready nature at the finish and ends up with a malt aftertaste, no acid and if there are hops, they are too well buried to be detected under the malt. Label identifies maker as Bavik Bavikhove.

CZECHOSLOVAKIA*

**Now politically divided into Czech and Slovak Republics.*

Crystal Pivovare

Brewery in **Cescké Budejovice**

CRYSTAL — bright deep gold, big bubble loosely knit head, medium body, skunky nose, hop and carbonation palate, malt finish, nutty hop aftertaste.

Jihoceske Pivovare K.P.

Samson Brewery in **Ceské Budejovice**

SAMSON 10º — bright gold, good head, pleasant balanced hop and malt aroma, sharp hops on front of palate, off-dry malt middle, crisp hop finish, very long dry and slightly sour hop aftertaste, also a faint trace of oxidation.

SAMSON 11º — tawny-gold, flowery hop aroma, moderately sweet hop flavor, malt shows well in the middle and finish, light nutty aftertaste shows both hops and malt, quite pleasant. There was also a trace of oxidation here, but it showed only in the nose.

Pivovare Karlovy Vary

Brewery in **Carlsbad (Karlovy Vary)**

KAREL SVELTE — brilliant deep tawny-gold, dense head, rich fruity aromatic slightly sweet nose, some background of pineapple, pleasant flavor is a bit too sweet up front, it dries toward the finish and ends with a dry hop aftertaste.

Pivovare a Sladovne Martin

Brewery at **Banska Bystrica**

URPIN — deep gold, hop nose, malt flavor, medium to light body, medium long dry malt and hop aftertaste.

MARTINSKY ZDROJ — brilliant gold, finely carbonated, delicious hop and malt aroma, big body, full flavored malt palate with good hop support, malt finish and long malt aftertaste.

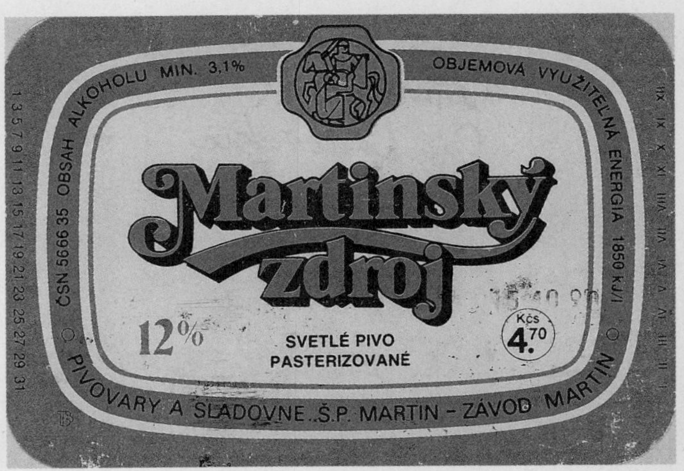

Pivovare Nosovice

Brewery at **Dageb Solna**

RADHOST — golden amber, hop nose, malt palate, smooth and fairly rich, long malt and hop aftertaste.

Praske Pivovare

Brewery in **Zavod Smichov**

SMICHOVSKY STAROPRAMEN — bright tawny-gold, big head, soapy nose, off-dry malt and light hop palate, touch of oxidation in front, long sour hop aftertaste.

Severoceske Pivovare

Brewery in Velke Brezno

BREZNAK SVETLY LEZAK — tawny-gold, slightly hazy, very little head, hop aroma, malt palate is sweetest in the middle, hops show in the finish as an edge, brief aftertaste is hops but not as pronounced as the finish.

Starobrno Brewery

Brewery in Brno, Moravia

STAROBRNO EXPORT LAGER BEER — deep gold, bright hop nose, very large hop flavor with plenty of malt in support, big body, strong hop finish and long hop aftertaste, bold, rich and long.

U Fleku

Brewpub/restaurant in Prague

FLEKOVSKY LEZAK — opaque brown, huge dense head that lasts to the bottom of the mug, slightly sweet dark and caramel malt palate, slightly underhopped, chewy rich flavor throughout, not complex, but rich and satisfying, very drinkable, high extract, low alcohol, very long malt aftertaste, a great deal of unfermented malt in solution and fairly high density (13°).

U SV. Tomase

Brewpub and restaurant in Letenska (Prague)

SPECIAL BRANIK — tawny-gold with a creamy head, well-hopped Hallertau (Zatek) nose, very dry bright and bitter palate that increases at the finish leading into a very long strong dry hop aftertaste, has a nutty quality that makes you feel like you had been eating peanuts with your beer.

TOMASOVSKY LEZAK — deep red-brown, light large bubble short-lived head, scorched malt aroma with hops in behind, pleasant fresh malt palate, low carbonation, long slightly off-sweet refreshing aftertaste with the hops on the sides of the tongue, very chewy and satisfying dark lager.

Urquell Brewery

Brewery in Pilsen

Facilities are shared with the Gambrinus Brewery.

PILSNER URQUELL — bright tawny-gold, good head, appetizing hop aroma, smooth well-balanced malt and hop flavor, refreshing and satisfying, long smooth dry hop aftertaste, excellent classic Pilsener beer. In Czechoslovakia it is called Prazdroj. Freshly bottled, it is almost not distinguishable from the fresh draft except for the thickness of the head, which is very dense on draft.

GAMBRINUS PILSEN — deep gold, appetizing hop nose, bright hop flavor with plenty of malt in support, malt emerges well at the finish and stays to balance a long dry hop aftertaste. Gambrinus Brewery, Pilsen.

WENZEL'S BRÄU — bright gold, roasted malt and hop aroma, palate has an off-dry front, but this quickly becomes big hops, some malt rejoins the hops at the finish, but the long aftertaste is dry hops backed with faintly sour malt. This is a pleasant lovely tasting brew when fresh. Gambrinus Brewery.

DIA PIVO — bright gold, low and short-lived head, sour malt aroma, light body, light malt flavor with noticeable carbonation, some tannin appears in the throat, short dry aftertaste. A low density (8°) beer made for diabetics with 3.5% alcohol. From Západoceske Pivovare Brewery, a Gambrinus affiliate.

SVETOVAR PUVODNI LEZAK — pale amber, thick head, grainy aroma, off-dry grainy palate, hops appear in the finish, light dry hop aftertaste with a nutty quality, 3.1% alcohol. Also from Západoceske Pivovare Brewery.

DENMARK

Ceres Breweries, Ltd.

Brewery in **Aarhus, Horsens**

CERES BEER — gold, faint apple-malt nose, light off-dry malt flavor, brief dry hop aftertaste.

RED ERIC MALT LIQUOR — yellow-gold, aroma of hops and off-dry toffee-malt, hops and toffee palate, good body, lots of character, long dry hop and malt aftertaste.

CERES STRONG ALE — gold, malt nose, very strong malt flavor shows the alcohol as well (7.7%), well hopped in back, very strong and very long, a real mouthful.

FRANCE

Brasserie Duyck

Brewery in **Jenlain**

JENLAIN FRENCH COUNTRY ALE — bright pale amber, fresh malt nose, finely carbonated, bright malt flavor like a delicate barley wine, fairly dry malt throughout, especially in the long aftertaste, very good with food.

LE MADELON FRENCH COUNTRY BEER — deep amber, roasted malt nose with a Kir-like background, winey dry roasted malt flavor, complex, soft and smooth, a bit like a porter but not enough to be named one, few hops, if any.

TRADER JOE'S RESERVE BROWN HOLIDAY ALE 1992 — brilliant amber, sour spicy nose, nutmeg, clove and ginger flavor, but malt still shows, good balance, very nicely done, medium length.

Brasserie Facon

Brewery in **Pont de Briques**

ALE DE GARDE DE SAINT ARNOULD — cloudy gold, fruity melon and malt nose, strong malt flavor, noticeable alcohol, long malt aftertaste.

Brasseries Kronenbourg, S.A.

Brewery in **Strasbourg**

KRONENBOURG 1664 IMPORTED BEER — medium gold, light malt aroma is almost fruity, vinous malt flavor, medium long dry hop aftertaste.

KRONENBOURG 1664 DARK BEER — deep copper color, extremely light malt aroma, malt flavor, light body, dull dry malt aftertaste.

KRONENBOURG 1664 MALT LIQUOR — bright amber-gold, good sour malt aroma, carbonation competes with the malt flavor, heavy body, long smooth malt aftertaste.

TOURTEL DE-ALCOHOLIZED BEER — gold, hop aroma is slightly skunky, grainy hop flavor, light body, short off-dry malt aftertaste.

Brasserie Mattiere du Pêcheur, S.A.

Breweries in **Schiltigheim** and **Strasbourg**

FISCHER BEER — pale gold, pleasant off-dry malt and hop nose, light body, pleasant slightly off-dry malt flavor, aftertaste is drier than the flavor and is still mostly malt, fairly short.

FISCHER ALE — pale gold, pleasant off-dry malt and hop nose is sweeter than above, but the malt flavor is nicely dry with the hops in back, good balance, long dry aftertaste like the flavor.

FISCHER D'ALSACE — bright gold, hop aroma, hop flavor has the malt sliding in from mid-palate on, very good balance, malt finish, good body, long dry malt and hop aftertaste, well-made beer.

FISCHER D'ALSACE BITTER — pale amber, hop nose, fairly bitter hop flavor that extends into a long dry aftertaste.

FISCHER D'ALSACE AMBER — light amber, aroma with plenty of off-dry malt and bright hops, flavor starts out with the malt, hops come in the middle and stay for the finish and long aftertaste, good hefty body, some complexity, a good very drinkable brew.

FISCHER LA BELLE STRASBOURGEOISE — deep gold, grainy malt nose, malt flavor seems to gain strength as it crosses the palate, hops join the malt at the finish, leading into a good long aftertaste with both components in harmony.

FISCHER PILS — pale gold, light malt nose, malt flavor gets hops as it approaches the finish, long fairly dry hop aftertaste.

FISCHER GOLD — gold, off-dry fruity malt aroma, strong vinous malt flavor, long malt aftertaste, heavy body.

36.15 PECHEUR LA BIERE AMOREUSE — bright gold, flowery, fruity, herbal, complex aroma (has added myrrh, ginger, cardamom, ginseng, cola, cinnamon, mango, licorice, myrtle and eleutherococque), fruity herbal flavor, almost cherry-like, good body, medium length, not beer-like.

ADELSHOFFEN BIERE SPECIALE D'ALSACE — deep yellow, off-dry fruity malt aroma with a touch of hops, very complex flavor of fruit and faint hops, a bit wine-like, not dry, long roasted malt aftertaste.

MÜNSTERHOF FRENCH BEER — deep gold, malt nose, light malt and hop flavor, sour malt finish and aftertaste.

ADELSHOFFEN TRADITION — medium deep gold, very pleasant fruity aroma, light body, pleasant slightly burnt fruity malt flavor, little depth, pleasant malt finish and short aftertaste.

ADELSCOTT SMOKED MALT LIQUOR — bright orange, butterscotch and smoky barbecue nose, smoky sweet malt palate, light body, some alcohol noticeable, very pleasant and very drinkable.

ADELSHOFFEN EXPORT — hazy tawny-gold, faint fruity malt nose, strange fruity malt flavor, light body, dull dry malt aftertaste.

ZELE — deep gold, lime aroma, light body, light lime flavor, not beer-like, probably flavored like the Canadian Zélé, light and brief.

Brasserie Schutzenberger, S.A.

Brewery in Schiltigheim

SANT'OR MALT BEVERAGE — very pale bright gold, faint hop nose, vegetal malt flavor, weak body, malt finish and aftertaste like the flavor.

SCHUTZ PILS LUXE BIERE D'ALSACE — tawny-gold, good hop and malt nose, good hop flavor up front, good malt in the middle, aftertaste has an unpleasant overly sour component that is not in the flavor.

SCHLOSS JOSEF ALSATIAN MALT BEVERAGE — gold, stinky hop nose, palate is faintly malty, but is impaired with oxidation.

SCHUTZENBERGER JUBILATOR FRENCH BEER- yellow-gold, good hop nose with off-dry malt in back, palate is mostly sharp bitter hops except for some malt at the very beginning and some off-dry malt in the finish, complex flavor, long dry aftertaste shows both hops and malt.

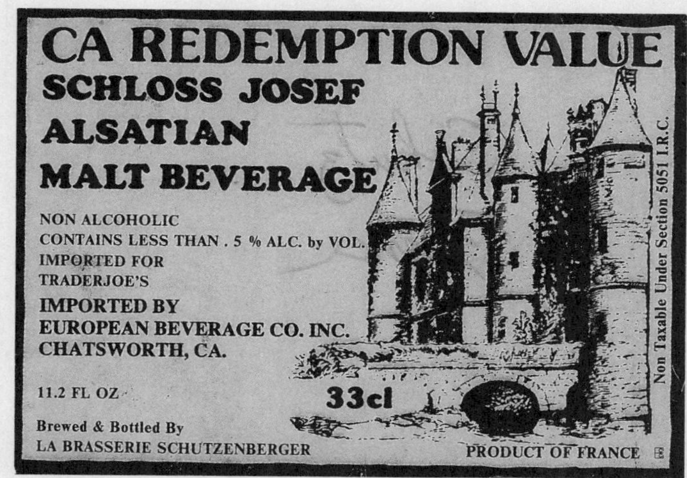

Brasserie de Saint Sylvestre

Brewery in St. Sylvestre

3 MONTS FLANDERS GOLDEN ALE — amber, malt nose with a citrus background, rich complex malt flavor, high alcohol, full bodied, long malt aftertaste.

ST. SYLVESTRE'S CHRISTMAS ALE 1992 — deep amber, concentrated malt aroma, strong flavor of concentrated malt well backed with hops, even and potent, big body, stays constant right through the finish and long aftertaste.

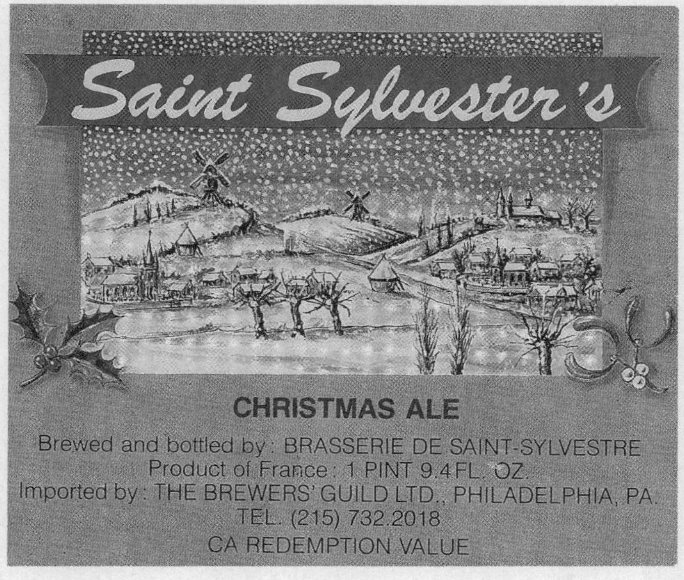

GERMANY

Aachener Burgerbauerei/ Peter Wiertz Gmbh.

Brewery in Aachen

BURGERBRÄU PILS — gold, faint malt and hop aroma, dull malt flavor with some hops in back, dull malt finish, short dry malt aftertaste.

Brauerei Albquell

Brewery-Gasthof in Trochtelfingen

ALBQUELL PILSNER —gold, big hop nose, bright sour hop flavor, dry hop finish, good body, long dry slightly sour hop aftertaste, nicely made classical Pils.

ALBQUELL URTRUNK — hazy gold, hop nose, big sour hop flavor, dry hop finish, good body, long dry hop aftertaste, a tad less sour than the Pils, but very similar and a little more balanced.

ALBQUELL EDELBIER EXPORT — gold, hop nose, big malt and hop flavor, good body, excellent balance, long dry hop aftertaste.

Notes:

Brauerei Aldersbach/ Frhr v. Aretin, K.G.

Brewery in Aldersbach

ALDERSBACHER KLOSTER HELL — gold, malt and hop aroma, very light malt flavor and finish, weak malt aftertaste.

ALDERSBACHER DUNKEL HEFE-WEIZEN — deep amber-brown, nice spicy hop and malt nose, bright fruity-spicy malt flavor, long dry malt aftertaste with the fruit and spice way in back, a tangy, tasty, drinkable beer.

Allgäuer Brauhaus

Brewery in Kempten

ALT KEMPTENER WEISSE DUNKEL — deep cloudy brown, terrific appetizing wheat and barley malt nose, zesty tangy flavor is smooth and drinkable, good body, great character, long long malt aftertaste.

ALLGÄUER BRAUHAUS URTYP EXPORT — gold, faint hop and malt nose, dull malt flavor, dry hop aftertaste, medium length.

ALLGÄUER BRAUHAUS DAS HELLE — gold, very faint hop nose, hop and malt flavor, not in balance, dry hop aftertaste, medium length.

ALLGÄUER BRAUHAUS FÜRSTADT WEIZEN — cloudy gold, big bright spicy nose, creamy, good malt and clove flavor, balanced, the malt softens the spicy nature, long aftertaste like the flavor.

ALLGÄUER BRAUHAUS EDELBRÄU — gold, big malt nose, strong malt flavor, tasty lip-smacking sipping beer, big body, long dry malt aftertaste, excellent balance, excellent beer.

TEUTSCH PILS — gold, malt and light hop nose, flavor is malt first, thence big hops to the finish, long dry hop aftertaste.

Alpirsbacher Klosterbrauerei/ C. Glauner

Brewery at Alpirsbach

ALPIRSBACHER KLOSTER DUNKEL — deep amber-brown, faint malt nose, medium body, very dry malt flavor, no complexity, light brief dry malt aftertaste.

ALPIRSBACHER KLOSTER HEFE WEIZEN — hazy tawny-gold, off-dry wheaty malt aroma, off-dry wheat and barley malt flavor, no spicy tang, very long aftertaste like the flavor but a bit drier, fresh and clean in the mouth, very pleasant and refreshing.

ALPIRSBACHER KLOSTER KRISTALLKLAR WEIZEN — bright gold, faint slightly sweet malt aroma that is very clean, full body, rich malt flavor, well-balanced, refreshing, long off-dry fairly delicate aftertaste.

ALPIRSBACHER KLOSTER SPEZIAL — bright tawny-gold, slightly sweet hop aroma, palate is off-dry malt up front, dry in the middle with a faint vegetal nature, finishes with both hops and malt leading into a long dry hop aftertaste with a faint sour vegetal malt background.

ALPIRSBACHER KLOSTER PILS — bright tawny-gold, creamy head, faintly off-dry malt aroma with a hop backing, slightly sour malt front palate, very dry middle, sour malt and dry hop aftertaste.

Notes:

Brauhaus Altenmünster-Weissenbrunn

Brewery in Altenmünster

ALTENMÜNSTER BRAUER BEER — deep gold, complex hop aroma, big hop flavor, creamy texture, slightly sour hop finish and aftertaste, pretty good except that it could use a bit more malt, especially in the finish.

ALTENMÜNSTER MAI-BOCK — beautiful deep gold, light toasted malt nose, pleasant big off-dry toasted malt flavor, rich and delicious, very smooth, big body, some alcohol noticeable, really feels good while it is in your mouth, short dry malt aftertaste.

Privatbrauerei Hellbräu Altöttinger

Brewery in Altötting

ALTÖTTINGER FEIN HERB HELL-BRÄU — gold , malt aroma, pleasant malty flavor, lightly hopped, dry malt and light hop aftertaste.

ALTÖTTINGER BAYRISCH DUNKEL — deep brown, big off-dry grainy malt nose, rich malt flavor is also grainy, big body, good balance, delicious, off-dry malt finish, long dry malt aftertaste, good complexity, and very drinkable, excellent dark pils.

Klosterbrauerei Andechs

Kloster Brewery in Erling-Andechs

ANDECHS SPEZIAL HELL — pale gold, complex off-dry malt and hop aroma, bright complex zesty very malty flavor, full bodied, rich, clean malt finish and fairly long aftertaste.

ANDECHS BERGBOCK HELL — brilliant deep gold, lovely nose is mostly hops but is well-backed with malt, big malt and hop flavor, really smooth, creamy, vinous, very long malt aftertaste.

ANDECHS DOPPELBOCK DUNKEL — deep amber-brown, extremely rich malt nose is very complex with all kinds of earthy notes, a very complex flavor that seems to flip back and forth from dry to off-dry, again with all kinds of flavors weaving in and out, some would say it had an earthiness (I like the word funky). Very long dry malt aftertaste. I believe this to be my favorite beer in all the world.

ANDECHS EXPORT DUNKEL — deep amber-brown, lovely toasted malt nose, good dry toasted malt flavor, complex with lots of underlying flavors like fruit, spices, aromatics, etc., medium body, dry malt finish, long lightly burnt malt aftertaste.

Arcobräu, Grafliches Brauhaus

Brewery in Moos

ARCOBRÄU MOOSER HELL — brilliant clear gold, big hop nose, balanced hop and malt flavor, good body, dry malt finish and aftertaste.

ARCOBRÄU PILSENER — pale gold, clean hop nose, big hop flavor in front, malt in middle, dry hop finish, long dry hop aftertaste, good body, fairly complex, good balance.

ARCOBRÄU URWEISSE — hazy gold, bright hop nose, big spicy clove, hop and malt flavor, very smooth, good body, light spicy finish, long spicy malt aftertaste.

GRAF ARCO GRAFEN HELL — gold, lovely malt and hop nose, zesty fresh flavor, big malt finish, long malt aftertaste with plenty of good hop support. Grafliches Brauereien Arco, Adldorf.

COUNT ARCO'S BAVARIAN WEISSBIER WITH YEAST — gold, spicy lactic nose, pleasant spicy flavor with off-dry wheat in back, good mouth feel, short dry spicy malt aftertaste.

COUNT ARCO'S BAVARIAN FESTBIER — gold, beautiful fresh rising malt aroma, fresh creamy medium dry malt flavor, good body, very drinkable, long medium dry lightly toasted malt aftertaste.

Augusta-Bräu

Brewery in Augsburg

BAYERISCH HELL VOLLBIER — deep gold, light aroma is mostly hops with faint malt in back, light malt and hop flavor, medium body, medium to short light dry malt and hop aftertaste.

Augustiner Brauerei, A.G.

Brewery in Munich

AUGUSTINER BRAÜ MUNICH EXPORT LIGHT BEER — beautiful bright gold, clean but very light aroma, slightly off-dry malt flavor with delicate hop background, clean light malt and hop finish, long mild dry hop aftertaste, very smooth and tasty.

AUGUSTINER BRAÜ MUNICH MAXIMATOR DARK EXPORT BEER — pale brown with copper tones, strong malt and hop nose, rich complex malt flavor with plenty of zest and character, slightly bitter and dry hop finish and aftertaste, a lovely double bock with lots of gusto.

AUGUSTINER BRÄU MÜNCHEN OKTOBERFEST BIER — bright gold, slightly off-dry malt aroma, very well-balanced malt and hop flavor, big body, alcohol seems high, very long slightly sour hop aftertaste, smooth and flavorful beer with good balance.

AUGUSTINER BRÄU EDELSTOFF EXPORT — pale gold, aroma and flavor like a packaged dry chicken noodle soup, had to be a bad bottle.

Schlossbrauerei Autenried

Brewery at Autenried

AUTENRIEDER WEIZEN — hazy gold, big thick head, clean malt aroma, smooth malt flavor, very refreshing, faint trace of cloves is way in back of nose and palate, good body, good balance, long dry malt aftertaste.

AUTENRIEDER PILSNER — gold, fragrant hop nose, good hop flavor, long dry hop aftertaste has a bit of sourness at the end.

AUTENRIEDER URTYP HELL — deep gold, light malt aroma, malt flavor, hops in back, dry malt aftertaste.

AUTENRIEDER URTYP DUNKEL — brown, off vegetal (garbage) nose, taste to match the bad aroma, dull dry malt aftertaste.

Brauerei Bavaria-St. Pauli

Brewery in Hamburg

ASTRA EXCLUSIVE — bright gold, dry faintly toasted malt nose, lightly sour and bitter hop flavor, one dimensional (hops) taste, short dry hop aftertaste.

GRENZQUELL GERMAN DARK PILSNER — deep copper, good hop and roasted malt aroma and flavor, thin body, some molasses in the finish, virtually no aftertaste.

GRENZQUELL GERMAN PILSENER — gold, good hop nose, bright well-hopped flavor well-backed with malt, good body, lots of hop character, long dry hop aftertaste, a big tasty brew.

JEVER PILSENER — bright tawny-gold, aroma is more malt than hops, big body, flavor starts out malt but gradually turns to hops, building bitterness as it goes until it finishes quite bitter, lingering bitter hop aftertaste.

JEVER MAIBOCK — deep amber, beautiful hop nose, big malt flavor but could use some hops for better balance, big body, but very short, there's just malt and alcohol on the palate and in this case the effect falls short.

ASTRA ALE — pale amber, good malt nose, pleasant malt flavor, but is too sweet and it becomes cloying after a while, long too sweet malt aftertaste.

ASTRA MEISTER BOCK — medium gold, good hop and malt aroma, light body, light malt flavor, faint molasses aftertaste has little length.

Brauerei Bayer

Brewpub in Viereth

BAYER MÄRZEN — deep amber-brown, strong malt nose with a fruity character, big fruity-malt flavor, long aftertaste like the flavor, would be better if drier as the fruit is sort of candy-like.

Bayerische Staatsbrauerei Weihenstephan

Brewery, school and yeast manufacturing facility in Freising

VITUS WEIZENBOCK — pale amber, pleasant malt-wheat nose, faint trace of lactic spice, good flavor much like the aroma with a hint of sweetness, balanced, complex, pleasant, refreshing, medium long aftertaste like the flavor, but drier.

WEIHENSTEPHAN KORBINIAN DUNKLES STARKBIER — amber-brown, malt nose, good body, rich malt flavor, dry hop finish, very good balance, long dry hop aftertaste, very satisfying.

WEIHENSTEPHAN WEIZENBIER KRISTALL EXPORT — bright gold, big head, fresh grainy wheat and barley malt aroma, quite fresh and zesty, very little acid in the malt flavor but enough for character, long malt aftertaste, bright, pleasant, refreshing, and very drinkable. Presently in U.S., this brew is labelled **WEIHENSTEPHAN WEIZENBIER CRYSTAL CLEAR.**

WEIHENSTEPHAN HEFE-WEISSBIER — hazy gold, lactic spicy clove nose, flavorful zesty clove flavor, spice strong in front, eases off in mid-palate enough for smooth slightly off-dry malt to rise up, finish and aftertaste are off-dry malt, with the spicy cloves coming again very late in the long aftertaste.

STEPHANSQUELL HELLES STARKBIER — medium deep gold, very rich malt aroma, huge malty flavor (like malted milk powder), a bit wine-like but has a good balance, long dry malt aftertaste. In the U.S., the brew is called WEIHENSTEPHAN ORIGINAL.

Privatbrauerei Beck

Brewery in Trabelsdorf

BECK UNSER DUNKLES — brown, toasted malt nose, light toasted malt flavor, medium body, dry toasted malt finish and aftertaste, not long.

Privatbrauerei Becker

Brewery in St. Ingbert

BECKER'S JUBILÄUMSBOCK — deep brown, big malt nose and taste, nice balance, has chocolate character, fairly complex, good body, very long malt aftertaste, nice drinkable brew.

Hofbrauhaus Berchtesgaden

Brewery in Berchtesgaden

BERCHTESGADENER BIER — gold, pleasant malt and hop nose, big flavorful dry malt and hop taste, good body and balance, long dry hop and malt aftertaste.

BERCHTESGADENER WEIZEN — hazy gold, nice clean spicy-fruity malt nose, tangy zesty clove and malt palate, long clean satisfying aftertaste like the flavor, feels good in your mouth, very tasty and refreshing.

Notes:

Binding Brauerei, A.G.

Brewery in Frankfurt

STEINHAUSER BEER — bright gold, light hop nose with good malt support, light body, smooth hop flavor and finish, good balance, long dry hop aftertaste.

RÖMER PILS — yellow-gold, sweet hop nose, brief off-dry malt flavor, light body, light medium dry malt aftertaste with hops in back.

CLAUSTHALER HERBFRISCHES SCHANKBIER — deep gold, grainy hop aroma, high carbonation, grainy hop and CO_2 flavor, long dry hop aftertaste. Version tasted in Europe.

CLAUSTHALER BIER — bright gold, fragrant honeyed malt aroma, off-dry malt palate, long off-dry malt aftertaste goes bitter at the end. Export version to the U.S.

CAROLUS DER STARKE DOPPELBOCK — very deep ruby-brown color, big rich sweet malt aroma with an unusual fruit-like component, big body, huge powerful dry malt flavor, complex, high alcohol, medium long dry malt aftertaste, very drinkable brew.

BINDING EXPORT — tawny-gold, sweaty sock and malt nose, tasty dry malt flavor shows none of the offishness of the aroma, slightly sour hop and malt aftertaste, good flavor but the nose is a spoiler.

Brauerei Bischofshof

Brewery in Regensburg

BISCHOFSHOF URHELL — gold, hop nose, pleasant bright hop flavor, good body, dry hop finish and long dry hop aftertaste.

BISCHOFSHOF HEFE-WEISSBIER HELL — hazy gold, big spicy clove and malt aroma, creamy and refreshing, good body, spicy malt finish, long aftertaste is dry malt.

Bräuwastl

Brewery in Weilheim

BRÄUWASTL KRISTALLWEIZEN — slightly hazy amber, big head, complex malt aroma was relatively dry, barley malt and wheat about 50-50 on the palate, nice balance, very smooth, brief malt aftertaste, but a good tasting brew.

Privatbrauerei Ambros Brütting

Brewery in Staffelstein

HOFLIEFERANT EXPORT EXQUISIT — tawny-gold, big toasted malt nose and flavor, dry malt finish, long dry malt and hop aftertaste, good body and good balance.

HOFLIEFERANT BAYRISCH HELL — gold, malt nose, high carbonation, flavor has only light malt and hops, dull malt finish, faint hops join the malt in the brief aftertaste.

HOFLIEFERANT BOCK BIER — amber-gold, big rich hop and toasted malt nose, huge rich roasted malt flavor, long rich aftertaste is a continuation of the flavor, high alcohol(7%) is not noticeable in the rich malt flavor, a finely balanced excellent bock.

Radbrauerei Gebr. Bucher

Brewery in Günzburg

GÜNZBURGER HEFE-WEIZEN — hazy gold, faint spicy nose, good well-spiced clove and malt flavor, high carbonation, flavor is on the light side and the carbonation interferes, smooth, light to medium body, light brief spicy aftertaste.

Notes:

Burger & Engelbrau A.G.

Brewery in Memmingen

BURGER & ENGELBRAU VOLLBIER HELL — pale gold, rich malt nose, beautifully balanced smooth flavor, more malt than hops, quite dry, a bit light, but fairly long and very drinkable.

Bürgerliches Brauhaus A.G.

Brewery in Ingolstadt

HERRN BRÄU AROMATOR DOPPELBOCK — pale brown, sour malt aroma and flavor, big body, long malt aftertaste is drier and less sour than the flavor.

Burgerbräu Bamberg

Brewery in Bamberg

SIMPATICO BEER — bright gold, faint off-dry hop aroma that sours as it goes, unbalanced hop palate, brief dry hop aftertaste.

BÜRGERBRÄU BAMBERG PILS — pale gold, faintly stinky hop nose at first, changed to apple and hop, disorganized flavor with the hops clashing with the malt, flat tasting in the middle, bitter finish, dull slightly sour aftertaste.

Brauerei Cluss A.G.

Brewery in Heilbronn

CLUSS BOCK DUNKEL — brilliant copper, big malt Ovaltine nose, very complex, a great nose, rich malt flavor but lighter than promised by the aroma, light to medium body, long dry light malt aftertaste.

CLUSS PILSENER — gold, malt nose, palate is mostly malt but there is high carbonation as well and some hops in back, there is plenty of both hops and malt at the finish leading into a long dry hop aftertaste.

CLUSS RATSHOF PILS — gold, hop and malt nose, pleasant light dry hop and malt flavor, hop finish, long dry hop aftertaste, very pleasant.

CLUSS EXPORT — gold, faint malt nose, fairly big malt flavor with plenty of hops in support, malt dominates the flavor especially as it crosses the palate, then the hops are alone in the fairly long aftertaste.

CLUSS KELLER PILS — hazy gold, big nose is mostly hops with malt in back, flavor and aftertaste are like the nose without the malt and hops ever coming together.

DUTTENBERGER ENGELBRÄU URTYP — gold, malt and hop aroma, big flavor is mostly malt, touch of soapiness, some hops appear in the finish, medium long dry hop aftertaste.

Dachsbräu

Brewery in Weilheim

DACHS WEIZEN — hazy brown, pleasant spicy malt aroma and flavor, long dry malt and spice aftertaste.

Weizenbrauerei Deggendorf

Brewery in Deggendorf

BAYER WEIZEN — hazy amber, big spicy-fruity malt nose and flavor, dry malt finish, fruit and spice return for the long aftertaste, good tasting brew.

Privatbrauerei Diebel

Brewery in Issum/Wiederrhein

DIEBEL'S ALT — brown, tangy ale-like nose, smooth zesty malt flavor with good hops in back, dry malt finish and long dry malt aftertaste, there is a spicy ale-like tang in the background all the way across the palate and through the aftertaste as well.

Dillinger Brauhaus, Gmbh./Brauerei Convikt

Brewery in Dillingen am Donau

CONVIKT MEISTER-SCHUTZ — gold, light malt nose, malt flavor, medium to short dry malt aftertaste, nice malt brew but lacks zest.

CONVIKT EGAUER ZWICK'L DUNKLES KELLERBIER — bright copper-amber, light roasted malt nose, faintly sweet and grainy malt flavor, quite pleasant, finely carbonated, good balance, medium body, finishes even better than it starts with a good long medium dry roasted malt aftertaste.

Dinkelacker Wülle, A.G.

Brewery in Stuttgart

DINKELACKER PRIVAT LIGHT BEER — gold, complex malt and hop aroma, great heft and plenty of zest, good body, plenty of character, good bright hop flavor, well-balanced, long dry hop aftertaste.

DINKELACKER BLACK FOREST LIGHT BEER — cloudy gold, blueberry malt aroma, off-dry malt flavor, dank finish and aftertaste.

DINKELACKER BOCK C.D. EXTRA — dark brown, big malt aroma and flavor, big body, rich malt flavor, long dry malt aftertaste.

DINKELACKER DARK IMPORT PRIVAT — brown, big malt nose, rich malt flavor with a yeasty nature, sour malt finish, long dry malt aftertaste, also seen labelled as DINKELACKER DARK C.D. EXTRA.

DINKELACKER WEIZENKRONE — yellow, huge head, pleasant light malt aroma, highly carbonated, sour malt finish, dry malt aftertaste.

DINKELACKER DARK BREW — amber-brown, big roasted malt nose and flavor, sour malt finish, long dry malt and hop aftertaste, good balance, drinkable.

PRO NON-ALCOHOLIC BEER — bright gold, hops first in the aroma then grainy malt, bright hop and off-dry malt flavor, slightly sour malt aftertaste.

DINKELACKER CD PILS — brilliant gold, faintly sweet hop nose, a little malty sweetness starts the flavor, but it is soon dry hops from mid-palate on, dry hop finish and aftertaste.

DINKELACKER WEIHNACHTSBIER SPEZIAL — deep gold, very nice hop and toasted malt nose, beautifully balanced malt and hop flavor, good body, long malt aftertaste ends dry hops very late, a delicious satisfying beer.

DINKELACKER VOLKSFESTBIER — brilliant gold, big dense head, huge hop nose, good body, big appetizing malt and hop flavor, clean and dry, long dry hop aftertaste, this seems to be available only at the Bad Canstatter Volksfest near Stuttgart.

DINKELACKER OKTOBERFEST PREMIUM GERMAN BEER — gold, stinky chemical aroma, dry metallic taste, out of balance, sour metallic aftertaste, all samples found were off.

SANWALD WEIZEN DUNKEL HEFETRUB — tawny-amber, big head, clean wheaty-malt nose, bright clean flavor is mostly wheat and malt with just a touch of lactic character, taste is just a little bit sweet, good balance between the sweetness and the lactic bite, long dry aftertaste.

SANWALD WEIZEN KRONE KRISTALLKLAR — bright gold, big head, faint wheaty-malt nose is on the sweet side, light flavor is also slightly sweet like the nose, acid is way in back, almost unnoticeable, light body, long off-dry malt aftertaste with lactic spice appearing at the end, drinkable but not much offered.

SANWALD HEFE WEISSE — bright gold, huge head, faint fruity-tart nose, light dry malt flavor with very little acidic tang, pleasant but brief.

SANWALD WEIZEN PERLSTARK — bright gold, clean weizen (wheat-malt-lactic) nose, not much lactic spice, smooth, well-balanced, slightly sour aftertaste.

Notes:

Brauerei Distelhäuser

Brewery in Distelhausen

DISTELHÄUSER PREMIUM PILS — gold, hop nose and flavor, long dry hop aftertaste, good body, but just hops.

DISTELHÄUSER EXPORT — gold, malt nose and flavor, good body, dry hop finish, long dry hop aftertaste.

DISTELHÄUSER MÄRZEN — gold, malt nose, strong malt flavor, good balance, good body, long dry hop and malt aftertaste.

Dortmunder Union Schultheiss

Brewing Conglomerate with breweries in Dortmund and Berlin. Includes Dortmunder Union Brauerei A.G., *Dortmunder Ritterbrauerei,* A.G., *and The Schultheiss Brauerei,* A.G.

DORTMUNDER UNION SIEGEL PILS — pale yellow-gold, good sour malt aroma with hops in back, fine malt and hop flavor, a very good pilsener-style beer, long dry hop aftertaste.

DORTMUNDER UNION PILSENER — tawny-gold, toasted malt aroma, pleasant toasted malt flavor, good balance, light body, a little sour malt in back but it doesn't mar the taste, toasted malt carries through the palate into the finish and aftertaste, light and not complex.

BERLINER WEISS SCHULTHEISS — pale cloudy white, foamy, yeasty nose and flavor, medium long semi-dry yeasty-malt aftertaste.

BERLINER UR-BOCK — hazy deep amber-gold, toasted malt nose and flavor, somewhat uninteresting dry malt aftertaste, lacks zest.

GERMANIA PREMIUM MALT BEVERAGE — yellow-gold,off-dry grainy malt nose, grainy palate is off-dry in front, dry in the middle, dry malt aftertaste has little duration, tastes like a light beer, which is good for a non-alcoholic brew.

DORTMUNDER UNION BEER — deep bright gold, toasted malt aroma and flavor, medium body, good flavor but not enough of it, fairly short dry malt aftertaste, lacks complexity and depth.

DORTMUNDER UNION MALT LIQUOR — bright tawny-gold, lovely rich roasted malt aroma, big malt flavor is especially good up front on the palate, finish is sour hops and this becomes the aftertaste, good length.

DORTMUNDER UNION SPECIAL — pale gold, intense and complex malt aroma, good malt flavor is strongly accented with hops, balanced, straightforward well-hopped beer, long dry hop aftertaste, an excellent pilsener.

DORTMUNDER UNION ORIGINAL — gold, hop nose, flavor starts out briefly as off-dry malt, then turns bitter hops with a metallic background, long aftertaste like the flavor.

DORTMUNDER UNION LIGHT BEER — bright gold, big hop nose, light body, flavor is carbonation and faintly sour malt, brief light dry aftertaste.

DORTMUNDER UNION DARK BEER — medium deep amber-brown, outstanding rich malt and hop aroma, medium body, finely carbonated, rich dark malt flavor, hops come in at the finish, pleasant dry malt and hop aftertaste, an excellent dark pilsener that goes very well with salamis and other cold wursts.

DORTMUNDER RITTER BRÄU LIGHT BEER — deep yellow, big hop and malt nose, huge hop flavor, big body, long sharp and dry hop aftertaste, a robust well-hopped brew.

DORTMUNDER RITTER PILS — gold, big hop nose, big hop flavor has a sour component in back, plenty of malt in back, good body, finishes dry hops without the bitterness, long dry hop aftertaste, a hearty brew, a good pils.

DORTMUNDER RITTER BRÄU BOCK — deep gold, beautiful toasted malt and hop aroma, very complex, delicious, rich toasted malt flavor, excellent balance, a blockbuster, long long rich malt and hop aftertaste.

DORTMUNDER RITTER EXPORT — deep gold, malt and hop nose, vegetal malt flavor, short dry malt aftertaste has a sourness in back.

DORTMUNDER RITTER DARK — medium deep brown, heavy malt nose with complex vegetal components (like celery seed and sage), hops join in for the flavor but the malt holds dominance and is somewhat sour, the sourness does get in the way, long dry and slightly sour malt aftertaste.

GASTHAUS SPECIAL —medium gold, creamy texture, pleasant mild hop nose, good body, bright hop flavor, very short dry hop aftertaste.

DORTMUNDER WESTFÄLIA SPECIAL — gold, faint malt and hop nose, sour malt flavor, hops seem out-of-balance, sharp hop finish and aftertaste.

DORTMUNDER WESTFÄLIA EXPORT BEER — bright pale gold, light hop nose, off-dry malt flavor, bitter hop finish and aftertaste.

BRINKHOFF'S NO. 1 — bright gold, extremely fresh hop aroma, palate is slightly bitter hops but there is enough malt for good balance, good body, very smooth, long malt aftertaste.

Brauerei Düll

Brewery-Gasthof in Gnodstadt

DÜLL BOCK — golden amber, very complex malt and hop nose, wonderfully appetizing, big strong malt flavor, big hops as well, high alcohol (6.8%), long and strong aftertaste like the flavor.

DÜLL PILS — gold, malt nose, malt flavor starts off-dry, finishes dry leading into a dry malt aftertaste, some hop sourness at the very end.

DÜLL MÄRZEN — gold, malt nose, dry malt flavor, long dry malt aftertaste has some tones of vegetable, herbs, and honey.

Ebelsbacher Klosterbräu

Brewery in Ebelsbach

EBELSBACHER KLOSTERBRÄU KLOSTER-HELL — deep gold, hop nose, plenty of malt support, big malt flavor, dry malt and hop aftertaste.

EBELSBACHER KLOSTERBRÄU KLOSTER-PILS — deep gold, hop nose, good hop and malt flavor, a bright taste, good body and balance, long dry hop and malt aftertaste, a likeable brew and easy to drink.

Notes:

Privaterbrauereigasthof Eck

Brewery Gasthof in **Böbrach-Eck**

ECKER BRÄU WILDERER DUNKEL — brown, light roasted malt nose, off-dry malt front palate, dry malt middle and finish, good body, good balance, long dry malt aftertaste, smooth, drinkable, and has zest.

ECKER BRÄU EDEL PILS — deep gold, fragrant hop aroma, complex rich hop and malt flavor, good body, complex dry hop and malt finish and aftertaste, long and very good, an excellent brew.

ECKER BRÄU FAHNDERL-WEISSE HEFE-WEISSBIER — clear gold, lovely light clove aroma, light clove and malt flavor, balanced, smooth, clean, dry malt finish and aftertaste.

ECKER BRÄU VOLLBIER HELL — brilliant gold, roasted caramel malt nose, smooth light roasted malt flavor, medium to long dry malt aftertaste, very likeable beer.

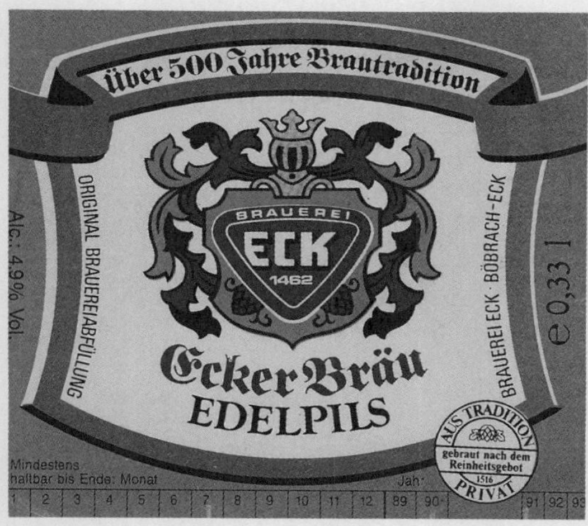

Privatbrauerei Eder

Brewery in **Grossostheim**

EDER PILS — hazy yellow, light hop nose, big hop flavor up front, sour malt in back, fair balance, long dry hop aftertaste.

BAVARIA BAYERISCH WEIZEN — gold, lactic spicy malt nose, clean wheat taste with only the faintest lactic spice, clean wheat and malt finish and aftertaste.

EDER PRIVAT EXPORT —hazy gold, grainy molasses nose, big body, big malt flavor, long and rich, ends dry malt.

EDER DOPPELBOCK DUNKEL — deep ruby-brown, big toasted malt nose, big creamy rich malt flavor, finely carbonated, huge body, very long and very satisfying.

BAVARIA DUNKLER STARKBIER — deep amber, lovely toasted malt nose, big malt flavor, rich and delicious, a heavy malt beer with lots of alcohol, long malt aftertaste continues to show the alcohol.

BAVARIA BAYERISCH MÄRZEN DUNKEL — deep amber-gold, lovely malt nose, big dry roasted malt flavor, very drinkable, dry malt aftertaste has a caramel nature, but is quite dry.

Privatbrauerei Ehnle

Brewery in **Lauterbach**

LAUTERBACHER HEFEWEIZEN — hazy gold, faint complex nose includes pine and cloves, very light spicy clove flavor, finish and aftertaste, medium to light body, pleasant and refreshing but brief.

LAUTERBACHER SCHLANKE WEISSE — hazy gold, faint spicy aroma, light spicy clove flavor, very light body, brief light spicy malt aftertaste.

LAUTERBACH BROTZEITBIER — deep gold, big hop and roasted malt nose, delicious flavor like the aroma, very good balance, good body, very drinkable tasty brew, an excellent beer for food or just plain sipping.

LAUTERBACHER URHELL — gold, stinky malt nose, very dry malt palate, long dry sour hop and malt aftertaste.

Eichbaum Brauerei, AG.

Brewery in **Mannheim**

EICHBAUM FESTBIER — pale amber, faint malt and hop nose, faintly sweet malt palate, some hops arrive for the finish, slightly sour and bitter long hop aftertaste.

EICHBAUM APOSTULATOR — brilliant pale ruby-brown, big toasted malt nose has a brief puff of cherry at the beginning, big complex fruity malt flavor, long malt aftertaste seems a bit smoky, a real lip smacking brew.

EICHBAUM EXPORT ALTGOLD — bright gold, good malt and hop aroma and flavor, fine balance, smooth and mellow, medium body, medium long aftertaste like the flavor.

EICHBAUM PILSENER EICHKRONE — bright pale gold, good well-hopped aroma, bright hop flavor, long complex aftertaste with both hops and malt.

EICHBAUM MAIBOCK — pale amber-gold, big toasted malt aroma, sense of alcohol as well (6.6%), rich malt flavor, great balance with the hops, good body, long off-dry malt and hop aftertaste.

EICHBAUM KRISTALL WEIZEN — bright gold, spicy lactic nose, fresh clove taste, clean and refreshing, medium length, a bit on the weak side.

EICHBAUM HEFE WEIZEN — cloudy yellow-gold, slightly yeasty and spicy nose, complex flavor has some of the yeast, fairly smooth, definitely mellow, good carbonation level to give it balance, fairly long.

EICHBAUM DUNKLES WEIZEN — hazy amber, light lactic-spice nose, light malt and spice flavor, light body, pleasant and drinkable, finishes quite well and has a long malt and clove aftertaste.

Einbecker Brauhaus, A.G.

Brewery in **Einbeck**

EINBECKER UR-BOCK STARKBIER — amber-gold, sour hop nose, pleasant hop palate up front, sour hop finish that goes into a long sour hop aftertaste.

EINBECKER UR-BOCK — pale amber-gold, roasted malt and hop aroma, pleasant malt and hop flavor has licorice and caramel in back, big body, a pervasive saltiness comes in at the finish and stays through the aftertaste and is detrimental to the flavors.

EINBECKER MAI-UR-BOCK — amber, mild complex malt aroma, big complex malt and hop flavor, noticeable alcohol (6.5%), long dry malt and hop aftertaste, big body.

Engel Brauerei

Brewery at **Schwäbische Gmund**

TYROLIAN BRÄU BEER — bright gold, good malt and hop nose, malt and hop flavor up front, goes to slightly sweet malt in mid-palate, finishes dry malt, long dry malt and hop aftertaste.

ST. BERNARD BRÄU BEER — bright gold, light malt aroma with faint hops, balanced malt and hop flavor, long dry hop aftertaste.

ANGEL BREW BEER — gold, big toasted malt aroma, rich malt and hop flavor, really feels good in your mouth, big body, long dry hop aftertaste has good malt support, a delicious and beautiful beer.

TROMPE LA MORT DOUBLEBOCK — deep gold with an amber tinge, rich malt aroma, very rich malt flavor, big body, huge, very strong and very long dry malt aftertaste.

BIERE DES DRUIDES — hazy yellow, toasted malt nose and flavor, malt finish and aftertaste, good while it is in your mouth, but it quits as soon as you swallow it.

Landbrauerei Ludwig Erl

Brewery in **Geiselhöring**

ERL-HELL HELLES EXPORT BIER — gold, big somewhat stinky hop nose, big hop flavor, good body, sour hop and off-dry malt aftertaste, poorly balanced.

Privatbrauerei Eschenbacher-Wagner Bräu

Brewery in **Eschenbach**

ESCHENBACHER EDEL MÄRZEN — hazy amber, roasted malt and dry hop aroma, complex palate exactly like the nose, excellent balance, very drinkable, full bodied and full flavored, long and satisfying.

Klosterbrauerei Ettal Gmbh.

Monastery brewery at Ettal

ETTALER KLOSTER DUNKEL — deep tawny-amber, light malt aroma, flavor is mostly malt except for a good hop finish, some complexity, good balance, long dry malt and hop aftertaste, very drinkable brew.

ETTALER CURATOR DUNKLER DOPPELBOCK — deep rosy-amber, rich off-dry malt nose (almost sweet) and flavor, good body, high alcohol, rich long slightly sour malt aftertaste.

ETTALER KLOSTER WEISSBIER — hazy gold, faint malt nose, delicate refreshing flavor of wheat, malt, and cloves, very good up front, softens a bit at the middle, but stays good, fairly long aftertaste like the flavor.

ETTALER KLOSTER WEISSBIER DUNKEL — medium deep amber, faint, slightly spiced wheat beer nose, light clove and malt flavor, light body, spicy finish, fairly long aftertaste like the flavor but quite light.

Ettl Bräu

Brewery in Teisnach

ETTL-HELL — gold, malt nose and flavor, somewhat flabby, medium long malt aftertaste, malt all the way through.

Privatbrauerei Fässla

Brewpub in Bamberg

FÄSSLA GOLD PILS — gold, very nice appetizing hop nose, plenty of malt in back, big malt and hop flavor, dry and delicious, big bodied, long dry hop aftertaste still has plenty of malt in support for good balance, good brew.

FÄSSLA HELL LAGER BIER — pale amber, light malt nose and flavor, medium body, medium long dry hop aftertaste.

ECHTES BAMBERGER ZWERGLA — brown, roasted malt nose, strong heavily roasted malt flavor, good body, extremely long roasted malt aftertaste (strongest flavored aftertaste I've experienced), fairly pleasant despite its almost overwhelming strength across the palate.

Notes:

Privatbrauerei Felsenkeller

Brewery in Beerfelden

MÜMLINGTHALER SCHANKBIER — pale bright gold, dank fruity nose, dry fruity malt taste, some sourness in the finish, long dry aftertaste.

BEERFELDER FELSENBOCK — amber, light malt nose has a chemical-like component, malt flavor is tasty but lacks zest, medium body, medium length malt aftertaste.

Felsenkeller Brauerei

Brewery in Monschau

ZWICKELBIER HEFETRÜB-DUNKEL — hazy amber, pleasant malt aroma, very dry malt flavor, light body, short dry malt aftertaste.

Privatbrauerei Frank

Brewery in Neunburg

NEUNBURGER WEIZEN HEFETRÜB — hazy gold, lightly spiced malt aroma, good bright spicy malt flavor, finish, and light aftertaste.

Notes:

Franken Brauerei

Brewery in Mitwitz

FRANKEN BRÄU PILSENER PREMIUM — gold, big hop nose and flavor, plenty of malt in support, very big body, solid flavor, very well-balanced, big long malt and hop aftertaste.

FRANKEN BRÄU KELLER GOLD DUNKEL — brown, rich roast malt aroma and flavor, no harshness, very smooth, good body and balance, long dry roasted malt aftertaste, a delicious brew.

FRANKEN BRÄU FEST BIER — gold, good hop and malt aroma, very appetizing nose, big flavor has hops but is mostly malt, very fine balance, rich tasting, good body, dry hop finish, long dry aftertaste has plenty of both hops and malt.

Brauerei Franz

Brewery in Rastatt

TURKENLOUIS BOCKBIER — pale amber, rich malt nose, big rich malt flavor, very full-bodied, some hops but mostly malt, very satisfying, filling brew, very long malt aftertaste.

Notes:

Brauerei Fuch

Brewery in **Windesheim**

FUCH'S FEST BOCK — amber, toasted malt nose, palate to match, medium body, very long toasted malt aftertaste, good balance between the malt and the hops.

Fürstlich Fürstenbergische Brauerei, K.G.

Brewery in **Donauschingen**

FÜRSTENBERG PILSENER — bright gold, malt aroma with hops in back, big hop flavor, nicely balanced, hops ease off a bit at the finish and the long aftertaste is smooth light dry hops, a nicely-made very serviceable clean tasting pilsener.

FÜRSTENBERG IMPORTED GERMAN BEER — deep bright gold, smooth hop aroma with a little roasted malt in back, palate is mostly malt but there is good hop support, very good balance, complex and interesting, long dry hop aftertaste.

Brauhaus Füssen

Brewery in **Füssen**

FÜSSENER EDEL PILS — brilliant deep gold, light hop nose, bright crisp hop flavor, malt finish, long pleasing aftertaste, well-balanced.

FÜSSENER FEST BOCK — medium deep brown color, malt nose and very rich malt flavor, big body, smooth, long rich malt aftertaste, very delicious and alcoholic (7.25%)

FÜSSENER EXPORT — tawny-gold, light malt and hop aroma, palate has plenty of hops in front, gets more malty from middle on, good balance, good body, long malt aftertaste, good but lacks the crispness of the Pils.

Notes:

Privatbrauerei Gambrinus Nagold

Brewery in **Hamburg**

BÖLK STOFF — gold, tangy hop and malt aroma, strong malt and big bright hop flavor, zesty and mouth-filling, complex and strong, very long dry hop and malt aftertaste, good strong sipping beer that lasts and lasts.

Brauerei Gampert.

Brewery in **Weissenbrunn/Kronach**

GAMPERTBRÄU FÖRSTER PILS — gold, unusual complex malt and carbonation nose, hop and off-dry malt flavor, long dry malt aftertaste.

Privatbrauerei Ganter

Brewery in **Freiburg**

GANTER EXPORT — deep gold, light malt nose, big malt flavor, very pleasant, light dry hop aftertaste has odd sour features.

Brauerei Gatzweilers

Brewery in **Dusseldorf**

GATZWEILERS ALT — medium brown, sour hop nose and front palate, dry hop middle and finish, dry hop aftertaste with some sour malt in back, medium body, medium length.

Gilden Brauerei

Brewery in **Köln**

GILDEN KÖLSCH — gold, light hop and malt aroma and flavor, smooth and balanced, light body, long aftertaste like the flavor.

Gold Ochsen, Gmbh.

Brewery in **Ulm**

GOLD OCHSEN PREMIUM BEER — gold, roasted malt and hop nose, tasty roasted malt flavor, lovely up front but weak at the finish, short dry roasted malt aftertaste.

GOLD OCHSEN HEFE WEIZEN — deep gold, lovely lightly toasted dry malt aroma, creamy head, pleasant slightly sweet smooth malt flavor with a wheaty background, virtually no spice or acid, very good duration and balance, lots of character, very refreshing.

GOLD OCHSEN KRISTALL WEIZEN — gold, big head, clean wheat and hop aroma with faint lactic spice, flavor is quite lactic with lots of cloves overriding the malt, very good front palate, but it doesn't last for long.

Brauerei Götx

Brewery in Geislingen/Altenstadt

DIE DUNKLE BARTELSTEINER WEISSE — hazy amber, light clove nose, spicy clove flavor, very dry finish and it sort of dies at that point, leaving only some faint sourness as an aftertaste.

Privatbrauerei Graf-Eder Gmbh. & Co., K.G.

Graf Brewery in Oberndorf

OBERNDORFER PRIVAT — gold, mild hop and malt nose, malt palate, light hops appear in the finish, dry wimpy hop aftertaste.

OBERNDORFER PILSENER — gold, big head, highly carbonated (you can even taste it), creamy, light malt and hop nose, dry malt flavor with a dry hop finish, medium long dry hop aftertaste.

Privater Brauereigasthof Greifenklau

Brewery-Gasthof in Bamberg

GREIFENKLAU EXPORT — amber-gold, good appetizing malt and hop aroma, delicately smoked malt flavor, long dry slightly smoked malt aftertaste, nicely done and very likeable.

Brauerei Grohe

Brewery in Darmstadt

GROHE BOCK — amber, lovely fresh fruity malt aroma, beautiful off-dry malt and hop flavor, excellent balance, medium to light body, dry hop finish, long off-dry malt aftertaste, a very pleasant easy-to-drink brew.

GROHE MÄRZEN — amber, fruity-malt nose, flowery fruit-like off-dry malt flavor, touch of banana, light to medium body, medium to long off-dry malt aftertaste.

Grüner Bräu

Brewery in Bad Tölz

GRÜNER BIER DUNKEL — dark brown, light malt aroma and taste, very little hop character, medium body, short malt aftertaste.

GRÜNER EXPORT — deep gold, light malt aroma, medium body, light malt flavor, smooth and drinkable, medium long malt aftertaste.

TÖLZER EDEL WEIZEN — hazy brown, light slightly lactic nose and flavor, very smooth and drinkable, medium body, medium length malt aftertaste with a trace of the lactic spice which is more pronounced at the end.

TÖLZER WEISSE — bright gold, very light smooth malt nose and taste, only a trace of actic-weizen character, very mild, medium body, mild malt aftertaste has medium length and little spiciness, pleasant enough but a bit weak for those who like their weizen to have zest.

Notes:

Burgerliches Brauhaus Zum Habereckl Pbh.

Brewery in Mannheim

HABERECKL MÄRZEN — hazy amber, big head, off-sweet faintly acidic fading nose, crisp malt flavor with no acidity, some yeast in the finish, short malt aftertaste.

HABERECKL FEUERIO TROPFEN JAHRGANG 1988 STARKBIER — deep ruby-brown, rich malt aroma, huge (no, enormous) rich malt flavor that lasts and lasts and lasts, one of the best examples found to prove what can be done with malt alone.

Hacker-Pschorr, A.G.

Brewery in Munich

HACKER EDELHELL EXPORT — gold, medium hop aroma, bright hop flavor with an off-dry malt background, good body, excellent balance, plenty of character, long dry hop aftertaste with a hint of malt in back, very nicely done.

HACKER-PSCHORR ORIGINAL OKTOBERFEST BIER BRÄUROSL-MÄRZEN — deep amber, big malty nose and taste, a beer to chew on, big in every way, but expertly balanced, long rich dry malt aftertaste, not to be missed.

HACKER-PSCHORR OKTOBERFEST MÄRZEN — pale amber, light malt aroma, bright malt-hop flavor, well-balanced, tasty complex malt and hop finish and aftertaste.

HACKER-PSCHORR LIGHT BEER — pale gold, beautiful clean malt and hop aroma, big malt and hop flavor, very good balance, more hops appear at the finish and stay for the aftertaste, stays clean and good throughout.

HACKER-PSCHORR DARK BEER — medium dark amber-brown, malt-hop aroma with molasses in back, good tasting toasted malt flavor, medium body, finish is a bit weak, but the medium long toasted malt aftertaste is excellent.

HACKER-PSCHORR WEISS BIER — foamy pale yellow-gold, yeasty nose, medium body, grainy dry flavor has a yeasty-spicy-smoky pine resin background, fairly bright, extremely complex, very pleasant and interesting, finish and aftertaste like the flavor but more dry, good duration.

PSCHORR-BRÄU WEISSE (WEISSBIER WITH YEAST) — cloudy gold, spicy clove nose, flavor starts tart and spicy, finishes a bit sweeter, good carbonation, medium body, fairly long off-dry malt aftertaste.

HACKER-PSCHORR MAIBOCK — brilliant deep tawny-gold, big smooth hop and malt aroma, good off-dry malt and hop flavor, extremely fine balance, very tasty, finish is off-dry malt and hops, and there is a long complex hop and malt aftertaste.

PSCHORR MUNICH — bright copper, caramel nose, light carbonation, wine-like malt flavor, heavy body, some hops show ightly in the finish and aftertaste, but they have trouble getting through the winy malt.

HACKER-PSCHORR FEST BEER — pale amber-gold, roasted malt and hop aroma, good hop and malt palate, but there is a faint sourness that carries through and does mar the aftertaste.

HACKER-PSCHORR BRAUMEISTER PILS — bright gold, toasted malt and hop nose, pleasant hop and toasted malt flavor, good body, finish is mostly malt, good long dry hop aftertaste.

HACKER-PSCHORR ANIMATOR DUNKLER DOPPELBOCK — deep ruby-amber-brown, rich malt aroma, fruity-malt flavor has a rich backtaste, complex, balanced, very satisfying, long long dry and rich malt aftertaste.

HACKER-PSCHORR HUBERTUS BOCK — deep gold, huge off-dry malt nose, big, smooth, rich, balanced clean malt flavor, high alcohol (6.8%), finely carbonated, very drinkable despite its heft, long rich malt aftertaste, super beer.

Notes:

Hannen Brauerei, Gmbh.

Brewery in **Monchengladbach**

HANNEN ALT — deep tawny-gold, sour cardboard nose, burnt cardboard taste, thin body, dull aftertaste.

Traditionsbrauerei Harklberg

Brewery in **Passau**

HARKLBERG HOCHFÜRST PILSENER — gold, fresh hop nose, hop flavor is a little sour, especially at the finish, dull aftertaste.

HARKLBERG URHELL — gold, stinky hop nose, zesty hop and malt flavor, flabby finish, dull aftertaste.

HARKLBERG JAKOBI WEIZEN — cloudy gold, malt nose, light slightly fruity-spicy malt flavor, long dull dry malt aftertaste has cloves way in back, medium body, not balanced.

HARKLBERG JAKOBI DUNKLE WEISSE — hazy brown, huge dense head like a fass (draft) beer, smooth spicy malt nose, fresh lightly spiced malty-fruity flavor, good body, slightly spicy malt finish, long dry malt and hop aftertaste, good tasting satisfying brew.

Schlossbrauerei Haselbach

Brewery in **Haselbach**

D'WIRTSDIRN SCHWARZE DUNKLES HEFEWEISSBIER — brown, big thick head, malt aroma has a spicy background, flavor is more roasted malt than spice (which is way in back), big tasty flavor, very smooth long malt aftertaste, with the spiciness still hiding far in back.

Hasen-Brau A.G.

Brewery in **Augsburg**

HASEN-BRÄU AUGSBURGER EXPORT — bright gold, malt aroma and flavor, well-balanced and smooth, medium long dry malt aftertaste, pleasant but not exciting.

HASEN-BRÄU DOPPELBOCK DUNKEL — brown, rich earthy malt aroma, rich full-flavored malt palate, very satisfying, sense of high alcohol, long rich malt aftertaste, real sipping beer.

HASEN-BRÄU EXTRA — gold, hop nose, faint dull off-dry malt and hop flavor, medium body, even fainter aftertaste like the flavor.

HASEN-BRÄU HELL — gold, light soapy hop nose, good malt and hop flavor, balanced, dry hop aftertaste with the malt laid back in behind.

BUNST BIER VOLLBIER HELL — gold, slightly soapy hop nose, soapy flavor, hop finish, medium length slightly dry hop aftertaste.

HASEN-BRÄU AUGSBURGER MÄRZEN — gold, zesty hop and malt nose, big balanced malt and hop flavor, perky and alcoholic (5.7%), richly malted, long dry hop aftertaste, more like a heller bock than a Märzen.

Hofbrauhaus Hatz

Brewery in **Rastatt**

BERNHARDUS BOCK — bright gold, visibly dense, viscous, beautiful hop nose, humungous body, very high density, great balance, high alcohol (6.9%), big malt flavor, clean hop finish, malt rolls back in to dominate the long aftertaste that is also well-balanced, and the overall impression is just great strength, and neither the sweetness of the malt or the bitterness of the hops, a magnificent brew.

AUGUST HATZ PRIVAT — gold, delightful hop aroma, very good hop and malt flavor, sour hop finish, long dry and faintly sour hop aftertaste, excellent balance, a really good tasting brew.

Gdbr. Hausmann

Brewery in Ramstein

RAMSTEINER EXCLUSIV PREMIUM PILSENER — gold, some particulate matter in suspension, lovely light flowery aromatic hop nose, big hop flavor, plenty of body, lots of malt in back, slightly oxidized, long dry hop aftertaste, very drinkable and very good with food.

RAMSTEINER EXCLUSIV PREMIUM DUNKEL — amber, big toasted malt aroma, malty flavor is off-dry in front, dry by the finish, good body, loads of flavor, long dry malt aftertaste, has a rich quality, feels good in your mouth.

Heidelberger Schlossquell Brauerei, A.G.

Brewery in Heidelberg

VALENTINS KLARES WEIZENBIER — bright gold, big head, clean grainy malt aroma with a touch of refreshing clove-lactic spice, clean fresh bright flavor is like the nose but better, lingering wheat and malt aftertaste, delicious and refreshing, very drinkable.

HEIDELBERGER SCHLOSSQUELL PILS — gold, complex hop and malt nose, zesty hop and malt flavor, long dry hop aftertaste.

Brauerei Heller

Brewery in Bamberg

AECHT SCHLENKERLA RAUCHBIER MÄRZEN — brown, appetizing smoked malt nose, not a meaty type smoke but more like the delicate smoking used with salmon, light fresh smoked flavor, hop finish, dry malt aftertaste has the smoke in behind, very nicely done.

Notes:

Henninger Brauerei KGuA

Brewery in Frankfurt

HENNINGER INTERNATIONAL — gold, faint sweet malt aroma, highly carbonated, light off-dry malt flavor, little hop character, light off-dry malt aftertaste, needs more hops.

HENNINGER BIER — deep gold, clean hop aroma with a touch of roasted malt in back, good dry hop flavor, big body, good balance, excellent finish and dry hop aftertaste, fresh tasting and refreshing.

HENNINGER DARK BIER — rosy-amber, dry roasted malt nose yields some hops when swirled, good malt and hop flavor, complex, balanced, long roasted malt and hop aftertaste, good beer with lots of character. More recently labelled CHRISTIAN HENNINGER DARK BEER.

HENNINGER KAISER PILSENER — deep gold, appetizing hop aroma, excellent malt and hop flavor, extremely dry, pleasant dry finish and long dry hop aftertaste, finely balanced, bright and refreshing.

HENNINGER KAISER EXPORT — tawny-gold, balanced hop and malt nose and taste, hops in front, malt middle, hop finish and aftertaste.

HENNINGER DOPPELBOCK DUNKLER BOCK — reddish-amber, aroma of hops, licorice, molasses, and roasted malt, big palate is mostly malt, quite complex, delicious, well-balanced, drinkable and satisfying.

GERSTEL BRÄU NON-ALCOHOLIC BEER — bright deep gold, rich grainy malt nose, pleasant grainy flavor, good but short, some hops appear in the aftertaste.

CHRISTIAN HENNINGER BEER — medium gold, soapy hop nose, bright hop flavor, good balance, good long dry hop aftertaste, but there is not much complexity.

KARAMALZ ALKOHOLFREIES MALZGETRÄNK — deep red, light smoky-sweet malt nose, slightly smoky sweet malt flavor, long sweet malt aftertaste.

HENNINGER HELLER BOCK — gold, lovely malt and hop aroma, big balanced malt and hop flavor, a tasty lip-smacking brew, very smooth, long malt aftertaste, beautifully made.

HENNINGER DOPPELBOCK — deep brown, big dry roasted malt aroma, very complex, huge flavor is dry rich malt, finishes big with off-dry malt, long dry malt aftertaste, so much flavor you don't even notice the 8.1% alcohol, an almost perfect double bock.

HENNINGER DUNKEL — deep brown, rich malt nose and taste, dry malt finish and long dry malt aftertaste, excellent balance, very well-made beer.

Heylands Brauerei Gmbh.

Brewery in **Aschaffenburg**

HEYLANDS FESTBOCK — brilliant deep gold, lovely sweet creamy roasted malt nose and taste, richness is maintained throughout, off-dry front, dry middle, sweet finish, long dry malt aftertaste, finely carbonated, a beautifully made delicious brew.

SEPPLS URBRÄU PREMIUM DUNKEL — medium deep amber, complex rich malt aroma, light malt flavor, medium body, medium long light dry malt aftertaste.

HEYLANDS SEPPL-BOCK DUNKEL — brown, dry toasted malt nose, flavor to match, very smooth, long dry malt aftertaste, richly flavored, and the 7% alcohol is barely noticeable amid all that malt.

SEPPLS URBRÄU DUNKEL — medium deep brown, good toasted malt nose, dry malt flavor, medium body, faintly sour dry malt aftertaste.

Privatbrauerei Karl Hintz

Brewery in **Marne i Holstein**

DITHSMARSCHER MAIBOCK — copper-amber, rich malt nose and zesty malt flavor, big body, long malt aftertaste, very rich and very good.

DITHSMARSCHER UR-BOCK— deep bright reddish copper, light malt aroma, big malt flavor, plenty of hops for balance, rich and big bodied, very long malt and hop aftertaste.

Hirsch Brauerei Honer

Brewery in **Wurmlingen**

HIRSCH HONER PILS — light gold, pleasant hop nose, smooth lightly hopped flavor, light body, light dry hop aftertaste, light everything.

HIRSCH GOLD EXPORT — pale gold, faint malt nose, pleasant light malt flavor, almost no hops at all, dry malt aftertaste has good lngth, but the brew simply needs more hop character.

JAEGERHOF PILS — gold, hop nose, very little flavor on the front of the palate, not much anywhere, dry hop finish and aftertaste, very short.

Hofbräuhaus Munich

Brewery in Munich

HOFBRÄU OKTOBERFEST BEER — amber, big hop nose with plenty of malt, big chewey palate with lots of hops and malt, big body, good balance, long dry malt and hop aftertaste.

HOFBRÄU MÜNCHEN DUNKELER MAI-BOCK — medium amber, light fruity malt and hop aroma, flavor like the nose, excellent balance, marvelous flavor, very mellow and very long, delightful, alcohol 6.4%, density 17.4º.

HOFBRÄU MÜNCHEN ROYAL EXPORT HELL — bright gold, fragrant roasted malt and hop aroma, delicious and complex malt and hop flavor, excellent balance, long and dry, good body, a brightly flavored good tasting brew.

HOFBRÄUHAUS MÜNCHEN DELICATOR — deep amber, light malt aroma, big dry malt flavor, big body, long dry malt aftertaste, a solid doublebock.

HOFBRÄUHAUS MÜNCHEN BOCK HELL — gold, great malt-hop aroma, huge hop and malt flavor, malt is a bit toasted, great balance, huge body, high density (16.3º), high alcohol (6.7%), delicious, long dry malt and hop aftertaste much like the flavor.

HOFBRÄUHAUS MÜNCHEN HELL — gold, marvelous hop and malt aroma, flavor to match, big and bright, complex and very well-balanced, long medium dry hop aftertaste, very drinkable and great with food.

HOFBRÄUHAUS MÜNCHEN DUNKEL — dark amber-brown, rich lightly toasted malt nose, flavor to match the nose, good body, fine balance, very drinkable, long dry malt aftertaste with the hops way in back but contributing to the balance, very good with German wursts.

Hofer Bierbrauerei

Brewery in Hof

FRÄNKISCH FEST BIER — deep gold, papery mnalt nose, big malt flavor, dull malt finish and aftertaste, a bit off-dry and somewhat flabby. Made for Marco Getränktmarkts of the Nürnberg-Kulmbach area.

Schlossbrauerei Hohenkammer

Brewery in Hohenkamm

HOHENKAMMER WEISSE — hazy gold, pleasant complex spicy-berry peach fruit nose, complex flavor with malt, spice, and fruit, creamy, light body, sags a bit at the finish, fruity aftertaste.

HOHENKAMMER SCHLOSSBIER SCHLOSS-BRÄU HELL — very deep gold, hop nose, good hop and malt flavor, highly carbonated, dry malt finish and aftertaste.

Holsten Brauerei

Brewery in Hamburg

SENATOR URBOCK MAIBOCK — pale amber, smoky caramel nose and taste,heavy body, long roasted malt aftertaste.

HOLSTEN LAGER — yellow-gold, hop nose has alittle malt in back, big hop flavor, too much for the malt and balance, long strong dry bitter hop aftertaste.

HOLSTEN PILS — gold, complex dry hop and faint malt nose, big flavor with plenty of hops and light malt, good body, long dry hop aftertaste, a classical north German pils.

HOLSTEN CERVEZA TIGRE — light gold, malt nose, sour and bitter hop palate, finishes quite sour, poor balance, long slightly sour hop aftertaste.

HOLSTEN EXPORT — bright gold, big roasted malt aroma, some hops in the back of the nose, lots of hops in the flavor, but they are neither sharp or unpleasant, good toasted malt appears at the finish and there is a pleasant long dry roasted malt aftertaste.

HOLSTEN DRY BIER— bright gold, rising malt aroma, dry malt flavor, dull dry hop finish and aftertaste.

HOLSTEN PREMIUM BEER — bright gold, vegetal malt nose, dry hop flavor, long dry hop aftertaste.

EXTRACTO DE MALTA HAMBURG MALT BEVERAGE — deep brown, lightly carbonated, malty ceral aroma, molasses-malt flavor, very heavy body, thick and chewey, sweet but not cloying, some hops creep in for the finish and aftertaste, but overall it stays malty, very long sweet malt aftertaste.

DRESSLER EXPORT BEER — yellow-gold, hop nose, strong bitter hop flavor, long dry and bitter hop aftertaste, very austere.

HOLSTEN PILSENER KRÄFTIG-HERB — bright tawny-gold, fine malt and hop aroma, palate is more malt than hops, slightly sour hop aftertaste.

HOLSTEN LIGHT — gold, malt nose, unbalanced malt and hop flavor, weak body, light dry hop finish and aftertaste.

Weissbierbrauerei Hans Hopf

Brewery in **Miesbach**

HOPF WEISSE EXPORT — clear gold, light spicy malt aroma (not the usual cloves), fruity background like apple and banana, sweet malt and faint lactic acid palate, a bit too sweet and not enough balancing factors to mitigate the sweetness, good body, long too sweet malt aftertaste.

HOPF DUNKLE SPEZIAL DUNKLES HEFEWEISSBIER — clean deep amber-brown, big head, hefty malt aroma, strong malt flavor but there is no follow-thru, weak off-dry malt aftertaste.

Hübsch & Koch

Brewery in **Bohlendamm, Hannover**

PUPASCH DUNKEL — amber, pleasant malt and hop nose, light toasted malt flavor, tasty and pleasant, light dry malt aftertaste, a flavorful easy drinking beer.

Ingobräu

Brewery in **Ingolstadt**

TILLY BRÄU HELL — gold, vegetal hop nose and flavor, sour vegetal finish, dry hop aftertaste, not likeable.

Schlossbrauerei Irlbach

Brewery in **Irlbach**

IRLBACHER VOLLBIER HELL — gold, pleasant malt and hop nose, smooth balanced flavor, long dry hop aftertaste, a good long refreshing brew.

IRLBACHER PILS — gold, nice hop and malt nose, balanced mostly hop flavor, long dry hop aftertaste, good body.

KUHL UND
DUNKEL LAGERN
SCHLOSS BRAUEREI IRLBACH
POSCHINGER
BRAY
IRLBACHER
Schloßherrn Weisse
EXPORT
aus hellem Malz
Original Flaschengärung mit feinster obergäriger Hefe
Gebraut nach dem Bayerischen Reinheitsgebot
AUS TRADITION
gebraut nach dem Reinheitsgebot 1516
PRIVAT
e 0,5 l
25 09 91
Mindestens haltbar bis:
alc. 5,4% Vol.

IRLBACHER SCHLOSSHERRN WEISSE — deep brown, thick head, light lactic-malt nose, flavor to match, medium long dry malt aftertaste, very drinkable.

IRLBACHER ECHT BAYERISCHES HEFE-WEIZEN — hazy gold, light spicy malt nose and taste, good balance, dry malt finish and aftertaste.

Irseer Klosterbrauerei

Brewery at **Irseer**

IRSEER KLOSTER STARKBIER — brownish amber, toasted malt nose, dry malt flavor, richer at the end than at the start, off-dry rich malt aftertaste is very long, excellent balance, a big beautiful strong brew.

Brauerei Jacob

Brewery in **Bodenwöhr**

BODENWÖRHER JACOB ALTBAYERISCH HELL — gold, malt nose, good body, dry malt flavor, finish, and aftertaste.

Privater Brauerei Gasthof Deutscher Rhein/Jankåbräu BRD

Brewery-Gasthof in **Zwiesel**

JANKÅBRÄU BÖHMISCHES BOHEME — gold, smooth pleasant hop nose and taste, plenty of supporting malt, long dry malt and hop aftertaste, a good tasting refreshing pils.

JANKÅBRÄU BÖHMISCHES KUPFER SPEZIAL — brown, light malt nose and flavorgood body, long dry malt aftertaste.

JANKÅBRÄU BÖHMISCHES SCHWARZESWEIZEN — dark brown, big tan head, typical rich spicy malt aroma and taste, good body, good balance, flavorful, long malt aftertaste.

Kaiser Bräu

Brewery in **Neuhaus/Pegnitz**

ECHT VELDENSTEINER LANDBIER — deep amber, toasted chocolate malt nose and flavor, good carbonation level, flavor is better than the aroma, tasty and very drinkable, seems to be a little smokiness in back, light body, fairly brief dry malt aftertaste.

KAISER WEISSE (WEIZENBIER MIT SEINER HEFE) — hazy gold, huge dense head, malt aroma, fruity malt flavor with no lactic spice, good body, very long malt aftertaste shows only the faintest trace of cloves at the end.

Privatbrauerei Kaiserhofbräu

Brewery in **Märkstetter Marktredwitz**

FRÄNKISCH WEIZEN HEFE DUNKEL — amber-brown, faint spicy malt nose, off chemical taste of banana and phenolic, sweet malt aftertaste with odd components. Brewed under contract for Marco Getränktmarkt of Kulmbach.

KAISERHOF FESTBIER — deep gold, lactic hop and malt aroma, smoked malt flavor, dry smooth smoked malt aftertaste.

KLOSTER-LANDBIER — dark brown, roasted malt nose with a little smoke, even more smoke flavor is almost burnt, long lightly smoked malt aftertaste.

Sclossbrauerei Kaltenberg/Irmingard Prinzessin von Bayern Gmbh.

Brewery at Schloss Kaltenberg

KÖNIG LUDWIG DUNKEL — deep red-brown, light off-dry malt nose, smoky malt flavor, smokiness becomes overdone in the aftertaste.

KALTENBERG HELL — gold, malt nose, high carbonation, vegetal malt flavor with hops in back, medium body, brief dull malt aftertaste.

PRINZREGENT LUITPOLD KÖNIGSLICHES DUNKLES WEISSBIER— very slightly hazy brown, pleasant spicy clove nose, well-spiced flavor, finishes malty with the cloves removing to a supporting position, fairly short malt and spice aftertaste.

PRINZREGENT LUITPOLD HEFE-WEISSBIER — hazy gold, faintly spicy malt nose, rich alcoholic malt flavor with the spiciness taking a back seat, long,dry malt and clove aftertaste.

Brauerei Karg

Brewery in Murnau am Staffelsee

KARG WEISSBIER — hazy gold, fresh spicy nose and taste, creamy, finishes malt, spicy malt aftertaste, long, clean, and refreshing.

SCHWARZER WOIPERLINGER DUNKLES HEFE-WEISSBIER — cloudy brown, spicy nose, spicy malt flavor is smooth and creamy, fine balance, long dry spicy malt aftertaste, good body, excellent beer with rich foods, and a marvelous beer just by itself.

Privatbrauerei Karl Olpp

Brewery at Bad Urach

URACHER OLPP HELL — bright gold, hop and grain nose and taste, very drinkable and refreshing, medium body, short duration, not done in a German style.

BAD URACH OLPP DOPPELBOCK — copper-brown, sweet malt nose, big malt and hop flavor, balanced, delicious, smooth, long malt and hop aftertaste, very likeable, and the 8.1% alcohol is not at all obtrusive.

BAD URACH OLPP MAIBOCK — brilliant gold, big rich dry malt aroma, excellent balance, great dry malt and hop flavor, unbelievably smooth, alcohol not really noticeable although 8.1%, just seems to smooth it off even more, long dry malt and hop aftertaste, a big winner.

Karlsberg Brauerei

Brewery in Homburg

KARLSBRÄU GERMAN LAGER — deep golden amber, faint hop and malt aroma, flavor of yeast and malt, mild hop background, sour hop finish and aftertaste.

WALSHEIM BEER — gold, beautiful malt and hop nose, flavor starts out on the sweet side, finishes dry and slightly sour hops, long dry hop aftertaste.

KARLSBRÄU MANNLICH — bright yellow-gold, nice hop nose, good balance, off-dry malt and hop palate, hop finish, medium long dry hop aftertaste, good tasting satisfying brew.

KARLSBERG BOCK — deep rose-amber, faint malt aroma, light to medium body, light dry malt flavor, pleasant long dry malt aftertaste.

Karmelitan Brauerei

Brewery at Straubing

KARMELITAN KLOSTER DUNKEL — deep amber, lovely off-dry toasted malt nose, medium dry toasted smoky malt flavor, medium body, dry malt finish, long dry malt aftertaste, not much complexity but very drinkable.

Brauerei Kauzen

Brewery in Ochsenfurt a. Main

KAUZEN DUNKELER KAUZ DUNKLES HEFE WEISSBIER — deep hazy amber, big head, rich wheat-malt nose, very complex with tobacco and chocolate, carbonation, grains, sour malt, faint spices, good while it lasts but it cuts off quickly once swallowed.

KAUZEN HEFE-WEISSBIER — cloudy gold, lightly spiced soapy malt nose, pleasantly spiced malt flavor, medium body, somewhat dull dry malt aftertaste.

Notes:

Privatbrauerei Kesselring

Brewery in Marksteft am Main

MARUHN PILS — bright gold, good hop aroma, medium dry hopped malt flavor, highly carbonated. slight papery mid-palate, dry finish and short dry hop aftertaste. Made for B. Maruhn of Die Grosste Biermarkt in Welt of Pfungstadt.

UR FRÄNKISCHES LANDBIER — amber, toasted malt nose, malt palate, no complexity, malt finish, short malt aftertaste.

KESSELRING PILS — gold, bright hop nose with malt in back, very bright flavor like the nose, malt rolls in at mid-palate and stays into the long rich malt aftertaste, good body, bright zesty brew, one of the better Pilseners encountered.

SCHLEMMER WEISSBIER MIT HEFE — hazy gold, dry malt nose, faintly spicy malt flavor, long dry malt aftertaste has no spicy component, very drinkable and refreshing.

Klosterbrauerei Gmbh.

Brewery in Metzingen (Metzingen Bräustätte Stuttgart)

BRÄUCHLE HELLER BOCK — pale golden amber, attractive lightly toasted malt aroma, big malt flavor, nicely carbonated and this balances the malt more than hops, big body, very long aftertaste.

SIGEL KLOSTER KRISTALL-WEIZEN — brilliant gold, big head, sweet nose with a clove background, also seemed to be a faint sense of acetone, flavor is somewhat candy-like with the lactic acid (cloves) in competition rather than balanced, finish is a bit sweet with citrus in behind, fairly short aftertaste has some banana.

SIGEL KLOSTER HEFE-WEIZEN — hazy amber, big head, dry malt aroma, dry malt flavor shows some cloves as well, fair to good body, complex, medium long dry aftertaste of malt and faint cloves.

SIGEL KLOSTER HEFE-WEISSBIER — gold, big hop nose, malt flavor, a bit dull, light dry malt aftertaste with medium length.

SIGEL KLOSTER PILSENER — gold, dull malt aroma and flavor, medium body, aftertaste like the flavor, not interesting.

Privatbrauerei Gebr. Krauss

Brewery in Riedbach

FRANKEN BRÄU SPEZIAL — gold, malt and spicy hop aroma, off-dry malt and spicy hop flavor, so-so balance, good body, off-dry malt aftertaste.

FRANKEN BRÄU PILS — gold, nice hop nose, palate is big bright hops, medium to good body, only fair balance, long sour hop aftertaste.

Notes:

Privatbrauerei A. Kropf

Brewery in Kassel

KROPF EDEL PILS — bright medium deep gold, faint malt nose, dull dry hop flavor, fairly light body, weak dull dry hop finish and aftertaste.

MEISTER PILS — pale gold, toasted malt nose, good toasted malt flavor, medium body, long pleasant dry toasted malt aftertaste.

KROPF GENUINE GERMAN DRAFT — bright gold, beautiful roasted malt nose, good hop palate well-backed with malt, good tasting, good body, short dry hop aftertaste.

KROPF DARK GERMAN BEER — brown, faint malt aroma, dry malt flavor, burnt finish, good balance but little zest, fair length.

KROPF GENUINE GERMAN LIGHT — pale gold, pleasant malt nose, sour hop flavor, light body, metAllic finish, long bitter hop aftertaste.

KROPF MAI-BOCK — deep gold, rich malt nose, big malt flavor, rich and full-bodied, long malt aftertaste.

KROPF MARTINATOR DOPPELBOCK — deep rosy-amber, malt nose, huge off-dry malt flavor, big body, complex throughout, very long malt aftertaste is a bit drier than the flavor, very good tasting brew.

Brauerei Krug

Brewery in Ebelsbach/Main

KRUG EDEL HELL — gold, sour hop nose and taste, good body, long aftertaste like the flavor.

KRUG GOLDEN PILS — gold, malt and hop nose, hop and malt flavor, good balance, dry hop finish is soften by a good level of malt, long dry hop and malt aftertaste.

KRUG ALT FRÄNKISCH — deep amber, roasted malt nose and taste, creamy, dry but rich, slightly toasted dry malt finish, long dry malt aftertaste.

KRUG HEILIG LÄNDER — golden amber, big malt nose and taste, malt finish, dry malt aftertaste, seems to be some faint hops in the aftertaste, but largely this is a malt only beer.

KRUG WEISSE — hazy gold, big spicy lactic nose, light spicy flavor, creamy, dry malt aftertaste has some length.

Brauerei Kurfürsten

Brewery in Köln

KURFÜRSTEN KÖLSCH — tawny-gold, dry hop nose, flavor is first hops, thence sour malt, long dry hop and sour malt aftertaste.

Brauerei Ladenburger

Brewery in **Neuler**

MEISTERBRÄU EXPORT — gold, faint malt nose, light malt flavor, touch of malty sweetness in the finish, short off-dry malt aftertaste.

Lamm Brauerei

Brewery in **Sindelfingen**

LAMM BRÄU PILS — brilliant gold, beautiful hop nose, bright hop flavor, bitter hop finish, long bitter hop aftertaste, a very good serviceable beer, especially with food.

LAMM BRÄU EXPORT — brilliant amber, balanced hop-malt aroma and taste, smooth, appetizing, malt dominant in mid-palate, hops in lead in front and at finish, long dry hop and malt aftertaste, another good beer with food.

WURTTEMBERG'S NATURTRUBE LAMM BRÄU — gold, highly carbonated, no nose, complex rich dry malt and hop flavor, dry hop finish, medium long dry malt aftertaste.

Privatbrauerei Lamm Bräu Rolf Goetz

Brewery-Gasthof in **Bingen** (near Sigmaringen)

LAMM BRÄU PILSENER — beautiful gold, hop and malt nose, good bright hop flavor well-balanced with malt, some complexity, medium long dry hop aftertaste.

LAMM BRÄU EDEL HELL — gold, pleasant hop nose, big hop flavor with plenty of malt in support, very malty in mid-palate, dry hop finish, long dry hop and malt aftertaste, nicely done brew.

Privatbrauerei Gasthof Landwehrbräu Fam. Wörner

Brewery-Gasthof in **Reichelshofen**

ROTHENBURGER LANDWEHR PILSNER — pale gold, great malt-hop nose, big hop flavor, wellbacked with malt, dry hop finish and aftertaste, very long. This is the draft version served at the brewery.

ROTHENBURGER LANDWEHR SCHANKBIER — pale gold, stinky hop nose, light body, very delicate malt and hop palate, light malt aftertaste has a faint hop background.

ALT FRÄNKISCH-DUNKEL — deep amber-brown, malt aroma, big malt flavor, heavy body but smooth on the palate, dry malt finish and aftertaste, very little hops in the aftertaste, a solid full-flavored malt brew. This is the draft version served at the brewery.

ROTHENBURGER LANDWEHR-BIER PILSNER — gold, malt nose, pleasant hop flavor, good malt backing, dry hop finish, very long dry hop aftertaste. This is the bottled version of the Pilsner described above.

ROTHENBURGER EXPORT EDELHELL — gold, malt aroma, hop and malt flavor, dry hop aftertaste has a sour component in behind the hops.

ROTHENBURGER LANDWEHR ALTFRÄNKISCH DUNKEL — beautiful deep amber-brown, pleasant faintly toasted malt aroma, mild dry malt flavor, somecomplexity at the finish, long dry malt aftertaste, very drinkable, excellent with food. This is the bottled version of the brew.

Brauerei Lang

Brewery in Schwäbische Gmünd

LA BIERE DE LA GRANDE ARMÉE — hazy yellow-gold, luscious malt aroma with some toasted quality and dry smoked sausage, creamy texture with small bubble carbonation, rich toasted malt flavor, long aftertaste like the flavor, but attenuated.

Brauerei Robert Leicht, A.G.

Brewery in Vahingen/Stuttgart

SCHWABEN BRÄU GERMAN PILSNER BEER — yellow-gold, light malt nose with some hops, dull malt flavor, bitter hop aftertaste.

SCHWABEN BRÄU PILSENER — gold, hop nose and taste, long dry hop aftertaste.

SCHWABEN BRÄU MEISTER PILS — bright gold, hop nose, pronounced hop flavor, hop finish, long dry hop aftertaste.

SCHWABEN BRÄU EXPORT — bright tawny-gold, balanced hop and malt nose and flavor, good body, fairly smooth,appetizing, long dry malt and hop aftertaste.

DAS ECHTE SCHWABEN BRÄU — tawny-gold, big hop nose, heavy body, big hop flavor, plenty of malt in support, long dry hop aftertaste.

SCHWABEN BRÄU URTYP 1878 — gold, dry hop nose and flavor, fairly long dry aftertaste features neither hops nor malt, just dry.

Brauerei Leikeim

Brewery in Altenkunstadt

LEIKEIM DAS ORIGINAL — gold, complex malt nose, tangy malt flavor is very hefty and well-backed with strong hops, big body, long aftertaste has plenty of both malt and hops, the malt dominates throughout this big flavored brew, yet there is harmony among the components, a lusty brew.

LEIKEIM WEISSE (MIT SEINER HEFE) — hazy gold, huge thick head, fruity-spicy malt nose, smooth creamy fruity-spicy malt flavor, dry malt aftertaste, good body and balance, very drinkable.

ALT KUNESTATER URSTOFF — amber-brown, malt nose, big dry roasted malt flavor, good body, long off-dry malt aftertaste.

Seit 1887
Leikeim
Das Original
Im kupfernen Sudkessel nach altem Rezept eingebraut, im offenen Gärbottich schonend vergoren und 3 Monate in kleinen Lagerfässern ausgereift. - Ein Bier, gebraut wie einst.

Notes:

Jhring-Melchior K.G./ Licher Privatbrauerei

Brewery in Lich

LICHER PILSNER PREMIUM — bright gold, pleasant light hop aroma, zesty hop flavor with plenty of malt in back, a little soapiness in the long malt aftertaste but not enough to be bothersome.

LICHER DOPPELBOCK PREMIUM — deep amber, big malt nose, chewey malt flavor, big and bold, very rich, full bodied, very long malt aftertaste, a clean and complex brew with lots of character.

Familienbrauerei Link

Link Brewery in Tuttlingen-Möhringen

MÖHRINGEN HERRENHAUS PILS — gold, big hop nose, big lusty flavor with an abundance of both hops and malt, rich long malt aftertaste, excellent balance, a super beer.

Löwenbräu Trier J. Mendgen

Brewery in Trier

PETRISBERGER PILSENER FEINER ART — pale yellow-gold, light hop nose, bright hop flavor, long dry hop aftertaste, some sour hops at the very end that lingers on for quite a time.

TRIERER LÖWENBRÄU EDELPILS — gold, light malt aroma, light hop and malt flavor, hop finish, long dry hop aftertaste.

TRIERER LøOWENBRÄU KURFURST EXPORT — pale gold, malt nose, malt front palate, dry hop finish, long hop aftertaste, very drinkable.

TREUERER ALT — brown, malt nose and big malt flavor, a bit sweet up front, drier at the middle and finish, long dry malt aftertaste.

Brauerei Löwenbräu

Brewery in Munich

LÖWENBRÄU MUNICH LIGHT SPECIAL — gold, lovely hop nose, marvelous complex hop and malt flavor, big body, chewey,very well-balanced, long dry hop aftertaste.

LÖWENBRÄU MUNICH DARK SPECIAL — deep brown with an amber tinge, very clean malt aroma with some hops, strong flavor starts out malt, finishes hops, long dry hop aftertaste has a little sour malt in back, gives it an earthy quality.

MUNICH OKTOBERFEST BEER — amber, beautiful hop aroma with a touch of caramel, big body, big hop flavor is well equipped with toasted malt, long rich and dry malt aftertaste.

LÖWENBRÄU OKTOBERFEST — brilliant deep gold, dense head lasts all the way to the bottom of the glass, big body, balanced malt and hop nose, delicious rich malt flavor well backed with hops, long delicious dry hop aftertaste. This is the brew served at the festhalle.

LÖWENBRÄU OKTOBERFEST — deep amber, lovely dry hop nose, quality clean hop nose, smooth balanced hop and malt palate, very drinkable, fairly long on the palate. This is the bottled version.

DER LÖWENBRÄU PREMIUM PILSENER— pale gold, nice thick head, clean hop nose, big fresh hop and malt flavor, high carbonation is more noticeable to the eye than the palate, creamy texture, delicious complex long dry hop aftertaste, excellent balance throughout.

LÖWEN WEISSE KLARES WEIZENBIER — bright clear gold, big head, pleasant clean off-dry malt nose, pleasant slightly sweet malt flavor with just a little lactic tang, really good balance, long pleasing aftertaste like the flavor.

TRIUMPHATOR DUNKLER DOPPELBOCK — deepred-brown, roasted malt aroma is complex and rich, big rich malt flavor is on the sweet side in front, dries at the middle, long medium dry malt aftertaste, very complex and very good.

LÖWENBRÄU HELLER BOCK — brilliant gold, beautiful hop nose, bug bright malt flavor, strong, rich, and complex, full body, finely carbonated, long malt and hop aftertaste, with hops coming on strongly at the very end.

LÖWENBRÄU SCHWARZEWEISSE DUNKLES HEFE-WEIZEN — slightly hazy deep copper-amber, wheat and malt aroma has a faint lactic acid character like clove spice, palate to match, nicely balanced, smooth, well-made, very drinkable.

LÖWENBRÄU BOCKBIER HELL — deep gold, fragrant hop nose, big hop and malt flavor, big body, finishes dry hops, aftertaste is dry hops and malt, this is a beer with plenty of everything including an excellent balance.

Privatbrauerei Löwenbräu Bamberg K.G.

Brewery in **Bamberg**

ST. STEPHANUS FEST BIER — amber, fruity malt aroma, pleasant malt and hop flavor, fairly dry, good balance, medium body, brief length.

BAMBERGER LÖWENBRÄU FRÄNKISCHES URBIER — deep amber, sweet clean malt nose, off-dry malt and hop flavor, plenty of alcohol, medium body, long malt aftertaste stays off-dry.

BAMBERGER LÖWENBRÄU EXPORT — deep gold, rich malt nose and flavor, complex and tasty, good body, long dry malt aftertaste, very good with food or by itself, one of Germany's best export style beers.

Brauerei Maisach

Brewery in **Maisach**

MAISACH RÄUBER-KNEISSL — copper-brown, dry malt aroma and palate, despite being dry it is quite rich, big body, long dry malt aftertaste, very satisfying and great with food.

MAISACH HELLER BOCK — deep tawny-gold, beautiful complex malt and hop aroma, so good it sends a shiver down your spine, big body, delicious long complex flavor of balanced hops and malt, wonderful long aftertaste is a continuation of the flavor gradually becoming more dry as it goes, this is about as good as a pale lager can get.

MAISACH BRAUEREI PILS — bright gold, well-hopped aroma, beautiful hop flavor, long dry hop aftertaste, good body, excellent balance, a classic pils.

Brauerei Märkelsteiner

Brewery in **Marktredwitz**

BRAUMEISTER HELL — deep gold, hop nose, light off-dry malt flavor, hops in back, long malt aftertaste is a little more dry.

Privatbrauerei Mittenwalder

Brewery in **Mittenwald**

MITTENWALDER DUNKEL — medium deep ruby-brown, lovely malt nose and flavor, magnificent balance, long malt aftertaste, very pleasant and satisfying.

MITTENWALDER WEIHNACHTSBOCK HELL — gold, perfumy malt nose, sour malt palate, short malt aftertaste.

MITTENWALDER JOSEFI BOCK DUNKEL — deep ruby-brown, rich malt nose, rich0ff-dry malt flavor, long malt aftertaste, good drinkable brew.

MITTENWALDER VOLLBIER HELL — gold, malt and faint hop aroma, malt flavor is off-dry and a little vegetal at first and becomes drier toward the finish, light dry malt aftertaste, somewhat dull.

Privatbrauerei Modscheidler KG

Brewery at Buttenheim

ST. GEORGEN BRÄU DUNKELER DOPPELBOCK — brown, excellent dry malt nose with good hops in support, big malt flavor again with plenty of hop backing, big body, complex, long long dry malt aftertaste with the hops dropping out early.

Brauerei Moninger

Brewery in Karlsruhe

MONINGER BERTHOLD BOCK DUNKEL — brown, lovely rich and roasted dry malt nose, good carbonation level, rich dry malt flavor, hops join with the carbonation to balance the richness of the malt, long rich malt aftertaste, excellent brew.

Mönchshof Brauerei Gmbh.

Brewery in Kulmbach

KULMBACHER MONKSHOF KLOSTER SCHWARZ BIER — deep copper-brown, light toasted malt aroma, mellow and smooth, lovely malt flavor, beautiful balance, long dry malt aftertaste, a lovely brew.

KULMBACHER MONKSHOF AMBER LIGHT BEER — gold, fragrant roasted malt and hop aroma, big body, big roasted malt and hop flavor, excellent balance, an excellent beer.

KULMBACHER MÖNCHSHOF FESTBIER — bright gold, subdued malt and hop aroma, smooth malt flavor has good hop backing, good balance, heavy body, long and delicious hop and malt aftertaste.

KULMBACHER MÖNCHSHOF PILSENER — bright pale gold, malt nose and flavor, medium to light body, dry hop finish, and long hop aftertaste which is a tad sour.

GREGORIUS WIESENFESTBIER — bright gold, delicious toasted malt nose is really malty (like malted milk-malty), delicious appetizing palate is first malt, then hops, all stays in balance right into the long complex malt and hop aftertaste, a very very nice drinkable brew.

MÖNCHSHOF URSTOFF DARK SPEZIAL STARKBIER — reddish brown, malt nose, huge strong smooth malt flavor, enormous body, you can taste the alcohol, very long pleasant strong malt aftertaste, a pleasure to sip.

MÖNCHSHOF URSTOFF SPEZIAL STARKBIER — deep amber, huge malt nose, concentrated malt palate, medium body, long dry malt aftertaste is like dry molasses.

KULMBACHER MONKSHOF DRY LIGHT BEER — pale gold, good malt nose with hops in back, a little toasted malt barely found in the nose is the good flavor, medium body, hops appear at the finish, long dry roasted malt aftertaste.

KULMBACHER MONKSHOF KLOSTERBOCK BEER— rosy-amber, fragrant roasted malt, caramel, and hop aroma, big body, front palate is off-dry roasted malt, finishes dry malt and hops, long pleasant malt and hop aftertaste leaves your mouth feeling god.

KULMBACHER MONKSHOF DARK BEER — tawny-brown, rich toasted malt aroma with hops in back, rich full toasted malt flavor, good balance, malty-molasses middle and finish, but the long aftertaste is tasty dry malt and the lasting memory is that dry malt rather than the sweeter malt earlier.

KULMBACHER MÖNCHSHOF OKTOBERBIER — brilliant gold, big toasted malt aroma with hops in back, light body, light flavor of hops and toasted malt, long dry hop aftertaste, not big but very drinkable.

KULMBACHER MONKSHOF HELLER BOCK — medium gold, rising toasted malt and hop aroma, big body, rich dark malt flavor has powerful hops in back trying to break through, strong, complex, and excellently balanced, very long complex dry hop and malt aftertaste.

KAPUZINER SCHWARZE HEFE-WEIZEN — amber-brown, big head, malt nose and fresh malt flavor, medium body, smooth rather than zesty, pleasant long dry malt aftertaste.

MÖNCHSHOF KLOSTER BOCK HELL — gold, good light malt and hop nose, big complex flavor has malt, hops, and alcohol (7%), good balance, very big with plenty of everything, long complex malt and hop aftertaste, a marvelous brew.

Brauerei D. Oechsner

Brewery in Ochsenfurt

OECHSNER PREMIUM PILS — deep gold, delightful hop nose, zesty malt and hop flavor, mostly hops but with great supporting malt, good body, excellent balance, rich and smooth, very refreshing, long dry hop aftertaste retains the malt as well, this is a perfect Pilsener.

OECHSNER MÄRZEN EXPORT — gold, big bright hop and malt aroma, very tasty rich hop and malt flavor, feels great in your mouth, good body, rich and very long hop and malt aftertaste, an absolute treasure, and perhaps the best Märzen in my experience.

OECHSNER HELLER BOCK — deep gold, extremely complex huge hop aroma, intense hop and malt flavor, expertly balance, a lip-smacking big complex brew that offers an abundance of everything but doesn't assault the palate, incredible brew, extremely long fine aftertaste much like the flavor.

Brauhaus Oettinger Gmbh.

Brewery in Oettingen

ORIGINAL OETTINGER DUNKLES HEFEWEIZEN — amber-brown, big head like a fass (draft) beer, light lactic nose, good malt-wheat-clove flavor, medium dry malt aftertaste.

ORIGINAL OETTINGER PILS — gold, big strong hop nose and flavor, dry hop finish, very long strong hop aftertaste, hops, hops, and more hops.

ORIGINAL OETTINGER EXPORT — gold, dry malt aroma, sour dry hop finish and aftertaste, highly carbonated.

ORIGINAL OETTINGER HEFEWEISSSBIER — hazy gold, faint clove and malt aroma, pleasant spicy malt flavor, light body, lightly flavored, dry malt aftertaste of medium duration.

Notes:

Bierbrauerei Ott

Brewery in Bad Schussenried

OTT URTYP — gold, good hop nose, malt-hop flavor, medium dry hop finish and aftertaste, not interesting.

SCHUSSENRIEDER PILSENER — gold, hop nose, pleasant hop flavor, dry hop finish and aftertaste.

OTT SPEZIAL — gold, pleasant hop and malt nose, plenty of both in the flavor, good body, good tasting, long dry hop and malt aftertaste, good brew.

Marburger Brauerei Otto Beyer

Brewery in Marburg

ALT MARBURGER DUNKEL — brilliant amber, dry malt nose and flavor, aftertaste is a continuation of the flavor as well and is only medium in duration, there is a touch of sourness at the very end, so-so beer, but it does grow on you if you keep drinking it.

Kronenbrauerei Otto Kimer Söhne

Brewery in Tuttlingen/Möhringen

KRONEN PILS — gold, hop nose with plenty of supporting malt, slightly sour hop flavor well-backed with malt, long dry sour hop aftertaste.

KRONEN GOLD EXPORT — gold, light malt and hop nose, off-dry malt flavor, dry hop finish, long hop and malt aftertaste.

KRONEN BRÄU VOLLBIER — gold, faint hop nose, fairly rich malt flavor, finishes dry hops like the Pils, long dry sour hop aftertaste.

KRONEN WEIZEN EXPORT — gold, big head, fresh clove aroma, clean and bright spicy clove and malt flavor, balanced, refreshing, feels good in your mouth, long dry spicy aftertaste, an excellent and very drinkable weizen.

KIRNER'S AECHT BADENER — gold, nice hop nose, some complexity, rather ordinary malt palate, smooth and only lightly hopped, not much of an aftertaste.

Brauerei Ottweiler

Brewery in Ottweil

KARLSKRONE EDEL PILS — gold, hop nose, dull malt flavor, long dry malt aftertaste.

Palmbräu Zorn Söhne

Brewery in Eppingen

PALMBRÄU PILSENER — gold, sour hop nose, bright hop flavor well-balanced with malt, hop finish and very long dry hop aftertaste.

PALMBRÄU KRAICHGAU EXPORT — gold, faint malt nose and taste, short weak dry malt aftertaste.

Parkbrauerei A.G.

Breweries in Pirmasens and Zweibrücken

PARKBRÄU EXPORT — pale gold, light but very good hop aroma well-backed with malt, good body,m creamy texture, bright tangy hop flavor and long dry hop aftertaste, good tasting refreshing brew.

PARKBRÄU PILS — medium gold, zesty hop and lightly toasted malt nose, well-balanced lively hop and toasted malt flavor, good body, lightly bitter dry hop finish and aftertaste, straightforward well-made brew.

PARKBRÄU PIRMINATOR — deep bright gold, toasted malt nose, big bright rich malt flavor, high alcohol, big body, huge but very well-balanced, long dry hop aftertaste has plenty of malt backing.

Patrizier-Bräu, A.G.

Brewery in **Nürnberg**

PATRIZIER EXPORT — deep amber, light hop nose, medium body, good malt flavor with the hops in back, long dry malt aftertaste.

PATRIZIER EDELHELL EXPORT — bright gold, nice complex hop aroma, big hop flavor up front, malt shows through in the finish, good balance, very good taste, complex, softens and gets better as you sip, pleasant long malt aftertaste.

PATRIZIER PILS — bright deep gold, toasted malt and hop aroma, light malt and hop palate, not exciting, brief malt aftertaste.

BAMBERGER HOFBRAU BEER — tawny-gold, slightly off-dry malt and grain aroma, grainy slightly toasted palate, very light body, virtually no finish or aftertaste.

PATRIZIER ZERO NON-ALCOHOLIC MALT BEVERAGE — amber-gold, grainy malt aroma like grapenuts, lightoff-dry grainy flavor, brief dry malt aftertaste.

PATRIZIER POCULATOR — pale brown, toasted malt aroma, intense dry malt flavor, big body, only medium duration but the feel of the strong flavor lasts in your mouth.

PATRIZIER BRÄU KUPFESTUBE — medium deep brilliant amber, toasted malt aroma and flavor, some smoke in the backtaste and in the finish, long toasted smoky malt aftertaste, very dry and very drinkable.

Paulaner Salvator Thomasbräu, A.G.

Brewery in **Munich**

PAULANER SALVATOR — deep brown, complex hop and malt aroma, huge fresh malt flavor, big body, very rich, clean and complex, extremely long dry malt aftertaste, noticeable alcohol (7.5%), a great double bock.

PAULANER HELL URTYP EXPORT — gold, rich malt aroma, strong hop flavor, sour malt and dry hop finish and aftertaste, good long palate.

PAULANER ALTBAYERISCHES HEFE WEISSBIER — bright gold, clean wheat nose with only the faintest trace of yeast, bright perky dry spicy flavor, big body, fresh, long dry hop aftertaste, this one is best with the twist of lemon.

PAULANER OKTOBERFEST BIER — bright deep gold, well-balanced hop and toasted malt aroma, complex toasted malt flavor, hop backing, good balance, good tasting, long pleasing rich and dry malt and hop aftertaste.

PAULANER URTYP 1634 — deep gold, toasted malt aroma, medium body, flavor is mostly malt but there are enough hops for good balance, slightly sour hop finish, medium long dry hop aftertaste, lacks the depth and character normally found with a Paulaner beer.

PAULANER MÜNCHENER MÄRZEN — copper-gold, toasted malt aroma, creamy texture, rich toasted malt flavor, hops are there but well in back, decent balance, good tasting flavor and finish, long refreshing dry malt aftertaste.

PAULANER ALT MÜNCHENER DUNKEL — deep reddish brown, very faint malt aroma, lovely malty flavor is a bit light, full bodied, light malt finish, lighter and brief malt aftertaste.

PAULANER FEST-BIER — bright gold, pleasant hop nose and flavor, good body, good feeling in the mouth, very long pleasant dry hop aftertaste.

PAULANER WIES'N-MÄRZEN — amber, delicate roasted malt aroma, pleasant toasted malt flavor, not much depth or character, but it is pleasant, dry malt finish and aftertaste.

PAULANER GERMAN PILS — yellow-gold, beautiful hop nose, delicious big hop flavor, long slightly sour dry hop aftertaste.

PAULANER MÜNCHENER UR-BOCK HELL — amber-gold, toasted malt and hop aroma, medium body, good tasting toasted malt and hop flavor, bright and hoppy up front, rich toasted malt at the finish, complex, balanced, long toasted malt aftertaste.

PAULANER MAIBOCK — bright tawny-gold, light roasted malt nose, light body, flavor is mostly hops, but there is malt and carbonation showing as well, bitter and dry hop finish and aftertaste.

PAULANER WEISSBIER ALTBAYERISCHES BRAUART — bright gold, foamy, clove-apple-wheat-citrus aroma, spicy-sweet palate is mostly cloves, malt finish and aftertaste shows little of the spiciness and is quite long.

PAULANER ORIGINAL MÜNCHENER HELL — pale gold, smooth malt and hop nose, hefty flavor has both malt and hops aplenty, very straightforward hop character, good balance, dry hop finish and long aftertaste.

PAULANER HEFE-WEIZEN — hazy gold, big head, off-dry tangy spicy nose with a caramel background, bright zesty flavor has good balance between the spice and the sweetness of the malt, good body, refreshing, good length, the touch of cloves in the nose and taste is just right for the balance.

PAULANER MÜNCHEN NR. 1 EXTRA PREMIUM LAGER — bright gold, hop nose and flavor, good body, long dry hop aftertaste, an excellent well-balanced brew that is most satisfying.

PAULANER OKTOBERFEST — amber, big malt nose, big toasted malt flavor, smooth and dry, long dry hop aftertaste, an excellent beer with food.

PAULANER UR-BOCK HELL — tawny-gold, strong aroma with plenty of both hops and lightly toasted malt, high alcohol (6.8%) adds to a rising nose, flavor is big malt and light hops, huge malt aftertaste is on the dry side, certainly drier than the flavor.

Brauerei Emil Petersen Gmbh. & Co., K.G.

Brewery in Flensburg

FLENSBURGER PILSENER — pale gold, pleasant light fresh malt aroma, malt palate with a flash of bitter hops in the middle that stay into a long dry bitter hop aftertaste.

Dampfbierbrauerei Zwiesel - W. Pfeffer

Brewpub in Zwiesel

PFEFFERBRÄU ZWIESEL SPEZIAL PILSENER — gold, big hop nose, very aromatic, smooth malt flavor, finishes weakly, pleasant dry malt aftertaste.

PFFERBRÄU MÄRZENBIER — amber, hop and malt aroma, spicy hop and malt flavor (more herbal than spice actually), low carbonation, dry spicy finish and aftertaste.

Notes:

Pflugbrauerei Rottweil

Brewery in Rottweil

SCHWARZWÄLDER URTYP-EXPORT — gold, very faint malt nose, faint malt flavor, brief malt aftertaste.

Privatbrauerei Hildebrand Gmbh. & Co., K.G.

Pfungstädter Brauerei
Brewery in Pfungstädt

PFUNGSTÄDTER — pale yellow-gold, hop and sour malt aroma, good flavor with a touch of roasted malt to give it richness, good tasting finish, good balance, long malt aftertaste.

BOCKALE PREMIUM CLASS — pale gold, faint hop and roasted malt aroma, highly carbonated, big hop flavor, and long hop aftertaste, could use more malt for a better balance.

ST. NIKOLAUS DUNKLES STARKBIER — copper-amber, caramel and roasted malt nose, delicious and appetizing, palate is big malt right from the start and it stays, a little smoky-toasty, faint sour hops join the malt in the long aftertaste, very attractive Christmas beer.

PFUNGSTÄDTER MAIBOCK — pale amber, lovely malt nose, hop flavor, well-balanced with malt, long dry hop aftertaste, a very nice appetizing May Bock.

Privatbrauereigasthof Prösslbräu

Brewery-Gasthof in Adlersberg

PRÖSSLBRÄU ADLERSBERG PALMATOR — dark reddish-brown, chocolate malt nose is smooth, a little smoky, and faintly buttery, very rich chocolate malt flavor, extremely rich yet dry, very complex, big body, long dry roasted malt aftertaste, the 6.3% alcohol is absorbed easily by the strength of the flavor and not even noticeable, this is a great beer.

PRÖSSLBRÄU ADLERSBERG VOLLBIER DUNKEL — deep red-brown, malt nose, very smooth rich dry malt flavor, good body, long dry malt aftertaste.

PRÖSSLBRÄU ADLERSBERG KLOSTER-PILS — gold, pleasant strong hop nose, big hop flavor, long dry hop aftertaste.

Püls-Bräu

Brewery in Weisman

PÜLS-BRÄU KRONE PILS — gold, big hop nose, zesty malt and hop flavor, as you sip it the hops gradually take a more and more prominent position on the palate, big body, long dry hop aftertaste.

Quenzer-Bräu Gmbh.

Brewery in Bad Urach

QUENZER SPEZIAL EXPORT — tawny-gold, beautiful hop nose, smooth malt flavor with a mild hop finish, long dry hop aftertaste.

Reichelbrauerei Kulmbach

Brewery in Kulmbach

KULMBACHER REICHELBRÄU HELL EXPORT DE LUXE — bright tawny-gold, big hop nose does have some malt in back, big hop flavor, malt shows well in the finish and stays through the long dry aftertaste.

KULMBACHER REICHELBRÄU FRANKISCHES URBIER — brilliant amber, pleasant toasted malt and hop nose, big body, big malt flavor has a coffee-like background, good balance, long dry malt and hop aftertaste.

KULMBACHER REICHELBRÄU EDELHERB PILS — bright deep gold, lovely flowery hop nose, bright hop palate, good balance and complexity, malt finish, medium body, long dry hop and malt aftertaste.

KULMBACHER REICHELBRÄU BAVARIAN DARK BEER — deep amber-brown, complex toasted malt aroma, medium body, lightly flavored dry toasted malt and hop taste, long dry malt aftertaste.

KULMBACHER REICHELBRÄU EISBOCK 24 — deep brown, rich complex off-dry aromatic malt nose, body so huge it seems thick, very rich heavy malt flavor, like a smooth malt tonic, very complex malt flavors, high alcohol, long concentrated malt aftertaste, an extraordinary beer.

Rhanerbräu

Brewery in Rhan

RHANER EXPORT HELL — gold, hop nose, malt flavor, good balance and body, off-dry malt finish and aftertaste.

Riedenburger Brauhaus Michael Krieger K.G.

Brewery in Riedenburg

RIEDENBURGER WEIZEN — clear amber-gold, light spicy malt nose, clean creamy spicy malt flavor, dry malt finish, faintly spicy long malt aftertaste.

Brauerei Riegeler

Brewery in Riegel/Kaiserstuhl

RIEGELER FELSEN PILS — gold, big hop nose and taste, good body, good flavor, hop finish and long dry hop aftertaste has a spiciness that would appear to be Tettnanger hops.

RIEGELER SPEZIAL EXPORT — gold, hop and malt nose, malt flavor, short dry malt aftertaste.

Privatbrauerei Johann Röck K.G.

Brewery in Nesselwang

BÄREN PILS — gold, hop aroma, mild malt-hop flavor, good body, very good balance, refreshing, complex, long dry hop aftertaste, a superb Pils.

BÄREN GOLD — gold, light malt nose and flavor, well balanced, dry hop finish and long aftertaste, a delicate brew with great finesse.

BÄREN BRÄU ALTBAYRISCH DUNKEL — brown, nice malr aroma, dry rich clean malt flavor, medium long dry malt aftertaste.

BÄREN BRÄU ALPEN BOCK — brown, rich malt nose has great complexity and earthiness, extremely big ricch roasted malt flavor, has a nut-like quality, quite complex, long dry roasted malt aftertaste continues the nutty taste, a most satifying bock and one of the best found.

BÄREN WEIZEN HEFETRUB — hazy gold, clean zesty nose, nice mild malt taste, very drinkable, medium body, good balance, dies at the finish, very little aftertaste.

Privatbrauerei Röhrl

Brewery in Frontenhausen

RÖHRL EXPORT BEER — gold, hop nose, hop flavor with plenty of malt, long bright malt aftertaste, balanced and bright, good tasting brew.

RÖHRL VILSTALER DUNKLES HEFE-WEIZEN — deep brown, very clear with all the yeast in the bottom, big malt nose, delicate spicy malt flavor, smooth and tasty, rich malt finish, long dry malt aftertaste, an excellent hefe-weizen.

Badische Staatsbrauerei Rothaus AG

Brewery at Rothaus, Hochschwarzwald

ROTHAUS DUNKEL EXPORT — deep amber, roasted malt aroma and big roasted malt flavor, not complex but very tasty, good body, tastes better as you continue to drink it, touch of sour malt at the finish, long malt aftertaste.

ROTHAUS MÄRZEN — bright gold, medium rich malt nose, extremely smooth pleasant malt flavor, some complexity, very drinkable, long malt aftertaste.

ROTHAUS PILS TANNEN ZÄPFLE — brilliant yellow-gold, big hop nose has plenty of malt in back, finely carbonated, good body, smooth dry malt flavor, creamy texture, hop finish, long dry hop aftertaste.

STAATSBRAUEREI ROTHAUS PILS — gold, pleasant malt nose, good malt flavor, very tasty, good body, fine balance, very clean and refreshing, long dry malt aftertaste.

Rotochsen Brauereigasthof Hermann Veit

Brewery Gasthof in Ellwangen

ROTOCHSEN EDEL EXPORT — deep gold, malt nose, smooth malt flavor has dry hops in back, good balance, long dry hop aftertaste.

ROTOCHSEN STIFTSHERREN PILS — pale gold, light dry hop aroma, dry hoppy flavor, long dry hop aftertaste, good body, good balance, very good with food.

ELLWANGER ROTOCHSEN TRADITIONSBOCK — deep gold, rich toasted malt nose, big rich creamy toasted malt flavor, big body, strong and long dry malt aftertaste, a real lip-smacker, high alcohol (6.6%) is not obtrusive, actua;lly it is just another component of the rich complex flavor.

ELLWANGER ROTOCHSEN KRISTALL-WEIZEN — clear gold, large bubble head, aroma is malt and faint cloves, lightly spiced malt flavor, medium body, aftertaste is a continuation of the flavor.

ELLWANGER ROTOCHSEN HEFE-WEIZEN — slightly hazy gold, light clove and malt nose, big well-spiced flavor, big body, long dry malt aftertaste with the cloves way in back.

ELLWANGER ROTOCHSEN DUNKLES HEFE-WEIZEN — hazy amber, big spicy clove and malt nose and taste, creamy texture, very complex, good body, complexity increases across the palate, the aftertaste is dry malt and the cloves stay all the way through.

Notes:

Privatbrauerei W. Rummel

Brewery in Darmstadt

DARMSTADTER UR BOCK DOPPELBOCK — amber, light malt nose, good malt flavor, finely carbonated, there is some complexity contributed by background hops, good body, hops show best in the finish and aftertaste, very well-balanced, long long dry hop and malt aftertaste.

Brauerei Franz Josef Sailer

Brewery in Marktoberdorf

SAILER PILS — pale gold, complex hop and toasted malt nose, light body, toasted malt front palate, tangy hop finish, long dry hop aftertaste.

SAILER WEISSE WITH YEAST— pale cloudy amber, huge head, good grainy nose, gives the sense of being smoky but isn't, sharp grainy flavor, fairly long grainy aftertaste with a bit of spice in back.

SAILER WEISSE — pale golden amber, foamy, lovely aroma is grainy, slightly sweet, and picquant, complex smoky-malty flavor, slightly sweet malt finish, balance is good, long off-dry malt aftertaste, pleasant and refreshing.

OBERDORFER WEISSE — brilliant gold, foamy, spicy-lactic nose, palate has only the faintest trace of lactic acid and is instead quite malty, pleasant and refreshing, very long malt aftertaste, has good zest.

OBERDORFER WEISSE WITH YEAST — hazy gold, foamy, wheat nose, creamy texture, frothy, pleasant and refreshing dry barley malt and wheat palate, grainy finish and aftertaste, good balance, a finely made wheat beer.

OBERDORFER DUNKLES HEFEWEIZENBIER — hazy deep amber, big head, light lactic and fruity wheat-malt aroma, good body, good complex flavor of cloves, wheat, malt, and hops, rich and satisfying, long pleasant malt aftertaste.

CHRISTKINDLBIER WEIHNACHTEN 1987 — deep gold, huge malt nose with some lactic spice, lactic acid and malt palate, flavor has an aromatic quality, very long sour hop and lactic malt aftertaste, interesting but there are better weizens.

FRANZ JOSEPH JUBELBIER — deep gold, dense head, charcoal nose, smoky-charcoal malt and lactic acid taste, acid eases toward the finish, long weizen aftertaste, a kristallklar.

URGÄUER WEIZEN — gold, spicy nose, bright clove spice and malt nose and flavor, fades a bit at the finish, very refreshing, medium dry wheat malt aftertaste.

Privatbrauerei Rudolf Schäff/ Schäffbräu

Brewery in Treuchtlingen

ALTMÜHLTALER PILSENER — pale gold, big hop nose, hefty body, strong hop and malt flavor, dry hop aftertaste has a sourness that causes it to end poorly.

ALTMÜHLTALER SCHLOSSBRAUEREI URTYP HELL — gold, big strong hop nose, dull hop flavor, off-dry soft dry hop aftertaste.

SCHÄFF FEUERFEST EDEL BIER — tawny port color, beautiful roasted malt aroma, extremely heavy body, almost syrupy, intense roasted smoked malt flavor, sweet sipping beer, very long smoky roasted malt aftertaste, no carbonation, a very long lived beer, almost impervious to mishandling.

SCHÄFF PILSENER — pale yellow-gold, light sour hop aroma, highly carbonated, palate starts off as strong hops, softens toward middle where some malt joins in to set the balance, malt finish, long sour malt and hop aftertaste.

SCHÄFFBIER — medium pale yellow-gold, lovely well-hopped aroma with a touch of roasted malt, god body, complex flavor is mostly hops, malt finish, good balance, long pleasant malt and hop aftertaste.

Privatbrauerei Scherdel

Brewery in Hof

SCHERDEL PILSNER PREMIUM — gold, complex malt and hop nose, big complex flavor like the aroma, spruce or pine in the finish, long dry malt aftertaste.

Klosterbrauerei Scheyern

Brewery at Scheyern

KLOSTERBRAUEREI SCHEYERN DUNKLER KLOSTERBOCK — deep amber-brown, light dry malt aroma, dry malt flavor, long pleasant off-dry malt aftertaste which gets a bit sweeter at the end, medium duration, very drinkable.

KLOSTERBRAUEREI SCHEYERN KLOSTER-DOPPELBOCK DUNKEL — deep brown, somewhat stinky-earthy roasted malt aroma, big dry roasted malt flavor, extremely rich and yet surprsingly dry, lush yet smooth, very long dry malt aftertaste, has great subtlety, a marvelous brew despite the offish start, and the 7.3% alcohol is barely noticeable.

KLOSTERBRAUEREI SCHEYERN KLOSTER-GOLD — gold, fragrant hop nose, sweet hop flavor, good body, fair balance, long dry hop aftertaste.

KLOSTERBRAUEREI SCHEYERN KLOSTER-WEISSE HELL — hazy gold, big head, grapefruit-like aroma, vegetal-grapefruit flavor, long dry malt aftertaste.

KLOSTERBRAUEREI SCHEYERN KLOSTER-WEISSE DUNKEL — hazy brown, nose of cloves, candy, and fruit, strong spicy-candy flavor, very assertive, flavor carries into the long aftertaste.

Schloss Bräu

Brewery in Stamsried

HERZOG PILSENER —gold, hop nose with a meaty background, big malt and hop flavor, finishes weakly, medium length dry hop aftertaste.

Notes:

Brauerei Schlösser

Brewery in **Dusseldorf**

SCHLÖSSER ALT — deep copper-amber, subdued malt nose, malt and carbonation on front palate, nothing but hops from then on, very bitter, especially the long aftertaste.

Privatbrauerei Gasthof Schmid/ Brauerei Biberach

Brewery-Gasthof in **Biberach-Roggenburg**

BIBERACHER UR-DUNKEL — dark brown, lovely malt nose, light body, smooth malt flavor, pleasant dry malt aftertaste.

BIBERACHER MÄRZEN — deep gold, hop nose with a faint yeasty-bready nature (but pleasantly so), good malt and hop flavor, balanced, rich tasting, good body, dry malt-hop finish and aftertaste, very good with German country wursts and patés. Draft version at the Gasthof.

BIBERACHER MÄRZEN — amber, light malt aroma and flavor, very little hops, low carbonation, pleasant and smooth, light short malt aftertaste. Bottled version.

Privatbrauerei Adolf Schmid

Brewery in **Usterbach**

REISCHENAU GOLD HELLES EXPORT — gold, hop nose, malt flavor wine fine hops in back, finish and long aftertaste are more malt than hops, good body, good balance, a fine beer.

USTERBACHER PILSNER — gold, hop nose, big hop flavor with plenty of support from the malt, dry hop finish, very well-balanced, long dry malt and hop aftertaste.

USTERBACHER BAYERISCH HEFE-WEIZEN — cloudy gold, big spicy malt nose and taste, plenty of cloves and cinnamon, good finish like the flavor leading into a long dry malt and hop aftertaste with a spicy background.

Privatbrauerei Schmucker

Brewery at **Mossautal**

SCHMUCKER DOPPEL-BOCK DUNKEL — deep amber-brown, rich dry malt nose, perfect balance, delicious dry roast malt palate, very long with great depth of flavor, excellent double bock.

Privater Brauereigasthof Schneider

Brewery-Gasthof in **Essing**

JOS. SCHNEIDER MAIBOCK — deep gold, hop nose, big hop taste with the malt in back, dry hop finish, long dry hop aftertaste, really good clean and bright flavor, good body and balance, very enjoyable.

JOS. SCHNEIDER MÄRZEN — pale amber, hop nose, big hop and malt flavor, finishes dry, long dry hop and malt aftertaste, excellent balance, good body, a very fine brew.

JOS. SCHNEIDER DUNKEL — brown, malt aroma, rich straightforward malt palate, dry malt finish and long dry malt aftertaste, good body and balance, well-made beer.

G. Schneider & Sohn K.G./Brauerei Kelheim

Brewery in Munich

SCHNEIDER WEISSE HEFE-WEIZENBIER — hazy amber, slight lactic nose but mostly a pleasant malt, mellow and smooth flavor, good balance, sour finish shows the lactic acid and spice promised by the nose, long faintly sour aftertaste.

AVENTIUS WEIZENSTARKBIER — hazy deep copper color, huge dense head, delightful appetizing malt-wheat-lightly lactic nose, big off-dry malt and lactic acid/spicy flavor, high alcohol, frothy, big body, heavy flavor, extremely tasty and balanced, very long complex aftertaste like the flavor, a dandy weizenbier, perhaps the best I ever tasted from a bottle.

L. Schönberger Sohne

Brewery at Gross-Bieberau

SCHÖNBERGER FEST BOCK — deep amber-brown, big roasted malt aroma, complex rich malt flavor up front on the palate, pungent hops in back that show best in the finish, good balance, medium to long malt and hop aftertaste, a marvelous tasting brew.

SCHÖNBERGER UR-BOCK — copper-amber, huge roasted malt aroma and flavor, flavor is drier than the nose and has many subtle nuances, long complex malt aftertaste, 6% alcohol, excellent brew.

SCHÖNBERGER ODENWALDER LANDBIER — gold, hop nose, palate has more malt than hops but the balance is very good, good body, long dry malt aftertaste has hops showing well at the very end.

Schwannen-Brauerei A.G. & Co., K.G.

Brewery in Schwetzingen

SCHÖFFERHOFER WEIZEN — pale yellow-gold, dusty clove and malt aroma, sweet malt and clove flavor, good body, spicy malt finish and aftertaste drier than the flavor.

SCHÖFFERHOFER HEFEWEIZEN — hazy gold, bright spicy hop nose, zesty spicy hop and malt flavor, creamy and smooth, long dry spicy malt aftertaste.

Schwarzbierbrauerei

Brewery in Bad Köstritz

KÖSTRITZER — opaque brown, brown head, big malt aroma, pure malt flavor like a finely carbonated malta, very sweet, big body, long strong malt aftertaste, it is drinkable, but too sweet.

Brauerei Schwarzbräu

Brewery in Zusmarshausen

SCHWARZBRÄU PILSENER — gold, hop nose, big hop flavor, good body and balance, very long good dry hop aftertaste.

SCHWARZBRÄU EXQUISIT SPEZIALBIER — gold, malt and hop nose, big malt flavor with a hop finish, dry hop aftertaste is very dry and very long, huge body, a big mouthful of flavor.

SCHWARZBRÄU DUNKLES EXPORT WEIZEN — hazy brown, head like a fass (draft) beer, clean spicy nose, very pleasant fruity-spicy flavor, nicely balanced, good body, long dry malt aftertaste.

Notes:

Brauerei zum Schwarze Adler

Brewery in Wassertrüdlingen

SCHWARZE ADLER PRIVAT WEIZEN HEFE-WEIZEN — cloudy gold, faint sour hop and malt aroma, some soapiness in back, light spicy malt and hop flavor, light to medium body, short aftertaste like the flavor.

Privatbrauerei Schweiger

Brewery in Markt Schwaben bei München

SCHWEIGER HELLES EXPORT — gold, malt nose, malt flavor with good hop support, off-dry hop finish, good body, good balance, hop aftertaste is similar to finish but drier, fairly long.

SCHWEIGER SCHMANKERL WEISSE — very slightly hazy gold, faint spicy nose, bright clove flavor, finish, and aftertaste, short, but good while it lasts.

Brauerei K. Silbernagel A.G.

Brewery in Bellheim

BELLHEIMERSILBER BOCK — gold, sweet malt and hop nose, malt palate with light hops, strong but not powerful, long medium dry malt aftertaste, stays very drinkable.

Schlossbrauerei Soldenau

Brewery in Soldenau

ORIGINAL ALT BAYERISCHE UR WEISSE — deep amber, big head, big aroma of malt with faint lactic-clove spice way in back, light picquant clove flavor, some soapiness in the finish, light body, dull soapy malt aftertaste. Bottled for Privatbrauerei Will, Motten.

SOLDENAUER SCHLOSS DUNKLES WEISSBIER — very slightly hazy amber, aroma is mostly malt but there is some faint spicy cloves in back, flavor is largely malt with some sourness in mid-palate, and a dry malt finish and aftertaste, the lactic stays in back but doesn't leave, an interseting brew.

Notes:

Spaten Franziskaner-Bräu KgaA

Brewery in Munich

SPATEN CLUB WEISS BIER — bright gold, big head, fresh clean fruity malt nose has only the faintest wheat component, very fresh slightly grainy flavor with a pleasant spicy tang, good balance, fairly short malt aftertaste and very little spicy-lactic character, but good and refreshing.

SPATEN OPTIMATOR DOPPELSPATEN — deep orange-brown, dry toast and malt aroma, very appetizing, heavy body, medium dry molasses and roasted malt flavor with sa hop tang in back, good tasting sour malt finish and long aftertaste, excellent balance, a wonderful smooth and rich dark doublebock that makes your mouth feel good. In Germany, may also be labelled a Frühjahrstarkbier

SPATEN MUNICH LIGHT — deep gold, toffee malt aroma, heavy body, big hop and malt flavor, the hops are bitter and the malt is off-dry, the balance is excellent, long bright hop aftertaste, a heavy handed brew, and a wonderful mouthful of beer.

SPATEN URMÄRZEN OKTOBERFEST BEER — copper-gold, good hop and roasted malt aroma, smooth well-balanced malt and hop flavor, flavorful and complex, long dry hop and malt aftertaste, rich satisfying brew.

SPATEN PILS — deep gold, good hop nose and flavor, sharp hop finish, long good hop aftertaste, a good appetizing brew, goes very well with food.

SPATEN FRANZISKUS HELLER BOCK — tawny-gold, toasted malt and hop aroma is very slightly on the off-dry side, big body, flavor like the nose, complex and balanced, slightly off-dry malt and bright hop finish, long malt and hop aftertaste is drier than the flavor, a very satisfying brew that also goes well with food.

SPATEN GOLD — bright gold, light malt and hop nose, good flavor throughout has both hops and malt, well-balanced, good complexity, long dry hop and malt aftertaste.

FRANZISKANER HEFE-WEISSBIER — cloudy gold, light wheat aroma, smooth light grainy palate, a touch of lactic acid is immediately noticeable on the front of the palate and again appears in the finish, otherwise it is not there, medium long aftertaste like the finish.

SPATEN DUNKEL — deep brown, malt aroma and flavor, good body, smooth and delicious, long malt aftertaste, very drinkable.

Spath Bräu

Brewery in Lohberg am Ossen

OSSER HELL — gold hop nose, big malt flavor, malt finish, long dry malt aftertaste, good body and balance.

OSSER GOLD — deep gold, malt aroma and big malt flavor, long malt aftertaste, hops very light throughout, but a nicely made pleasant tasting brew.

OSSER WEISSE (MIT SEINER HEFE) — clear gold, light aroma of hops and spicy cloves, zesty clove flavor, very sparkly and creamy, refreshing, finishes with the spice leading the flavor into a lightly spiced malt aftertaste with good duration.

Burgerliches Brauhaus Spessart

Brewery in Wiesen

WIESENER RÄUBER BOCK — amber, big very rich malt nose, huge malt flavor, big body, rich, strong, smooth, and very long.

Brauerei Spezial

Brewpub in Bamberg

SPEZIAL RAUCHBIER LAGER — amber, meaty smoked malt nose, very dry smoked malt flavor, dry malt finish and aftertaste has the smoke but it gradually sets in far to the back.

SPEZIAL RAUCHBIER MÄRZEN — deep amber, meaty smoked malt aroma, big flavor like the nose, smooth, very tasty and very drinkable, there's a hidden sweetness in there also, complex and interesting, medium dry long malt aftertaste with a faint smoky background. Now, I see why the Bambergers like rauch bier.

St. Martin Brauerei Fohr OHG.

Brewery in Lahnstein/Rhein

SCHNEE BOCK — deep amber, both hops and malt in nose, strong malt and hop flavor, good balance, plenty of alcohol as well (7.5%), long malt aftertaste, good tasting bock.

LAHNSTEINER JÄGER-BOCK — amber, very complex nose with hops, banana fruit, and malt, strong malt flavor, very intense, big body, lots of alcohol (you can feel it in your mouth, nose, and sinuses), very long strong malt aftertaste, a blockbuster bock.

Privatbrauerei Jacob Stauder

Brewery in Essen

STAUDER BEER — bright tawny gold, faint roasted malt nose and taste, light body, brief dry malt aftertaste.

STAUDER PILS — deep gold, hop aroma, slightly sour hop flavor with plenty of malt backing, good body, decent balance, long dry hop aftertaste is a bit sour.

Stiftungsbrauerei

Brewery in Erding

DIE SCHWARZE DUNKLES WEISSBIER — brown, malt nose with a lactic-spice background, flavor like the nose but even spicier, dry malt finish and aftertaste.

Privat Landbrauerei Strössner

Brewery in Ahornberg

AHORNBERGER MAIBOCK — bright gold, malt nose, big rich malt flavor, slightly bitter hop finish, long light malt aftertaste, very pleasant.

Brauerei Stumpf

Brewery in Lohr

ORIGINAL 1878 LOHRER BEER — golden amber, pleasant roasted malt and hop aroma, light off-dry roasted malt flavor, hops show well in the finish, long caramel malt and dry bitter hop aftertaste has good length and complexity.

BAVARIAN ABBEY LAGER — pale amber, light roasted malt nose and taste, very light on the hops, brief malt aftertaste, lacks zest without enough hops to balance.

BAVARIAN ABBEY LIGHT LAGER NON-ALCOHOLIC MALT BEVERAGE — gold, dull malt nose, light grainy very malty flavor, straight malt finish and aftertaste.

KEILER WEISSBIER DUNKEL — amber, light wheat beer nose (some malt, some wheat, some cloves), light spicy clove flavor, very mild, highly carbonated, light body, fairly long aftertaste like the flavor.

Stuttgarter Hofbrau

Brewery in Stuttgart

STUTTGARTER HOFBRAU HERRN PILS — bright gold, aroma of wet wool, hop flavor, plenty of supporting malt, slightly sour hop finish, long dry hop aftertaste.

STUTTGARTER HOFBRAU PILSNER — slightly tawny-gold, good hop nose is sort of sweet, austere dry hop palate, good body, long dry hop aftertaste.

STUTTGARTER HOFBRAU WEIHNACHTS-BIER — pale gold, strange offish nose, dull flavor that isn't particularly like hops or malt, uninteresting, medium long aftertaste like the flavor.

Stuttgarter Lokalbrauerei

Brewpub in Stuttgart

CALWER-ECK-BRÄU NATURTRUB — cloudy gold, yeasty hop aroma, good flavor of yeast, malt, and hops, interesting, good body, smooth, not rough or coarse in any way, a little off-dry in front, but dry by the finish, long dry malt and hop aftertaste.

FLORIANO MAIBOCK — cloudy brown, thick brown head, very little nose, smooth malty flavor starts out off-dry and dires toward the finish, medium long dry malt aftertaste.

Herzoglich Bayerisches Brauhaus Tegernsee

Brewery in Tegernsee

QUIRINUS DUNKELER DOPPELBOCK — light brown, rich soft malt nose, velvety sweet malt in the mouth, sweetest at the finish, yet has a dry malt aftertaste that fades very slowly, a very tasty brew. Bottled version.

QUIRINUS DUNKELER DOPPEL-BOCK — brown, lightly toasted malt nose and flavor, on the sweet side but very complex and earthy, dry malt finish, off-dry malt aftertaste, big body, excellent balance, absolutely delicious and very drinkable. Draft versionat the Brauhaus Tegernsee.

DER BLAU PAGE HELLER BOCK — hazy yellow-gold, lovely off-dry malt aroma, huge malt flavor is drier than the nose, very big body, honeyed texture, long dry malt aftertaste, well-made brew, good balance, but the hops aren't quite enough for the malt.

TEGERNSEE HELLER BOCK — hazy amber-gold, pleasant toasted malt nose, rich toasted malt and hop flavor, complex, very good balance, rich, delicious, and very long. Bottled version.

TEGERNSEE HELLER BOCK — bright gold, hop nose, big hop and malt flavor, balanced and rich, complex malt and hop finish leads into a long dry malt aftertaste. Draft version at the Brauhaus Tegernsee.

BRAUHAUS TEGERNSEE DUNKLER DOPPELBOCK — deep amber-brown, malt aroma and flavor, palate is sweet in front, off-dry in the middle, and stays off-dry thereafter, good body, very good of the type, long off-dry malt aftertaste, quite enjoyable, but not one of the blockbusters.

TEGERNSEE DUNKEL EXPORT — dark amber-brown, pleasant malt aroma, lovely roasted malt flavor, refreshing and drinkable, good body, good balance, very satisfying, medium long dry malt aftertaste.

TEGERNSEE SPEZIAL — gold, hop aroma, excellent balanced hop and malt flavor, long dry hop aftertaste, good body, and about as good a balance as you can imagine, this is the best in a German export style that I have tasted.

TEGERNSEER HELL — gold, lovely hop aroma, good hop and malt flavor, excellent balance, good body, long dry hop and malt aftertaste, a really good beer superbly balanced.

Postbrauerei Thannhausen

Brewery in Thannhausen

POSTBRÄU BERNHARDI GOLD SPEZIAL MÄRZEN — gold, big hop aroma, malt flavor has plenty of hop support, big body, richness goes all the way through the palate into the aftertaste, long rich malt aftertaste goes dry at the end.

POSTBRÄU HEFE-WEIZEN — hazy gold, odd dull malt aroma, pleasant bright and clean spicy clove and malt palate, medium body, short dry malt aftertaste.

Fürstliche Brauerei Thurn und Taxis

Brewery in Regensberg

THURN U TAXIS HEFEWEIZEN — cloudy amber, sweet wheaty weizen nose, much sweeter than usual for a wheat beer, spicy-fruity palate, complex, long off-dry malt aftertaste with only the faintest hint of cloves.

THURN U TAXIS POSTMEISTER DOPPELBOCK — medium brown, big malt nose, strong malt flavor but very smooth, excellent balance, well rounded, quite long and very delicious.

SCHIERLINGEN ROGGEN OBERGÄRIG HEFETRUBE — hazy deep amber, big head, sweet and sour lactic nose with a buttery background, buttery malt taste up front, lactic spice finish and aftertaste. Made for A.D. Laber Fürstliches Specialtätes-Brauhaus zu Schierling.

THURN U TAXIS DAS FURSTLICHE PILSENER — gold, hop nose, hop flavor balanced well with malt, good body, long and strong dry hop aftertaste shows no malt whatever.

THURN U TAXIS EXPORT — gold, hop nose, good hefty hop and malt flavor, nicely balanced, big body, long malt aftertaste.

Hofbrauhaus Traunstein

Brewery in Traunstein

HOFBRAUHAUS TRAUNSTEIN FÜRSTEN QUELL — gold, hop nose, dull malt flavor, dry malt and hop finish and aftertaste, uninteresting.

HOFBRAUHAUS TRAUNSTEIN ALBAIRISCH DUNKEL — deep amber-brown, pleasant toasted malt aroma, creamy roasted malt flavor, dull dry malt finish and aftertaste.

HOFBRAUHAUS TRAUNSTEIN ALTBAIRISCH UR-WEIZEN — deep amber-brown, faint malt nose, big spicy malt flavor, medium long malt aftertaste with a clove background, pleasant but lacks depth and strength.

HOFBRAUHAUS TRAUNSTEIN HOFBRÄU WEISSE — cloudy gold, clean faintly spicy malt nose, big clove and malt flavor, lemony finish, good body, fine balance, very complex and delicious, long fresh cinnamon and clove aftertaste, very interesting and very good sipping beer.

Tucher Bräu A.G.

Brewery in Nürnberg

TUCHER UBERSEE EXPORT BEER — tawny-gold, malt aroma, medium body, very lightly dry toasted malt and hop flavor, dry slightly sour hop finish, light dry hop and toasted malt aftertaste. Also **TUCHER UBERSEE EXPORT** (domestic version), same as foregoing except that there is no toasted nature to the malt and the hops are not sour, giving a smoother and cleaner taste.

BRÄUHAUS ROTHENBURG GERMAN PILSENER — gold, light hop nose, harsh bitter hop flavor, sour metallic finish and aftertaste.

TUCHER GERMAN PILSENER — bright gold, nice hop nose with some malt support, big hop flavor, long dry and bitter hop aftertaste. **TUCHER PILSENER** (the domestic version) is identical except for the name on the label.

TUCHER WEIZEN — bright deep gold, foamy, beautiful malt nose, zesty picquant flavor up front, dry very fresh and crisp wheaty middle, long clean off-dry malt finish and medium long aftertaste, a very fine brew that is a pleasure to drink.

TUCHER HEFE WEIZEN — brilliant deep gold, foamy, good malt aroma with some wheat and yeast in back, picquant spicy flavor starts up front and stays throughout, a bit yeasty in the middle, slightly off-dry raspberry malt finish, medium long dry malt aftertaste keeps much of the picquancy of the flavor, very nicely done.

TUCHER HEFE-WEIZEN DUNKLES — amber, malt nose, high carbonation, hop, spice, and malt flavor (in that order), refreshing and drinkable, fairly light handed, short malt aftertaste.

TUCHER IMPORTED GERMAN BEER LIGHT — medium deep gold, hop and faintly roasted malt aroma, complex palate of hops and dry roasted malt, roasted malt finish, long slightly sour malt aftertaste.

TUCHER IMPORTED GERMAN BEER DARK — pale copper, faint toasted malt nose and flavor, weak body, faintly sweet short malt aftertaste.

TUCHER LORENZI BOCK HELL — bright gold, malt and corn nose, toasted malt and corn flavor, finishes cleaner and better with just the malt, long dry malt aftertaste.

TUCHER ALT FRANKEN EXPORT DUNKEL — deep amber, pleasant malt aroma, good tasting light malt flavor, light body, almost nothing at the finish, faint brief malt aftertaste.

TUCHER MAIBOCK HELL — deep gold, lovely toasted malt nose, big zesty hop and toasted malt flavor, fairly intense, very long aftertaste like the flavor, an excellent beer.

TUCHER FESTBIER MÄRZEN — tawny-gold, pleasant toasted malt aroma, highly carbonated, good toasted malt flavor, sour hop aftertaste.

TUCHER BAJUVATOR DOPPELBOCK — deep red-amber, roasted malt nose and taste, delicious, rich, and clean, very drinkable, long roasted malt aftertaste is medium dry, very drinkable.

TUCHER BAYERISCHES WEISSBIER HEFE-WEIZEN — tawny, faint citrus nose, spicy lactic flavor on front of the palate, medium dry malt in the middle, and a touch of lactic with the malt in the finish, medium body, very brief dry malt aftertaste with no spice at all at the end.

SEBALDUS WEIZENBOCK DUNKEL — rich brown color, big creamy head and creamy texture, bright spicy clove aroma, zesty spicy rich malt flavor, complex and refreshing, long bright aftertaste like the flavor.

Ulmer Münster Brauerei

Brewery in Ulm

MÜNSTER WEIHNACHTS BIER — deep gold, rich toasted malt aroma, full rich malt flavor, very complex and smooth, finely balanced, creamy, fairly long dry malt aftertaste.

ULMER MÜNSTER ZUNFTMEISTER SPEZIAL DUNKEL — medium pale amber, nice toasted malt nose, palate has a big malt front, smooth middle making the transition to a hop finish, delicious, long complex dry hop and malt aftertaste, good body, good beer.

alc. 5,1% vol.
℮ 0,5 L
101
RATS
KRONE
HELL
Ein Bier gebraut nach deutschem
Reinheitsgebot
Hergestellt in der Ulmer Münster Brauerei, Ulm/Donau
Mindestens haltbar
bis Ende: | 1 | 2 | 3 | 4 | 5 | 6 | 7 | 8 | 9 | 10 | 11 | 12 | 91 | 92 | 93 |

ULMER MÜNSTERKANZLERGOLD HELLES STARKBIER — faintly hazy amber-gold, complex malt nose with chocolate, Ovaltine, Postum features, equally complex malt flavor, pleasant and very long malt aftertaste.

SCHLOSSHERR PILS — gold, malt and hop nose, dry malt flavor, finish, and aftertaste, good hop support, pleasant and refreshing, seems to be virtually identical to **RATS KRONE PILS** below.

RATS KRONE HELL — gold, good, malt-hop nose, smooth malt flavor with the hops in back, good dry malt finish, long dry malt and hop aftertaste.

RATS KRONE PILS — gold, beautiful hop nose, good flavor with plenty of both malt and hops, long dry malt and hop aftertaste, good tasting beer.

LÖWENBRÄU NEU-ULM WEIZEN — gold, bright big spicy nose, creamy, big sparkle on the tongue, clean flavor feels good and is refreshing, plenty of spice and zest, long bright spicy aftertaste, a delightful beer.

WAPPEN PILS — gold, big malt nose and flavor, hardly any hops except in the aftertaste, pleasant but not exciting, brief aftertaste.

HIRSCH BIER URHELL — medium deep gold, vegetal-malt nose, malt flavor, dry malt finish and aftertaste, not much offered.

SCHLOSS EXPORT — medium deep gold, light hop nose, very light hop and malt flavor, high carbonation, light to medium body, short dry hop aftertaste.

Fürstlicher Brauerei Schloss Wächtersbacher

Brewery in Wächtersbach

WÄCHTERSBACHER JUBILAUMSBIER 400 PREMIUM — tawny-gold, roasted malt nose, malt flavor, nutty candy finish, long somewhat dull malt aftertaste, lacks zest.

WÄCHTERSBACHER FÜRSTEN PILS CLASSIC — pale gold, faint malt nose, dry malt palate, bone dry finish, fairly long dry malt aftertaste.

Privatbrauerei Wagner/ Weiss Rössl Bräu

Brewery in Eltmann-Rosstadt

WEISS RÖSSL LEONARDI BOCK — brown, lovely lightly toasted malt nose, big malt flavor, excellent balance, good body, good tasting long malt aftertaste.

WEISS RÖSSLE RATSHERREN DUNKEL — brown, ceral malt aroma and flavor, good body, long dry malt aftertaste.

WEISS RÖSSLE FESTBIER — deep gold, pleasant malt aroma, good dry malt flavor, medium long very dry malt aftertaste, good hop balance.

WEISS RÖSSL MÄRZEN — deep gold, toasted malt nose, very nice, lovely toasted malt flavor finishes richly, smooth dry medium long malt aftertaste.

WEISS RÖSSL FRANKEN RAUCHBIER — deep amber, aroma like smoked bacon, smoked salty meat flavor, fades a bit at the finish but remains on the palate for a very long time.

WEISS RÖSSL URSTOFF — pale gold, complex malt aroma, pleasant straightforward malt flavor, light body, pleasant and very drinkable, medium long dry malt aftertaste.

KARLSKRONE — gold, hop and toasted malt aroma, flavor to match, sour hop finish and long dry sour hop aftertaste. Made for ALDI, Mulheim A.D., Ruhr.

Klosterbrauerei Weltenburg Gmbh.

Monastery Brewery at **Weltenburg**

WELTENBURGER KLOSTER SPEZIAL DUNKEL — amber-brown, big malt nose, rich malt flavor, light body, very little hops (if any), no complexity, medium to short aftertaste of malt with a bit of sour at the end.

WELTENBURGER KLOSTER ASAM-BOCK — deep ruby-brown, excellent earthy toasted malt nose, very complex palate of chocolate, acid, malt, and hops, rich, big, and interesting, gets better as it goes, long medium dry malt aftertaste is interesting in itself considering the way the palate starts out, an absolutely delicious experience.

WELTENBURGER KLOSTER BAROCK DUNKEL — deep rich amber, light toasted malt nose, smooth toasted malt flavor, good body, medium intensity, long light and dry malt aftertaste.

WELTENBURGER KLOSTER HEFE-WEISSBIER DUNKEL — deep amber, huge dense head, lactic clove spice nose, light clove and malt flavor, light body, medium long light dry aftertaste like the flavor, overall seems a bit puny, at least compared to other Weltenburger brews.

Werner-Bräu

Brewery in **Poppenhausen**

WERNER PILSENER — gold, malt and hop aroma and flavor, quite tasty, excellent balance, long dry hop and malt aftertaste.

Privatbrauerei Gasthof Wichert

Brewery-Gasthof in **Lichtenfels**

WICHERT PILSENER — gold, aromatic hop nose, hop and malt flavor, dry hop finish, long dry hop aftertaste.

WICHERT DUNKLES — brown, malt aroma, lightly smoked malt flavor, long and dry malt aftertaste, a pleasant good tasting brew.

Wildbräu

Brewery in **Grafing**

LANDPILS NACH ALTER BRÄUHERRN ART — pale gold, light hop aroma, mild hop flavor, long dry sour hop aftertaste.

Brauhaus Wilhermsdorf

Brewery in **Wilhermsdorf**

ALT WILHERMSDORFER DUNKEL — very deep amber, smooth dry malt aroma, dry malt palate, finishes off-dry malt, there is a back taste of alcohol although the alcohol rating is not high (4.1%), soft texture, long malt aftertaste, it has a good flavor and it grows on you.

Notes:

Privatbrauerei Wilhelm Mayer

Brewery in Rottweil

ORIGINAL ROTTWEILER SCHWARZBIER — deep rosy-brown, pleasant dry lightly toasted malt nose, burnt nature on the palate gives the moalt more complexity, faint dry malt aftertaste, dies immediately as it is swallowed leaving little after, also the balance is questionable.

E. Winkels KG

Brewery in Karlsruhe

WINKELS MEISTER BRÄU PILSENER — gold, big hop nose that was extremely fragrant, you could smell it a good foot away, lusty malt flavor well-balanced with hops, long bitter hop aftertaste, best described as a big rough and tumble brew.

WINKELS MEISTER BRÄU EXPORT — gold, big malt and hop nose, finely carbonated, balanced malt and hop flavor, smooth and delicious, long bright hop aftertaste.

WINKELS MEISTER BRÄU HEFE WEIZEN — hazy gold, medium head, pleasAnt malt nose with a tartness in back, zesty malt and clove flavor,good balance set between the sweetness of the malt and the tartness of the lactic acid, complex and refreshing, long aftertaste follows the flavor in kind.

Privatbrauerei Oberäu Wochinger K.G.

Brewery in Holzkirchen

HOLZKIRCHNER OBERÄU PILS — gold, hop nose, big hop flavor, well backed with malt, highly carbonated, good body, long dry malt and hop aftertaste.

HOLZKIRCHNER OBERÄU EDEL EXPORT — very deep gold, faint malt nose, fairly big malt flavor, big body, long malt aftertaste.

HOCHLAND HELL — gold, malt-hop nose and flavor, off-dry malt finish, long drier malt aftertaste.

HOLZKIRCHNER OBERÄU URTYP HELL — gold, malt and hop aroma, flavor is mostly malt with some hops in back, dry malt-hop finish, and long dry hop aftertaste.

HOLZKIRCHNER WEISSE DUNKEL — deep amber-brown, citrus lemony-grapefruit malt nose, creamy, light spicy clove and malt flavor, dry malt finish, long dry malt aftertaste shows little of the spiciness.

HOLZKIRCHNER WEISSE BAYERISCHES HEFEWEIZEN — hazy gold, faint lactic spice in behind a malt aroma, mild spicy flavor, medium body, long mild spice and malt aftertaste.

HOLZKIRCHNER LAURENZI EXPORT DUNKEL — good deep brown, roasted malt nose, rich roasted malt flavor, finishes dry, long dry malt aftertaste, medium body, good balance.

Woinemer Hausbrauerei

Brewpub in Weinheim

WOINEMER HELL — hazy amber, hop nose, bright hop flavor, excellent balance with the malt that takes the lead in the long aftertaste, a delightful bright beer that goes very well with food or can stand by itself.

WOINEMER MAI BOCK — hazy amber, faint malt and hop nose, huge malt flavor with plenty of hops for balance and complexity, big body, long dry malt and hop aftertaste.

WOINEMER DUNKEL — deep amber-brown, soft malt nose and flavor, medium body, brief medium dry malt aftertaste.

Wolfstetter Bräu George Huber

Brewery in Vilshofen

WOLFERSTETTER VOLLBIER HELL — gold, sour hop nose, very sour hop taste, dry hop finish and aftertaste.

WOLFSTETTER HERREN PILS — gold, zesty hop nose, malt flavor with a hop finish, long dry hop aftertaste.

WOLFSTETTER EXPORT HEFE-WEIZEN — hazy gold, pleasant spicy malt nose, big spicy malt flavor, huge palate, big body, has to be taken in small sips, no guzzling this one, spicy malt finish and aftertaste, a brute of a beer.

WOLFSTETTER RATSHERREN WEISSBIER — brown, pleasant spicy malt aroma, creamy malt and spicy cloves on the palate, fairly big, good body, smooth and creamy, dry malt finish and aftertaste.

J. Wörner & Sohne KG Erbacher Brauhaus

Brewery at Erbach

ERBACHER PRÄDIKATOR DOPPELBOCK — deep amber-brown, delightful rich sweet malt nose, big rich malt with a sour background, excellent background, medium dry long malt, a delicious brew.

Brauerei Zoller-Hof

Brewery in Sigmaringen

ZOLLER BRENZKOFER DUNKEL — amber, light hop nose, medium body, dry malt flavor, short dry malt aftertaste.

ZOLLER FURSTEN HEFE-WEIZEN — hazy gold like grpaefruit juice appearance, spicy clove nose, creamy feel in the mouth, clean light clove and malt flavor, refreshing and balanced, long clean fruity-malty aftertaste, a pleasure to drink.

ZOLLER FURSTEN KRISTALL WEIZEN — pale gold, light malt aroma and flavor, smooth, light, and refreshing, light body, medium long light dry malt aftertaste, excellent wheaty malt character throughout and no spiciness.

ZOLLER FURSTEN PILS — pale gold, big head, light hop nose, dry hop flavor, long dry hop aftertaste.

ZOLLER SPEZIAL- EXPORT — gold, dense head, clean hop nose, smooth hop flavor with a touch of malty sweetness, off-dry malt finish, long slightly off-dry malt and hop aftertaste.

ZOLLER BÖCKLE DUNKLES BOCK BIER — deep amber, thick tan head, faint malt nose, rich dry malt flavor, big body, very long rich dry malt aftertaste with some hops at the end, a delicious bock.

ZOLLER FIDELIS WEIZEN — cloudy brown, fresh spicy malt nose, very rich flavor of malt and cloves, creamy texture, good body, long aftertaste like the flavor except the lactic acid is more noticeable.

Zwiefalter Klosterbrauerei

Brewery at Zwiefalt

ZWIEFALTER KLOSTERBRÄU PILSNER EDELTYP — gold, faintly roasted malt aroma, malt flavor with good hop support, a big lusty flavor, good body, long dry malt and hop aftertaste.

GREAT BRITAIN

Adnams Sole Bay Brewery

Brewery in Southwold, Suffolk

ADNAMS BROADSIDE STRONG PALE ALE — amber, spicy nose, fruity ale flavor, high alcohol (6.3%), creamy, smooth, balanced, quite malty throughout, long dry malt and hop aftertaste.

Notes:

Allied Breweries (U.K.), Ltd.

Breweries include Ind Coope, Tetley-Walker, Lorimer, Beskins, Warrington & Ansells, with locations in Burton-on-Trent and Leeds, England; Edinburgh; Scotland; et al.

DOUBLE DIAMOND ORIGINAL BURTON ALE — deep amber, beautiful rich off-dry roasted malt nose, dry bitter palate up front, off-dry malt finish, long very dry hop aftertaste that borders on bitter, excellent balance, medium body, has a sense of high alcohol, delicious.

DOUBLE DIAMOND PILSENER BEER — amber, big pungent hop aroma, big dry hop flavor, creamy, finely carbonated, long dry hop aftertaste, flavor could use more malt.

TETLEY BITTER — pale amber, nice hop aroma, finely carbonated, tart ale flavor with lots of hop character, fruity malt finish, long dry hop aftertaste. From Joseph Tetley & Son, Leeds.

TETLY SPECIAL PALE ALE — medium amber, toasted malt aroma, flavor starts out like the nose, but the hop intensity increases across the palate to a sharp bitter hop aftertaste, with the roasted malt sliding into the background.

LORIMER'S TRADITIONAL SCOTCH ALE — golden amber, beautiful roasted malt aroma with good hops and a beneficial touch of sour malt that gives balance, intense roasted malt flavor, lingering dry malt aftertaste, big and powerful brew that has plenty of alcohol (7.2%/vol). From Lorimer's Breweries, Ltd. of Edinburgh.

LORIMER'S SCOTTISH BEER — golden amber, big hop nose, huge mouth-filling malt and hop flavor, good balance, dry hop aftertaste has a touch of sour malt. From Lorimer's Breweries, Ltd. of Edinburgh.

ST. CHRISTOPHER NON-ALCOHOLIC BEER — amber, slightly sweet grainy aroma, watery, dry flavor that shows neither malt nor hops, odd dry aftertaste.

JOHN BULL BEER — tawny-gold, bright hop and malt aroma, zesty big hop flavor well-backed with malt, full-bodied, good balance, long dry hop aftertaste.

CHESTER GOLDEN ALE — amber, malt nose and flavor, some off-dry malt at the finish, dull dry malt aftertaste. The Cheshire, Chester, and Mitchell brews were previously made by Greenall Whitley Co., Ltd. in Warrington, Cheshire, England.

CHESHIRE ENGLISH PUB BEER — deep amber, light roasted malt nose with an apricot background, big body, off-dry malt flavor, finishes dry malt, long dry faintly hopped malt aftertaste.

MITCHELL'S CENTENARY ALE — deep copper-amber, complex malt aroma with a tangy hop background, tangy off-dry complex malt and hop flavor, good body, balanced sipping beer, dry middle and finish, excellent lightly sweet long malt aftertaste.

MITCHELL'S BITTER — amber, light hop and malt nose, light hop and malt flavor, weak middle, light sour hop finish and aftertaste.

MITCHELL'S BROWN ALE — ruby-brown, complex toasted malt nose has scents of licorice and bread as well, weak flavor is only faint malt, medium body, little or no aftertaste.

Bass Charrington, Ltd.

A conglomerate of breweries comprised of the Bass, Worthington, Tennent Caledonian, Mitchells & Butler, and Charrington United. Breweries are in Burton-on-Trent, Birmingham, Sheffield, Tadcaster, and Runcorn, England; Belfast, North Ireland; and Glasgow and Edinburgh, Scotland.

BASS PALE ALE — brilliant copper color, big malt and hop aroma, full rich malty flavor, excellent balnce, marvelous long rich and dry aftertaste. Draft version.

BASS PALE ALE I.P.A. — brilliant copper, pleasant malt aroma, good malt flavor with plenty of hop support, well-bodied, excellent balance, long dry hop aftertaste. Bottled version.

WORTHINGTON E BRITISH BEER — pale amber, toasted malt nose, smoky well-hopped roasted malt flavor, complex and long, good flavor but a bit shallow.

WORTHINGTON'S ORIGINAL PALE ALE (WHITE SHIELD) — yellow-gold, yeasty aroma, delicate and complex malt and hop flavor, some yeast in the background, smooth and rich, long dry hop aftertaste.

TENNENT'S LAGER BEER — tawny-gold, creamy, clean malty aroma and malt flavor, faintly soapy backtaste, clean fresh malt finish, long dry malt aftertaste.

TENNENT'S EXTRA — deep gold, mild very good malt and hop aroma, good hop flavor with enough malt for balance, good body, malt finish, long satisfying dry hop aftertaste.

TENNENT'S MILK STOUT — opaque brown, rich malt nose with a smoky-burnt background, rich off-sweet malt flavor, medium body, pleasant long dry malt aftertaste

PIPER EXPORT ALE — deep amber color, roasted mash aroma, burnt toffee-apple flavor, sour in back, assertive at the beginning with the scorched malt and this mars the pleasant aspects, long dry off aftertaste.

BARBICAN NON-ALCOHOLIC MALT BEVERAGE — deep bright gold, dull toasted grainy nose, very light body, light grainy flavor, tartmess in mid-palate, brief dry hop aftertaste.

BASS NO. 1 BARLEY WINE — amber, tart citrus-cherry-licorice nose, palate is sweet malt in front, briny middle, and cuts off quickly at the finish, very complex but surprisingly brief, also the saltiness doesn't go well with the other flavors.

CHARRINGTON BARLEY WINE — very deep red-brown, rich complex nose of malt, coffee, and licorice, complex and rich malt flavor is a little too sweet in the middle, heavy body, off-sweet finish and aftertaste, very long duration, a complex malt sipping beer with hops faintly in the background.

George Bateman & Son

Brewery in Wainfleet

BATEMAN'S VICTORY ALE — amber-brown, malt nose is a bit winy, big flavor starts out dry malt but finishes with a touch of caramel, concentrated taste with a hint of licorice, full bodied, long malt aftertaste like the flavor, the hops stay in back but are there, very tasty and very drinkable.

BATEMAN'S XXXB ALE — amber, fruity malt and alcohol aroma, flavor like the aroma, malt finish, long malt aftertaste shows some alcohol, not complex but very warming and enjoyable.

Carlsberg Brewery

Brewery in Northampton, England

CARLSBERG SPECIAL BREW — bright amber-gold, big malt and malt aroma, big mouthful of flavor, lots of both malt and hops, big body, wine-like and alcoholic (8%), complex and balanced, extremely long malt aftertaste has some hops in back for balance, nicely made beer.

Courage, Ltd.

Breweries in London, Reading, Plymouth, and Bristol, England

COURAGE LAGER EXPORT BEER — yellow-gold, high carbonation, hops dominate the nose and taste, long sour hop aftertaste.

JOHN COURAGE EXPORT — tawny-gold, foamy, off-dry malt nose, bitter hop flavor, doubtful balance, slightly off-dry malt aftertaste.

BULLDOG PALE ALE — pale yellow, hop nose, dull hop flavor up front, light hop finish, very brief dry hop aftertaste, almost none at all.

BULLDOG LAGER BEER — bright pale gold, intense fruity-malt aroma, big body, lots of hops in the flavor all the way through, long dry hop aftertaste, very good brew.

JOHN COURAGE AMBER LAGER — amber, light toasted malt nose, toasted malt flavor, smooth, medium body, long dry malt aftertaste.

IMPERIAL RUSSIAN STOUT 1983 — opaque brown, buttery roasted malt aroma, palate starts dry malt, gets intensely sweet in the middle, finishes sour, and this sourness carries into the long malt aftertaste.

MARTIN'S PALE ALE — amber, big head, pine needle and citrus aroma, big hop, malt and pine flavor, very zesty, pine most noticeable at the finish and goes with the malt into the aftertaste, very big body, rich flavor, long malt aftertaste. Made by Courage for John Martin of Antwerp, Belgium.

Edwin Holden, Ltd.

Burton Bridge Brewery in Dudley, England

BURTON BRIDGE BURTON FESTIVAL ALE — copper-amber, toasted malt nose, huge malt flavor, big body, hops are present but only in back, fruity off-dry apple-like finish, lightly hopped malt aftertaste.

BURTON BRIDGE BITTER ALE — hazy amber, complex hop and malt aroma, finely carbonated, light body, flavorful malt-hop palate, good balance, long smooth aftertaste has a cider-like quality.

BURTON BRIDGE XL BITTER — amber, complex nose of cantelope, melon, shellac, and cider, flavor is off-dry malt at first then linseed and woody oxidation, bad sample.

BURTON BRIDGE BURTON PORTER — tawny-brown, light off-dry malt nose, zesty hop and malt flavor, light but balanced, dry hop finish, long dry hop aftertaste.

Felinfoel Brewing Co., Ltd.

Brewery in Llanelli, Wales

DRAGON ALE — amber, fairly strong hop nose is a little stinky, light body, thin hop flavor, malt finish, light malt and hop aftertaste is medium to long.

Felinfoel
Festive
Ale
CONTENTS 1 PT. 2.5 FL. OZ. (U.S.A.) 550ml
Product of Great Britain, Brewed and Bottled by
The Felinfoel Brewery, Llanelli, Wales, U.K.

DOUBLE DRAGON ALE — very deep amber, zesty hop nose, big sweet hop flavor, good body, zesty hop finish, long spicy hop aftertaste, tastes like a good brewpub ale.

JOHN BROWN ALE — copper-brown, faint malt aroma and flavor, short dry malt aftertaste.

FELINFOEL BITTER ALE — gold, hop nose, sharp hops up front on the palate, the flavor gradually softens until it is weak sour hops at the finish, thin body, weak watery aftertaste, just a quick burst of hops and thats that.

FELINFOEL CREAM STOUT — almost opaque red-brown, faint burnt licorice and malt nose, bitter and dry licorice flavor, finish, and aftertaste.

ST. DAVID'S PORTER — deep red-brown, faint malt aroma, malt flavor with a licorice finish, dry licorice aftertaste.

HERCULES ALE — copper, candy nose, sweet licorice flavor, complex and alcoholic but overwhelmingly sweet right through the aftertaste, 7-8% alc/vol.

WELSH ALE — deep amber, nose a bit off at first, then exotic spicy hops, very strong almost overwhelming malt and hop flavor, sweet then tart then sweet again, finishes sweet leading into a long off-dry aftertaste.

WELSH BITTER BEER — frr[s,nrt. mpdr s noy pgg sy gotdy. yjrm rcpyov d[ovu jp[d. brtu dytpmh. s;,pdy pbrtejr;,omh ,s;y smf jp[g;sbpt. derry yjrm ysty yjrm derry shsom. gomodjrd derry ;rsfomh omyp s ;pmh ;gg=ftu sgyrtysdyr.

FELINFOEL HERITAGE ALE — deep bright copper, light candy sweet nose, tart candy flavor, sour hop finish, good body, long dry hop aftertaste.

PRINCESS PORTER — deep ruby-amber, chicken coop aroma, dull watery malt flavor, mercifully brief.

FELINFOEL FESTIVE ALE — hazy amber, faintly acetone aroma, a big malt flavor, noticeable alcohol, very strong and very long.

Notes:

BREWED BY THE OLD BREWERY OAKHILL, SOMERSET, ENGLAND.
FARMERS ALE
THE OLD BREWERY OAKHILL
330 ml
BOTTLED BY GIBBS MEW PLC. SALISBURY, ENGLAND.
11.2 fl oz US
IMPORTED BY BRITBEER IMPORT CORPORATION, CARSON, CA90745, USA

Gibbs Mews, PLC

Brewery in Salisbury, England

OLD THUMPER EXTRA SPECIAL ALE — medium amber, marvelous smooth complex slightly sweet hop aroma, bright smooth complex roasted malt and hop flavor, good body and balance, finishes off-dry malt, extremely long malt aftertaste, very drinkable. Made for Ringwood Brewery, Ringwood.

FORTY-NINER FINEST ALE — pale amber, beautiful hop nose, complex with good malt support, good zesty malt and hop flavor, malt stays through the finish, but mostly the palate is hops, long dry hop aftertaste. Made for Ringwood Brewery.

THE BISHOP'S TIPPLE — deep amber, beautiful complex sweet berries and hop nose, well balanced with malt, good body, big smooth creamy rich malt flavor, off-dry in front, dry at finish, very long medium dry malt sort of sherry-like aftertaste (perhaps because it is 6.5% alcohol), excellent balance, very likeable.

FARMER'S VELVET STOUT — extremely deep opaque brown, brown head, dry smoky-coffee nose, light body for a stout, dry smoky malt flavor and aftertaste. Brewed by the Old Brewery, Oakhill, Somerset, bottled by Gibbs Mews of Salisbury.

FARMER'S ALE — hazy pale amber, big fruity malt aroma, dry malt flavor with a burnt component, bitter hop finish, short dry hop aftertaste, medium body, faint citrus background is present throughout. Also brewed by Old Brewery and bottled by Gibbs Mews.

SARUM SPECIAL FINE PALE ALE — hazy dark amber, fruity malt nose, sweet malt front palate, dry middle, bitter finish, light body, faintly sweet malt aftertaste, doesn't quite come together.

Greenall Whitley Co., Ltd.

Brewery in Warrington, Cheshire, England

CHESTER GOLDEN ALE — amber, malt nose and flavor, some off-dry malt at the finish, dull dry malt aftertaste.

CHESHIRE ENGLISH PUB BEER — deep amber, light roasted malt nose with an apricot background, big body, off-dry malt flavor, finishes dry malt, long dry faintly hopped malt aftertaste.

MITCHELL'S CENTENARY ALE — deep copper-amber, complex malt aroma with a tangy hop background, tangy off-dry complex malt and hop flavor, good body, balanced sipping beer, dry middle and finish, excellent lightly sweet long malt aftertaste.

MITCHELL'S BITTER — amber, light hop and malt nose, light hop and malt flavor, weak middle, light sour hop finish and aftertaste.

MITCHELL'S BROWN ALE — ruby-brown, complex toasted malt nose has scents of licorice and bread as well, weak flavor is only faint malt, medium body, little or no aftertaste.

Greene King, Ltd.

Breweries in Bury St. Edmunds and Biggleswade, England

GREENE KING ALE — bright amber, faint sour malt nose, light body, light bitter hop flavor, weak slightly sour malt and hop aftertaste.

ABBOT ALE — pale amber, apple-malt aroma, bitter hop flavor, long dry and bitter hop aftertaste. Another sample had a distinct pine character instead of the apple. It too lacked balance.

ST. EDMUND SPECIAL PALE ALE — fairly deep tawny-gold, candylike ale nose, sweet with a resiny background, sharp tangy hop-ale flavor, heavy body, big malt finish and aftertaste but there are unlikeable components.

SUFFOLK DARK ENGLISH ALE — deep red-brown, big ale aroma with an off-dry berry-like background, very complex malt and hop flavor with an acidic finish and aftertaste.

Brewers Guinness PLC

Brewery in London, England; affiliate of Arthur Guinness of Ireland

GUINNESS DRAFT BITTER — amber, big thick head, faintly fruity malt aroma, malt flavor, weak body, lightly carbonated, weak dry and harsh malt aftertaste. This is packaged in a can.

PUB DRAUGHT GUINNESS — deep brown, pleasant hop and malt aroma, very dry mild hop flavor, medium body, dry hop finish, long dry hop aftertaste, packaged in a can this seems to be a lot lighter than the bottled or draft versions.

Harvey & Son (Lewes) Ltd.

Bridge Wharf Brewery in Lewes, England

HARVEY'S ELIZABETHAN ALE — hazy amber, big bubble head, toasted malt nose, strong sweet-ale palate, complex but has balance problems with many flavors coming at you from many directions, noticeable alcohol (>8%), sour licorice aftertaste.

Mansfield Brewery

Brewery in Mansfield, England

MANSFIELD BEST BITTER — brilliant amber, faint complex burnt vegetal-butter nose, burnt malt and bitter hop palate, malt finish, and a long malt aftertaste has hops arriving at the end. Sounds worse than it is, and it actually grows on you as you drink it.

KINGPIN ENGLISH LAGER BEER — hazy amber, nice toasted malt nose, good malt flavor is somewhat light, faintly sour malt aftertaste.

OLD BAILY STRONG BITTER — deep amber, flat, well-hopped toasted malt flavor, long dry toasted malt aftertaste, needs the missing carbonation.

McMullen & Son Ltd.

Brewery in Hertford, England

CASTLE SPECIAL PALE ALE — medium amber, light complex off-dry hop aroma with interesting fruity notes like papaya and citrus, light body, light off-dry hop flavor, complex middle and finish, long light medium dry hop aftertaste.

Norwich Brewery Co.

Brewing Company in **Norwich, England**

ANGLICAN STRONG ALE — hazy amber, big bubble head, crisp off-dry and citrus ale nose, crisp tart flavor is strong hops in front, medium dry hops in the middle and finish, lots of bite on the sides of your tongue, dry hop aftertaste. Made in Manchester for Norwich.

Eldridge Pope & Co., Ltd.

Brewery in **Dorchester, England**

THOMAS HARDY'S OLD ALE— bright reddish persimmon color, intense hop nose, very heavy body, robust malty-herbal hop flavor that carries through to a rich finish, long strong malt and hop aftertaste, a concentrated ale, luxuriously flavored. This is the description of the **1979** bottling.

THOMAS HARDY'S ALE 1982 — deep cherry-amber, strong fruity-malt nose with melon, papaya, and acid, heavy body, intensely sweet malt flavor is a little salty at first, extremely long malt and hop aftertaste, quite different from the 1979.

THOMAS HARDY' ALE 1989 — hazy amber, beautiful roasted malt aroma with a definite sense of alcohol, taste is extremely rich malt heavily flavored with alcohol, but the very long aftertaste is dry malt, big bodied, aging very well, and has an excellent balance.

THOMAS HARDY'S ALE 1991 — cloudy amber, most appetizing rich malt nose with little apparent alcohol,body is huge, flavor is strong rich malt, particularly good on the front of the palate, but a bit coarse at the finish, aftertaste is already becoming dry but its strength is as yet unabated.

THOMAS HARDY'S ALE 1986 — dark amber and hazy, aroma transcends normal bounds with herbs, spices, flowers, smoke, leather, and tobacco, even scents normally found in fine old Bugundies and Barolos, the palateis like the nose but the features are greatly attenuated and underlie the malt, body is medium and there is a delicacy of flavors that is not there in younger samples, finish is very much like fine sweet sherry, almost like Pedro Ximenez grapes after they have been dried to raisins in the hot Spanish sun.

THOMAS HARDY ALE 1984 — paler than the '86 (more like the '89) and, by the aroma, the development of the brew is troubled. There is an acidic sparkle that masks most of the subtle complexities, all but the malt, herbs, and spices. On the palate, the same effect obtains, but the brew is bright and tasty with the spicy lightly acidic tang. Body is only medium, but the brew is very good to sip and ends with a smooth semi-dry spicy malt aftertaste.

THOMAS HARDY'S ALE 1988 — deep hazy amber, concentrated malt nose, flavor like a malt syrup, very low carbonation, at the finish there is a salty-sweet-salty feeling on the palate as the flavor seems to flip around in confusion (or because the flavors are so strong the palate flips around in confusion), big long malt aftertaste.

POPE'S "1880" BEER — bright amber, complex roasted off-dry malt, orange peel, and hop aroma, complex creamy licorice, molasses, and toasted malt flavor, very dry and very long malt aftertaste. This is the bottled **POPE'S DORSET INDIA PALE ALE.**

ROYAL OAK PALE ALE— brilliant deep amber, complex rich off-dry malt and hop ale nose that favors the malt, big delicious malt flavor, fairly intense but still smooth, big body, finishes gently, long slightly off-dry mild malt aftertaste, not a whole lot of complexity but very well-balanced, and a very very drinkable ale.

Robinwood Breweries & Vintners

Microbrewery in **Todmorden**

OLD FART — dark amber, very foamy, lactic nose and harsh acidic taste.

The Old Brewery

Samuel Smith's Brewery in **Tadcaster, England**

SAMUEL SMITH'S OLD BREWERY GOLDEN BROWN ALE — medium deep amber, burnt malt aroma with a trace of something like orange oil, smooth fruity-toffee malt flavor, well-balanced and mellow, pleasant and appetizing dry malt aftertaste.

SAMUEL SMITH'S OLD BREWERY PALE ALE — pale amber, pale copper head, lovely roasted malt and molasses aroma, big hop flavor with plenty of roasted malt in support, big body, finely carbonated, long dry hop and roasted malt aftertaste, another lovely ale.

SAMUEL SMITH'S NUT BROWN ALE — red-brown, complex off-dry toasted malt nose with an apple backing, medium body, big complex ale flavor, slightly sweet finish, very long dry malt aftertaste.

SAMUEL SMITH'S OATMEAL STOUT — deep ruby-brown, almost opaque, complex fruity-malt aroma, palate is dry malt in fruit, off-dry malt at the finish, rich and full-bodied, soft and smooth, no bite whatever, long fairly dry malt aftertaste.

TADDY PORTER — brilliant deep red-brown, generous brown head, complex dry coffee bean aroma, dry rich clean malt and hop flavor has a mocha background, delicious and satisfying, long long clean dry malt aftertaste, a beautiful brew.

SAMUEL SMITH'S IMPERIAL STOUT — deep brown, intensely sweet malt nose, big sweet malt flavor but not cloying, good flavor, good body, good balance, dry malt aftertaste, well-made brew.

SAMUEL SMITH'S PURE BREWED LAGER BEER — hazy gold, hop nose, dry hop flavor has good malt backing, good balance, high carbonation, medium long dry hop aftertaste.

SAMUEL SMITH'S WINTER WELCOME ALE 1990-1991 — hazy gold, faintly skunky nose, big hop flavor, big body, malt rolls in at mid-palate and is there in quantity, alcoholic finish, long dry malt aftertaste.

SAMUEL SMITH'S WINTER WELCOME ALE 1991-1992 — peach color, strong hop nose is almost skunky, finely carbonated, strong hop flavor, assertive and alcoholic, dull malt and sour hop aftertaste.

SAMUEL SMITH'S WINTER WELCOME ALE 1992-1993 — hazy amber, well-hopped alelike aroma, slightly toasted, big rich toasted malt flavor, big body, very long and rich toasted malt aftertaste.

Scottish and Newcastle Breweries, Ltd.

Conglomerate comprised of MacEwan's, Younger's, and Newcastle Breweries in Edinburgh, Scotland, Newcastle-on-Tyne, England, et al.

MacEWAN'S SCOTCH ALE — deep amber, creamy, big picquant malt nose, big body, distinctive meal and malt flavor with good bittering hops in back, long dry hop and malt aftertaste.

MacEWAN'S TARTAN ALE — dark brown with reddish hues, creamy texture, strong off-dry malt taste, licorice and malt finish and aftertaste, quite long and very good.

MacEWAN'S EDINBURGH ALE — deep brown, creamy, rich very complex malt nose, beautiful rich roasted -smoky malt flavor, long smoky aftertaste, easily the best of the MacEwan ales.

MacEWAN'S STRONG ALE —deep amber-gold, clean delicate malt nose, rich full-flavored off-dry malt taste, very heavy body, long malt aftertaste.

MacEWAN'S MALT LIQUOR — extremely deep brown color, almost opaque, light toffee aroma, heavy body, rich very sweet malt flavor, bitter hop finish, long dry coffee aftertaste, high alcohol (7.8%).

MacEWAN'S STRONG MALT LIQUOR — deep dark brown, slightly sweet roasted malt aroma, sweet caramel and toasted malt flavor with a touch of licorice, big body, balanced, lingering malt aftertaste.

MacEWAN'S EXPORT — amber, off-dry malt nose with some odd background, malt flavor, light body, brief dry malt aftertaste with some sweetness at the end.

NEWCASTLE BROWN ALE — dark amber-brown, nutty malt aroma, smooth and mellow malt flavor, some bitter hops at the finish, long dry hop and malt aftertaste, a delightful brew.

NEWCASTLE LIGHT ALE — medium copper-gold, off-dry malt nose, slightly sweet malt flavor, softens and fades at the finish, very little aftertaste.

YOUNGER'S TARTAN BITTER — amber, strange off nose with malt hidden beneath, sort of like burnt candy, bitter hop flavor, dry bitter hop aftertaste with little length.

YOUNGER'S KESTREL LAGER — bright amber-gold, good hop and malt aroma, strong bitter hop flavor up front, hops fade a bit and are replaced by malt in the mid-palate, medium body, soft and pleasant malt finish, medium length dry malt and light hop aftertaste, very drinkable.

YOUNGER'S KESTREL SUPER STRENGTH VERY STRONG LAGER — gold, stinky strong hop nose, wine-like with noticeable alcohol (9.5%), strong and sweet (strong hops and sweet malt), heavy body, long off-dry hop and malt aftertaste, gets better as you continue to drink it, very much like drinking a malt whiskey.

GORDON HIGHLAND SCOTCH ALE — deep rose-brown, extremely dense small bubble long lasting brown head, well-balanced rich roasted malt and hop aroma and flavor, full body, high density, high alcohol (8%), extremely long rich malt aftertaste. Brewed by Scottish Brewers Ltd. and bottled by John Martin of Antwerp, Belgium.

GORDON DOUGLAS SCOTCH BRAND ALE — deep amber, light dry malt aroma, concentrated malt flavor, big body, aftertaste is briefly off-dry malt but quickly goes and stays dry, a big brew that feels good in your mouth. Made for John Martin of Antwerp, Belgium.

THEAKSTON OLD PECULIER YORKSHIRE ALE — brown, aroma of canned brown bread, dry malty-molasses flavor, malt finish, light malt aftertaste, tastes a whole lot better than it sounds. Theakston brews were previously made by T & R Theakston, Ltd. with breweries at Masham and Carlisle, England.

THEAKSTON BEST BITTER ALE — tawny-gold, fragrant hop aroma with a touch of apple cider, light carbonation, good tasting malt and hop flavor, good balance, bitter hop finish, long dry hop aftertaste.

Notes:

Shepherd Neame Ltd.

Canterbury Brewery in Faversham, England

CANTERBURY HOP PICKER'S PALE ALE — copper-amber, dry complex ale aroma with a buttery component, dry sour hop flavor and aftertaste.

CANTERBURY PREMIUM ALE — amber, light hop and malt aroma (with a faint background of paint thinner), flavor starts out with hops, but a chemical taste develops and the hops turn sour, must be bad sample.

CANTERBURY REGIMENTAL DINNER ALE — amber, aroma of sweet malt, hops, apple, and cardboard, strong hop flavor has plenty of supporting malt, but the balance is questionable, hops go from bitter to salty then sour.

Watney-Mann & Truman Brewers, Ltd.

Brewing Company comprised of nine regional companies: Watney, Combe & Reid, Truman, Usher, Bryborough, Wilson, Webster, Phoenix, Norwich, and Mann. Breweries in Norwich, Mortlake, London, Edinburgh, Halifax, Manchester, and Trowbridge.

WATNEY'S RED BARREL — bright amber, tangy malt nose, zesty malt and hop flavor, bright and well-balanced, tangy in front, off-dry malt in the middle, dry at the finish, complex and long. This beer has also been labelled WATNEY'S TRADITIONAL BEER in the U.S. Widely available on draft.

WATNEY'S STINGO DARK ALE — opaque brown, all-malt treacle nose with a faint sourness in back, taste of heavy malty-molasses, tenacious long sweet malt aftertaste, despite all that sweet malt, the balance is fairly good, an interesting barleywine style with 7% alc/vol.

WATNEY'S STINGO CREAM STOUT — opaque brown, off-dry concentrated malt nose, big smoky (very much burnt) malt flavor, big body, pleasant,decent balance, overall fairly dry, not filling, long dry malt aftertaste.

WATNEY'S CREAM STOUT — deep brown, tan head, malty nose doesn't yield expected roasted barley or chocolate malt, but the roast barley is there on the palate, very smooth and soft, but not long.

MANN'S THE ORIGINAL BROWN ALE — brown, good rich coffee aroma with a charcoal background, finely carbonated, full all-malt flavor, no hops noticeable, smooth and mellow, good balance, lightly sweet long malt aftertaste, a delightful "mild".

USHER'S WINTER ALE — medium brown, light malt nose, dry and robust malt flavor, you can really sink your teeth into it, long flavored dry malt aftertaste, marvelous sipping beer.

TRUMAN'S CHRISTMAS ALE — medium deep amber, beautiful complex citrus-ale nose that reminds you of Marguerita mix, malt and hop flavor with an ale-like character, excellent balance, complex, long, and satisfying.

SCOTTISH PRIDE LIGHT BEER — deep tawny-gold, malt nose with a sourness in back, light dry malt flavor, light body, very little aftertaste. From Drybrough & Co., Ltd., Edinburgh.

LONDON LIGHT LAGER BEER — bright gold, malt nose, weak malt flavor, thin body, weak brief malt aftertaste.

WATNEYS LIGHT — deep gold, lovely malt nose with good hop backing, light body, light malt flavor is faintly sour, short dull malt aftertaste. From Watney, Combe, Reid & Co., Ltd.

WATNEY'S LIGHT BEER — hazy gold, slightly stinky soapy hop aroma, strange light sour vegetal malt flavor, reminds you of cabbage, short sour malt aftertaste. From Watney-Truman, Ltd.

Whitbread & Co., Ltd.

A large brewing conglomerate with breweries in Cheltenham, Leeds, Liverpool, Luton, Faversham, Durham, Salford, Sheffield, Samlesbury, Marlow, Portsmouth, Tiverton, Wateringbury, and Romsey, England.

WHITBREAD TANKARD LONDON ALE — tawny-brown, caramel and yeast nose, good malty flavor, good balance, short dry malt aftertaste.

WHITBREAD ALE — deep tawny-brown, beautiful rich and smooth caramel-malt aroma, caramel taste, very pleasant and appetizing, finely balanced, long malt aftertaste, a mellow enjoyable brew.

WHITBREAD BREWMASTER — brownish gold, highly cabonated, malt aroma and flavor, dry malt finish and medium aftertaste, not well-balanced.

MACKESON STOUT — very deep dark brown, alomost opaque, rich malt aroma, heavy body, syrup-like, rich coffee-malt flavor, excellent stout and a worthy rival of Guinness, perhaps not as dry but in some respects a bit richer.

MACKESON TRIPLE STOUT — extremely deep opaque brown, roasted malt aroma, off-dry malt flavor, very rich and very big, long rich off-dry malt aftertaste, quite drinkable for a heavy brew.

GOLD LABEL NO. 1 SPARKLING BARLEY WINE — rosy-orange, sweet candy-apple nose, assertive aroma and flavor much like some of the strongly flavored fruity cough medecines, but not medicinal, strong hops really bite the corners of your mouth and back of the tongue, long bitter hop aftertaste, a powerfully strong sipping beer.

CAMPBELL'S CHRISTMAS — deep copper, big sweet rising malt nose, rich, complex, intensely flavored malt, big bodied, long off-dry malt aftertaste, an incredible beer made for the Belgian market, a must try for any serious beer drinker.

CAMPBELL'S SCOTCH ALE— very deep amber-brown, fresh and tangy ale nose, big malt and hop flavor, very insistent, almost overwhelming, complex, strong, aftertaste like the flavor but a bit less intense and drier, very long. Also made for the Belgian market.

CAMPBELL'S GOLD LABEL — deep amber, huge head, light complex toasted malt and hop aroma, big malt and hop flavor, excellent balance, big body, long delicious complex malt and hop aftertaste, a huge brew. wine-like and alcoholic (10%), great sipping beer. Made for the Belgian market.

BODDINGTON'S BITTER BEER — deep bright gold, strong roasted malt aroma, pleasant roasted malt flavor, light body, very light dry hop aftertaste. This brew was previously made by Boddinton's Breweries, Ltd. in Manchester, England.

GREECE

Atalanti Brewery/ Henninger

Breweries in Athens and Hellas

AEGEAN HELLAS BEER — gold, malt aroma with just a touch of hops, malt flavor with little complexity, light body, sour malt aftertaste.

SPARTAN LAGER EXPORT — bright yellow-gold, pleasant malt nose with good hop background, dull off-dry malt flavor, dry and bitter hop aftertaste.

SPARTAN PREMIUM BEER — gold, fragrant malt nose, hop palate, creamy, dry malt finish, good body, medium length "honeyed" hop aftertaste.

Notes:

HOLLAND

Abdij Van Koningshoeven

Brewery at Tilburg

LA TRAPPE ALE — amber-gold, faint fruity alcoholic nose, strong spicy clove palate with noticeable alcohol, long spicy aftertaste. Made for John Martin of Antwerp, Belgium. Strangely, it is labelled as a product of Belgium.

HUNGARY

Borsod Brewery

Brewery in Bocs

BORSOD PREMIUM — gold light malt and hop aroma, very dry malt and hop flavor, almost too dry, long dry hop aftertaste.

ICELAND

Brewery Egill Skallagrimsson Ltd.

Brewery at Reykjavik

POLAR BEER — pale amber-gold, toasted malt nose, light body, pleasant toasted malt flavor, hops come in at the finish, long dry hop aftertaste, good balance.

IRELAND

Arthur Guinness Son & Co., Ltd.

St. James's Gate Brewery in Dublin, Dundalk, et al.

Also some beers (like Extra Stout) are brewed in Scotland, England and in many countries throughout the world for local markets.

GUINNESS EXTRA STOUT — opaque red-brown color, creamy tawny head, very full-bodied, dense and thick, complex Worcestershire sauce nose, dry coffee-toffee flavor with a chocolate finish, long dry complex malt aftertaste, excellent stout — the baseline description of the classic stout. On draft, it seems to be darker in color, less carbonated, spicier and smoother than the bottled version. It is very mellow, excellently balanced and the head stays on right to the bottom of the glass.

GUINNESS CREAM STOUT — extremely deep brown, low carbonation, strong scorched malt flavor, bitter and flat, harsh long hop aftertaste.

HARP LAGER — deep gold, pungent hop nose, bitter hop flavor, long bitter hop aftertaste, great for true "hop-heads." Version exported to the U.S..

HARP LAGER BEER — pale gold, lovely well-hopped aroma, finely carbonated, bright strong hop flavor, good balance, more hops than malt but done right. This is the version shipped to Canada; it is higher in alcohol, has better balance and I find it much tastier than the version above.

GUINNESS GOLD LAGER BEER — pale gold, good well-balanced hop and malt nose, good crisp hop flavor, good balance, clean dry hop finish, long dry hop aftertaste, very drinkable and refreshing.

Notes:

KALIBER ALL NATURAL NON-ALCOHOLIC BEER — tawny-gold, grainy sweet malt nose, sour grainy palate, slightly roasted character, gets stronger at the finish, very long tenacious dry roasted malt aftertaste.

PUB DRAUGHT GUINNESS — the so-called draft version in a can, deep brown, pleasant hop and malt aroma, very dry mild hop flavor, medium body, dry hop finish, long dry hop aftertaste, seems to be a lot lighter than the bottled or draft versions.

KILKENNY IRISH BEER — deep amber, big bright hop aroma, big hop flavor, very big bodied, hefty and very long dry hop aftertaste, very well hopped throughout, but there is no lack of malt either, fairly good balance, big and brightly flavored brew. Smithwick & Sons, Kilkenny, St. Francis Abbey Brewery from Guinness.

ITALY

Birra Moretti S.p.A.

Brewery in Udine

Also Castello Brewery in San Giorgio di Nogaro.

MORETTI PILSENER — deep gold, clean malt and hop aroma and taste, excellent balance, light body, long aftertaste like the flavor, very tasty and very drinkable.

SCHLOSS-BIER EXPORT LAGER — gold, creamy, nice hop and malt aroma, faint malt flavor and aftertaste, medium to light body.

MORETTI EXPORT BEER (BIRE FURLANE) RESERVA CASTELLO — brilliant gold, pleasant malt and hop aroma, off-dry apple and malt flavor, palate drops off rapidly after a good start, short faint dry malt aftertaste.

MORETTI BIRRA FRIULANA — bright gold, grainy aroma, grainy malt flavor with a good hop background, long dry malt aftertaste.

CASTELLO BEER — pale bright gold, off-dry fruity malt and apple nose, pleasant light malt flavor, light fruity malt finish, dry malt aftertaste.

SAN SOUCI DOUBLE MALT — pale gold, light beery nose, fresh malt flavor with good hop balance, long dry hop aftertaste, very drinkable.

MORETTI LA ROSSA DOUBLE MALT BEER — rosy amber, big toasted malt nose, huge rich and complex toasted malt flavor with plenty of hop support, good body, alcoholic, long aftertaste like the flavor, a little clumsy, but there is a lot to it.

MORETTI DOUBLE MALT DARK (BIRRA DOPPIO MALTO BRUNA) — deep reddish amber, big sweet malt aroma, buttery brown sugar flavor, light body, long malt aftertaste is a bit flabby.

OLD VENICE ITALIAN PILSENER — yellow-gold, pleasant malt aroma, sour malt and hop palate, bitter hop finish, light body, short dry hop aftertaste.

D'AQUINO ITALIAN BEER — pale gold, very faint grapey-malt aroma, strange fruity-malt flavor, light body, medium long odd dry malt aftertaste.

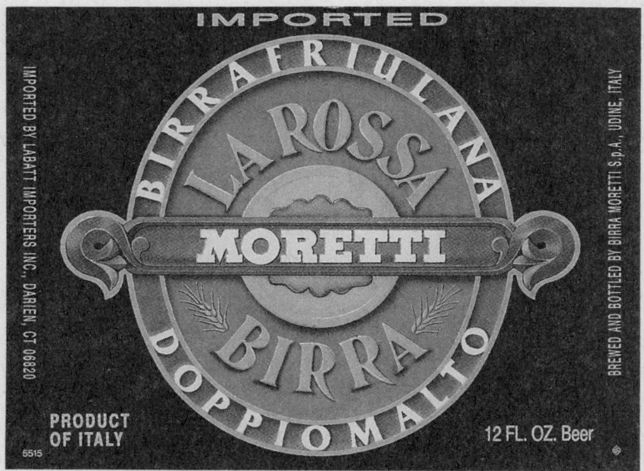

NORWAY

Ringnes Brewery

Brewery in Oslo

RINGNES SPECIAL BEER — tawny-gold, strong hop nose and big hop flavor, lots of hops and malt and loaded with character, good malt finish and aftertaste, long and delicious.

RINGNES MALT LIQUOR — deep gold, off-dry malt nose, very sweet malty taste and aftertaste, sharp hop bitterness at the very end.

RINGNES EXPORT — gold, aroma of hops and caramel, really good hop and malt flavor up front, but it sags in the middle, and finishes poorly of sour celery, short dry offish aftertaste.

RINGNES SPECIAL BOCK BEER — dark red-brown, strong roasted malt, molasses and prune nose, very heavy body, good molasses-treacle flavor that is really delightful, long rich malt aftertaste, excellent.

RINGNES LOW — bright gold, slightly skunky nose at first, this evolved into hops and tuna salad, very light slightly malty flavor, light body, grainy finish and aftertaste.

RINGNES ZERO PLUS — bright gold, skunky nose at first but the malt soon fights its way through, high carbonation, grainy malt flavor, little body, dry malt finish and aftertaste, medium length.

RINGNES DARK — bright red-brown, sweet malt aroma, light body, pleasant off-dry malt flavor, long off-dry malt aftertaste, nice but could use more heft.

RINGNES SPECIAL CHRISTMAS ALE— deep amber, faintly smoky malt aroma, there is some sweetness in behind, zesty smooth pleasant malt flavor, good balance throughout, medium body, touch of caramel in back, long dry malt aftertaste, didn't find any hops to mention.

NORSK NON-ALCOHOLIC MALT BEVERAGE — pale yellow-gold, faint malt nose, faint grainy malt and CO_2 palate, sour light metallic aftertaste.

RINGNES ALE SPECIAL JUBILEE — bright amber, toasted malt nose, good off-dry malt flavor is like brown sugar, finish and aftertaste are drier malt than the flavor, mellow and long.

RINGNES PILSENER ØL — pale gold, big hop aroma and flavor, good body, very long dry hop aftertaste.

RUSSIA

Russian Breweries

The situation of Russian breweries is still in a confused state (at least to me) so I have lumped them together under a single heading with any identification included with the write-up.

ALDARA ALUS — hazy gold, sour creamy malt nose, sour malt palate with a hop bite in back, rough hop aftertaste, not a pleasant brew. No brewery cited but a brewery origin date of 1865 given. Alus means ale.

PORTERIS — hazy amber-brown, off-dry roasted malt nose, lovely big roasted malt flavor, rich, delicious and very long, an excellent porter (porteris). Label says 20%, which I presume to be 20 degrees density. Porteris is labelled almost identically to Aldara so it is further presumed they are from the same brewery.

RUSSKOYE PREMIUM RUSSIAN LAGER BEER — bright deep gold, soapy malt nose, dry malt flavor, hop finish, soapy malt aftertaste has good length. From Obolon Brewery, Kiev.

MOSCOVA BEER OF RUSSIA— hazy gold, very fruity malt and European hop nose, pleasant fruity malt flavor and finish, lightly hopped, good body, long dry malt aftertaste, bigger in the front than at the finish. Moscow Brewery, Moscow-since 1863.

RUSKI IMPORTED RUSSIAN BEER — gold, mango-papaya tropical fruit aroma and flavor, finish is even more fruit-like, dry malt aftertaste. From Oboken Brewery, Kiev.

TROIKA ORIGINAL RUSSIAN BEER — gold, dank aroma is mostly cardboard with faint hop and malt background, dank malt flavor, sour finish, short aftertaste. From the Moscow Brewery.

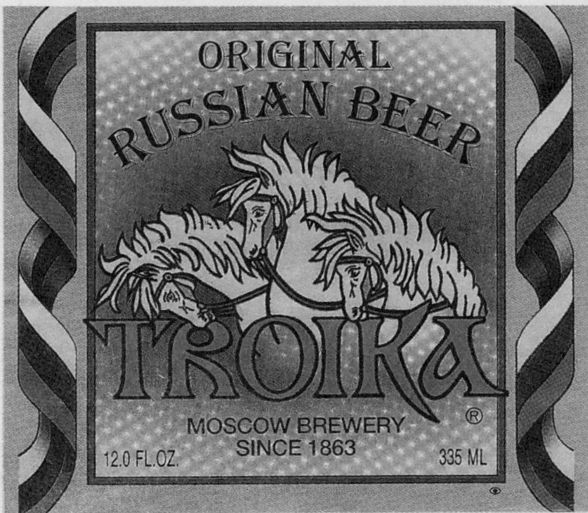
ORIGINAL
RUSSIAN BEER
TROIKA
MOSCOW BREWERY
SINCE 1863
12.0 FL.OZ.
335 ML

GOVERNMENT WARNING: (1) ACCORDING TO THE SURGEON GENERAL WOMEN SHOULD NOT DRINK ALCOHOLIC BEVERAGES DURING PREGNANCY BECAUSE OF THE RISK OF BIRTH DEFECTS. (2) CONSUMPTION OF ALCOHOLIC BEVERAGES IMPAIRS YOUR ABILITY TO DRIVE A CAR OR OPERATE MACHINERY, AND MAY CAUSE HEALTH PROBLEMS.
PRODUCT OF U.S.S.R.
Ruski
IMPORTED RUSSIAN BEER
500 ml. 1 PINT.9 FL. OZ.
PRODUCED BY OBOKEN BREWERY, KIEV, USSR
IMPORTED BY BLAIR IMPORTERS LTD.
LAKE SUCCESS, N.Y.
0 44286 44095 2

Notes:

CONGO

SCBK (Congo Brewing)

Brewery in **Pointe Noire**

N'GOK IMPORTED BEER — gold, hop nose, almost skunky, high carbonation, light hop flavor, medium long dry hop aftertaste.

Notes:

ETHIOPIA

Asmara Brewery

Brewery in **Asmara**

ASMARA LAGER BEER — deep bright gold, big malt nose, good body, big malt flavor, long dry hop aftertaste.

Ethiopian Beverage Co.

Brewery in **Harar**

HARAR BEER — pale gold, slightly toasted malt aroma and flavor, burnt malt appears in the fairly long aftertaste.

Notes:

Notes:

CHINA

Beijing Brewery

Brewery in Beijing (Peking)

MON-LEI BEER — gold, off-dry malt nose and flavor, fairly dry hop finish, long dry aftertaste, good balance, good body.

FIVE STAR BEER — pale gold, off-dry malt nose, toasted (a bit burnt) malt flavor and long aftertaste. Also has been seen as SPECIALLY BREWED FIVE STAR BEER.

NINE STAR PREMIUM BEER — gold, hop nose, good malt and hop flavor, good body, some complexity, off-dry finish, long dry hop aftertaste. Brewery named as being Five Star Brewery.

BEIJING PREMIUM BLACK LAGER EXPORT BEER — amber-gold, malt and light hop aroma, big body, big malt flavor with lots of hops in back, dry hop finish, long dry hop aftertaste shows some malt.

Hangzhou Brewery

Brewery in Hangzhou

EMPERORS GOLD BEER — gold, malt nose, faintly oxidized and slightly sour malt flavor, dry finish, off-dry malt aftertaste reminds you of molasses.

Hua Du Brewery

Brewery in Beijing

LONGXIANG BEER — pale gold, hoppy nose is almost skunky, light hop flavor has malt in back and is drinkable and refreshing, light body, dry hop finish and fairly long aftertaste.

Shenyang Brewery

Brewery in Shenyang

CHINA GOLD BEER — bright deep gold, hoppy ale-like nose, bright hop and malt flavor, good balance, low carbonation, good balance, some hop bite in the finish and long malt aftertaste.

SNOWFLAKE BEER — gold, light malt and hop nose, malt and hop flavor, medium body, malt finish drops off to nothing, virtually no aftertaste.

SHENYANG EXPORT SPECIAL BEER — deep gold, malt nose, lightly toasted off-dry malt flavor, light body, long off-dry malt aftertaste.

Notes:

Zhujiang Brewery

Brewery in **Zhujiang (Shanghai)**

YI KING CHINESE BEER — medium gold, malt nose, off-dry malt front palate, hop middle and finish, good body, dry hop aftertaste.

GOLDEN DRAGON BEER — pale gold, light fruity-malt aroma, off-dry light malt flavor, almost no hops, off-dry malt aftertaste.

ZHU JIANG BEER — pale gold, faint malt aroma, clean crisp pleasant dry malt flavor, light to medium body, dry hop aftertaste.

SHANGHAI BEER — brilliant gold, toasted malt aroma and flavor, creamy, light body, unbalanced sweet-sour aftertaste, overall pleasant. Also seen as SHANGHAI GOLDEN BEER.

YUCHUAN BEER — yellow-gold, pleasant hop nose and taste, off-dry malt finish, hops return in the long aftertaste.

CHUNG HUA BEER — pale gold, faint malt and hop nose, hops start off the palate yielding soon to off-dry malt with a spicy background, the finish and aftertaste are almost too sweet malt. Brewery named is Cian Jiang Brewery of Zhe Jiang. I feel there may be something amiss with the spelling.

CHINA LIGHT BEER — pale gold, dusty fruity malt aroma, dry hop flavor, malt reappears in the aftertaste, some complexity and some length.

TAIWAN

Taiwan Tobacco & Wine Monopoly Bureau

Brewery in **Taipeh**

DYNASTY TAIWAN BEER — deep yellow-gold, rich appetizing malt aroma, clean malt flavor is lightly toasted, long clean malt aftertaste, pleasant drinkable brew when fresh.

DYNASTY PREMIUM DRY BEER — pale gold, pleasant malt nose with good hops, good tasting off-dry malt flavor, light body, pleasant butterscotch and honeyed finish, clean long malt aftertaste.

CHINA BEER — hazy pale amber, toasted malt aroma, good toasted malt flavor, finish and aftertaste, fairly well-balanced. From Chien-Kuo Brewery.

TAIWAN DRAFT BEER — gold, hop aroma, big hop flavor, style of an English bitter, austere, long dry hop aftertaste.

INDIA

Associated Breweries & Distilleries

Brewery in **Bombay**

MAHARAJA LAGER BEER — gold malt nose with a trace of chocolate, dull malt flavor, medium body, light malt finish and aftertaste, dry and short.

Notes:

KOREA

Chosun Brewery Co., Ltd.

Brewery in Seoul

CROWN LAGER BEER — pale gold, faint malt and hop nose, faint sweetness way in back, flavor is off-dry malt with hops, medium body, fair duration.

CROWN DRY — gold, faint malt and hop nose, light weak malt flavor, light body, short dry aftertaste.

LEBANON

Almaza Brewery

Brewery in Almaza

ALMAZA PILSENER — gold, a little skunky first, but this soon cleared to a malt and hop nose, light body, light malt and hop flavor, dull malty aftertaste.

Notes:

Notes:

Notes:

Notes:

COLOMBIA

Cerveceria Aguila, S.A.

Brewery in **Barranquilla**

CERVEZA AGUILA — gold, hop and malt aroma, flavor just like the nose, dry finish and dry hop aftertaste.

JAMAICA

Desnoes & Geddes, Ltd.

Brewery in **Kingston**

RED STRIPE LAGER BEER — pale tawny-gold, good bright hop and malt nose, full-flavored dry malt and hop palate, hops dominate, pleasant and very drinkable, long dry hop aftertaste.

DRAGON STOUT — opaque, brown head, rich off-dry malt nose, big body, lightly sweet malt palate, very tasty, long dry malt aftertaste.

Notes:

PANAMA

Cerveceria Panama, S.A.

Brewery in **Panama City**

CERVEZA SOBERANA — pale gold, faint dry malt aroma, papery malt flavor, metallic aftertaste, light body, low carbonation.

GUINNESS EXTRA STOUT — opaque brown, brown head, big malt and hop nose, dry and bitter hop and malt flavor, not much character, long dry and bitter aftertaste.

Cerveceria Nacional, S.A.

Brewery in **Panama City**

HB CERVEZA NEGRA — bright brown, light dry malt nose and taste, dry finish, little aftertaste, overall a pleasant dark beer.

CERVEZA BALBOA — medium gold, off-dry banana fruit nose, light body, light banana flavor with a sense of acetone, long sour metallic banana aftertaste.

ATLAS CERVEZA LAGER — bright gold, pleasant malt aroma, good malt and hop flavor, nicely balanced, light body, not much of an aftertaste, but a refreshing hot weather brew.

Notes:

Notes:

Notes:

1993 UPDATE

Appendix

the BEER log

BY JAMES D. ROBERTSON

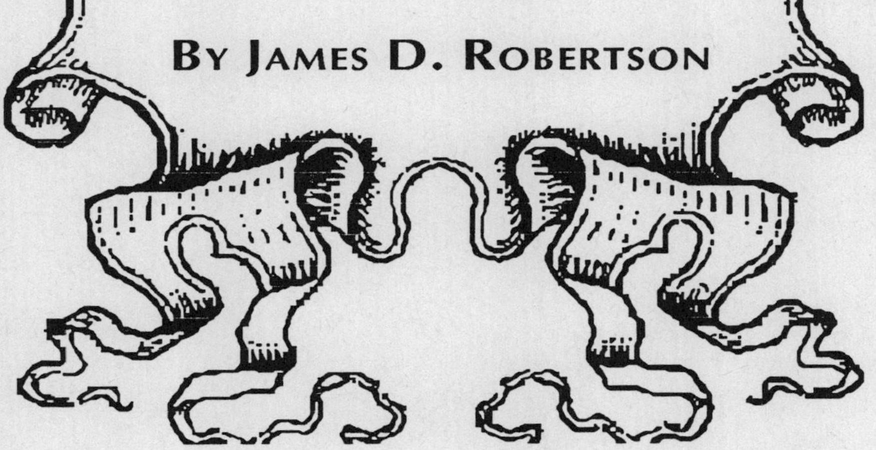

The Beer Log Update: Appendix

All inquiries should be addressed to Bosak Publishing Company, 4764 Galicia Way, Oceanside, CA 92056, (619) 724-4447.

ISBN: 0-9635332-4-X

Printed in the United States of America

APPENDIX I

Alphabetical Listing of Beers Tasted with Ratings by Taste Panel

This alphabetical list gives a shortened form of the brand name; the type of beverage (A-ale, B-beer, BK-bock, BW-barley wine, D-dry, IPA-India pale ale, L-lambic, LO-low calorie, M-malt beverage/malta, ML-malt liquor, NA-non-alcoholic, P-porter, RA-reduced alcohol, ST-steam, S-stout, W-wheat); the manufacturer for U.S., Canadian, and Mexican beers, country of origin for others; and, a taste panel rating on a scale of 0-90 according to the "About This Book" section at the beginning of this book. The list is divided into separate sections for the United States, Canada, Mexico, Central & South America/Caribbean, Australia/Asia/Africa/Oceania, and Europe.

The reader is advised to view the numerical scores with some caution. They are the upper figures of scores given by a panel of tasters and must simply be regarded as quantitative measures of a very subjective subject, personal taste and preference. The same set of tasters examining the same set of beers conceivably could come up with different results at any time. That they did not ever come up with substantially different scores in retrials of a brew does not mean that the numbers applied are hard and fast. Where two brews achieved greatly different scores, the reader may safely assume that the higher scoring item is the better of the pair. Where the scores differ only by a small amount, like within 10-15 percent, no such assumption should be made.

UNITED STATES

Brand	Type	Brewer	Rating
A-1	B	HEILEMAN	36
ABBEY TRAPPISTE	A	NEW BELGIUM	72
ABC ALE	B	FLORIDA	42
ABC BEER	B	FLORIDA	42
ABC LIGHT	LO	FLORIDA	26
ABC MALT LIQUOR	ML	FLORIDA	42
ABERDEEN AMBER	A	WEINKELLER	35
ABITA AMBER	B	ABITA	55
ABITA ANDYGATOR	A	ABITA	75
ABITA BOCK	BK	ABITA	66
ABITA FALL FEST	F	ABITA	67
ABITA GOLDEN	B	ABITA	53
ABITA TURBO DOG	B	ABITA	59
ACADIA AMBER ALE	A	ACADIA	51
ACADIA PALE ALE	A	ACADIA	60
ACE AMBER ALE	A	HUBCAP	52
ACE'S STRONG ALE	A	SEABRIGHT	75
ACME	B	HEILEMAN	21
ACME LIGHT	LO	BOSTON BEER WORKS	48
ADAMSTOWN AMBER	B	STOUDT	73
ADLER BRAU AMBER	B	APPLETON	41
ADLER BRAU BOCK	BK	APPLETON	43
ADLER BRAU LAGER	B	APPLETON	42
ADLER BRAU LIGHT	LO	APPLETON	24
ADLER BRAU OATMEAL	S	APPLETON	50
ADLER BRAU OKT	B	APPLETON	49
ADLER BRAU PILSNER	B	APPLETON	48
ADLER BRAU PORTER	P	APPLETON	43
ADLER BRAU PUMPKIN	B	APPLETON	47
ADLER BRAU WEISS	W	APPLETON	44
AIREDALE PALE ALE	A	FLYING DOG	50
ALASKAN AMBER	B	ALASKAN	84
ALASKAN ARTIC ALE	A	ALASKAN	57
ALASKAN AUTUMN	A	ALASKAN	66
ALASKAN BREAKUP	BK	ALASKAN	63
ALASKAN PALE ALE	A	ALASKAN	68
ALASKAN SPRING WHEAT	W	ALASKAN	43
ALBANY AMBER	B	MATT	50
ALBATROSS LAGER	B	SAN FRANCISCO	51
ALBEMARLE ALE	A	DILWORTH	36
ALBERT DAMM BITTER	A	COOPERSMITHS	38
ALPINE PEARL PALE	A	TIED HOUSE	45
ALPINE V. BOCK	BK	SO. CALIFORNIA	66
ALPINE V. FEST	B	SO. CALIFORNIA	54
ALPINE V. LAGER	B	SO. CALIFORNIA	50
ALPINE V. LIGHT	LO	SO. CALIFORNIA	46
ALPINE V. PILS	B	SO. CALIFORNIA	54
ALPINE V. RED ALE	A	SO. CALIFORNIA	58
ALPINE V. SPECIAL RES.	B	SO. CALIFORNIA	54
ALPINE V. WHEAT	W	SO. CALIFORNIA	53
ALPS BRAU	B	HUBER	21
ALT DEUTSCH	B	PITTSBURGH	37
ALTA	LO	HEILEMAN	30
ALTES	B	HEILEMAN	30
AMBER VIENNA STYLE	B	BREWMASTERS'	47
AMBIER	B	HUBER	64
AMERICA'S FINEST PILS	B	KARL STRAUSS	44
AMERICAN	B	PITTSBURGH	28
AMERICAN LIGHT	LO	PITTSBURGH	22
ANCHOR PORTER	P	ANCHOR	83
ANCHOR SPRUCE	B	ANCHOR	43
ANCHOR STEAM	ST	ANCHOR	57
ANCHOR WHEAT	W	ANCHOR	48
ANDEKER	B	S&P	42
ANHEUSER MARZEN	B	ANHEUSER-BUSCH	62
APRICOT ALE	A	SAN ANDREAS	57
ARAPAHOE AMBER	A	ROCK BOTTOM	57
ARCH AMBER	A	HARTFORD	55
ARIZONA PILSENER	B	BLACK MOUNTAIN	24
ARROWHEAD	B	COLD SPRING	36
ARROYO AMBER	A	CROWN CITY	61
ARTIC ALE	A	GORKY	64
ASPEN SILVER CITY	A	BOULDER	57
ATLANTIC AMBER	B	NEW ENGLAND	57
ATLANTIC CITY	B	LION	53
ATLAS AMBER	A	BIG TIME	42
AUBURN DARK LAGER	B	SCHELL	41
AUGSBURGER	B	STROH	72
AUGSBURGER BOCK	BK	STROH	68
AUGSBURGER DARK	B	STROH	50
AUGSBURGER LIGHT	LO	STROH	44
AUGUST SCHELL BOCK	BK	SCHELL	59
AUGUST SCHELL EXPORT	B	SCHELL	24
AUGUST SCHELL OKT.'91	B	SCHELL	76
AUGUST SCHELL PILS	B	SCHELL	60
AUGUST SCHELL WEIZEN	W	SCHELL	39
AUGUSTINER	B	PITTSBURGH	36
AUTUMN FEST ALE	A	SPANISH PEAKS	54
AVALANCHE ALE	A	BRECKENRIDGE	50
AVENUE	B	SCHELL	46
AVID BARLEY BREE WEE	BW	VERMONT	70
AZTEC ALE	A	ROCK BOTTOM	37
AZTEC AMBER ALE	A	BREWSKI'S	65
BACH'S BOCK	BK	KESSLER	71
BACHELOR BITTER	A	DESCHUTES	50
BADERBRAU	B	PAVICHEVICH	58
BALLANTINE ALE	A	S&P	55
BALLANTINE	B	S&P	48

Brand	Type	Brewer	Rating
BALLANTINE BOCK	BK	S&P	25
BALLANTINE DRAFT	B	S&P	34
BALLANTINE INDIA PALE	IPA	S&P	59
BALLANTINE LIGHT LAGER	LO	S&P	20
BALLARD BITTER	A	RED HOOK	48
BALTIC LIGHT	A	GORKY	43
BALTIMORE AMBER	B	BALTIMORE	52
BALTIMORE LAGER	B	BALTIMORE	53
BALTIMORE PILS	B	BALTIMORE	50
BANDERSNATCH MILK	S	BANDERSNATCH	44
BANKS BEER	B	HUDEPOHL-SCHOENLING	32
BAR HARBOR REAL ALE	A	ACADIA	37
BARLEYHOPPER BROWN	A	M.J. BARLEYHOPPER	42
BARNEY FLATS OATMEAL	S	ANDERSON VALLEY	78
BARTEL'S	B	LION	34
BASICS	B	LION	32
BAVARIAN CLUB	B	HUBER	37
BAVARIAN DARK	B	HEILEMAN	26
BAVARIAN TYPE	B	YUENGLING	25
BAVARIAN WEISS	W	WATER STREET	66
BAVARIAN'S SELECT	B	GENESEE	24
BEACH BREW NA	NA	S&P	24
BEACON BARLEYWINE	BW	SANTA CRUZ	60
BEANTOWN BROWN	A	BOSTON BEER WORKS	65
BEAR DOWN BROWN	A	GENTLE BEN	34
BEAVER TAIL BROWN	A	HUBCAP	49
BEER	B	PITTSBURGH	28
BEER	B	S&P	26
BEERGUY	B	ZELE	44
BELL'S AMBER ALE	A	KALAMAZOO	60
BELL'S BEER	B	KALAMAZOO	54
BELL'S CHERRY STOUT	S	KALAMAZOO	52
BELL'S PORTER	P	KALAMAZOO	56
BELL'S SPECIAL	S	KALAMAZOO	69
BEN FRANKLIN'S GOLDEN	B	SAM ADAMS BREWHOUSE	39
BERGHEIM	B	HEILEMAN	33
BERGHOFF ALE	A	BERGHOFF	50
BERGHOFF	B	BERGHOFF	51
BERGHOFF	B	HUBER	66
BERGHOFF BOCK	BK	HUBER	38
BERGHOFF DARK	B	BERGHOFF	61
BERGHOFF DARK	B	HUBER	42
BERGHOFF LIGHT	LO	HUBER	39
BERGHOFF LITE	LO	BERGHOFF	30
BERGHOFF WEISS	W	BERGHOFF	48
BEST OF SHOW '89	IPA	BOULDER	71
BEST OF SHOW 1988 OKT.	B	BOULDER	47
BHAGWANS BEST IPA	A	BIG TIME	54
BIG FOOT (PRE-86)	A	SIERRA NEVADA	72
BIG FOOT 1986	A	SIERRA NEVADA	60
BIG FOOT 1987	A	SIERRA NEVADA	68
BIG FOOT 1988	A	SIERRA NEVADA	44
BIG HORN ALE	A	BANDERSNATCH	67
BIG HORN BITTER	A	WALNUT	43
BIG JUG	B	HUDEPOHL-SCHOENLING	43
BITTER END	A	PACIFIC BEACH	42
BLACK BEAR LAGER	B	VERMONT	42
BLACK BEAR PORTER	P	SAN JUAN	54
BLACK BUTTE PORTER	P	DESCHUTES	49
BLACK CHERRY PORTER	P	BOULDER	22
BLACK CLOUD OATMEAL	S	CROWN CITY	67
BLACK CLOUD	P	RUSSELL	51
BLACK DIAMOND STOUT	S	ROCK BOTTOM	54
BLACK DOG BITTER	A	SPANISH PEAKS	45
BLACK FLY STOUT	S	GRITTY MC DUFFS	52
BLACK FOREST	B	CHAMPION	54
BLACK FOREST	B	CRESCENT CITY	66
BLACK FOREST PORTER	P	COLUMBUS	42
BLACK HAWK STOUT	S	MENDOCINO	58
BLACK HORSE ALE	A	GENESEE	54
BLACK HORSE ALE	A	HEILEMAN	65
BLACK LABEL 11-11	B	HEILEMAN	32
BLACK MTN. GOLD	B	BLACK MOUNTAIN	62
BLACK'S BEACH	A	KARL STRAUSS	36
BLACKENED VOO DOO	B	DIXIE	51
BLACKHOOK PORTER	P	RED HOOK	48
BLACKWELL STOUT	S	NEW HAVEN	54
BLARNEY STONE	S	PACIFIC BEACH	31
BLATZ	B	HEILEMAN	43
BLATZ LA	RA	HEILEMAN	24
BLATZ LIGHT CREAM ALE	A	HEILEMAN	26
BLATZ LIGHT	LO	HEILEMAN	33
BLDR OKT CASK COND.	B	BOULDER	51
BLITZ-WEINHARD	B	HEILEMAN	36
BLITZEN'S GNARLY BW	BW	FLYING DOG	69
BLIZZARD BOCK	BK	BUFFALO	56
BLOND DOUBLEBOCK	BK	CLEMENT	54
BLOODHOUND RASP ST.	S	FLYING DOG	54
BLUE HEN	B	LION	42
BLUE HERON	A	BRIDGEPORT	66
BLUE HERON PALE ALE	A	MENDOCINO	68
BLUE NOTE AMBER	A	WALNUT	45
BLUE RIBBON	B	S&P	45
BLUE RIBBON BOCK	BK	S&P	37
BLUE RIBBON DRY	D	S&P	30
BLUE RIBBON LIGHT	LO	S&P	45
BLUE RIVER BOCK	BK	BRECKENRIDGE	71
BLUE WHALE ALE	A	PACIFIC COAST	66
BLUEBEERY ALE	A	MARIN	62
BLUEBERRY ALE	A	BOSTON BEER WORKS	51
BLUEBONNET LAGER	B	DALLAS	33
BOAR HEAD STOUT	S	HEILEMAN	45
BOCK N' ROLL	BK	HUBCAP	54
BOH BOHEMIAN	B	S&P	24
BOHEMIAN CLUB	B	HUBER	56
BOHEMIAN PILSNER	B	S&P	62
BOLSA CHICA BITTER	A	HUNTINGTON BEACH	70
BOND ST BROWN	A	DESCHUTES	54
BONDI BEACH BLONDE	B	MELBOURNE	58
BONE DRY	D	KESSLER	46
BONZO'S BROWN ALE	A	SAN FRANCISCO	46
BOOMERANG BROWN	A	SAN JUAN	62
BOONT AMBER	A	ANDERSON VALLEY	53
BOSCH	B	LEINENKUGEL	24
BOSTON LIGHTSHIP	LO	BOSTON	50
BOSTON RED	A	BOSTON BEER WORKS	74
BOSTON STOCK ALE	B	BOSTON	75
BOULDER AMBER	A	BOULDER	42
BOULDER AMBER ALE	A	BOULDER	33
BOULDER BITTER	B	BOULDER	55
BOULDER ENGLISH ALE	A	BOULDER	32
BOULDER EXTRA PALE	A	BOULDER	55
BOULDER LIGHT ALE	LO	BOULDER	24
BOULDER OKTOBERFEST	B	BOULDER	60
BOULDER PORTER	P	BOULDER	48
BOULDER SPORT	B	BOULDER	17
BOULDER STOUT	S	BOULDER	50
BOULDER XMAS 1986	S	BOULDER	36
BOUNDARY WATERS	B	JAMES PAGE	48
BOUNDARY WATERS BOCK	BK	JAMES PAGE	38
BOUNDARY WATERS RICE	B	JAMES PAGE	39
BOXER PREMIUM	ML	HUBER	52
BRAUMEISTER	B	HUBER	17
BRAUMEISTER BOCK	BK	HUBER	32
BRAUMEISTER LIGHT	LO	HUBER	16
BRECKENRIDGE IPA	A	BRECKENRIDGE	70
BRECKENRIDGE MÄRZEN	B	BRECKENRIDGE	47
BRECKENRIDGE OATMEAL	S	BRECKENRIDGE	52
BREW 102	B	S&P	41
BREW HOUSE BROWN ALE	A	SAM ADAMS BREWHOUSE	36
BREW HOUSE CRANBERRY	W	SAM ADAMS BREWHOUSE	63
BREWER'S GOLD	A	S&P	39
BREWMASTER SPECIAL	A	KELMER	6
BRICHSHOT RED	A	HUNTINGTON BEACH	39
BRICKSKELLER	B	PITTSBURGH	20
BRIDALVEIL ALE	A	BUTTERFIELD	48
BROAD RIPPLE ESB	A	BROAD RIPPLE	51
BROAD RIPPLE IPA	A	BROAD RIPPLE	45
BROAD RIPPLE KÖLSCH	K	BROAD RIPPLE	48
BROAD RIPPLE PORTER	P	BROAD RIPPLE	37
BROOKLYN BRAND	B	MATT	58
BROOKLYN BROWN	B	MATT	54
BROWN COW ALE	A	FIREHOUSE	45
BROWN DERBY	B	S&P	27
BROWN DERBY LIGHT	LO	S&P	54
BROWN DOG	A	NORTHAMPTON	53
BRUCKS JUBILEE	B	HUDEPOHL-SCHOENLING	42
BUCKEYE BOCK	BK	HOSTER	62
BUCKEYE OATMEAL ST.	S	BOSTON BEER WORKS	66
BUCKHORN	B	HEILEMAN	37
BUCKHORN	B	S&P	38
BUCKS WHEAT	W	CRESTED BUTTE	51
BUDWEISER	B	ANHEUSER-BUSCH	51
BUDWEISER DRY	D	ANHEUSER-BUSCH	36
BUDWEISER LIGHT	LO	ANHEUSER-BUSCH	32
BUFF. BILL DOUBLE CR.	A	BUFFALO BILL	30
BUFFALO BILL'S	B	BUFFALO BILL'S	40
BUFFALO BITTER	A	FIREHOUSE	35
BUFFALO GOLD	A	BOULDER	68
BUFFALO GOLD	B	WALNUT	27
BUFFALO LAGER	B	BUFFALO	48
BUFFALO PILS	B	BUFFALO	58
BULLDOG STOUT	S	FLYING DOG	42
BULLMASTIFF	A	FLYING DOG	33

Brand	Type	Brewer	Rating
BULLSHOOTERS	B	ZELE	64
BUNKERHILL	B	LION	22
BURGEMEISTER	B	HUBER	31
BURGEMEISTER	B	S&P	24
BURGER	B	HUDEPOHL	20
BURGIE LIGHT GOLDEN	LO	S&P	20
BURNING RIVER	B	GREAT LAKES	68
BUSCH BAVARIAN	B	ANHEUSER-BUSCH	34
BUSCH LIGHT DRAFT	LO	ANHEUSER-BUSCH	35
BUSCH PREMIUM	B	ANHEUSER-BUSCH	32
BUTTERFIELD IMP. ST.	S	BUTTERFIELD	42
BUTTERFIELD MAIBOCK	BK	BUTTERFIELD	51
CACTUS LAGER	B	ELEC. DAVE/SAN FRAN BAR	48
CADILLAC MTN. STOUT	S	BAR HARBOR	61
CAJUN	B	CAJUN	32
CALIENTE	B	MINNESOTA	8
CALIFORNIA CONDOR	A	OKIE GIRL	48
CALISTOGA GOLDEN	B	NAPA	50
CALISTOGA RED ALE	A	NAPA	51
CALISTOGA WHEAT ALE	W	NAPA	34
CALLAHAN RED	A	CALLAHAN	42
CALLAN'S ENGLISH RED	A	WATER STREET	54
CAMP HALE GOLDEN	A	HUBCAP	44
CAPITAL BOCK	BK	CAPITAL	60
CAPITAL DARK	B	CAPITAL	58
CAPITAL GARTEN BRAU	B	CAPITAL	69
CAPITAL LAGER	B	CAPITAL	60
CAPITAL MAIBOCK	BK	CAPITAL	58
CAPITAL OKTOBERFEST	B	CAPITAL	73
CAPITALSPECIAL	B	CAPITAL	65
CAPITAL WILD RICE	B	CAPITAL	28
CAPSTONE ESB	A	OASIS	47
CARDINAL PALE ALE	A	BANDERSNATCH	60
CARLING 71	LO	HEILEMAN	20
CARLING BL LIGHT	LO	HEILEMAN	49
CARLING BLACK LABEL	B	HEILEMAN	51
CARLING LA	RA	HEILEMAN	20
CARLING RED CAP	A	HEILEMAN	53
CARLING'S BL NA	NA	HEILEMAN	18
CASCADE AMBER	A	TIED HOUSE	42
CASCADE GOLDEN ALE	A	DESCHUTES	43
CAT TAIL ALE	A	DEAD CAT ALLEY	27
CATALINA ALE	A	GENTLE BEN	60
CATAMOUNT AMBER	B	CATAMOUNT	50
CATAMOUNT GOLD	B	CATAMOUNT	74
CATAMOUNT OCTOBER	B	CATAMOUNT	65
CATAMOUNT PORTER	P	CATAMOUNT	50
CATAMOUNT XMAS '90	A	CATAMOUNT	71
CATAMOUNT XMAS '91	A	CATAMOUNT	83
CATAMOUNT XMAS '92	A	CATAMOUNT	75
CAVE CREEK CHILI	B	MINNESOTA	17
CELEBRATION ALE 1982	A	SIERRA NEVADA	60
CELEBRATION ALE 1983	A	SIERRA NEVADA	63
CELEBRATION ALE 1984	A	SIERRA NEVADA	65
CELEBRATION ALE 1985	A	SIERRA NEVADA	66
CELEBRATION ALE 1986	A	SIERRA NEVADA	83
CELEBRATION ALE 1987	A	SIERRA NEVADA	86
CELEBRATION ALE 1988	A	SIERRA NEVADA	80
CELEBRATION ALE 1989	A	SIERRA NEVADA	78
CELEBRATION ALE 1990	A	SIERRA NEVADA	82
CELEBRATION ALE 1991	A	SIERRA NEVADA	82
CELEBRATION ALE 1992	A	SIERRA NEVADA	78
CELIS GOLDEN	A	CELIS	48
CELIS PALE BOCK	BK	CELIS	45
CELIS WHITE	A	CELIS	69
CELTIC ALE	A	YAKIMA	35
CENTENNIAL 100 ALE	A	NORTH COAST	69
CENTENNIAL PALE ALE	A	COEUR D'ALENE	34
CHAMPALE	ML	HEILEMAN	40
CHANNEL ISLANDS	A	SHIELDS	48
CHARGER GOLD	A	BREWSKI'S	53
CHARTER OAK	B	CHARTER OAK	27
CHARTER OAK XMAS '91	A	CHARTER OAK	44
CHAU TIEN EMPEROR ALE	A	ST. STANISLAUS	45
CHAU TIEN EMPEROR	B	ZELE	63
CHEERS	NA	S&P	19
CHEROKEE CHOICE	B	OKIE GIRL	38
CHICKEN KILLER BW	BW	SANTA FE	60
CHIEF OSHKOSH	B	STEVENS POINT	37
CHILKOOT CHARLIE	W	SPENARD	14
CHIPPEWA FALLS	B	LEINENKUGEL	38
CHIPPEWA PRIDE	B	LEINENKUGEL	29
CHR. MOERLEIN BOCK	BK	HUDEPOHL-SCHOENLING	25
CHR. MOERLEIN SELECT	B	HUDEPOHL-SCHOENLING	35
CHRISTIAN M. DARK	B	HUDEPOHL-SCHOENLING	54
CHRISTIAN MOERLEIN	B	HUDEPOHL-SCHOENLING	60
CHURCHYARD ALE	A	WYNKOOP	41

Brand	Type	Brewer	Rating
CLEMENT'S AMBER	B	CLEMENT	44
CLEMENT'S BLOND DBL	BK	CLEMENT	56
CLEMENT'S COLE PORTER	P	CLEMENT	57
CLEMENT'S DARK DBL BK	BK	CLEMENT	75
CLEMENT'S DBL BOCK	BK	CLEMENT	48
CLEMENT'S OKTOBER	B	CLEMENT	70
CLEMENT'S PILSENER	B	CLEMENT	44
CLEMENT'S PORTER	P	CLEMENT	50
COAL PORTER	P	ACADIA	52
COHO PACIFIC LIGHT	A	BRIDGEPORT	66
COLD BRAU	B	COLD SPRING	40
COLD SPRING	B	COLD SPRING	38
COLD SPRING EXPORT	B	COLD SPRING	42
COLD SPRING SELECT	B	COLD SPRING	21
COLDERS 29	B	MILLER	21
COLDERS 29 LIGHT	LO	MILLER	18
COLE'S SPECIAL BITTER	A	SALT LAKE	51
COLLIN COUNTY EMERALD	B	DALLAS	42
COLLIN COUNTY GOLD	B	DALLAS	53
COLLIN CTY BLACK GOLD	B	DALLAS	32
COLT .45 DRY	D	HEILEMAN	28
COLT .45	ML	HEILEMAN	51
COLT .45 SILVER	ML	HEILEMAN	18
COLT.45 POWERMASTER	ML	HEILEMAN	57
COLUM. NUT BROWN	A	COLUMBUS	36
COLUMBIA	B	HEILEMAN	33
COLUMBUS 1492	B	MATT	54
COLUMBUS NUT BROWN	A	COLUMBUS	45
COLUMBUS PALE ALE	A	COLUMBUS	54
COMMODORE PERRY IPA	A	GREAT LAKES	61
COMMONWEALTH BURTON	A	CATAMOUNT	14
COMMONWEALTH IPA	A	COMMONWEALTH	36
COOK'S GOLDBLUME	B	HEILEMAN	33
COOK'S LIGHT	LO	HEILEMAN	29
COOL COLT	ML	HEILEMAN	22
COOPERSMITH'S DUNK WZ.	W	COOPERSMITHS	45
COORS	B	COORS	59
COORS CUTTER	NA	COORS	36
COORS DRY	D	COORS	34
COORS EXT. GOLD DRAFT	B	COORS	42
COORS EXTRA GOLD	B	COORS	46
COORS LIGHT	LO	COORS	26
COORS WINTERFEST '87	B	COORS	38
COORS WINTERFEST '88	B	COORS	38
COORS WINTERFEST '89	B	COORS	33
COORS WINTERFEST '90	B	COORS	50
COORS WINTERFEST '91	B	COORS	63
COORS WINTERFEST '92	B	COORS	41
COPPER CREEK ALE	A	MILL-CHARLOTTE	41
COPPERHEAD ALE	A	GENTLE BEN	72
COQUI 900	ML	HEILEMAN	24
COUNTRY CLUB ALE	B	S&P	23
COUNTRY CLUB	ML	S&P	20
COWBOY LAGER	B	DALLAS	42
COWBOY PREMIUM	B	DALLAS	35
COY	B	DIXIE	46
COY	B	HEILEMAN	38
COYOTE GOLD	B	COYOTE SPRINGS	50
COYOTE OATMEAL ST.	S	COYOTE SPRINGS	61
COYOTE XMAS	A	COYOTE SPRINGS	60
CRANBERRY ALE	A	SAN ANDREAS	34
CRANBERRY NOEL	A	SAN ANDREAS	41
CRAZY HORSE	ML	HEILEMAN	40
CRESC. CITY MARDI GRAS	B	CRESCENT CITY	42
CRESC. CITY PILSNER	B	CRESCENT CITY	54
CROFT ALE	A	S&P	33
CROSSROADS	B	SCHELL	29
CRYSTAL	B	LION	33
CYNIC'S ELECTION LAGER	B	KARL STRAUSS	30
D'AGOSTINO	B	MATT	57
DAKOTA	W	MILLER	46
DALLAS GOLD	B	DALLAS	33
DANA PORTER	P	HERITAGE	60
DANIEL SHAY'S BITTER	A	NORTHAMPTON	56
DARK HORSE	B	VIRGINIA	70
DE LIGHT BREW	NA	S&P	9
DEAD CAT LAGER	B	DEAD CAT ALLEY	50
DEAD HORSE IPA	A	MC NEILL'S	57
DEEP ENDERS PORTER	P	ANDERSON VALLEY	48
DEL RICO	ML	BLACK MOUNTAIN	26
DEMPSEY'S	A	HUBER	48
DESCHUTES DUNK WEIZ	W	DESCHUTES	42
DESCHUTES FEST. PILS	B	DESCHUTES	48
DET & MAC IPA	A	DETROIT & MACKINAC	36
DET & MAC RED ALE	A	DETROIT & MACKINAC	42
DEVIL	B	SPOETZL	23
DEVIL'S BREW PORTER	P	DEVIL MOUNTAIN	68

Brand	Type	Brewer	Rating
DEVIL'S THUMB STOUT	S	WALNUT	53
DIAMOND HEAD DRY	D	HONOLULU	39
DICTATOR'S LIT. SISTER	BK	HOPS! SCOTTSDALE	42
DILWORTH PORTER	P	DILWORTH	32
DIXIE AMBER LIGHT	B	DIXIE	34
DIXIE	B	DIXIE	33
DIXIE LAGER	B	DIXIE	47
DIXIE LIGHT	LO	DIXIE	48
DOCK ST.	B	MATT	75
DOCK ST. BARLEY WINE	BW	DOCK STREET	81
DOCK ST. BOHEMIAN	B	DOCK STREET	50
DOCK ST. CREAM ALE	A	DOCK STREET	42
DOCK ST. DORTMUNDER	B	DOCK STREET	44
DOCK ST. HELLES	B	DOCK STREET	55
DOCK ST. IMPERIAL	S	DOCK STREET	45
DOCK ST. OLD ALE	A	DOCK STREET	49
DOCK ST. PALE ALE	A	DOCK STREET	68
DOCK ST. WEISS	W	DOCK STREET	45
DOG HOUSE WHEAT	W	FLYING DOG	24
DOGGIE STYLE	A	FLYING DOG	58
DOMINATOR WHEAT	W	MANHATTAN BEACH	45
DOMINION ALE	A	OLD DOMINION	51
DOMINION LAGER	B	OLD DOMINION	42
DOMINION STOUT	S	OLD DOMINION	48
DOUBLE BOCK WEIZEN	BK/W	TWENTY TANKS	50
DOUBLE K	B	S&P	32
DOUBLIN STOUT	S	WEINKELLER	60
DOWN AND OUT STOUT	S	PORTLAND	33
DOWN UNDER	B	MELBOURNE	55
DOWNTOWN BROWN	A	UMPQUA	12
DOWNTOWN CHESTNUT	A	BREWSKI'S	48
DRAKE'S ALE	A	LIND	39
DRAKE'S GOLD	A	LIND	45
DREWRY'S	B	HEILEMAN	30
DREWRY'S DRAFT	B	HEILEMAN	33
DRUMMOND BROS	B	EVANSVILLE	39
DRY GULCH STOUT	S	COYOTE SPRINGS	66
DRY HOPPED BROWN	A	KARL STRAUSS	36
DUBOIS BOCK	BK	PITTSBURGH	46
DUBUQUE STAR	B	ZELE	34
DUCK'S BREATH BITTER	A	MC NEILL'S	54
DUESSELDORFER DRAFT	A	INDIANNAOPLIS	32
DUKE	B	HEILEMAN	29
DUKE'S BOCK	BK	FULLERTON	48
DUNKEL WEIZEN BOCK	W-BK	GOOSE ISLAND	72
DUNKELWEIZEN	A	BREWSKI'S	24
DUNRAVIN ALE	A	COOPERSMITHS	46
DUQUESNE BAVARIAN	B	HEILEMAN	44
DURANGO COLORFEST	B	DURANGO	36
DURANGO DARK	B	DURANGO	39
DUTCH TREAT	B	HEILEMAN	33
DÜSSELDORFER DOPPEL	BK	WEINKELLER	50
EAGLE	B	STEVENS POINT	35
EAGLE DARK	B	HOSTER	47
EAGLE LIGHT	LO	HOSTER	34
EAGLE PREMIUM	ML	EVANSVILLE	38
EARL'S ALE	A	FULLERTON	55
EARTHQUAKE PALE	A	SAN ANDREAS	32
EARTHQUAKE PORTER	P	SAN ANDREAS	50
EAST SIDE DARK	A	LAKEFRONT	43
EASTSIDE	B	S&P	35
ECONO BUY	B	S&P	26
ECONOMY CORNER	B	LION	21
ED DEBEVIC	B	HUBER	41
EDDIE MC STIFF'S AMBER	A	EDDIE MC STIFF'S	42
EDELWEISS	B	ZELE	29
EDINBREW	A	BANDERSNATCH	64
EDMUND FITZGERALD	P	GREAT LAKES	55
EL PASO LIGHT	LO	MATT	12
ELECTRIC BEER	B	ELECTRIC DAVE	66
ELIOT NESS (VIENNA)	B	GREAT LAKES	64
ELM CITY CT. ALE	A	NEW HAVEN	50
ELM CITY GOLDEN	A	NEW HAVEN	45
ELVIS BRAU	B	WYNKOOP	51
EMERALD ALE	A	PACIFIC COAST	60
EMIGRATION AMBER ALE	A	SALT LAKE	41
EMPEROR NORTON	B	SAN FRANCISCO	53
ENGLISH SETTER BITTER	A	FLYING DOG	70
ERIE LIGHT	LO	HEILEMAN	23
ERIN BREW	B	CLEVELAND	72
ERLANGER MARZEN	B	ZELE	39
ESQUIRE	B	JONES	30
ESQUIRE EXTRA DRY	B	JONES	13
ESQUIRE LIGHT	LO	JONES	11
ESQUIRE PREMIUM PALE	B	JONES	39
ESSLINGER	B	LION	41
ETHAN ALLEN ALE	A	CATAMOUNT	28
ETNA ALE	A	ETNA	45
ETNA DARK	B	ETNA	49
ETNA EXPORT	B	ETNA	47
ETNA WEIZEN	W	ETNA	50
EUGENE ALE	A	KESSLER	45
EUGENE CELEB 88	BK	KESSLER	41
EUGENER WEIZEN	W	KESSLER	55
EUREKA AMBER	B	LOS ANGELES	41
EUREKA AMBER UNFIL.	B	LOS ANGELES	49
EUREKA	B	LOS ANGELES	45
EUREKA DARK	B	LOS ANGELES	53
EUREKA UNFILTERED	B	LOS ANGELES	54
EXPEDITION	S	KALAMAZOO	63
EYE OF THE HAWK	A	MENDOCINO	54
EYE OF THE ROCKIES	W	SPANISH PEAKS	46
FAIR DINKUM AMBER	A	BARLEY'S	18
FALCON PALE ALE	A	ROCK BOTTOM	38
FALLS CITY LIGHT	LO	EVANSVILLE	24
FALSTAFF 96	LO	S&P	36
FALSTAFF	B	S&P	45
FALSTAFF FINE LIGHT	B	S&P	27
FALSTAFF LITE	LO	S&P	27
FAMOUS PORTER	P	MATT	35
FARMALL WHEAT	W	VERMONT	54
FAT CAT PORTER	P	DEAD CAT ALLEY	74
FAT TIRE AMBER	A	NEW BELGIUM	48
FEHR'S XL	B	HUDEPOHL-SCHOENLING	54
FESTIVAL DARK	A	COEUR D'ALENE	27
FIESTA ALE	A	SANTA FE	57
FIREHOUSE PALE	A	MC NEILL'S	39
FIRESTONE	NA	FIRESTONE & FLETCHER	22
FISCHER'S ALE	A	HEILEMAN	38
FISCHER'S BEER	B	HEILEMAN	39
FISCHER'S LIGHT	LO	HEILEMAN	31
FISHER	B	S&P	20
FITGER	B	HUBER	44
FITGER FLAGSHIP	B	JAMES PAGE	53
FITGER'S	B	SCHELL	18
FLYING MC DOG	S	FLYING DOG	19
FOECKING LIGHT	LO	HUBER	24
FOECKING PREMIUM	B	HUBER	38
FORT PITT	B	JONES	20
FORT SCHUYLER	B	MATT	42
FORTY-NINER GOLD	A	MILL-CHARLOTTE	45
FOX DE LUXE	B	COLD SPRING	26
FRAGATI	A	HERITAGE	48
FRANKENMUTH BOCK	BK	FRANKENMUTH	76
FRANKENMUTH DARK	B	FRANKENMUTH	75
FRANKENMUTH LIGHT	LO	FRANKENMUTH	18
FRANKENMUTH PILSENER	B	FRANKENMUTH	76
FRANKENMUTH WEISSE	W	FRANKENMUTH	38
FREEPORT USA	NA	MATT	6
FRENCH PETE'S PORTER	P	STEELHEAD	42
FRONTIER BROWN	B	COYOTE SPRINGS	69
FRONTIER TOWN	BK	KESSLER	53
FULL MOON STOUT	S	COEUR D'ALENE	33
FULL SAIL AMBER	A	HOOD RIVER	68
FULL SAIL GOLDEN	A	HOOD RIVER	69
FYFE & DRUM	LO	GENESEE	40
GALISTEO WIESS	W	SANTA FE	42
GALLOPING GOOSE GOLD	A	SAN JUAN	54
GAMBRINUS GOLD	B	PITTSBURGH	10
GAMBRINUS GOLD LABEL	B	PITTSBURGH	28
GARDEN ALLEY AMBER	B	SAN LUIS OBISPO	51
GASLAMP GOLD ALE	A	KARL STRAUSS	54
GAYLE'S PALE ALE	A	DEVIL MOUNTIAN	31
GEARY'S	A	D.L. GEARY	68
GEMEINDE	B	SCHELL	40
GEMEINDE BRAU	B	COLD SPRING	29
GENESEE	B	GENESEE	47
GENESEE BOCK	BK	GENESEE	50
GENESEE CREAM ALE	A	GENESEE	49
GENESEE CREAM LIGHT	A	GENESEE	42
GENESEE LIGHT	LO	GENESEE	26
GENESEE NA	NA	GENESEE	33
GENESEE OKTOBERFEST	B	GENESEE	49
GEO. WASHINGTON'S	P	SAM ADAMS BREWHOUSE	51
GHOSTLY PALE	A	PACIFIC BEACH	43
GIBBONS ALE	A	LION	26
GIBBONS	B	LION	34
GIBBONS PORTER	P	LION	18
GIBBY'S GOLD	B	COLUMBUS	44
GINGER BELLS	A	STEELHEAD	45
GLEN WALTER WEE HVY	BW	VERMONT	65
GLUEK	B	COLD SPRING	26
GOEBEL	B	STROH	44
GOETZ	B	S&P	44

Brand	Type	Brewer	Rating
GOETZ PALE	NA	S&P	23
GOLD COAST	B	SHIELDS	50
GOLD CUP	B	VIRGINIA	55
GOLD CUP EXPORT	B	VIRGINIA	44
GOLD FINCH	B	LION	51
GOLD NECTAR ALE	A	HUMBOLDT	48
GOLD RUSH	A	HUMBOLDT	24
GOLD TOP	B	HOSTER	49
GOLD TOP	B	HOSTER	51
GOLDEN ANNIVERSARY	B	GENESEE	20
GOLDEN CHAMPALE	ML	HEILEMAN	16
GOLDEN CROWN	B	S&P	32
GOLDEN EXPORT	B	MATT	57
GOLDEN HARPOON	B	MATT	69
GOLDEN LAGER	B	COORS	25
GOLDEN LION PALE	A	HAPPY VALLEY	58
GOLDEN PACIFIC BITTER	A	GOLDEN PACIFIC	54
GOLDEN RAIL	B	CHERRYLAND	40
GOLDFINCH AMBER	B	LION	51
GOOSE ISL OATMEAL ST	S	GOOSE ISLAND	49
GOOSE ISL RUSSIAN IMP	S	GOOSE ISLAND	42
GOOSE ISL. PILSNER	B	GOOSE ISLAND	50
GORD. BIERSCH DBL BOCK	BK	GORDON BIERSCH	71
GORD. BIERSCH MAERZEN	BK	GORDON BIERSCH	61
GORDON BIERSCH AMBER	B	GORDON BIERSCH	54
GORDON BIERSCH PILS	B	GORDON BIERSCH	55
GORKY RUSSIAN IMP	S	GORKY	53
GORKY'S IMPERIAL	S	GORKY	60
GR. LAKES DORTMUNDER	B	GREAT LAKES	84
GRAFFITI ALT 1990	A	ST. STANS	32
GRAFITTI 1992	A	ST. STAN'S	41
GRAIN BELT	B	HEILEMAN	34
GRAIN BELT	B	MINNESOTA	21
GRAIN BELT LIGHT	LO	MINNESOTA	28
GRAIN BELT PREM. LIGHT	LO	MINNESOTA	42
GRAIN BELT PREMIUM	B	HEILEMAN	26
GRAND SLAM BASEBALL	B	VERMONT	39
GRANITE STATE GOLDEN	A	FRANK JONES	41
GRANT'S INDIA PALE ALE	A	YAKIMA	60
GRANT'S SCOTTISH ALE	A	YAKIMA	66
GRANT'S SPICED ALE	A	YAKIMA	44
GRANT'S WEIS BEER	W	YAKIMA	75
GRAY WHALE ALE	A	PACIFIC COAST	34
GREAT LAKES AMBER	A	KALAMAZOO	48
GREAT LAKES CHERRY	S	KALAMAZOO	27
GREAT LAKES VIENNA	B	GREAT LAKES	72
GREEN LEPRECHAUN ALE	A	SAN ANDREAS	48
GREYHOUND HONEY ALE	A	FLYING DOG	45
GRIESEDIECK GB LIGHT	B	S&P	30
GRIPMAN'S PORTER	P	SAN FRANCISCO	26
GROWLIN' GATOR	B	FLORIDA	33
GUNTHER	B	STROH	39
H.C. BERGER IPA	A	BERGER	48
H.WEINHARD PRIV. RES	B	HEILEMAN	45
HAFFENREFFER	B	S&P	47
HAFFENREFFER ML	ML	S&P	35
HAIR OF THE DOG	P	FLYING DOG	48
HAMM'S	B	S&P	48
HAMM'S BIG BEAR	ML	S&P	32
HAMM'S DRAFT	B	S&P	29
HAMM'S GEN. DRAFT	B	S&P	35
HAMM'S NA	NA	S&P	8
HAMM'S SPECIAL LIGHT	LO	S&P	32
HAMPSHIRE ALE '89	A	GEARY	84
HAMPSHIRE ALE '90	A	GEARY	82
HAMPSHIRE ALE '91	A	GEARY	72
HAMPSHIRE ALE '92	A	GEARY	64
HANLEY	B	S&P	54
HAPPY VALLEY WEIZEN	W	HAPPY VALLEY	53
HARBOR LIGHT ALE	A	BAR HARBOR	59
HARBOR LIGHTS	A	PIZZA DELI	42
HARD ROCK CAFE	B	PITTSBURGH	27
HARD TIMES SELECT	B	OLD DOMINION	65
HARLEY DAVIDSON'90	B	HUBER	48
HARLEY-DAVIDSON '88	B	HUBER	42
HARLEY-DAVIDSON '89	B	HUBER	38
HARPOON	A	MASS BAY	68
HARPOON OKTOBERFEST	B	MATT	39
HARPOON WINTER '88	A	MASS BAY	64
HARPOON WINTER '90	B	MATT	60
HARPOON WINTER '91	B	MATT	43
HARVEST GOLD	LO	BEACH/MILL	36
HARVEST MOON LIGHT	A	GENTLE BEN	42
HAUENSTEIN	B	HEILEMAN	45
HEAD LIGHT	A	BREWHOUSE MAN.	47
HEARTLAND WEISS	W	CHICAGO	58
HEFERYZEN	A	BIG TIME	55
HEIDEL BRAU	B	HEILEMAN	20
HEIDELBERG	B	HEILEMAN	35
HEIDELBERG LIGHT	LO	HEILEMAN	27
HEILEMAN'S LIGHT	LO	HEILEMAN	50
HEILEMAN'S OLD STYLE	B	HEILEMAN	50
HEISMAN (DORTMUNDER)	B	GREAT LAKES	66
HELENBOCH	B	SCHELL	39
HELENBOCH OKT 1992	B	SCHELL	62
HENRY W. LIGHT	LO	HEILEMAN	27
HENRY W. PRIV. RES	B	HEILEMAN	35
HENRY WEINHARD DARK	B	HEILEMAN	27
HERCULES STRONG ALE	A	BOSTON WORKS	84
HERITAGE HOUSE	B	PITTSBURGH	39
HERMAN JOSEPH 1868	B	COORS	68
HERMAN JOSEPH DRAFT	B	COORS	56
HERMAN JOSEPH LIGHT	LO	COORS	33
HI-BRAU	B	HUBER	24
HIGH ROLLERS	W	ANDERSON VALLEY	54
HIGHLAND AMBER	A	BREWHOUSE MAN.	48
HINKY DINK KENNA	B	JONES	55
HOBOKEN SPECIAL	A	NEW HAVEN	52
HOF-BRAU	B	S&P	30
HOFBRAU	B	HUDEPOHL-SCHOENLING	49
HOLIDAY ALE 1988	A	PACIFIC COAST	79
HOLIDAY BARLEYWINE '90	BW	PACIFIC COAST	81
HOLIDAY STRONG 1991	A	PACIFIC COAST	52
HOLY MOSES ALE	A	GREAT LAKES	54
HOME RUN ALE	A	CHAMPION	54
HONKER'S ALE	A	GOOSE ISLAND	63
HOP OF THE ROCK IPA	A	TRIPLE ROCK	70
HOPE BOCK	BK	LION	58
HOPE LAGER	B	LION	46
HOPE LIGHT	LO	LION	45
HOPPY HOLIDAYS '92	A	SANTA CRUZ	56
HOPPY HOLIDAYS 1988	A	SANTA CRUZ	59
HOPPY HOLIDAZE '92	A	MARIN	47
HOPPY HOLIDAZE ALE	A	MARIN	55
HOPS! AMBER ALE	A	HOPS!SCOTTSDALE	50
HOPS! BARLEYWINE	BW	HOPS!SCOTTSDALE	60
HOPS! ESB	A	HOPS! LA JOLLA	49
HOPS! EXPORT LAGER	B	HOPS! LA JOLLA	53
HOPS! HEFE-WEIZEN	W	HOPS! LA JOLLA	55
HOPS! HEFE-WEIZEN	W	HOPS! SCOTTSDALE	58
HOPS! OATMEAL STOUT	S	HOPS! LA JOLLA	71
HOPS! OATMEAL STOUT	S	HOPS! SCOTTSDALE	81
HOPS! OCTOBERFEST	B	HOPS! SCOTTSDALE	60
HOPS! PILSNER	B	HOPS! LA JOLLA	47
HOPS! PILSNER	B	HOPS! SCOTTSDALE	48
HOPS! RASPBERRY	A	HOPS! SCOTTSDALE	47
HOPS! RASPBERRY	B	HOPS! LA JOLLA	37
HOPS! XMAS	A	HOPS! SCOTTSDALE	68
HORNET'S TAIL	A	BEACH/MILL	62
HORSETOOTH STOUT	S	COOPERSMITHS	43
HORST'S OKTOBERFEST	B	O'FALLON	24
HORTON'S HOOTCH	B	KARL STRAUSS	36
HOSTER AMBER	B	HOSTER	59
HUBER BOCK	BK	HUBER	42
HUBER CLASSIC	B	HUBER	54
HUBER PREMIUM	B	HUBER	45
HUDEPOHL 14K	B	HUDEPOHL-SCHOENLING	24
HUDEPOHL	B	HUDEPOHL-SCHOENLING	18
HUDEPOHL GOLD	B	HUDEPOHL-SCHOENLING	44
HUDSON LAGER	B	WOODSTOCK	54
HUDY DE LIGHT	LO	HUDEPOHL-SCHOENLING	14
HUMBOLDT OATMEAL ST.	S	HUMBOLDT	67
HÜBSCH BRAU DARK	B	HÜBSCH	54
HÜBSCH BRÄU	B	HÜBSCH	54
HÜBSCH LAGER	B	HÜBSCH	51
HÜBSCH MÄRZEN	B	HÜBSCH	51
HÜBSCH PILS	B	HÜBSCH	50
HÜBSCH WEIZEN	W	HÜBSCH	56
I.C. DRY	D	PITTSBURGH	29
I.C. GOLDEN LAGER	B	PITTSBURGH	36
IMPERIAL STOUT	S	GORKY	46
IMPERIAL STOUT	S	HERITAGE	60
IMPERIAL STOUT	S	YAKIMA	62
INDEGO PALE ALE	A	BERGER	55
INDEPENDENCE ALE	A	KELMER	42
INDEPENDENCE ALE	A	MANHATTAN	44
INDIA PALE ALE	A	PIZZA PORT	60
INDIAN PEAKS PALE ALE	A	WALNUT	38
INDICATOR DOPPELBOCK	BK	TWENTY TANKS	62
IRISH RED ALE	A	MELBOURNE	50
IRISH SETTER STOUT	S	FLYING DOG	48
IRON CITY	B	PITTSBURGH	46
IRON CITY DARK	B	PITTSBURGH	49
IRON CITY DRAFT	B	PITTSBURGH	41

Brand	Type	Brewer	Rating
IRON CITY LIGHT	LO	PITTSBURGH	11
IRONHORSE ALT	A	DEVIL MOUNTAIN	48
IRONS ALE	A	IRONS	46
IRONS AMBER LAGER	B	IRONS	45
IRONSIDE	A	OLDENBERG	59
IROQUOIS	B	GENESEE	50
ISLAND GOLD	B	FRANKENMUTH	9
J. PAGE PRIV. STOCK	B	JAMES PAGE	54
J.R.EWING	B	S&P	46
JAGUAR	ML	ANHEUSER-BUSCH	42
JAMES BOWIE	B	HEILEMAN	39
JAX	B	S&P	42
JAZZBERRY	A	ROCK BOTTOM	43
JEFF & JER'S HOOTCH	B	KARL STRAUSS	59
JEFFERSON BLUE RIDGE	B	SCHELL	73
JERSEY LAGER	B	LION	29
JOHN BARLEYCORN	BW	MAD RIVER	51
JOHNSON'S HONEY LAGER	B	BREWMASTERS'	42
JOLIEBLONDE	B	S&P	46
JUBEL ALE 91	A	DESCHUTES	60
JUBILEE 100	B	HUDEPOHL-SCHOENLING	72
JUDGE BALDWIN'S AMBER	A	JUDGE BALDWIN	42
JUDGE BALDWIN'S PALE	A	JUDGE BALDWIN	40
JUDGE BALDWIN'S PORT.	P	JUDGE BALDWIN	45
JUDGE BALDWIN'S WHEAT	W	JUDGE BALDWIN	42
K&B PILSENLAGER	B	DIXIE	20
K-9 CLASSIC PALE	A	FLYING DOG	37
KALAMAZOO STOUT	S	KALAMAZOO	70
KAPPY'S	B	LION	30
KAPPY'S	B	S&P	35
KARL STRAUSS AMBER	B	KARL STRAUSS	64
KARLSBRAU	B	COLD SPRING	20
KASSEL	B	S&P	38
KATZ	B	S&P	44
KEG BRAND	B	S&P	25
KEGLE BRAU	B	COLD SPRING	54
KELMER'S KLASSIC	A	KELMER	53
KENMORE KÖLSCH	K	BOSTON BEER WORKS	55
KENOSHA GOLD	B	BREWMASTERS'	45
KESSLER	B	KESSLER	62
KESSLER BOCK	BK	KESSLER	45
KESSLER LORELEI	BK	KESSLER	53
KESSLER WHEAT	W	KESSLER	26
KESSLER WINTER	BK	KESSLER	58
KEYSTONE	B	COORS	27
KEYSTONE DRY	D	COORS	23
KEYSTONE LIGHT	LO	COORS	14
KIDDER'S PALE ALE	A	KIDDER'S	51
KIDDER'S SCOTTISH	A	KIDDER'S	53
KILLER WHALE	A	MONTEREY	24
KILLER WHALE STOUT	S	PACIFIC COAST	42
KILLIAN IRISH RED	B	COORS	38
KING COBRA	ML	ANHEUSER-BUSCH	48
KING'S LAGER	B	FULLERTON	50
KINGSBURY	B	HEILEMAN	17
KINGSBURY BREW	NA	HEILEMAN	21
KINNIKINICK IMPERIAL	S	TWENTY TANKS	67
KIT FOX AMBER	A	SAN ANDREAS	16
KLASSIC AMBER	A	KELMER	33
KNICKERBOCKER	B	HEILEMAN	32
KNIGHT LIGHT	LO	BEACH/MILL	34
KNIGHT'S LIGHT	LO	FULLERTON	45
KOCH GOLD. ANNIV. LIGHT	LO	GENESEE	23
KOCH GOLDEN ANNIV.	B	GENESEE	25
KOCH HOLIDAY	B	GENESEE	17
KOCH JUBILEE	P	GENESEE	44
KOCH'S LIGHT	LO	GENESEE	33
KOEHLER	B	HEILEMAN	39
KOEHLER LAGER	B	HEILEMAN	36
KOEHLER PILSENER	B	HEILEMAN	32
KOLONIE BRAU	B	COLD SPRING	45
KOOLAU	BK	KOOLAU	41
KOYOTE KÖLSCH	K	COYOTE SPRINGS	47
KRIS KRINGLE 1990	A	KELMER	61
KRIS KRINGLE 1992	A	KELMER	15
KRUEGER PILSENER	B	S&P	59
KRYSTAL WHEAT	W	KELMER	44
KUFNERBRAU	BK	KUFNERBRAU	NR
KYLE'S LIGHT BROWN	A	WYNKOOP	39
LA CANADA	A	RUSSELL	54
LA	RA	ANHEUSER-BUSCH	15
LA-VE CON COP	B	WINCHESTER	40
LAGERHEAD	B	ROCK BOTTOM	40
LANDMARK	B	MINNESOTA	45
LANDMARK BOCK	BK	MINNESOTA	40
LANDMARK LIGHT	LO	MINNESOTA	33
LANDMARK OCTOBERFEST	B	MINNESOTA	54

Brand	Type	Brewer	Rating
LANDRY'S	B	ABITA	49
LANTERN BAY BLONDE	A	HERITAGE	48
LAS BRISAS	B	OLDENBERG	39
LEGACY	B	CHICAGO	75
LEGACY RED ALE	B	CHICAGO	68
LEINENKUGEL	B	LEINENKUGEL	41
LEINENKUGEL BOCK	BK	LEINENKUGEL	29
LEINENKUGELS LTD.	B	LEINENKUGEL	48
LEINIE'S LIGHT	LO	LEINENKUGEL	27
LIBERTY ALE	A	ANCHOR	78
LIEBOTSCHANER ALE	A	LION	37
LIEBOTSCHANER BOCK	BK	LION	20
LIGHTHOUSE AMBER	B	SANTA CRUZ	51
LIGHTHOUSE LAGER	B	SANTA CRUZ	57
LIMERICK'S	A	BUFFALO	61
LION'S PRIDE	A	GRITTY MC DUFFS	47
LIONSHEAD	B	LION	44
LITE	LO	MILLER	43
LITE ULTRA	LO	MILLER	32
LITTLE KINGS	B	HUDEPOHL-SCHOENLING	35
LITTLE KINGS CR. ALE	B	HUDEPOHL-SCHOENLING	47
LITTLE POINT PALE	A	LA JOLLA	44
LIVE OAK GOLD	A	MANHATTAN BEACH	34
LODI	B	S&P	48
LONE STAR	B	HEILEMAN	35
LONE STAR BOCK	BK	HEILEMAN	42
LONE STAR DRAFT	B	HEILEMAN	44
LONE STAR LIGHT	LO	HEILEMAN	32
LONG BEACH CRUDE	P	BELMONT	53
LONG TRAIL ALE	A	MOUNTAIN	54
LONG TRAIL IPA	A	MOUNTAIN	68
LONG TRAIL LIGHT	LO	MOUNTAIN	23
LONG TRAIL STOUT	S	MOUNTAIN	21
LORD CHESTERFIELD	A	YUENGLING	59
LORELEI	B	KESSLER	46
LOST COAST AMBER	A	LOST COAST	83
LOST COAST DOWNTOWN	A	LOST COAST	57
LOST COAST PALE ALE	A	LOST COAST	47
LOST COAST STOUT	S	LOST COAST	53
LOW ALCOHOL GOLD	RA	S&P	21
LOWENBRAU DARK	B	MILLER	48
LOWENBRAU LIGHT	LO	MILLER	31
LOWENBRAU SPECIAL	B	MILLER	54
LUCKY 50	LO	S&P	15
LUCKY 96 EXTRA LIGHT	LO	S&P	18
LUCKY BOCK	BK	S&P	40
LUCKY DRAFT	B	S&P	42
LUCKY LAGER	B	S&P	44
LUDWIG HUDEPOHL BOCK	BK	HUDEPOHL-SCHOENLING	50
LUDWIG HUDEPOHL OKT.	B	HUDEPOHL-SCHOENLING	59
M.W. BRENNER	B	MATT	38
MACHO 1200	B	SCHELL	35
MAD LUDWIG'S OKT.	A	HARTFORD	61
MAGIC BREW	A	BEACH/MILL	57
MAGNA CARTA CR. ALE	B	PITTSBURGH	18
MAGNUM	ML	MILLER	18
MAIN ST. GOLDEN	B	INDIANNAPOLIS	11
MALTA INDIA	M	LION	15
MAN. PREM. AMBER	A	MANHATTAN	66
MAN. ROYAL AMBER	A	MANHATTAN	56
MANHATTAN DRY IRISH	S	MANHATTAN	51
MANHATTAN GOLD	A	MANHATTAN	66
MANHATTAN GOLD	B	MATT	64
MANHATTAN PORTER	P	MANHATTAN	68
MANHATTAN SPECIAL	A	MANHATTAN	54
MANHATTAN STOUTS	S	MANHATTAN	69
MARATHON PALE ALE	A	BELMONT	41
MARBLE PILSENER	B	SISSONS	45
MARK V	B	PITTSBURGH	34
MARKET ST. GOLDEN	B	BOHANNON	50
MARKET ST. OKTOBER	B	BOHANNON	57
MARKET ST. WHEAT	W	BOHANNON	45
MARKET STREET	B	BOHANNON	62
MARTINS MELLOW-GLOW	A	TWENTY TANKS	50
MATT TRAD. 1986	B	MATT	48
MATT TRAD. 1990	B	MATT	50
MATT TRAD. 1991	B	MATT	40
MATT TRAD. 1992	B	MATT	27
MATT'S LIGHT	LO	MATT	51
MATT'S PREMIUM	B	MATT	32
MATT'S SPECIAL DRY	D	MATT	20
MAUI	B	PACIFIC	60
MAXIMUS SUPER	ML	MATT	52
MAXX	B	S&P	42
MC DUFF'S BEST BITTER	A	GRITTY MC DUFFS	45
MC GINTY'S OLD IRISH	S	M.J. BARLEYHOPPER	42
MC GUIRE'S IRISH STOUT	S	MC GUIRE'S	49

Brand	Type	Brewer	Rating
MC GUIRE'S PORTER	P	MC GUIRE'S	54
MC NEILL'SPALE BOCK	A	MC NEILL'S	48
MC NEILL'S SPEC. BITTER	A	MC NEILL'S	60
McGUIRES IRISH ALE	A	McGUIRES	55
McGUIRES IRISH ALE	A	OLDENBERG	44
McGUIRES LITE	LO	McGUIRES	54
McGUIRES PORTER	P	McGUIRES	60
McGUIRES STOUT	S	McGUIRES	52
McSORLEY'S CREAM ALE	A	HEILEMAN	44
McTARNAHAN'S ALE	A	PORTLAND	50
MEDALLION	B	S&P	43
MEISTER BRAU	B	MILLER	39
MEISTER BRAU LIGHT	LO	MILLER	26
MESA PALE ALE	A	CALLAHANS	55
METBRAU/METBREW	NA	HEILEMAN	16
METBREW LIGHT	NA	HEILEMAN	16
MEXICALI ROUGE	A	ROGUE	60
MICH. GOLD DRFT LIGHT	LO	ANHEUSER-BUSCH	22
MICHAEL SHEA	B	GENESEE	20
MICHELOB	B	ANHEUSER-BUSCH	66
MICHELOB DARK	B	ANHEUSER-BUSCH	19
MICHELOB DRY	D	ANHEUSER-BUSCH	27
MICHELOB GOLD. DRAFT	B	ANHEUSER-BUSCH	35
MICHELOB LIGHT	LO	ANHEUSER-BUSCH	47
MICKEY'S	ML	HEILEMAN	61
MID. DRAGON LAGER	B	HEILEMAN	23
MID. DRAGON MALTA	M	LION	30
MIDNIGHT DRAGON ALE	B	HEILEMAN	57
MIDNIGHT DRAGON ALE	B	HUDEPOHL-SCHOENLING	23
MIDNIGHT DRAGON	ML	HUDEPOHL-SCHOENLING	35
MIDNIGHT DRAGON ML	ML	HEILEMAN	47
MILL NUT BROWN ALE	A	MILL-CHARLOTTE	29
MILL PALE ALE	A	MILL-ORLANDO	72
MILLER DRAFT	B	MILLER	40
MILLER GEN. DRAFT LIGHT	LO	MILLER	9
MILLER GENUINE DRAFT	B	MILLER	26
MILLER HIGH LIFE	B	MILLER	58
MILLER MALT LIQUOR	ML	MILLER	29
MILLER RESERVE	B	MILLER	38
MILLER RESERVE LIGHT	LO	MILLER	24
MILLER SPECIAL RES.	B	MILLER	27
MILLSTREAM	B	MILLSTREAM	44
MILLSTREAM WHEAT	W	MILLSTREAM	18
MILW. BEST LIGHT	LO	MILLER	20
MILWAUKEE 1851	B	HEILEMAN	37
MILWAUKEE 1851 LIGHT	LO	HEILEMAN	32
MILWAUKEE GERMANFEST	B	S&P	42
MILWAUKEE'S BEST	B	MILLER	26
MIRROR POND PALE ALE	A	DESCHUTES	44
MISSION CREEK	P	BREWHOUSE GRILL	55
MIWOK WEIZENBOCK	W	MARIN	34
MKT. ST. HONEY WHEAT	W	MARKET STREET	49
MOERLEIN'S BOCK	BK	HUDEPOHL-SCHOENLING	34
MOLLY'S TITANIC BROWN	A	ROCK BOTTOM	41
MONTAUK LIGHT	LO	MATT	25
MONTEZUMA'S CHILI	B	WYNKOOP	31
MOODY'S HI-TOP	A	TWENTY TANKS	49
MOON DOG ALE	A	GREAT LAKES	69
MOONBEAM PALE ALE	A	WINDHAM	60
MOOSE JUICE STOUT	S	OTTO BROS.	51
MOUNTAIN AVENUE	W	COOPERSMITHS	55
MOUNTAIN WHEAT	W	BRECKENRIDGE	42
MR. MIKE'S LIGHT ALE	LO	NEW HAVEN	28
MT. EVEREST	ML	HUDEPOHL-SCHOENLING	20
MT. HOOD	B	PORTLAND	42
MT. TAM PALE ALE	A	MARIN	45
MT. WILSON WHEAT	W	CROWN CITY	51
MULATE'S	B	ABITA	50
MULLIGAN'S BREW	A	MOUNTAIN	49
MUSTANG	ML	PITTSBURGH	51
N.ENGL. ATLANTIC AMBER	A	NEW ENGLAND	65
N.ENGL. GOLD STOCK	A	NEW ENGLAND	75
N.ENGL. HOLIDAY'90	A	NEW ENGLAND	48
N.ENGL. HOLIDAY'91	A	NEW ENGLAND	41
N.ENGL. HOLIDAY'92	A	NEW ENGLAND	39
N.ENGL. OATMEAL ST.	S	NEW ENGLAND	63
NAMELESS NUT BROWN	A	CALLAHAN	36
NARRAGANSETT 96	LO	S&P	40
NARRAGANSETT	B	S&P	45
NARRAGANSETT BOCK	BK	S&P	26
NARRAGANSETT CR.ALE	A	S&P	15
NARRAGANSETT PORTER	P	S&P	42
NATHAN HALE	B	LION	42
NATIONAL BOHEMIAN	B	HEILEMAN	57
NATIONAL LIGHT	LO	HEILEMAN	35
NATIONAL PREMIUM	B	HEILEMAN	45
NATURAL LIGHT	LO	ANHEUSER-BUSCH	40

Brand	Type	Brewer	Rating
NATURAL PILSENER	B	ANHEUSER-BUSCH	30
NEUWEILER BLK & TAN	P	LION	38
NEUWEILER PORTER	P	LION	28
NEUWEILER TRADITIONAL	B	LION	34
NEVADA CITY DARK	B	NEVADA CITY	55
NEVADA CITY GOLD	B	NEVADA CITY	59
NEW AMSTER. WINTER	B	MATT	56
NEW AMSTERDAM ALE	B	MATT	78
NEW AMSTERDAM AMBER	B	OLD NEW YORK	58
NEW OR. BEST LIGHT	LO	DIXIE	35
NEW ORLEANS BEST	B	DIXIE	24
NEW YORK HARBOR	A	STEVENS POINT	51
NEWMAN SARATOGA	B	CATAMOUNT	44
NINE HUNDRED CNTRY CL.	ML	PEARL	45
NINE-0-FIVE	B	HEILEMAN	16
NINE-0-FIVE LIGHT	LO	PITTSBURGH	30
NINETY SHILLING ALE	A	O'DELL	62
NITTANY LAGER	B	HAPPY VALLEY	57
NO DOUBT STOUT	S	UMPQUA	42
NO FRILLS	B	LION	28
NO. COAST XMAS '89	A	NORTH COAST	26
NO. COAST XMAS '90	A	NORTH COAST	85
NO. COAST XMAS '91	A	NORTH COAST	72
NO. COAST XMAS '92	A	NORTH COAST	53
NORTH STAR	B	COLD SPRING	31
NORTHAMPTON AMBER	A	NORTHAMPTON	48
NORTHAMPTON GOLDEN	A	NORTHAMPTON	55
NORTHERN	B	COLD SPRING	39
NOT BROWN ALE	A	COOPERSMITHS	42
NUMBSKULL AMBER	B	O'FALLON	23
NUT BROWN	A	BREWHOUSE MAN.	69
NUTS TO YOU	A	COYOTE SPRING	22
O'DELL'S GOLDEN ALE	A	O'DELL	39
O'DELL'S SPECIAL BITTER	A	O'DELL	39
O'DOULS	NA	ANHEUSER-BUSCH	21
O'FEST	B	VERMONT	42
OASIS OKTOBERFEST	B	OASIS	33
OASIS PALE ALE	A	OASIS	30
OATMEAL STOUT	S	BREWHOUSE MAN.	67
OATMEAL STOUT	S	BREWSKI'S	66
OATMEAL STOUT	S	GENTLE BEN	54
OATMEAL STOUT	S	KARL STRAUSS	30
OBRIEN'S LONG TRAIL	S	MOUNTAIN	45
OBSIDIAN STOUT	S	DESCHUTES	61
OCEAN CITY	B	JONES	25
OERTEL'S 92	B	HUBER	36
OKIE GIRL WINTERFEST	B	OKIE GIRL	69
OKTOBER QUAKE ALE	A	SAN ANDREAS	11
OKTOBERFEST ALT	A	BREWMASTERS'	51
OL' YELLER	A	FLYING DOG	43
OLD 55 PALE ALE	A	BIRD CREEK	64
OLD BAWDY BARLEYWINE	BW	PIKE PLACE	60
OLD BAY AMBER	B	CLEMENT	43
OLD BROWN DOG	A	PORTSMOUTH	55
OLD CHERRY ALE	A	NEW BELGIUM	47
OLD CHICAGO	B	HUBER	12
OLD CHICAGO DARK	B	HUBER	60
OLD CLYBOURN PORTER	P	GOOSE ISLAND	55
OLD CROWN ALE	A	HUBER	32
OLD CROWN	B	HUBER	26
OLD DETROIT	B	FRANKENMUTH	42
OLD DIPSEA	BW	MARIN	60
OLD DUTCH BRAND	B	PITTSBURGH	21
OLD ELK BROWN ALE	A	WALNUT	34
OLD ENGLISH 800	ML	HEILEMAN	24
OLD EXPORT	B	PITTSBURGH	6
OLD FAITHFUL ALE	A	OTTO BROS.	45
OLD FOGHORN	A	ANCHOR	69
OLD FROTHINGSLOSH	B	PITTSBURGH	42
OLD GERMAN	B	HUBER	21
OLD GERMAN	B	YUENGLING	42
OLD GERMAN BRAND	B	PITTSBURGH	20
OLD GUILFORD PORTER	P	WINDHAM	54
OLD HEIDELBRAU	B	S&P	26
OLD KNUCKLEHEAD	BW	BRIDGEPORT	49
OLD LEATHER MAN ALE	A	CHARTER OAK	38
OLD MACLUNK'S SCOT.	A	BOULDER CREEK	46
OLD MIL. GEN, DRAFT	B	STROH	27
OLD MIL. GEN. DFT LIGHT	LO	STROH	32
OLD MILWAUKEE	B	STROH	56
OLD MILWAUKEE LIGHT	LO	STROH	20
OLD MILWAUKEE NA	NA	STROH	31
OLD NO. 38	S	NORTH COAST	60
OLD POJOAQUE	P	SANTA FE	66
OLD RIP	S	BIG TIME	44
OLD SHAY ALE	B	JONES	17
OLD STYLE CLASS. DRAFT	B	HEILEMAN	34

Brand	Type	Brewer	Rating
OLD STYLE DRY	D	HEILEMAN	30
OLD STYLE SPECIAL DRY	D	HEILEMAN	28
OLD TANKARD ALE	B	S&P	61
OLD TOWN ALE	A	O'DELL	51
OLD TOWN PALE	A	BREWHOUSE GRILL	57
OLD WOOLY	P	BIG TIME	51
OLD WORLD OKTOBER	B	WATER STREET	60
OLDE BUCKEYE DRAFT	B	MATT	24
OLDE BUCKEYE LIGHT	LO	MATT	19
OLDE ENG. 800 GEN DFT	ML	S&P	26
OLDE HEURICH	B	PITTSBURGH	65
OLDE HEURICH MAERZEN	BK	MATT	60
OLDENBERG BLONDE	B	OLDENBERG	35
OLDENBERG CELEB. ALE	A	OLDENBERG	54
OLDENBERG PREM.	B	OLDENBERG	48
OLDENBERG WEISS	W	OLDENBERG	32
OLDENBERG WINTER ALE	A	OLDENBERG	64
OLYMPIA	B	S&P	50
OLYMPIA DARK	B	S&P	27
OLYMPIA DRY	D	S&P	23
OLYMPIA GENUINE DRAFT	B	S&P	44
OLYMPIA GOLD	LO	S&P	34
OLYMPIA LIGHT	LO	S&P	29
ORCA PORTER	P	PACIFIC COAST	59
OREGON STATE FAIR '89	A	KESSLER	53
ORIGINAL BEACH	B	S&P	24
ORTLEIB'S BOCK	BK	HEILEMAN	23
ORTLIEB'S	B	HEILEMAN	36
OUR	B	HUBER	42
OUR SPECIAL ALE 1978	A	ANCHOR	45
OUR SPECIAL ALE 1979	A	ANCHOR	26
OUR SPECIAL ALE 1980	A	ANCHOR	81
OUR SPECIAL ALE 1981	A	ANCHOR	63
OUR SPECIAL ALE 1982	A	ANCHOR	68
OUR SPECIAL ALE 1983	A	ANCHOR	63
OUR SPECIAL ALE 1984	A	ANCHOR	69
OUR SPECIAL ALE 1985	A	ANCHOR	80
OUR SPECIAL ALE 1986	A	ANCHOR	80
OUR SPECIAL ALE 1987	A	ANCHOR	56
OUR SPECIAL ALE 1988	A	ANCHOR	48
OUR SPECIAL ALE 1989	A	ANCHOR	63
OUR SPECIAL ALE 1990	A	ANCHOR	57
OUR SPECIAL ALE 1991	A	ANCHOR	64
OUR SPECIAL ALE 1992	A	ANCHOR	60
OUTBACK LAGER	B	DALLAS	20
OVER THE LINE STOUT	S	PACIFIC BEACH	50
OXFORD CLASS AMBER	A	BRITISH	20
PABST BLUE RIBBON DR.	B	S&P	28
PABST EXTRA LIGHT	LO	S&P	20
PABST GEN DRAFT	B	S&P	15
PABST GENUINE DRAFT	B	S&P	29
PABST SPECIAL DARK	B	S&P	42
PAC. COAST IMPER. ST.	S	PACIFIC COAST	39
PAC. COAST TRAD. IPA	A	PACIFIC COAST	45
PACE	RA	HUDEPOHL	21
PACIFIC BEACH BLONDE	B	PACIFIC BEACH	53
PACIFIC CASCADE	A	GOLDEN PACIFIC	9
PACIFIC COAST	BK	KESSLER	29
PACIFIC CREST ALE	A	HART	74
PACIFIC PORTER	P	SANTA CRUZ	39
PACIFICA PALE ALE	A	MANHATTAN BEACH	49
PADRE	B	S&P	29
PALE BOCK	B	FULLERTON	69
PALI	B	HONOLULU	45
PALOUSE WEIZEN	W	M.J. BARLEYHOPPER	24
PANDORA'S PORTER	P	TELLURIDE	12
PARADISE PALE ALE	A	M.J. BARLEYHOPPER	45
PARLEY'S PORTER	P	SALT LAKE	42
PASSION PALE	A	TIED HOUSE	45
PBC CL. DRAFT LIGHT	LO	PITTSBURGH	21
PBC CLASSIC DRAFT	B	PITTSBURGH	9
PEACH WHEAT	W	COOPERSMITHS	45
PEARL	B	S&P	64
PEARL CREAM ALE	A	S&P	52
PEARL LIGHT LAGER	B	S&P	27
PEARL NA	NA	S&P	16
PEARL WHEAT	W	PACIFIC COAST	31
PECAN STREET	B	SCHELL	60
PENN DARK	B	PENNSYLVANIA	30
PENN LIGHT LAGER	B	PENNSYLVANIA	42
PENN OKTOBERFEST	B	PENNSYLVANIA	34
PENN PORTER	P	HAPPY VALLEY	49
PENNSYLVANIA PILS	B	JONES	59
PETE'S GOLD COAST	B	SCHELL	81
PETE'S PACIFIC DRY	D	SCHELL	41
PETE'S WICKED ALE	A	SCHELL	56
PETER HAND	B	HUBER	35
PETER HAND EXT. LIGHT	LO	HUBER	42
PETER'S PORTER	P	HOPS! SCOTTSDALE	42
PFEIFFER	B	HEILEMAN	26
PICKWICK ALE	A	S&P	35
PIELS	B	STROH	48
PIELS LIGHT	LO	STROH	45
PIELS REAL DRAFT	B	STROH	32
PIER PALE ALE	A	HUNTINGTON BEACH	54
PIG'S EYE	B	MINNESOTA	27
PIGS EYE PILSNER	B	MINNESOTA	40
PIKE PLACE EAST IPA	A	PIKE PLACE	49
PIKE PLACE PALE ALE	A	CATAMOUNT	50
PIKE PLACE PALE ALE	A	PIKE PLACE	53
PIKE PLACE XXXXX ST.	S	PIKE PLACE	61
PILBOX PALE ALE	A	PIZZA PORT	54
PILSENER CLUB	B	S&P	41
PINK CHAMPALE	ML	HEILEMAN	36
PINNACLE PALE	A	TRIPLE ROCK	66
PIONEER DAYS 1982	A	SIERRA NEVADA	22
PIONEER DAYS 1985	A	SIERRA NEVADA	82
PIONEER PORTER	P	BREWSKI'S	54
PITBULL GOLDEN	A	HARTFORD	69
PITTS BEER	B	OLDENBERG	48
PLAYER'S	LO	MILLER	14
PMD MILD ALE	A	GOOSE ISLAND	61
POINT BOCK	BK	STEVENS POINT	51
POINT LIGHT	LO	STEVENS POINT	35
POINT REYES PORTER	P	MARIN	72
POINT SPECIAL	B	STEVENS POINT	48
POLEEKO GOLD	A	ANDERSON VALLEY	28
POOR RICHARD'S AMBER	B	SAM ADAMS BREWHOUSE	50
PORT'S PORTER	P	PIZZA PORT	66
PORTLAND ALE	A	PORTLAND	56
PORTLAND DRY HONEY	B	PORTLAND	64
PORTLAND HEAD LIGHT	A	GRITTY MC DUFFS	40
PORTLAND PORTER	P	PORTLAND	32
PORTLAND PORTER	P	PORTLAND	43
PORTSMOUTH ALE	A	FRANK JONES	45
PORTSMOUTH AMBER	B	PORTSMOUTH	49
PORTSMOUTH BLONDE	A	PORTSMOUTH	44
PORTSMOUTH GOLDEN	B	PORTSMOUTH	46
PORTSMOUTH PALE ALE	A	PORTSMOUTH	54
POST ROAD	A	CATAMOUNT	69
POTRERO COMMONS ALE	A	ANCHOR	80
PRIME TIME	A	BIG TIME	45
PRIMO	B	STROH	24
PRINCE'S PILSENER	B	FULLERTON	52
PRIOR DOUBLE DARK	B	MATT	55
PROSPECTOR JOE	B	LOS ANGELES	81
PROSPECTOR JOE DARK	B	LOS ANGELES	68
PROSPECTOR PALE	B	COYOTE SPRINGS	62
PT. LOMA LIGHTHOUSE	LO	KARL STRAUSS	55
PULASKI PIVO	B	S&P	27
PUMP HOUSE PORTER	P	LA JOLLA	44
PUMPKIN ALE	A	BUFFALO BILL	62
PUNJABI PALE ALE	A	COOPERSMITHS	35
PUNKIN ALE	A	BUFFALO BILL'S	65
PYRAMID AMBER WHEAT	W	HART	54
PYRAMID PALE	A	HART	73
PYRAMID SPHINX STOUT	S	HART	51
PYRAMID WHEATEN	W	HART	36
QUEEN CITY	B	LION	45
RAF BETTER BITTER	A	GOOSE ISLAND	54
RAILROAD ALE	A	DEVIL MOUNTAIN	75
RAINBOW TROUT STOUT	S	HUBCAP	59
RAINIER ALE	A	HEILEMAN	49
RAINIER	B	HEILEMAN	27
RAINIER DRAFT	B	HEILEMAN	15
RAINIER DRY	D	HEILEMAN	18
RAINIER LIGHT	LO	HEILEMAN	13
RASPBERRY ALE	A	BOSTON BEER WORKS	59
RASPBERRY OATMEAL	S	CRESTED BUTTE	27
RASPBERRY TRAIL	A	MARIN	59
RASPBERRY WHEAT ALE	W	CARVER	41
RASPBERRY WHEAT	W	EDDIE MC STIFF'S	50
RATTLESNAKE	B	SPOETZL	37
RAUCH BEER	B	BUFFALO BILL	13
RAY'S CLASSIC	B	OLDENBERG	54
READING	B	HEILEMAN	50
RED BULL	ML	STROH	20
RED CAT AMBER	A	GENTLE BEN	48
RED DOG GINGER	A	FLYING DOG	48
RED FEATHER PALE ALE	A	ARROWHEAD	66
RED HAWK ALE	A	ROCK BOTTOM	33
RED HOOK ESB	A	RED HOOK	62
RED LADY ALE	A	CRESTED BUTTE	58
RED LIGHT	LO	CHAMPION	48

Brand	Type	Brewer	Rating
RED MTN GOLDEN ALE	A	BIRMINGHAM	45
RED MTN GOLDEN LAGER	B	BIRMINGHAM	52
RED NECTAR ALE	A	HUMBOLDT	78
RED OKTOBER	A	MILL-CHARLOTTE	54
RED ROCK	B	BEACH/MILL	60
RED ROCK STRONG ALE	A	TRIPLE ROCK	34
RED ROCKS RED	A	ROCK BOTTOM	53
RED ROOST ALE	A	LA JOLLA	42
RED ROOSTER	A	LION	69
RED SAILS ALE	A	BREWSKI'S	47
RED SEAL ALE	A	NORTH COAST	55
RED STALLION	B	CRESCENT CITY	52
RED STAR	A	GORKY	50
RED TAIL ALE	A	MENDOCINO	64
RED TROLLEY ALE	A	KARL STRAUSS	51
RED WARLOCK RASP	A	FLYING DOG	41
RED WH. &BLUE LIGHT	LO	S&P	32
RED WHITE & BLUE	B	S&P	42
REED'S GOLD	A	DILWORTH	34
REGAL	B	HEILEMAN	52
REGAL BRAU	B	HUBER	36
REGAL SELECT	B	S&P	34
REIDENBACH	B	S&P	27
RHEINGOLD	B	HEILEMAN	37
RHEINGOLD EXT. LIGHT	LO	HEILEMAN	29
RHEINLANDER	B	HUBER	44
RHEINLANDER BOCK	BK	HUBER	68
RHEINLANDER EXPORT	B	HUBER	35
RHINO CH. AMERICAN	A	MINNESOTA	55
RHINO CHASERS AMBER	A	ANGELES	69
RHINO CHASERS LAGER	B	ANGELES	32
RILEY'S RYE	A	STEELHEAD	40
RIN TIN TAN	A	FLYING DOG	66
RIVER BOTTOM STOUT	S	OKIE GIRL	62
RIVERMOUTH RASPBERRY	A	PIZZA PORT	48
RJ'S GINSENG	B	STEVENS POINT	45
ROBIN HOOD CREAM ALE	A	PITTSBURGH	40
ROCK & ROLL	B	DIXIE	47
ROCKIES PREMIUM	A	BOULDER	48
ROCKIES PREMIUM	B	ROCK BOTTOM	65
ROCKY MTN. WHEAT	W	SALT LAKE	44
ROGUE BARLEYWINE	BW	ROGUE	74
ROGUE GOLDEN ALE	A	ROGUE	66
ROGUE IMPERIAL STOUT	S	ROGUE	64
ROGUE MOGUL ALE	A	ROGUE	64
ROGUE NEW-PORTER	P	ROGUE	67
ROGUE SPRINGBOCK	BK	ROGUE	56
ROLLING BAY BOCK	BK	THOMAS KEMPER	15
ROLLING ROCK	B	LATROBE	50
ROLLING ROCK LIGHT	LO	LATROBE	29
ROUGHRIDER	B	HUBER	20
RUBICON AMBER ALE	A	RUBICON	52
RUBICON HEFE WEIZEN	W	RUBICON	49
RUBICON IPA	A	RUBICON	54
RUBICON STOUT	S	RUBICON	51
RUBICON WHEAT	W	RUBICON	45
RUNNER'S HIGH	B	TELLURIDE	51
RUSHMORE STOUT	S	FIREHOUSE	37
S. ADAMS CRANBERRY	L	BOSTON	31
S. ADAMS DOUBLE BOCK	BK	BOSTON	78
S. ADAMS OKTOBER	B	BOSTON	64
S. ADAMS WHEAT	W	BOSTON	41
S. ADAMS WINTER '89	B	BOSTON	72
S. ADAMS WINTER '90	B	BOSTON	75
S. ADAMS WINTER '91	B	BOSTON	80
S. ADAMS WINTER '92	B	BOSTON	68
S.V. OUR HOLIDAY 1990	A	KESSLER	63
S.V. SAWTOOTH GOLD	BK	KESSLER	57
S.V. WHITE CLOUD	B	KESSLER	59
SAGEBRUSH STOUT	S	WYNKOOP	42
SAIL ALE	A	HERITAGE	65
SAINT MICHAEL'S	NA	PITTSBURGH	12
SAINT NICK'S DARK ALE	A	KESSLER	72
SALOON LIGHT LAGER	LO	SCHELL	18
SAM ADAMS CR. STOUT	S	BOSTON	49
SAM ADAMS DUNK. WEIZ.	W	BOSTON	56
SAMUEL ADAMS	B	BOSTON	71
SAMUEL MIDDLETON	A	WILD GOOSE	22
SAN JOAQUIN ALE	A	BUTTERFIELD	38
SAN QUENTIN BREAKOUT	S	MARIN	74
SAN RAFAEL	A	J&L	54
SAN RAFAEL AMBER	A	J&L	71
SAN RAFAEL GOLDEN	A	J&L	45
SAN RAFAEL TRAD.	A	J&L	55
SANGRE DE FRAMBUESA	A	SANTA FE	67
SANTA FE NUT BROWN	A	SANTA FE	65
SANTA FE PALE ALE	A	SANTA FE	56
SARANAC 1888	B	MATT	43
SARANAC	B	MATT	60
SARANACK ADIRONDACK	B	MATT	54
SCHAEFER	B	STROH	48
SCHAEFER BOCK	BK	STROH	20
SCHAEFER CREAM ALE	A	STROH	31
SCHAEFER LA	RA	STROH	20
SCHAEFER LIGHT	LO	STROH	18
SCHELL DEER BR. EXP.	B	SCHELL	56
SCHELL DEER BRAND	B	SCHELL	18
SCHELL OCTOBER '90	B	SCHELL	69
SCHELL OKTOBERFEST '92	B	SCHELL	68
SCHELL PILS	B	SCHELL	36
SCHELL PILSENER	B	SCHELL	69
SCHELL WEISS	W	SCHELL	30
SCHELL WEIZEN	W	SCHELL	20
SCHELL'S 1979 BOCK	BK	SCHELL	31
SCHELL'S EXPORT LIGHT	B	SCHELL	27
SCHELL'S GRAND OLD	B	SCHELL	38
SCHELL'S HUNTER'S	B	SCHELL	24
SCHELL'SXMAS	B	SCHELL	18
SCHILD BRAU	B	MILLSTREAM	72
SCHLITZ	B	STROH	39
SCHLITZ LIGHT	LO	STROH	25
SCHLITZ MALT LIQUOR	ML	STROH	49
SCHMIDT	B	HEILEMAN	31
SCHMIDT LIGHT	LO	HEILEMAN	36
SCHMIDT SELECT	NA	HEILEMAN	17
SCHMIDT'S	B	HEILEMAN	46
SCHMIDT'S BAVARIAN	B	HEILEMAN	30
SCHMIDT'S BOCK	BK	HEILEMAN	40
SCHMIDT'S LIGHT	LO	HEILEMAN	17
SCHMIDT'S OKTOBERFEST	B	HEILEMAN	46
SCHOENLING BIG JUG	B	HUDEPOHL-SCHOENLING	30
SCHOENLING BOCK	BK	HUDEPOHL-SCHOENLING	26
SCHOENLING CREAM ALE	A	HUDEPOHL-SCHOENLING	33
SCHOENLING DRAFT	B	HUDEPOHL-SCHOENLING	11
SCHWARZ HACKER	B	ROCK BOTTOM	44
SCHWEGMANN	B	DIXIE	16
SCOTCH ALE	A	HAPPY VALLEY	72
SCOTCH BUY	B	S&P	38
SCOTCH BUY LIGHT	LO	S&P	36
SCOTTIE	A	FLYING DOG	55
SCRIMSHAW	B	NORTH COAST	63
SEA LION	S	MONTEREY	48
SEABR. BANTY ROOSTER	A	SEABRIGHT	53
SEABRIGHT AMBER	A	SEABRIGHT	60
SEABRIGHT CENTURY RED	A	SEABRIGHT	59
SEABRIGHT ESB	A	SEABRIGHT	65
SEABRIGHT OATMEAL	S	SEABRIGHT	72
SEABRIGHT PALE ALE	A	SEABRIGHT	65
SEABRIGHT PELICAN	A	SEABRIGHT	85
SEABRIGHT PORTER	P	SEABRIGHT	71
SEABRIGHT WEIZEN	W	SEABRIGHT	54
SEALANE AMBER	A	LA JOLLA	40
SEALANE STEAM	A	LA JOLLA	50
SEBAGO LIGHT ALE	A	GRITTY MC DUFFS	38
SEISMIC ALE	A	SAN ANDREAS	33
SGA	B	HEILEMAN	42
SGA GOLD LABEL	B	PITTSBURGH	20
SHAKESPEARE STOUT	S	ROGUE	54
SHAN SUI YEN SUM	B	MATT	38
SHARKBITE RED ALE	A	PIZZA PORT	73
SHARP'S LA	RA	MILLER	23
SHARP'S NA	NA	MILLER	23
SHEEPDOG STOUT	S	FLYING DOG	24
SHIELDS STOUT	S	SHIELDS	46
SHINER	B	SPOETZL	38
SHINER BOCK	BK	SPOETZL	41
SIERRA NEV. PALE ALE	A	SIERRA NEVADA	58
SIERRA NEV. PORTER	P	SIERRA NEVADA	57
SIERRA NEV. STOUT	S	SIERRA NEVADA	40
SIERRA NEV. SUMMER '91	B	SIERRA NEVADA	52
SIERRA NEV. SUMMER '92	B	SIERRA NEVADA	46
SIERRA NEV.PALE BK '91	BK	SIERRA NEVADA	87
SIERRA NEV.PALE BK '92	BK	SIERRA NEVADA	73
SIERRA NEV.SUMMERFEST	A	SIERRA NEVADA	69
SIERRA OLD CHICO	A	SIERRA NEVADA	66
SIGDA'S GREEN CHILI	B	COOPERSMITHS	32
SILVER RAIL	B	CHERRYLAND	42
SILVER THUNDER	ML	STROH	50
SIMPATICO AMBER	B	ZELE	65
SIMPATICO GOLDEN	B	ZELE	54
SIR EDWARD STOUT	B	SCHOENLING	29
SIR FRANCIS STOUT	S	LIND	44
SKIPJACK	B	LION	52
SLIM PRICE	B	GENERAL	33

Brand	Type	Brewer	Rating
SLIM PRICE LIGHT	LO	GENERAL	22
SLO AMBER ALE	A	SAN LUIS OBISPO	55
SLO NUT BROWN ALE	A	SAN LUIS OBISPO	60
SLO PALE ALE	A	SAN LUIS OBISPO	47
SLO PORTER	P	SAN LUIS OBISPO	49
SLOPBUCKET BROWN	A	MC NEILL'S	42
SMITH & REILLY	B	S&P	51
SMOKED PORTER 88	P	ALASKAN	60
SNAKE BITE	B	HUBER	23
SNOW CAP ALE '89	A	HART	75
SNOW CAP ALE '90	A	HART	84
SNOW GOOSE WINTER	A	WILD GOOSE	78
SNOW WHEAT	W	TELLURIDE	55
SNOWBIRD TRAM ALE	A	SCHIRF	44
SOLSTICE ALE	A	HUBCAP	47
SOUTH BAY BITTER	A	MANHATTAN BEACH	39
SOUTH SISTER SCOTCH	A	DESCHUTES	52
SPANISH PEAKS PORTER	P	SPANISH PEAKS	66
SPECIAL EDITION	B	STEVENS POINT	42
SPECIAL EXPORT	B	HEILEMAN	64
SPECIAL EXPORT DARK	B	HEILEMAN	20
SPECIAL EXPORT LIGHT	LO	HEILEMAN	30
SPECIAL OLD ALE	B	MATT	47
SPHINX STOUT	S	HART	33
SPIRIT OF ST. LOUIS	A	SIGNATURE	45
SPLATZ PORTER	P	WYNKOOP	48
SPORTS LIGHT	LO	MATT	27
SPRECHER BLK BAV.	B	SPRECHER	45
SPRECHER DUNK.WEIZEN	W	SPRECHER	48
SPRECHER MAI BOCK	BK	SPRECHER	67
SPRECHER MILW. WEISS	W	SPRECHER	15
SPRECHER OKT.	B	SPRECHER	22
SPRECHER SPEC.AMBER	B	SPRECHER	58
SPRECHER WINTER	B	SPRECHER	46
SPRING	B	S&P	15
SPUD PREMIUM	B	STEVENS POINT	20
ST. BRENDAN'S IRISH RED	A	MARIN	27
ST. CHARLES ESB	A	WYNKOOP	40
ST. PATS STOUT	S	KELMER	49
ST. ROGUE RED	A	ROGUE	61
ST. SEVERINS KÖLSCH	K	BOULDER CREEK	47
ST. STAN'S ALT	A	ST.STANS	46
ST. STAN'S DARK ALT	A	ST.STANS	22
ST. STAN'S FEST ALT	A	ST. STANS	78
ST.IDES PREMIUM	ML	HEILEMAN	38
STAG	B	HEILEMAN	47
STAG LIGHT	LO	HEILEMAN	17
STALLION TEN	ML	MATT	34
STEAMER LANE	B	S&P	35
STEELHEAD AMBER	A	STEELHEAD	54
STEELHEAD	B	MAD RIVER	67
STEELHEAD CREAM ALE	A	STEELHEAD	45
STEELHEAD EXTRA ST.	S	MAD RIVER	63
STEELHEAD NUT BROWN	A	PIZZA DELI	43
STEELHEAD OATMEAL	S	STEELHEAD	45
STEELHEAD PORTER	P	PIZZA DELI	55
STEGMAIER 1857	B	LION	35
STEGMAIER 1857 DRY	D	LION	39
STEGMAIER 1857 LIGHT	LO	LION	39
STEGMAIER	B	LION	27
STEGMAIER LIGHT	LO	LION	24
STEGMAIER PORTER	P	LION	27
STEINBRAU LIGHT	LO	S&P	12
STEINBRAU	NA	S&P	22
STEINHAUS	B	SCHELL	18
STENGER	B	HUBER	49
STINSON BEACH PEACH	A	MARIN	62
STITE	ML	HEILEMAN	31
STOCKADE AMBER	B	SISSONS	55
STONEY'S	B	JONES	26
STONEY'S LIGHT	LO	JONES	33
STORMCELLAR PORTER	P	HUMBOLDT	62
STOUDT'S ANNIV. ALE	A	STOUDT	47
STOUDT'S BEERFEST BK	BK	STOUDT	50
STOUDT'S BOCK	BK	STOUDT	50
STOUDT'S BULL ALE	A	STOUDT	37
STOUDT'S DBL. BOCK	BK	STOUDT	8
STOUDT'S DOPPELBOCK	BK	STOUDT	39
STOUDT'S FASCHING	B	STOUDT	29
STOUDT'S FEST	B	STOUDT	18
STOUDT'S GOLDEN LAGER	B	STOUDT	65
STOUDT'S HEFE-WEIZEN	W	STOUDT	51
STOUDT'S HOLIDAY ALE	A	STOUDT	78
STOUDT'S HOLIDAY BOCK	BK	STOUDT	42
STOUDT'S OCTOBER BEER	B	STOUDT	31
STOUDT'S OKT. MAERZEN	BK	STOUDT	27
STOUDT'S OKTOBERFEST	B	LION	42
STOUDT'S OKTOBERFEST	BK	STOUDT	39
STOUDT'S PILSENER	B	STOUDT	50
STOUDT'S RASPBERRY	W	STOUDT	52
STOUDT'S RED ALE	A	STOUDT	41
STOUDT'S SOUR MASH	A	STOUDT	10
STOUDT'S STOUT	S	STOUDT	55
STOUDT'S STOUT	S	STOUDT	56
STOUDT'S WINTERFEST	B	STOUDT	60
STOUT STREET STOUT	S	CHAMPION	42
STRAND AMBER	A	MANHATTAN BEACH	51
STRAUB ALL GRAIN	B	STRAUB	42
STRAUB	B	STRAUB	63
STRAUSS STOUT	S	KARL STRAUSS	59
STROH BOHEMIAN	B	STROH	43
STROH SIGNATURE	B	STROH	56
STROH'S BOCK	BK	STROH	62
STROH'S LIGHT	LO	STROH	45
SUMMER ALE 1990	A	NORTH COAST	73
SUMMER ALE	A	BOULDER	53
SUMMER ALE CASK COND	A	BOULDER	50
SUMMER PALE LAGER	B	SCHELL	33
SUMMER WHEAT	W	UMPQUA	20
SUMMERTIME WHEAT	W	LOST COAST	42
SUMMIT EXTRA PALE ALE	A	SUMMIT	46
SUMMIT GREAT NORTHERN	P	SUMMIT	40
SUMMIT SPARKLING	A	SUMMIT	36
SUMMIT WINTER ALE	A	SUMMIT	40
SUN V. OUR HOLIDAY 91	A	KESSLER	84
SUN VALLEY OUR HOLIDAY	A	KESSLER	75
SUNSET RED	A	PACIFIC BEACH	65
SUNSHINE WHEAT	W	NEW BELGIUM	52
SWHEAT HEART	W	TRIPLE ROCK	66
SWISS TRAIL WHEAT	W	WALNUT	50
T.W. FISHER'S LIGHT	LO	COEUR D'ALENE	13
TAHOE	B	LEINENKUGEL	26
TANKER ALE	A	BOULDER	33
TANZEN GANS KÖLSCH	K	GOOSE ISLAND	65
TAP	B	HUDEPOHL	33
TAYLOR JANE RASP.	W	GENTLE BEN	60
TECH LIGHT	B	PITTSBURGH	30
TELLURIDE	B	HUBER	54
TETON ALE	A	OTTO BROS.	55
TEXAS LIGHT DARK	NA	S&P	17
TEXAS LIGHT	NA	S&P	26
TEXAS PRIDE	B	S&P	40
TEXAS PRIDE LIGHT	LO	S&P	40
TEXAS SELECT	NA	S&P	15
TGIF PREM. AMBER	B	ZELE	5
THE JAMES IRISH RED	A	WALNUT	33
THIRD COAST BEER	B	KALAMAZOO	18
THIRD COAST OLD ALE	A	KALAMAZOO	60
THOMAS KEMPER PILS	B	THOMAS KEMPER	34
THOMAS POINT	B	WILD GOOSE	68
THOS. KEMPER MAIBOCK	BK	THOMAS KEMPER	70
THREE CLUBS RED	B	SO. CALIFORNIA	37
THREE PIN GRIN PORTER	P	CRESTED BUTTE	23
TIED HOUSE AMBER	B	TIED HOUSE	60
TIED HOUSE WHEAT BOCK	BK	TIED HOUSE	54
TIME WARP WEIZ. BOCK	W	STEELHEAD	45
TIVOLI	B	HEILEMAN	23
TOMBOY BITTER	A	SAN JUAN	42
TOO BERRY	A	BREWSKI'S	36
TOP HAT	B	HUDEPOHL-SCHOENLING	41
TOP SAIL AMBER ALE	A	BELMONT	43
TOWER DARK ALE	A	BUTTERFIELD	28
TRADITIONAL BOCK	BK	NORTH COAST	83
TREE FROG STRONG ALT	A	TRIPLE ROCK	42
TRESTLES	B	ZELE	68
TRICK PALE ALE	A	COYOTE SPRING	30
TRIPEL THREAT	A	CAMBRIDGE	62
TRIPPEL TRAPPISTE	A	NEW BELGIUM	50
TRUPERT	B	LION	58
TUBORG DARK	B	HEILEMAN	68
TUBORG GOLD	B	HEILEMAN	56
TUT BROWN ALE	A	OASIS	31
TWELVE HORSE ALE	A	GENESEE	63
ULMER BRAUN	B	SCHELL	40
UTICA CLUB CREAM ALE	B	MATT	30
UTICA CLUB LIGHT	LO	MATT	24
UTICA CLUB NA	NA	MATT	40
UTICA CLUB PILS	B	MATT	42
VAIL ALE	A	OLDENBURG	42
VAN LAUTER BAVARIAN	B	HEILEMAN	40
VAN MERRITT	B	HUBER	15
VERMONT BICENT. ALE	A	MOUNTAIN	70
VERMONT SMOKED PORT.	P	VERMONT	55
VICE WEIZEN	W	GOOSE ISLAND	64

Brand	Type	Brewer	Rating
VICTORIA	B	HUBER	43
VICTORIA LIGHT	B	HUBER	48
VICTORIA MORENA	B	HUBER	38
VIENNA	B	HUBER	62
VIKING VIENNA STYLE	B	THOMAS KEMPER	63
WASATCH CHRISTMAS	A	SCHIRF	65
WASATCH IRISH STOUT	S	SCHIRF	69
WASATCH PREMIUM ALE	A	SCHIRF	65
WASATCH SLICKROCK	B	SCHIRF	50
WASATCH STOUT	S	SCHIRF	45
WASATCH WEIZENBIER	W	SCHIRF	39
WASATCH WHEAT	W	SCHIRF	33
WASSAIL WINTER ALE	A	FULL SAIL	51
WATER ST. PALE ALE	A	WATER STREET	67
WEEPING RADISH FEST	B	WEEPING RADISH	41
WEEPING RADISH HELLES	B	WEEPING RADISH	46
WEINHARD'S ALE	A	HEILEMAN	37
WEINKELLER BAV. WEISS	W	WEINKELLER	48
WEINKELLER OKTOBER.	B	WEINKELLER	45
WEIZEN ALE	A	BREWSKI'S	27
WELCOMMEN RAUCH	B	ROGUE	41
WEST CANFIELD ALE	A	DETROIT & MACKINAC	22
WEST END LAGER	B	DALLAS	19
WEST END LAGER	B	DALLAS	41
WESTERN	B	COLD SPRING	45
WHALE ALE	A	BELMONT	38
WHALE'S TALE	A	BREWSKI'S	50
WHEATHOOK	W	RED HOOK	35
WHEATLAND WHEAT	W	O'DELL	45
WHETSTONE GOLDEN	B	WINDHAM	54
WHISTLEPIN WHEAT	W	BERGER	45
WHITE LABEL	B	COLD SPRING	39
WHITE RIVER WHEAT	W	HUBCAP	45
WIDMER HEFE-WEIZEN	W	WIDMER	37
WIDMER OKTOBERFEST	B	WIDMER	68
WIEDEMANN	B	EVANSVILLE	34
WIEDEMANN	B	HEILEMAN	47
WIEDEMANN LIGHT	LO	EVANSVILLE	41
WIEDEMANN LIGHT	LO	HEILEMAN	21
WILD BOAR	B	ZELE	69
WILD GOOSE AMBER	B	WILD GOOSE	60
WILDERNESS WHEAT	W	WYNKOOP	42
WILLAMETTE ALE	A	BUTTERFIELD	39
WILLIAM PENN	B	HUDEPOHL-SCHOENLING	50
WINCHESTER RED ALE	A	WINCHESTER	32
WINCHESTER XMAS '91	A	WINCHESTER	23
WIND 'N SEA	W	LA JOLLA	50
WINTER ALE 1991	A	PORTLAND	19
WINTER STOCK 1990	A	ALASKAN	87
WINTER WARMER BW	BW	GOOSE ISLAND	50
WINTERHOOK 1990	A	RED HOOK	70
WINTERHOOK 1991	A	RED HOOK	63
WINTERHOOK 1992	A	RED HOOK	39
WISCONSIN AMBER	B	CAPITOL	42
WISCONSIN CLUB	B	HUBER	40
WISCONSIN GOLD LABEL	B	HUBER	35
WISCONSIN HOLIDAY	B	HUBER	38
WISCONSIN PREMIUM	B	HEILEMAN	33
WOLFHOUND STOUT	S	FLYING DOG	54
WOMBAT WHEAT	W	MELBOURNE	56
WOODRUFF ALE	A	SAN ANDREAS	41
WRIGLEY RED	A	BOULDER	36
WYCHICK WEIZEN	W	DESCHUTES	37
WYNKOOP IPA	A	WYNKOOP	42
WYNKOOP IRISH CREAM	S	WYNKOOP	51
YELLOW JACKET ALE	A	PACIFIC COAST	42
YELLOWSTONE PALE ALE	A	SPANISH PEAKS	60
YUENGLING LIGHT	LO	YUENGLING	24
YUENGLING PORTER	P	YUENGLING	42
YUENGLING PREMIUM	B	YUENGLING	59
YUENGLING TRADITIONAL	B	YUENGLING	33
YULETIDE PORTER	P	MENDOCINO	58
ZATEC RED	B	VERMONT	34
ZIP CITY DUNKEL	B	ZIP CITY	48
ZIP CITY HELLES	B	ZIP CITY	40
ZIP CITY MAIBOCK	B	ZIP CITY	55
ZIP CITY MÄRZEN	B	ZIP CITY	32
ZIP CITY OKTOBERFEST	B	ZIP CITY	42
ZIP CITY PILSENER	B	ZIP CITY	64
ZIP CITY VIENNA	B	ZIP CITY	66
ZODIAC	ML	HUBER	15
ZOSER OATMEAL STOUT	S	OASIS	60
ZUMA LIGHT	LO	ZELE	23

CANADA

Brand	Type	Brewer	Rating
ADLY'S ALE	A	HEUTHER	47
ALGONQUIN COUNTRY	B	ALGONQUIN	28
ALGONQUIN CDN LIGHT	LO	ALGONQUIN	25
ALGONQUIN LIGHT	LO	ALGONQUIN	27
ALGONQUIN SPEC. RES	A	ALGONQUIN	23
ALPINE	B	MOOSEHEAD	36
ALPINE COLD FILT.	B	MOOSEHEAD	22
ALPINE LITE	LO	MOOSEHEAD	24
ALTA 3.9	LO	MOLSON	22
AMBER DRY	D	BRICK	34
AMSTEL	B	AMSTEL	40
AMSTEL LIGHT	LO	AMSTEL	24
BANKS	B	UPPER CANADA	9
BEAVER VALLEY AMBER	B	THORNBURY	39
BENNETT'S DOMINION	A	MOLSON	47
BIG ROCK BITTER PALE	A	BIG ROCK	60
BIG ROCK PALE ALE	A	BIG ROCK	39
BIG ROCK TRADITIONAL	A	BIG ROCK	25
BIG ROCK XO LAGER	B	BIG ROCK	46
BLACK HORSE ALE	A	MOLSON	51
BLACK HORSE BEER	B	MOLSON	29
BLENDED OLD STOCK ALE	A	MOLSON	45
BLUE STAR	B	LABATT	46
BOHEMIAN LAGER	B	MOLSON	20
BRADING	A	MOLSON	33
BRADOR	ML	MOLSON	45
BREW LIGHT	LO	AMSTEL	21
BRICK	B	BRICK	48
BUCKEYE	A	MOLSON	23
BUD LIGHT	B	LABATT	14
BUDWEISER	B	LABATT	48
BULLDOG	B	PACIFIC WESTERN	36
BUZZARD BREATH	A	BIG ROCK	43
CALGARY AMBER LAGER	B	MOLSON	33
CALGARY EXPORT	B	MOLSON	32
CANADA COUNTRY	B	CANADA COUNTRY	35
CANADIAN 55	B	NORTHERN	48
CANADIAN GOLD	B	CDN NATIONAL	39
CANADIAN GOLD	B	PACIFIC WESTERN	22
CANADIAN NORTHERN	B	NORTHERN	15
CANADIAN RED CAP	A	MOLSON	37
CARLING BLACK LABEL	B	MOLSON	33
CARLING PILSENER	B	MOLSON	27
CARLSBERG	B	MOLSON	41
CARLSBERG BOCK	BK	MOLSON	49
CARLSBERG GOLD	ML	MOLSON	71
CARLSBERG LIGHT	LO	MOLSON	15
CERVOISE	A	LABATT	29
CHAMPLAIN PORTER	P	MOLSON	20
CHARRINGTON TOBY	A	MOLSON	35
CINCINNATI CREAM	B	MOLSON	53
COCK O' THE ROCK	P	BIG ROCK	60
COLD COCK WINTER	P	BIG ROCK	60
COLT .45	B	MOLSON	18
COLUMBIA	ML	LABATT	35
CONNERS ALE	A	DON VALLEY	47
CONNERS BEST BITTER	A	DON VALLEY	51
CONNERS SPEC. DRAFT	A	DON VALLEY	29
COOL SPRING	LO	LABATT	27
COORS	B	LABATT	29
COORS LIGHT	LO	MOLSON	27
CREEMORE PREMIUM	B	CREEMORE SPRINGS	35
DOW BLACK HORSE ALE	A	MOLSON	22
DOW CREAM PORTER	P	MOLSON	66
DRUMMOND	B	DRUMMOND	39
DRUMMOND DRY	D	DRUMMOND	31
DRUMMOND LIGHT	LO	DRUMMOND	11
EDELBRAU	B	NORTHERN	43

Brand	Type	Brewer	Rating
ENGLISH ALE	A	HEUTHER	62
FORMOSA SPRINGS DRAFT	B	ALGONQUIN	37
FORMOSA SPRINGS LIGHT	LO	ALGONQUIN	23
FOSTER'S LAGER	B	MOLSON	32
GLACIER BAY	B	VICTORIA STREET	41
GOLD KEG	B	LABATT	58
GOLD PEAK	B	ROCKY MOUNTAIN	38
GOLDEN LIGHT	LO	MOOSEHEAD	42
GRAND PRIX	A	LABATT	27
GREAT LAKES	B	GREAT LAKES	30
GREAT WESTERN	B	GREAT WESTERN	36
GREAT WESTERN LIGHT	LO	GREAT WESTERN	28
GRITSTONE	B	NIAGARA FALLS	27
GRIZZLY	B	AMSTEL	53
GUINNESS EXTRA STOUT	S	LABATT	57
HANSHAUS	B	BAVARIAN SPECIALTIES	53
HEIDELBERG O-B BREW	B	HEIDELBERG	24
HEIDELBERG	B	MOLSON	32
HENNINGER EXPORT	B	AMSTEL	39
HENNINGER MEIST. PILS	B	AMSTEL	29
HEUTHER'S PREMIUM	B	HEUTHER	75
INDIA	B	MOLSON	58
ISLAND BOCK	BK	GRANVILLE	78
ISLAND LAGER	B	GRANVILLE	26
JAMES READY	B	MOOSEHEAD	30
JOCKEY CLUB	B	LABATT	58
KEELE'S	B	SAXON	40
KEITH'S	IPA	LABATT	54
KEITH'S DRY	D	LABATT	37
KEITH'S LIGHT	LO	LABATT	32
KINGSBEER	B	MOLSON	39
KOKANEE	B	LABATT	39
KOOTENAY	A	LABATT	48
KRONENBRAU 1308	B	MOLSON	27
LABATT .5	NA	LABATT	20
LABATT CLASS. LIGHT	LO	LABATT	14
LABATT CLASSIC	B	LABATT	12
LABATT DRAFT	B	LABATT	28
LABATT EXTRA DRY	D	LABATT	25
LABATT SPECIAL LITE	LO	LABATT	29
LABATT'S 50	A	LABATT	47
LABATT'S BEER	B	LABATT	39
LABATT'S "BLUE"	B	LABATT	38
LABATT'S BLUE DRAFT	B	LABATT	55
LABATT'S BLUE LIGHT	LO	LABATT	17
LABATT'S CDN ALE	A	LABATT	32
LABATT'S CRYSTAL	B	LABATT	51
LABATT'S DRY	D	LABATT	30
LABATT'S DRY LIGHT	D	LABATT	18
LABATT'S EXTRA STOCK	ML	LABATT	69
LABATT'S IPA	IPA	LABATT	41
LABATT'S SUPER BOCK	ML	LABATT	35
LAKER LAGER	B	AMSTEL	27
LAKER LIGHT	LO	AMSTEL	20
LAURENTIDE	A	MOLSON	48
LETHBRIDGE	B	MOLSON	20
LION DRY	D	HEUTHER	42
LION LAGER	B	HEUTHER	53
LION LITE	B	HEUTHER	45
LISTWIN'S KODIAK	B	GREAT WESTERN	36
LONDON STOUT	S	MOOSEHEAD	52
LOWENBRAU SPECIAL	B	MOLSON	50
MAGNUM ALE	A	MOLSON	41
MASTER'S ALE	A	MASTER	50
MASTER'S LAGER	B	MASTER	46
MCNALLY'S EXTRA	A	BIG ROCK	56
MILLER HIGH LIFE	B	MOLSON	15
MILLER LITE	LO	MOLSON	22
MOLSON ALE	A	MOLSON	62
MOLSON BOCK	BK	MOLSON	24
MOLSON CANADIAN	B	MOLSON	68
MOLSON CDN LIGHT	LO	MOLSON	19
MOLSON CLUB ALE	A	MOLSON	16
MOLSON DRY	D	MOLSON	51
MOLSON EXEL	NA	MOLSON	15
MOLSON EXPORT	A	MOLSON	63
MOLSON EXPORT LIGHT	LO	MOLSON	29
MOLSON GOLDEN	B	MOLSON	32
MOLSON LIGHT	LO	MOLSON	27
MOLSON LITE	LO	MOLSON	24
MOLSON MALT LIQUOR	ML	MOLSON	30
MOLSON OKTOBERFEST	B	MOLSON	42
MOLSON PORTER	P	MOLSON	65
MOLSON SPECIAL DRY	D	MOLSON	21
MOLSON SPECIALE	B	MOLSON	30
MOLSON STOCK ALE	A	MOLSON	50
MOOSEHEAD CDN LAGER	B	MOOSEHEAD	50
MOOSEHEAD EXPORT ALE	A	MOOSEHEAD	54
MOOSEHEAD LIGHT	LO	MOOSEHEAD	30
MOOSEHEAD PALE ALE	A	MOOSEHEAD	33
MOOSEHEAD PREM. DRY	D	MOOSEHEAD	54
MOOSEHEAD SPEC. ALE	A	MOOSEHEAD	54
MOUNTAIN CREST	B	GLACIER	38
NATURAL POINT NINE	RA	UPPER CANADA	12
NORTHERN ALE	A	NORTHERN	18
NORTHERN EXTRA LIGHT	LO	NORTHERN	12
NORTHERN GOOSE	NA	NORTHERN	12
O'BRUNSWICK	ML	BAVARIAN SPECIALTIES	78
O'KEEFE CAN. EXP. ALE	A	MOLSON	22
O'KEEFE CAN. GOLDEN	LO	MOLSON	32
O'KEEFE CANADIAN ALE	A	MOLSON	54
O'KEEFE EXT. OLD STOCK	ML	MOLSON	50
O'KEEFE LIGHT	LO	MOLSON	17
O'KEEFE OLD VIENNA	B	MOLSON	52
OKANAGAN WHEAT	W	OKANAGAN SPRING	50
OLAND EXPORT ALE	A	LABATT	64
OLAND EXTRA STOUT	S	LABATT	58
OLAND LITE	LO	LABATT	36
OLD ENGLISH	P	OKANAGAN	59
OLD SCOTIA ALE	A	LABATT	54
OLD STYLE PILSNER	B	MOLSON	60
OLD VIENNA BOCK	BK	MOLSON	62
OLDE JACK	A	NIAGARA FALLS	47
PACIFIC GOLD	B	PACIFIC WESTERN	44
PACIFIC REAL DRAFT	B	PACIFIC WESTERN	32
PERONI	B	AMSTEL	51
PUBLICAN'S BITTER	A	UPPER CANADA	38
RALLYE	A	MOLSON	42
REBELLION	A	UPPER CANADA	63
RED BARON	B	BRICK	43
ROYAL BLUE	B	LABATT	39
ROYAL CANADIAN	B	PACIFIC WESTERN	35
SABRE	B	CANADA COUNTRY	42
SCHOONER	B	LABATT	47
SLEEMAN CREAM ALE	B	SLEEMAN	38
SLEEMAN SILVER CREEK	B	SLEEMAN	33
SPRING EXT. SPEC. PALE	A	OKANAGAN SPRING	36
SPRING PREMIUM	B	OKANAGAN SPRING	47
SPRINGBOK	BK	BIG ROCK	62
ST. AMBROISE PALE	A	MC AUSLAND	69
STANDARD LAGER	B	MOLSON	34
STEELER	B	AMSTEL	20
STEVESTON HERITAGE	B	CANADIAN HERITAGE	14
STROH'S	B	SLEEMAN	23
SUPERIOR	B	NORTHERN	25
TEN-PENNY	A	MOOSEHEAD	42
TOBY	A	MOLSON	24
TORONTO LIGHT	LO	SLEEMAN	24
TRILIGHT	LO	MOLSON	15
U. C. ALE	A	UPPER CANADA	35
U. C. DARK	A	UPPER CANADA	42
U. C. LAGER	B	UPPER CANADA	28
U. C. NATURAL LIGHT	LO	UPPER CANADA	22
U. C. TRUE LIGHT	LO	UPPER CANADA	24
U. C. WHEAT	W	UPPER CANADA	22
UNICORN ALE	A	GREAT LAKES	39
UPPER CANADA	A	UPPER CANADA	36
VELVET CREAM	P	LABATT	24
W.J. MACKAY	B	SUMMIT	34
WELLINGTON ARKELL BITTER	B	WELLINGTON COUNTY	39
WELLINGTON COUNTY LAGER	B	WELLINGTON COUNTY	60
WELLINGTON COUNTY ALE	A	WELLINGTON COUNTY	58
WELLINGTON IRON DUKE	A	WELLINGTON COUNTY	62
WELLINGTON SPEC. PALE	A	WELLINGTON COUNTY	46
WESTNER'S	B	BAVARIAN SPECIALTIES	24
YORK PILSNER	B	YORK	36
YUKON CREAM ALE	A	PACIFIC WESTERN	23
YUKON GOLD	B	PACIFIC WESTERN	46
ZELE DRY	B	PACIFIC WESTERN	42
ZELE DRY LIGHT	LO	PACIFIC WESTERN	16

MEXICO

Brand	Type	Brewer	Rating
BOHEMIA	A	CUAUHTEMOC	4[illegible]
BRISA LIGERA	LO	CUAUHTEMOC	18
CARTA BLANCA	B	CUAUHTEMOC	34
CARTA BLANCA DARK	B	CUAUHTEMOC	28
CHIHUAHUA	B	CRUZ BLANCA	24
CORONA	B	MODELO	54
CORONA EXTRA	B	MODELO	41
CORONA LIGHT	LO	MODELO	36
CRUZ BLANCA	B	CRUZ BLANCA	28
DOS EQUIS	B	MOCTEZUMA	54
DOS EQUIS LIGHT	LO	MOCTEZUMA	33
DOS EQUIS SPECIAL	B	MOCTEZUMA	45
HOMBRE	B	CRUZ BLANCA	12
HUSSONG'S	B	MOCTEZUMA	26
INDIO OSCURA	B	CUAUHTEMOC	41
MODELO ESPECIAL	B	MODELO	14
MONTEJO DARK	B	YUCATECA	29
MONTEJO PREMIUM	B	YUCATECA	29
NAVIDAD 1984	B	CUAUHTEMOC	37
NEGRA MODELO	B	MODELO	68
NOCHE BUENA	B	MOCTEZUMA	75
NUDE	B	CRUZ BLANCA	17
PACIFICO CLARA	B	PACIFICO	30
SIMPATICO	B	CRUZ BLANCA	20
SOL ESPECIAL	B	MOCTEZUMA	33
SUPERIOR	B	MOCTEZUMA	32
TECATE	B	CUAUHTEMOC	51
TRES EQUIS DARK	B	MOCTEZUMA	18
TRES EQUIS LIGHT	B	MOCTEZUMA	42

CARIBBEAN, CENTRAL & SOUTH AMERICA

Brand	Type	Brewer	Rating
AGUILA	B	COLOMBIA	29
ANDES	B	CHILE	42
ANDES	B	VENEZUELA	49
ANTARCTICA	B	BRAZIL	28
ATLAS	B	PANAMA	40
BALBOA	B	PANAMA	13
BANKS	B	BARBADOS	27
BAVARIAN GOLD	B	COSTA RICA	23
BELIKIN BEER	B	BELIZE	45
BELIKIN STOUT	S	BELIZE	32
BIECKERT ETIQUETA	B	ARGENTINA	36
BIECKERT LIVIANA	B	ARGENTINA	32
BIECKERT PILSEN ESP	B	ARGENTINA	68
BOHEMIA	B	DOMINICAN REP.	33
BRAHMA	B	BRAZIL	30
BRAHMA BRAZILIAN	B	BRAZIL	14
BRAHMA CHOPP	B	BRAZIL	27
BREW MASTER'S	B	PUERTO RICO	22
CABRO EXTRA	B	GUATEMALA	30
CALLAO	B	PERU	56
CALLAO DARK	B	PERU	34
CARACU	B	BRAZIL	33
CARDENAL	B	VENEZUELA	26
CARIB LAGER	B	TRINIDAD	41
CARIBE	B	TRINIDAD	31
CLAUSEN	B	COLOMBIA	39
CLUB	B	ECUADOR	9
CLUB COLOMBIA	B	COLOMBIA	31
COLUMBIAN GOLD	B	COLUMBIA	21
CORDOBA DORADA	B	ARGENTINA	35
CORONA	B	PUERTO RICO	33
CORONA CERVEZA	B	PUERTO RICO	20
CRISTAL	B	CHILE	47
CRISTAL	B	PANAMA	29
CRISTAL	B	PERU	14
CUZCO	B	PERU	38
DOBLE URUGUAYA	B	URUGUAY	18
DRAGON	S	JAMAICA	50
DURANGO	B	PERU	27
EBONY	B	BARBADOS	26
ESCUDO	B	CHILE	42
FAMOSA	B	GUATEMALA	43
GUINNESS EXTRA STOUT	S	PANAMA	36
HB CERVEZA NEGRA	B	PANAMA	27
INDIA	B	PUERTO RICO	45
INGLESINHA	S	BRAZIL	23
KALIK	B	BAHAMAS	37
LEON DE ORO	B	ARGENTINA	58
MEDALLA	B	PUERTO RICO	19
MEDALLA DE ORO	B	GUATEMALA	28
MONTE CARLO	B	GUATEMALA	36
MOZA BOCK	BK	GUATEMALA	25
PACEÑA	B	BOLIVIA	26
PANAMA	B	PANAMA	36
PILSEN	B	URUGUAY	9
PILSENER EL SALVADOR	B	EL SALVADOR	34
POLAR	B	VENEZUELA	46
POLAR DARK	B	VENEZUELA	44
PORT ROYAL	B	HONDURAS	21
PRESIDENTE	B	DOMINICAN REP.	48
QUILMES EXPORT	B	ARGENTINA	26
QUILMES IMPERIAL	B	ARGENTINA	54
QUISQUEYA	B	DOMINICAN REP.	56
RED STRIPE	B	JAMAICA	44
SANTA FE	B	ARGENTINA	26
SKOL	B	BRAZIL	34
SOBERANA	B	PANAMA	16
TAQUINA	B	BOLIVIA	43
TIJUCA	B	BRAZIL	23
XINGU	B	BRAZIL	45

AUSTRALIA, ASIA, AFRICA & OCEANIA

Brand	Type	Brewer	Rating
ABBOTS LAGER	B	AUSTRALIA	20
ABC EXTRA STOUT	S	SINGAPORE	53
ALMAZA	B	LEBANON	33
AMARIT	B	THAILAND	30
AMSTEL	B	SOUTH AFRICA	37
ANCHOR	B	SINGAPORE	35
ASAHI DRAFT	B	JAPAN	29
ASAHI LAGER	B	JAPAN	48
ASAHI SUPER DRY	D	JAPAN	22
ASAHI "Z" DRAFT	B	JAPAN	37
ASMARA	B	ETHIOPIA	50
AUSTRALIA	B	AUSTRALIA	31
BAIYUN	B	CHINA	25
BANGKOK	B	THAILAND	12
BEERSHEBA	B	ISRAEL	14
BEIJING BLACK	B	CHINA	50
BEST BREW	B	ISRAEL	10
BIG BARREL	B	AUSTRALIA	21
BOAGS ALE	A	AUSTRALIA	30
BOAGS DRAUGHT	B	AUSTRALIA	24
BOAGS LAGER	B	AUSTRALIA	32
BOAGS LIGHT	LO	AUSTRALIA	19
BOAGS PREMIUM	B	AUSTRALIA	17
BOMBAY	B	INDIA	13
BUDWEISER	B	JAPAN	40
CANTON	B	CHINA	21
CARBINE STOUT	S	AUSTRALIA	45
CARLTON DRAUGHT	B	AUSTRALIA	47
CARLTON LIGHT	B	AUSTRALIA	27
CASCADE BITTER	A	AUSTRALIA	44
CASCADE DRAUGHT	B	AUSTRALIA	29
CASCADE PALE	A	AUSTRALIA	50
CASTLE	B	SOUTH AFRICA	32
CASTLEMAINE BITTER	A	AUSTRALIA	63
CASTLEMAINE DRAUGHT	B	AUSTRALIA	18
CASTLEMAINE LAGER	B	AUSTRALIA	18
CHANGLEE	B	CHINA	36
CHINA	B	CHINA	44
CHINA CLIPPER	B	CHINA	36
CHINA GOLD	B	CHINA	61
CHU SING	B	CHINA	24
CHUNG HUA	B	CHINA	37
COOPER EXTRA STOUT	S	AUSTRALIA	60
COOPER GOLD CROWN	B	AUSTRALIA	30
COOPER LAGER	B	AUSTRALIA	40
COOPER'S REAL ALE	A	AUSTRALIA	47
COORS	B	JAPAN	43
COURAGE DRAUGHT	B	AUSTRALIA	42
CREST	B	AUSTRALIA	22
CROWN	B	KOREA	46
CROWN DRY	D	KOREA	18
DB EXPORT	B	NEW ZEALAND	33
DOUBLE BROWN	B	NEW ZEALAND	24
DOUBLE HAPPINESS	B	CHINA	30
DOWN UNDER	B	AUSTRALIA	12
DYNASTY	B	TAIWAN	62
DYNASTY DRY	D	CHINA	46
EAGLE	B	INDIA	10
EMPEROR'S GOLD	B	CHINA	32
FESTIVAL PILSENER	B	AUSTRALIA	21
FIJI BITTER	B	FIJI	33
FIVE STAR	B	CHINA	17
FIVE STAR SPECIAL	B	CHINA	22
FOSTER'S LAGER	B	AUSTRALIA	60
FOSTERS LIGHT	LO	AUSTRALIA	15
GOLD STAR	B	ISRAEL	40
GOLDEN EAGLE	B	INDIA	45
GREAT WALL	B	CHINA	35
GULDER	B	NIGERIA	8
HANSA	B	SOUTH AFRICA	44
HARAR	B	ETHIOPIA	37
HINANO	B	TAHITI	30
HUA NAN	B	CHINA	39
INDIAN GURU	B	INDIA	38
KANGAROO	B	AUSTRALIA	25
KINGFISHER	B	INDIA	27
KIRIN	B	JAPAN	60
KIRIN DRAFT	B	JAPAN	11
KIRIN DRY DRAFT	D	JAPAN	32
KIRIN FINE MALT	B	JAPAN	48
KIRIN ICHIBAN	B	JAPAN	39
KIRIN LIGHT	LO	JAPAN	25
KIWI	B	NEW ZEALAND	50
LEOPARD EXPORT	B	NEW ZEALAND	14
LEOPARD LAGER	B	NEW ZEALAND	17
LEOPARD STRONG	B	NEW ZEALAND	26
LION LAGER	B	SOUTH AFRICA	36
LONGXIANG	B	CHINA	55
MACCABEE	B	ISRAEL	40
MAHARAJA	B	INDIA	8
MAMBA	ML	IVORY COAST	57
MANILA GOLD	B	PHILIPPINES	22
MELBOURNE BITTER	B	AUSTRALIA	36
MON-LEI	B	HONG KONG	22
MURREE	B	PAKISTAN	14
NEW ZEALAND PREMIUM	B	NEW ZEALAND	39
NEXT ONE	B	JAPAN	23
NGOK'	B	CONGO	29
NGOMA AWOOYO	B	TOGO	47
NGOMA CASTEL	B	ZAIRE	38
NGOMA TOGO PILS	B	TOGO	45
NINE STAR	B	CHINA	56
OB DRY	D	KOREA	35
OLD AUSTRALIA STOUT	S	AUSTRALIA	64
ORIENTAL OB	B	KOREA	21
ORION	B	JAPAN	9
PANDA	B	CHINA	26
PAYAK	B	THAILAND	29
PEKING	B	CHINA	42
RAINMAKER	B	SAMOA	30
RAZOR'S EDGE	B	AUSTRALIA	36
RED BACK	W	AUSTRALIA	33
RED CENTRE	B	AUSTRALIA	54
RED HORSE	B	PHILIPPINES	30
RESCHS PILSENER	B	AUSTRALIA	33
ROGUE	B	SOUTH AFRICA	31
SAN MIGUEL	B	INDONESIA	22
SAN MIGUEL	B	NEW GUINEA	10
SAN MIGUEL	B	PHILIPPINES	60
SAN MIGUEL DARK	B	INDONESIA	76
SAN MIGUEL DARK	B	PHILIPPINES	78
SAN MIGUEL NEGRA	B	NEW GUINEA	44
SAN MIGUEL PALE PILS	B	PHILIPPINES	26
SAPPORO BLACK	B	JAPAN	44
SAPPORO CLEAN MALT	B	JAPAN	45
SAPPORO DRAFT	B	JAPAN	12
SAPPORO DRAFT DRY	D	JAPAN	28
SAPPORO LAGER	B	JAPAN	20
SAPPORO MALT 100	B	JAPAN	57
SAPPORO WINTER'S TALE	B	JAPAN	39
SHANGHAI	B	SHANGHAI	38
SHANGHAI GOLDEN	B	SHANGHAI	44
SHEAF	ST	AUSTRALIA	67
SHEN YANG	B	CHINA	36
SIAM ALE	A	THAILAND	12
SIMBA	B	SWAZILAND	21
SINGHA	B	THAILAND	36
SINGHA STOUT	B	THAILAND	14
SNOWFLAKE	B	CHINA	12
SONG HAY	B	CHINA	24
SOUTH PACIFIC SPECIAL	B	NEW GUINEA	44
SOUTHWARK BITTER	B	AUSTRALIA	29
SOUTHWARK EXPORT	B	AUSTRALIA	54
SOUTHWARK GOLD	B	AUSTRALIA	33
SOUTHWARK PREMIUM	B	AUSTRALIA	39
SOVEREIGN	B	INDIA	38
STAR	B	NIGERIA	5
STEINLAGER	B	NEW ZEALAND	54
SUN-LIK	B	HONG KONG	47
SUNTORY DRAFT	B	JAPAN	3
SUNTORY MALT'S	B	JAPAN	35
SWAN EXPORT	B	AUSTRALIA	38
SWAN PREMIUM	B	AUSTRALIA	58
SWEET CHINA	B	CHINA	21

Brand	Type	Brewer	Rating
TAIWAN	B	TAIWAN	22
TAJ MAHAL	B	INDIA	33
TASMANIAN LAGER	B	AUSTRALIA	41
THOS. COOPER ALE	A	AUSTRALIA	30
THOS. COOPER STOUT	S	AUSTRALIA	50
TIENTAN	B	CHINA	26
TIGER GOLD	B	SINGAPORE	29
TOOHEY'S DRAUGHT	B	AUSTRALIA	29
TOOHEY'S LAGER	B	AUSTRALIA	53
TOOHEY'S LITE	LO	AUSTRALIA	20
TOOTH KB	B	AUSTRALIA	26
TRAK	B	AUSTRALIA	26
TROPICAL	B	CANARY ISLANDS	26
TSING-TAO	B	CHINA	36
TSING-TAO PORTER	P	CHINA	38
TUSKER	B	KENYA	23
VICTORIA BITTER	A	AUSTRALIA	33
WEST END BITTER	B	AUSTRALIA	42
WEST END EXPORT	B	AUSTRALIA	45
YEBISU	B	JAPAN	42
YEBISU PREMIUM DRAFT	B	JAPAN	49
YEBISU STOUT	S	JAPAN	4
YI KING	B	CHINA	45
YUCHUAN	B	CHINA	38
ZHU JIANG	B	CHINA	46

EUROPE

Brand	Type	Brewer	Rating
AASS AMBER	B	NORWAY	54
AASS BOK	BK	NORWAY	45
AASS EXPORT	B	NORWAY	57
AASS JUBILEE	B	NORWAY	38
AASS JULE OL	A	NORWAY	62
AASS NORWEGIAN	B	NORWAY	33
AASS PILSENER	B	NORWAY	65
AASS WINTER	B	NORWAY	70
ABBAYE DE BORNEM DBL	A	BELGIUM	55
ABBAYE DE BROGNE XMAS	A	BELGIUM	65
ABBAYE DE FLOREFF	A	BELGIUM	56
ABBEY DE LEFFE	B	BELGIUM	29
ABBEY OF LEFFE BLOND	A	BELGIUM	34
ABBOT ALE	A	ENGLAND	22
ADAM CLASSIC	B	AUSTRIA	43
ADAM DUNKEL	B	AUSTRIA	33
ADAM FESTBIER	B	AUSTRIA	75
ADAM HELLES EXPORT	B	AUSTRIA	24
ADELSCOTT	ML	FRANCE	48
ADELSHOFFEN	B	FRANCE	24
ADELSHOFFEN EXPORT	B	FRANCE	17
ADLER BEER	B	BELGIUM	48
ADLER BRAU	B	AUSTRIA	44
ADLER BRAU	B	GERMANY	52
ADLER PREMIUM LUXUS	B	BELGIUM	38
AECHT SCHLENKERLA	B	GERMANY	61
AEGEAN HELLES	B	GREECE	40
AERTS 1900	A	BELGIUM	69
AFFLIGEM	A	BELGIUM	63
AGUILA DORADA	B	SPAIN	19
AGUILA IMPERIAL	B	SPAIN	66
AHORNBERGER MAIBOCK	BK	GERMANY	36
AKTIEN EDEL AUSSTICH	B	GERMANY	47
AKTIEN FRUNDSBERG	B	GERMANY	26
AKTIEN HEFE-WEIZEN	W	GERMANY	42
AKTIEN HELL	B	GERMANY	49
AKTIEN JUBILAUMS	B	GERMANY	39
AKTIEN ST. MARTIN	BK	GERMANY	60
AKTIEN TÄNZELFEST	B	GERMANY	45
ALBANI EXPORT	B	DENMARK	41
ALBANI JULE BRYG	B	DENMARK	56
ALBANI PILSENER	B	DENMARK	41
ALBANI PORTER	P	DENMARK	90
ALBANI PÅSKEBRYG	B	DENMARK	54
ALBQUELL EDELBIER	B	GERMANY	64
ALBQUELL PILSNER	B	GERMANY	59
ALBQUELL URTRUNK	B	GERMANY	61
ALDARA ALUS	A	USSR	10
ALDERSBACHER DUNKEL	W	GERMANY	72
ALDERSBACHER HELL	B	GERMANY	21
ALEXANDER RODENBACH	A	BELGIUM	58
ALFA DORTMUNDER	B	HOLLAND	71
ALFA EDEL	B	HOLLAND	51
ALFA LAGER	B	HOLLAND	50
ALLGÄUER DAS HELLE	B	GERMANY	29
ALLGÄUER EDELBRÄU	B	GERMANY	78
ALLGÄUER EXPORT	B	GERMANY	34
ALLGÄUER FÜRSTADT	W	GERMANY	72
ALPENSTEIN	NA	SWITZERLAND	42
ALPINE AYINGERBRAU	B	ENGLAND	22
ALPIRS. KR. KL. WEIZEN	W	GERMANY	54
ALPIRSBACHER KL. DNK	B	GERMANY	42
ALPIRSBACHER KL. HW	W	GERMANY	60
ALPIRSBACHER PILS	B	GERMANY	50
ALPIRSBACHER SPEZIAL	B	GERMANY	48
ALT BAYER DUNKLES	W	GERMANY	59
ALT FRuANKISCH DUNK.	B	GERMANY	84
ALT KEMPTENER	W	GERMANY	67
ALT KUNESTATER	B	GERMANY	53
ALT MARBURGER	B	GERMANY	46
ALT WETZLAR	B	GERMANY	30
ALT WILHERMSDORFER DK	B	GERMANY	72
ALTENMUNSTER	B	GERMANY	33
ALTENMUNSTER MAIBOCK	BK	GERMANY	77
ALTMUNSTER	B	LUXEMBOURG	64
ALTMÜHLTALER HELL	B	GERMANY	26
ALTMÜHLTALER PILS	B	GERMANY	42
ALTÖTTINGER DUNKEL	B	GERMANY	82
ALTÖTTINGER DUNKEL	B	GERMANY	82
ALTÖTTINGER FEIN HERB	B	GERMANY	51
ALTÖTTINGER HELL	B	GERMANY	51
ALTSEIDELBRAU	B	GERMANY	13
AMBAR	B	SPAIN	42
AMOS	B	FRANCE	28
AMPERTHALER LT.HW	W	GERMANY	47
AMSTEL LIGHT	LO	HOLLAND	18
ANDECHS BERGBOCK HELL	BK	GERMANY	73
ANDECHS DOPPELBOCK	BK	GERMANY	90
ANDECHS EXPORT DUNK.	B	GERMANY	39
ANDECHS HELL	B	GERMANY	65
ANDREAS	B	GERMANY	32
ANGEL ALE	A	ENGLAND	46
ANGEL BEER	B	ENGLAND	32
ANGEL BREW	B	GERMANY	78
ANGEL HELL	B	GERMANY	33
ANGLICAN	A	ENGLAND	34
ARCO GRAFEN HELL	B	GERMANY	60
ARCOBRÄU MOOSER HELL	B	GERMANY	53
ARCOBRÄU PILSENER	B	GERMANY	60
ARCOBRÄU URWEISSE	W	GERMANY	42
ARNOLD	B	GERMANY	46
ARNOLD DARK	B	GERMANY	40
ARTEVELDE GR. CRU	A	BELGIUM	65
ASTRA ALE	A	GERMANY	48
ASTRA EXCLUSIVE	B	GERMANY	40
ASTRA MEISTER BOCK	BK	GERMANY	30
ATHENIAN	B	GREECE	45
ATLAS	B	GREECE	33
AUGSBURGER EXPORT	B	GERMANY	48
AUGUST HATZ PRIVAT	B	GERMANY	72
AUGUST.MAXIMATOR	BK	GERMANY	72
AUGUSTIJN	A	BELGIUM	36
AUGUSTINER EXPORT	B	GERMANY	6
AUGUSTINER LIGHT	B	GERMANY	50
AUGUSTINER OKT.	B	GERMANY	48
AUSTRIAN GOLD	B	AUSTRIA	33
AUTENREIDER DUNKEL	B	GERMANY	40
AUTENREIDERHELL	B	GERMANY	51
AUTENREIDER PILSNER	B	GERMANY	52
AUTENRIEDER WEIZEN	W	GERMANY	70
AVENTIUS WEIZEN	W	GERMANY	81
AYINGER ALTBAYER.	B	GERMANY	71
AYINGER DUNKEL	B	GERMANY	78
AYINGER EXPORT WEISS	W	GERMANY	49
AYINGER FEST MARZEN	B	GERMANY	38
AYINGER HEFE WEISS	W	GERMANY	25

Brand	Type	Brewer	Rating
AYINGER JAHRHUNDERT	B	GERMANY	26
AYINGER MAIBOCK	BK	GERMANY	74
AYINGER OKT. MÄRZEN	B	GERMANY	65
AYINGER UR-WEIZEN	W	GERMANY	43
AYINGER WEIHNACHTS	BK	GERMANY	56
BAD URACH OLPP DOPPEL	BK	GERMANY	86
BAD URACH OLPP MAIBK	BK	GERMANY	89
BADGER ALE	A	ENGLAND	44
BAMBERGER HOFBRAU	B	GERMANY	28
BAMBERGER KRONEN	B	GERMANY	22
BAMBERGER LOWEN FRK	B	GERMANY	45
BAMBERGER LÖWEN EXP.	B	GERMANY	77
BARBAROSSA GOLD	B	GERMANY	24
BARBAROSSA KAISER	B	GERMANY	48
BARBICAN	NA	ENGLAND	14
BARON VON FUNK	ML	GERMANY	42
BARTELSTEINER WEISSE	W	GERMANY	36
BASS NO. 1	A	ENGLAND	28
BASS OLD BARLEY	S	BELGIUM	56
BASS PALE ALE	A	ENGLAND	78
BATEMAN'S VICTORY	A	ENGLAND	48
BATEMAN'S XXXB	A	ENGLAND	39
BAVARIA LAGER	B	HOLLAND	28
BAVARIA MALT	M	HOLLAND	30
BAVARIA MARZEN	B	GERMANY	41
BAVARIA WEIZEN	W	GERMANY	42
BAVARIAN ABBEY	B	GERMANY	41
BAVARIAN ABBEY	NA	GERMANY	25
BAVARIAN DUNK. STARK	B	GERMANY	70
BAYER MÄRZEN	B	GERMANY	45
BAYER WEIZEN	W	GERMANY	55
BAYERISCH MÄRZEN DK.	B	GERMANY	64
BAYRISCH HELL VOLLBIER	B	GERMANY	30
BÄREN ALPEN BOCK	BK	GERMANY	89
BÄREN DUNKEL	B	GERMANY	65
BÄREN GOLD	B	GERMANY	60
BÄREN PILS	B	GERMANY	78
BÄREN WEIZEN	W	GERMANY	54
BBK PILS	B	GERMANY	24
BEAMISH CREAM	S	IRELAND	26
BEAMISH	S	IRELAND	18
BEAVER	B	ENGLAND	14
BECK UNSER DUNKLES	B	GERMANY	35
BECK'S	B	GERMANY	56
BECK'S DARK	B	GERMANY	58
BECKER'S EXPORT	B	GERMANY	28
BECKER'S EXTRA	B	GERMANY	27
BECKER'S JUBIL.	B	GERMANY	67
BECKER'S PILS	B	GERMANY	30
BEERFELDER FELSEN BK	BK	GERMANY	44
BELGRADE GOLD	B	YUGOSLAVIA	82
BELHAVEN	A	SCOTLAND	43
BELHAVEN LAGER	B	SCOTLAND	22
BELLE-VUE CREAM	L	BELGIUM	36
BELLE-VUE KRIEK	L	BELGIUM	33
BELLHEIMER SILBER BK	BK	GERMANY	60
BERCHESGADENER BIER	B	GERMANY	74
BERCHESGADENER WEIZ.	W	GERMANY	60
BERLINER KINDL PILS	B	GERMANY	30
BERLINER KINDL WEISS	W	GERMANY	18
BERLINER PILS EXPORT	B	GERMANY	30
BERLINER UR BOCK	BK	GERMANY	24
BERLINER WEISS	W	GERMANY	38
BERNHARDUS BOCK	BK	GERMANY	84
BIBERACHER MÄRZEN	B	GERMANY	82
BIBERACHER UR-DUNKEL	B	GERMANY	63
BIERE DE PARIS	A	FRANCE	60
BIERE DES DRUIDES	B	GERMANY	27
BIG BEN	B	ENGLAND	41
BINDING	B	GERMANY	29
BINDING EXPORT	B	GERMANY	33
BIOS	A	BELGIUM	33
BIRELL	NA	SWITZERLAND	42
BISCHOFF	B	GERMANY	29
BISCHOFF PILS	B	GERMANY	25
BISCHOFSHOF HEFE-W	W	GERMANY	63
BISCHOFSHOF URHELL	B	GERMANY	50
BISHOP'S ALE	A	ENGLAND	74
BISHOP'S TIPPLE	A	ENGLAND	86
BITBURGER	B	GERMANY	35
BLANC DE NEIGES	A	BELGIUM	24
BOCHOLTER KWIK PILS	B	BELGIUM	44
BOCKALE	B	GERMANY	30
BODDINGTON'S BITTER	B	ENGLAND	26
BODEN WÖHRER JACOB	B	GERMANY	31
BOLD GOLD	ML	GERMANY	28
BORSOD	B	HUNGARY	36
BÖLK STOFF	B	GERMANY	72
BRACHLE HELLER BOCK	BK	GERMANY	72
BRAINS RED DRAGONIP	A	ENGLAND	74
BRAND	B	HOLLAND	58
BRASSIN DE GARDE	A	FRANCE	60
BRAUGOLD	B	GERMANY	20
BRAUMEISTER HELL	B	GERMANY	37
BRAUNFELS PILS	B	GERMANY	8
BRAUNFELSER 1868	B	GERMANY	15
BRAUWASTLE KRISTAL	W	GERMANY	54
BRÄUCHLE HELLER BK	BK	GERMANY	72
BREDA	B	HOLLAND	9
BREMER DOM-BRAU	B	GERMANY	14
BREZNAK SVETLY LEZA	B	CZECHOSLOVAKIA	24
BRIGAND	A	BELGIUM	32
BRIGAND	A	BELGIUM	72
BRINKHOFF'S NO. 1	B	GERMANY	50
BROCK	B	ENGLAND	4
BROYHAN	B	GERMANY	41
BUCKLER	NA	HOLLAND	31
BUDVAR BUDWEISER	B	CZECHOSLOVAKIA	55
BULLDOG	B	ENGLAND	54
BULLDOG PALE ALE	A	ENGLAND	26
BUNST VOLLBIER HELL	B	GERMANY	24
BURGER & ENGELBRÄU	B	GERMANY	27
BURGERBRAU BAMBERG	B	GERMANY	25
BURGERBRÄU PILS	B	GERMANY	36
BURKE'S STOUT	S	ENGLAND	47
BURTON BR. XL BITTER	A	ENGLAND	17
BURTON BRIDGE BITTER	A	ENGLAND	55
BURTON BRIDGE FEST	A	ENGLAND	65
BURTON BRIDGE PORTER	P	ENGLAND	52
BUSH BEER	A	BELGIUM	87
BUSH BEER STRONG ALE	A	BELGIUM	84
BUUR	B	DENMARK	62
CALWER ECK BRÄU	B	GERMANY	72
CAMPBELL'S CHRISTMAS	A	ENGLAND	82
CAMPBELL'S GOLD LABEL	A	ENGLAND	74
CAMPBELL'S SCOTCH	A	ENGLAND	76
CAMPBELL'S XMAS 91	A	ENGLAND	80
CANTERBURY HOP PICKER	A	ENGLAND	35
CANTERBURY PREMIUM	A	ENGLAND	17
CANTERBURY REGIMENT.	A	ENGLAND	38
CARDINAL AMBER	LO	SWITZERLAND	20
CARDINAL	B	SWITZERLAND	75
CARLSBERG	B	DENMARK	42
CARLSBERG ELEPHANT	ML	DENMARK	22
CARLSBERG LIGHT	LO	DENMARK	23
CARLSBERG ROYAL	B	DENMARK	54
CARLSBERG SPECIAL	B	ENGLAND	73
CARLSBERG SPECIAL DK	B	DENMARK	46
CAROLUS DOPPELBOCK	BK	GERMANY	65
CASSEL SCHLOSS	B	GERMANY	64
CASTELAIN	B	FRANCE	61
CASTLE ALE	A	ENGLAND	33
CELEBRATOR	BK	GERMANY	57
CERES	B	DENMARK	24
CERES STRONG ALE	A	DENMARK	70
CHARRINGTON BW	BW	ENGLAND	50
CHAS WELLS BOMBARD.	A	ENGLAND	34
CHAS WELLS LIGHT	A	ENGLAND	15
CHESHIRE ENGLISH PUB	A	ENGLAND	50
CHESTER GOLDEN	A	ENGLAND	34
CHIC	B	FRANCE	35
CHIC LITE	LO	FRANCE	12
CHIMAY	A	BELGIUM	32
CHIMAY BLUE CAP 1985	A	BELGIUM	57
CHIMAY CINQ CENTS	A	BELGIUM	70
CHIMAY RED CAP	A	BELGIUM	68
CHIMAY RESERVE	A	BELGIUM	75
CHIMAY TRAPPISTES	A	BELGIUM	23
CHRIST. HENNINGER	B	GERMANY	46
CHRIST.HENNINGER DK	B	GERMANY	54
CHRISTKIND WEIHNACHT	W	GERMANY	14
CHRISTOFFEL	B	HOLLAND	66
CHURCHILL AMBER	B	ENGLAND	28
CHURCHILL DRY	D	ENGLAND	29
CHURCHILL LAGER	B	ENGLAND	31
CINEY 10 SPECIALE	A	BELGIUM	59
CINEY CHEVTOGNE	A	BELGIUM	55
CLAUSTHALER	NA	GERMANY	48
CLUB WEISSE	W	GERMANY	63
CLUSS BOCK DUNKEL	BK	GERMANY	45
CLUSS EXPORT	B	GERMANY	49
CLUSS KELLER PILS	B	GERMANY	34
CLUSS PILSENER	B	GERMANY	66
CLUSS RATSHOF PILS	B	GERMANY	52

Brand	Type	Brewer	Rating
COLUMBUS FEST DARK	B	AUSTRIA	40
COLUMBUS GOLDEN BK	BK	AUSTRIA	40
COLUMBUS MÄRZEN	B	AUSTRIA	50
COLUMBUS PILS	B	AUSTRIA	36
CONRADIN KÖLSCH	A	GERMANY	34
CONVIKT EGAUER ZWICKL	B	GERMANY	69
CONVIKT MEIST. SCHUTZ	B	GERMANY	45
CORSENDONK AGNUS	A	BELGIUM	62
CORSENDONK MONK'S BR.	A	BELGIUM	70
CORSENDONK MONK'S PA.	A	BELGIUM	74
CORSENDONK PATER	A	BELGIUM	69
COURAGE LAGER	B	ENGLAND	24
CRISTAL	B	PORTUGAL	36
CRYSTAL	B	CZECHOSLOVAKIA	39
CRYSTALL WUHRER	B	ITALY	50
CUPIDO	A	BELGIUM	17
CUVEE DE CINEY BLONDE	A	BELGIUM	22
CUVEE DE L'HERMITAGE	B	BELGIUM	51
CUVEE L'HERM. XMAS 87	A	BELGIUM	55
D'AQUINO	B	ITALY	13
D'WIRTSDIRN SCHWARZE	W	GERMANY	45
DAB ALT	A	GERMANY	28
DAB EXPORT	B	GERMANY	48
DAB KRAFT PERLE	NA	GERMANY	8
DAB LIGHT	LO	GERMANY	11
DAB MEISTER PILS	B	GERMANY	76
DAB ORIGINAL	B	GERMANY	48
DAB TRAD. DARK	B	GERMANY	12
DACHS WEIZEN	W	GERMANY	56
DAHL'S EXPORT	B	NORWAY	60
DAHL'S PILS	B	NORWAY	48
DAMM	B	SPAIN	27
DANISH DYNAMITE	B	DENMARK	55
DANISH GOLD	B	DENMARK	16
DANISH LIGHT	NA	DENMARK	6
DARK STAR	B	ENGLAND	60
DARMSTADTER URBOCK	BK	GERMANY	76
DART MORKT STARKOL	B	SWEDEN	57
DAS ECHTE SCHWABEN	B	GERMANY	55
DAVENPORT	A	ENGLAND	78
DB URTYB	B	GERMANY	50
DEKONINCK	A	BELGIUM	22
DEININGER HEFE WEISS	W	GERMANY	78
DEMPSEY'S	A	IRELAND	18
DER BLAU PAGE	BK	GERMANY	68
DER LOWENBRAU	B	GERMANY	72
DER LÖWENBRÄU PILS	B	GERMANY	68
DIE SCHWARZE DUNKLES	W	GERMANY	36
DIEBELS ALT	A	GERMANY	62
DIEKIRCH MALT LIQUOR	ML	LUXEMBOURG	48
DIEKIRCH ML EXCLUSIVE	ML	LUXEMBOURG	26
DIEKIRCH PILS	B	LUXEMBOURG	61
DIESTER'S	A	BELGIUM	44
DINKEL. BLK FOREST	B	GERMANY	45
DINKEL. VOLKSFEST	B	GERMANY	74
DINKEL. WEIHNACHTS	B	GERMANY	73
DINKEL. WEIZENKRONE	W	GERMANY	21
DINKELACKER BOCK	BK	GERMANY	80
DINKELACKER DARK	B	GERMANY	31
DINKELACKER DARK C.D.	B	GERMANY	61
DINKELACKER DK BREW	B	GERMANY	35
DINKELACKER PILS CD	B	GERMANY	51
DINKELACKER PRIVAT	B	GERMANY	61
DISTELHÄUSER EXPORT	B	GERMANY	50
DISTELHÄUSER MÄRZEN	B	GERMANY	56
DISTELHÄUSER PILS	B	GERMANY	45
DITHSMARSCH. MAIBOCK	BK	GERMANY	67
DITHSMARSCH. UR-BOCK	BK	GERMANY	66
DOM KÖLSCH	A	GERMANY	40
DOMFURSTEN	B	GERMANY	24
DORT. IMP. OKTOBERFEST	B	GERMANY	52
DORT. KRONEN ALT DK	A	GERMANY	26
DORT. KRONEN CLASSIC	B	GERMANY	69
DORT. KRONEN PILS	B	GERMANY	34
DORT. RITTER BOCK	BK	GERMANY	76
DORT. RITTER DARK	B	GERMANY	45
DORT. RITTER EXPORT	B	GERMANY	9
DORT. RITTER LIGHT	B	GERMANY	64
DORT. RITTER PILS	B	GERMANY	54
DORT. UNION BEER	B	GERMANY	39
DORT. UNION DARK	B	GERMANY	51
DORT. UNION LIGHT	B	GERMANY	22
DORT. UNION ML	ML	GERMANY	30
DORT. UNION ORIGINAL	B	GERMANY	13
DORT. UNION PILSENER	B	GERMANY	30
DORT. UNION SIEGEL	B	GERMANY	68
DORT. UNION SPECIAL	B	GERMANY	72

Brand	Type	Brewer	Rating
DORT. WESTFALIA EXP	B	GERMANY	29
DORT. WESTFALIA SPEC	B	GERMANY	29
DORTMUNDER HANSA EXP	B	GERMANY	45
DORTMUNDER IMP. ALT	A	GERMANY	32
DORTMUNDER IMPERIAL	B	GERMANY	56
DORTMUNDER STIFTS	B	GERMANY	26
DOUBLE DIAMOND	A	ENGLAND	48
DOUBLE DIAMOND PILS	B	ENGLAND	51
DOUBLE DRAGON	A	WALES	55
DRAGON ALE	A	WALES	34
DREHER	B	ITALY	22
DREHER EXPORT	B	ITALY	33
DREHER FORTE	B	ITALY	59
DRESSLER EXPORT	B	GERMANY	10
DRIBECK'S LIGHT	LO	GERMANY	32
DUTTENBERGER ENGEL	B	GERMANY	50
DUVEL	A	BELGIUM	42
DÜLL BOCK	BK	GERMANY	74
DÜLL MÄRZEN	B	GERMANY	33
DÜLL PILS	B	GERMANY	30
EBELSBACHER HELL	B	GERMANY	45
EBELSBACHER PILS	B	GERMANY	57
ECHT VELDENSTEINER	B	GERMANY	39
ECHT VELDENSTEINER	B	GERMANY	48
ECHTES BAM. ZWERGLA	B	GERMANY	60
ECKER EDEL PILS	B	GERMANY	81
ECKER FAHNDERL	W	GERMANY	63
ECKER VOLLBIER HELL	B	GERMANY	70
ECKER WILDERER DUNKEL	B	GERMANY	69
EDEL WEISS	ML	GERMANY	30
EDELWEISS DUNKEL	W	AUSTRIA	22
EDELWEISS HEFE-WEIZ.	W	AUSTRIA	56
EDELWEISS KRISTALL	W	AUSTRIA	23
EDER	B	GERMANY	39
EDER DOPPELBOCK DUNK	BK	GERMANY	85
EFES PILS	B	TURKEY	62
EFES PILSEN	B	TURKEY	42
EGER URBIER	B	CZECHOSLOVAKIA	32
EGGENBERGER PILS	B	AUSTRIA	15
EGGENBERGER URBK 17	BK	AUSTRIA	66
EGGENBERGER URBK 23	BK	AUSTRIA	80
EGGER NATUR BRAU	B	AUSTRIA	42
EGGER PILS	B	AUSTRIA	50
EICHBAUM ALTGOLD	B	GERMANY	53
EICHBAUM APOSTULATOR	BK	GERMANY	75
EICHBAUM DUNKL WEIZEN	W	GERMANY	65
EICHBAUM EICHKRONE	B	GERMANY	47
EICHBAUM FESTBIER	B	GERMANY	27
EICHBAUM HEFEWEIZEN	W	GERMANY	61
EICHBAUM KRISTALL	W	GERMANY	54
EICHBAUM MAIBOCK	BK	GERMANY	76
EINBECKER MAIBOCK	BK	GERMANY	69
EINBECKER UR-BOCK	BK	GERMANY	40
EKU DARK RESERVE	B	GERMANY	28
EKU EDELBOCK	BK	GERMANY	34
EKU HEFE WEIZEN	W	GERMANY	26
EKU HEFE-WEISS DUNK	W	GERMANY	55
EKU HEFE-WEIZEN DUNK	W	GERMANY	38
EKU JUBILAUMSBIER	B	GERMANY	72
EKU KULMBACHER EXP.	B	GERMANY	52
EKU KULMIN. DK DBL BK	BK	GERMANY	68
EKU KULMINATOR 28	B	GERMANY	45
EKU MAIBOCK	BK	GERMANY	82
EKU OKTOBERFEST	B	GERMANY	44
EKU PILS	B	GERMANY	26
EKU RUBIN	B	GERMANY	58
EKU SPECIAL	B	GERMANY	38
EKU WEIZENBK DUNK	W	GERMANY	51
ELAN	NA	SWITZERLAND	44
ENGHEIN SAISON DBL	A	BELGIUM	39
EPHESUS	B	TURKEY	35
ERBACHER DOPPELBOCK	BK	GERMANY	77
ERDINGER PIKANTUS	W	GERMANY	63
ERDINGER WEISS DUNK.	W	GERMANY	41
ERDINGER WEISS	W	GERMANY	48
ERIKOIS	B	FINLAND	50
ERL-HELL	B	GERMANY	27
ERZQUELL	B	GERMANY	27
ESCHENBACHER MARZEN	B	GERMANY	80
ESPECIAL	B	AZORES	30
ESTRELLA DORADA	B	SPAIN	50
ETTALER CURATOR	BK	GERMANY	7O
ETTALER KL WEISSBIER	W	GERMANY	51
ETTALER KL. WEISS DUNK	W	GERMANY	43
ETTALER KLOST.DUNK	B	GERMANY	46
ETTL-HELL	B	GERMANY	19
EULER LANDPILS	B	GERMANY	34

Brand	Type	Brewer	Rating
EX BIER	NA	SWITZERLAND	14
EXTRACTO DE MALTO	M	GERMANY	40
FALCON EXPORT	B	SWEDEN	24
FARMER'S ALE	A	ENGLAND	30
FARMER'S STOUT	S	ENGLAND	47
FARO LAMBIC	L	BELGIUM	40
FARSON'S SHANDY	ML	ENGLAND	32
FASSL GOLD	B	AUSTRIA	82
FASSL GOLD PILS	B	AUSTRIA	26
FÄSSLA GOLD PILS	B	GERMANY	68
FÄSSLA HELL	B	GERMANY	42
FELDSCHLOSSEN	B	SWITZERLAND	68
FELINFOEL BITTER	A	ENGLAND	31
FELINFOEL CREAM STOUT	S	WALES	18
FELINFOEL FESTIVE	A	WALES	62
FELINFOEL HERITAGE	A	WALES	28
FEST BRAU	B	GERMANY	25
FIEDLERS BOCK	BK	GERMANY	48
FIEDLERS PILS	B	GERMANY	53
FINLANDIA GOLD	B	FINLAND	74
FINLANDIA LIGHT	B	FINLAND	26
FISCHER AMBER	B	FRANCE	57
FISCHERBELLE STRASB.	B	FRANCE	42
FISCHER BITTER	B	FRANCE	8
FISCHER D'ALSACE	B	FRANCE	62
FISCHER GOLD	B	FRANCE	48
FISCHER MARCH	B	FRANCE	18
FISCHER PILS	B	FRANCE	41
FIX	B	GREECE	45
FIX SPEZIAL	B	GREECE	21
FLANDERS FARMERS ALE	A	BELGIUM	64
FLANDERS GR. CRU TRIP.	A	BELGIUM	71
FLEKOVSKY LEZAK	B	CZECHOSLOVAKIA	80
FLENSBURGER	B	GERMANY	50
FLENSBURGER PILS	B	GERMANY	62
FLORIANO MAIBOCK	BK	GERMANY	59
FOHRENBURGER BLONDES	B	AUSTRIA	30
FOHRENBURGER JUBILÄUM	B	AUSTRIA	44
FORST DUNKEL	B	GERMANY	34
FORST EXPORT	B	GERMANY	35
FORST HEFE-WEISSBIER	W	GERMANY	47
FORST PILS	B	GERMANY	36
FORST WEISSBIER	W	GERMANY	36
FRANKEN BRÄU DUNKEL	B	GERMANY	81
FRANKEN BRÄU FEST	B	GERMANY	59
FRANKEN BRÄU PILS	B	GERMANY	75
FRANKENBRÄU PILS	B	GERMANY	40
FRANKENBRÄU SPEZIAL	B	GERMANY	36
FRANZ JOSEF JUBIL	W	GERMANY	20
FRANZISKANER H-W DK	W	GERMANY	65
FRANZISKANER H-W	W	GERMANY	50
FRÄNKISCH FEST	B	GERMANY	27
FRÄNKISCH WEIZEN DK	W	GERMANY	12
FRYDENLUND'S EXPORT	B	NORWAY	30
FRYDENLUND'S NORWEIG.	B	NORWAY	28
FRYDENLUND'S PILSENER	B	NORWAY	21
FUCHS FEST BOCK	BK	GERMANY	59
FULLER'S LONDON PRIDE	A	ENGLAND	30
FULLER'S PALE ALE	A	ENGLAND	24
FULLERS ESB	A	ENGLAND	80
FÜRSTENBERG IMPORTED	B	GERMANY	55
FÜRSTENBERG PILSENER	B	GERMANY	44
FÜSSENER EDEL PILS	B	GERMANY	65
FÜSSENER EXPORT	B	GERMANY	55
FÜSSENER FEST BOCK	BK	GERMANY	65
GAFFEL KÖLSCH	K	GERMANY	20
GAMBRINUS PILSEN	B	CZECHOSLOVAKIA	42
GAMPERTBRÄU FÖRSTER	B	GERMANY	36
GANTER EXPORT	B	GERMANY	48
GASTHAUS SPECIAL	B	GERMANY	38
GATZWEILERS ALT	A	GERMANY	32
GEISLINGER KAISER	B	GERMANY	49
GEO. GALE ESB BITTER	A	ENGLAND	76
GERMAN STAR	M	GERMANY	12
GERMANIA	M	GERMANY	16
GERSTEL BRAU	NA	GERMANY	36
GILDE EDEL-EXPORT	B	GERMANY	81
GILDE PILSENER	B	GERMANY	44
GILDE RATSKELLER	B	GERMANY	20
GILDEN KOLSCH	A	GERMANY	36
GINDER ALE	A	BELGIUM	51
GIRAF	ML	DENMARK	59
GLARNER	B	SWITZERLAND	48
GOLD EAGLE BITTER	A	ENGLAND	51
GOLD LABEL NO. 1	BW	ENGLAND	18
GOLD OCHSEN H-W	W	GERMANY	56
GOLD OCHSEN KR-W	W	GERMANY	35
GOLD OCHSEN PILS	B	GERMANY	45
GOLD OCHSEN WEIZEN	W	GERMANY	57
GOLD STAR	B	ISRAEL	40
GOLDEN HORN	B	YUGOSLAVIA	41
GOLDHORN CLUB	B	YUGOSLAVIA	30
GORD.DOUGLAS SCOTCH	A	SCOTLAND	66
GORDON DOUGLAS	A	ENGLAND	66
GORDON HIGHLAND	A	SCOTLAND	77
GOSSER	B	AUSTRIA	24
GOSSER EXPORT	B	AUSTRIA	47
GOSSER GOLDEN ROCK	B	AUSTRIA	20
GOSSER STIFTSBRAU	B	AUSTRIA	24
GOUDEN CAROLUS	A	BELGIUM	46
GOUDEN CAROLUS	A	BELGIUM	69
GÖSSER MÄRZEN	B	AUSTRIA	24
GRAFEN WALDER	B	GERMANY	55
GRAND ARMEE	B	GERMANY	38
GRÄNGES	B	SWEDEN	45
GRÄNGES BLONDE	B	SWEDEN	54
GREEN ROOSTER	ML	DENMARK	58
GREENE KING	A	ENGLAND	10
GREGORIUS WIESENFEST	B	GERMANY	75
GREIFENKLAU EXPORT	B	GERMANY	60
GRENZQUELL DARK	B	GERMANY	48
GRENZQUELL PILSENER	B	GERMANY	40
GRIMBERGEN DUBBEL	A	BELGIUM	68
GRIMBERGEN TRIPLE	A	BELGIUM	83
GROLSCH	B	HOLLAND	43
GROLSCH DARK	B	HOLLAND	42
GROLSCH DRY	B	HOLLAND	18
GROLSCH LAGER	B	HOLLAND	50
GRÖHE BOCK	BK	GERMANY	68
GRÖHE MÄRZEN	B	GERMANY	39
GRUNER DUNKEL	B	GERMANY	40
GRUNER EXPORT	B	GERMANY	40
GUEUZE BELLE-VUE	L	BELGIUM	40
GUEUZE DE NEVE	L	BELGIUM	22
GUEUZE LAMBIC	L	BELGIUM	43
GUEZE ST. LOUIS	L	BELGIUM	63
GUILDER	B	HOLLAND	30
GUINNESS CREAM STOUT	S	IRELAND	16
GUINNESS DR. BITTER	A	ENGLAND	21
GUINNESS EXTRA STOUT	S	IRELAND	67
GUINNESS GOLD	B	IRELAND	54
GUINNESS PUB DRAUGHT	S	ENGLAND	17
GULDEN DRAAK	A	BELGIUM	60
GULPENER	B	HOLLAND	51
GÜNZBURGER HEFE-WEIZ.	W	GERMANY	42
HAAKE BECK	NA	GERMANY	41
HABERECKL FEUERIO	B	GERMANY	84
HABERECKL MÄRZEN	B	GERMANY	56
HACKER ANIMATOR	BK	GERMANY	78
HACKER BRAUMEISTER	B	GERMANY	60
HACKER DARK	B	GERMANY	48
HACKER EDELHELL	B	GERMANY	37
HACKER EDELHELL EXP.	B	GERMANY	55
HACKER FEST BIER	B	GERMANY	25
HACKER HUBERTUS	BK	GERMANY	84
HACKER PSCH. OKT MÄRZ	B	GERMANY	72
HACKER PSCHORR LIGHT	B	GERMANY	67
HACKER PSCHORR MAIBK	BK	GERMANY	74
HACKER PSCHORR OKT	B	GERMANY	61
HACKER PSCHORR WEISS	W	GERMANY	57
HANNEN ALT	A	GERMANY	13
HANSA DARK	B	NORWAY	34
HANSA EXPORT	B	NORWAY	35
HANSA FJORD	B	NORWAY	82
HANSA PILS	B	NORWAY	42
HANSA PILSENER	B	NORWAY	38
HARBOE BEAR	ML	DENMARK	42
HARBOE GOLD	B	DENMARK	37
HARKLBERG HOCHFÜRST	B	GERMANY	27
HARKLBERG JAK. DK.	W	GERMANY	57
HARKLBERG JAKOBI	W	GERMANY	24
HARKLBERG URHELL	B	GERMANY	24
HARP	B	IRELAND	38
HARVEY'S ELIZABETHAN	A	ENGLAND	32
HASEN-BRÄU EXTRA	B	GERMANY	24
HASEN-BRÄU HELL	B	GERMANY	33
HASEN-BRÄU MÄRZEN	B	GERMANY	76
HEIDELBERGER PILS	B	GERMANY	53
HEINEKEN	B	HOLLAND	65
HEINEKEN DARK	B	HOLLAND	68
HENNINGER	B	GERMANY	61
HENNINGER DARK	B	GERMANY	72
HENNINGER DOPPELBOCK	BK	GERMANY	89
HENNINGER DUNKEL	B	GERMANY	78

Brand	Type	Brewer	Rating
HENNINGER HELLER BK	BK	GERMANY	88
HENNINGER INTL	B	GERMANY	17
HENNINGER KAISER	B	GERMANY	54
HENNINGER KAISER EXP	B	GERMANY	45
HERCULES ALE	A	WALES	2
HERFORDER PILS	B	GERMANY	26
HERFORDER PILSNER	B	GERMANY	22
HERITAGE	A	ENGLAND	78
HERRENBRÄU AROMATOR	BK	GERMANY	51
HERRENBRÄU LIGHT	B	GERMANY	30
HERRENBRÄU PILSNER	B	GERMANY	38
HERRENBRÄU WEIZEN	W	GERMANY	12
HERRENHAUSEN	B	GERMANY	45
HERZOG PILSENER	B	GERMANY	33
HET KAPITTEL	A	BELGIUM	53
HEYLANDS FESTBOCK	BK	GERMANY	65
HEYLANDS SEPPL-BOCK	BK	GERMANY	80
HIRSCH GOLD EXPORT	B	GERMANY	42
HIRSCH HONER PILS	B	GERMANY	36
HIRSCH URHELL	B	GERMANY	28
HOCHLAND HELL	B	GERMANY	36
HOEGAARDEN GRAND CRU	A	BELGIUM	74
HOEGAARDEN TRIPLE	A	BELGIUM	70
HOEGAARDEN WHITE ALE	A	BELGIUM	23
HOEGAARDEN WHITE BEER	B	BELGIUM	56
HOFB MUN DELICATOR	BK	GERMANY	75
HOFB MUN DK MAI-BOCK	BK	GERMANY	75
HOFB MUN ROYAL EXP.	B	GERMANY	64
HOFBRAU DARK RES.	B	GERMANY	46
HOFBRAU LIGHT RES.	B	GERMANY	45
HOFBRAU MUN. BK HELL	BK	GERMANY	86
HOFBRAU MÜNCHEN DUNK.	B	GERMANY	78
HOFBRAU MÜNCHEN HELL	B	GERMANY	78
HOFBRAU OKTOBERFEST	B	GERMANY	48
HOFLIEFERANT BOCK	BK	GERMANY	87
HOFLIEFERANT EXQUISIT	B	GERMANY	79
HOFLIEFERANT HELL	B	GERMANY	24
HOFMARK	B	GERMANY	46
HOFMARK FEINE HERB	B	GERMANY	60
HOFMARK FEINE MILD	B	GERMANY	47
HOFMARK GOLD	B	GERMANY	53
HOGERBRAU HELLES	B	GERMANY	45
HOHENKAMMER SCHLOSS	B	GERMANY	35
HOHENKAMMER WEISSE	W	GERMANY	62
HOLSTEN CERVEZA TIGRE	B	GERMANY	32
HOLSTEN DRY	D	GERMANY	30
HOLSTEN EXPORT	B	GERMANY	65
HOLSTEN KRAFTIG HERB	B	GERMANY	34
HOLSTEN LAGER	B	GERMANY	30
HOLSTEN LIGHT	LO	GERMANY	19
HOLSTEN PILS	B	GERMANY	36
HOLSTEN PREMIUM	B	GERMANY	29
HOLZKIRCHNER DUNKEL	W	GERMANY	47
HOLZKIRCHNER EXPORT	B	GERMANY	36
HOLZKIRCHNER HEFE-W	W	GERMANY	48
HOLZKIRCHNER HELL	B	GERMANY	41
HOLZKIRCHNER LAURENZI	B	GERMANY	63
HOLZKIRCHNER PILS	B	GERMANY	41
HOPF DUNKLE HEFE-WEIZ.	W	GERMANY	32
HOPF WEISSE EXPORT	W	GERMANY	30
HORNECKER HELL	B	GERMANY	43
HORSE ALE	A	BELGIUM	45
HORSY	B	GERMANY	69
HUMMER	B	GERMANY	26
HÜRLIMANN DARK	B	SWITZERLAND	33
HÜRLIMANN STERN	B	SWITZERLAND	46
IMPERIAL RUSSIAN ST.	S	ENGLAND	12
IMPERIAL STOUT	S	DENMARK	60
INNSBRUCK	B	AUSTRIA	23
IRLBACHER HEFE-WEIZ.	W	GERMANY	53
IRLBACHER HELL	B	GERMANY	70
IRLBACHER PILS	B	GERMANY	41
IRLBACHER WEISSE	W	GERMANY	42
IRSEER KL.STARKBIER	B	GERMANY	78
ISENBECK EXPORT	B	GERMANY	30
ISENBECK EXTRA DRY	B	GERMANY	62
ISI 08 SPECIAL	NA	GERMANY	21
ITALA PILSEN	B	ITALY	66
ITALA PILSEN GOLD	B	ITALY	77
JACOBINS KRIEK	L	BELGIUM	34
JACOBINS LAMBIC	L	BELGIUM	43
JADRAN	B	YUGOSLAVIA	30
JAEGER	B	HOLLAND	14
JAEGERHOF PILS	B	GERMANY	41
JANKABRÄUBOHEME	B	GERMANY	72
JANKABRÄU DK WEIZEN	W	GERMANY	51
JANKABRÄU KUPFER	B	GERMANY	57
JENLAIN ALE	A	FRANCE	47
JEVER	B	GERMANY	21
JEVER LIGHT	L	GERMANY	36
JEVER MAIBOCK	BK	GERMANY	35
JOHN BROWN ALE	A	ENGLAND	33
JOHN BULL	B	ENGLAND	28
JOHN COURAGE AMBER	B	ENGLAND	44
JOHN COURAGE EXPORT	B	ENGLAND	28
JOHN PEEL EXPORT	B	ENGLAND	65
JOS. SCHNEIDER DUNK.	B	GERMANY	69
JOS. SCHNEIDER MAIBOCK	BK	GERMANY	73
JOS. SCHNEIDER MÄRZEN	B	GERMANY	72
JOSEPH MEENS	B	HOLLAND	33
JULIUS ECHTER	W	GERMANY	67
JUPILER	B	BELGIUM	45
KAASTAR	A	BELGIUM	54
KAISER BAVARIA	B	GERMANY	62
KAISER KUR PILS	B	AUSTRIA	24
KAISER MÄRZEN FASSTYP	B	AUSTRIA	50
KAISER PREMIUM	B	AUSTRIA	60
KAISER WEISS	W	GERMANY	44
KAISER WEISSE	W	GERMANY	57
KAISERDOM EXTRA DRY	D	GERMANY	24
KAISERDOM HEFE-WEISS	W	GERMANY	50
KAISERDOM PILSENER	B	GERMANY	68
KAISERDOM RACHBIER	B	GERMANY	58
KAISERDOM UR-BOCK	BK	GERMANY	76
KAISERHOF FESTBIER	B	GERMANY	36
KALBACK	B	SWEDEN	30
KALIBER	NA	IRELAND	43
KALTENBERG HELL	B	GERMANY	33
KANTERBRAU	B	FRANCE	45
KAPUZINER SCHW. HEFE	W	GERMANY	48
KARAMALZ	M	GERMANY	24
KAREL SVELTE	B	CZECHOSLOVAKIA	27
KARG WEISSBIER	W	GERMANY	63
KARJALA EXPORT	B	FINLAND	54
KARLOVACKO LIGHT	B	YUGOSLAVIA	15
KARLOVACKO SPECIAL	B	YUGOSLAVIA	24
KARLSBEER	B	YUGOSLAVIA	68
KARLSBERG	B	GERMANY	45
KARLSBERG BOCK	BK	GERMANY	50
KARLSBRAU	B	GERMANY	39
KARLSBRAU MANNLICH	B	GERMANY	64
KARLSKRONE	B	GERMANY	51
KARLSKRONE EDEL PILS	B	GERMANY	45
KARMELITEN KL. DUNKEL	B	GERMANY	65
KASTEEL	B	BELGIUM	57
KAUZEN DUNKELER	B	GERMANY	35
KAUZEN HEFE-WEISS	W	GERMANY	42
KEILER WEISSBIER	W	GERMANY	37
KELLERBRAU	B	ENGLAND	13
KEO PILSENER	B	CYPRUS	19
KESSELRING PILS	B	GERMANY	79
KESTREL	B	ENGLAND	42
KESTREL SUPER STRONG	B	ENGLAND	67
KETJE PALE ALE	A	BELGIUM	46
KIESEL EXPORT	B	GERMANY	51
KIESEL FESTBIER	B	GERMANY	63
KIESEL HEFE-WEISSE	W	GERMANY	47
KIESEL MÄRZEN	B	GERMANY	33
KIESEL PERL BOCK	BK	GERMANY	57
KIESEL PILS	B	GERMANY	71
KIESEL WEISS	W	GERMANY	44
KILKENNY	B	IRELAND	65
KILLIAN'S BIERE ROUSSE	A	FRANCE	77
KINDL WEISS	W	GERMANY	48
KINGPIN	B	ENGLAND	41
KINROSS	A	ENGLAND	56
KIRNER'S ECHT BADENER	B	GERMANY	40
KLOSTER ALTENBERG	B	GERMANY	24
KLOSTER LANDBIER	B	GERMANY	42
KLOSTER PILS	B	GERMANY	30
KOFF	B	FINLAND	42
KOFF IMPERIAL	S	FINLAND	48
KORBINIAN DUNKLES	B	GERMANY	76
KOSTRITZER	B	GERMANY	60
KÖNIG LUDWIG DUNKEL	B	GERMANY	24
KÖNIG-PILSENER	B	GERMANY	36
KÖNIGSBACHER ALT	A	GERMANY	46
KÖNIGSBACHER MALZ	M	GERMANY	24
KÖNIGSBACHER PILS	B	GERMANY	44
KÖNIGSBACHER UR-BOCK	BK	GERMANY	90
KRAKUS	B	POLAND	52
KROMBACHER PILS	B	GERMANY	48
KRONEN ALT	A	GERMANY	16
KRONEN BRÄU VOLLBIER	B	GERMANY	57

Brand	Type	Brewer	Rating
KRONEN GOLD EXPORT	B	GERMANY	54
KRONEN PILS	B	GERMANY	51
KRONEN WEIZEN EXPORT	W	GERMANY	75
KRONENBOURG	B	FRANCE	34
KRONENBOURG DARK	B	FRANCE	15
KRONENBOURG ML	ML	FRANCE	39
KRONENTHALER	NA	AUSTRIA	20
KROPF DARK	B	GERMANY	37
KROPF EDEL	B	GERMANY	29
KROPF GENUINE	B	GERMANY	51
KROPF LIGHT	LO	GERMANY	38
KROPF MAI-BOCK	BK	GERMANY	78
KROPF MARTINATOR	BK	GERMANY	86
KROPF MEISTER PILS	B	GERMANY	57
KRUG ALT FRÄNKISCH	B	GERMANY	67
KRUG HEILIG LÄNDER	B	GERMANY	42
KRUG HELL	B	GERMANY	36
KRUG PILS	B	GERMANY	55
KRUG WEISSE	W	GERMANY	46
KULM. MONK KL. BOCK	BK	GERMANY	75
KULM. MONK KL. SCHWARZ	B	GERMANY	75
KULM. MONK. DRY LIGHT	B	GERMANY	59
KULM. MONK. HELLER BK	BK	GERMANY	68
KULM. MONKSHOF DARK	B	GERMANY	69
KULM. MONKSHOF OKT	B	GERMANY	74
KULM. MÖNCH. AMBER	B	GERMANY	72
KULM. MÖNCH. FEST	B	GERMANY	76
KULM. REICH	B	GERMANY	46
KULM. REICH. EDELHERB	B	GERMANY	68
KULM. REICH. EISBOCK	BK	GERMANY	80
KULM. REICH. FRANK.	B	GERMANY	62
KULM. REICHELBRAU DK	B	GERMANY	45
KULM. SCHWEIZ.	B	GERMANY	38
KULM. SCHWEIZ. BOCK	BK	GERMANY	87
KUPPERS KÖLSCH	K	GERMANY	56
KURFURSTEN KÖLSCH	K	GERMANY	34
KWAK PAUWEL	A	BELGIUM	51
LA GAULOISE	A	BELGIUM	66
LA MADELON	B	FRANCE	24
LA TRAPPE ALE	A	BELGIUM	62
LAHNSTEINER JAGER BK	BK	GERMANY	84
LAMM BRAU EXPORT	B	GERMANY	50
LAMM BRAU PILS	B	GERMANY	54
LAMM BRÄU EDEL HELL	B	GERMANY	66
LAMM BRÄU PILSNER	B	GERMANY	57
LAMOT PILSOR	B	BELGIUM	22
LANDPILS BRAUHERRN	B	GERMANY	26
LANDSKRON	B	GERMANY	23
LAUTERBACH BROTZEIT	B	GERMANY	80
LAUTERBACH. SCHLANKE	W	GERMANY	42
LAUTERBACHER HEFE-W	W	GERMANY	43
LAUTERBACHER URHELL	B	GERMANY	40
LEDERER EXPORT	B	GERMANY	33
LEDERER EXPORT LIGHT	B	GERMANY	25
LEEUW	B	HOLLAND	36
LEFFE BLONDE	A	BELGIUM	46
LEFFE DARK	A	BELGIUM	73
LEFFE RADIEUSE	A	BELGIUM	50
LEIKEM ORIGINAL	B	GERMANY	69
LEIKEM WEISSE	W	GERMANY	75
LEOPOLD	B	BELGIUM	12
LIBERO	NA	SWITZERLAND	18
LICHER DOPPELBOCK	BK	GERMANY	81
LICHER EXPORT	B	GERMANY	46
LICHER PILS	B	GERMANY	50
LIEFMAN'S FRAMBOISE	L	BELGIUM	75
LIEFMAN'S GOUDENBAND	A	BELGIUM	62
LIEFMAN'S GOUDENBAND	B	BELGIUM	55
LIEFMAN'S KRIEK	L	BELGIUM	57
LINDEBOOM	B	HOLLAND	33
LINDEMANFRAMBOISE	L	BELGIUM	59
LINDEMAN'S GUEUZE	L	BELGIUM	38
LINDEMAN'S KRIEK	L	BELGIUM	37
LINDEMAN'S PECHE	L	BELGIUM	56
LOBURG	B	BELGIUM	30
LOHRER	B	GERMANY	38
LOLLAND FALSTERS	B	DENMARK	23
LONDON LIGHT	LO	ENGLAND	30
LÖWEN SWISS SPECIAL	B	SWITZERLAND	38
LÖWEN WEISSE H-W	W	GERMANY	50
LÖWEN WEISSE	W	GERMANY	60
LÖWEN. ALKOHOLFREI	NA	GERMANY	45
LÖWEN. ALT MÜNCH DUNK	B	GERMANY	51
LÖWEN. MUNICH LIGHT	B	GERMANY	54
LÖWEN. SCHWARZE	W	GERMANY	51
LÖWEN. ZURICH DARK	B	SWITZERLAND	28
LÖWEN. ZURICH LIGHT	LO	SWITZERLAND	46
LÖWEN.MUN.HELL BK	BK	GERMANY	78
LÖWENBRAU MUN. DARK	B	GERMANY	36
LÖWENBRAUOKT	B	GERMANY	79
LÖWENBRAU PILS	B	GERMANY	54
LÖWENBRÄU BOCK HELL	BK	GERMANY	75
LÖWENBRÄU NEU-ULM WZ.	W	GERMANY	82
LUCIFER	A	BELGIUM	68
LUTECE	A	FRANCE	72
MAC QUEEN'S NESSIE	B	AUSTRIA	77
MACANDREW'S SCOTCH	A	SCOTLAND	66
MACEWAN'S EDINBURGH	A	SCOTLAND	82
MACEWAN'S EXPORT	A	SCOTLAND	24
MACEWAN'S ML	ML	SCOTLAND	45
MACEWAN'S SCOTCH	A	BELGIUM	59
MACEWAN'S SCOTCH	A	SCOTLAND	70
MACEWAN'S STRONG	A	SCOTLAND	71
MACEWAN'S TARTAN	A	SCOTLAND	72
MACK POLAR	B	NORWAY	17
MACKESON	S	ENGLAND	80
MACKESON TRIPLE	S	ENGLAND	52
MAES PILS	B	BELGIUM	46
MAGNUS	A	BELGIUM	62
MAIS. RAUBER-KNEISSL	B	GERMANY	60
MAISACH BOCKBIER HELL	BK	GERMANY	82
MAISACH PILS	B	GERMANY	61
MAISEL BAYRISCH	B	GERMANY	42
MAISEL DAMPFBIER	B	GERMANY	28
MAISEL DUNKEL	B	GERMANY	22
MAISEL EXPORT	B	GERMANY	42
MAISEL FEST BEER	B	GERMANY	83
MAISEL HEFE WEISSE	W	GERMANY	63
MAISEL HEFE WEIZEN	W	GERMANY	38
MAISEL PILSNER	B	GERMANY	47
MAISEL SPEZIAL	B	GERMANY	24
MAISEL TRADITIONAL	B	GERMANY	39
MAISEL WEIZEN	W	GERMANY	29
MAISEL'S 1887	B	GERMANY	72
MAISEL'S PILSNER	B	GERMANY	54
MAISEL'S WEIZEN BOCK	W	GERMANY	56
MANN'S BROWN ALE	A	ENGLAND	55
MANSFIELD BITTER	A	ENGLAND	39
MARATHON	B	GREECE	45
MARCUS	B	YUGOSLAVIA	22
MAREDSOUS 6	A	BELGIUM	23
MAREDSOUS 8	A	BELGIUM	68
MAREDSOUS 9	A	BELGIUM	68
MAREDSOUS	A	BELGIUM	84
MARIESTADS FESTIVAL	B	SWEDEN	33
MARKSMAN	B	ENGLAND	29
MARTIN'S PALE ALE	A	ENGLAND	60
MARTINSKY	B	CZECHOSLOVAKIA	64
MARUHN	B	GERMANY	32
MATEEN TRIPLE	A	BELGIUM	84
MAXIMILIAN	BK	GERMANY	58
MEISTERBRÄU EXPORT	B	GERMANY	24
MESSINA	B	ITALY	45
METEOR PILS	B	FRANCE	29
MITCHELL'S BITTER	A	ENGLAND	24
MITCHELL'S BROWN	A	ENGLAND	29
MITCHELL'S CENTENARY	A	ENGLAND	78
MITTENWALDER DUNKEL	B	GERMANY	72
MITTENWALDER HELL	B	GERMANY	36
MITTENWALDER JOSEFI	BK	GERMANY	47
MITTENWALDER WEIH.	BK	GERMANY	24
MONINGER BERTHOLD	BK	GERMANY	82
MORAVIA	B	GERMANY	41
MORAVIA DARK	B	GERMANY	18
MORETTI DBL MALT DK	B	ITALY	30
MORETTI EXPORT	B	ITALY	35
MORETTI FRIULANA	B	ITALY	32
MORETTI LA ROSSA	B	ITALY	80
MORETTI PILSENER	B	ITALY	51
MORETTI SANS SOUCI	B	ITALY	51
MORT SUBITE	L	BELGIUM	52
MOSCOVA	B	RUSSIA	48
MOUSEL	B	LUXEMBOURG	30
MOUSSY	NA	SWITZERLAND	35
MOY EDELWEIZEN	W	GERMANY	50
MOY JAEGER	B	GERMANY	54
MOY REGENT	B	GERMANY	57
MÖHRINGER HERRENHAUS	B	GERMANY	78
MÖNCH. KAPUZ. H-W	W	GERMANY	24
MÖNCH. KAPUZINER KR.	W	GERMANY	33
MÖNCHSHOF FESTBIER	B	GERMANY	28
MÖNCHSHOF KL. BK. HELL	BK	GERMANY	86
MÖNCHSHOF KLOSTER.	BK	GERMANY	40
MÖNCHSHOF OKT.	B	GERMANY	20

Brand	Type	Brewer	Rating
MÖNCHSHOF PILSENER	B	GERMANY	33
MÖNCHSHOF URSTOFF	B	GERMANY	72
MÖNCHSHOF URSTOFF DK	B	GERMANY	66
MUNICH OKTOBERFEST	B	GERMANY	45
MUNSTER WEIHNACHTS	B	GERMANY	60
MUNSTERHOF	B	FRANCE	23
MURPHY EXPORT	S	IRELAND	23
MUTZIG	B	FRANCE	6
MÜMLINGTALER SCHANK	LO	GERMANY	16
NASTRO AZZURRO	B	ITALY	26
NEKTAR	B	YUGOSLAVIA	24
NEPTUN GOLDEN BROWN	B	DENMARK	16
NEPTUN PILSNER	B	DENMARK	42
NEPTUN PINSE BRYG	B	DENMARK	52
NEPTUN PÅSKE BRYG	B	DENMARK	52
NEU HAUS KAISER	B	GERMANY	43
NEUNBURGER WEIZEN	W	GERMANY	60
NEWCASTLE BROWN	A	SCOTLAND	65
NEWCASTLE LIGHT	A	ENGLAND	36
NIKSICKO PIVO	B	YUGOSLAVIA	16
NORDIK WOLF	LO	SWEDEN	21
NORSK	B	NORWAY	32
NORSK NA	NA	NORWAY	6
OBERDORF H-W DUNKLES	W	GERMANY	58
OBERDORF HEFE WEISS	W	GERMANY	54
OBERDORF WEISS	W	GERMANY	54
OBERNDORFER PILSNER	B	GERMANY	45
OBERNDORFER PRIVAT	B	GERMANY	45
OECHSNER HELLER BOCK	BK	GERMANY	90
OECHSNER MÄRZEN	B	GERMANY	85
OECHSNER PILS	B	GERMANY	90
OETTINGER DUNK. H-W	W	GERMANY	54
OETTINGER EXPORT	B	GERMANY	51
OETTINGER HEFE-WEISS	W	GERMANY	36
OETTINGER PILS	B	GERMANY	57
OKOCIM FULL LIGHT	B	POLAND	42
OKOCIM PORTER	P	POLAND	32
OLD BAILY	B	ENGLAND	32
OLD BEDFORD ALE	A	ENGLAND	57
OLD FART	A	ENGLAND	7
OLD NICK	A	ENGLAND	56
OLD PECULIER	A	ENGLAND	46
OLD THUMPER	A	ENGLAND	78
OLD VENICE	B	ITALY	24
ORANJEBOOM	B	HOLLAND	40
ORIG. ALT BAYER. WEISSE	W	GERMANY	33
ORIGINAL OKTOBER	B	GERMANY	42
ORVAL	A	BELGIUM	34
OSSER GOLD	B	GERMANY	54
OSSER HELL	B	GERMANY	51
OSSER WEISSE	W	GERMANY	69
OTT SPEZIAL	B	GERMANY	63
OTT URTYP	B	GERMANY	45
OTTAKRINGER HELLES	B	AUSTRIA	33
OUD HOEGAARDS	W	BELGIUM	47
PADERBORNER	B	GERMANY	35
PADERBORNER LIGHT	LO	GERMANY	2
PADERBORNER PILSENER	B	GERMANY	18
PAINE'S PALE ALE	A	ENGLAND	15
PALM ALE	A	BELGIUM	57
PALM BOCK	BK	BELGIUM	47
PALMBRÄU KRAICHGAU	B	GERMANY	21
PALMBRÄU PILSENER	B	GERMANY	50
PANACH	B	FRANCE	10
PANTHER	NA	FRANCE	24
PARKBRAU EXPORT	B	GERMANY	59
PARKBRAU PILS	B	GERMANY	61
PARKBRAU PIRMINATOR	BK	GERMANY	75
PARKBRÄU PILS	B	GERMANY	54
PATRIZ. KÖNIGSTRUNK	B	GERMANY	51
PATRIZ. KUPFERSTUBE	B	GERMANY	62
PATRIZIER EDELHELL	B	GERMANY	54
PATRIZIER EXPORT	B	GERMANY	45
PATRIZIER PILS	B	GERMANY	29
PATRIZIER POCULATOR	B	GERMANY	74
PATRIZIER ZERO	NA	GERMANY	15
PAUL. ALT MUNCH DK	B	GERMANY	42
PAUL. MÜNCHENER MÄRZ	B	GERMANY	58
PAUL. PREM. LEICHT	LO	GERMANY	40
PAUL.WEIS'N-MARZEN	W	GERMANY	45
PAULANER ALT DUNKEL	B	GERMANY	35
PAULANER EDELWEISS	W	GERMANY	68
PAULANER FEST BIER	B	GERMANY	62
PAULANER HEFE WEIZEN	W	GERMANY	39
PAULANER HELL	B	GERMANY	51
PAULANER HELL URTYP	B	GERMANY	52
PAULANER MAIBOCK	BK	GERMANY	28
PAULANER MÜNCH NR.1	B	GERMANY	65
PAULANER OKTOBERFEST	B	GERMANY	67
PAULANER PILS	B	GERMANY	30
PAULANER SALVATOR	BK	GERMANY	85
PAULANER UR-BOCK	BK	GERMANY	56
PAULANER UR-BOCK HELL	BK	GERMANY	87
PAULANER URTYP 1634	B	GERMANY	36
PAULANER WEISSBIER	W	GERMANY	53
PECHEUR 36.15	B	FRANCE	15
PELFORTH	B	FRANCE	54
PERONI BEER	B	ITALY	74
PERONI BIRRA	B	ITALY	33
PETER'S BRAND	B	HOLLAND	54
PETRISBERGER PILSENER	B	GERMANY	52
PETRUS	A	BELGIUM	43
PFEFFERBRÄU MÄRZEN	B	GERMANY	47
PFEFFERBRÄU SPEZIAL	B	GERMANY	51
PFUNGSTADTER	B	GERMANY	44
PFUNGSTADTER MAIBK	BK	GERMANY	55
PIEDBOEUF BLONDE	B	BELGIUM	46
PIEDBOEUF TRIPLE	B	BELGIUM	48
PINKUS ALT	A	GERMANY	10
PINKUS MALZ BIER	M	GERMANY	6
PINKUS PILS	B	GERMANY	23
PINKUS UR PILS	B	GERMANY	66
PINKUS WEIZEN	W	GERMANY	59
PIPER EXPORT	A	SCOTLAND	25
POLAR	B	ICELAND	53
POPE'S "1880"	B	ENGLAND	68
POPPER	NA	GERMANY	36
PORETTI ORO	B	ITALY	15
PORTER 39	P	FRANCE	52
PORTERIS	P	USSR	72
POSTBRÄU BERNHARDT	B	GERMANY	81
POSTBRÄU HEFE-WEIZEN	W	GERMANY	51
PREMINGER WEISS	NA	GERMANY	12
PRIMUS HAACHT PILS	B	BELGIUM	34
PRINCESS PORTER	P	WALES	1
PRINZEXPORT	B	ITALY	30
PRINZ REGENT LUITPOLD	W	GERMANY	40
PRINZREG. LUITPOLD H-W	W	GERMANY	57
PRIPPS EXPORT	B	SWEDEN	68
PRIPPS JUBILEE	B	SWEDEN	56
PRIPPS LAGER	B	SWEDEN	45
PRIZE OLD ALE	A	ENGLAND	54
PRO	NA	GERMANY	39
PROSTEL	NA	GERMANY	16
PRÖSSLBRÄU DUNKEL	B	GERMANY	80
PRÖSSLBRÄU PALMATOR	BK	GERMANY	88
PRÖSSLBRÄUPILS	B	GERMANY	54
PSCHORR MUNICH	B	GERMANY	13
PSCHORRWEISSE HW	W	GERMANY	43
PUNTIGAM	B	AUSTRIA	45
PUNTIGAMER MÄRZEN	B	AUSTRIA	42
PUNTIGAMER PANTHER	B	AUSTRIA	54
PUPASCH DUNKEL	B	GERMANY	56
PÜLS-BRÄU KRONE PILS	B	GERMANY	49
QUENZER SPEZIAL EXP.	B	GERMANY	55
QUIRINUS DOPPELBOCK	BK	GERMANY	64
QUIRINUS DUNK. DOPPEL	BK	GERMANY	78
RADEBERGER	B	GERMANY	28
RADHOST	B	CZECHOSLOVAKIA	53
RAFFO	B	ITALY	12
RAMSTEINER DUNKEL	B	GERMANY	70
RAMSTEINER PILS	B	GERMANY	54
RATS KRONE HELL	B	GERMANY	67
RATS KRONE PILS	B	GERMANY	73
RAUCHENFELS	B	GERMANY	40
RED BARREL	A	ENGLAND	29
RED ERIC	ML	DENMARK	33
REISCHENAU GOLD	B	GERMANY	63
REISSDORF KÖLSCH	K	GERMANY	66
RHANER EXPORT HELL	B	GERMANY	59
RICHMODIS KÖLSCH	K	GERMANY	12
RIEDENBURGER WEIZEN	W	GERMANY	59
RIEGELER FELSEN PILS	B	GERMANY	81
RIEGELER SPEZIAL EXP.	B	GERMANY	60
RINGNES BOCK	BK	NORWAY	56
RINGNES CHRISTMAS	A	NORWAY	62
RINGNES DARK	B	NORWAY	42
RINGNES EXPORT	B	NORWAY	55
RINGNES LOW	LO	NORWAY	16
RINGNES MALT LIQUOR	ML	NORWAY	18
RINGNES PILS ØL	B	NORWAY	38
RINGNES SPECIAL	B	NORWAY	66
RINGNES ZERO	NA	NORWAY	33
RINGWOOD 49ER	A	ENGLAND	53

Brand	Type	Brewer	Rating
RIVA 2000	B	BELGIUM	56
RIVA BLANCHE	W	BELGIUM	29
RIVA CHRISTMAS 1983	B	BELGIUM	60
ROCHEFORT TRAPP. 6	A	BELGIUM	68
ROCHEFORT TRAPP. 8	A	BELGIUM	70
ROCHEFORT TRAPP. 10	A	BELGIUM	80
RODENBACH RED BEER	A	BELGIUM	45
ROEMER	B	FRANCE	36
ROLAND	LO	GERMANY	16
ROMAN SPECIALE MATER	A	BELGIUM	68
ROMER PILS	B	GERMANY	32
ROT. TANNEN ZAPFLE	B	GERMANY	74
ROTHAUS DUNKEL	B	GERMANY	72
ROTHAUS MÄRZEN	B	GERMANY	77
ROTHAUS PILS	B	GERMANY	63
ROTHENBERGER PILS	B	GERMANY	75
ROTHENBURG	B	GERMANY	27
ROTHENBURGER ALT DK.	B	GERMANY	54
ROTHENBURGER EDELHELL	B	GERMANY	42
ROTHENBURGER PILSNER	B	GERMANY	60
ROTHENBURGER SCHANK	LO	GERMANY	18
ROTOCHSEN BOCK	BK	GERMANY	86
ROTOCHSEN DK. H-W	W	GERMANY	69
ROTOCHSEN EDEL EXP.	B	GERMANY	55
ROTOCHSEN HEFE-WEIZ.	W	GERMANY	55
ROTOCHSEN KRISTALL	W	GERMANY	49
ROTOCHSEN STIFTSHERR	B	GERMANY	60
ROTTWEILER SCHWARZ	B	GERMANY	34
ROYAL DUTCH	B	HOLLAND	12
ROYAL DUTCH KOSHER	B	HOLLAND	14
ROYAL OAK	A	ENGLAND	60
RÖHRL EXPORT	B	GERMANY	54
RÖHRL VILSTALER	W	GERMANY	80
RUDDLE'S COUNTRY ALE	A	ENGLAND	24
RUDDLES BITTER	A	ENGLAND	23
RUDDLES COUNTY	A	ENGLAND	36
RUSKI	B	RUSSIA	29
RUSSKOYE	B	RUSSIA	27
SAGRES	B	PORTUGAL	6
SAGRES DARK	B	PORTUGAL	46
SAILER HEFE WEISSE	W	GERMANY	41
SAILER PILS	B	GERMANY	36
SAILER WEISSE	W	GERMANY	57
SAINT ARNOUD	A	FRANCE	27
SAISON REGAL	A	BELGIUM	60
SAISON REGAL XMAS 82	A	BELGIUM	53
SAISON SILLY	A	BELGIUM	54
SAM. SMITH GOLD BROWN	A	ENGLAND	65
SAM. SMITH NUT BROWN	A	ENGLAND	34
SAM. SMITH WINTER '90	A	ENGLAND	24
SAM. SMITH WINTER '91	A	ENGLAND	36
SAMICHLAUS DARK '86	A	SWITZERLAND	48
SAMICHLAUS DARK '87	A	SWITZERLAND	54
SAMICHLAUS PALE '86	A	SWITZERLAND	79
SAMICHLAUS PALE '87	A	SWITZERLAND	47
SAMICHLAUS PALE '89	A	SWITZERLAND	80
SAMICHLAUS PALE '90	A	SWITZERLAND	80
SAMICHLAUS PALE '91	A	SWITZERLAND	80
SAMSON 10	B	CZECHOSLOVAKIA	30
SAMSON 11	B	CZECHOSLOVAKIA	44
SAMUEL SMITH OATMEAL	S	ENGLAND	70
SAMUEL SMITH PALE	A	ENGLAND	77
SAMUEL SMITH'S LAGER	B	ENGLAND	46
SAN MARTIN	B	SPAIN	13
SAN MIGUEL	B	SPAIN	32
SAN MIGUEL SELECTA	B	SPAIN	60
SANDLERBRAU	B	GERMANY	21
SANWALD HEFE WEIZEN	W	GERMANY	39
SANWALD WEIZEN DUNK	W	GERMANY	49
SANWALD WEIZEN KRONE	W	GERMANY	23
SANWALD WEIZEN PERL	W	GERMANY	42
SARUM	A	ENGLAND	30
SATAN	A	BELGIUM	31
SCALDIS	A	BELGIUM	42
SCANDIA GOLD	B	DENMARK	62
SCHAFF FEUERFEST	B	GERMANY	59
SCHAFF PILSENER	B	GERMANY	41
SCHAFFBIER	B	GERMANY	57
SCHERDEL PILSENER	B	GERMANY	37
SCHEYERN DOPPELBK	BK	GERMANY	83
SCHEYERN DUNKLER BK	BK	GERMANY	60
SCHEYERN GOLD	B	GERMANY	48
SCHEYERN WEISSE DUNK.	W	GERMANY	36
SCHEYERN WEISS HELL	W	GERMANY	24
SCHIERLINGEN ROGGEN	W	GERMANY	30
SCHLEMMER WEISS	W	GERMANY	45
SCHLOSS EXPORT	B	GERMANY	43

Brand	Type	Brewer	Rating
SCHLOSS-BIER	B	ITALY	21
SCHLOSSER ALT	A	GERMANY	36
SCHLOSSHERR PILS	B	GERMANY	67
SCHMUCKER DOPPEL DK	BK	GERMANY	83
SCHNEE BOCK	BK	GERMANY	69
SCHNEIDERHEFEWEIZEN	W	GERMANY	32
SCHOFFERHOFER HEFE W	W	GERMANY	55
SCHOFFERHOFER WEIZEN	W	GERMANY	45
SCHONBERGER FEST	B	GERMANY	80
SCHOUS	B	NORWAY	16
SCHÖFFERHOFER H-W	W	GERMANY	49
SCHÖFFERHOFER WEIZEN	W	GERMANY	46
SCHÖNBERGER ODENWALD	B	GERMANY	57
SCHÖNBERGER UR-BOCK	BK	GERMANY	83
SCHUSSENRIEDER PILS	B	GERMANY	49
SCHUTER'S RED STAR	B	GERMANY	12
SCHUTZ	B	FRANCE	15
SCHUTZENBERGER JUBIL	B	FRANCE	25
SCHWABEN BRAU	B	GERMANY	21
SCHWABEN BRAU EXP.	B	GERMANY	35
SCHWABEN BRAU MEIST.	B	GERMANY	29
SCHWABEN PILS	B	GERMANY	29
SCHWABEN URTYP 1878	B	GERMANY	29
SCHWARZ, WOIPERLINGER	W	GERMANY	80
SCHWARZBRÄU DUNK WZ.	W	GERMANY	84
SCHWARZBRÄU EXQUISIT	B	GERMANY	73
SCHWARZBRÄU PILS	B	GERMANY	71
SCHWARZE ADLER H-W	W	GERMANY	36
SCHWARZWALDER EXPORT	B	GERMANY	21
SCHWEIGER EXPORT	B	GERMANY	50
SCHWEIGER SCHMANKERL	W	GERMANY	51
SCOTTISH PRIDE	B	SCOTLAND	24
SEBALDUS WEIZENBOCK	BK	GERMANY	78
SENATOR	BK	GERMANY	15
SEPPL'S URBRAU DUNK.	B	GERMANY	49
SEPPLS DUNKEL	B	GERMANY	40
SEPTANTE 5	ML	FRANCE	73
SEPTANTE ROUGE	A	FRANCE	49
SEPTANTE VERTE	A	FRANCE	49
SESTER KÖLSCH	K	GERMANY	20
SEZOENS	A	BELGIUM	34
SIEGL PILSNER	B	AUSTRIA	60
SIGEL KLO.KRISTALL	W	GERMANY	21
SIGEL KLOSTERH-W	W	GERMANY	54
SIGEL KLOSTER PILS	B	GERMANY	43
SILVER PILS	B	BELGIUM	50
SIMPATICO	B	GERMANY	30
SKANSEN	B	FRANCE	24
SKI	B	NORWAY	24
SKOL	B	HOLLAND	22
SKOPSKO	B	YUGOSLAVIA	42
SLAVIA	B	FRANCE	47
SMICHOVSKY STARO	B	CZECHOSLOVAKIA	17
SOLDENAUER WEISSE	W	GERMANY	35
SPARTAN	B	GREECE	39
SPARTAN PREMIUM	B	GREECE	48
SPATEN DUNKEL	B	GERMANY	52
SPATEN FRANZISKUS	BK	GERMANY	70
SPATEN FRUHJAHR	B	GERMANY	62
SPATEN LIGHT	B	GERMANY	48
SPATEN LIGHT SCHANK	LO	GERMANY	38
SPATEN OPTIMATOR	B	GERMANY	70
SPATEN PILS	B	GERMANY	36
SPATEN URMARZEN	B	GERMANY	65
SPATENGOLD	B	GERMANY	36
SPECIAL BRANIK	B	CZECHOSLOVAKIA	71
SPECIALE AERTS	B	BELGIUM	62
SPEZIAL RAUCH. LAGER	B	GERMANY	43
SPEZIAL RAUCH. MÄRZEN	B	GERMANY	67
SPLUGEN BOCK	BK	ITALY	84
SPLUGEN DRY	B	ITALY	21
SPLUGEN ORO	B	ITALY	24
ST. BERNARD	B	GERMANY	39
ST. CHRISTOPHER	NA	ENGLAND	12
ST. DAVID'S PORTER	P	WALES	10
ST. EDMUND	A	ENGLAND	18
ST. FEUILLIEN XMAS	BK	GERMANY	74
ST. GEORGEN BRÄU	BK	GERMANY	74
ST. NIKOLAUS DUNKLES	B	GERMANY	59
ST. PAUL DOUBLE	A	BELGIUM	56
ST. PAUL TRIPLE	A	BELGIUM	68
ST. PAULI GIRL	B	GERMANY	56
ST. PAULI GIRL DARK	B	GERMANY	62
ST. PAULINA	NA	GERMANY	38
ST. SEBASTIAAN CROCK	A	BELGIUM	66
ST. SIXTUS ABDY	A	BELGIUM	45
ST. SIXTUS ABT	A	BELGIUM	55

Brand	Type	Brewer	Rating
ST. SIXTUS PATER	A	BELGIUM	42
ST. SIXTUS PRIOR	A	BELGIUM	41
ST. STEPHANUS FEST	B	GERMANY	53
ST.SEBASTIAAN GOLDEN	A	BELGIUM	66
STAR PILS EXCELSIOR	B	BELGIUM	45
STAROBRNO	B	CZECHOSLOVAKIA	55
STAUDER	B	GERMANY	24
STAUDER PILS	B	GERMANY	51
STEENDONK BRABANT	W	BELGIUM	28
STEFFL EXPORT	B	AUSTRIA	20
STEINBOCK 17	BK	AUSTRIA	88
STEINGADENER DUNKEL	W	GERMANY	12
STEINHAUSER	B	GERMANY	42
STELLA ARTOIS	B	BELGIUM	46
STER ALE	A	BELGIUM	36
STERN PREMIUM	B	GERMANY	60
STIEGL COLUMBUS	B	AUSTRIA	53
STIEGL GOLDBRAU	B	AUSTRIA	39
STIEGL WEIHNACHTS	BK	AUSTRIA	75
STRASBRAU	B	GERMANY	48
STUTT. HOF HERREN	B	GERMANY	29
STUTT. HOF. WEIZEN	W	GERMANY	53
STUTT. HOFBRAU LIGHT	LO	GERMANY	29
STUTT. HOFBRAU PILS	B	GERMANY	42
STUTT. WEIHNACHTEN	B	GERMANY	23
STUTTGARTER HOF H-W	W	GERMANY	35
SUFFOLK	A	ENGLAND	40
SUPER 49	B	FRANCE	23
SVETOVAR PUVODNI	B	CZECHOSLOVAKIA	33
SWINKEL LIGHT	LO	HOLLAND	15
SWINKELS EXPORT	B	HOLLAND	32
SWINKELS IMPORTED	B	HOLLAND	24
TADDY PORTER	P	ENGLAND	84
TARTAN BITTER	A	ENGLAND	5
TEGERNSEE DUNK. DOPPEL	BK	GERMANY	75
TEGERNSEE DUNK. EXPORT	B	GERMANY	76
TEGERNSEE HELLER BOCK	BK	GERMANY	81
TEGERNSEE PILS	B	GERMANY	60
TEGERNSEE SPEZIAL	B	GERMANY	45
TEGERNSEE SPEZIAL	B	GERMANY	75
TEGERNSEER HELL	B	GERMANY	78
TENNENT MILK STOUT	S	ENGLAND	42
TENNENT'S	B	SCOTLAND	75
TENNENT'S EXTRA	B	SCOTLAND	44
TERKEN BLONDE	B	FRANCE	47
TERKEN BRUNE	B	FRANCE	75
TETLEY	A	ENGLAND	27
TETLEY BITTER	B	ENGLAND	50
TEUTSCH PILS	B	GERMANY	50
TH. U. TAXIS EXPORT	B	GERMANY	56
TH. U. TAXIS FURSTLICHE	B	GERMANY	51
TH.U TAXIS POSTMEISTER	BK	GERMANY	79
THEAKSTONBITTER	A	ENGLAND	44
THIRTY-THREE EXPORT	B	FRANCE	62
THIRTY-THREE EXT. DRY	B	FRANCE	75
THIRTY-THREE RECORD	B	FRANCE	62
THOMAS HARDY 1984	A	ENGLAND	61
THOMAS HARDY 1986	A	ENGLAND	85
THOMAS HARDY 1989	A	ENGLAND	77
THOMAS HARDY 1991	A	ENGLAND	75
THOMAS HARDY 1982	A	ENGLAND	75
THOMAS HARDY 1983	A	ENGLAND	46
THOMAS HARDY 1986	A	ENGLAND	33
THOMAS HARDY 1987	A	ENGLAND	37
THOMAS HARDY 1988	A	ENGLAND	21
THOR	B	DENMARK	37
THREE HORSES	B	HOLLAND	29
THREE MONTS	A	FRANCE	50
THREE TOWNS	B	SWEDEN	46
THURN U TAXIS H-W	W	GERMANY	54
TILLY BRÄU HELL	B	GERMANY	20
TIMMERMAN'S FRAMBOISE	L	BELGIUM	63
TIMMERMAN'S KRIEK	L	BELGIUM	47
TIMMERMAN'S PECHE	L	BELGIUM	64
TIROL	B	AUSTRIA	51
TOLLY	A	ENGLAND	38
TOLZER DUNKEL WEIZEN	W	GERMANY	55
TOLZER EDEL WEIZEN	W	GERMANY	50
TOLZER WEISSE	W	GERMANY	47
TOMASOVSKY LEZAK	B	CZECHOSLOVAKIA	51
TONGERLO NORBERTIJNER	A	BELGIUM	49
TOPAZIO	B	PORTUGAL	15
TOURTEL	NA	FRANCE	29
TRADER JOE'S HOLIDAY	A	FRANCE	59
TRAQUAIR HOUSE	A	SCOTLAND	81
TRAUNSTEIN ALTBAIR.	B	GERMANY	45
TRAUNSTEIN FÜRSTEN	B	GERMANY	30
TRAUNSTEIN UR-WEIZEN	W	GERMANY	63
TRAUNSTEIN WEISSE	W	GERMANY	83
TREUERER ALT	A	GERMANY	53
TRIER LÖWEN KURFURST	B	GERMANY	48
TRIERER LÖWEN PILS	B	GERMANY	50
TRIPLE TOISON D'OR	A	BELGIUM	59
TRIUMPHATOR	BK	GERMANY	70
TROMPE LA MORTE	BK	GERMANY	65
TRUMAN CHRISTMAS	B	ENGLAND	77
TUBORG	B	DENMARK	27
TUBORG PORTER	P	DENMARK	74
TUBORG ROYAL DANISH	B	DENMARK	39
TUCHER ALT FRANKEN	B	GERMANY	50
TUCHER	B	GERMANY	36
TUCHER BAJUVATOR	BK	GERMANY	81
TUCHER BAYER H-W	W	GERMANY	44
TUCHER DARK	B	GERMANY	28
TUCHER FEST MÄRZEN	B	GERMANY	47
TUCHER H-WEIZEN DUNK	W	GERMANY	41
TUCHER HEFE WEIZEN	W	GERMANY	69
TUCHER LIGHT	B	GERMANY	60
TUCHER LORENZI	BK	GERMANY	36
TUCHER MAIBOCK HELL	BK	GERMANY	79
TUCHER PILS	B	GERMANY	33
TUCHER UBERSEE	B	GERMANY	42
TUCHER WEIZEN	W	GERMANY	62
TUDOR HORNDEAN	A	ENGLAND	75
TURKENLOUIS BOCK	BK	GERMANY	66
TURMER	B	GERMANY	26
TYROLIAN	B	GERMANY	39
ULM MUN. KANZLERGOLD	B	GERMANY	70
ULM MUN.ZUNFMEISTER	B	GERMANY	70
UNION EXPORT	B	YUGOSLAVIA	45
UNION EXPORT STOUT	S	YUGOSLAVIA	41
UNION SVETLO PIVO	B	YUGOSLAVIA	34
URACHER OLPP HELL	B	GERMANY	50
URFRANKISCHES LAND	B	GERMANY	41
URGÄUER WEIZEN	W	GERMANY	58
URQUELL	B	CZECHOSLOVAKIA	71
USHER'S WINTER	A	ENGLAND	83
USTERBACHER HEFE-W	W	GERMANY	60
USTERBACHER PILSNER	B	GERMANY	52
VALENTINS KLARES	W	GERMANY	81
VANDER LINDEN FRAMB.	L	BELGIUM	48
VAUX DOUBLE MAXIM	A	ENGLAND	30
VELDENSTEIN KAISER	B	GERMANY	67
VELTINS	B	GERMANY	40
VERY DIEST	NA	BELGIUM	34
VIENNA LAGER	B	AUSTRIA	24
VIEUX TEMPS	A	BELGIUM	43
VIKING	B	SWEDEN	15
VILLACHER GOLD	B	AUSTRIA	42
VITUS WEIZENBOCK	W	GERMANY	72
VONDEL TRIPLE	A	BELGIUM	18
WACHTERSBACH FURST	B	GERMANY	39
WACHTERSBACH JUBIL	B	GERMANY	33
WAGNER BRAU BOCK	BK	GERMANY	8
WAGNER BRAU MÄRZEN	B	GERMANY	20
WALSHEIM	B	GERMANY	37
WAPPEN PILS	B	GERMANY	40
WARD'S ENGLISH	A	ENGLAND	41
WARD'S GOLDEN	A	ENGLAND	59
WARSTEINER	B	GERMANY	57
WARTECK LAGER	B	SWITZERLAND	48
WARTECK LIGHT	LO	SWITZERLAND	24
WARTECK	NA	SWITZERLAND	26
WATNEY CREAM STOUT	A	ENGLAND	32
WATNEY STINGO	A	ENGLAND	30
WATNEY'S TRADITIONAL	A	ENGLAND	68
WATNEYS LIGHT	LO	ENGLAND	18
WEIHEN. KRISTALLKLAR	W	GERMANY	54
WEIHEN. STEPHANSQUELL	B	GERMANY	78
WEIHENSTEPHAN H-W	W	GERMANY	48
WEISS RÖS. RATSHERREN	B	GERMANY	43
WEISS RÖSSL FESTBIER	B	GERMANY	60
WEISS RÖSSL LEONHARDI	BK	GERMANY	76
WEISS RÖSSL MÄRZEN	B	GERMANY	77
WEISS RÖSSL RAUCH	B	GERMANY	48
WEISS RÖSSL URSTOFF	B	GERMANY	46
WEIZ. GOLD CHAMPAGNER	W	AUSTRIA	65
WEIZ. GOLD CHAMPAGNER	W	GERMANY	65
WEIZEN GOLD DUNK. H-W.	W	GERMANY	31
WEIZEN GOLD	W	AUSTRIA	72
WEIZEN GOLD	W	GERMANY	72
WELSH ALE	A	WALES	65
WELTENBURGER ASAM	BK	GERMANY	80
WELTENBURGER BAROCK	B	GERMANY	61

Brand	Type	Brewer	Rating
WELTENBURGER H-W DK	W	GERMANY	49
WELTENBURGER KL. DK	B	GERMANY	50
WELTENBURGER KL. SPEZ	B	GERMANY	46
WENZELS BRÄU	B	CZECHOSLOVAKIA	36
WERNER PILSENER	B	GERMANY	60
WESTFALEN PILS	B	GERMANY	41
WESTMALLE DUBBEL	A	BELGIUM	82
WESTMALLE TRIPLE 8%	A	BELGIUM	65
WESTMALLE TRIPLE 9%	A	BELGIUM	61
WHITBR. BREWMASTER	B	ENGLAND	30
WHITBREAD PALE	A	ENGLAND	70
WHITBREAD TANKARD	A	ENGLAND	62
WHITE OF BRUGES	A	BELGIUM	38
WICHERT DUNKLES	B	GERMANY	57
WICHERT PILSENER	B	GERMANY	51
WICKÜLER PILSENER	B	GERMANY	62
WIEL'S	B	BELGIUM	54
WIENINGER EXPORT HELL	B	GERMANY	53
WIESENER RAUBER BK	BK	GERMANY	79
WIEZE	B	BELGIUM	68
WINKELS EXPORT	B	GERMANY	50
WINKELS HEFE WEIZEN	W	GERMANY	53
WINKELS PILS	B	GERMANY	47
WITTEKOP	W	BELGIUM	54
WOHLBAUER	B	GERMANY	48
WOINEMER DUNKEL	B	GERMANY	48
WOINEMER HELL	B	GERMANY	74
WOINEMER MAI BOCK	BK	GERMANY	68
WOLFBRAU	B	GERMANY	38
WOLFERSTETTEN HELL	B	GERMANY	27
WOLFERSTETTEN PILS	B	GERMANY	48
WOLFERSTETTER H-W	W	GERMANY	50
WOLFERSTETTER WEISS	W	GERMANY	42
WOLTER'S PILS	B	GERMANY	45
WORTHINGTON ALE	A	ENGLAND	65
WORTHINGTON E	B	ENGLAND	46
WREXHAM	B	ENGLAND	30
WURMHÖRINGER MÄRZEN	B	AUSTRIA	78
WURMHÖRINGER SPEZIAL	B	AUSTRIA	77

Brand	Type	Brewer	Rating
WURTTEMBERG'S NATUR.	B	GERMANY	63
WÜNSTER 14	B	ITALY	51
WÜNSTER 18	B	ITALY	81
WÜRZBURGER BOCK	BK	GERMANY	59
WÜRZBURGER DARK	B	GERMANY	59
WÜRZBURGER HOLIDAY	B	GERMANY	86
WÜRZBURGER LIGHT	B	GERMANY	72
WÜRZBURGER MAY BK	BK	GERMANY	70
WÜRZBURGER NA	NA	GERMANY	8
WÜRZBURGER OKT.	B	GERMANY	72
WÜRZBURGER PILS	B	GERMANY	28
X-PERT	B	HOLLAND	28
YOLL DAMM	B	SPAIN	28
YOUNG'S OATMEAL ST.	S	ENGLAND	42
YOUNG'S ORIG. LONDON	P	ENGLAND	27
YOUNG'S RAM ROD	A	ENGLAND	42
YOUNG'S SPEC.LONDON	A	ENGLAND	76
YOUNG'S WINTER '88	A	ENGLAND	52
YOUNG'S WINTER '90-91	A	ENGLAND	43
ZAPADOCESKE DIA	B	CZECHOSLOVAKIA	31
ZIEGELHOF	NA	SWITZERLAND	42
ZIPFER BIER	B	AUSTRIA	30
ZIPFER JOSEFI BOCK	BK	AUSTRIA	81
ZIPFER MÄRZEN	B	AUSTRIA	48
ZIPFER URTYP	B	AUSTRIA	45
ZOLLER BÖCKLE DUNKLES	BK	GERMANY	80
ZOLLER BRENZKOFER	B	GERMANY	57
ZOLLER FIDELIS WEIZEN	W	GERMANY	75
ZOLLER FURSTEN HEFE-W	W	GERMANY	81
ZOLLER FURSTEN KRIST.	W	GERMANY	72
ZOLLER FURSTEN PILS	B	GERMANY	69
ZOLLER SPEZIAL EXPORT	B	GERMANY	69
ZULTE	A	BELGIUM	44
ZWICKELBIER	B	GERMANY	37
ZWIEFALTER KLOS. PILS	B	GERMANY	60
ZYWIEC	B	POLAND	37
ZYWIEC FULL LIGHT	B	POLAND	51
ZYWIEC PIAST	B	POLAND	31
ZYWIEC POLISH LAGER	B	POLAND	50

Taster's Notes

BEER NAME ____________________

Type (Ale, Stout, etc.) ____________________

Country of Origin ____________________

Bottled by ____________________

Container (can, bottle, etc.) ____________________

Serving Temperature ________ Cold ________ Room ________

Where Purchased ____________ Date ________

Quantity Purchased ____________ Price ________

PERSONAL EVALUATION

Appearance ________ Clear ________ Cloudy ________

Visible Sediment ________ Yes ________ No ________

Color _____ Pale _____ Amber _____ Brown _____ Dk. Brown _____

Head _____ None _____ Little _____ Full _____ Too Much _____

Aroma ______ Good ______ Bad ______ None ______

Other ____________________

Flavor ______ Good ______ Too Much Body ______

Too Little Body ______ Flat ______

Does Flavor Taste ______ Sweet ______ Sour ______

Bitter ______ Malty ______ Yeasty ______

Metallic ______ Salty ______ Other ______

After Taste _____ None _____ Mild _____ Strong _____

Would you purchase more? ____________________

Would you recommend it to others? ____________________

____

Taster's Notes

BEER NAME ____________________

Type (Ale, Stout, etc.) ____________________

Country of Origin ____________________

Bottled by ____________________

Container (can, bottle, etc.) ____________________

Serving Temperature ________ Cold ________ Room ________

Where Purchased ____________ Date ________

Quantity Purchased ____________ Price ________

PERSONAL EVALUATION

Appearance ________ Clear ________ Cloudy ________

Visible Sediment ________ Yes ________ No ________

Color _____ Pale _____ Amber _____ Brown _____ Dk. Brown _____

Head _____ None _____ Little _____ Full _____ Too Much _____

Aroma ______ Good ______ Bad ______ None ______

Other ____________________

Flavor ______ Good ______ Too Much Body ______

Too Little Body ______ Flat ______

Does Flavor Taste ______ Sweet ______ Sour ______

Bitter ______ Malty ______ Yeasty ______

Metallic ______ Salty ______ Other ______

After Taste _____ None _____ Mild _____ Strong _____

Would you purchase more? ____________________

Would you recommend it to others? ____________________

____

Notes: ____________________

____

____

____

____

____

Taster's Notes

BEER NAME ____________________

Type (Ale, Stout, etc.) ____________________

Country of Origin ____________________

Bottled by ____________________

Container (can, bottle, etc.) ____________________

Serving Temperature ________ Cold ________ Room ________

Where Purchased ____________ Date ________

Quantity Purchased ____________ Price ________

PERSONAL EVALUATION

Appearance ________ Clear ________ Cloudy ________

Visible Sediment ________ Yes ________ No ________

Color _____ Pale _____ Amber _____ Brown _____ Dk. Brown _____

Head _____ None _____ Little _____ Full _____ Too Much _____

Aroma ________ Good ________ Bad ________ None ________

Other ____________________

Flavor ________ Good ________ Too Much Body ________

Too Little Body ________ Flat ________

Does Flavor Taste ________ Sweet ________ Sour ________

Bitter ________ Malty ________ Yeasty ________

Metallic ________ Salty ________ Other ________

After Taste ______ None ______ Mild ______ Strong ______

Would you purchase more? ____________________

Would you recommend it to others? ____________________

____

Taster's Notes

BEER NAME ____________________

Type (Ale, Stout, etc.) ____________________

Country of Origin ____________________

Bottled by ____________________

Container (can, bottle, etc.) ____________________

Serving Temperature ________ Cold ________ Room ________

Where Purchased ____________ Date ________

Quantity Purchased ____________ Price ________

PERSONAL EVALUATION

Appearance ________ Clear ________ Cloudy ________

Visible Sediment ________ Yes ________ No ________

Color _____ Pale _____ Amber _____ Brown _____ Dk. Brown _____

Head _____ None _____ Little _____ Full _____ Too Much _____

Aroma ________ Good ________ Bad ________ None ________

Other ____________________

Flavor ________ Good ________ Too Much Body ________

Too Little Body ________ Flat ________

Does Flavor Taste ________ Sweet ________ Sour ________

Bitter ________ Malty ________ Yeasty ________

Metallic ________ Salty ________ Other ________

After Taste ______ None ______ Mild ______ Strong ______

Would you purchase more? ____________________

Would you recommend it to others? ____________________

____

Notes: ____

____

____

____

____

____

Taster's Notes

BEER NAME ____________________

Type (Ale, Stout, etc.) ____________________

Country of Origin ____________________

Bottled by ____________________

Container (can, bottle, etc.) ____________________

Serving Temperature ________ Cold ________ Room ________

Where Purchased ____________ Date ________

Quantity Purchased ____________ Price ________

PERSONAL EVALUATION

Appearance ________ Clear ________ Cloudy ________

Visible Sediment ________ Yes ________ No ________

Color _____ Pale _____ Amber _____ Brown _____ Dk. Brown _____

Head _____ None _____ Little _____ Full _____ Too Much _____

Aroma ________ Good ________ Bad ________ None ________

Other ____________________

Flavor ________ Good ________ Too Much Body ________

Too Little Body ________ Flat ________

Does Flavor Taste ________ Sweet ________ Sour ________

Bitter ________ Malty ________ Yeasty ________

Metallic ________ Salty ________ Other ________

After Taste ______ None ______ Mild ______ Strong ______

Would you purchase more? ____________________

Would you recommend it to others? ____________________

____

Taster's Notes

BEER NAME ____________________

Type (Ale, Stout, etc.) ____________________

Country of Origin ____________________

Bottled by ____________________

Container (can, bottle, etc.) ____________________

Serving Temperature ________ Cold ________ Room ________

Where Purchased ____________ Date ________

Quantity Purchased ____________ Price ________

PERSONAL EVALUATION

Appearance ________ Clear ________ Cloudy ________

Visible Sediment ________ Yes ________ No ________

Color _____ Pale _____ Amber _____ Brown _____ Dk. Brown _____

Head _____ None _____ Little _____ Full _____ Too Much _____

Aroma ________ Good ________ Bad ________ None ________

Other ____________________

Flavor ________ Good ________ Too Much Body ________

Too Little Body ________ Flat ________

Does Flavor Taste ________ Sweet ________ Sour ________

Bitter ________ Malty ________ Yeasty ________

Metallic ________ Salty ________ Other ________

After Taste ______ None ______ Mild ______ Strong ______

Would you purchase more? ____________________

Would you recommend it to others? ____________________

____

Notes: ____________________

____

____

____

____

____

Taster's Notes

BEER NAME ______________________

Type (Ale, Stout, etc.) ______________________

Country of Origin ______________________

Bottled by ______________________

Container (can, bottle, etc.) ______________________

Serving Temperature ______ Cold ______ Room ______

Where Purchased ______________ Date ______

Quantity Purchased ______________ Price ______

PERSONAL EVALUATION

Appearance ______ Clear ______ Cloudy ______

Visible Sediment ______ Yes ______ No ______

Color ____ Pale ____ Amber ____ Brown ____ Dk. Brown ____

Head ____ None ____ Little ____ Full ____ Too Much ____

Aroma ______ Good ______ Bad ______ None ______

Other ______________________

Flavor ______ Good ______ Too Much Body ______

Too Little Body ______ Flat ______

Does Flavor Taste ______ Sweet ______ Sour ______

Bitter ______ Malty ______ Yeasty ______

Metallic ______ Salty ______ Other ______

After Taste ______ None ______ Mild ______ Strong ______

Would you purchase more? ______________________

Would you recommend it to others? ______________________

____

Taster's Notes

BEER NAME ______________________

Type (Ale, Stout, etc.) ______________________

Country of Origin ______________________

Bottled by ______________________

Container (can, bottle, etc.) ______________________

Serving Temperature ______ Cold ______ Room ______

Where Purchased ______________ Date ______

Quantity Purchased ______________ Price ______

PERSONAL EVALUATION

Appearance ______ Clear ______ Cloudy ______

Visible Sediment ______ Yes ______ No ______

Color ____ Pale ____ Amber ____ Brown ____ Dk. Brown ____

Head ____ None ____ Little ____ Full ____ Too Much ____

Aroma ______ Good ______ Bad ______ None ______

Other ______________________

Flavor ______ Good ______ Too Much Body ______

Too Little Body ______ Flat ______

Does Flavor Taste ______ Sweet ______ Sour ______

Bitter ______ Malty ______ Yeasty ______

Metallic ______ Salty ______ Other ______

After Taste ______ None ______ Mild ______ Strong ______

Would you purchase more? ______________________

Would you recommend it to others? ______________________

____

Notes: ____

PERFECT BOUND EDITION OF

The Beer Log

Great Gift Idea!

The Paperback Edition of Jim Robertson's wildly popular book, *The Beer Log*, is now available. Included with this original 1992 version are the 1993 Updates for North America and Foreign beers.

Price: **$43.70** ($3.75 shipping/handling Continental U.S. included in price).

Send payment to: **Bosak Publishing Inc., 4764 Galicia Way, Oceanside, CA 92056**

Name: ____________________

Address: ____________________

City: ____________ State: ______ Zip: ________

Method of payment: ❑ Check ❑ Money Order ❑ Credit Card

Card #: ____________________ Exp. Date ________

Signature: ____________________

PRICE GOOD THRU JANUARY 1, 1995

YES! I want the '94 Update

Presented in two sections, **The Beer Log Update 1994** is designed for insertion in your looseleaf binder. **Section I:** North America — Descriptions of new beers and revisions to descriptions of beers previously rated. **Section II:** Foreign — Describes hundreds of interesting new beers found abroad. A completely updated rating list accompanies every order. In all, over 1,000 new beers are described and rated. Approximate shipping date for '94 Update is October 1994.

$16.00 + $3.00 S/H Continental U.S.

Send payment to: **Bosak Publishing Inc., 4764 Galicia Way, Oceanside, CA 92056**

Name: ____________________

Address: ____________________

City: ____________ State: ______ Zip: ________

Method of payment: ❑ Check ❑ Money Order ❑ Credit Card

Card #: ____________________ Exp. Date ________

Signature: ____________________

PRICE GOOD THRU JANUARY 1, 1995

Running out of binder space?

Spare binders for *The Beer Log*, featuring the same handsome design as the original, are available to hold additional pages.

Price: **$7.75** + $3.75 shipping/handling (Continental U.S.)

Send payment to: **Bosak Publishing Inc., 4764 Galicia Way, Oceanside, CA 92056**

Name: ____________________

Address: ____________________

City: ____________ State: ______ Zip: ________

Method of payment: ❑ Check ❑ Money Order ❑ Credit Card

Card #: ____________________ Exp. Date ________

Signature: ____________________

PRICE GOOD THRU JANUARY 1, 1995

Introducing the Latest Book by America's Foremost Beer Authority...

James D. Robertson

TRAVEL DEEP INTO THE FORESTS OF SOUTHERN GERMANY...

...to find beers that taste so great you'll scarcely believe your good fortune.

Covers Southern Germany from Frankfurt to the borders of Czechoslovakia, Austria, Switzerland and France.

$9.95 + $3.75 S/H Continental U.S.

Send payment to: **Bosak Publishing Inc., 4764 Galicia Way, Oceanside, CA 92056**

Name: ____________________

Address: ____________________

City: ____________ State: ______ Zip: ________

Method of payment: ❑ Check ❑ Money Order ❑ Credit Card

Card #: ____________________ Exp. Date ________

Signature: ____________________

PRICE GOOD THRU JANUARY 1, 1995

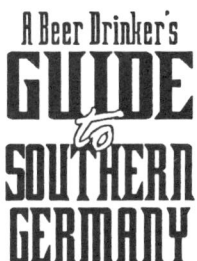

NO POSTAGE
IF MAILED
IN THE
UNITED STATES

BUSINESS REPLY MAIL
FIRST CLASS MAIL PERMIT NO. 12 OCEANSIDE CA
POSTAGE WILL BE PAID BY ADDRESSEE

1994 Beer Log Update
c/o Bosak Publishing Inc.
4764 Galicia Way
Oceanside, CA 92056

NO POSTAGE
IF MAILED
IN THE
UNITED STATES

BUSINESS REPLY MAIL
FIRST CLASS MAIL PERMIT NO. 12 OCEANSIDE CA
POSTAGE WILL BE PAID BY ADDRESSEE

The Beer Log Paperback Edition
c/o Bosak Publishing Inc.
4764 Galicia Way
Oceanside, CA 92056

NO POSTAGE
IF MAILED
IN THE
UNITED STATES

BUSINESS REPLY MAIL
FIRST CLASS MAIL PERMIT NO. 12 OCEANSIDE CA
POSTAGE WILL BE PAID BY ADDRESSEE

Guide To Southern Germany
c/o Bosak Publishing Inc.
4764 Galicia Way
Oceanside, CA 92056

NO POSTAGE
IF MAILED
IN THE
UNITED STATES

BUSINESS REPLY MAIL
FIRST CLASS MAIL PERMIT NO. 12 OCEANSIDE CA
POSTAGE WILL BE PAID BY ADDRESSEE

Spare Binder Offer
c/o Bosak Publishing Inc.
4764 Galicia Way
Oceanside, CA 92056